SUN, WIND & LIGHT

ARCHITECTURAL DESIGN STRATEGIES

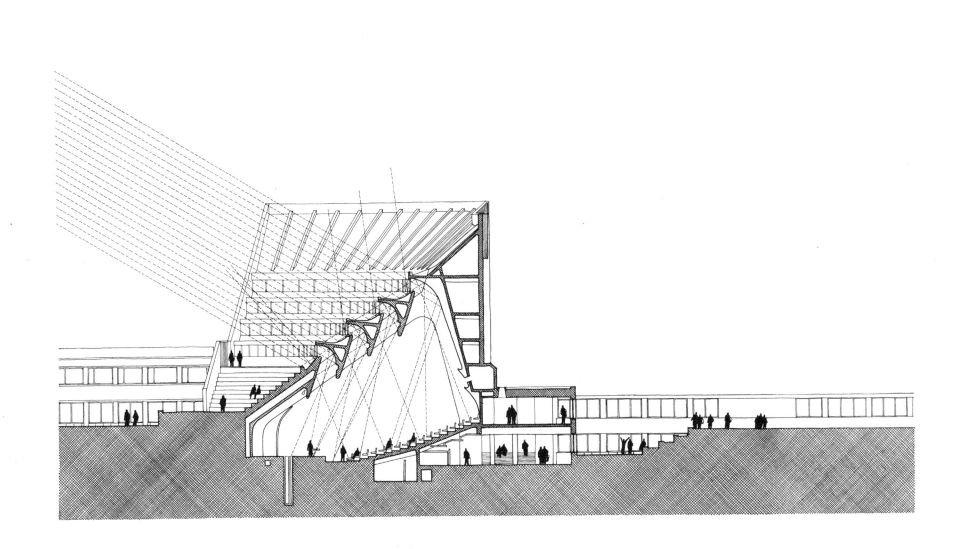

SUN, WIND & LIGHT

ARCHITECTURAL DESIGN STRATEGIES

second edition

G. Z. Brown

Department of Architecture
University of Oregon

Mark DeKay

School of Architecture
Washington University in St. Louis

Illustrations
Virginia Cartwright
Mark DeKay
Chi-Wen Hung
Pallavi Kalia
Arjun Mande

JOHN WILEY & SONS, INC.

New York · Chichester · Weinheim · Brisbane · Singapore · Toronto

This publication is designed to provide accurate and authoritative information in regard to the subject matter covered. It is sold with the understanding that the publisher is not engaged in rendering professional services. If professional advice or other expert assistance is required, the services of a competent professional person should be sought.

Library of Congress Cataloging-in-Publication Data
Brown, G. Z.
    Sun, wind & light: architectural design strategies / G.Z. Brown, Mark DeKay ; illustrations, V. Cartwright ... [et al.] ; research team, D. Barbhaya ... [et al.].-- 2nd ed.
        p. cm.
    Includes bibliographical references and indexes.
    ISBN 0-471-34877-5 (pbk. : alk. paper)
    1. Architecture and energy conservation. 2. Architecture and solar radiation. 3. Interior lighting. I. Title: Sun, wind, and light. II. DeKay, Mark. III. Barbhaya, D. IV. Title.

NA2542.3 .B76 2000
720'.472--dc21   00-026334

Printed in the United States of America.

10 9 8 7 6 5 4 3 2 1

First Edition Dedication
To ASB: for what it's worth

Second Edition Dedication
**To H.T., Martha, Mona, and all those creating
ecologically sustainable places**

CONTENTS

CONTENTS

vii

DETAILED CONTENTS

DETAILED CONTENTS

PART 3 STRATEGIES FOR SUPPLEMENTING PASSIVE SYSTEMS   276

PREFACE

The purposes of this second edition are identical to those outlined in the first edition preface: to help architectural designers who are not energy experts understand the energy consequences of their most basic design decisions and to give them information so that they can use energy issues to generate form rather than simply as limits that must be accommodated. The consciousness of the resource-side "energy crisis," out of which much of the concern for energy-conscious architecture was born, has faded somewhat in the 15 years since *Sun, Wind, and Light* was first published. However, the finite limits of our planet have not changed. We have become much more aware not only that resources are finite, but also that the capability of natural systems to absorb society's wastes may be even a more stringent limit. In other words, while saving energy has a high social benefit because it slows the depletion of finite reserves of fossil fuels, it is equally important in reducing the pollution caused by the extraction and burning of these fuels and, therefore, in reducing acid rain, the potential for global climate change, and the localized ecological impact of such practices as strip coal mining.

The relationships between architectural form and energy explored in this book are one example of a larger idea: the relationship of form and process. If we are to create an ecologically sustainable society, then every aspect of what we do will have to follow the underlying order of all living systems. That underlying order is always a *process* order. As Fritjof Capra explains so well in *The Web of Life,* the forms we perceive are really patterns. The patterns are configurations of relationships, and the relationships are each processes involving the exchange, processing, and storage of energy, matter, and information.

Each form, then, whether architectural or any other type, is both a contingent phenomenon manifesting underlying processes and a shaper of the process it contains and guides. My interest in the energy–form relationship is to explore how architectural form is in part a manifestation of the energy flows that are always present in a building. The designer can, with some experience, create form that guides and shapes those energy flows of sun, wind, and light.

Beyond just making buildings functional energy processors, I hope that designers using this book will also look for ways to reveal these processes and to give them meaning in the lives and experiences of building occupants. In a time where most of our buildings conceal their environmental control systems and segregate occupants from the rhythms of life in our outdoor environment, many of the strategies in this book can be used to reconnect, to, as John T. Lyle puts it, "shape form to manifest process." In simple and beautiful ways, each act of building can serve to heal the relationship between people and the living systems of which we are all a part. The effect, while nonquantifiable, of designing a building that helps another person to heal or discover that important relationship, to the extent that care leads to action, may have a far greater indirect impact on ecological health than the direct impact of conserved energy.

This edition, while greatly revised and expanded, has retained the critical organizational structure of the first edition. This structure, as described in the Introduction, allows the user to think about heating, cooling, and lighting within the context of thinking about architectural elements and their relationships. Often, we have cited the original source of theory or data used to generate a tool or graphic, even if the result is much different than it appears in the original. Where possible, geographic coverage has been extended beyond the temperate latitudes of the United States, and Dual Inch–Pound (I-P) and Standard International metric (SI) units have been included throughout. The text has been updated to reflect new codes and standards, and references to orientation now include clarifications for both Northern and Southern Hemisphere latitudes.

Cross-referencing between strategies is now included in the text of each section, and each strategy and technique has been given a memorable name, so it is easy to find in the contents and index. The number of strategies has increased by 35, and some of the first-edition strategies have been combined or renamed. This represents, in part, the vast increase since 1985 in both research and applications in the field of climatic design, especially in the areas of passive cooling and daylighting.

I would like to gratefully acknowledge the people who have been most helpful in making this second edition possible and in supporting me through the process of writing. My wife, Mona Shiber De Kay, deserves a great deal of thanks both for initiating much of my interest in ecology and for supporting me with great enthusiasm, for the four years the process has taken. She also provided graphic design consultation and helped with the typography and the cover deisgn.

Thanks to G. Z. Brown for trusting in me enough to take me on board for the second edition of what was undoubtedly a very personal creation and for his continued and generous mentorship over the years. A book like this takes a lot of perspective, more than I imagined. For me, that perspective was shaped by a few major agents. My understanding of architecture and of climatic design in particular has been greatly influenced by my study with Ginger Cartwright and John Reynolds while at the University of Oregon, and by my years in the practice of David Sellers in Warren, Vermont. In the two years I spent at Virginia Tech, I had the pleasure of working with Bob Schubert, Donald Sunshine, and Fernando Ruiz, all of whom taught me more than they will ever realize. A special thanks goes to my comrade Micheal O' Brien, whose insights into "the patterns that connect" I am still processing.

Dean Cynthia Weese of the Washington University School of Architecture has done everything I asked in support of the book, including starting a funded student research assistant program and giving me a paid research leave in the fall of 1998 to work on the project. While at Washington University, Carl Safe, Gay Goldman Lorberbaum, Jo Noero, and Davis van Bakergem have been particularly supportive, both personally and professionally.

The project was also funded in part by a grant from the Graham Foundation for Advanced Studies in Architecture. Some of the data used in the Appendix have been borrowed from work done in the Teaching Architecture + Energy Project, funded by the U.S. Department of Education's Fund for the Improvement of Postsecondary Education and by Washington University. Support for making much of these data accessible on-line and for extending the analysis to make the information more usable by designers has been provided by the Hay Fund of the Renewable Energy Institute at Cal Poly, San Luis Obispo.

Numerous research assistants have been a part of the team that produced the analyses in each strategy and the climate data. The assistants have worked very hard, and without their assistance the tasks could never have been done. They are Dhaval Barbhaya, Utsav Chakrabarti, Doyle Cozadd, Neena Gupta, Chi-Wen Hung, David Meyers, and Mujihad Sherdil. Dhaval oriented me to the many climatic-responsive examples in Indian architecture. Doyle worked on early forms of the climate analyses and scanned and laid out in digital form the entire first edition. Utsav and Mujihad did much of the detail scanning and layout of the illustrations and worked on climate analyses. David spent lots of time and talent developing computer tools that helped create the climate analyses in the Appendix. Several illustrators have also worked on the project. As readers of the first edition will notice, many of Virginia Cartwright's illustrations have been retained in this edition. She set a high standard, difficult to equal. Hong (Henry) Zeng began the second edition illustrations. Thanks Henry. Pallavi Kalia and Arjun Mande have worked tirelessly (or at least continuously) and with excellence on the illustrations for nine months. They stuck with the project to the end, committing much more time than any of us anticipated. Chi-Wen Hung was most helpful in completing the illustrations, taking charge of much of the Appendix. Each of these wonderful people has done an excellent job. I am proud to have worked with them.

John Hoag, Walter Grondzik, Fuller Moore, Allison Kwok, Bruce Haglund, and Paul Clark expertly reviewed the manuscript in record time, offering the detailed observations of lifetimes of collective experience with the topics.

Lastly, Ken Botnick and H. T. DeKay have heightened my awareness of graphic design principles, in addition to providing critical consulting on the book design and typography. The legibility and coherence of this edition are due to their invaluable advice.

MdK

1st EDITION PREFACE

My purpose in writing this book is to help architectural designers who are not energy experts understand the energy consequences of their most basic design decisions and to give them information so that they can use energy issues to generate form rather than simply as limits that must be accommodated. It is not that energy is important in and of itself, but that the processes of making energy that depend on fossil fuels are damaging to the natural environment to which we are inextricably bound. So, in the long run at least, environmental cost equals social cost; conversely, environmental benefit equals social benefit. It seems then that energy issues should be of professional concern to architects, whose goal is to improve the quality of life.

If energy is the concern, why cover only daylighting and passive solar heating and cooling? Certainly energy use in architecture can and should be addressed more broadly than it is in this book. My reason for narrowing the focus is to concentrate on the relationship between architectural *form* and energy use. Therefore, some important energy issues that do not have major architectural form consequences have been excluded. It also means that some architectural concerns have been addressed from an extremely narrow perspective. Daylighting, for example, which some say is the essence of architecture, is treated simply as a strategy for reducing electric lighting levels. It is because daylighting is of such broad concern in architecture that this narrow perspective is valuable: it lets the designer know both the good and bad energy consequences of certain approaches to daylighting and shows how those consequences change with building type and climate.

I have concentrated on *passive* means of heating, cooling, and lighting because they are more closely tied to building form than active systems are. However, the line between passive and active systems has not been rigorously drawn, and many of the illustrations are hybrid in nature. I have concentrated on heating, cooling, and lighting because they are the most important energy uses in buildings, and because they demonstrate a strong influence on form. My preoccupation with the connections between architectural form and energy is not because I think that all energy issues should profoundly affect architectural form but because architectural form can profoundly affect energy use. Those effects should be known and taken into consideration in the design process.

Throughout this book I have tried to credit original sources for data and ideas even if they appear here greatly revised. However, much of this information is of my own devising, so no references are cited.

I would like to acknowledge the people who helped make this book possible. First, I want to thank the students who have been in my architectural design studios. It was through their eyes that I first saw the need for a book structured like this one. It has been through their struggles that I have learned to identify what is meaningful and useful at the beginning of the design process. Four former students, Jeff Stark, Marla Fritzlen, Don Harton, and Ronda Thompson, did research that was crucial to this project. Don Harton also prepared and tested pieces of the analysis section on generic heating and cooling patterns.

A major influence on this book came from the curriculum development project initiated by the University of Pennsylvania and the U.S. Department of Energy. I would particularly like to thank Harrison

Fraker, Don Prowler, and Bob Shibley. Several documents that resulted from that program have been used in this book. But more important, that project and the continued efforts of those individuals have gone a long way toward establishing the ongoing dialogue about energy and architecture that exists within schools of architecture today.

Since coming to the University of Oregon, I have established regular working relationships with two people, Bobby-Jo Novitski and John Reynolds, who have greatly influenced my perception of architecture. I see their influence over and over again in this book. I would like to especially thank Bobby-Jo, who has carefully reviewed the entire manuscript and has made innumerable valuable suggestions on both style and content. Without her help I would never write anything readable.

Many of the ideas in this book were first considered while Susan Ubbelohde, John Reynolds, and I were developing *INSIDEOUT, Design Procedures for Passive Environmental Technologies* for publication, and I would like to acknowledge the importance of our discussions in the development of this book.

I would also like to thank Ginger Cartwright, who illustrated the book. She has gone far beyond the role of illustrator in her suggestions on book layout and organization and thoughts about effective communication. Her familiarity with the design process and energy issues made her judgments about what should be included extremely valuable. I also want to thank her for her willingness to do far more illustrations than were originally envisioned. I would like to thank Heidi Humphrey for her thoughts on book design.

Several people within the School of Architecture and Allied Arts deserve thanks: Mary Williams, who typed the manuscript and was the first line of defense in spelling and grammar; and Jerry Finrow, Department Head, and Bill Gilland, Dean, who are generous with their release time but who, more important, help establish the school as an enjoyable and productive work place.

I owe a great deal to Mike Pyatok, who has helped me clarify my values about architecture and who has a systematic and rigorous way of thinking about architecture that I admire and try to emulate.

I would also like to thank Ron Kellett, who stepped in at a moment of doubt to help me restructure and reorganize and to give me encouragement.

For their thoughtful review of the manuscript and many useful suggestions, I would like to thank Susan Ubbelohde of Florida A & M, Jack Kremers of Kent State University, Harvey Bryan of the Massachusetts Institute of Technology, Bruce Haglund of the University of Idaho, and Jerry Finrow of the University of Oregon.

And last, I want to thank April Shelley Brown for her support and endless trips to the library and the copy center as the deadline drew near.

GZB

INTRODUCTION

A basic premise of this book is that most decisions that affect a building's energy use occur during the schematic design stage of the project. Furthermore, the effort required to implement those decisions at the beginning of the design process is small compared to the effort that would be necessary later on. Therefore, if energy issues are going to receive an appropriate level of consideration at the beginning of the design process, they must be presented in a way that is useful to the designer and fits with other things the designer is considering at that time. At first, the designer works primarily in a synthesis mode, bringing ideas together, not in an analysis mode. Therefore, information and problem analysis must be presented in a way that is generative of architectural form and that helps the designer understand how the forms generated by energy concerns fit with forms generated by other architectural issues. The schematic design stage is one in which things proceed very rapidly, involving experimentation with many ideas and combinations of ideas. The considerations are broad and conceptual rather than detailed and fine. Therefore, information should be accessible and quick to use.

It is anticipated that the users of this book will have some background in energy issues and techniques, so the book is not meant to be a complete, self-sufficient reference or textbook. These considerations have had a profound effect on the character of this book. The information presented is at a rule-of-thumb level. Its in tention is to give only general ideas about architectural elements and their size and relationship to other elements. Precision of the information is sacrificed somewhat so that speed of use may be increased. The approximation methods are founded on certain assumptions about the elements under consideration. If those assumptions do not apply to the considerations of the moment, then the approximations probably won't either. So, along with the speed of use comes a certain need for caution, though no more so than with many of the other concerns in the schematic stage. It is important to realize that, to **develop** a design based on the ideas in this book, the designer must also go to other sources.

Most of the ideas in this book are presented in a format of a few pages. Each spread contains a statement of the idea, a brief explanation of the phenomenon and its architectural implications, and an illustration of how the idea has been used elegantly by architects. The brevity is aimed at increasing speed of use, and the illustrations are a means of helping the designer translate ideas into architectural form.

This book is organized in three parts: 1) Analysis Techniques, 2) Design Strategies, and 3) Strategies for Supplementing Passive Systems.

The first part, on Analysis Techniques, plays a crucial but supporting role to the second part. The analysis techniques help the designer define the context of the problem, by understanding the sun, wind, and light resources of a particular site and climate. They also help the designer understand the design problems: Are they heating, cooling, or daylighting? How do they change over the day and from season to season, and how are they affected by changes in the building's form and envelope construction? With this information the designer can form an idea of what kinds of strategies are likely to be important.

The heart of the book is the second part, on Design Strategies. It is the section that designers will find the most useful while formulating a basic design concept for a project. The design strategies are organized into sections

first in terms of scale: Building Groups, Buildings, and Building Parts. This helps a designer understand a particular principle like sun movement at a scale of consideration that is similar to the project. Within the scale organization, the strategies are organized by the architectural elements, such as streets, blocks, rooms, windows, and walls, and by the relationships between those elements, such as layers and zones. This approach was used because architectural elements are the common denominator of the issues under consideration at the scheming stage. They are what the designer manipulates to develop a design concept. For example, when considering the role of windows, the designer can find heating, cooling, and daylighting strategies together organized under the categories of window orientation, size, location, and shape. These strategies can be considered together and with other window considerations such as view or display.

The third part of the book, on Strategies for Supplementing Passive Systems, is the shortest, but it addresses an important consideration of how passive design strategies should be integrated with more conventional electrical and mechanical systems in buildings. This integration is complex, especially in large buildings, and could easily fill a book by itself. Our intention in Part Three is to identify recurring considerations, like how to extend the heat storage capacity of passive systems, and to explain their potential architectural impact, not to give detailed methods for sizing systems.

Readers should understand that this book deals primarily with temperate climates like those within the United States. Many of the design strategies will be useful in other climates, but there is a distinct bias towards those that address the changing nature of temperate climates rather than the more consistent needs of extremely hot or cold regions. We have, however, in the second edition, attempted to extend the range of coverage wherever possible to cover latitudes from the equator to the poles.

The strategies use language for northern latitude sun positions, with southern latitude references given paren-

thetically. Many of the strategies assume a sun position to the south of the building that stays low in the winter sky. These assumptions are inappropriate for regions near the equator, so the reader should use caution.

The book is organized in several ways to help the user find a particular piece of information. First, the table of contents lists all of the techniques and strategy statements under their major headings and subheadings so that in a few minutes one can get a feeling for what is covered in the entire book. The same statements occur **in bold type** at the beginning of the discussion of that technique or strategy. Each statement is followed by a subject, either heating, cooling, daylighting, or power, that it concerns. Within the strategy statements, the discussion of the illustration and the sizing rule-of-thumb are *highlighted* so that they can be easily found. Within the text, sources that contain a more detailed explanation of the idea or the example are identified by author and page number where appropriate. These sources frequently aren't the original source but are a convenient place to find more information. A complete citation for all sources mentioned in the text can be found in the bibliography.

Each section has an introductory overview and gives an example of how the techniques and strategies are related to each other and to techniques and strategies in other sections.

The book is also indexed by subject, architect, building, and selected tables and graphs so that after you've read about an idea it will be easy to retrieve. A glossary provides definitions for technical terms used in the text.

Appendix A includes climate data organized by city and keyed to the technique or strategy where the data are needed. That way, most of the information needed to design in a particular place is in one location in the book. Appendix B includes more general climate data that are not specific to a particular city, such as data in the form of maps; it is also keyed to the organization of techniques and strategies.

Part I ANALYSIS TECHNIQUES

The purpose of Part 1 is to present techniques that enable the designer to understand, *before* the building is designed, how the building is likely to use energy, so that appropriate architectural design strategies for daylighting and passive solar heating and cooling can be a basic and integral part of the initial design idea. In some cases, they are also used to provide climatic data or energy loads as inputs to tools presented in Parts 2 and 3. To formulate these analysis techniques, a distinction was made between analysis techniques, design strategies, and evaluation techniques.

Analysis techniques are used to understand the problem and its context. They characterize the important variables and establish their relative importance. Design strategies are form-generating; they concentrate on revealing the relationship between architectural form and space and energy use. Evaluation techniques differ from analysis techniques in that they follow the design proposition. They are used to evaluate the performance of a design. While their content might be quite similar to analysis techniques, their use is fundamentally different, and their potential impact on the initial design idea is much smaller because they cannot inform that initial idea. Granted, design is a reiterative process of analysis, design, evaluation, redesign, and reevaluation. There is an opportunity for evaluation to affect design; however, the role of evaluation is always to force change in the initial idea rather than to be an integral part of its formulation. Because a building must be envisioned before its energy use can be understood, evaluation techniques have tended to play a more important role than either design strategies or analysis tools in the design process as it relates to energy use. Therefore, energy considerations have played a less formative role in the initial conception of a design than they potentially could.

The analysis techniques are subdivided into five groups: A, Climate as a Context (Techniques 1–11); B, Program and Use (Techniques 12–14); C, Form and Envelope (Techniques 15–17); D, Combining Climate, Program, and Form (Techniques 18–23); and E, Electric and Hot Water Loads (Techniques 24–25). The climate analysis techniques are directed at establishing the context. They allow the designer to determine what resources of sun, wind, and light are available on the site and how they interact over the course of the day and year. The severity of the climate can be assessed to help to determine the building's role in providing for human comfort.

The program and use analysis techniques concentrate on revealing how the type of building and the intensity and rate of use affect the rate of internal heat production and therefore the heating and cooling requirement. The form and envelope techniques show how a building's shape, size, orientation, and skin construction affect its ability to both lose and gain heat and thus affect its heating and cooling requirements.

Section D is perhaps the most important because those techniques show how the interaction of climate, program, and form affect heating and cooling requirements. Considered separately, the design implications of climate, program, and form are intuitively understandable, but when combined and considered over diurnal and seasonal cycles, they are complex and frequently counterintuitive.

While the analysis techniques can be used in any order, depending on one's design goal, a possible sequence is the following: first, a comfort analysis using the Bioclimatic Chart (Technique 11) from the climate section; then an analysis of sun and wind using Technique 3, Solar Radiation, and Technique 5, Wind Square, as they relate to the comfort analysis; then an extension of those techniques to the site using the Sundial, Air Movement Principles, and Site Microclimates techniques (numbers 1, 6, and 7).

The designer should then proceed to the section on Combining Climate, Program, and Form. If the project is residential or residential-like in terms of size and internal loads, the next step is to use the Building Bioclimatic Chart (Technique 18) or to see what is required to develop Balance Point Profiles of heating and cooling patterns (Technique 23). To generate heating and cooling patterns, analysis techniques from the Program and Use and the Form and Envelope sections are required.

If daylighting is important, the Sky Cover and Daylight Availability analysis in the Light section (Techniques 8 and 9) should be considered after the patterns have been completed. If earth contact is being considered, its potential can be evaluated in Technique 19.

The Shading Calendar (Technique 20) establishes the times and dates when shading is needed and therefore whether it is a major or minor issue in the design process. Technique 24 provides a quick method for estimating the Total Heat Gains needed to design most of the passive cooling strategies in Part 2.

The Total Heat Losses method in the same technique gives a quick check on the energy conservation performance of the building and assures that a design meets the assumptions of the passive solar design strategies in Part 2.

The techniques in the Electric and Hot Water Loads section (Techniques 24 and 25) help estimate, before details of the building are known, the consumption rates needed for preliminary sizing of solar hot water and photovoltaic systems.

The analysis techniques presented in this section, like the following sections on design strategies, are designed to be easy and quick to use. Therefore, their precision is quite limited in some cases, and they shouldn't be used beyond the initial stages of the design process.

IA   Climate as a Context

These analysis techniques are directed at understanding a context that greatly influences how much energy buildings use, and when they use it, for heating, cooling, and lighting. The techniques are divided into five sections: sun, wind, sun and wind together, light, and comfort. All of the techniques allow the designer to evaluate the resources of the site without the inconvenience of actual on-site measurements. The methods in the sun section allow the designer to evaluate sun availability using two techniques. The first, the Sundial (Technique 1), is three dimensional; the second, the Sun Path Diagram (Technique 2), is graphic. The section also helps the designer estimate the amount of solar radiation available to offset low temperatures, for use later in the Comfort section.

The Wind techniques are geared toward translating tabular data from the weather bureau into a graphic format so that wind direction, speed, and frequency can be more easily visualized by the designer. The first two wind analysis techniques are similar, but the Wind Rose (Technique 4) emphasizes direction and frequency, while the Wind Square (Technique 5) emphasizes time

of day and change over the year. The Wind section ends with an explanation of Air Movement Principles for adjusting the weather bureau data to a particular site (Technique 6).

The Sun and Wind analysis section includes techniques for analyzing the combined effects of these elements on a site and helps the designer evaluate alternate locations for the building and exterior spaces.

The Light section contains three techniques. Sky Cover (Technique 8) analyzes weather data to determine whether the conditions are clear, partly cloudy, or overcast; how they change over the year; and which condition predominates, so that minimum design conditions can be established. Daylight Availability (Technique 9) helps the designer determine what percentage of the year a given level of daylight will be available in an overcast sky and what level of outside illuminance to use for design under a clear sky. Daylight Obstructions (Technique 10) helps predict the effects of surrounding buildings, landforms, and trees on the amount of daylight that reaches the building. The Light section, like the Sun and Wind section, is primarily concerned with

determining the availability of resources, not with how those resources will be used.

The Comfort section evaluates the interaction of temperature, relative humidity, radiation, and wind speed in terms of human comfort, using the Bioclimatic Chart (Technique 11) to suggest to the designer how the resources of the sun, wind, and light may be used. It is the single most important technique in the Climate section; this chart probably should be filled in first, then supported by a wind analysis and a radiation availability analysis. These analyses can be applied to a particular site using the Air Movement Principles (Technique 6) and sun availability techniques, the Sundial and Sun Path Diagram (Techniques 1 and 2) and summarized using the Site Microclimates technique (#7). The lighting techniques are more frequently used after the desirability of daylighting has been demonstrated using Techniques 18–23 in the section Combining Climate, Program, and Form, though if the Bioclimatic Charts (Techniques 11 and 18) indicate a substantial overheating period, it is likely that daylighting will be important.

1
The *SUNDIAL* used with a model simulates the changing position of sun and shade over the course of the day and throughout the year.

A sundial may be used to evaluate the effects of existing site conditions, impacts of building massing alternatives, the extent of sun penetration into buildings, and the effectiveness of shading devices.

From Appendix A, select the sundial with a latitude closest to that of the building's site. The model must be made to scale and should show significant topography, vegetation, buildings, fences, etc.—anything that will cast a shadow. Mount a copy of the sundial on a model of the site with north on the sundial corresponding to north on the model. The sundials are designed to work for both north and south latitudes. The sundials are printed with north as up for the Northern Hemisphere. For use in the Southern Hemisphere, turn the sundial 180°, so that the label for south latitude reads correctly.

Make sure that the sundial is on a horizontal (not sloping) surface. Mount a peg of the size indicated at the cross marker. The cross marker will be somewhere along the vertical noon line; depending on latitude, it may be above or below the Jun 21 line (Dec 21 in the Southern Hemisphere) on the sundial. By tilting the model in the sun one can make the end of the peg's shadow fall on any intersection of the sundial. Only the real sun will work; desk lamps do not have parallel rays, and thus will give splayed shadows. Each intersection represents the time of day and the day of the year corresponding to the two lines that meet at that intersection. When the shadow extends to a given intersection, the shadows and sun penetration in the model simulate the actual condition for that time of day and date (Lynch, 1971, p. 71).

The example shows a hypothetical site located in St. Louis, Missouri at 39° N latitude. For this site, the 40° sundial has been used to cast shadows for 9 AM, 12 noon, and 3 PM, on January 21 (coldest month) and on July 21 (hottest month). In January, sun angles are low and shadows long, casting shadows from the steeper topography. In summer, the sun is higher and shadows are much shorter; no shadows are cast from the landform. Patterns of sun and wind can be combined in Technique 7 to determine the site's microclimates.

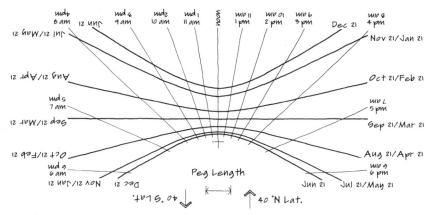

Sundial, 40° Latitude

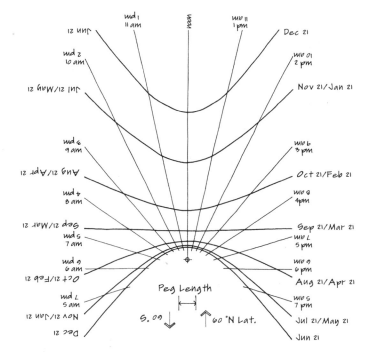

Sundial, 60° Latitude

To determine times and dates that the building needs shade, see Technique 20. Shading periods are different for outdoor rooms, for skin-load-dominated buildings, and for internal-load-dominated buildings.

In dense urban sites, a building's footprint often fills the site to its property line. In this case, shadows can be evaluated on a vertical plane at the site boundaries, to assess the shading by surrounding buildings. Portions of the elevation in shade during times when the building requires shade will not need to shade themselves with shading devices. Portions of the elevations in winter sun between 10 AM and 2 PM may be opportunities for locating solar collection apertures.

The relative resources of sun and wind on the surfaces of urban buildings may also suggest zoning strategies for heating, cooling, or lighting reasons. For instance, rooms may be located in the building based on the match of their need for heat, with rooms needing the most heat located on sunny orientations and rooms with high internal loads on the shady orientations (see Strategies 46, 57, 58, and 59).

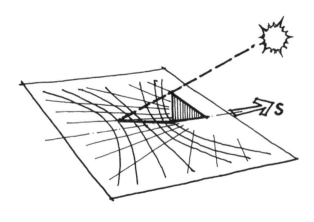

Use of Sundial

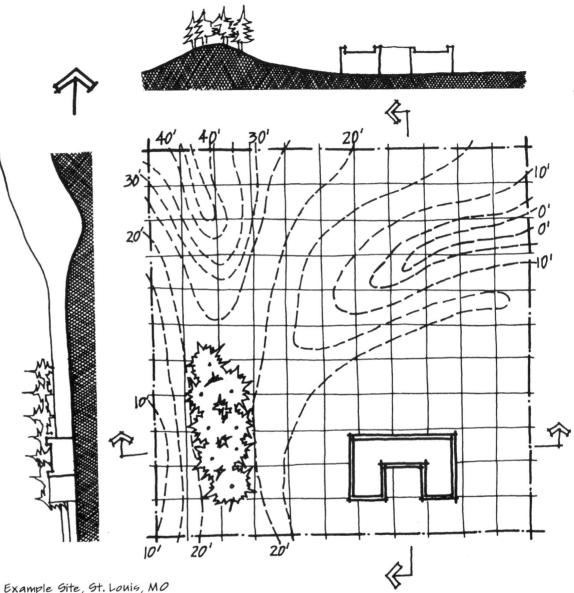

Example Site, St. Louis, MO

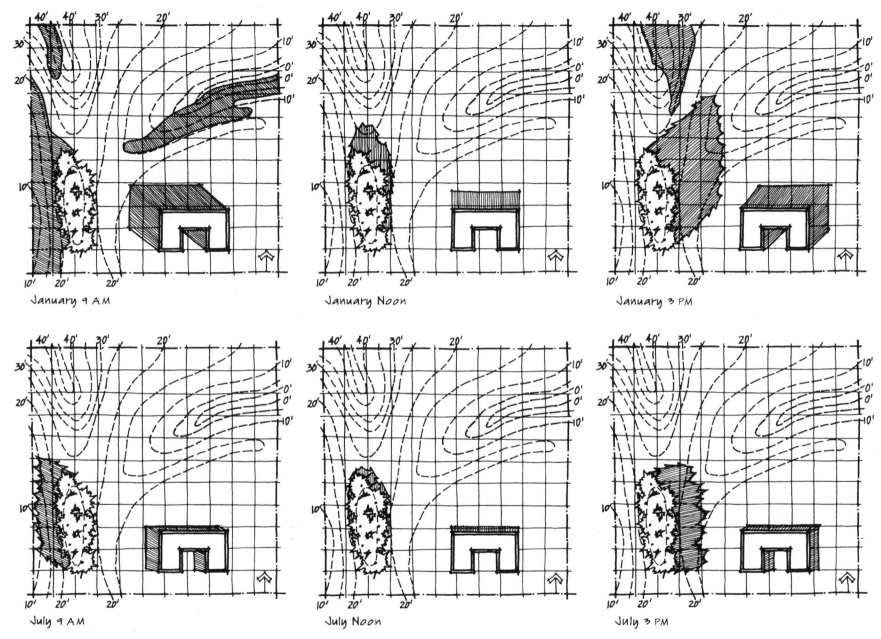

January 9 AM

January Noon

January 3 PM

July 9 AM

July Noon

July 3 PM

Shadows on a Hypothetical Site, St. Louis, MO

2 **The *SUN PATH DIAGRAM,* with existing site objects plotted, can determine the times of the day and year in which the sun will be available on a particular site.**

Sun path diagrams show the path of the sun in the sky dome as projected onto a horizontal surface (Libbey-Owens-Ford, 1974; Olgyay, 1963, p. 35; Hoke, 1996). The heavy lines running from east to west represent the path of the sun on the 21st day of each month of the year. The heavy lines running perpendicular to the sun path lines indicate hours of the day. The light lines radiating from the center of the diagram indicate the sun's azimuth. The concentric light lines indicate the sun's altitude. Sun path diagrams for 4° increments of latitude can be found in Appendix A.

The sun path diagram for a given latitude can be used to determine the sun's position in terms of altitude and azimuth for any hour of the year. For example, to determine the sun's position at 40 °N latitude, at 8 AM on Aug 21, find the intersection of the heavy 8 AM line and the heavy sun path line for Aug 21. Then follow the radial line that runs through the intersection to the outside circle and read the azimuth of 80° east of south. Finally, follow the concentric ring that runs through the intersection to the north/south line and read the sun altitude of 30°. Dates, times, altitudes,

and azimuths may all be interpolated between values given.

The same diagram of altitudes and azimuths may also be used to describe the position and size of objects from a particular viewpoint on a site. Trees, buildings, and hills can be described in terms of their altitude and azimuth from that viewpoint. By plotting them on the sun path diagram, one can tell when they will obstruct the sun and therefore shade the reference point on the site.

During overheated periods shading by such obstructions may be advantageous (Strategy 27), but during

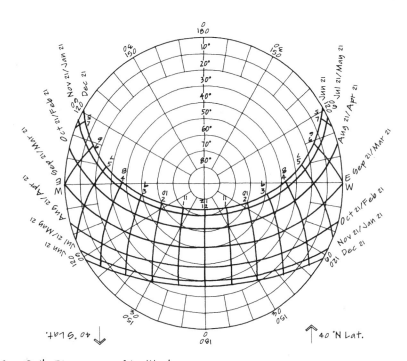

Sun Path Diagram, 40° Latitude

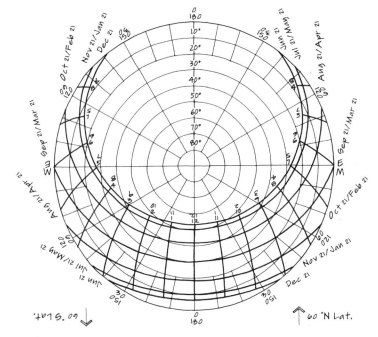

Sun Path Diagram, 60° Latitude

underheated periods it may be disadvantageous (Strategies 29 and 42).

The altitude and azimuth of site objects can be measured on the site using a compass and an altitude finder such as a transit or adjustable triangle, or they can be determined geometrically from a site map that shows the location and height of objects.

The example establishes a point A on the site plan, for which for solar access will be evaluated. To determine the potential obstruction of the existing building, draw a line from point A to the corner of the building, point B. Measure the azimuth angle between that line and a due south line. Measure the distance x from point A to point B and the height, y, of the building. The altitude of point C, which is directly above point B on the edge of the building, can then be determined by the formula.

If the building height, y, is 20 ft (6.1 m) and the distance from point A to B, x, is 36 ft (11.0 m), the altitude of point C is 29°. The altitude of point B is 0° because it lies in the horizontal plane of the reference point A. The azimuth for both points B and C is 34° west of south.

Points B and C may now be plotted on the sun path diagram. The line connecting them represents the building edge on the diagram. Plot enough significant points for each object on the site so that those objects can be represented on the sun path diagram. The places where the objects on the diagram cover the sun path show the times when point A will be in shade.

In the example, the building will shade point A from *about* 1:30 PM to 4 PM between Nov 21 and Jan 21 and 2 PM to 3 or 3:30 PM between Oct 21 and Nov 21 and between Jan 21 and Feb 21. The ridge line will shade point A for some time in the morning throughout the year.

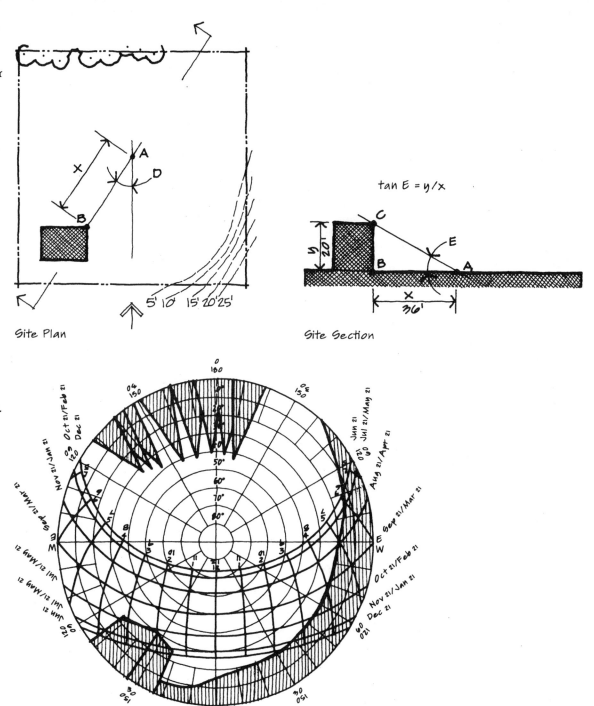

tan E = y/x

Site Plan

Site Section

Plot of Site Obstructions

3 *SOLAR RADIATION* available each hour can be used to determine times when comfort can be achieved outdoors and to estimate potential for solar heating in buildings.

The hourly solar radiation available on a horizontal surface can be used along with the temperature, relative humidity, and wind speed on the Bioclimatic Chart (Technique 11) to determine the potential for human comfort at a particular time and date.

Average hourly solar radiation data for 80 cities are in Kusuda & Ishii (1977), still the only available hourly radiation data in print for the United States. Hourly mean radiation in the form of the Radiation Square, is given for representative cities in Appendix A.

The Radiation Square chart at right shows hourly solar radiation on a horizontal surface for Columbia, Missouri (data from Kusuda & Ishii, 1977). The Radiation Square can be rendered to identify times of low radiation, when shading of a building's glazing is unnecessary, and times of very high radiation, when shading of the opaques surfaces of the building might be considered beneficial. The example codes low radiation as less than 75 Btu/hr, ft^2 and high radiation as over 200 Btu/hr, ft^2; other cutoff criteria could be used. The sun path diagram on the following page shows these times of various radiation levels plotted. This information can be combined with overheated times plotted on the same sun path diagram in Technique 20 to determine specific times and dates for which shading should be designed.

Measured hourly radiation for the building's location is the best source to use. If not available, a rough method is to estimate hourly solar radiation as a percentage of the total daily radiation available on a horizontal surface by using the percentages in the Percentage of Total Daily Radiation table. The variation within each range results from slight differences between latitudes. Total average daily radiation can be estimated from the maps in Appendix B. Multiply the daily radiation by the values from the table. Lastly, plot the hourly radiation values on the Bioclimatic Chart (Technique 11) to estimate how the comfort zone can be expanded due to radiation.

	J	F	M	A	M	J	J	A	S	O	N	D
1 am												
2 am												
3 am												
4 am												
5 am					2	6	2					
6 am				17	36	44	37	17	1			
7 am		10	36	63	87	94	90	69	39	9		
8 am	24	52	85	110	137	144	143	124	96	56	25	14
9 am	60	93	128	152	180	187	189	173	149	104	66	49
10 am	90	126	162	184	214	221	225	211	189	142	100	78
11am	109	146	184	205	236	242	247	235	215	166	121	97
12 noon	115	153	191	212	243	249	255	243	224	175	129	104
1 pm	109	146	184	205	236	242	247	235	215	166	121	97
2 pm	90	126	162	184	214	221	225	211	189	142	100	78
3 pm	60	93	128	152	180	187	189	173	149	104	66	49
4 pm	24	52	85	110	137	144	143	124	96	56	25	14
5 pm		10	36	63	87	94	90	69	39	9		
6 pm				17	36	44	37	17	1			
7 pm					2	6	2					
8 pm												
9 pm												
10 pm												
11 pm												
12 mid												

Radiation Square: Hourly Solar Radiation on a Horizontal Surface, Columbia, MO

Specific values for average daily solar radiation on a horizontal surface for each month for 239 cities in the United States can be found in Marion and Wilcox (1994, 1995).

Radiation data, together with degree day data, which indicate the severity of the heating season, can be used to estimate the potential for solar heating in the building's climate. The graph shows annual heating degree days (HDD) plotted against January radiation on a vertical surface (VS) for a number of U.S. and Canadian cities. The diagonal lines show the ratio between HDD65 and VS (in Wh/ft², day); the ratio can be used as an indicator of solar heating potential. HDD and VS conditions for the building's climate can be plotted on the chart, for comparison with other cities.

Hour	Northern Hemisphere, Temperate Latitudes		
	January	Mar/Sep	June
6am / 6pm	0%	0%	1-2%
7am / 5pm	0%	1-3%	4-5%
8am / 4pm	0-4%	5-6%	6-7%
9am / 3pm	6-9%	8-9%	8-9%
10am / 2pm	13-14%	11-12%	10-11%
11am / 1pm	15-19%	13-15%	11-12%
12 noon	16-21%	14-15%	11-12%
Hour	June	Mar/Sep	January
	Southern Hemisphere, Temperate Latitudes		

Percentage of Total Daily Radiation on a Horizontal Surface Available Each Hour

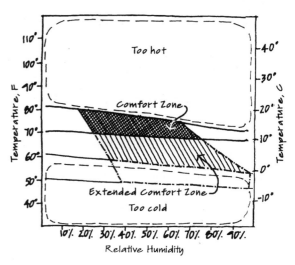

Extension of Comfort Zone With Sun

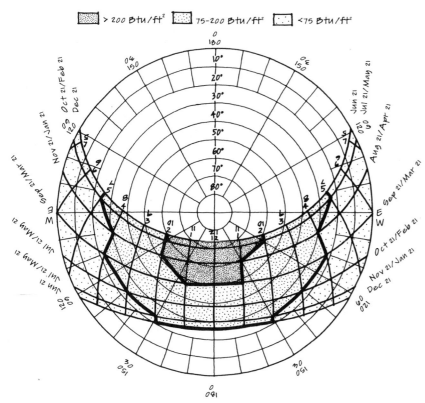

> 200 Btu/ft²   75-200 Btu/ft²   <75 Btu/ft²

Radiation Plotted on Sun Path Diagram
St. Louis, MO, 40 °N Latitude

These values for representative cities can be found in Appendix A, along with maps of heating degree days in Appendix B. The plots show that cities such as Phoenix and Los Angeles have low heating requirements and high solar radiation, whereas cities in Alaska have high annual degree days and very little winter sun. In between these extremes, are cities such as Boulder, CO, with a significant winter climate and high levels of winter sun, and other cities, such as Eugene, OR, with a moderate winter, but low radiation. Low levels of radiation do not exclude a climate from effectively using solar heating strategies. The implications are for increased insulation (Strategy 76) and larger solar collection areas (Strategy 93). Even buildings at high latitudes can benefit from the much higher solar radiation available in spring and fall months, when outside conditions are still well below the comfort zone.

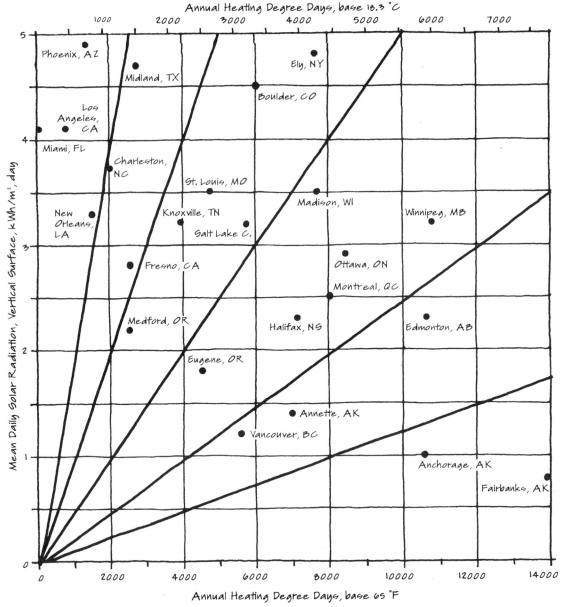

Heating Season Severity vs. January Radiation as an Indicator of Solar Heating Potential
Diagonal lines show the ratio Degree Days/Radiation; Lower ratios indicate better solar heating potential.

4 A *WIND ROSE* can be used to characterize the direction, speed, and frequency of wind in a particular location by month or year.

The wind rose gives detailed information about wind direction and frequency for a month or a whole year. It can be prepared with data from the *Airport Climatological Summary* (U.S. Dept. of Commerce) or other sources listed in Changery et al. (1977). Although the paper summaries for U.S. airports are still available from the National Climatic Data Center, the most accessible source for many users will be the *International Station Meteorological Summary CD-ROM* (NCDC, 1996), which covers most major airports around the world.

Using data from the table, Wind Direction vs. Wind Speed, in one of these sources, determine the relative frequency for each direction from the Total Mean % column. For example, the wind blows from the south 13.8% of the year in Eugene, Oregon. Plot this total percentage for each direction on the wind rose.

Note that the data indicates the direction from which the wind blows. For example, a wind direction marked NNE means that the wind blows from the north-northeast towards the south-southwest. The percentages for each wind speed group can also be plotted on the wind rose.

The annual wind rose for Eugene, Oregon, indicates that the wind comes predominantly from the north and south with the greatest frequencies in the speed group of 4 to 6 knots. Wind roses for the months of January and July for Eugene reveal that south winds occur in the winter and north winds in the summer.

Remember that the wind data from an airport site may not be exactly the same as the wind on the building's site. See Technique 6, Air Movement Principles. If detailed tabulated wind data, such as from the sources mentioned above, are not available, maps with simplified monthly and annual graphic surface wind roses are available in the *Climatic Atlas of the United States* (NOAA, 1993, pp. 75–78; ESSA, 1975, pp. 237–249) and the *Climatic Atlas Canada* (Environment Canada, 1988, Map series 5: Wind).

DIRECT.	1-3	4-6	7-10	11-16	17-21	22-27	28-33	34-40	41-47	48-55	>56	Total Mean %	Mean Speed
N	.9	4.0	6.1	3.2	.3							14.1	8.3
NNE	.5	2.1	2.4	1.1	.1							6.5	7.8
NE	.4	1.2	.6	.1								2.4	6.3
ENE	.2	.6	.1									1.0	4.9
E	.3	.7	.1									1.2	4.0
ESE	.2	.8	.4	.1								1.5	5.5
SE	.6	2.1	2.0	.3								5.1	6.7
SSE	.5	2.7	2.6	.9	.1							7.3	7.5
S	1.3	4.7	4.7	2.8	.6	.1						13.8	8.1
SSW	.7	3.0	2.6	1.1	.2							7.9	7.4
SW	.8	3.0	2.7	1.1	.1							8.0	7.5
WSW	.6	2.0	2.0	1.0	.1							5.8	7.6
W	.6	1.5	1.4	.8	.1							4.2	7.3
WNW	.3	1.0	.6	.2								2.3	6.7
NW	.4	1.4	.9	.1								2.9	6.5
NNW	.5	2.1	2.2	.7								5.8	7.4
VAR	0											0	0
CALM												10.3	0
ALL	8.7	33.4	31.8	13.7	1.7	.2						100	6.7

EUGENE ANNUAL: Frequency of Surface WIND DIRECTION vs SPEED (knots)

Wind Rose, Eugene, January (direction)

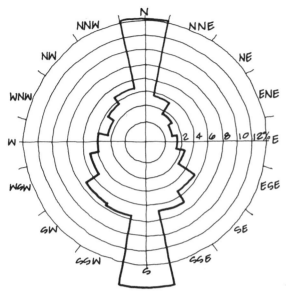

Wind Rose, Eugene, Oregon, Annual (Direction)

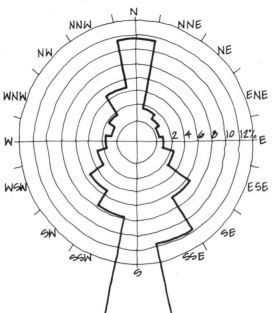

Wind Rose Eugene, Oregon, July (Direction)

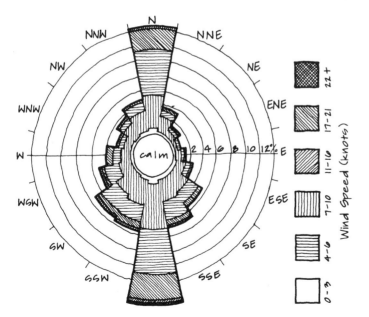

Wind Speed (knots)

22 +

17-21

11-16

7-10

4-6

0-3

Wind Rose, Eugene, Oregon,
Annual (Direction and Speeds)

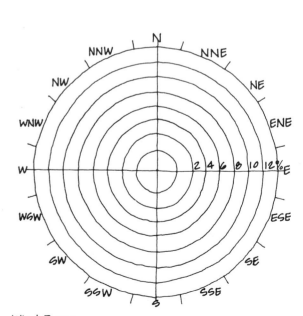

Wind Rose
Month: City:

5 The *WIND SQUARE* represents patterns of wind direction and speed by time of day and month of the year for a particular location.

The Wind Square gives more time-specific information than does the Wind Rose (Technique 4). It tabulates, for 3-hr periods (or 1-hr, depending on data source) and for each month, the predominant wind speed, the predominant wind direction at that speed, and the percentage of time that the wind blows from that direction.

Several conclusions can be drawn from the wind square. Because it is organized by month and time it can be used in conjunction with the bioclimatic chart to anticipate the speed and direction of the wind when the temperature and humidity are above or below the comfort zone.

From the St. Louis, MO, wind square, one can determine that the wind comes from the west-northwest during the winter and from the south in the summer, so there is little conflict on the site between blocking the chilling winter winds and admitting the ventilating summer winds. Also, wind speed is greatest during the daytime and lowest at night. Wind speeds are faster during the winter than during the summer.

Wind data are collected by several organizations in varying formats, and breakdowns by time, speed, direction, and month are frequently limited. Data available by state and city are listed in Changery et al. (1977). A separate *Airport Climatological Summary* is published by NOAA (U.S. Dept. of Commerce) for each of 130 major airports. The *Summary of Hourly Observations* (U.S. Dept. of Commerce, 1974) is available for many locations and gives hourly wind data for each month. Although the paper summaries for U.S. airports are still available from the National Climatic Data Center, the most accessible source for many users will be the *International Station Meteorological Climate Summary (ISMCS) CD-ROM* (NCDC, 1996), which covers most major airports around the world.

To make a wind square using the data from ISMCS, from the data options menu for the building's city, select the data group, "Wind Direction vs. Speed by Hour–Month." For each of the 3–hr intervals, in each month, examine the data table given (for instance, January tables for the 000, 003, 006 hours, etc.).

Record the mean wind speed for "All" observations. Then, in the Total Percent column, find and record the highest percentage and its associated wind direction. Also record the second highest percentage and its associated wind direction. If the second highest percentage comes from very near the same direction as the highest figure, choose the highest number that varies by more than one compass point from the highest percentage. This will give a measure of the most common secondary direction from which the wind blows during that hour. Repeat the process for each 3-hr interval in each month. Record the data as shown in the table on the next page.

Use these data to construct the wind square as shown, determining wind speed categories appropriate for your climate and application. You may wish to draw the length of the wind direction arrow in the wind square in proportion to the percentage of time the wind blows from the predominant direction.

Keep in mind that wind data are usually collected at airports and the wind speed and direction on your site may be quite different (Robinette, 1972, p. 73; Technique 6). The graph of **Wind Speed Variation With Height for Various Terrains** can be used to estimate the difference between wind speed measured at the airport and the likely reduction on your site (Chandra et al., 1986, p. 29). The profiles are derived from data for strong winds; low wind speeds used for natural ventilation will likely show even smaller ratios (greater difference) for local-to-airport wind speeds.

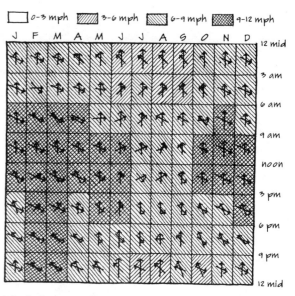

Wind Square, St. Louis, MO
Speed (mph) & Direction

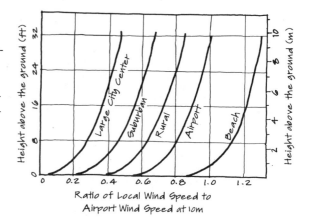

Wind Speed Variation with Height & Terrains

HR	JAN	FEB	MAR	APR	MAY	JUN	JUL	AUG	SEP	OCT	NOV	DEC
12 mid	8.6 WNW/S 13/9%	8.5 WNW/S 11/9%	8.9 WNW/S 10/10%	8.4 S/SE 11/8%	6.6 S/SE 13/10%	6.2 S/W 14/9%	5.8 S/SE 15/8 %	5.5 S/SSE 14/9%	5.8 S/SE 14/9%	6.5 S/SE 13/9%	8 S/WNW 13/10%	8.4 WNW/S 11/11%
3 am	8.3 WNW/S 14/8%	8.2 NW/W 11/8%	8.6 WNW/S 11/8%	7.9 WNW/S 9/9%	6.2 S/W 11/8%	5.9 S/SW 12/10%	5.3 S/SW 12/9 %	5 S/W 11/8%	5.4 S/SE 11/8%	6.1 S/SE 10/9%	7.7 WNW/S 12/11%	8 WNW/S 12/9%
6 am	8.4 WNW/S 14/8%	8.3 WNW/SE 12/7%	8.6 WNW/SE 11/9%	8 WNW/S 10/8%	6.7 W/S 11/9%	6.3 S/WSW 12/9%	5.5 S/SW 10/10%	4.9 S/ESE 10/8%	5.5 S/ESE 10/8%	6.2 SE/W 11/10%	7.8 WNW/S 11/11%	8.2 WNW/S 12/9%
9 am	9.5 WNW/S 15/8%	9.9 WNW/S 14/8%	11 WNW/S 11/8%	10.6 WNW/S 10/10%	9 S/WNW 11/8%	8.3 S/WSW 11/10%	7.4 WSW/S 12/9 %	7.1 WSW/SSW 10/8%	7.9 S/SE 10/8%	8.6 S/WNW 11/9%	9.6 NWN/S 14/13%	9.4 WNW/S 12/11%
12 n	10.2 WNW/SE 14/8%	10.6 WNW/WSW 15/7%	11.8 WNW/SE 13/9%	11.5 WNW/SSE 12/9%	9.9 S/WNW 11/9%	9.1 S/W 11/9%	8.1 WSW/NW 10/9 %	7.7 S/WSW 9/8%	8.7 S/WNW 11/8%	9.4 S/WNW 12/10%	10.5 WNW/S 14/10%	10.2 WNW/S 14/9%
3 pm	10.3 WNW/SSE 16/8%	10.9 WNW/SE 16/7%	12 WNW/SSE 13/9%	11.8 WNW/S 10/9%	10.3 S/NW 10/10%	9.4 S/SW 13/8%	8.4 NW/S 10/9 %	8 S/NW 9/8%	9 S/NW 11/10%	9.5 SSE/WNW 11/10%	10.5 WNW/SSE 14/10%	10.2 WNW/SSE 15/9%
6 pm	8.8 WNW/SE 14/8%	9.4 WNW/SE 15/8%	10.6 WNW/SE 12/9%	10.6 WNW/SE 11/10%	9.1 S/NW 11/9%	8.7 S/NW 14/7%	7.8 S/NW 12/7 %	7.4 S/E 11/8%	7.3 S/SE 12/9%	7.4 SSE/NW 13/9%	8.7 WNW/SSE 12/11%	8.8 WNW/SE 12/10%
9 pm	8.7 WNW/S 13/9%	9.1 WNW/SE 12/9%	9.5 WNW/SE 10/9%	9.5 ESE/SSE 10/10%	7.2 SSE/ESE 11/10%	6.7 S/SE 16/8%	6.2 S/ESE 14/8 %	6.1 S/SE 13/12%	6.5 SSE/ESE 14/8%	7.1 SSE/WNW 13/7%	8.6 S/WNW 13/11%	8.8 WNW/S 12/10%

Wind Speed Data for Wind Square, St. Louis, MO
mean wind speed mph / wind direction / percentage of observations from direction

6 **Use *AIR MOVEMENT PRINCIPLES* to adjust airport wind data to approximate wind flow on a site.**

The information in wind squares and wind roses, Techniques 5 and 4, frequently comes from an airport, which may have wind flow patterns quite different than those of nearby sites.

The wind flow patterns for a particular site can be understood in relation to airport data by simulating the way the site modifies the wind in a wind tunnel (Aynsley et al., 1977, p. 71). When wind tunnel tests aren't feasible, the designer can estimate wind direction and speed by using three principles that govern air movement and by becoming familiar with the way wind interacts with natural and built forms.

The first of the three principles is that, as a result of friction, air velocity is slower near the surface of the earth than higher in the atmosphere. The reduction in velocity is a function of the ground's roughness, so wind velocity profiles are quite different for different terrain types (Melaragno, 1982, p. 45). The diagrams show, for the three terrain types, the height at which the gradient velocity is reached. Wind velocities measured at a site near the ground are frequently lower than those measured at the airport towers and presented in most climatological data. Likewise, exposed sites or buildings at altitudes higher than the airport tower are likely to experience higher velocities. Assuming that the airport wind velocities were measured at 30 ft (10 m) above the ground, use the curves in Technique 5 to approximate the adjusted velocity for any height and any terrain.

The second principle is that, as a result of inertia, air tends to continue moving the same direction when it meets an obstruction. Therefore, it flows around objects, like water flows around a rock in a stream, rather than bouncing off the object in random directions.

Third, air flows from areas of high pressure to areas of low pressure. For example, when solar radiation heats the air in a meadow, reducing its pressure and causing it to rise, air will then flow into the meadow area from the surrounding forest, where the air is at a relatively lower temperature and higher pressure.

Using these principles and realizing that air acts like a fluid, like water, it is often possible to visualize how wind flow on a site might differ from wind flow at a nearby airport.

In addition to these air movement principles, there are several microclimate phenomena that often occur on building sites (Olgyay, 1963, pp. 45, 94; Robinette, 1972, p. 73). The diagrams of the Influence of Terrain on Wind Flow show the patterns of wind flows for a variety of landforms, in part derived from wind tunnel tests (McClenon & Robinette, 1975, pp. 94–97).

When wind meets an object like a building or a hill, it creates a high-pressure zone of increased velocity on the windward side of the object (the side the wind is blowing toward) and a low-pressure zone of lower velocity on the leeward side of the object. The velocity is increased as the wind sweeps around the sides and over the top of the object. Wind striking a landform, such as a hillside, is deflected, but not stopped.

Wind is accelerated when constricted, according to the Venturi effect, such as when it flows through a gap between buildings, or through a saddle between two

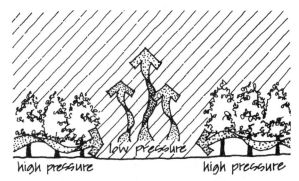

Wind Flow From High to Low Pressure Zones

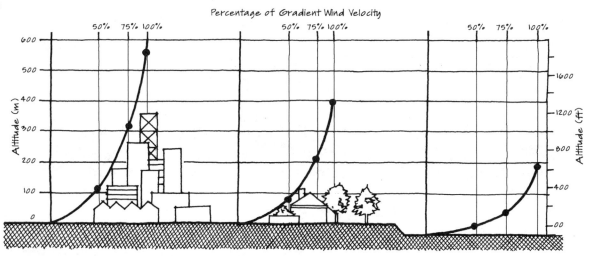

Effect of Terrain on Wind Velocity Profiles

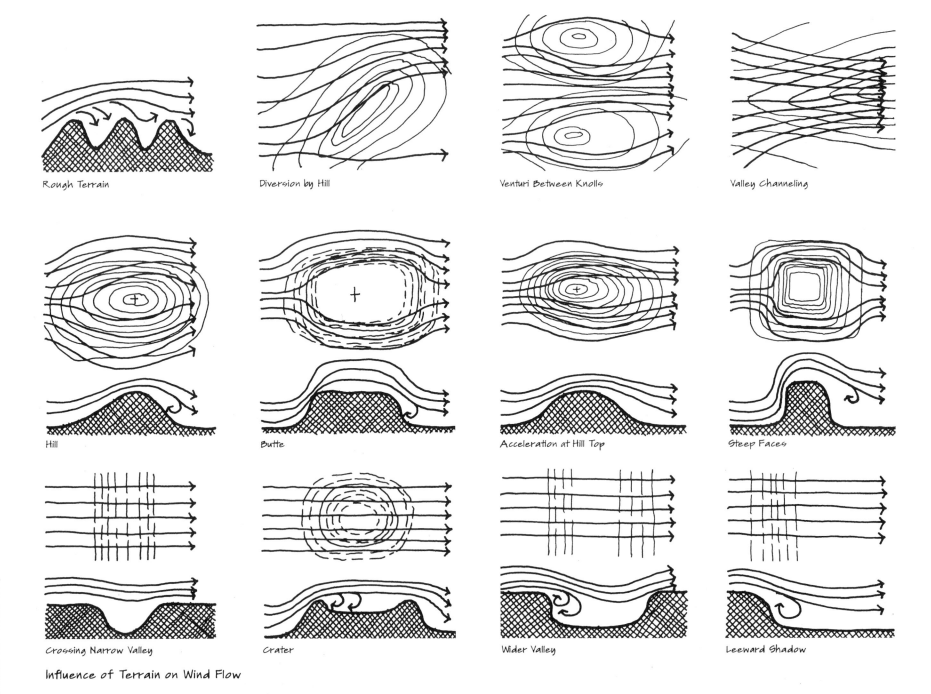

Rough Terrain

Diversion by Hill

Venturi Between Knolls

Valley Channeling

Hill

Butte

Acceleration at Hill Top

Steep Faces

Crossing Narrow Valley

Crater

Wider Valley

Leeward Shadow

Influence of Terrain on Wind Flow

knolls, or when it is channelized by flowing parallel to the ridges of a canyon.

Wind diverted by a landform will increase in turbulence and decrease in velocity behind the obstruction. Wind moving crosswise over a depression will tend to carry over narrow valleys and gradually fall into wider ones.

Near bodies of water, the breeze blows off the water toward the land during the day. The land heats up more rapidly than the water, causing the air over the land to rise and be replaced by the air from over the water. At night the flow is reversed, with the breeze blowing from the land, which has cooled more rapidly than the water, to the water, which is relatively warmer than the land, as the air over it rises and is replaced by the cooler air from over the land.

In valleys, the wind blows uphill during the day because the sun warms the air, causing it to rise. Upward currents form on sunny slopes in the morning. By midday, upvalley winds follow ascending valley floors. At night the air flow reverses because cold ground surfaces cool the surrounding air, making it heavier and causing it to flow down the valley, beginning with flows down valley walls. Different orientations of valley profiles create complex thermal wind patterns. The phenomenon of cool air falling also results in cool air flowing down hills at night and collecting in pockets formed by topography or vegetation.

Wind patterns are altered by their interaction with built form in complex ways. The diagrams of **Wind Flows Around Buildings** are adapted from results of wind tunnel studies (Evans, 1957). Arrows represent wind flow patterns, with closer lines indicating increased wind speed. Circular arrows indicate eddies. The low-pressure eddy zones will have markedly decreased wind speeds and are sometimes termed areas of "wind shadow." In most all cases, high pressure occurs on the windward side and low pressure on the leeward side, while wind constricted as it moves around the edges of a building increases in velocity.

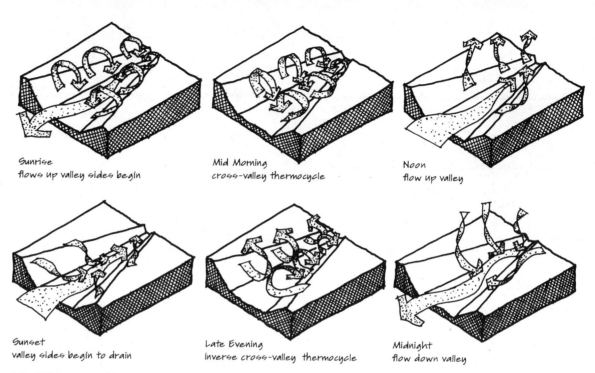

Sunrise
flows up valley sides begin

Mid Morning
cross-valley thermocycle

Noon
flow up valley

Sunset
valley sides begin to drain

Late Evening
inverse cross-valley thermocycle

Midnight
flow down valley

Wind Flows in a Valley Over a Daily Cycle

The sectional diagrams show the impact of roof slope and building height for the same width building. Steeply pitched roofs deflect wind higher, extending the height and length of the low-pressure zone. Increasing building heights show very similar wind patterns above the building, while the length of the wind shadow increases proportional to the building's height.

The lower set of plan diagrams shows the impact of varied building widths for the same height building. Similar patterns occur at the sides of narrow and wide buildings, while the length of the eddy zone increases with width, but not in direct proportion. It takes a large increase in building width to create a small increase in eddy length.

The upper set of plan diagrams shows the patterns created by different building configurations and orientations. Using these basic patterns, it is possible to fit basic design alternatives to the climate and the building's need for admitting or blocking wind. It is also possible to predict the impact on outdoor rooms of wind in different seasons.

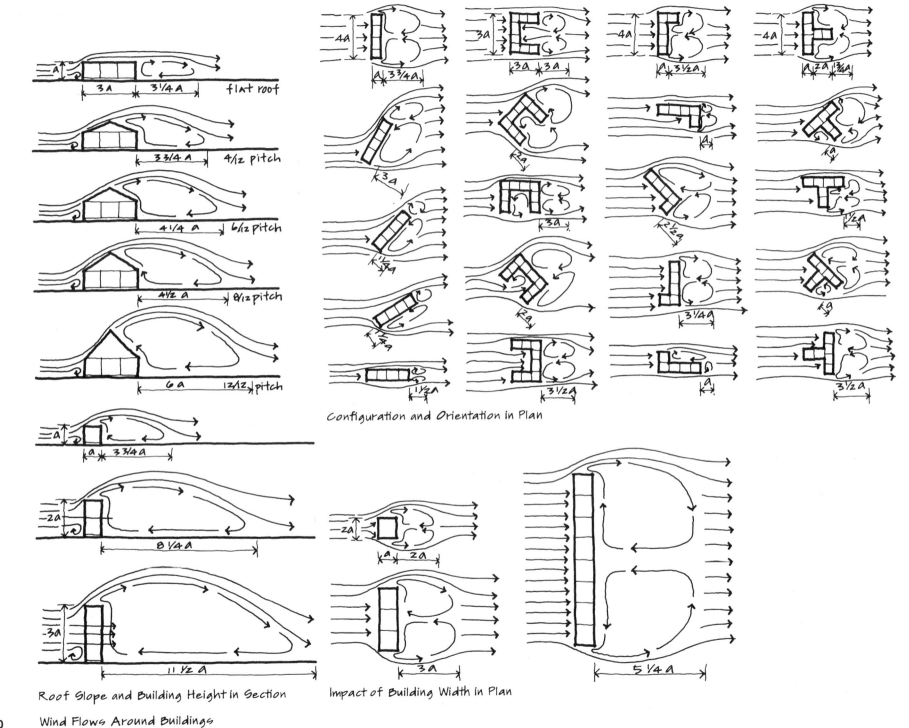

flat roof

3 A | 3¼ A

4½ pitch

3¾ A

6½ pitch

4¼ a

8½ pitch

4½ a

12/12 pitch

6 a

a | 3¾a

−2a

8¼ a

−3a

11½ a

Configuration and Orientation in Plan

Roof Slope and Building Height in Section

Impact of Building Width in Plan

Wind Flows Around Buildings

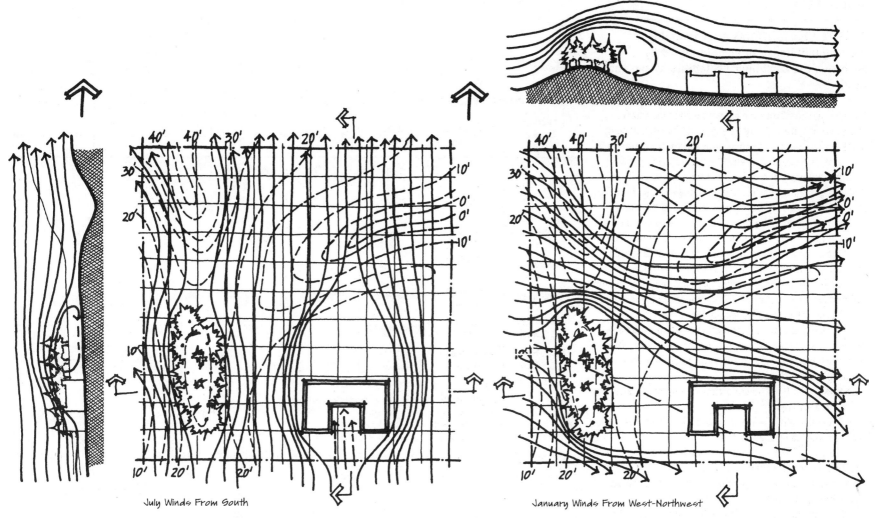

July Winds From South

January Winds From West-Northwest

Wind Microclimatic Patterns, July, St. Louis, Missouri

Wind Microclimatic Patterns, January, St. Louis, Missouri

The example shows a hypothetical site with wind patterns projected using wind principles. In St. Louis, the wind blows from the south in summer and from the west-northwest in the winter. In summer, the wind blows into the courtyard building, creating a high-pressure zone in the court and separating around and over the building. The calmer eddy zone extends about 3½ times the building height, while the wind speed is reduced for a longer distance. Crossing the narrow valley, it passes over the depression. The wind also separates around the trees and remains separated as it splits around the ridge.

In winter, a wind shadow is created by the trees, with the airstream staying aloft over the building. Moving oblique to the ridge, the air pattern is deflected around the end of the smooth ridge. Prevailing wind is also channelized by being deflected down the valley wall.

7 The *SITE MICROCLIMATES* most favorable for locating buildings can be determined by analyzing the combined availability of sun and wind.

The thermal comfort zone shown on the bioclimatic chart, Technique 11, may be expanded by admitting or blocking the wind and sun at appropriate temperature and relative humidity levels. The permutations of admitting and blocking sun and wind are represented in Table B. As an example, the condition of Sun + Lee (Admit Sun–Block Wind) is a response that would be appropriate for an exterior space if the temperature were below the standard comfort zone. Throughout the year all four matrix conditions may occur at various locations on a site as a result of sun position, wind direction, site topography, vegetation, and existing buildings. They may create more or less favorable building sites, depending on the climate conditions with which they coincide.

This method can be used before any buildings are proposed to see where favorable sites exist and after buildings are proposed to see what microclimates are created around the buildings.

• SUN + WIND = The condition in which sun and wind are admitted.

• SHADE + WIND = The condition in which sun is blocked and wind is admitted.

• SUN + LEE = The condition in which sun is admitted and wind is blocked.

• SHADE + LEE = The condition in which both sun and wind are blocked.

Different climatic conditions have differing importance for comfort, depending on the type of climate and the season. At the site scale, admitting a desired resource is more important than blocking an undesirable force. For instance, in a cold climate, admitting sun is more important than blocking wind, because design strategies at the building and element scales can be used to block wind, but nothing can be done to solar heat the building if access to the sun is blocked. Table A gives **Recommended Values for Individual Microclimate Variables by Climate and Season,** on a scale of 0 to 3. As an example, St. Louis is a temperate climate; so admitting summer wind and admitting winter sun are both given high values of 3.

CLIMATE / BUILDING TYPE			SHADE			SUN			LEE			WIND		
Internal-Loaded Building	Skin-Loaded Building	Outdoor Rooms	W	F/S	Su	W	F/S	Su	W	F/S	Su	W	F/S	Su
		Cold	0	0	0	3	3	3	2	2	2	1	1	1
	Cold	Cool	0	0	2	3	3	1	2	2	0	1	1	3
Cold	Cool	Temperate	0	0	2	3	3	1	2	2	0	1	3	3
Cool-Arid	Temperate Arid	Hot-Arid	0	2	2	3	1	1	2	2	0	1	1	3
Cool-Humid	Temperate Humid	Hot-Humid	0	2	2	3	1	1	2	0	0	1	3	3
Temp.-Arid & Hotter	Hot-Arid & Hotter	Tropical-Arid	2	2	2	1	1	1	2	2	2	1	1	1
Temp.-Humid & Hotter	Hot-Humid & Hotter	Tropical-Humid	2	2	2	1	1	1	0	0	0	3	3	3

Scale:
0 --- desirable force blocked (worst condition)
1 --- undesirable force admitted
2 --- undesirable force blocked
3 --- desirable force admitted (best condition)

TABLE A. Recommended Values for Individual Microclimatic Variables by Climate and Season

Internal-Loaded Building	Skin-Loaded Building	Outdoor Rooms	SUN + WIND			SUN + LEE			SHADE + WIND			SHADE + LEE		
			W	F/S	Su	W	F/S	Su	W	F/S	Su	W	F/S	Su
		Cold	4	4	4	5	5	5	1	1	1	2	2	2
	Cold	Cool	4	4	4	5	5	1	1	1	5	2	2	2
Cold	Cool	Temperate	4	6	4	5	5	1	1	3	5	2	2	2
Cool-Arid	Temperate-Arid	Hot-Arid	4	2	4	5	3	1	1	3	5	2	4	2
Cool-Humid	Temperate-Humid	Hot-Humid	4	4	4	5	1	1	1	5	5	2	2	2
Temperate-Arid	Hot-Arid & Hotter	Tropical-Arid	2	2	2	3	3	3	3	3	3	4	4	4
Temp.-Humid & Hotter	Hot-Humid & Hotter	Tropical-Humid	4	4	4	1	1	1	5	5	5	2	2	2

CLIMATE / BUILDING TYPE

Scale:
1 = worst microclimate
6 = best microclimate
values = sum of climatic element values from Table A

TABLE B. Values of Microclimatic Conditions Combinations by Climate and Season

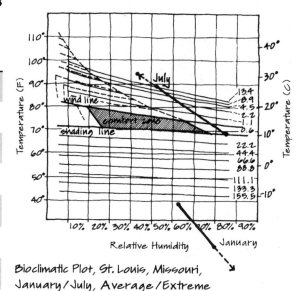

Bioclimatic Plot, St. Louis, Missouri, January / July, Average / Extreme

These values can then be added together to determine the relative importance of microclimatic variables found in the matrix. Table B shows **Values for Microclimatic Conditions Combinations by Climate and Season,** on a scale of 1–6. Looking at a Temperate winter condition in an outdoor room, for instance, the combination of Sun + Lee conditions has a relative value of 5, whereas Shade + Lee has a value of 2.

Select time periods to be analyzed from the bioclimatic chart, Technique 11. The following example shows a method for determining microclimates on a site, using the weightings for climatic elements by climate and season.

For the St. Louis example, the coldest month, January, and the hottest month, July, are used. The July average conditions call for admitting the wind and blocking the sun all day. The January average conditions call for admitting the sun and blocking the wind all day.

To analyze microclimates on a building site:

1) Determine shadow patterns using the sundial in Technique 1, and a site model to plot the shaded areas of the site for the time periods under consideration. 9 AM, 12 noon, and 3 PM are standard times to evaluate. A different drawing for each time is required.

2) Determine wind flow patterns for the site using Technique 6, with summer winds and winter wind directions. There should generally be one wind pattern for each season, unless there is a predictable daily change in wind direction (requires analysis of hourly data).

3) Convert the site shadow and wind pattern drawings to a grid cell system. Give each climatic condition (sun, shade, lee, wind) a different graphic representation.

4) Overlay the sun layer for each hour with wind layer to determine the combination of microclimatic conditions in each grid cell, for each of the drawings. You will typically have three "sun + wind" drawings for each season, one for each hour. Use the graphic designations shown, or your own symbols, to shade each cell.

5) Assign numerical values to the combination of conditions in each cell, based on the values in Table B.

6) Overlay the hourly combination layers for each season, adding the three values of each cell to obtain a map of composite ratings. Higher numbers indicate more favorable microclimates for the season indicated on each seasonal composite drawing. The composite drawings may then be rendered graphically for clarity.

7) If desired, the composite ratings for each season can be added to get an annual microclimate rating, and, if desired, values of each layer can be weighted. For instance, if annual heating degree days are twice as high as annual cooling degree days, the values of the winter microclimate could be doubled before they are added to the summer values. If siting is biased toward one season, consider what other design strategies could be used to mitigate for the opposite season.

The example on the next page shows a **Microclimate Analysis for a Hypothetical Site in St. Louis.** The wind patterns shown are from Technique 6. The shadow patterns shown are a composite of the shadow studies from Technique 1. Values used in the microclimate analysis were for the location of an outdoor room for summer and winter in a temperate climate. The higher values show the most advantageous locations.

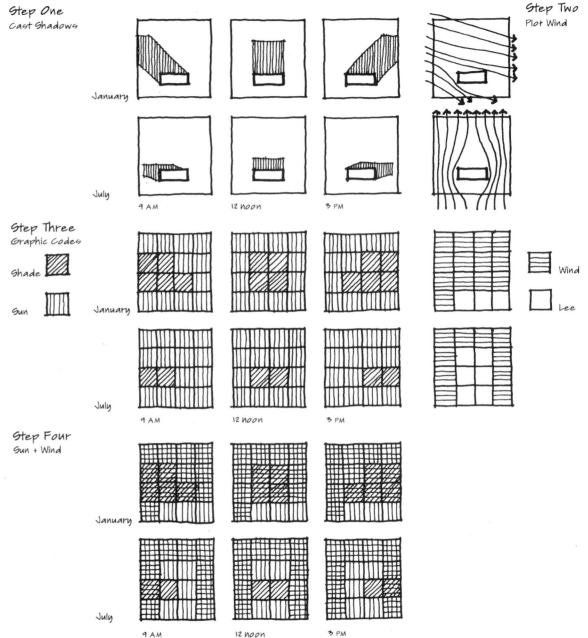

Step One
Cast Shadows

January

July

9 AM 12 noon 3 PM

Step Two
Plot Wind

Step Three
Graphic Codes

Shade

Sun

January

July

9 AM 12 noon 3 PM

Wind

Lee

Step Four
Sun + Wind

January

July

9 AM 12 noon 3 PM

Microclimate Analysis Method, Steps 1-4

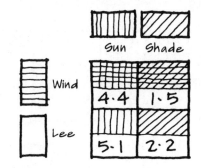

Sun   Shade

Wind

Lee

| 4·4 | 1·5 |
| 5·1 | 2·2 |

Key: Combined Values

Values in cells = Winter value/Summer value

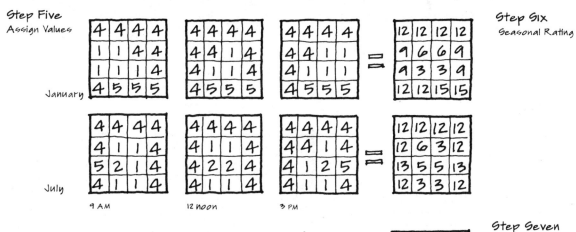

Step Five
Assign Values

Step Six
Seasonal Rating

January

9 AM   12 noon   3 PM

July

Step Seven
Annual Rating

24	24	24	24
21	12	9	21
22	8	8	22
24	18	18	27

Microclimate Analysis Method, Steps 5-7

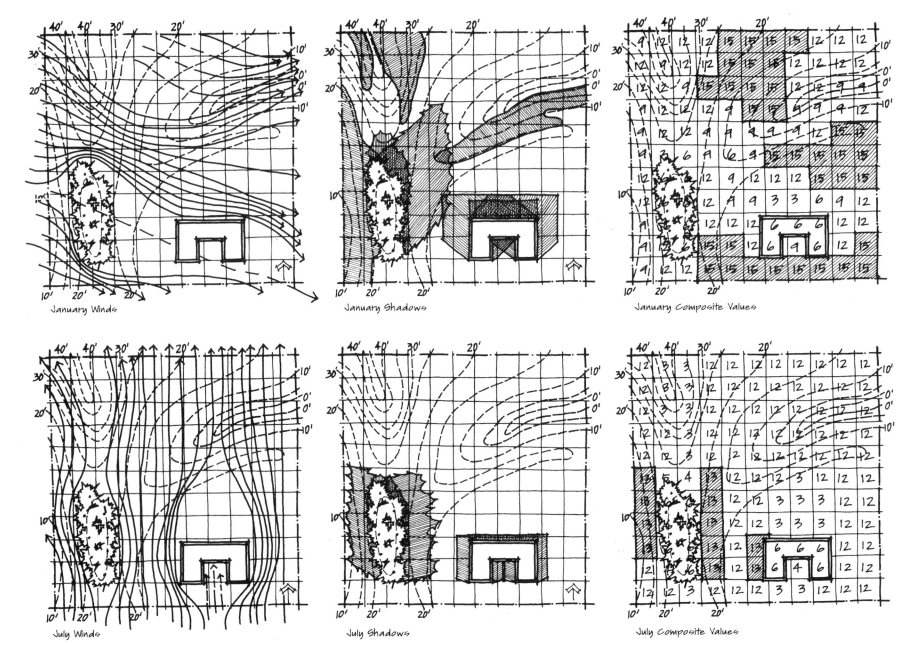

January Winds

January Shadows

January Composite Values

July Winds

July Shadows

July Composite Values

Microclimatic Analysis for a Hypothetical Site in St. Louis, Missouri

8 **Plotting *SKY COVER* can determine the dominant daylighting design condition for each month.**

For daylighting purposes, sky conditions are classified as either overcast, clear, or partly cloudy. Each classification has characteristics that influence daylighting design. (For a more extensive discussion, see Hopkinson et al., 1966, pp. 29–58, and B. H. Evans, 1981, pp. 95–105.) The overcast sky is defined as one in which the position of the sun cannot be determined due to density of cloud cover; the light is diffuse and relatively even over the sky dome. The overcast sky is three times brighter at the zenith than at the horizon, and the illumination is evenly distributed around the zenith. Therefore, the top of the sky dome is the source of the most illumination. The overcast sky is frequently used as the minimum design condition, though the actual amount of illumination can vary from a few hundred to several thousand foot-candles, depending on the altitude of the sun and the density of the cloud cover.

Illumination from the sun's direct rays is extremely powerful compared to that reflected from the sky dome; however, not including the sun, the clear sky is less bright than the overcast sky. The distribution of light from a clear sky, with the exception of the sun and the area immediately around it, is opposite that of the overcast sky—three times brighter at the horizon than at the zenith. Therefore, building openings that face the top of the sky dome, do not face reflective surfaces, and do not admit direct light may receive less light on clear days than on overcast days.

The illumination from a clear sky varies with the position of the sun, the season, and the amount of water vapor in the atmosphere. Therefore, the amount of illumination available to any surface will change throughout the day and year and may vary considerably depending on local conditions.

Sunlight reflected from the ground usually represents 10–15% of the total illumination reaching a vertical

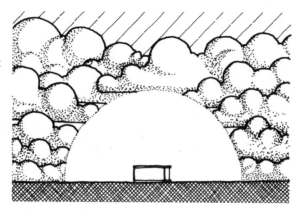

Overcast Sky

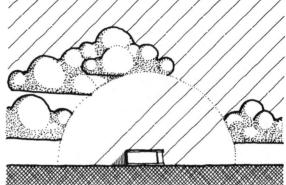

Partly Cloudy Sky

window, though it can account for more than 50% when the window is shaded from direct radiation. Reflected light from the ground can be a good source of daylighting during clear sky conditions because it reflects again off the usually lighter ceiling and penetrates deeply into the room. Because direct sunlight is so powerful, it is a potential source of glare and may introduce an undesirable source of heat gain.

The third classification, the partly cloudy sky, describes the most common condition. Days that are either uniformly overcast or perfectly clear are the exception in most regions of the United States. Most skies are partly cloudy and fall somewhere between the extremes of overcast skies that have a few clear spots and mostly clear skies that have a few clouds. Overcast skies with bright spots take on some of the character of clear skies in that illumination levels depend on sun position. Clear skies with clouds are frequently very bright if both direct sunlight and light reflected from clouds are

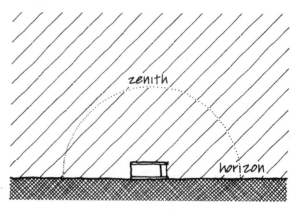

Clear Sky

available at the same time. Partly cloudy skies frequently exhibit very different amounts of illumination across the sky dome as the cloud cover changes over time. As a result, estimation procedures must be regarded as preliminary approximations. For more information on illumination levels, see IES (1993, pp. 366-7).

Daylighting conditions for your climate can be estimated by plotting the average number of clear, cloudy, and partly cloudy days as a percentage of the total days in the month. Sky cover "normals" can be found in a number of sources (NOAA, 1993, 1995).

To illustrate, in St. Louis, Missouri, the overcast condition predominates from November to June. Partly cloudy and clear days increase in summer, with September and October being the clearest months. The overcast condition is the primary concern in daylighting design, while the clear and partly cloudy days must also be accommodated.

If sky cover data are not readily available, the maps of Mean Sky Cover for the United States (Appendix B) can be used to determine the typical sky cover, and thus the daylight design condition, for each season.

Illumination resulting from a variety of cloud conditions can be approximated from the three graphs. Determine the solar altitude from a Sun Path Diagram (Technique 2) for the hour and month in question. Select the graph for the appropriate sky condition. Enter the chart at the altitude, move vertically to the appropriate curve, and then horizontally to read illumination.

	CLR DAYS 0/8-2/8	PT CD DAYS 3/8-6/8	OVR DAYS 7/8-8/8	% CLR	% PT CD	% OVR
Jan	7	7	17	23	23	55
Feb	7	6	15	25	21	54
Mar	7	8	16	23	26	52
Apr	7	8	15	23	27	50
May	7	10	14	23	32	45
Jun	7	11	12	23	37	40
Jul	9	11	11	29	35	35
Aug	10	11	10	32	35	32
Sep	11	8	11	37	27	37
Oct	12	8	11	39	26	35
Nov	8	7	15	27	23	50
Dec	7	7	17	23	23	55
Ann	101	101	164	28	28	45

Sky Cover Normals Data, St. Louis, MO

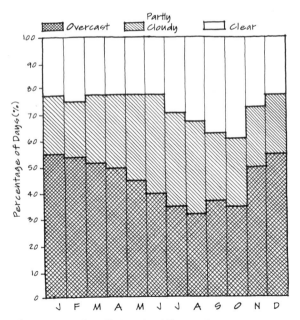

Sky Cover for St. Louis, Missouri

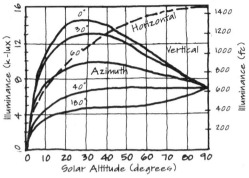

Clear Sky

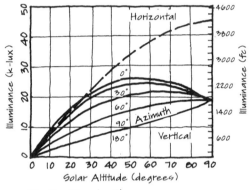

Partly Cloudy Sky

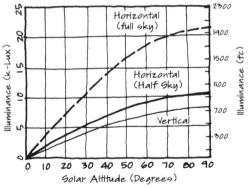

Overcast Sky

Illuminance Levels for Various Sky Conditions as a Function of Solar Altitude

HRS	CLR 0/10	SCT 1-5/10	BRK 6-9/10	OVR 10/10
0	32.8	11.2	10.2	45.9
3	33.5	11.0	10.8	44.7
6	30.8	12.8	8.9	47.6
9	18.3	12.6	17.2	51.9
12	17.5	15.4	19.6	47.5
15	19.9	15.4	18.4	46.3
18	23.3	15.0	15.0	46.7
21	30.9	12.1	11.6	45.4
ALL	25.9	13.2	13.9	47.0

Sky Cover vs. Hour , January, St. Louis, MO,
percentage of observations

HRS	CLR 0/10	SCT 1-5/10	BRK 6-9/10	OVR 10/10
0	45.2	21.7	16.1	17.0
3	42.6	22.4	15.0	20.0
6	23.4	26.8	23.9	25.9
9	25.2	24.5	24.4	25.9
12	9.8	32.6	33.7	23.9
15	6.9	37.5	34.9	20.7
18	16.7	36.1	27.7	19.5
21	33.2	29.3	20.9	16.6
ALL	25.4	28.9	24.6	21.2

Sky Cover vs. Hour , July, St. Louis, MO,
percentage of observations

A more detailed analysis of sky cover can be prepared with a sky cover square that relates varying sky cover to time of day and month of the year (Loftness, 1981, p. 41). Three-hour interval sky cover data can be found for most air force bases in the *Airport Climatological Summary* (U.S. Dept. of Commerce) for individual cities and in the *International Station Meteorological Climate Summary* (NCDC, 1996). Different sources will use different classifications for the fraction of sky cover assigned to a sky classification. The data example tables show sky cover data for four conditions in the months of January and July in St. Louis, Missouri (NCDC,1996). Appendix A has hourly average sky cover data for representative cities.

To construct the Sky Cover Square using the data from the International Station Meteorological Climate Summary, select the sky condition with the largest percentage for each 3-hr row. For example, in St. Louis during July 12 noon, "broken" (6/10 to 9/10 clouds) is the most common condition, while at midnight in July, "clear" (0/10 clouds) is the most common condition. Establish a graphic key for each condition and fill in each cell in the square.

The **Sky Cover Square for St. Louis** shows overcast conditions dominant from November to April during all hours, with decreasing cloudiness in late summer and fall. From June to October, there is a pattern of clear nights and cloudiness increasing to midday.

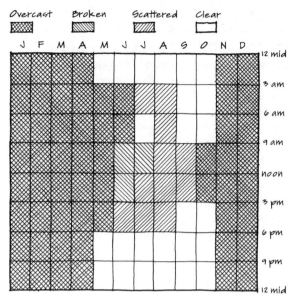

Sky Condition Square, St. Louis, Missouri

9 *DAYLIGHT AVAILABILITY* **data can be used to determine required daylight factors for design.**

The percentage of exterior illumination available inside the building is called the "daylight factor." It is a function of window size and placement (Strategies 94 and 92), sky obstructions (Strategy 10), glazing transmission (Strategy 101), and interior reflectances (Strategy 78). The total amount of exterior illumination available is a function of weather conditions and latitude. Based on the daylight design condition as determined in Technique 8, the required daylight factor can be determined from data for either cloudy days or for clear days.

Exterior illuminance under clear skies varies with season and with orientation. A horizontal plane receives much more light in summer than a vertical one. In winter at temperate latitudes, the south facade (north in the Southern Hemisphere) receives the most light. Whereas under overcast skies, orientation is relatively insignificant, under clear skies, the amount of illumination available to light buildings varies over the course of the day as the sun moves. North facades (S in SH) generally have stable light conditions throughout the day, while illumination on east and west orientations varies greatly.

There are two basic approaches to daylighting under clear skies: using small windows in direct sun and using moderately sized windows that "see" an external reflector but are shaded from direct sun. In the first approach, design daylight factors should be determined using the total illuminance, including direct sunlight. In the second, since the window and reflector have different orientations, two illuminance values must be used, as described in Strategy 92.

Illuminance values for either clear or overcast skies can be graphed to find the appropriate design values. Illuminance data for U.S. cities, given in kilolux, for five times during the day in four seasons can be found in Marion and Wilcox (1995) and are excerpted in the Appendix A for representative cities.

"Mostly Cloudy" conditions have more than 50% cloud cover, and "Mostly Clear" have less than 50% cover. These illuminance levels are total incident illuminance, including both the direct-beam solar, diffuse sky,

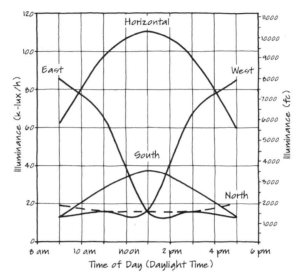

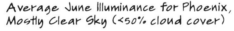

Average June Illuminance for Phoenix, Mostly Clear Sky (<50% cloud cover)

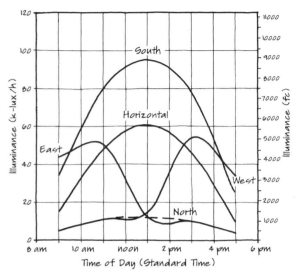

Average December Illuminance for Phoenix, Mostly Clear Sky (<50% cloud cover)

		June					December				
		9am	11am	1pm	3pm	5pm	9am	11am	1pm	3pm	5pm
HORIZ.	M.Clear	62	97	110	97	60	15	48	61	46	10
	M.Cloudy	50	81	95	84	50	10	34	45	33	8
NORTH	M.Clear	19	16	16	16	20	5	11	12	10	4
	M.Cloudy	19	19	18	19	19	4	11	14	11	4
EAST	M.Clear	86	65	16	16	13	44	50	12	10	4
	M.Cloudy	62	55	19	19	14	18	30	14	11	4
SOUTH	M.Clear	13	28	37	28	13	34	80	95	78	25
	M.Cloudy	14	28	36	29	14	15	44	57	44	11
WEST	M.Clear	13	16	17	67	85	5	11	15	54	34
	M.Cloudy	14	19	19	58	62	4	11	15	32	14
M.Clear	(% hrs)	82	83	84	83	83	55	57	54	54	53

Example Data for Phoenix, Arizona, Average Incident Illuminance (klux-hr)

and ground-reflected components. Hourly clear and cloudy sky illuminance data for 77 U.S. locations can be found in Robbins (1986).

The **Example Data for Phoenix, Arizona** shows an excerpt from Marion and Wilcox. The graphs of **Average Illuminance for Phoenix** show these illuminance data plotted for clear skies during summer and winter.

Using the graphs generated for the building's climate, for each orientation, considering the occupancy schedule of the building, choose the lowest illuminance value that occurs in any season.

For example, in a Phoenix office building operating 9 AM to 5 PM, a south window would receive about 13 kilolux (1200 foot-candles) in June and 25–34 klux (2300–3150 fc) in December, for the lowest illuminance hours of 9 AM and 5 PM local time. So 13 klux (1200 fc) should be used as the design value. If windows are sized using these values, then there will be more than enough daylight available indoors when the sky is brighter. In this case, shading devices should be provided for reducing the amount of light admitted during the middle of the day and during brighter seasons. Alternatively, a lesser daylight goal, with fewer work hours fully daylit, would make windows that were undersized for the lowest light conditions, but less oversized for the bright sky times.

To determine the required design daylight factor (DF%), divide the required interior illuminance by the available exterior illuminance and multiply by 100%. Interior illuminance recommendations can be found in Technique 13. With the design daylight factor known, windows can be then be sized in Strategy 94.

If local data are not available, typical values for the site's latitude can be used (Appendix B). Hourly illuminance can also be estimated from the graphs in Technique 8, using the sun's position.

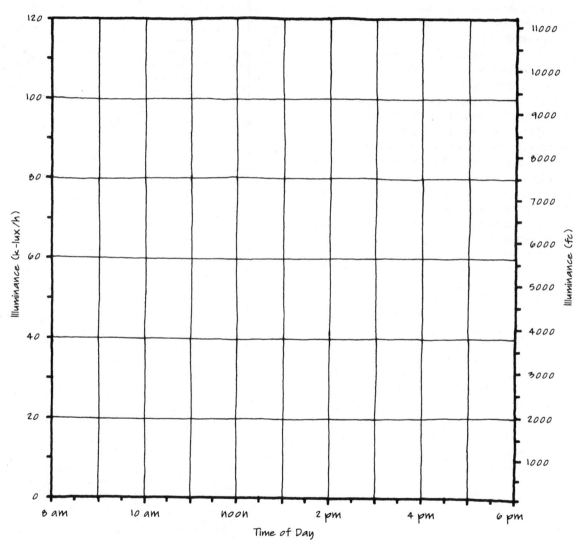

Sky Illuminance Graph

In climates that cycle seasonally from predominantly clear to predominantly cloudy, both clear and overcast illuminance levels, for the hours you want to provide full interior daylight, should be checked and the lowest value used.

If a daylight factor is assumed, then daylight availability curves can be used to determine the percentage of time that illumination level will be available for a given latitude and set of working hours (CIE, 1970, p. 5). This method may be used in the absence of local data for overcast conditions.

To find the daylight factor (DF) required to meet interior illumination goals, enter the chart at the latitude of your site and move down until intersecting the curve for the desired goal of daylit hours. Then read horizontally left to find the outdoor foot-candles (fc) available. Curves A through F correspond to the percentage of time the desired illumination levels will be met or exceeded for a given time interval. Time intervals and curve percentages can be determined from the lower table.

For example, entering the chart at 40° latitude, moving down to the C curve, for a goal of 90% annual daylit hours between 9 AM and 5 PM, reading horizontally left, we get about 650 fc (7000 lux) minimum outside. At this exterior illuminance level, a 10% DF is required to provide an average of 65 fc inside. It follows that a 1% DF provides 6.5 fc; a 2% DF, 13 fc, etc. For a building requiring 30 fc average, the minimum daylight factor that should be designed for the space is derived as follows: $DF_{req} = 30\ fc \div 650\ fc \times 100\% = 4.6\%$.

The daylight availability curves are based on average overcast weather conditions for typical climates; therefore, some years will have more or less light than the average condition, and some dry climates will have higher illumination levels.

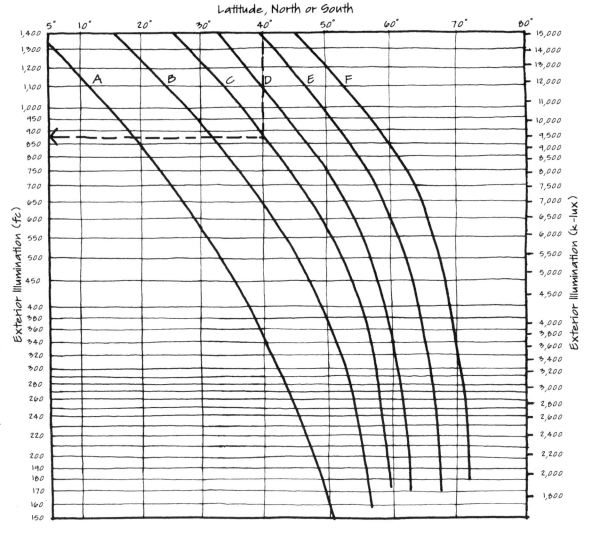

Percentage of Hours when Levels of Illumination Will Be Exceeded						
Curves	A	B	C	D	E	F
09.00 – 17.00	95	90	85	80	70	60
0.7.00 – 15.00	95	90	85	80	70	60
08.00 – 16.00	100	100	95	85	70	60
07.00 – 17.00	95	85	75	65	55	45
06.00 – 18.00	75	70	65	60	50	40

Key to Curves

Daylight Availablity Under Overcast Skies, by Latitude and Percentage of Hours

10 **The effect of DAYLIGHT OBSTRUCTIONS on a site can be estimated using daylight dot charts in conjunction with a sun path diagram.**

The amount of daylight available to a building is a function of the sky condition and, under clear skies, the sun position, which varies by latitude, date, and time. On a particular site, the available light is reduced by obstructions to the sky dome as seen from the building. These obstructions can be terrain, such as nearby hills, trees, or other buildings. Once the obstructions have been plotted on the sun path diagram using Technique 2, the Daylight Dot Charts can be used to estimate the light available on site as a fraction of the light available to an unobstructed site.

Daylight available to a building is usually considered to have two components: the sky component (SC), which is light from the diffuse sky; and the external reflected component (ERC), which is light bounced from the ground and other surfaces outside the building. The dot charts given in this technique are for both the sky and external components under CIE standard clear and overcast sky conditions (Moore, 1991, pp. 194–196, 234–242). For the clear sky condition, a different chart is given for 15° increments of solar altitude (Appendix B).

The dots on the accompanying charts are distributed based on the sky luminance distribution. Overcast skies are three times brighter at the zenith than at the horizon, while clear skies, neglecting light from the solar disk, are three times brighter at the horizon than at the zenith. Under clear skies, there is more light from the sky in the region near the sun.

To use the overcast SC dot chart, first prepare an obstruction mask of your site conditions as in Technique 2. This technique may also be used to plot an obstruction mask for a particular elevation from a point outside on the elevation (or at its base to be conservative), or for a particular window, with the mask drawn from a point inside a room.

Next, overlay the obstruction mask on the dot chart. For overcast conditions, the sky luminance is equal for all azimuths, so orientation is not important. Count the dots in the exposed part of the sky that are not covered by obstructions. Each dot repre-

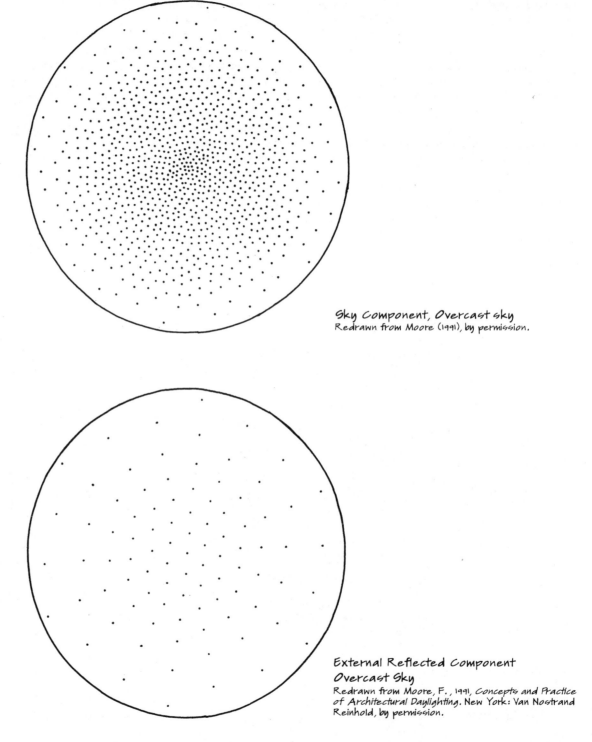

Sky Component, Overcast sky
Redrawn from Moore (1991), by permission.

External Reflected Component
Overcast Sky
Redrawn from Moore, F., 1991, Concepts and Practice of Architectural Daylighting. New York: Van Nostrand Reinhold, by permission.

sents a 0.1% daylight factor. Divide the number of dots by 10 (or multiply by 0.1) to determine the sky component as a percentage of unobstructed exterior illuminance.

The overcast SC dot chart works in exactly the same way. Daylight factor results from the SC and ERC charts can be added. The ERC chart assumes an average obstruction reflectance of 20%. If the reflectance of your external surfaces is not 20% (0.2), multiply the ERC daylight factor result by the actual exterior reflectance times 5.

The dot charts assume unglazed openings and must be reduced by factors to account for the glazing transmittance, window framing, and maintenance (dirt). See Strategy 10 for detail on glazing transmittance.

The clear sky SC charts work similarly to the overcast charts, except that orientation must be taken into account. The clear sky ERC chart is not specific to orientation.

From the sun path diagram, determine the solar altitude for the date and time being analyzed. From Appendix B, pick the clear SC dot chart that is closest to this altitude. Overlay the dot chart with the sun path diagram. Rotate the dot chart to the solar azimuth for the date and time you are analyzing. Count the visible dots and divide by 10, as described above.

For overcast skies, the daylight factor derived using the dot chart can be used for design. To do this, reduce the outdoor illuminance found in Technique 9 by the sum of SC and ERC components. For instance, if an unobstructed location has 1000 fc under overcast sky, the site in the example would have 1000 x (0.871 + 0.076) = 947 fc.

For clear skies, the available daylight varies considerably over the day and seasons. One design approach would be to evaluate the daylight available on each orientation of the building separately, using the dot chart for the lowest solar altitude that occurs during dates and hours when daylight is desired, such as 9 AM and 3 PM at the winter solstice. This would require a different obstruction mask for each orientation. For instance, an east-facing window can never be exposed to the western hemisphere of the sky dome, so that portion of the sun path diagram would be drawn as obstructed. With this strategy, one could size windows for low light conditions and then provide shading to reduce excess light and heat levels when the sky is brighter. Note that the sky is less bright opposite the sun. Since the sun is in a particular position only a short period each day, direct-beam light from the sun is most often ignored in architectural approaches to daylight design.

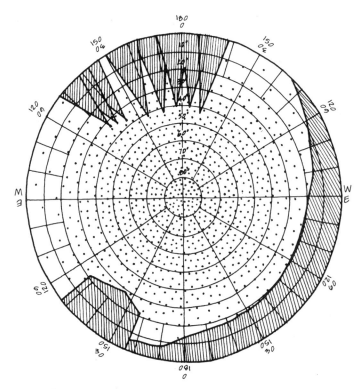

SC = 871 dots x 0.1% = 87.1%

Sky Component Dot Chart,
Overlaid With Site Obstructions

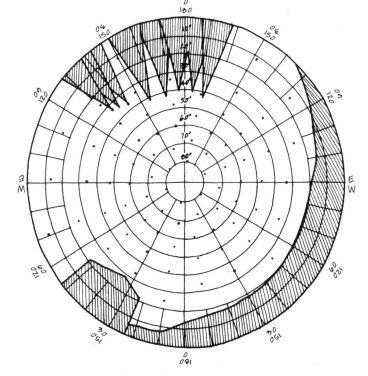

ERC = 76 dots x 0.1% each = 7.6%

External Reflected Component Dot Chart,
Overlaid With Site Obstructions

11 The *BIOCLIMATIC CHART* determines appropriate climatic responses that produce thermal comfort in a particular climate.

The bioclimatic chart shows the relationship of the four major climate variables that determine human comfort (Arens et al., 1980, p. 1202; Olgyay, 1963, p. 19). By plotting temperature and relative humidity, one can determine if the resulting condition is comfortable (within the comfort zone), too hot (above the top of the comfort zone), or too cold (below the bottom of the comfort zone). The chart shown, based on work by Arens et al., assumes a 0.8 clo level, which is typical for winter clothing, and an activity level of 1.3 Met, equivalent to slow walking or office work. Furthermore, if the temperature–humidity combination falls above the shading line, then shading is assumed. If the temperature–humidity combination is below the wind line, still air is assumed.

Point A corresponds to a temperature of 48 °F (8.9 °C) and a relative humidity of 52%, a condition usually described as too cold for comfort. Because point A is below the wind line, it is assumed that the wind is blocked. If the wind were not blocked, the condition would feel even colder due to the chilling effect of the wind.

The horizontal lines below the shading line indicate increments of solar radiation falling on a horizontal surface that can compensate for successively lower ambient air temperatures. At point A, if there were approximately 130 Btu/hr, ft² (410 W/m²) of solar radiation available, this would provide enough warmth to offset the low temperature, and a person would feel comfortable if there were no air movement.

At point B, with a temperature of 80 °F and 70% relative humidity, if a person were in the shade and a wind of 2.2 mph (2.0 m/s) were available, the cooling effect of the wind would produce comfort.

At point C, with a temperature of 92 °F (33.3 °C) and 15% relative humidity, conditions can be made comfortable by evaporating water into the air, thereby cooling it. The dotted lines indicate the amount of evaporation required per pound (or per kg) of dry air.

One of the most useful ways of analyzing a climate is to plot an average day for each month of the year on the bioclimatic chart. Temperature and humidity can be plotted hourly, in three-hour intervals, or in twelve-hour intervals. Because average maximum and minimum temperatures and humidities are easily available for many locations, twelve-hour intervals are usually the simplest to plot. A good source of information, usually in the local library, is *Climates of the States* (NOAA, 1985). This type of data can also be found in *Local Climatological Data, Annual Summary with Comparative Data,* for individual cities (U.S. Dept. of Commerce); in NOAA (1994 &1995); in Environment Canada (1993) for Canadian cities; and in NCDC (1996) for airports worldwide.

When using the average maximum and minimum, plot the maximum temperature paired with the minimum relative humidity and the minimum temperature paired with the maximum relative humidity. Draw a line connecting these two points. This line approximates the change in temperature and humidity over the day. By assuming that the high temperature occurs at 4 PM and the low temperature occurs at 4 AM, the line may be subdivided into equal increments that can be used to approximate the temperature and relative humidity at any time of the day.

Remember that this is only an approximation—the highs and lows do not occur at twelve-hour intervals in all seasons, and temperature does not change at a constant rate (Loftness, 1981, p. 13; Watson & Glover, 1981, p. 35).

Several types of information can be gathered from a plot of twelve months. For example, the bioclimatic chart for Phoenix indicates that while the climate is cold in the winter, it rarely gets below the point that can be offset by solar radiation. The amount of solar radiation available can be approximated by the methods outlined in Technique 3. The temperature–humidity lines for each day are long and fairly steeply inclined,

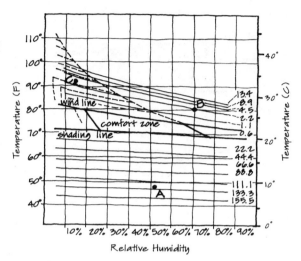

Bioclimatic Chart-Example Points

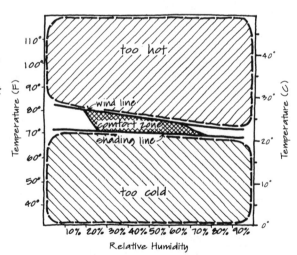

Interpreting the Bioclimatic Chart

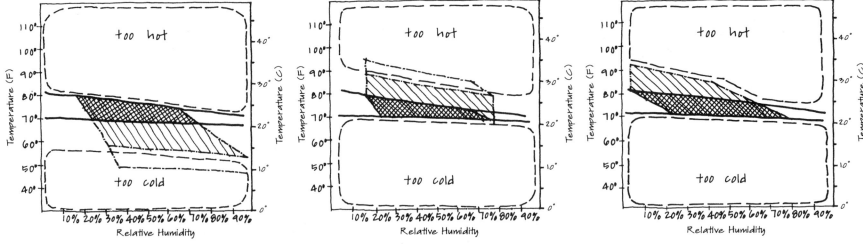

Extension of Comfort Zone With Sun

Extension of Comfort Zone With Wind

Extension of Comfort Zone With Evaporation

indicating large daily temperature swings. This indicates that heating and cooling techniques that store heat or cold from one time of the day to use in another may be effective. Evaporation alone will work as a cooling strategy in the months of May and June. To a limited extent, wind can be used to cool. The availability of wind can be estimated from the Wind Square (Technique 5).

Remember, these plots represent outdoor conditions. A building changes its internal microclimate by virtue of the thermal lag of its materials, its controlled infiltration rate, etc. This is especially true of large buildings, which generate a lot of internal heat and are therefore less affected by climate than smaller buildings. See Techniques 20, 22, and 23.

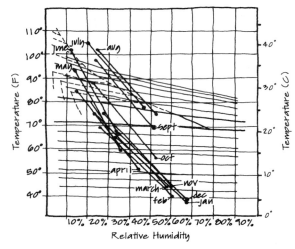

Monthly Temperatures-Phoenix, Arizona

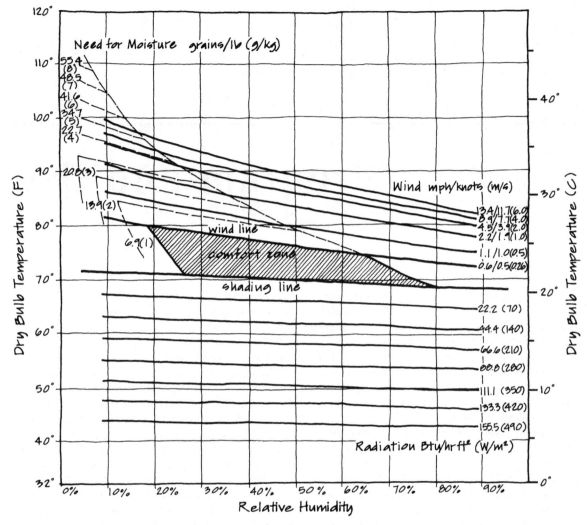

Bioclimatic Chart

IB   Program and Use

Knowing how and when a building is used is critical in determining the building's heating and cooling requirements. Buildings that have low levels of use generate little internal heat, and their heating and cooling needs depend on the climate's characteristics. If the climate is cold, buildings need heating; if it's warm, they need cooling. Buildings that have high levels of use may generate so much internal heat that no matter how cold it gets, they still need cooling. In most buildings, the rate and timing of internal heat generation is closely linked to occupancy. People give off heat, which is especially important when they are densely packed. But more importantly, when people enter a building, they turn on lights and equipment, both of which are sources of heat in a room. There are buildings in which equipment runs without many people, like computing centers or automated factories, but these are the exceptions, not the rule.

Because the internal heat gain is normally so closely linked to how people use the building, the rate of gain changes over the day and week. For example, an office building may experience its greatest gain in the morning and the afternoon, with a reduction at noon when people leave for lunch and a larger reduction at night and on weekends. Apartment buildings might experience quite a different pattern, generating heat in the early evening and on weekends. However, this gain is probably at a lesser rate than in an office building because there are fewer people and lights and less equipment per unit of floor area.

Cooling requirements for a building are frequently accentuated when the timing of internal heat gain coincides with heat gain from the climate. This is often the case in office buildings that experience intense use in the afternoon, coinciding in warm climates with the maximum outside temperatures and intense radiation on vertical west-facing surfaces. This occurs frequently in some areas, so that utility companies that supply electricity to those areas experience their peak loads in the afternoon. Design strategies that can reduce cooling loads during these peak periods not only reduce the building's need for energy, but also help reduce the area's need to build more electricity-generating capacity. Since many utilities set power rates based on a building's peak demand or on the utility's peak times, reducing the building's peak loads can also save an owner money on the most expensive power.

The analysis techniques in this section are divided into three groups: Occupancy, Electric Lighting, and Equipment. They are directed primarily at supplying information for Heating and Cooling Patterns, Techniques 22 and 23, and should be used in conjunction with them. However, because they reveal the most important major sources of internal heat generation, they can suggest design strategies to reduce these gains. For example, daylighting reduces the electric-lighting load and is usually available in the afternoon when the electric utility may be reaching its peak. The total rate of heat gain from people and equipment is also listed by building type in Technique 21. Heat gain from lights, taking into account reductions due to daylighting is similarly covered in Technique 21.

12 **Estimate _OCCUPANCY HEAT GAIN_ to understand the contribution of people to the building's heating and cooling requirements.**

The metabolic energy of people can contribute substantially to the amount of heat generated in the building. This heat may increase the cooling requirement in a hot climate or in a building that has a cooling load due to other internal sources of heat gain, or it may decrease the heating requirements of a building in a cool climate.

The amount of heat and moisture generated by people is a function of sex, age, activity, and other factors. Most passive cooling systems cannot remove water vapor from the air; therefore, only the sensible heat (that which raises the air temperature) gains are considered in determining the internal heat gains from people. Conventional mechanical refrigeration systems that remove moisture from the air in the cooling process require additional energy to condense the water vapor, to prevent an uncomfortable increase in humidity at the lower temperature. This additional load on the cooling system is called latent heat (Reynolds & Stein, 2000, p. 277) and should be added to the sensible heat gain to determine the total heat gain for systems that remove water vapor in addition to cooling the air.

The total sensible heat gain from people is found by multiplying the occupant density of the building by the rate of heat gain per person (ASHRAE, 1997, p. 28.8). The occupant density of a building may be determined for either peak or average conditions. The peak condition indicates the maximum requirements of the systems, frequently a passive plus backup system; the average occupancy indicates the capacity of the systems under normal conditions.

**The Rate of Heat Gain From People, per person, based on activity level, can be found from the table on the right. The approximate Occupant Density, in people per unit area, can be found from the table on the next page.**

In the **Occupant Density** table, the bold figures represent gross occupant densities for the entire building. Other figures, in regular type, such as for auditorium spaces or classrooms, represent net occupant densities for a single room. Figures in the Average column are for typical conditions, while the Maximum columns are for

Degree of Activity	Typical Occupancy	Sensible Heat Gain		Latent Heat Gain	
		Btu/hr	Watts	Btu/hr	Watts
Seated at rest, Seated very light work	Theatre	225–245	66–72	105–155	31–45
Moderately active office work, Walking slowly	Office, Bank Hotel, Retail, Apartment, Drugstore	250	73	200	59
Sedentary work, Light bench work	Restaurant, Factory	275	81	275–475	81–139
Moderate dancing	Dance hall	305	89	545	160
Walking fast, Moderately heavy work	Factory	375	110	625	183
Bowling, Heavy work, lifting	Factory, Bowling Alley	580–635	170–186	870–965	255–283
Athletics	Gymnasium	710	208	1090	319

Rate of Heat Gain from People, per person

peak load conditions, based on building code egress requirements, which may rarely occur. Figures from the two tables can be used to find the total rate of heat gain from people using the graph on the following page.

To determine the rate of internal gain from occupants, first locate on the horizontal axis the number of people per 100 ft² (100 m²) of occupied area (from the Occupant Density table). Then move vertically to the diagonal line corresponding to the people's activity level (from the Rate of Heat Gain From People table). Next move horizontally to the vertical axis, which indicates the rate of internal gain from people per unit of floor area.

Different occupancies for different parts of the building and different activity levels can be done separately and then summed.

Typical heat gain from people, lights, and equipment by building type is listed in Technique 21.

OCCUPANCY TYPE	OCCUPANT DENSITY			
	people/100 ft²		people/100 m²	
	Average	Maximum	Average	Maximum
Retail Bldgs.	0.7	3.0	8	32
Mall		2.0		22
Office Bldgs	0.4	0.7	4	8
Assembly Bldgs.	2.0		22	
Auditorium spaces	12.5	14.0	135	151
Conference rooms		5.0		54
Warehouse	0.1	0.5	1	5
Restaurant Bldgs.	0.7		8	
Dining rooms		7.0		75
Fast food, bars		10.0		108
Kitchens		2.0		22
Education Bldgs.	1.0	3.0	11	32
Classroom		5.0		54
Laboratory		3.0		32
Libraries		2.0		22
Grocery Stores	0.8	2.0	9	22
Lodging Bldgs.	0.4	0.5	4	5
Hospital patient rms.		1.0		11
Jail cells		2.0		22
Residential, multifamily	0.3	0.3	3	3
Dormitory sleeping rms.		2.0		22
Recreation Facilties				
Spectator areas		15.0		161
Gymnasium		3.0		32
Ball room		10.0		108

Occupant Density

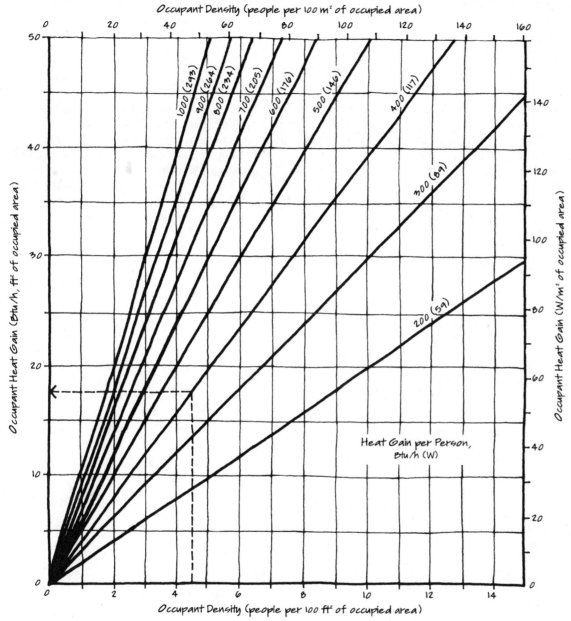

Estimating Heat Gain From Occupants

13 **Estimate *ELECTRIC LIGHTING HEAT GAIN* to understand its contribution to the building's heating and cooling requirements.**

Electric lighting contributes heat to occupied spaces as an inevitable by-product of its function as illumination. Unless special heat removal techniques are used, almost all of the electrical power fed into the lights eventually generates heat in the occupied space. The amount of heat generated from lights is a function of the illumination level and the efficiency of the light source.

To the degree that daylighting with an automated daylight-sensing control system is used to meet the desired illumination level, electric lighting levels may be reduced (Technique 21, Strategy 103). Lighting energy use, and thus heat gains, can also be reduced with automated switching systems, such as occupancy sensors and schedulers. In intermittent occupancy spaces (private offices, toilet rooms, etc.) or building types (warehouses, storage), energy savings and heat gain reduction from automatic switching of lights is in the range of 20–75%, with 35–45% typical (Eley Assoc., 1993, pp. 10-10 to 10-11).

To determine the heat gain from lights, assuming no daylighting contribution, first select the illuminance level appropriate for the building, space, or activity (IES, 1993, pp. 460, 459–78). Find this level on the vertical axis of the graph, then move horizontally until intersecting the zone representing the lighting type to be used. Finally, move vertically to the horizontal axis and read the heat gain per unit of lighted floor area.

The zones for each lighting type represent a range of average to high lamp/ballast efficacy. The luminous efficacy of lamps varies with their wattage and manufacturer and so some lamps and luminaires may have substantially more heat gains than the graph indicates. Lighting system efficiencies vary with the reflectances of room surfaces and the proportions and size of the room. The graph assumes light-colored surfaces and a fairly large room, about the size of a classroom. For more detailed estimation of gains from lights with different daylight factors and latitudes, see Technique 21.

Illuminance levels in buildings depend on both the desired subjective experience of a space and more objective, task-oriented criteria. In general, more light is required for tasks with higher difficulty, longer duration, lower contrast, higher risk, and smaller size; older people will also require more light.

Illuminance categories E and F are usually met with localized task lights covering small areas (see Strategy 102). Task areas, such as desks in an office, may often cover less than half of the total floor area, so task lighting levels should be applied only to specific task areas. To promote visual comfort and ease of adaptation, ambient light levels should be no less than one third of task illumination levels. For instance, a task level of 150 fc should have at least a 50-fc ambient illuminance level. For an extensive listing of illuminance recommendations, see IES (1993, pp. 459–478).

IES Category	Type of Activity	Illuminance (foot-candles)			Illuminance (lux)		
		low	mean	high	low	mean	high
	General Lighting						
A	Public spaces with dark surroundings	2	3	5	20	30	50
B	Simple orientation for short stay	5	7.5	10	50	75	100
C	Working spaces, occasional visual task	10	15	20	100	150	200
D	Visual task, high contrast of large size	20	30	50	200	300	500
	Illumination on Task						
E	Visual taks, medium contrast of small size	50	75	100	500	750	1000
F	Visual task, low contrast or very small size	100	150	200	1000	1500	2000

Illumination Levels by Activity Type

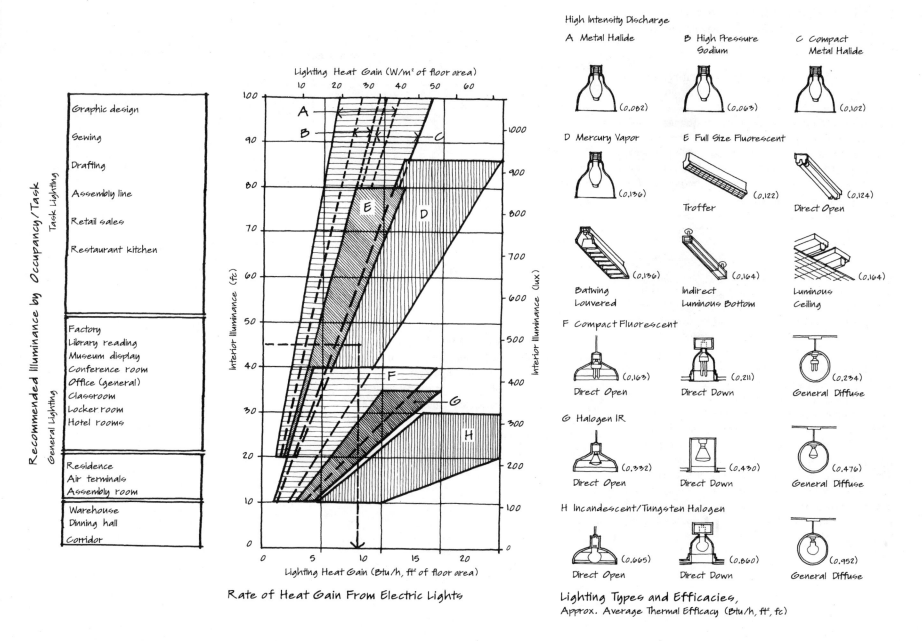

Recommended Illuminance by Occupancy/Task

Task Lighting

- Graphic design
- Sewing
- Drafting
- Assembly line
- Retail sales
- Restaurant kitchen

General Lighting

- Factory
- Library reading
- Museum display
- Conference room
- Office (general)
- Classroom
- Locker room
- Hotel rooms

- Residence
- Air terminals
- Assembly room

- Warehouse
- Dinning hall
- Corridor

Lighting Heat Gain (W/m² of floor area)

Interior Illuminance (fc)

Interior Illuminance (lux)

Lighting Heat Gain (Btu/h, ft² of floor area)

Rate of Heat Gain From Electric Lights

High Intensity Discharge

A Metal Halide (0.082)

B High Pressure Sodium (0.063)

C Compact Metal Halide (0.102)

D Mercury Vapor (0.136)

E Full Size Fluorescent

Troffer (0.122)   Direct Open (0.124)

Batwing Louvered (0.136)   Indirect Luminous Bottom (0.164)   Luminous Ceiling (0.164)

F Compact Fluorescent

Direct Open (0.163)   Direct Down (0.211)   General Diffuse (0.234)

G Halogen IR

Direct Open (0.332)   Direct Down (0.430)   General Diffuse (0.476)

H Incandescent/Tungsten Halogen

Direct Open (0.665)   Direct Down (0.860)   General Diffuse (0.952)

Lighting Types and Efficacies,
Approx. Average Thermal Efficacy (Btu/h, ft², fc)

14 **Estimate *EQUIPMENT HEAT GAIN* to understand its contribution to the building's heating and cooling requirements.**

Electrical equipment and appliances operating in a space contribute heat to that space as a by-product of their operation. The amount of heat generated is a function of the type and efficiency of equipment used, the amount of equipment, and how often it is operated.

All of the electric energy that goes into equipment, such as electric motors and computers, ends up as waste heat in the space. Heat gain from equipment can be reduced by selecting more efficient equipment and equipment designed to turn itself off or go into a low-power mode when not in use, such as products with EPA Energy Star ratings.

Typical equipment heat gains for some building types are given in the table. "High" values are based on surveys of existing building stock up to the early 1990s; these figures represent average values for existing buildings, and can reasonably be equated with low-efficiency/high-energy-use equipment installed in new construction. The "low" column represents equipment that is 40% more energy efficient than the higher energy use levels. This roughly corresponds to the difference between typical efficiencies and the highest efficiency products generally available on the market.

Figures include the sensible component of space heat gains from service hot water systems inside conditioned spaces, including standby losses from storage and distribution and tap water heat retained. Insulating hot water storage, using tankless, on-demand hot water heaters, and insulating hot water pipes are ways to reduce heat gains from hot water systems. In warm climates, locate hot water heaters and storage in unconditioned spaces.

Building Type	Heat Gain, Btu/hr, ft²		Heat Gain, W/m²	
	low	high	low	high
Mercantile & Sales	3	5	10	17
Office	3	5	10	17
Assembly	1	2	4	7
Warehouse	2	4	8	13
Restaurant	10	16	31	52
Education	4	7	14	23
Grocery	8	13	24	42
Lodging	3	5	10	17
Residential	1	2	3	6

Heat Gain From Equipment

When the exact equipment and operating schedule are known, their heat contribution may be estimated from the tables in *ASHRAE Handbook of Fundamentals* (1997, pp. 28.9–28.14). These more specific heat gain estimates are especially useful for special building types, such as laboratories and factories, or for areas within buildings, such as kitchens, with a high concentration of equipment.

Typical heat gain from equipment, lights, and people by building type is listed in Technique 21.

IC   # Form and Envelope

The building itself is the third basic factor that influences the heating and cooling requirements. Its shape and construction greatly influence how much of the climate and internal loads are actually translated into heating or cooling requirements. For example, a building located in a sunny, hot climate experiences a tremendous load from the sun per unit area of surface. However, if the building is shaped and oriented so as to reduce the area exposed to the sun, the glazing is shaded, and the walls are insulated, much of that solar load can be prevented from increasing the cooling requirements.

Like the techniques in the Program and Use section, these techniques are primarily directed at supplying information to Heating and Cooling Patterns (Techniques 22 and 23) and probably will be used most often in conjunction with them. Technique 15, Skin Heat Flow, estimates how fast the heat will flow through the building's skin for each degree of temperature difference between inside and outside temperatures. The designer can understand how the ratio of skin area to floor area, percentage of window area, and wall construction affect the rate of heat flow. Because this rate of heat flow depends on a temperature difference, it is not important for some passive systems, like natural ventilation, which do not depend on creating a difference in temperature between inside and out. The rate of heat flow is also related to occupancy because the inside temperature is determined by human comfort criteria. When the building isn't occupied, the inside temperature can be allowed to float at or nearer to the outside temperature, thereby reducing the temperature difference between inside and out and the magnitude of heat flow.

Technique 17, Ventilation/Infiltration Gain and Loss, is related to both occupancy and envelope construction. When outside air enters the building it must be either heated or cooled if a difference in temperature is being maintained between inside and out. Air that leaks in (infiltration) is not related to occupancy but the amount of ventilation air required is, and therefore heating or cooling that air can be greatly reduced when the building isn't occupied.

Heat gain from the sun, analyzed with Technique 16, Window Solar Gain, is very dependent on the building's form, orientation, and amount of glazing, as well as the climate, which determines the sun's availability. Estimating solar impact is somewhat time-consuming and, if the glazing area is very small or if the climatic and internal gains are such that conditions are only accentuated, not changed, then heat gain through glazing may be omitted. This technique will demonstrate to the designer the degree of importance to the building's heat gain rate of design variables such as the amount of glazing, its orientation, and its shading.

Typical skin and ventilation loss/gain and solar gain can be estimated by building type in Technique 21, Total Heat Gains and Total Heat Losses.

15 Estimate *SKIN HEAT FLOW* to understand its contribution to the building's heating and cooling requirements.

The amount of heat that flows through a building's skin due to a temperature difference between inside and outside is a function of the magnitude of that difference, the resistance to heat flow by the skin materials, and the area of the skin. Because heat flows from hot to cold, if the inside is warmer than the outside, the heat will flow outward. If the inside is cooler than the outside, the heat will flow inward.

The rate of heat flow through building materials is usually described in terms of resistance *(R)*. *R* is the number of hours needed for 1 Btu to flow through one square foot of skin, given a temperature difference of 1 °F. The units for *R* are ft², °F, h/Btu (or m², K/W). The reciprocal of *R,* the *U*-value, is the number of Btu's that will flow through one square foot of building skin in one hour, given a temperature difference of 1 °F. The units for *U* are Btu/hr, °F, ft² (or W/K, m²) (Reynolds & Stein, 2000, p. 128).

Glass has a much lower resistance to heat flow than other building materials. For example, single glazing has a *U*-value of 1.13 Btu/hr, °F, ft² (*R* = 0.88) or in metric, USI = 6.41 W/K, m² (RSI = 0.15), while an uninsulated wood stud wall has a *U*-value of 0.24 Btu/hrr, °F, f² (*R* = 4.17) or in metric, USI = 1.36 (RSI = 0.73). The resistance of opaque walls increases dramatically as insulation is added to the wall, at a rate of approximately *R* = 3–4 /in of insulation (RSI = 0.2–0.3/cm of insulation). Therefore, the amount of insulation after the first inch (2.5 cm) or so becomes much more important in determining the overall *U*-value of the skin than the rest of the skin assembly. (See ASHRAE, 1997, pp. 24.4–24.7 for a listing of the thermal resistance of building materials, or Reynolds & Stein, 2000, pp. 147–174.)

For insulation recommendations in your climate, see Strategy 76 (See Balcomb et al., 1984, pp. 2–1 to 2–7, for more discussion of balancing energy conservation with the use of solar energy.) In skin-load-dominated, passively cooled buildings, insulation may be more important for reducing solar heat gain than for reducing temperature-caused loads through the skin. Therefore,

the roof, with its large solar load, may be very well insulated, while the walls may be only moderately insulated. Buildings in cool climates that have a cooling load because they generate so much internal heat can be "poorly" insulated to increase the rate of heat loss, but when using low levels of insulation in cold climates, keep in mind that the insulation also plays a role in keeping wall surface temperatures warm. Warm walls increase comfort by reducing drafts and reducing the area of cold surfaces within the occupants' radiant field.

Because glazing is more thermally conductive than insulated skin, much more heat flows through the glazing, per unit of area, than through the insulated skin.

The overall **U***-value for a combination of insulated and double-glazed skin may be found in the nomograph. Enter the left-hand horizontal axis with an area-weighted average* **U***-value of the opaque skin. Move vertically to the diagonal line that represents the percentage of skin area in double glazing. Then move horizontally to the vertical axis to find the overall* **U***-value of the glazed and opaque wall. Continue horizontally to the diagonal line that represents the ratio of the exposed skin area to floor area; then vertically again to the right-hand horizontal axis to determine the heat flow through the skin per unit of building floor area.*

Since double glazing insulates about twice as well as single glazing, one can use this graph for single glazing by assuming a percentage of glazing equal to twice that of the actual glazing area. This graph can also be used in the reverse order; starting from the overall heat flow (such as a maximum allowable heat loss criteria) one can determine the required *U*-value for the opaque skin.

Total heat gain through the skin can be calculated based on outdoor temperature in Technique 21.

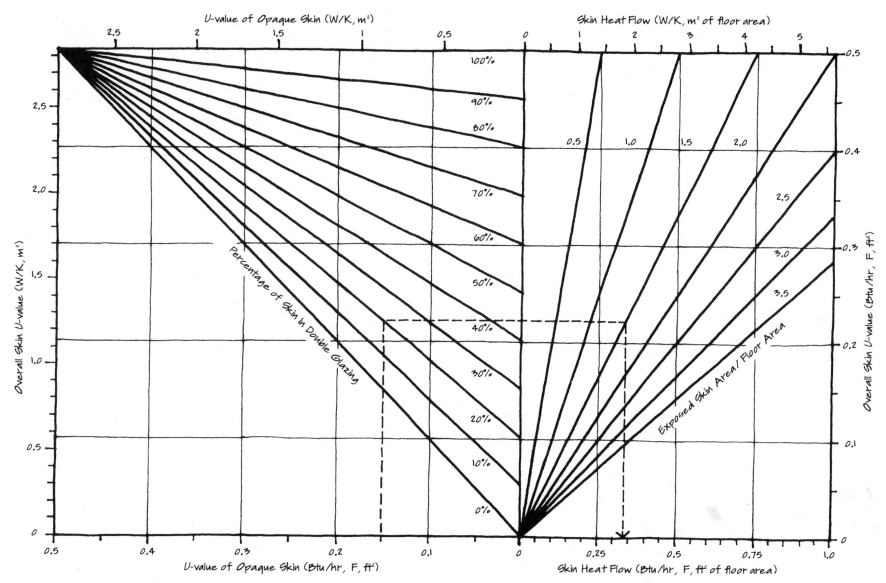

Estimating Heat Flow Through the Skin

16 Estimate *WINDOW SOLAR GAIN* to understand the sun's contribution to the building's heating and cooling requirements.

The amount of solar radiation transmitted through the skin of a building is a function of the available radiation and the area, orientation, and heat transmission characteristics of the exposed skin. If the skin is opaque, 0–12% of the available solar heat will eventually reach the interior spaces, depending on the color of the exterior surface and its insulating qualities.

While solar heat gain through opaque surfaces can be large, especially through poorly insulated roofs, it is usually small compared to the solar gain through glazing, which can be as high as 85% of the incident radiation. The amount of radiation gained through single-pane clear glass under clear skies, known as the Solar Heat Gain Factor (SHGF) can be found in ASHRAE (1997, pp. 29.29–29.35) for 16°–64° lat., Mazria (1979, pp. 444–492) for 28°–56° lat., and in Reynolds & Stein (2000, pp. 1636–1645) for 16°–64° lat., conventional and SI units. Values are tabulated by latitude, month, time of day, and orientation and are given in Btu/hr, ft^2 or W/m^2. One of the quickest and easiest ways to find SHGFs is the *PEC Solar Calculator* (Benton & Marcial, 1993).

Clear-day radiation data are used to calculate the SHGF. These data can be used without modification to predict the heat gain through windows for the worst-case cooling situation. Average conditions can be roughly approximated by adjusting the SHGF by the percentage of possible sunshine for the month, as listed in *Local Climatological Data, Annual Summary with Comparative Data* (U.S. Dept. of Commerce) for individual locations or NOAA (1995). For example, if the SHGF is 300 Btu/hr, ft^2 and the percentage of possible sunshine for the building's location is 60%, multiply 300 by 0.60 to find the average radiation of 180 Btu/hr, ft^2. Maps of percentage of mean possible sunshine can be found in NOAA (1993) and Environment Canada (1988).

The SHGF for clear single glass should be reduced by the shading coefficient of the glazing itself (if of any other type) and of the internal and external shading devices (ASHRAE, 1997, p. 29.28; Olgyay, 1963, p. 68).

Shading coefficients for typical windows are listed in the table. Windows in the upper section of the table show the shading coefficient for operable windows, including the reductions from the window's frame (ASHRAE, 1997, pp. 29.24–29.26). Therefore, gross window area should be used with these figures. The lower section of the table shows shading coefficients for various other glazings, without the effect of frames. If these glazings are used in conventional window situations, with frames and mullions, the shading coefficient should be multiplied by about 0.8.

Shading coefficients for internal and external shading can be estimated from the chart on the next page.

The shading value of interior drapes varies substantially with color, and fabric, while other interior devices vary with color and degree of translucency (Strategy 100). The shading coefficient within the range indicated for fixed shading elements depends on the exact design used. Trees are especially variable by species, season if deciduous, and climate (see Strategy 99). Movable vertical and horizontal shading devices can achieve very low shading coefficients, but view and potentially daylight will be blocked when fully employed.

To determine the solar heat gain through windows in a particular roof or wall, enter the graph on the left side horizontal axis with the SHGF (clear or average day) for the appropriate orientation, slope, hour, latitude, and month. Draw a line vertically until it intersects the diagonal line corresponding to the percentage of glazing in the roof or wall. Next, move horizontally until intersecting the diagonal line corresponding to the product of the shading coefficient for the glazing and shading devices. (If only the glazing or only shades are present, use just the one shading coefficient corresponding to either the glass or shade.) Move vertically to the horizontal axis to read the solar heat gain through the windows per unit of skin area. These values do not include the gain through the opaque section of the skin.

GLASS TYPE	SHADING COEFFICIENT
GLASS + FRAME	
Single, clear	0.69- 0.73
bronze	0.53 -0.62
green	0.50- 0.61
gray	0.48 -0.60
reflective	0.17 - 0.28
Double, clear	0.60- 0.70
bronze	0.43 - 0.53
green	0.40 -0.52
gray	0.38- 0.51
HP green	0.33
reflective	0.12 - 0.20
Double - Low E, clear	0.32 - 0.60
bronze	0.23 - 0.48
green	0.27 - 0.47
gray	0.21 - 0.46
HP green	0.25 - 0.39
Triple, clear	0.52 - 0.58
HP green	0.30
Triple – 1 low E layer	0.45 - 0.53
Triple – 2 low E layers	0.28 - 0.39
GLASS ONLY	
Single Acrylic, clear	0.98
bronze	0.46 - 0.90
gray	0.52 - 0.89
Single polycarbonate, clear	0.98
bronze	0.74
gray	0.74
Double Clear, shading inbetween	
w/ venetian blinds between	0.33 - 0.36
w/ sun screen between	0.43 - 0.49
Domed Skylights, clear	0.81 -0.99
Glass Block, clear	0.65
gray	0.24
reflective	0.16
Kalwall	0.99

Shading Coefficients of Windows and Glazings

Shading Coefficient

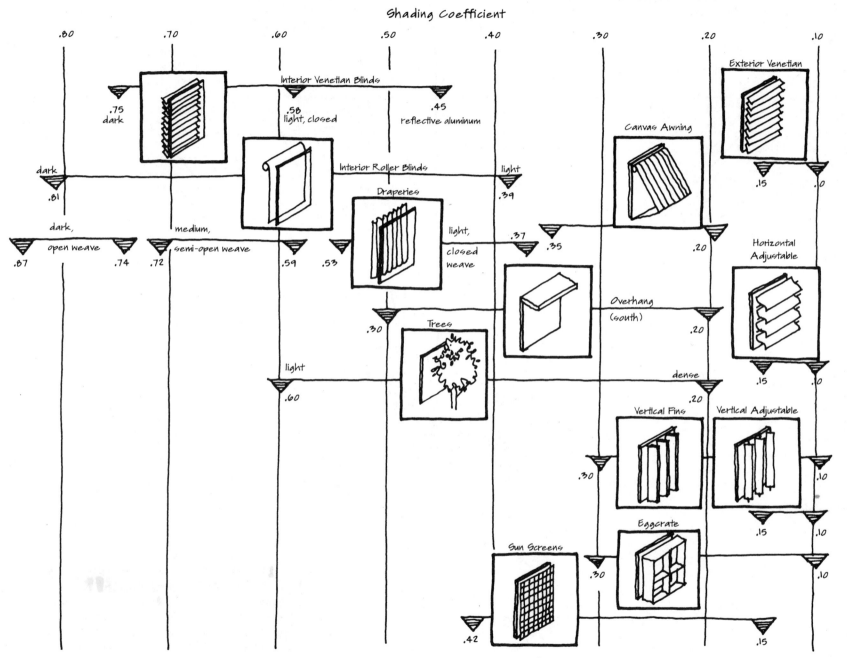

.80   .70   .60   .50   .40   .30   .20   .10

Interior Venetian Blinds

.75 dark   .58 light, closed   .45 reflective aluminum

Exterior Venetian

.15   .0

dark   Interior Roller Blinds   light

.81   .39

Canvas Awning

dark, open weave   medium, semi-open weave   Draperies   light, closed weave   Horizontal Adjustable

.87   .74   .72   .59   .53   .37   .35   .20

Overhang (south)

.30   Trees   .20   .15   .0

light   dense

.60   .20

Vertical Fins   Vertical Adjustable

.30   .15   .10

Eggcrate

Sun Screens   .30   .15   .10

.42   .15

Shading Coefficients of Different Internal and External Shading Devices

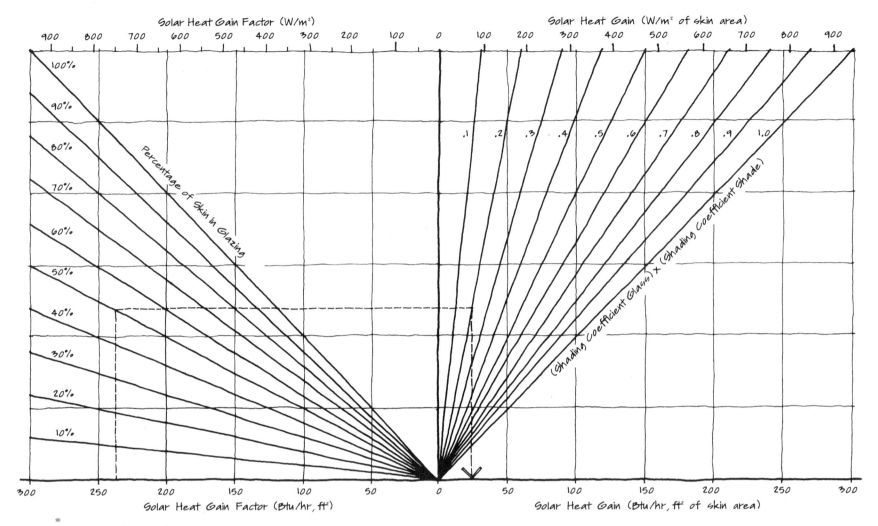

Estimating Solar Heat Gain

Multiply the heat gain in Btu/hr, ft² (or W/m²) of skin by the area of skin to determine the solar heat gain for that entire surface. Complete this procedure for each surface for the same time and date. Then add these solar heat gains and divide the sum by the number of square feet (or m²) in the building to determine the solar heat gain per unit of floor area for that particular month and time of day.

A quick estimated method for the solar heat gain rate per unit of floor area can be found in Technique 21.

17 Estimate *VENTILATION or INFILTRATION GAIN AND LOSS* to understand their contribution to the building's heating and cooling requirements.

Whenever the inside temperature of a building is higher or lower than the outside temperature, air that leaks into the building (infiltration) or is drawn into it for fresh air (ventilation) must be either heated or cooled. In passively heated or cooled buildings that are well insulated and maintain a substantial difference in temperature between inside and outside and in buildings with a high occupancy level, the heating and cooling of outside air can become a significant percentage of the thermal load.

The table for Heat Gain/Loss From Ventilation in Commercial and Multifamily Buildings presents the heat loss and gain in Btu/hr, °F, ft² of building floor area (W/K, m²) by building type.

Average values are for typical conditions, while Maximum values represent peak occupancy conditions. These figures can be reduced by 60–80% if a heat recovery ventilation system is used (Strategy 108) or by about 50% if air flow windows are used (Strategy 95).

The table is developed based on occupant densities as presented in Technique 12, and ventilation volume rates from ASHRAE Standard 62-1989, *Ventilation for Acceptable Indoor Air Quality* (ASHRAE, 1989b). Recommended ventilation rates can also be found in Reynolds and Stein (2000, pp. 180–187) and in Tao and Janis (1997, pp. 61–62).

The table for Heat Gain/Loss From Residential Ventilation/Infiltration presents the heat loss and gain in Btu/hr, °F, ft² of building floor area (W/K, m²) by different levels of attention to construction detailing, which affects the building's air tightness (see Balcomb et al., 1984, pp. 6–5).

Average values are for typical conditions, assuming a 7.5-mph (3.4-m/s) wind; while Maximum values represent peak heat loss or gain conditions under a 15-mph (6.7-m/s) wind. Higher wind speeds create more wind pressure on the building envelope, driving more air through cracks. The infiltration rate for a building can vary by 50% or more from these values, depending on climatic conditions and construction details. The heat gain/loss rate for a building with a heat recovery sys-

Building Type / Room	Ventilation Heat Gain/Loss Btu/hr, F, ft²		Ventilation Heat Gain/Loss W/K, m²	
	Average	Maximum	Average	Maximum
Retail Bldgs.	0.08	0.32	0.43	1.84
Mall		0.22		1.23
Office Bldgs.	0.09	0.15	0.49	0.86
Assembly Bldgs.	0.32		1.84	
Auditorium spaces	2.03	2.27	11.49	12.87
Conference rooms		1.08		6.13
Warehouse	0.01	0.05	0.06	0.31
Restaurant Bldgs.	0.15		0.86	0.00
Dining rooms		1.51		8.58
Fast food, bars		3.24		18.38
Kitchens		0.32		1.84
Education Bldgs.	0.16	0.49	0.92	2.76
Classroom		0.81		4.60
Laboratory		0.65		3.68
Libraries		0.32		1.84
Grocery Stores	0.13	0.32	0.74	1.84
Lodging Bldgs.	0.06	0.08	0.37	0.46
Hospital patient rms.		0.27		1.53
Residential, multifamily	0.05	0.05	0.28	0.28
Dormitory sleeping rms.		0.32		1.84
Auto Repair Shop		1.62		9.19
Recreation Facilities				
Spectator areas		2.43		13.79
Gymnasium		0.65		3.68
Ball room		2.70		15.32

Heat Gain/Loss From Ventilation in Commercial and Multifamily Buildings

tem represents the effective rate, including the effects of the heat exchanger. Homes with an infiltration rate less than 0.5 air changes per hour (ACH) should generally use mechanical ventilation, to insure good indoor air quality. ASHRAE recommends a minimum fresh air volume of 0.35 ACH, or 15 cubic feet per minute per occupant (ASHRAE, 1997, p. 25.20; 1989b).

For heat gain that imposes a cooling load on the building, the values in both tables are for sensible heat only and do not include the energy that would be necessary for dehumidification. Dehumidification is not possible in most passive cooling systems but would be an important part of cooling loads in conventional refrigeration systems. Rule-of-thumb estimated heat gains from ventilation for different summer outdoor design temperatures are also covered in Technique 21, Total Heat Gains.

Residential Construction Type	Infiltration Heat Gain Btu/hr, F, ft²		Infiltration Heat Gain W/K, m²	
	Average (7.5 mph)	Maximum (15 mph)	Average (3.4 m/s)	Maximum (6.7 m/s)
Older buildings with leaky doors and windows	0.18	0.36	1.02	2.04
Conventional insulated frame construction	0.14	0.27	0.77	1.53
+ plastic vapor barrier	0.09	0.18	0.51	1.02
+ sealed joints & foamed cracks	0.05	0.09	0.26	0.51
+ advanced sealing & heat recovery unit/ system	0.02	0.05	0.13	0.26

Heat Gain/Loss From Residential Ventilation/Infiltration

ID   Combining Climate, Program, and Form

While each of the analysis techniques outlined in this book may be used separately, many of them are designed to be used together to form the base of data for Technique 23, Balance Point Profiles. Because climate and occupancy change over the day and the season and because they both interact with the building form, heating and cooling requirements are difficult to predict, making it hard to select appropriate daylighting and passive solar heating and cooling strategies. Analysis Technique 23 helps the designer identify which of three generic heating and cooling patterns applies for different times of the year and under different occupancy conditions. Once the generic patterns have been identified, the appropriate heating, cooling, and daylighting strategies can be determined.

Analysis Technique 22, Balance Point Temperature, helps the designer determine the exterior temperature at which the building makes the transition from a heating need to a cooling need for the particular conditions of climate, form, and program. This temperature can then be compared to the outside temperature to see if

the building needs heating or cooling. Technique 21, Total Heat Gains and Total Heat Losses, allows a quick estimation of rates used to calculate the balance point. These same rates can be used to develop the generic patterns in Technique 23. The total rate of heat gain is needed to size passive cooling design strategies in Part Two. The total heat loss rate can be compared to conservation criteria that are assumed to be met by the passive solar heating design strategies in Part Two.

If the building is residential or does not generate much internal heat, Technique 18, the Building Bioclimatic Chart, can be used to determine the most appropriate passive solar heating and cooling strategies. Technique 19, Earth Contact, can be used to identify issues and appropriateness of earth sheltering design strategies.

The balance point temperature is used again in Technique 20, Shading Calendar, to identify the dates and times that are above the balance point and therefore, become the criteria for shading design.

18 The *BUILDING BIOCLIMATIC CHART,* when plotted with monthly temperatures and relative humidities, identifies potential passive solar heating and cooling strategies appropriate for the building's climate.

On the bioclimatic chart, plot two points: first, the average minimum temperature for one month by the maximum relative humidity; second, maximum temperature by minimum relative humidity. Connect these points with a straight line and repeat the process for each month of the year. Each line represents the change in temperature and relative humidity over an average day. (See Technique 11 for a more complete explanation of this procedure and the bioclimatic chart.)

The bioclimatic chart is subdivided into zones that define passive solar heating and cooling strategies, based on the work of Milne and Givoni (in Watson, 1979, pp. 96–113) and later work by Givoni (1998, pp. 22–45). This version of the chart differs in form but not in concept from the version by Arens et al. (1980), shown in Technique 11. The zones crossed by the lines plotted indicate strategies that may be appropriate for that climate. In most temperate climates, there will be a seasonal change from one strategy to another. Furthermore, some months lend themselves to several different strategies. In most cases, to reduce costs, the designer should select a few strategies that are compatible with each other and with other design issues. The design strategies are illustrated and described in more detail in Part Two.

The design strategies suggested by this version of the bioclimatic chart are appropriate only for residences and those other buildings with small internal heat gains. A residential rate of heat gain is assumed to be about 20 kBtu/day per person (21,100 kJ/day per person).

Passive solar heating is usually an appropriate strategy for months when the plotted lines fall below the comfort zone. The solar heating zone is based on certain assumptions about glazing areas and insulation levels. It may be extended to lower temperatures depending on building design, radiation levels, and the desired solar savings fraction.

COMBINING CLIMATE, PROGRAM, & FORM/ Design Strategies 18

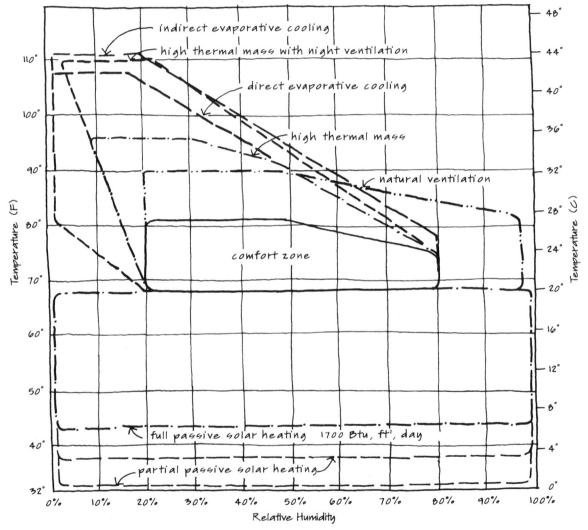

Building Bioclimatic Chart (for skin-load-dominated buildings)

There are five cooling strategies represented by the five somewhat overlapping zones above the comfort zone: 1) natural ventilation, which depends solely on air movement to cool occupants; 2) large thermal mass, which depends on the building's materials to store heat during the day and reradiate it at night; 3) large thermal mass combined with night ventilation, which relies on mass heat storage during the day and ventilation at night to cool the mass; and two types of evaporative cooling, 4) direct, and 5) indirect. Direct evaporative cooling raises the humidity and lowers the temperature of the indoor space. Indirect evaporative cooling, such as the cooling of the outside of a roof or wall by evaporating water on its surface, lowers the temperature of a building element, which then becomes a heat sink for the adjacent space (Givoni, 1994, p. 147). To assess the appropriateness of earth sheltering strategies in the building's climate, see Technique 19.

All of these strategies fall into one of three general categories: open, closed, or open/closed. The open building depends on its connection to the outside wind environment, the closed building depends on its isolation from the exterior temperature environment, and the open/closed building operates in different modes at different times of the day.

As the annual plots for Charleston, South Carolina, Phoenix, Arizona, and Madison, Wisconsin, indicate, the appropriate design strategies are quite different for each climate. In Charleston, natural ventilation and solar heating are most appropriate. In Phoenix, high mass with night ventilation and evaporative cooling are good strategies for cooling, and heating can be done effectively by the sun. In Madison, natural ventilation will meet cooling needs and the sun will meet some of the heating needs.

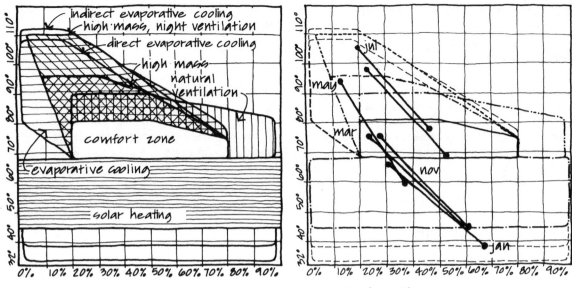

Bioclimatic Chart-Design Strategy Zones

Bioclimatic Chart-Phoenix

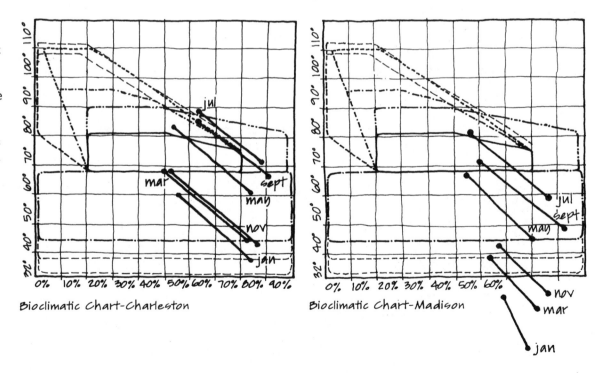

Bioclimatic Chart-Charleston

Bioclimatic Chart-Madison

19 *EARTH CONTACT* effectiveness for load reduction and as a heat sink depends on regional climate.

Energy for space heating can be reduced by using earth contact strategies if appropriate conditions exist on the building's site. Earth sheltering reduces heat loss and heat gain by increasing the resistance of the envelope and by reducing the temperature difference between inside and outside. Since the ground is massive, its temperature lags behind the seasonal changes of the air. In some climates, cooler ground temperature may be a heat sink for passive summer cooling. With proper materials and detailing, the thermal storage capacity of earth-sheltered buildings can be quite large. Design strategies for earth contact are covered in Strategy 72. Additionally, air may be passed through buried ducts and thus used to cool or heat incoming fresh ventilation air (Strategy 109).

The appropriateness of earth contact strategies in a particular climate is based on the building's need for heating and cooling, the difference between ground and air temperatures, and summer humidity levels, which can potentially contribute to condensation.

The matrix identifies earth shelter suitability for

several climate-related factors in 16 cities representing a range of continental U.S. climate zones (Sterling et al., 1982, pp. 34–36). To use the matrix, first find the zone and representative city for the building's site from the map of U.S. climate zones. Then find the same city in the climate suitability matrix. Darker tones mean that the issue is an important consideration in earth-sheltered design.

Reduce Winter Heating Column: Earth shelter strategies will significantly reduce winter heating loads. Darker ratings indicate the severity of the climate's heating season.

Promote Passive Cooling Column: Darker ratings indicate the appropriateness of earth sheltering for passive cooling, based on a correspondence between the severity of the cooling season, sufficient temperature differentials, and humidity conditions.

Reduce Mechanical Cooling Column: Darker ratings indicate the ability for earth shelter to reduce loads on mechanical cooling systems by reducing conduction and infiltration, indicating a significant need for nonpassive

and nonventilative cooling.

Summer Condensation Column: Darker ratings indicate high summer dewpoint temperatures and a significant need for dehumidification above 80% relative humidity (RH). Proper detailing of insulation and ventilation control on RH cycles are mitigation options.

Summer Ventilation Column: Darker ratings indicate the importance of ventilation for cooling in this climate. Earth sheltering strategies must not compromise the ability of the building to be naturally ventilated.

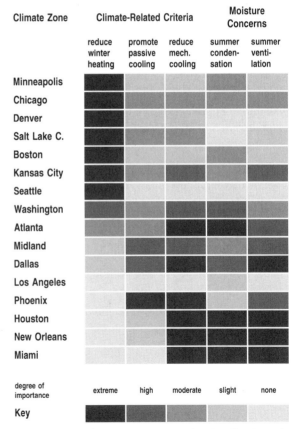

Climate Zone	Climate-Related Criteria			Moisture Concerns	
	reduce winter heating	promote passive cooling	reduce mech. cooling	summer condensation	summer ventilation
Minneapolis					
Chicago					
Denver					
Salt Lake C.					
Boston					
Kansas City					
Seattle					
Washington					
Atlanta					
Midland					
Dallas					
Los Angeles					
Phoenix					
Houston					
New Orleans					
Miami					

degree of importance	extreme	high	moderate	slight	none
Key					

Climate Suitability Matrix for Earth-Sheltered Buildings in Different Climates

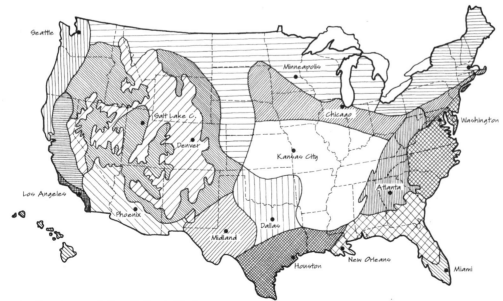

Climatic Regions of the United States

20   *SHADING CALENDAR* times and dates plotted on the sun path diagram determine sun angles that require shade.

To design effective shading, a designer needs to know when to admit and when to block sun. For a given latitude, these admit/block times and dates can be associated with specific sun angles. Because the earth stores heat seasonally, two dates with the same sun angles, such as March 21 and September 21, may require different shading responses. At temperate latitudes, spring dates are usually underheated and fall dates with the same sun angles are usually overheated.

Shading is desirable for an outdoor space whenever the outdoor conditions are within or above the bioclimatic chart's comfort zone (Technique 11). Buildings require shading whenever the outdoor temperature is above the building's balance point temperature, T_b (Technique 22). The balance point is the outdoor temperature at which a building changes from a need for cooling to a need for heating, or vice versa. Buildings with high levels of internal heat loads from lights, people, and equipment have lower balance points, so they shift to heating at a lower outdoor temperature and thus require a longer season for shading.

The daily cycles of temperature for average days in each month can be used to determine when shade is desirable. Long-term mean hourly temperature data are not currently available in the United States. Hourly data are available in large data sets in Typical Meteorological Year files (TMY) used for computer simulations (Marion & Urban, 1995). Currently there is no user-friendly software available to process or display this data in the format required, although it can be manipulated by spreadsheet software. Hourly temperature squares developed from TMY for representative cities are given in Appendix A.

The example shows the shading calendar developed for St. Louis, Missouri from the approximate shading calendar method. Details are given in Appendix B. Depending on clothing and activity levels, shading is required outdoors beginning somewhere between 65 and 70 °F (18 and 21 °C). The shading calendar for outdoor rooms shows shading required for four hours on April afternoons, starting at 10 AM in May, all day long from

	J	F	M	A	M	J	J	A	S	O	N	D
1	26	30	39	49	58	68	72	70	62	51	41	30
2	24	28	37	47	56	66	70	68	60	49	39	29
3	23	27	36	46	55	65	69	67	59	48	38	28
4	22	26	35	46	55	65	69	67	59	48	37	27
5	21	25	34	46	55	65	69	67	59	48	36	26
6	21	25	34	48	57	67	71	69	61	50	36	26
7	22	26	35	50	59	68	72	70	63	52	37	26
8	23	27	36	52	61	71	75	73	65	54	38	28
9	26	30	39	55	64	74	78	76	68	57	41	30
10	28	32	42	58	67	76	80	78	71	60	43	33
11	32	36	46	61	70	79	83	81	74	63	47	35
12	35	39	49	63	72	82	86	84	76	65	50	38
13	37	41	52	65	74	83	87	85	78	67	52	40
14	38	42	53	67	76	85	89	87	80	69	53	42
15	39	43	54	67	76	85	89	87	80	69	54	42
16	39	43	54	67	76	85	89	87	80	69	54	42
17	38	42	53	66	75	84	88	86	79	68	53	41
18	37	41	52	64	73	82	86	84	77	66	52	40
19	36	40	51	62	71	81	85	83	75	64	51	39
20	35	39	49	60	69	79	83	81	73	62	50	38
21	33	37	47	58	67	76	80	78	71	60	48	36
22	31	35	45	55	64	74	78	76	68	57	46	35
23	29	33	43	53	62	71	75	73	66	55	44	33
24	27	31	41	51	60	69	73	71	64	53	42	32

65 F	66-79 F	80 F

Shading Calendar, Outdoor Rooms
Balance Point = 65 °F (18.3 °C), St. Louis, Missouri

June to September, and on October afternoons starting at noon. The next two shading calendars also represent the St. Louis climate, but are based on lower balance points. The outdoor temperatures are the same on all charts, but they have been shaded differently. A skin-load-dominated building (SLD) with T_b = 55 °F (12.8 °C) requires heating below 55° and shade above 55°.

The SLD shading calendar shows a larger overheated zone and shading required for the building all day long from April to October. The internal-load-dominated building (ILD) shading calendar shows that a building with high internal loads would have a much longer cooling season and needs shading on March and November mornings beginning at 11 AM and extending the rest of the day. Shade is desirable during all sun hours from April to October.

If the periods requiring shade are plotted on the Sun Path Diagram (Technique 2), a picture of the sky sector that the shading design must block is readily revealed. It is useful to distinguish sun angles that require shade on both dates from those that require shade on the fall side of the summer equinox and sun on the spring side.

To plot the shading times on the sun path diagram:

1) Begin by plotting the fall morning hour at which comfort conditions begin (October, 12 noon in the St. Louis example for outdoor rooms). Place a dot at that point. Then plot the earliest comfort hour for the previous month (September, 8 AM for St. Louis).

2) Continue plotting dots for the earliest hour in preceding months until the earliest comfort hour occurs before sunrise. For the St. Louis example, the last point in this series occurs at sunrise in August.

3) Repeat this process for the afternoon boundaries of the comfort zone. In the St. Louis example, the last hour of comfort in September and October occurs after sunset, therefore shading is required all afternoon and the plots fall off of the diagram.

4) Connect the dots with a smooth curve. This repre-

	J	F	M	A	M	J	J	A	S	O	N	D
1	26	30	39	49	58	68	72	70	62	51	41	30
2	24	28	37	47	56	66	70	68	60	49	39	29
3	23	27	36	46	55	65	69	67	59	48	38	28
4	22	26	35	46	55	65	69	67	59	48	37	27
5	21	25	34	46	55	65	69	67	59	48	36	26
6	21	25	34	48	57	67	71	69	61	50	36	26
7	22	26	35	50	59	68	72	70	63	52	37	26
8	23	27	36	52	61	71	75	73	65	54	38	28
9	26	30	39	55	64	74	78	76	68	57	41	30
10	28	32	42	58	67	76	80	78	71	60	43	33
11	32	36	46	61	70	79	83	81	74	63	47	35
12	35	39	49	63	72	82	86	84	76	65	50	38
13	37	41	52	65	74	83	87	85	78	67	52	40
14	38	42	53	67	76	85	89	87	80	69	53	42
15	39	43	54	67	76	85	89	87	80	69	54	42
16	39	43	54	67	76	85	89	87	80	69	54	42
17	38	42	53	66	75	84	88	86	79	68	53	41
18	37	41	52	64	73	82	86	84	77	66	52	40
19	36	40	51	62	71	81	85	83	75	64	51	39
20	35	39	49	60	69	79	83	81	73	62	50	38
21	33	37	47	58	67	76	80	78	71	60	48	36
22	31	35	45	55	64	74	78	76	68	57	46	35
23	29	33	43	53	62	71	75	73	66	55	44	33
24	27	31	41	51	60	69	73	71	64	53	42	32

Legend: 65 F | 66-79 F | 80 F

Shading Calendar, Skin-Load-Dominated Buildings (SLD)
Balance Point = 55 °F (12.8 °C), St. Louis, Missouri

	J	F	M	A	M	J	J	A	S	O	N	D
1	26	30	39	49	58	68	72	70	62	51	41	30
2	24	28	37	47	56	66	70	68	60	49	39	29
3	23	27	36	46	55	65	69	67	59	48	38	28
4	22	26	35	46	55	65	69	67	59	48	37	27
5	21	25	34	46	55	65	69	67	59	48	36	26
6	21	25	34	48	57	67	71	69	61	50	36	26
7	22	26	35	50	59	68	72	70	63	52	37	26
8	23	27	36	52	61	71	75	73	65	54	38	28
9	26	30	39	55	64	74	78	76	68	57	41	30
10	28	32	42	58	67	76	80	78	71	60	43	33
11	32	36	46	61	70	79	83	81	74	63	47	35
12	35	39	49	63	72	82	86	84	76	65	50	38
13	37	41	52	65	74	83	87	85	78	67	52	40
14	38	42	53	67	76	85	89	87	80	69	53	42
15	39	43	54	67	76	85	89	87	80	69	54	42
16	39	43	54	67	76	85	89	87	80	69	54	42
17	38	42	53	66	75	84	88	86	79	68	53	41
18	37	41	52	64	73	82	86	84	77	66	52	40
19	36	40	51	62	71	81	85	83	75	64	51	39
20	35	39	49	60	69	79	83	81	73	62	50	38
21	33	37	47	58	67	76	80	78	71	60	48	36
22	31	35	45	55	64	74	78	76	68	57	46	35
23	29	33	43	53	62	71	75	73	66	55	44	33
24	27	31	41	51	60	69	73	71	64	53	42	32

Legend: 65 F | 66-79 F | 80 F

Shading Calendar, Internal-Load-Dominated Buildings (ILD)
Balance Point = 45 °F (7.2 °C), St. Louis, Missouri

sents the boundary of the zone requiring shading on only one date.

5) Apply a similar process to create a new series of plots based on the Spring comfort zone boundary. For the St. Louis example, the critical points are April, 1 PM and May, 10 AM. When the points are connected, the line follows the August/April date line up to 1 PM, passes through 10 AM, and finishes at the next hour, June 9 AM. This is the boundary of the period when shade is required on both dates for a given angle.

7) Render the diagram with color or a graphic pattern to distinguish the different zones.

Fixed shading is appropriate for the upper, midsummer zone, while moveable or otherwise responsive shading is more appropriate for the lower zone where the building would sometimes require shade, and sometimes sun. The examples below show the substantial difference in these requirements for spaces with three different balance points, indicating the need for much more shade in buildings with high internal loads.

The same shading times and dates from the shading calendar for various balance points can be plotted on the Sundial (Technique 1) and used to evaluate building sites and

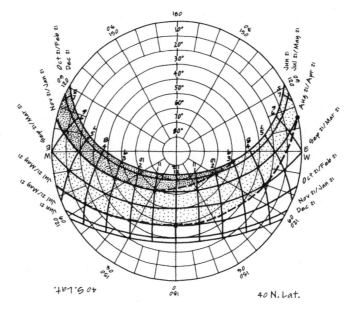

Sun Path Diagram, 40 Degrees Latitude

Shading Angles, Outdoor Rooms,
Balance Point = 65 °F (18.3 °C), St. Louis, MO

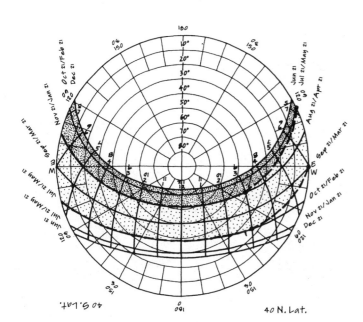

Sun Path Diagram, 40 Degrees Latitude

Shading Angles, Skin-Load-Dominated Building;
Balance Point = 55 °F (12.8 °C), St. Louis, MO

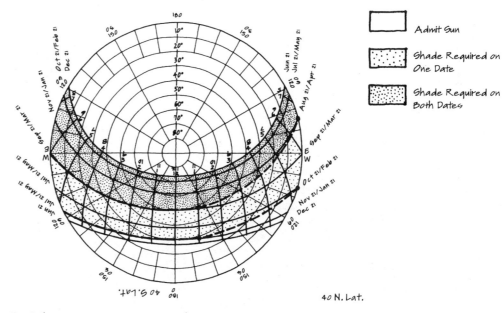

Sun Path Diagram, 40 Degrees Latitude

Shading Angles, Internal-Load-Dominated Building;
Balance Point = 45 °F (7.2 °C), St. Louis, MO

☐ Admit Sun

▨ Shade Required on One Date

▨ Shade Required on Both Dates

shading designs. With the shading period plotted on the Sundial, one can determine whether a shadow pattern cast on a site is an asset or a liability. A designer can also easily evaluate potential building sites, the effectiveness of a shading element design, or a building massing intended to provide shade between buildings. The procedure for plotting shading times is the same as when using the sun path diagram.

Even though, in terms of bioclimatic comfort, shading may be called for on a particular date and time, there may not be enough radiation during many hours, such as the hour or two after sunrise and before sunset, to have a significant heat gain effect. Solar radiation is covered in Technique 3. The last set of diagrams in this technique shows the shading times applied to the sundial and sun path diagrams, as before, but then reduced by a 75-Btu/hr, ft² (236-W/m²) cutoff. This relieves the designer, in many cases, of the difficult task of shading very low sun angles for little improvement in solar load reduction. However, local user-controlled moveable shading should still be provided to allow occupants to control glare from low angle sun. Shading design is covered in Strategies 98, 99, and 100.

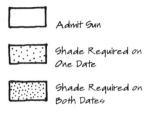

Admit Sun

Shade Required on One Date

Shade Required on Both Dates

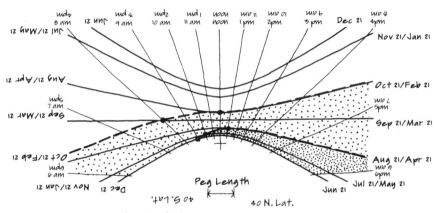

40 Degrees Latitude Sundial

Shading Angles, Outdoor Rooms
Balance Point = 65 °F (18.3 °C), St. Louis, MO

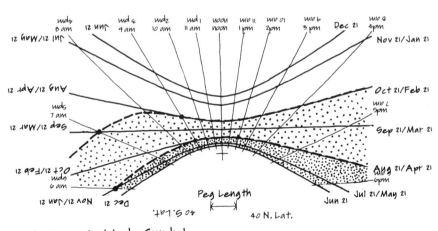

40 Degrees Latitude Sundial

Shading Angles, Skin-Load-Dominated Buildings
Balance Point = 55 °F (12.8 °C), St. Louis, MO

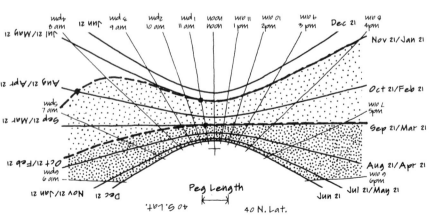

40 Degrees Latitude Sundial

Shading Angles, Internal-Load-Dominated Buildings
Balance Point = 45 °F (7.2 °C), St. Louis, MO

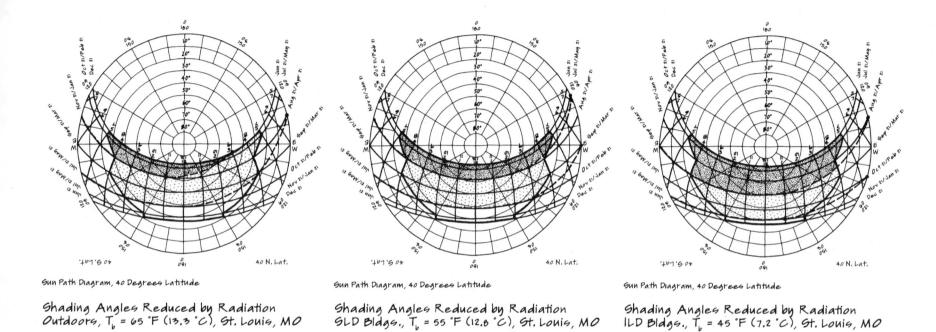

Sun Path Diagram, 40 Degrees Latitude

Shading Angles Reduced by Radiation
Outdoors, T_b = 65 °F (13.3 °C), St. Louis, MO

Sun Path Diagram, 40 Degrees Latitude

Shading Angles Reduced by Radiation
SLD Bldgs., T_b = 55 °F (12.8 °C), St. Louis, MO

Sun Path Diagram, 40 Degrees Latitude

Shading Angles Reduced by Radiation
ILD Bldgs., T_b = 45 °F (7.2 °C), St. Louis, MO

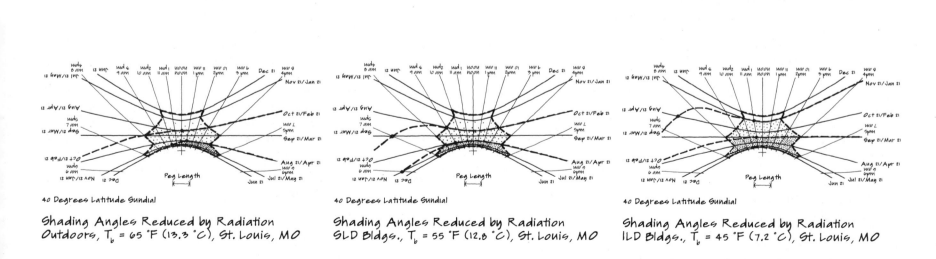

40 Degrees Latitude Sundial

Shading Angles Reduced by Radiation
Outdoors, T_b = 65 °F (13.3 °C), St. Louis, MO

40 Degrees Latitude Sundial

Shading Angles Reduced by Radiation
SLD Bldgs., T_b = 55 °F (12.8 °C), St. Louis, MO

40 Degrees Latitude Sundial

Shading Angles Reduced by Radiation
ILD Bldgs., T_b = 45 °F (7.2 °C), St. Louis, MO

21 *TOTAL HEAT GAINS* **can be estimated to determine the loads used to size passive cooling strategies.** *TOTAL HEAT LOSSES* **can be compared against energy conservation criteria.**

Knowing the total rate of heat gain in the building, or in a zone of the building, is essential to being able to size passive cooling systems, such as the depth of a roof pond, the size of cross-ventilation windows, or the height of a ventilation stack. Knowing the building's total rate of heat loss on a unit area basis allows buildings to be compared against each other or to a standard for energy efficiency per unit of floor area. Both the rate of heat gain and the rate of heat loss can be used to calculate the building balance point (Technique 22).

A building's rate of heat gain is the sum of internal heat gains from lights, people, and equipment, gains from heat transfer through the envelope, solar gains on the envelope and through windows, and gains from infiltration and ventilation. The rate of heat gain changes constantly with the outdoor temperature, occupancy patterns, and the variable heat from the sun. Because only passive systems are being considered here, only sensible heat is included in the calculations.

To determine the building's total rate of heat gain, use the four-part, rule-of-thumb estimating method.

1) Determine the heat gain sources for your building. Thermally "closed" strategies, such as roof ponds, radiant cooling, evaporative cooling, and earth tubes have gains from people, equipment, electric lighting, the building envelope, and infiltration/ventilation. Thermally "open" strategies have all of these gains except infiltration/ventilation. Night ventilation of mass is an open/closed strategy; during thermally closed hours, include infiltration/ventilation gains and during open hours, exclude them. During the night hours before the building is opened to ventilation, also exclude solar gains through windows.

2) Find the total rate of heat gain from People and Equipment from the Part A table, **Internal Heat Sources—People and Equipment** (Btu/hr, ft^2 or W/m^2). Bold numbers for building types should be used for the total floor area of the building. Equipment gains represent a range of efficiencies from very efficient to

average. Gains from people represent a range of average to maximum (building code) occupant densities. For "P + E" totals, the Low figure represents efficient equipment combined with average occupancy; High figures represent average equipment efficiencies combined with peak occupant density. For more on occupant loads, see Technique 12; for equipment loads, see Technique 14.

3) Find the rate of heat gain from Electric Lights from the Part B table, **Internal Heat Sources—Electric Lighting.** Enter the table in the row for the building type and latitude. Find the column for the average daylight factor (DF) of the building and read the heat gain from lights (See Strategy 94 for information on DF calculation.) The table assumes that automatic controls switch off electric lights when enough daylight is present in the room. It also assumes 80% of the gross floor area is daylit, electric light is provided during work hours of 9 AM–5 PM all year, and a control effectiveness/dimming factor of 80%. If the building has no daylight controls, use the column for DF < 1.5; also use this column for calculating peak loads. The Low and High figures represent a range of lighting power densities, with the high being the maximum allowed under ASHRAE/IES 90.1-1989 standard (ASHRAE, 1989a). For more on gains from electric lights, see Technique 13.

4) Find the rate of heat gain through the envelope from the Part C table, **Heat Gain Through Envelope.** Summer outdoor design temperatures for the building's climate can be found in ASHRAE (1997, Chapter 26) and in Reynolds and Stein (2000, pp. 1623–1633).

a. For gains through externally shaded windows, find the ratio of window area ÷ floor area, then multiply by the constant for the site's outdoor design temperature.

The constants assume a shading coefficient of 0.25 (Technique 16). If your windows are not shaded, as a rule of thumb, multiply the calculated heat gains from windows by 4. For partially shaded windows, multiply by 2.

b. For gains through opaque walls, find the ratio of wall area ÷ floor area, then multiply by the *U*-value of the wall (Technique 15 and Strategy 76) and then by the constant for the site's outdoor design temperature.

c. For gains through roofs, find the ratio of roof area ÷ floor area, then multiply by the *U*-value of the roof (see Technique 15 and Strategy 76) and then by the constant for the site's outdoor design temperature.

5) Find the rate of heat gain from infiltration OR ventilation from the Part D table, **Heat Gain From Infiltration/Ventilation of Thermally Closed Buildings.** Choose gains from either infiltration OR ventilation. For houses and small buildings without mechanical ventilation, choose infiltration. For commercial buildings, choose ventilation. From Technique 17, find the building's rate of heat gain from infiltration or ventilation in Btu/hr, °F, ft^2 (or W/K, m^2). Then multiply by the constant for the site's outdoor design temperature.

6) Add the rate of heat gains from each of the contributing elements relevant to your passive cooling system to obtain the total average hourly rate of heat gain. Units should be Btu/hr, ft^2 (or W/m^2).

To determine the building's total rate of heat loss add the rates of heat loss from the envelope, as calculated in Technique 15, and from infiltration/ventilation, as calculated in Technique 17. Values will be in units of Btu/hr, °F, ft^2 (or W/K, m^2). Note that the heat loss rate is kept in loss per degree of temperature difference between inside and outside.

BUILDING TYPE	SENSIBLE HEAT GAIN (Btu/hr, ft² of Floor Area)		Total: People + Equipment			SENSIBLE HEAT GAIN (W/m² of Floor Area)		Total: People + Equipment		
	People	Equipment	Low (Efficient Equip. + Ave. Occupancy)	Mid	High (Average Equip. + Peak Occupancy)	People	Equipment	Low (Efficient Equip. + Ave. Occupancy)	Mid	High (Average Equip. + Peak Occupancy)
Assembly Bldgs.	**5**	**3-5**	**8**	**10**		**16**	**10-17**	**26**	**33**	
Auditoria	28	1		29		88	3		91	
Standing space	32	0-0.5		33		101	0-2	101	103	
Conference rooms	up to 11	3-5	8	12	16	up to 35	10-17	28	32	35
Education Bldgs.	**3-8**	**4-7**	**7**	**11**	**15**	**10-25**	**13-23**	**23**	**36**	**48**
Classroom	up to 13	3-4	10	14	17	up to 41	10-13	30	42	54
Laboratory	up to 8	4-7	8	12	15	up to 25	13-23	26	37	48
Libraries	up to 5	3-4	6	8	9	up to 16	10-13	18	24	29
Grocery Stores	**2-5**	**8-13**	**10**	**14**	**18**	**6-16**	**24-42**	**30**	**44**	**58**
Lodging Bldgs.	**1**	**3-5**	**4**	**5**	**6**	**3**	**10-17**	**13**	**20**	
Healthcare Bldgs.										
Sleeping (hospital)	1-2	1-2	2	3	4	3-6	3-6	6	9	12
In-patient (clinic)	2	2-4	4	5	6	6	6-13	12	16	19
Office Bldgs.	**1-2**	**3-5**	**4**	**6**	**7**	**3-6**	**10-17**	**13**	**18**	**23**
Recreation Bldgs.										
Spectator areas	up to 34	0	17	26	34	up to 107	0	54	81	107
Gymnasium	up to 19	1-2	10	16	21	up to 60	3-6	33	50	66
Ballroom	up to 31	1-2	17	25	33	up to 98	3-6	52	78	104
Residential Bldgs.	**1-2**	**1-2**	**2**	**3**	**4**	**3-6**	**3-6**	**6**	**9**	**12**
Dormitory sleeping	up to 5	1-2	3	5	7	up to 16	3-6	11	17	22
Apartments	1-2	1-2	2	3	4	3-6	3-6	6	9	12
Restaurant Bldgs.	**2**	**10-16**	**12**	**18**		**6**	**31-52**	**37**	**48**	
Fast food, dining	up to 23	3-5	15	22	28	up to 73	10-17	47	69	90
kitchen, refrigeration	up to 6	17	20	22	23	up to 19	54	64	69	73
Sit-down	up to 16	4-6	12	17	22	up to 50	13-19	38	54	69
kitchen, refrigeration	up to 6	7	10	12	13	up to 19	22	32	36	41
Retail Bldgs.	**2-8**	**3-5**	**5**	**9**	**13**	**10-25**	**10-17**	**20**	**31**	**42**
Warehouse Bldgs.	**0-2**	**2-4**	**2**	**4**	**6**	**0-6**	**8-13**	**8**	**14**	**19**

Heat Gain Totals
Part A Internal Heat Sources-People and Equipment

BUILDING TYPE	LATITUDE	SENSIBLE HEAT GAIN (Btu/hr, ft² of Floor Area) Average Daylight Factor																				SENSIBLE HEAT GAIN (W/m² of Floor Area) Average Daylight Factor										
		DF < 1.5		1.5 < DF < 2		2 < DF < 3		3 < DF < 5		DF > 5		DF < 1.5		1.5 < DF < 2		2 < DF < 3		3 < DF < 5		DF > 5	
		lo	hi	lo	hi	lo	hi	lo	hi	lo	hi	lo	hi	lo	hi	lo	hi	lo	hi	lo	hi
Assembly	20	2.8	4.8	1.2	2.1	1.1	1.8	0.8	1.3	NR	NR	9	15	4	6	3	6	2	4	NR	NR
	30	2.8	4.8	1.4	2.3	1.2	2.1	1.1	1.8	0.8	1.3	9	15	4	7	4	6	3	6	2	4
	40	2.8	4.8	1.6	2.6	1.4	2.3	1.2	2.1	1.1	1.8	9	15	5	8	4	7	4	6	3	6
	50	2.8	4.8	1.8	3.0	1.6	2.6	1.4	2.3	1.2	2.1	9	15	6	10	5	8	4	7	4	6
	60	2.8	4.8	NR	NR	1.8	3.0	1.6	2.6	1.4	2.3	9	15	NR	NR	6	10	5	8	4	7
Education	20	4.0	6.5	1.7	2.8	1.5	2.5	1.1	1.8	NR	NR	13	20	5	9	5	8	3	6	NR	NR
	30	4.0	6.5	1.9	3.1	1.7	2.8	1.5	2.5	1.1	1.8	13	20	6	10	5	9	5	8	3	6
	40	4.0	6.5	2.2	3.6	1.9	3.1	1.7	2.8	1.5	2.5	13	20	7	11	6	10	5	9	5	8
	50	4.0	6.5	2.5	4.1	2.2	3.6	1.9	3.1	1.7	2.8	13	20	8	13	7	11	6	10	5	9
	60	4.0	6.5	NR	NR	2.5	4.1	2.2	3.6	1.9	3.1	13	20	NR	NR	8	13	7	11	6	10
Grocery	20	3.8	7.8	1.6	3.4	1.4	3.0	1.0	2.1	NR	NR	12	25	5	11	5	9	3	7	NR	NR
	30	3.8	7.8	1.8	3.8	1.6	3.4	1.4	3.0	1.0	2.1	12	25	6	12	5	11	5	9	3	7
	40	3.8	7.8	2.1	4.3	1.8	3.8	1.6	3.4	1.4	3.0	12	25	7	14	6	12	5	11	5	9
	50	3.8	7.8	2.4	4.9	2.1	4.3	1.8	3.8	1.6	3.4	12	25	7	16	7	14	6	12	5	11
	60	3.8	7.8	NR	NR	2.4	4.9	2.1	4.3	1.8	3.8	12	25	NR	NR	7	16	7	14	6	12
Lodging	20	2.9	4.1	1.2	1.8	1.1	1.6	0.8	1.1	NR	NR	9	13	4	6	3	5	2	3	NR	NR
	30	2.9	4.1	1.4	2.0	1.2	1.8	1.1	1.6	0.8	1.1	9	13	4	6	4	6	3	5	2	3
	40	2.9	4.1	1.6	2.3	1.4	2.0	1.2	1.8	1.1	1.6	9	13	5	7	4	6	4	6	3	5
	50	2.9	4.1	1.8	2.6	1.6	2.3	1.4	2.0	1.2	1.8	9	13	6	8	5	7	4	6	4	6
	60	2.9	4.1	NR	NR	1.8	2.6	1.6	2.3	1.4	2.0	9	13	NR	NR	6	8	5	7	4	6
Healthcare	20	6.8	9.2	2.9	4.0	2.6	3.5	1.8	2.5	NR	NR	22	29	9	13	8	11	6	8	NR	NR
	30	6.8	9.2	3.3	4.4	2.9	4.0	2.6	3.5	1.8	2.5	22	29	10	14	9	13	8	11	6	8
	40	6.8	9.2	3.8	5.1	3.3	4.4	2.9	4.0	2.6	3.5	22	29	12	16	10	14	9	13	8	11
	50	6.8	9.2	4.3	5.8	3.8	5.1	3.3	4.4	2.9	4.0	22	29	14	18	12	16	10	14	9	13
	60	6.8	9.2	NR	NR	4.3	5.8	3.8	5.1	3.3	4.4	22	29	NR	NR	14	18	12	16	10	14
Office	20	4.4	5.1	1.9	2.2	1.7	1.9	1.2	1.4	NR	NR	14	16	6	7	5	6	4	4	NR	NR
	30	4.4	5.1	2.1	2.5	1.9	2.2	1.7	1.9	1.2	1.4	14	16	7	8	6	7	5	6	4	4
	40	4.4	5.1	2.4	2.8	2.1	2.5	1.9	2.2	1.7	1.9	14	16	8	9	7	8	6	7	5	6
	50	4.4	5.1	2.8	3.2	2.4	2.8	2.1	2.5	1.9	2.2	14	16	9	10	8	9	7	8	6	7
	60	4.4	5.1	NR	NR	2.8	3.2	2.4	2.8	2.1	2.5	14	16	NR	NR	9	10	8	9	7	8

Heat Gain Totals
Part B Internal Heat Sources-Electric Lighting

BUILDING TYPE	LATITUDE	SENSIBLE HEAT GAIN (Btu/hr, ft² of Floor Area) Average Daylight Factor										SENSIBLE HEAT GAIN (W/m² of Floor Area) Average Daylight Factor									
		DF < 1.5		1.5 < DF < 2		2 < DF < 3		3 < DF < 5		DF > 5		DF < 1.5		1.5 < DF < 2		2 < DF < 3		3 < DF < 5		DF > 5	
		lo	hi	lo	hi	lo	hi	lo	hi	lo	hi	lo	hi	lo	hi	lo	hi	lo	hi	lo	hi
Recreation	20	5.5	13.3	2.3	5.7	2.1	5.1	1.5	3.6	NR	NR	17	42	7	18	7	16	5	11	NR	NR
	30	5.5	13.3	2.6	6.4	2.3	5.7	2.1	5.1	1.5	3.6	17	42	8	20	7	18	7	16	5	11
	40	5.5	13.3	3.0	7.3	2.6	6.4	2.3	5.7	2.1	5.1	17	42	9	23	8	20	7	18	7	16
	50	5.5	13.3	3.4	8.4	3.0	7.3	2.6	6.4	2.3	5.7	17	42	11	26	9	23	8	20	7	18
	60	5.5	13.3	NR	NR	3.4	8.4	3.0	7.3	2.6	6.4	17	42	NR	NR	11	26	9	23	8	20
Residential	20	0.7	4.1	0.3	1.8	0.3	1.6	0.2	1.1	NR	NR	2	13	1	6	1	5	1	3	NR	NR
	30	0.7	4.1	0.3	2.0	0.3	1.8	0.3	1.6	0.2	1.1	2	13	1	6	1	6	1	5	1	3
	40	0.7	4.1	0.4	2.3	0.3	2.0	0.3	1.8	0.3	1.6	2	13	1	7	1	6	1	6	1	5
	50	0.7	4.1	0.4	2.6	0.4	2.3	0.3	2.0	0.3	1.8	2	13	1	8	1	7	1	6	1	6
	60	0.7	4.1	NR	NR	0.4	2.6	0.4	2.3	0.3	2.0	2	13	NR	NR	1	8	1	7	1	6
Restaurant	20	2.4	4.8	1.0	2.1	0.9	1.8	0.6	1.3	NR	NR	8	15	3	6	3	6	2	4	NR	NR
	30	2.4	4.8	1.1	2.3	1.0	2.1	0.9	1.8	0.6	1.3	8	15	4	7	3	6	3	6	2	4
	40	2.4	4.8	1.3	2.6	1.1	2.3	1.0	2.1	0.9	1.8	8	15	4	8	4	7	3	6	3	6
	50	2.4	4.8	1.5	3.0	1.3	2.6	1.1	2.3	1.0	2.1	8	15	5	10	4	8	4	7	3	6
	60	2.4	4.8	NR	NR	1.5	3.0	1.3	2.6	1.1	2.3	8	15	NR	NR	5	10	4	8	4	7
Retail	20	3.4	11.3	1.5	4.8	1.3	4.3	0.9	3.0	NR	NR	11	36	5	15	4	14	3	10	NR	NR
	30	3.4	11.3	1.6	5.4	1.5	4.8	1.3	4.3	0.9	3.0	11	36	5	17	5	15	4	14	3	10
	40	3.4	11.3	1.9	6.2	1.6	5.4	1.5	4.8	1.3	4.3	11	36	6	20	5	17	5	15	4	14
	50	3.4	11.3	2.1	7.1	1.9	6.2	1.6	5.4	1.5	4.8	11	36	7	22	6	20	5	17	5	15
	60	3.4	11.3	NR	NR	2.1	7.1	1.9	6.2	1.6	5.4	11	36	NR	NR	7	22	6	20	5	17
Warehouse	20	0.3	3.1	0.1	1.3	0.1	1.2	0.1	0.8	NR	NR	1	10	0	4	0	4	0	3	NR	NR
	30	0.3	3.1	0.2	1.5	0.1	1.3	0.1	1.2	0.1	0.8	1	10	1	5	0	4	0	4	0	3
	40	0.3	3.1	0.2	1.7	0.2	1.5	0.1	1.3	0.1	1.2	1	10	1	5	1	5	0	4	0	4
	50	0.3	3.1	0.2	2.0	0.2	1.7	0.2	1.5	0.1	1.3	1	10	1	6	1	5	1	5	0	4
	60	0.3	3.1	NR	NR	0.2	2.0	0.2	1.7	0.2	1.5	1	10	NR	NR	1	6	1	5	1	5

Part B Internal Heat Sources-Electric Lighting (continued)

Method: developed based on lighting power densities from EIA (1992, Table 7, p. 42); PSIC (1998, based on EIA surveys, 1989, 1990, 1994); and summaries from ASHRAE (1989a) as found in Tao and Janis (1997, p. 355). Daylight savings estimated from Daylight Nomographs (Selkowitz & Gabel, 1984) as found in Moore (1991, pp. 140-141).

*NR = Not Recommended.

For residential buildings and nonresidential buildings with low internal loads, the building's rate of heat loss can be compared against conservation criteria. Passive solar heated buildings should meet these criteria if the sizing methods in Part Two are to be accurate.

To calculate the building's conservation performance, multiply the rate of total heat loss, in Btu/hr, °F, ft^2 (or W/K, m^2) by 24 hr to get Btu/DD, ft^2 of floor area (W/DD, m^2). Compare this value to the criteria listed in the **Building Conservation Criteria Based on Total Heat Loss Rate** table. If the building's heat loss rate is greater than the criteria, it may be reduced by increasing insulation levels (Strategies 76, 97, and 101), reducing skin area (Strategy 49), tightening construction detailing to reduce infiltration (Technique 17), or using a heat exchanger to improve ventilation efficiency (Strategy 109).

		Outdoor Design Temperature		Outdoor Design Temperature	
		90 F	100 F	32 C	38 C
I. Gains through externally shaded windows: (window area) ÷ (floor area)	x _____	16	21	50	66
II. Gains through opaque walls: {[(opaque wall area) (U_{wall})] ÷ (floor area)}	x _____	15	25	8	14
II. Gains through roofs: {[(opaque roof area) (U_{roof})] ÷ (floor area)}	x _____	35	45	19	25

Part C Heat Gain Through Envelope
Method adapted from Reynolds & Stein (2000, p. 277).

CHOOSE Infiltration OR Ventilation		Outdoor Design Temperature		Outdoor Design Temperature	
		90 F	100 F	32 C	38 C
Infiltration					
(infiltration load from Technique 17, Btu/hr, F, ft^2)	x _____	16	27	---	---
OR					
(infiltration load from Technique 17, W/K, m^2)	x _____	---	---	9.6	16.8
Ventilation					
(ventilation load from Technique 17, Btu/hr, F, ft^2)	x _____	16	27	---	---
OR					
(ventilation load from Technique 17, W/K, m^2)	x _____	---	---	9.6	16.8

Part D Heat Gain From Infiltration/Ventilation of Thermally Closed Buildings

Annual Heating Degree Days (base 65 F)	Maximum Heat Loss (Btu/DDF, ft^2)		Annual Heating Degree Days (base 18 C)	Maximum Heat Loss (W/DDK, m^2)	
	Conventional Buildings	Passively Solar Heated Buildings, Exclusive of Solar Wall		Conventional Buildings	Passively Solar Heated Buildings, Exclusive of Solar Wall
<1000	9	7.6	<550	51	43
1000–3000	8	6.6	550–1650	45	37
3000–5000	7	5.6	1650–2800	40	32
5000–7000	6	4.6	2800–3900	34	26
>7000	5	3.6	>3900	28	20

Building Conservation Criteria Based on Total Heat Loss Rate

22 *BALANCE POINT TEMPERATURE:* **The outside temperature at which the building makes a transition from a heating need to a cooling need determines when heating and cooling are required.**

The "balance point" for a building is defined as the outdoor temperature at which the heat generated inside the building balances the building's heat loss, to maintain a desired inside temperature. If the balance point of a building is 50 °F, then the building must be cooled when the outside temperature is above 50 °F and heated when the temperature is below 50 °F. The balance point is a function of the rate of heat gain in the building from people, equipment, lights, and solar radiation and the rate of heat loss by ventilation and skin transfer. (ASHRAE, 1997, p. 30.17).

Since the amount of heat loss is a function of the difference in temperature between the inside and outside, the building will lose as much heat as it produces at a sufficiently low temperature, the balance point. The rate of heat gain inside the building changes over the day, week, or year due to occupancy patterns and available solar radiation. The rate of heat loss may also change due to varying ventilation rates related to occupancy or changes in the insulating quality of the skin from day to night.

Once the balance point has been determined, it can be compared to the outside temperature for any time period to see how the building's need for heating and cooling changes. This information can be used to determine when to use design strategies for passive solar heating, cooling, and daylighting (see Technique 23).

To determine the balance point temperature (T_b) of a building, enter the graph on the vertical axis with the rate of heat gain in Btu/hr, ft² (W/m²) of building floor area. Move horizontally to intersect the diagonal for the building's rate of heat loss in Btu/hr, °F, ft² (W/K, m²) of building floor area. From that point, move vertically to the horizontal axis and read there the temperature difference (ΔT) between inside and outside at which heat gains balance heat losses. To determine the exterior balance point temperature, subtract the ΔT found on the horizontal axis from the desired interior temperature (T_i).

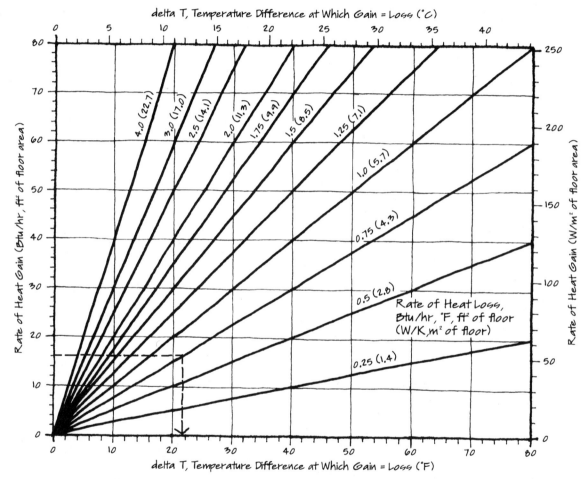

Estimating Balance Point Temperature Difference

$$T_i - \Delta T = T_b$$

The total rates of heat gain and loss can be approximated by using Technique 21.

23

BALANCE POINT PROFILES: The characteristics of the climate, the building's use, and the building's form can be used to develop daily heating and cooling patterns that represent the building's performance over a year and help identify climatic design strategies.

The purpose of identifying the generic heating and cooling patterns that apply to a building is to establish appropriate design strategies while the design is still in its most formative stages. Graphs may be generated using precise data or rough approximations. They will only be as accurate as the data used to generate them, but they take much more time to do precisely than roughly. Since at the beginning of the design process we are interested in identifying the basic types of patterns and their related design strategies, the extra effort required for precision may not be worth the time it takes. By doing the graph roughly the first time and with increasing precision and detail for successive trials, one can get an idea of the relationship between effort in and usable information out.

The process for generating the generic heating and cooling patterns has ten steps. 1) Select months of the year to analyze. 2) Plot the outside temperature for an average day in those months. 3) Assume a hypothetical building form. 4) For that building, determine the heat gain from people, lights, equipment, and the sun. 5) Determine heat transfer through the envelope and infiltration/ventilation. 6) Determine when the building is occupied so that one can tell when lights, equipment, etc. will be turned on. 7) Determine the heat gain and loss at 4-hr intervals during the day. 8) Use the heat gain and loss to determine the balance point temperature for each 4-hr interval. 9) Plot the balance point temperatures on the same graphs as the average outside temperature, and develop the generic heating and cooling patterns. 10) Use the patterns to identify appropriate types of design strategies.

STEP 1: Select Months

Select the months that are representative of the building's climate. Do the bioclimatic plots shown in Technique 11 if there is doubt about which months may be important. Four months will be analyzed as representa-

tive of the St. Louis, Missouri climate: January, April, July, and October.

STEP 2: Plot Outside Temperature

For each month, plot the average high temperature at 4 PM and average low temperature at 4 AM. In St. Louis, January has an average high of 39 °F (3.9 °C) and an average low of 21 °F (-6.1 °C). Connect the high and low points with a straight line. The intersection of this line with each vertical time line approximates the temperature at those times. The temperature profile is assumed to be symmetrical around 4 PM, so use the noon temperature to plot the 8 PM temperature, and the 8 AM temperature to plot the midnight temperature (twice).

STEP 3: Assumed Building Form

First, develop a simple rectangular shape that represents the building. Consider as much about the site and program as possible without going beyond the most basic diagrammatic relationships. Remember the purpose of this analysis is to inform the design, *not* to evaluate after it is finished. For example, the building under construction for the St. Louis site is a 1500-ft² (139-m²) office building. A rectangle 20 × 75 × 15 ft high (6.1 × 22.9 × 4.6 m) was used to represent a single-loaded corridor scheme. The building will need good lighting; therefore it's assumed that 20% of the wall area will be glazing.

STEP 4: Gain From People, Lights, Equipment, and Sun

This determination will include sensible gains only, for passive systems. In office spaces the maximum occupancy is 0.7 people/100 ft² (8 people/100 m²) and the average occupancy is 0.4 people/100 ft² (4 people/100 m²). Assuming an occupancy of 0.5 people/100 ft² (5.4 people/100 m²) and a sensible heat gain of a moderately active office of 250 Btu/hr (73 W) per person, the graph from Technique 12 indicates that heat gain from people will be approximately 1.25 Btu/hr, ft² (3.9 W/m²).

The visual tasks in the office are assumed to be of high contrast, corresponding to IES category D, with a recommended 20–50 foot-candles (fc) (215–540 lux), so a general illumination level of 30 fc (325 lux) is selected from the table in Technique 13. Fluorescent lighting will be the predominant light source. The graph in Tech-

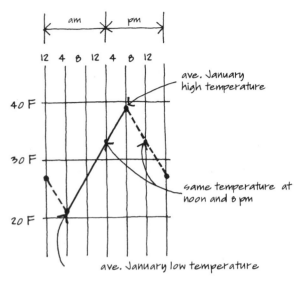

Exterior Temperatures, January, St. Louis, MO

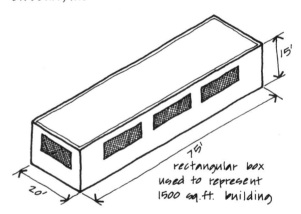

rectangular box used to represent 1500 sq.ft. building

east and west elevations —glazing 20% of area or 60 sq.ft.

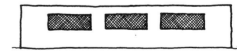

north and south elevations —glazing 20% of area or 225 sq.ft.

Hypothetical Building, 1500 ft²

nique 13 indicates that 30 fc of light from average efficiency full-size fluorescent lights produces approximately 4.5 Btu/hr, ft² (14.2 W/m²). This rate assumes no contribution from daylighting in reducing electric lighting use. If automated daylight controls are used, see Technique 21 to determine the appropriate rate of heat gain from lights. From the chart in Technique 14, we estimate the heat gain from office equipment to be 4 Btu/hr, ft² (12.5 W/m²).

Using data from Kusuda and Ishii (1977) for the nearest city, Columbia, Missouri, the radiation levels in Btu/hr, ft² for January are shown in the table. If the building's city is not listed in Kusuda and Ishii, this information can be approximated using Technique 16.

Vertical Radiation, January (Btu/hr, ft² of vertical surface)

	8 AM	Noon	4 PM
South facing	49	152	49
West facing	9	33	67
North facing	9	33	9
East facing	67	33	9
Horizontal	24	115	24

The hypothetical building design has 20% windows on all elevations and no skylights in the roof. The shading coefficient of the window is assumed to be 0.65 and there are no interior or exterior shades. Using the graph from Technique 16, enter the horizontal axis with the radiation from one hour and one orientation in the above table. Move vertically to the diagonal line that represents 20% glazing; reflect horizontally to the diagonal 0.65 shading coefficient line; then reflect vertically to the horizontal axis and read the heat gain per ft² (or m²) of skin for that time and wall orientation. Usingthat process, the following heat gain in Btu/hr, ft² was determined for each elevation for each hour.

Solar Heat Gain, January (Btu/hr, ft² of skin area)

	8 AM	Noon	4 PM
South elevation	6	20	6
West elevation	1	4	9
North elevation	1	4	1
East elevation	9	4	1
Roof (no glazing)	0	0	0

The next step is to multiply the heat gain per ft² (or m²) of skin times the area of skin in each elevation. In the hypothetical example, the area of the north and south elevations is 1125 ft² (104.5 m²) and the east and west elevations are 300 ft² (27.9 m²). The solar heat gain in Btu's is as follows:

Solar Heat Gain, January (Btu)

	8 AM	Noon	4 PM
South elevation	6,750	22,500	6,750
West elevation	300	1,200	2,700
North elevation	1,125	4,500	1,125
East elevation	2,700	1,200	300
Roof	0	0	0
TOTAL	10,875	29,400	10,875

Next, divide the total heat gain for all skin areas for each hour by the floor area, 1500 ft² (139 m²) to determine the heat gain per unit area of building.

Heat Gain, January (Btu/hr, ft² of floor area)

	8 AM	Noon	4 PM
	7.3	19.6	7.3

STEP 5: *Infiltration/Ventilation and Skin*

From Technique 17, the average ventilation heat loss rate for offices of 0.09 Btu/hr, °F, ft² (0.49 W/K, m²) was used as the rate of heat loss (or gain, if the outside air were hotter than inside).

The office is assumed to be well-insulated, with an average opaque skin *U*-value of 0.04 Btu/hr, °F, ft² (0.23 W/K, m²) (Technique 15). The floor slab has been neglected because its losses are assumed to be small. To adjust this value to include the glazing, which is 20% of the exposed skin area, use the graph from Technique 15 to determine the overall *U*-value of 0.12 Btu/hr, °F, ft² (0.68 W/K, m²). Next determine the ratio of the exposed skin area to the floor area. The wall area is (2 × 20' × 15') + (2 × 75' × 15') or 2850 ft² (256 m²). The roof is 1500 ft² (139 m²), making a total exposed skin area of 4350 ft² (404 m²). The skin area divided by the floor area is 4350/1500 = 2.9. Use the graph from Technique 15 to determine the heat loss of 0.35 Btu/hr, °F, ft² (1.99 W/K, m²) of building floor area.

The total rate of heat loss from the office is the ventilation/infiltration rate plus the loss through the skin: 0.09 + 0.35 = 0.44 Btu/hr, °F, ft² (2.5 W/K, m²).

STEP 6: *Schedule Internal Loads*

Once the rates of heat gain and loss have been determined, an average occupancy schedule should be completed for the hours of the day for each month of the year under consideration. (Any hours of the day can be used, and unusual conditions as well as average ones can be graphed.) The 4-hr intervals on the daily graphs are used in this example.

Schedule of Heat Gains, January (Btu/hr, ft² of floor area)

	People	Lights	Equip.	Solar	Total
12 mid	0	1.1	0	0	1.1
4 am	0	0⁺	0	0	0
8 am	0.7*	2.3**	4	7.3	14.3
12 n	1.3	4.5	4	19.6	29.4
4 pm	1.3	4.5	4	7.3	17.1
8 pm	0.7*	2.3**	4	0	7.0
12 mid	0	1.1⁺	0	0	1.1

* One-half the people have arrived or left
⁺ 25% of the lights are on for cleaning.
** 50% of the lights are on as people arrive and leave.

STEP 7: *Total Gains*

Sum the heat gains for each time period. Next, determine the average inside temperature. Plot the average inside temperature on the daily graph. For our example, an interior temperature of 75 °F (24 °C) all day is assumed.

STEP 8: *ΔT and Balance Point Temperatures*

Use the rate of heat gain for each hour, the total rate of heat loss, and the balance point chart from Technique 22 to determine the ΔT and balance point temperature for each hour. For example, at 8 PM in January, the rate of gain is 7.0 Btu/hr, ft² and the rate of loss is 0.45 Btu/hr, ft². The balance point chart reveals that the ΔT is 15 °F. Subtracting 15° from the inside temperature of 75 °F, the balance point is determined to be 60 °F. The following balance points were determined in a similar manner.

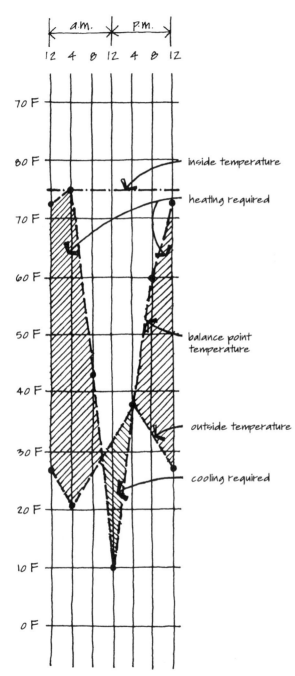

Combined Exterior and
Balance Point Temperature,
January, St. Louis

Balance Point Temperatures, January (F)

	Gain	Loss	ΔT	Inside	Bal. Pt.
12 mid	1.1	0.45	2	75-2	**73**
4 am	0	0.45	0	75-0	**75**
8 am	14.3	0.45	32	75-32	**43**
12 n	29.4	0.45	65	75-65	**10**
4 pm	17.1	0.45	38	75-38	**37**
8 pm	7.0	0.45	15	75-15	**60**
12 mid	1.1	0.45	2	75-2	**73**

STEP 9: Plot Balance Points

Plot the balance points on the same graph on which the outside temperatures were plotted.

STEP 10: Interpretation

When the balance point temperature exceeds the outside temperature, the building needs to be heated; when the outside temperature exceeds the balance point temperature, the building needs to be cooled. For the hypothetical building in St. Louis in January, the heat gain from people, lights, equipment, and the sun exceeds the heat loss during the sunny middle part of the day, and the heat loss exceeds the heat gain during the early morning, late afternoon, and all night.

Following the same procedures, graphs have been prepared for the three remaining months. The graphs for April, July, and October illustrate different patterns. In April, daytime net gains are roughly equal to night time losses, while in July and October, the building is clearly overheated much of the time. In July, there is almost no night cooling resource, while in October there is much more night cooling potential. The building load is clearly internally dominated—what happens inside the building in terms of heat gain is more important than what happens outside in terms of climate.

The process of creating balance point graphs is much faster using the *BPgraph* spreadsheet (Utzinger & Wasley, 1997a). *BPgraph* allows quick studies of "what-if" scenarios. The *Building Balance Point Resource Package* from the Vital Signs curriculum project offers an in-depth discussion of balance point concepts and methods (Utzinger & Wasley, 1997b). The two sets of balance point graphs following show the output as drawn by *BP-graph* for the same example building located in both St. Louis and Minneapolis. Note that there are some minor differences between the hand-calculated graphs and those drawn by *BPgraph*. This is because the months for analysis are fixed and some of the calculation methods are more sophisticated than the hand methods. The balance point line is broken into two parts: the balance point drop due to internal gains and the balance point drop due to solar gains. The solar curve is added to the bottom of the internal gains curve. The composite balance point graph is the lowest point of the two for any hour.

The building, when located in Minneapolis, Minnesota, performs differently and is more greatly influenced by the climate. In December the building needs to be heated all the time. In March and September it needs to be heated some of the time and cooled some of the time, and in June it needs to be cooled most of the time. Note that the balance point curves for St. Louis and Minneapolis are very similar because the building design and occupancy loads are the same and the solar gains have only minor differences in magnitude. However, the cooler outdoor temperatures shift the *relationship* between the balance point and temperature curves, shifting the building's needs more toward heating.

The matrix of **Energy Conservation Strategies Based on Balance Point Profiles** shows the three basic generic patterns: 1) heating need alone, 2) cooling need alone, and 3) both heating and cooling needs together in one day. For each pattern there is an associated set of strategies for energy conservation. ***First, identify the patterns that are appropriate for the building and then look across the row to see which strategies are appropriate. There are six groups of strategies, each of which is divided into two parts.***

The first strategy, ***adjust the interior temperature***, is based on the simple idea that the smaller the temperature difference between inside and out, the less energy will be required to heat or cool the building. This can be accomplished by allowing the temperature to fluctuate during unoccupied periods, say between 50 and 90 °F (10 and 32 °C); grouping activities together that have a high tolerance for temperature fluctuations, say between 60 and 80 °F (16 and 27 °C); and allowing the interior temperature to vary with the season, say 65 °F (18 °C) in the winter and 78° (26 °C) in the summer.

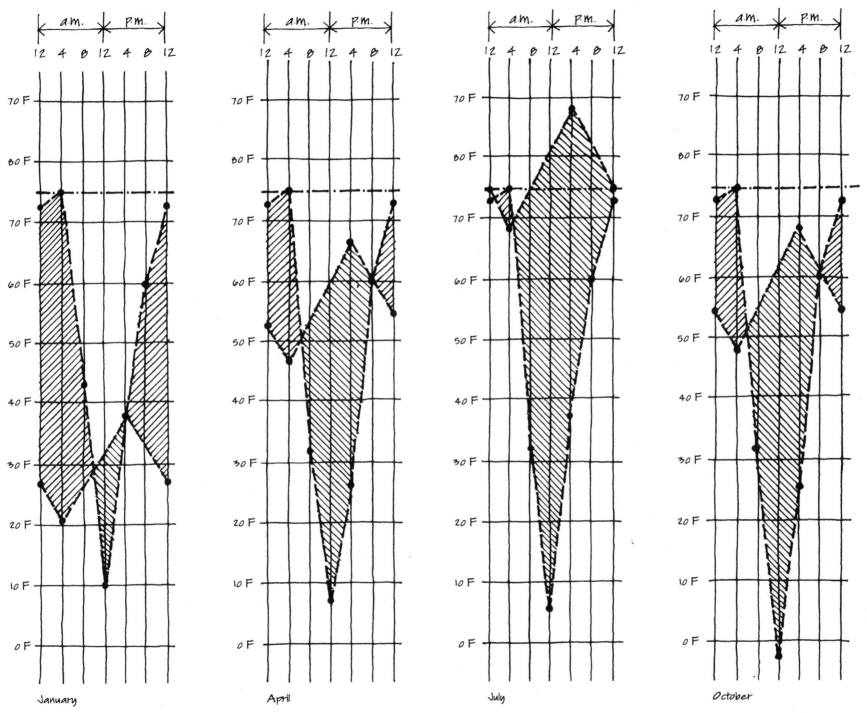

Balance Point Graphs for 1500-ft² Hypothetical Building in St. Louis, Missouri

In the second strategy, ***internal heat generation,*** internal sources of heat can be increased to help offset the heating load and decreased to reduce the cooling load. Daylighting is an excellent example of reducing the internal heat gains by decreasing the heat generated by electric lights.

The third strategy, ***solar heat gain,*** indicates that solar heat can be used to offset the heating load by, for example, increasing the area of south-facing glazing. It can also be decreased by shading devices to reduce the cooling requirements.

The fourth strategy, ***rate of heat flow through the envelope—gain or loss,*** indicates that the rate of heat flow can be increased by reducing the amount of insulation. This is an advantage if the building has a cooling requirement and the outside temperature is lower than the inside temperature. It is a disadvantage if the outside temperature is higher than the inside temperature. When the outside temperature is less than the inside temperature and heating is required, it is an advantage to decrease the heat flow through the envelope.

The fifth strategy, ***rate of heat transfer by ventilation—gain or loss,*** is similar to manipulating the rate of flow through the envelope. It is affected by envelope tightness, wind breaks or site channeling of wind, and whether or not heat recovery is used.

The sixth strategy, ***storage,*** is useful when a building has both a heating and cooling requirement in the same day. When excess heat is available during the cooling phase, it can be stored in the mass of the structure, or stored remotely, and used to heat the structure later in the day. When the outside temperature is sometimes below the inside temperature in buildings that always have a cooling load, the cold may be stored in the building's structure (or remotely) to help offset the cooling load when the outside temperature rises above the inside temperature.

A more detailed listing of energy conversation strategies in each of the six categories is found in the U.S. Department of Energy's (1980) publication *Predesign Energy Analysis*. See Utzinger and Wasley (1997b) for details on interpreting patterns of balance point graphs.

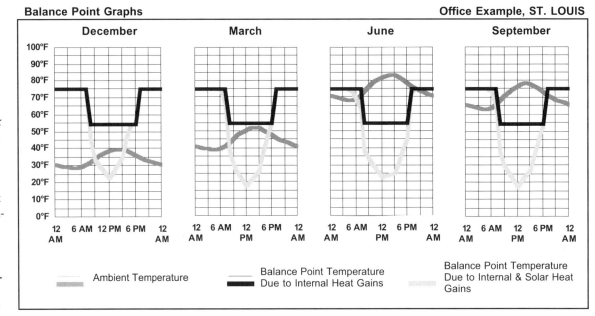

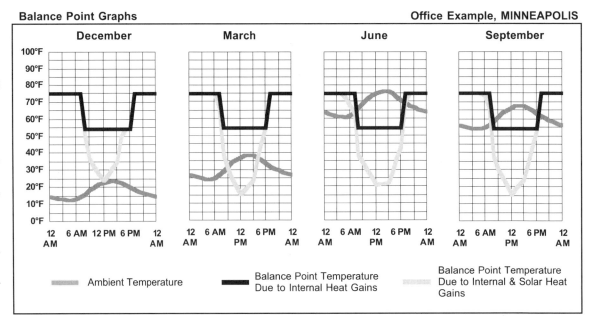

Balance Point Profiles From BPgraph Spreadsheet

Energy Conservation Strategies Based on Balance Point Profiles

All the strategies suggested for a particular pattern are not necessarily compatible with each other, and over the course of the year, different months or days will exhibit different patterns that have mutually exclusive design strategies. The designer's goal should be to identify the strategies that address the problems that occur the most often and have the potential for addressing multiple problems.

cooling always required		heating and cooling required			heating always required	Energy Conservation Strategies		Related Design Strategies in Parts 2 & 3
outside temperature below inside	outside temperature above inside	cooling – outside temperature below inside	cooling – outside temperature above inside	heating				
X	X	X	X			1. increase	interior temperature	+ increase/decrease: 11, 18, 46, 57
				X	X	2. decrease		+ decrease: 56
				X	X	3. increase	internal heat generation	+ increase/decrease: 12, 13, 14
X	X	X	X			4. decrease		+ decrease (daylighting): 51, 54, 55, 58, 70, 71, 78, 85, 89, 92, 94, 96, 98, 101, 102, 103
				X	X	5. increase	solar heat gain	+ increase: 52, 53, 59, 60, 61, 62, 63, 64, 82, 89, 93
X	X	X	X			6. decrease		+ increase/decrease: 17, 101 + decrease: 20, 48, 75, 81, 82, 98, 99, 100
X			X			7. increase	rate of heat flow through the envelope gain or loss	+ increase/decrease: 15, 19, 57, 63, 72, 76, 79, 88, 101
	X		X	X	X	8. decrease		+ decrease: 49, 81, 91, 97
X			X			9. increase	rate of heat transfer by ventilation gain or loss	+ increase (cooling): 50, 59, 65, 67, 68, 69, 73, 74, 90, 105, 106
	X		X	X	X	10. decrease		+ increase/decrease: 89, 95, 108, 109 + decrease: 87
		X	X			11. store heat	storage	+ store heat: 77
X				X		12. store cold		+ store heat/cold: 83, 88, 104 + store cold: 68

Energy Conservation Strategies Based on Balance Point Profiles

IE   Electric and Hot Water Loads

The two techniques in this section provide information used to design two types of building service systems that use the sun to reduce the building's use of energy for power and hot water. While they address issues other than heating, cooling, and daylighting, and are not purely passive in nature, they are included here because of their potentially significant impact on the design of roofs and walls.

Technique 24, Electric Loads, uses statistics on typical electric consumption for various building types and end uses to predict loads to be met by Photovoltaic Roof and Walls (Strategy 80). Photovoltaic cells convert sunlight directly into electricity.

Technique 25 uses similar data for hot water consumption rates in buildings to predict the loads to be met by Solar Hot Water systems (Strategy 86), one of the most cost-effective uses of solar energy.

24 The *ELECTRIC LOADS* required for sizing photovoltaic surfaces can be estimated from data on commercial and residential electricity consumption.

The sizing of photovoltaic roofs and walls (Strategy 80) is based on two important variables, the amount of solar radiation available from the sun and the electric load of the building. In designing for photovoltaic-supplied electricity, it is important to reduce both the total average daily load and the building's peak load.

There are four basic strategies for reducing electric loads: 1) choosing efficient equipment, 2) reducing the hours that equipment is used, 3) substituting equipment that uses a nonelectric fuel, and 4) supplying some or all of the need with renewable energy, such as capturing sun to heat water and using daylight instead of electric lights.

For lighting and appliance uses, electric load (and equipment heat gains) can be reduced by choosing efficient equipment. Fluorescent lights, for instance, use about one-fourth the energy of incandescent lights and reduce heat gains from lights by the same margin (Technique 13). Good daylighting design (Technique 21) can significantly reduce electricity use if lights are ar-

ranged properly and if automated daylight controls are used (Strategy 103).

In most buildings electricity is used for refrigeration, although gas-fired refrigeration is also available. Refrigeration equipment varies widely in efficiency and insulation levels. Some uses, such as clothes drying, cooking, and water heating, may be accomplished with either electricity or some form of combustible fuel, such as natural gas, propane, or heating oil. The price per Btu (per MJ) for electricity is several times higher than

OCCUPANCY TYPE	Hot Water			Lighting				Cooking		Refrigeration		Office Equip.		Other Uses		Total all uses		
	typ.	cons.	solar	typ.	best	med DF	hi DF	typ.	best	typ.	best	typ.	best	typ.	best	typ.	cons.	best
Assembly	0.88	0.44	0.22	12.54	5.01	3.01	2.01	0.24	0.14	0.40	0.24	0.24	0.18	1.04	0.63	15.35	6.02	2.68
	9.5	4.8	2.4	134.9	54.0	32.4	21.6	2.6	1.6	4.3	2.6	2.6	1.9	11.2	6.7	165.1	64.8	28.9
Education	1.21	0.60	0.30	12.46	4.98	2.99	1.99	0.16	0.10	0.64	0.39	1.81	1.29	1.37	0.82	17.64	7.35	3.91
	13.0	6.5	3.2	134.0	53.6	32.2	21.4	1.7	1.0	6.9	4.2	19.5	13.9	14.7	8.8	189.8	79.1	42.1
Food Sales	6.67	3.33	1.67	22.42	8.97	5.38	3.59	0.88	0.53	67.46	40.48	1.26	0.47	5.22	3.13	103.92	53.78	45.90
	71.8	35.9	17.9	241.2	96.5	57.9	38.6	9.5	5.7	725.9	435.5	13.6	5.0	56.2	33.7	1118.2	578.6	493.8
Food Service	2.09	1.04	0.52	14.87	5.95	3.57	2.38	10.69	6.41	9.08	5.45	1.75	0.66	2.49	1.49	40.97	19.51	15.16
	22.5	11.2	5.6	160.0	64.0	38.4	25.6	115.0	69.0	97.7	58.6	18.9	7.1	26.8	16.1	440.8	209.9	163.1
Health Care	0.80	0.40	0.20	23.87	9.55	5.73	3.82	1.12	0.67	2.65	1.59	1.26	0.82	8.12	4.87	37.82	13.04	7.01
	8.6	4.3	2.2	256.8	102.7	61.6	41.1	12.1	7.3	28.5	17.1	13.6	8.8	87.3	52.4	407.0	140.3	75.4
Lodging	2.89	1.45	0.72	17.68	7.07	4.24	2.83	1.37	0.82	1.04	0.63	0.74	0.44	4.34	2.60	28.06	10.40	5.07
	31.1	15.6	7.8	190.2	76.1	45.7	30.4	14.7	8.8	11.2	6.7	8.0	4.7	46.7	28.0	301.9	111.9	54.6
Mercantile	3.37	1.69	0.84	15.03	6.01	3.61	2.40	0.24	0.14	0.96	0.58	1.73	0.96	1.77	1.06	23.10	9.38	4.51
	36.3	18.2	9.1	161.7	64.7	38.8	25.9	2.6	1.6	10.4	6.2	18.6	10.3	19.0	11.4	248.6	100.9	48.5
Office	2.57	1.29	0.64	15.19	6.07	3.64	2.43	0.08	0.05	0.24	0.14	4.88	3.15	3.13	1.88	26.09	10.70	6.09
	27.7	13.8	6.9	163.4	65.4	39.2	26.1	0.9	0.5	2.6	1.6	52.5	33.9	33.7	20.2	280.7	115.2	65.6
Warehouse	1.29	0.64	0.32	11.49	4.60	2.76	1.84	0.00	0.00	0.88	0.53	1.21	1.01	1.21	0.72	16.07	6.78	3.54
	13.8	6.9	3.5	123.6	49.5	29.7	19.8	0.0	0.0	9.5	5.7	13.0	10.9	13.0	7.8	172.9	73.0	38.1
Other	2.01	1.00	0.50	12.86	5.14	3.09	2.06	0.00	0.00	0.08	0.05	0.74	0.52	2.41	1.45	18.10	6.72	2.88
	21.6	10.8	5.4	138.3	55.3	33.2	22.1	0.0	0.0	0.9	0.5	8.0	5.6	25.9	15.6	194.7	72.3	31.0

Commercial Building Electrical Energy Intensities, Wh/ft², day (Wh/m², day)

that for natural gas, and free solar energy can be used to heat hot water (Strategy 86).

Because space conditioning loads are large relative to the capacity of photovoltaic systems, the method presented below ignores space heating and cooling loads.

To determine the electric load for nonresidential buildings, use the table. For the occupancy type that most closely matches the building, choose one figure from each of the applicable end use categories; then add the total of all end use loads to get the total daily electric load for the building. The columns on the right end of the chart give the total of all end uses. Bold figures are I-P units; nonbold figures are in SI units. The total electric load, in Wh/ft², day (or Wh/m², day), may then be used in Strategy 80 to size photovoltaics.

Electricity for hot water is generally not recommended and will yield higher life cycle costs. The column "typ" represents typical average use for that occupancy. The columns labeled "cons" are for buildings that use water-conserving fixtures to reduce flow requirements for hot water by 50%. Values in the "solar" columns assume conserving fixtures and that 50% of the heat needed is supplied by a solar hot water system.

Lighting values are given for typical (typ.) commercial rates (installed base, 1993), for the best available lighting technology (best), and for two values of daylighting design, a medium level (best + med DF), representing an average daylight factor of 2–4%, and a high level (best + hi DF), for buildings with an average daylight factor greater than 4%. Loads for refrigeration, office equipment, and other equipment range from average commercial levels (typ.) to the most efficient technology on the market (best). For more information on electicity use in non-residential buildings, see EIA (1994); Koomy, et al. (1995); and Vine and Crawley (1991).

To estimate the electric load of residential buildings, choose one of four load profiles that most closely matches the building. For buildings where nonelectric appliances are used, subtract the load for those appliances from the total.

For more information on electicity use in residential buildings, see Reynolds, et al. (1994); EIA (1995); Vine and Crawley (1991); and Koomy (1995).

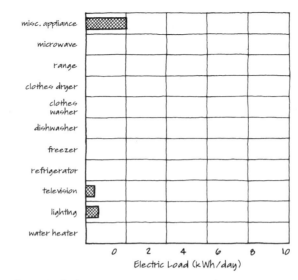

1) Best Technology + Appliance Substitution
(very low use, off-the-grid, with gas appliances)
Total Load: 3.0 kWh/day

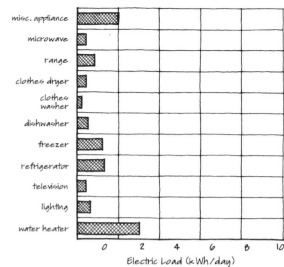

2) Best Electric Technology
(very conserving appliances)
Total Load: 10.7 kWh/ day

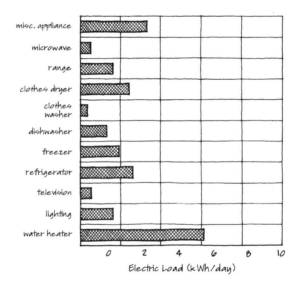

3) Typical USA All-Electric Household Loads
Total Load: 22.2 kWh/day

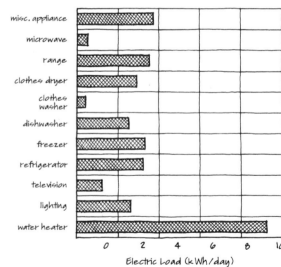

4) Very Generous Electricity Use
(above national average, older appliances)
Total Load: 33 kWh/day

Four Residential Electric Load Profiles

25 SERVICE HOT WATER LOADS required for sizing solar hot water collectors can be estimated from end use consumption data.

The size of a building's south-facing roof (north in Southern Hemisphere) for service hot water collectors is based in part on the magnitude of the annual hot water load (Strategy 86).

To determine the hot water load of a residential building, begin at the bottom of the residential graph with the number of residents and move up to the diagonal zone. Use the bottom of the zone for highly efficient fixtures and the top of the zone for older, less efficient fixtures. From the intersection move horizontally to read the annual load.

For a nonresidential building's hot water load, use a consumption value from the table that represents the building's occupancy and conservation level. Use this value to enter the nonresidential building's graph on the horizontal axis. Move vertically to the curve for the building floor area; from the intersection, move horizontally to read the annual load. These loads are used as input to Strategy 86.

Occupancy	Nonresidential Hot Water Load gal/ft², yr (L/m², yr)	
	Conserving	Conventional
Elem School	0.5 (20)	0.8 (35)
Office	0.7 (30)	1.2 (50)
Secondary School	0.9 (40)	1.6 (65)
Assembly	1.7 (70)	3.3 (135)
Mercantile & Service	2.5 (100)	4.1 (170)
Gymnasium	5.3 (215)	11.3 (460)
Residential	6.5 (265)	11.9 (485)
Clinic	7.5 (305)	8.9 (365)
Lodging	10.5 (430)	13.3 (540)
Hospital	14.1 (575)	18.4 (750)

Annual Nonresidential Hot Water Consumption

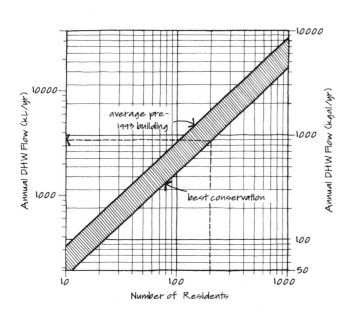

Residential Buildings Annual Hot Water Flow

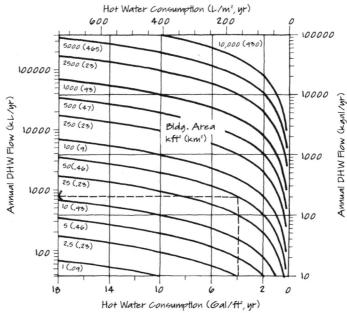

Nonresidential Buildings Annual Hot Water Flow

II DESIGN STRATEGIES

The goal of this section is to identify a comprehensive yet limited set of design strategies to use in the schematic part of the design process. They must be comprehensive so that no major opportunities are missed, but they also have to be few enough in number that they are memorable and do not bury the designer in too much information. We used five criteria to evaluate whether a design strategy should be included in this book. First, of course, it must deal with energy. Second, it must be primarily passive in nature. The term "passive" is defined rather loosely, and many of the illustrations are hybrid schemes, using some energy for pumps, fans, and controls. Third, the strategies must reveal major form and organizational relationships. This criterion eliminates a large number of very good energy-conservation strategies. For example, it eliminates the strategy of using plastic vapor barriers to reduce infiltration. This is an extremely important consideration in the design of any solar-heated building because infiltration is a major source of heat loss. However, because vapor barriers are thin and usually concealed in the wall, their consideration can easily be left to later stages of the design process. In many cases, if things don't take much space or have very specific locations they don't require exacting consideration in the scheming stage because the consequences of changing them later in the design process are not very great.

As a fourth criterion, even if a strategy doesn't reveal a major form or organizational relationship, it is included if it has a potentially major impact on the appearance of the building. Two examples are the way certain daylighting strategies limit the possible solid/void relationships on the facades and the way masonry tends to be used for thermal storage on the interior surfaces rather than on exterior surfaces.

Fifth, some small-scale strategies are included if ignoring them at the schematic stages would require redesign in later design stages. An example of this is night insulation—certainly an important energy-conserving strategy but probably not one that reveals major relationships. However, because storing the insulation can prove to be such a sticky problem later on in the design process, it is worth taking into account at the beginning.

The design strategies are organized first by three scales: building groups, buildings, and building parts. Most of the principles underlying energy phenomena do not change much within this scale range but their manifestations can. For example, while the sun's movement remains the same at all scales, the designer's thoughts about the sun's movement might be quite different at each scale. At the building groups scale, the concern might be how to arrange buildings and streets to provide solar access; at the building scale, how to arrange major living areas to receive the sun; and at the building parts scale, how to arrange the windows so that the sun penetrates deep into the room. All have to do with sun position and movement but the elements and issues under consideration are quite different at each scale. Some principles are developed in strategies at all scales, but in most cases the principles affect the strategies at just those one or two scales where the principles reveal major form and organizational relationships. With some imagination, the designer can easily extend a strategy from one scale to any other.

One might well expect a book about energy to be organized by categories like daylighting, heating, and cooling, and by subjects like ventilation and shading. These organizations are important and the indexes provide access to the contents by energy subject. However, in the schematic design stage, designers aren't thinking in an orderly fashion about a list of single isolated subjects, but are thinking about multiple subjects simultaneously; furthermore, designers are thinking about the subjects as secondary while primarily studying the arrangement of architectural elements such as streets, plazas, rooms, and windows. Therefore, in addition to scales, the other major organizing devices for this book are the architectural elements the designer works with.

At the building groups scale these elements are streets, open spaces, and buildings; at the building scale, rooms and courtyards; at the building parts scale, they are walls, roofs, floors, and windows. The architectural elements are grouped by form characteristics, such as shape, orientation, location, edge, enclosure, size, material, and color, and by organizational characteristics, like thin, compact, elongated, dispersed, zoned, and layered.

One way to use this book, when you are considering a particular problem—perhaps how to arrange a group of rooms—is to pursue the strategies at the building scale having to do with organizing rooms as a source of ideas to be included in your design. Another way to use the book, when working with a particular design idea like a compact organization of rooms, is to look up the characteristics of compact arrangements in terms of their potential for heating, cooling, and lighting.

Each design strategy is limited to a few pages, containing a strategy statement, an explanation of the phenomenon related to the strategy, a sizing rule of thumb or tool, and an illustration of the strategy in an architectural application. Each strategy was developed in light of three questions whose answers are necessary to design any physical object: What are the architectural elements involved? What is the relationship between those elements? How big are the elements? The questions of, "How big?", "What magnitude?" and "What configuration?" were consistently the most difficult to answer appropriately at the schematic design stage. With a couple of exceptions, all strategies where the "How big?" question is important have a sizing rule of thumb. Some useful energy-conservation strategies have been discarded because there was no rule of thumb for their sizing.

The strategy statements aren't directive; they don't say that one must do this to conserve energy. They do say that if one does this, that will probably be the result. They are stated this way first because the strategies are frequently redundant—the problem can be solved at several scales or with different elements. The strategy that fits with the designer's other concerns should be selected. Second, there is no single right way to do something without the agreement of the people involved and affected; therefore, the strategies are stated as possibilities, not as absolutes.

IIA   Building Groups

The strategies in the Building Groups section deal with the range of scales that extends beyond the single building to a cluster, block, town, or city. The major architectural elements they address are buildings, streets, and open spaces, which are the primary pieces that make up building groups. The strategies are mostly concerned with relationships between those pieces, either between buildings or between buildings and open spaces/streets.

The Building Groups scale strategies are among the most neglected by architects and urban designers, yet they are among the most important design strategies in the book. Larger scale strategies can be difficult to implement because the designer frequently does not have control over the larger site or urban pattern. However, these strategies are critical to passive design at the building scale because they control access to the site resources of sun, wind, and, light—and because they can have a major impact on reducing or magnifying the heating, cooling, and lighting loads to which buildings are subjected. The Building Groups strategies should be considered whenever one is charged with designing more than one building on a site, with neighborhood planning or guidelines, or with urban design. However,

even for projects of single-building scope the designer should consider Building Groups strategies because each building and site contributes incrementally over time to create a larger urban pattern. Also, even though a designer may control only one building on one site, the form and placement of that building creates a particular set of relationships with the street and with neighboring buildings, configures open space between buildings, and creates distinct microclimates around the building.

Several of the strategies (Strategies 20, 21, 26, and 27) are concerned with insuring access for individual areas to the basic ingredients for daylighting and passive solar heating and cooling, that is, the sun, wind, and light. These include four strategies concerned with access to wind in hot climates: Strategy 26, Converging Ventilation Corridors; 35, Loose Urban Patterns; 36, Breezy Streets; and 37, Dispersed Buildings. Three strategies address winter access to sun, both for buildings under the designers control and for neighboring sites: Strategy 29, Solar Envelopes; 38, East–West–Elongated Groups; and 42, Neighborhood Sunshine. Strategy 35, Daylight Envelopes, addresses the relationship of urban form to daylight access from the sky, as distinct from direct beam solar radiation from the sun. A related

strategy, 32, Glazed Streets, further details one approach to lighting in a dense urban context.

Conversely, four strategies address the need to block sun or wind to streets, open spaces and buildings when it is a liability: Strategy 27, Shared Shade; 33, Dense Urban Patterns; 43, Windbreaks; and 45, Overhead Shades.

Strategy 28, Topographic Microclimates, helps the designer locate building groups in terms of the effects of topography on modifying the regional macroclimate.

The remaining strategies involve forming building groups to manipulate the sun and the wind to improve the microclimates near the buildings. Three of these strategies involve manipulating the relationships between buildings and plants or water to cool air by shading or evaporation. These are Strategy 39, Interwoven Buildings and Plantings; 40, Interwoven Buildings and Water; and 44, Green Edges. Strategies 30, Tall Buildings, and 34, Gradual Height Transitions, show means of reducing the street level negative impacts of urban winter wind patterns on pedestrian comfort. Strategy 41, Winter Outdoor Rooms, combines admitting sun and blocking wind to extend the season of outdoor comfort.

26 *RADIAL VENTILATION CORRIDORS* **of streets or open space can take advantage of cool air drainage and night thermal currents. [cooling]**

Cities have a significant impact on metropolitan regional wind patterns in two ways. First, when regional wind currents are calm, the urban heat island effect, active mostly at night, causes centripetal wind patterns moving from areas of low density to areas of high density. These winds can be significantly stronger than those of the surrounding countryside (Givoni, 1998, pp. 285-286).

Second, because areas of higher development density produce and store more heat during the day than low density areas, and retain it longer, the temperature differential between high density areas and the surrounding countryside increases as the surrounding areas cool at night. Warmer, polluted city air then tends to rise, creating a negative pressure that sucks cooler air from the city perimeter toward the center.

Both of these effects, which are particularly pronounced on calm summer nights, can potentially be utilized to help flush dense areas of heat and pollutants. Two main urban design elements are required: 1) a band of undeveloped, preferably vegetated land at the perimeter that can serve as a cool air source, and 2) wide corridors to provide a pathway for the air to move from less dense to more dense areas. This implies a system of linear greenways or boulevards in a converging organization, with one or more centers.

As a rule, use wide vegetated avenues and open linear parks of 100 m (328 ft) or more in width to enhance urban cooling on calm nights. Orient some of these wind corridors parallel to the prevailing breezes to bring wind deep into dense, built-up areas. Locate the corridors to connect perimeter greenbelts with centers of built-up density. The area of the greenbelt should be 40–60% of the size of the urban area to be cooled. See Strategy 39 and 44 for details on sizing evapotranspiring areas.

To minimize wind velocity reduction in urban environments, organize streets and blocks into neighborhoods spaced perpendicular to summer winds and interspersed with open spaces of 400 × 400 m (1300 × 1300 ft) minimum size, which allow wind to reach its

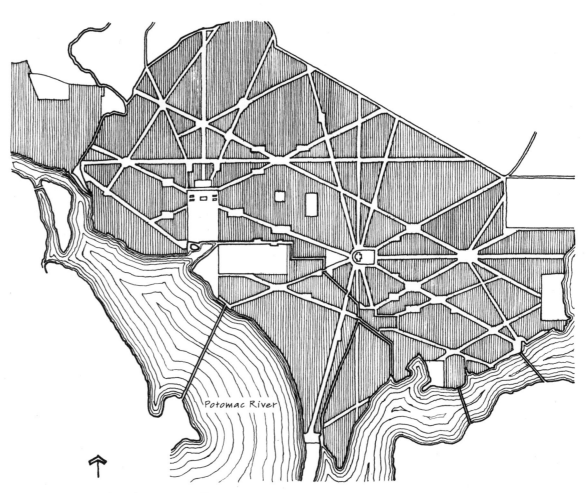

Potomac River

1856 Plan of Washington, DC

unobstructed velocity (Thurow, 1983, p. 27).

The **Plan of Washington, DC,** planned by Pierre L' Enfant in 1791, while not climatically derived, may serve as an example of city planning with wide axial avenues leading from edge to center. In this case, avenues lead to squares intended as nodes for development

(Reps, 1991, p. 79). Summer wind in Washington is from the south, and thus able to enter the city over the open space of the Potomac River. Other similar examples of this urban type include Canberra, Australia (Vale, 1992; Turnbull, 1999) and Belo Horizonte, Brazil (Lemos, 1995; Barreto, 1950).

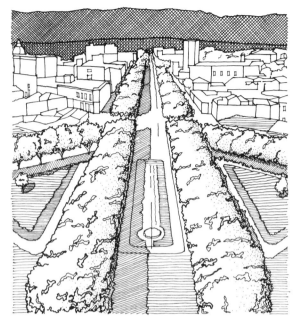

Shaded Boulevard, Belo Horizonte, Brazil

High Density Settlement

Low Density Settlement

Parks/Woods/ Cemeteries

Agriculture/ Undeveloped

→ Tributary Night Air Flow

⇨ Primary Night Air Flow

—·— River

Regional Plan of Stuttgart, Germany
Showing Topography, Open Space, and Night Air Drainage

In regions of significant topographic variation, terrain modifies prevailing winds to create local wind patterns. Additionally, gravity-driven air drainage often dominates during calm nights. Cooler, more dense air moves downslope in a pattern analogous to water. See Technique 6 for a discussion of microclimate air movement principles.

To make use of this resource in urban areas, locate undeveloped, vegetated areas on higher slopes to provide a cool air source to displace rising air in lower elevation developed areas. Connect the green cool air source with unobstructed downhill corridors leading to areas of high density.

The **city of Stuttgart, Germany,** an inland valley city with frequent calm winds and temperature inversions, has implemented a comprehensive land use plan based on wind and topography (Spirn, 1984, pp. 82–84; Hough, 1995, pp. 278–281; Hinweise für die Bauleitplanung, 1998). A system of open-space corridors channels cooler air down preserved, undeveloped park areas on hillsides and through low-density developed areas, con-

necting rural areas with the city center. Land use within the green corridors and on the slopes is strictly regulated; the preferred width is a minimum of 100 m. Within the city, shaded parks are connected to the air flow channels wherever possible, providing cooling for local neighborhoods.

27 *SHARED SHADE:* **Buildings can be arranged to shade each other and adjacent exterior spaces. [cooling]**

Narrow streets with tall buildings are characteristic of vernacular layouts of hot-arid cities. They create more shade than wide streets, and are useful for shading east and west facades on north/south-oriented streets. Since midday sun has a high altitude angle, it is usually difficult to use one building to shade the south-facing (north in Southern Hemisphere) facade of another building, except for very high building height to street width *(H/W)* proportions of 4:1 or greater. When the sun is high, horizontal shading elements like roofs, pergolas, or tree canopies are extremely effective. This may also be an effective strategy in hot-humid climates where buildings are placed farther apart to encourage cross-ventilation (Strategy 33 and 37). When facades are shaded, their surface temperatures are lower, thus the building gains less heat and uses less energy for cooling. When streets and sidewalks are shaded in summer, daytime mean radiant temperatures are lower, creating more comfort for pedestrians.

In hot-arid climates, which rely less on cross-ventilation cooling strategies, buildings are placed very close together, as they are in **Tunis, Tunisia,** to shade each other and adjacent streets. Hassan Fathy's design for **New Bariz, Egypt** organizes narrow streets oriented in the north–south direction to maximize morning and afternoon shade, deviating from this principle only as necessary to conform to topography (Steele, 1988, pp. 92–95).

During the day, the tops of facades along urban streets are warmer than the street level, because they receive more solar radiation than the lower portions. At night, the opposite is true; the street cools slower than the tops of the facades because, having a smaller sky view angle, it "sees" less of the heat-absorbing cool sky. Late at night, streets may collect stratified cooler air that settles, moving downslope or from roofs sloped toward the street. For similar building heights, wider streets create greater daily temperature swings on street and building surfaces than do narrow streets. The graph, derived from scale model tests, shows the signifi-

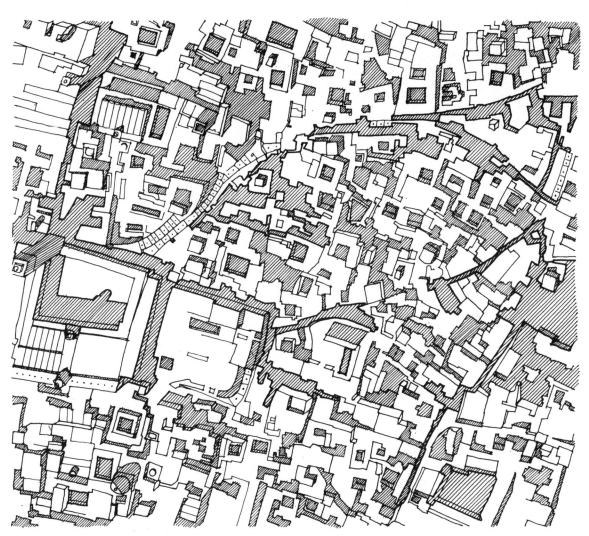

Aerial View of Tunis, Tunisia

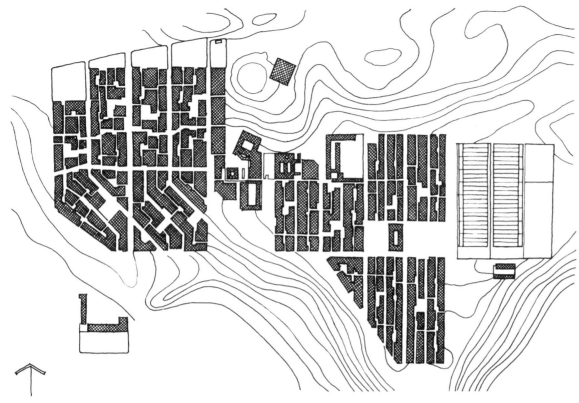

Site Plan for New Bariz, Egypt, 1967, Hassan Fathy

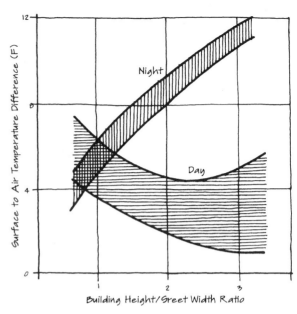

Impact of Cross-Section on Surface Temp.,
North-South Canyons Under Clear Sky

cant **Impact of Cross Section on Surface Temperatures** (El Sioufi & Boonyatikarn, 1987; El Sioufi, 1987). Studies of Dhaka, Bangladesh (23° N. lat.) indicate that streets with an *H/W* ratio of 1:1 can have a summer daily high temperature 4 °C (7 °F) higher than streets with an *H/W* ratio of 3:1 (Ahmed, 1994).

The space formed by the street and building walls on either side is often called an "urban canyon." North-south axis canyons benefit the most from shadows cast by buildings. The diagrams of the **Impact of Cross Section on Shading Patterns** show that these canyons will have their west-facing facade in shade all morning (also, their east-facing facade in shade all afternoon). Depending on the ratio of building height to street width, more or less of the street and the facade facing the sun will be in shadow. The effectiveness of shading varies with the canyon's proportions. The shadow line

moves up on facades as the *H/W* ratio increases. Taller buildings on narrower streets create more shade.

The amount of shade cast by a building onto the street and the opposite building is a function of the street orientation and width, the building heights, and the sun angles. The diagrams on the next page show shadows cast on a north–south canyon for a range of sun angles at three latitudes.

The profile angle of the sun for a given latitude, orientation, and time is used to cast shadows in section. To find the Profile Angles for Street Section Shading Design on a north–south street, use the value from the table for the combination of the site's latitude and the desired shading time criteria. Then draw the angle from the top of the east side building to find the morning shadow line, or draw starting at the top of the west side building to find the afternoon shadow line.

Notice that profile angles are low early in the morning when the sun is low and the azimuth is farther from south (N in SH), and that the profile increases to a maximum of 90° at noon, when the sun shines from the south. While at midday there is little shade of east and west facades, there is also little heat gain to those walls because of the acute angle of incidence. Profile angles for any combination of orientation and sun position can be found using the *LOF Sun Angle Calculator* (Libbey-Owens-Ford, 1974) or the *PEC Solar Calculator* (Benton and Marcial, 1993).

In hot climates, narrow, better shaded streets are more appropriate for pedestrian circulation, outdoor living areas, and shopping. Since east-west streets are difficult to shade by buildings, they may be wider and thus appropriate to vehicular traffic, while being shaded by arcades, awnings, or other element scale shading devices (Strategies 45 and 99). Since at least one side of north–south streets is always shaded, arcades for shading purposes are redundant there.

Narrow streets may also be associated with higher pollution concentrations, more noise, and lower wind speeds. Since radiant night sky cooling is less effective, for narrow streets, it is necessary to ensure adequate

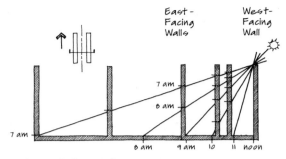

East-Facing Walls / West-Facing Wall

7 am
8 am
7 am
8 am 9 am 10 11 noon

0° Latitude (equator)

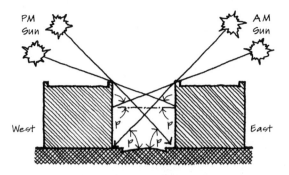

Profile Angle for North-South Canyons

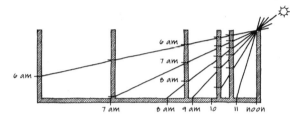

6 am
7 am
8 am
6 am
7 am 8 am 9 am 10 11 noon

24° Latitude

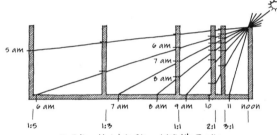

5 am
6 am
7 am
8 am
6 am   7 am   8 am 9 am 10 11 noon
1:5   1:3   1:1   2:1 3:1

Building Height: Street Width Ratio

48° Latitude

Impact of Cross-Section on Shading Patterns, North-South Canyons on Jun 21

night ventilation to cool the streets and exterior building surfaces (Strategies 26 and 36). Take care in locating buildings, such that shading does not extend into the cool season when solar heat is desirable (Strategies 29, 31, and 38).

Latitude	6 AM / 6 PM	7 AM / 5 PM	8 AM / 4 PM	9 AM / 3 PM	10 AM / 2 PM	11 AM / 1 PM	12 noon
0°	0	15	30	45	60	75	90
4°	2	17	31	46	61	75	90
8°	3	18	33	47	61	76	90
12°	5	20	34	48	62	76	90
16°	7	21	35	49	62	76	90
20°	8	22	36	49	63	76	90
24°	10	23	36	49	63	76	90
28°	12	24	37	50	63	76	90
32°	13	25	37	50	63	76	90
36°	14	26	37	49	62	76	90
40°	16	26	37	49	62	76	90
44°	17	27	37	49	62	75	90
48°	18	27	37	48	61	75	90
52°	19	27	37	48	60	75	90
56°	20	28	36	47	59	74	90
60°	21	28	36	46	58	73	90
64°	21	28	35	45	57	72	90
68°	22	27	34	43	55	71	90
72°	22	27	33	42	54	70	90

Profile Angles (degrees) for Shading Design in Section of North-South-Oriented Streets
Jun 21 (Northern Hemisphere), Dec 21 (Southern Hemisphere)

28 Favorable *TOPOGRAPHIC MICROCLIMATES* can be used to locate building groups. [heating and cooling]

On a large scale, topography, solar radiation, and wind combine to produce microclimates that accentuate certain characteristics of the area's macroclimate. These microclimates make some locations within the topography more desirable than others, depending on the macroclimate and season. Building group location can thus enhance comfort and productivity, change the length of heating or cooling seasons, and reduce energy used for heating and cooling.

These considerations are much more important for exterior spaces or skin-load-dominated buildings, in which heating and cooling loads are affected primarily by climate, than for internal-load-dominated buildings in which heating and cooling requirements are affected primarily by how much heat is generated in the building and which have a cooling requirement much of the time.

The southeastern **Turkish city of Mardin,** located in a hot-arid climate with mild, but still cool winters, is sited on a 20–25° slope above a steeper rise that abuts the plain below. Streets are organized to follow topography, giving the whole city a southeasterly orientation that reduces afternoon solar heat gain. Densely packed buildings give self-shading on east and west orientations, while allowing good winter solar access to south facades. On summer nights, differences in air density create a downhill flow of cool air that pools in low areas, between buildings and behind walls. Such cool pools are often used for outdoor sleeping. Calculations indicate that building groups in this region located on a 20% south-facing slope require approximately 50% less heat to maintain the same indoor temperatures than the same settlement on a flat plain (Turan, 1983).

Several principles can be applied to predict the microclimate on a site:

1) Air movement is driven by density. Cool air flows downhill because it is more dense than warm air. At night, a cool layer forms near the ground, settling into low areas and depressions and behind anything that will form a "dam." Convex, higher elevation landforms shed cool air, while low elevation, concave forms collect it.

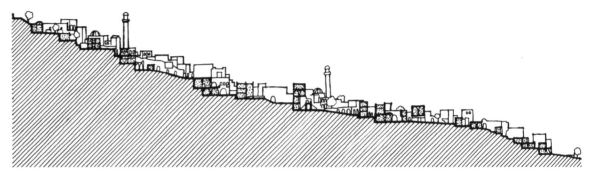

Cross-Section, City of Mardin, Turkey

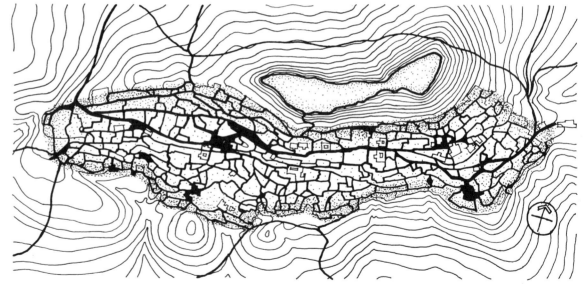

Site Plan, City of Mardin, Turkey

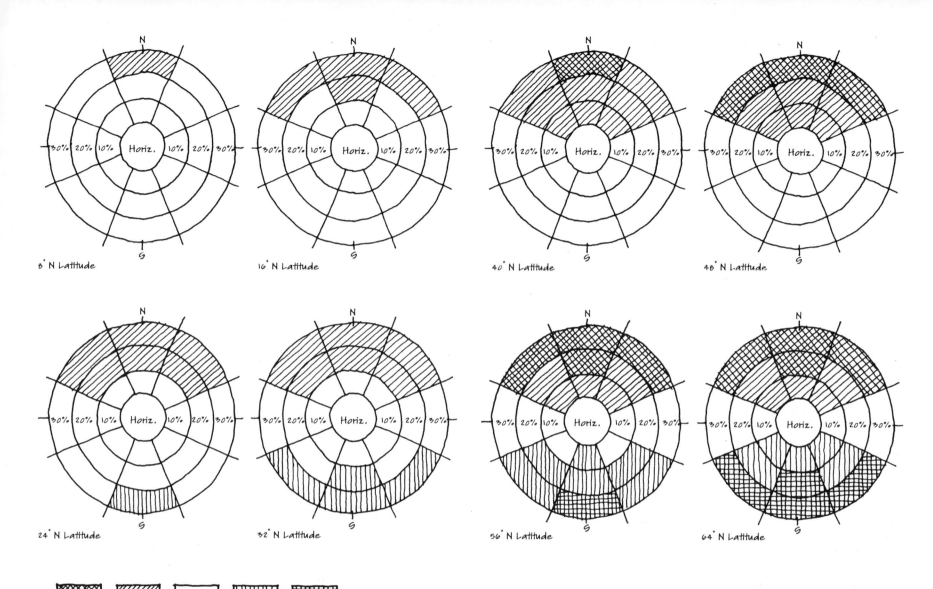

Legend:

| 75–85% | 85–95% | 95–105% | 105–115% | 115–125% |

Percentatage of Radiation on a Horizontal Surface

0° N Latitude

16° N Latitude

40° N Latitude

48° N Latitude

24° N Latitude

32° N Latitude

56° N Latitude

64° N Latitude

Combined Effect of Slope and Orientation on Annual Radiation

Developed from calcualtions by the METEORNORM software (Meteotest, 1997) using midcontinent locations, low elevation, and northern latitudes in the Western Hemisphere.

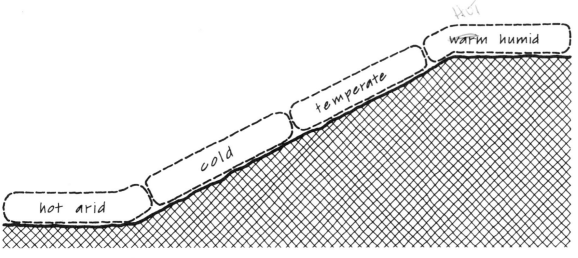

Slope Location Based on Climate

mer daytime high temperatures are lower near water. This nonlinear effect gives great differences in microclimate over relatively short distances, especially within 20 km (12 miles) of a sea. (Givoni, 1998, p. 277).

5) High mountains create wet windward slopes, while low hills create wet leeward slopes. Humid air masses caused to rise rapidly when striking mountainous slopes cause cooling and rain on windward slopes as the air reaches its dewpoint. Crossing the ridge, the air descends and warms, lowering its relative humidity and leaving the leeward slopes drier. The situation is reversed for smaller differences in elevation, where the air is carried over a hill by increased wind velocity, allowing precipitation to drop on the leeward side where currents are more irregular.

The general design objectives for each climatic region are
• Cold: Maximize the warming effects of solar radiation. Reduce the impact of winter wind.
• Temperate: Maximize warming effects of the sun in winter. Maximize shade in summer. Reduce the impact of winter wind but allow air circulation in summer.
• Hot-Arid: Maximize shade and minimize hot, dust-laden winds.
• Hot-Humid: Maximize shade and wind.

These principles, combined with those of the interaction of air movement and terrain (Technique 6), create distinct microclimates that have advantages or disadvantages, depending on the region (Robinette, 1977, p. 69; Zeren, 1982, p. 35).

As the diagrammatic section of Slope Locations Based on Climate shows, the most favorable microclimate location for each region is
• Cold: *Low on a south-facing slope (N in SH)* to increase solar radiation; low enough to give wind protection but high enough to avoid cold air collection at the bottom of the valley.
• Temperate: *In the middle to upper part of the slope* with access to both sun and wind, but protected from high winds.
• Hot-Arid: *At the bottom of the slope* for exposure to cold air flow at night and *on east orientations* for decreased solar exposure in the afternoons.
• Hot-Humid: *At the top of the slope* for exposure to wind and *on east orientations* for decreased solar exposure in the afternoons.

2) Temperate varies with elevation. The cooling rate near the ground is about 0.8 °C (1.4 °F) for each 100 m (328') of elevation. Higher elevations are cooler than low elevations, and air moving down slope will thus be cooler than air it replaces lower down, and vice versa. (Givoni, 1998, p. 276)

3) Solar radiation varies with terrain aspect. Aspect is the combined slope and orientation of a surface in relation to the sun. A surface perpendicular (normal) to the sun's rays receives the most radiation per unit of surface area. Therefore, south-facing slopes (north in Southern Hemisphere) receive more sun than other orientations, easterly slopes receive more morning sun, and western slopes receive more afternoon sun. However, slope has little impact on total daily radiation for east and west orientations. Steeper slopes generally receive more sun that flat areas, except north-facing slopes (S in SH), which receive minimum radiation. The diagrams of the **Combined Effect of Slope and Orientation on Annual Radiation** show that aspect has very little impact on radiation levels at tropical latitudes, and that the effect increases with latitude. The amount of radiation on a site will affect its temperature microclimate, the rate of snowmelt, the length of its growing season, frost dates, and the deciduous plant cycles. At temperate latitudes on a south slope of 20°, spring will arrive about 2 weeks earlier than on a flat site (Olgyay, 1963, p. 49).

4) Large water bodies moderate the daily and annual temperature range. Sites near oceans and large lakes have both less variation between day and night and less between summer and winter than inland sites. Sum-

29 *SOLAR ENVELOPES* **can be used to ensure access to the sun for buildings, streets, and open spaces. [heating and daylighting]**

The solar envelope defines the maximum buildable volume for a given site that will not shade adjacent sites, thereby assuring the availability of solar energy to those sites. The size and shape of the solar envelope varies with site size, orientation, and latitude, the times of day solar access is desired, and the amount of allowable shading on adjacent streets and buildings (Knowles, 1981, p. 51).

Once the shape and orientation of the site have been determined, the geometry of the solar envelope is determined by the time period during which solar access must be maintained. For example, to construct a solar envelope for a site at 40° N latitude that provides solar access to adjacent sites between 9 AM and 3 PM all year, select the month when the sun is lowest in the sky (December) to determine the slope of the north part of the envelope and the month when the sun is highest in the sky (June) to determine the slope of the south part of the envelope. Assuming that before 9 AM and after 3 PM shading adjacent sites is permitted, the sun positions at 9 AM and 3 PM on Dec 21 and Jun 21 define the maximum size of the solar envelope. At 40° N latitude the sun positions at those times are

- Dec 21, 9 AM and 3 PM:
  Altitude 14°, Azimuth +/– 42°
- Jun 21, 9 AM and 3 PM:
  Altitude 49°, Azimuth +/– 80°

The diagonal line to the northwest corner is defined by the sun's angle at 9 AM; the diagonal to the northeast corner, is defined by the angle at 3 PM. The intersection of the morning and afternoon diagonals forms one end of a potential ridge line. But because the sun at 40° N latitude between 9 AM and 3 PM doesn't get to the north of east or west, it never casts a shadow to south. Therefore, it is assumed that the south face of the solar envelope rises vertically from the edge of the site. If the sun is ever north of east and west at the cutoff times, then the southwest and southeast diagonals are defined by the sun's angle at 9 AM and 3 PM. The

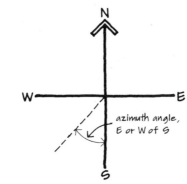

a) Azimuth Angle

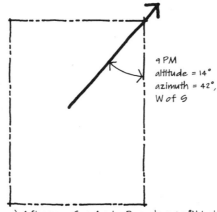

c) Afternoon Sun Angle, December 40 °N Lat.

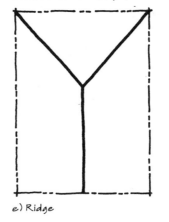

e) Ridge

Construction of Solar Envelope

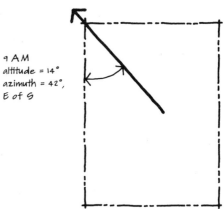

b) Morning Sun Angle, December 40 °N Lat.

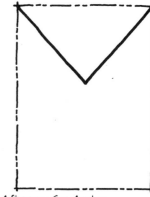

d) Combined Morning and Afternoon Sun Angles

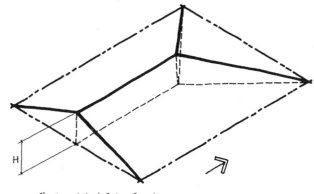

f) Completed Solar Envelope

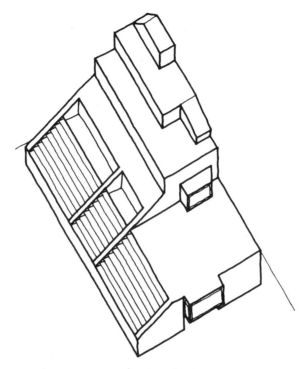

Hypothetical Building Within Solar Envelope,
View From Northwest

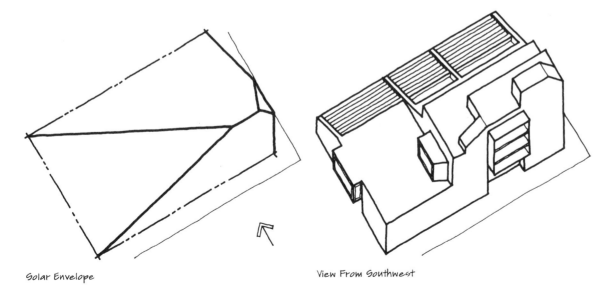

Solar Envelope

Solar Envelope Example

View From Southwest

ridge line is formed by the intersection of either the winter diagonals or the summer diagonals, whichever is lower in height. The completed envelope defines the maximum building height at any point on the site that will not shade an adjacent site from 9 AM to 3 PM from Dec 21 to Jun 21.

Ralph Knowles and his students at the University of Southern California have done extensive design exercises using the solar envelope at various scales (Knowles, 1981, pp. 179–282). The **Hypothetical Solar Envelope Example** shows a small building developed for a corner site using a complex solar envelope that extended beyond the site boundaries.

In a study of **Solar Envelopes to Control Massing in the City of Toronto, Canada,** three different sunlight criteria were used in different parts of the city: 3, 5, and 7 hr of sunlight for the commercial streets in the central district, shopping streets and tourist areas, and residential areas on the edge of downtown, respectively. The drawing shows allowable building envelopes to ensure 3 hr of sunlight on at least one sidewalk of all streets between 10:30 AM and 1:30 PM on Sep 21. While all of the study's recommendations were not adopted by the city, height and bulk controls were implemented for all main streets leading from the city core into neighborhoods (Bosselmann et al., 1995).

To construct the solar envelope for a given rectangular block of cardinal (0°) or 45° street orientations, providing solar access at specified targets times and dates:

1) Determine the site's latitude and the criteria for the period of solar access. Select from one of the combinations of dates and times in the tables for **Ridge Heights of Solar Envelopes** on the following pages.

2) Determine or assume the dimensions of the site; the street width or any open space may be included in the shadow-protected area.

3) From the table for the site's orientation, find the plan angles of the solar envelope for the correct latitude and time; draw these angles on a plan of the block. North and south latitudes use the same angles, but the envelopes will be mirror images.

4) Connect the points of intersection of the plan angles; this represents the ridge.

5a) Cardinal orientation: if the ridge runs north-south, find its height in the table as a function of the X or east–west dimension of the site; if there is no ridge

STREETS, OPEN SPACES, & BUILDINGS: Space and Orientation

or if the ridge runs east–west, find its height in the table as a function of the *Y*, the north–south dimension of the site.

5b) 45° orientation: find the ridge height in the table as a function of the shortest dimension.

Variables that affect the configuration of the envelope are the latitude, the period of solar access (shading protection), the size of the site, its proportions, slope, and orientation, and the nature of its edge conditions. Because the winter sun at high latitudes is very low, sometimes even below the horizon, solar access all winter can be difficult, if not impossible. Therefore, the tables show a range of more practical solar access criteria appropriate for each latitude. For the same shading criteria, high latitudes allow less height and therefore less volume than low latitudes. Reducing the period of solar access will result in a higher but sharper peak. Increasing the size of the site will decrease the skin-to-volume ratio of the envelope. If the proportions of the site result in a north–south ridge, the envelope will contain less volume to be developed than if the proportions of the site result in an east–west ridge.

On a slope, if the ridge of the envelope runs with the direction of the slope, the ridge height will remain the same. If the ridge runs across the direction of the slope, the ridge height will vary; a south slope will increase the height and all other slopes will decrease the height.

Changing the orientation of a level site, that is, rotating its alignment to 30°, 45°, or 60° off the cardinal orientations, reduces the envelope height and volume.

Finally, the edge condition of the block may be varied to increase the volume of the envelope. The point of solar access may be taken to begin a distance horizontally from the edge of the block (across the street). It may also be taken a distance vertically from street level (the top of a fence or the top of a lower story). In either case, the effect is to lift the envelope onto a platform. This is particularly viable in dense, multiuse, vertical zoning where higher residential floors may require solar access for heating, while lower commercial floors do not. Existing sites often have complex edge conditions that allow a variety of manipulations of the envelope.

Solar envelopes can also be constructed from the point of view of the site being protected, such as when the massing of neighboring buildings is limited to preserve solar access to an open space, such as a square or garden.

Solar access criteria for the open space depends on the use of the space and its climate. For gardens, sun access during the growing season is critical, while center city plazas may use criteria that support midday pedestrian use. Warm climates will have longer growing seasons than cool climates. Solar radiation can also improve outdoor comfort in cool seasons (Technique 11). From the sun path on the critical times and dates, a maximum building envelope may be constructed.

Many plants need at least 6 hr of direct sunlight, so this may be taken as the minimum planning goal for vegetated open space. The best hours are centered around solar noon; for the 6 hr goal, protecting solar access from 9 AM to 3 PM is sufficient. The growing season is usually assumed to be the period between the first and last frosts for a particular site (Splittstoesser, 1984). Although many plants will continue to grow after frost has set in, the first frost date (last frost-free date) is a reasonable goal for urban situations. Since the sun is almost always lower in the sky at the first frost in the fall than at the last frost in the spring, this date may be used as the controlling solar access criteria. Dates for the first frost, or the end of the growing season, may be roughly determined from the maps in Appendix B. Criteria for winter warming of open space by the sun are similar to those for other solar envelopes. The most radiation occurs in the middle of the day, from 10 AM to 2 PM.

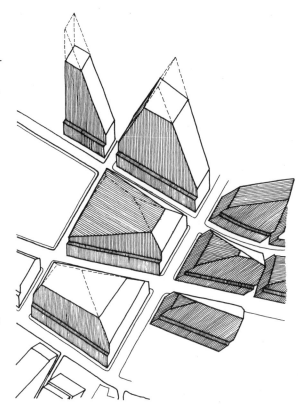

Solar Envelopes to Control Massing in Toronto, Canada

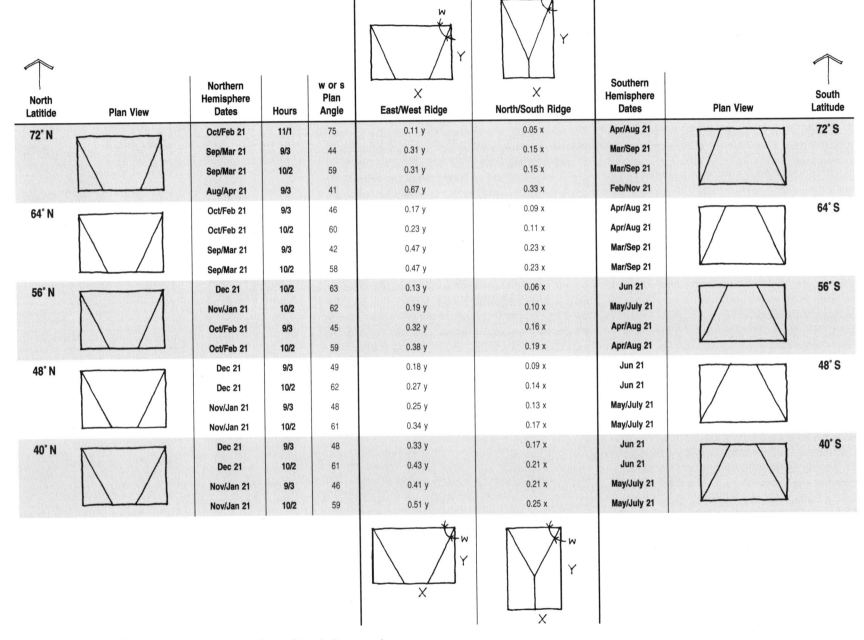

North Latitide	Plan View	Northern Hemisphere Dates	Hours	w or s Plan Angle	East/West Ridge	North/South Ridge	Southern Hemisphere Dates	Plan View	South Latitude
72° N		Oct/Feb 21	11/1	75	0.11 y	0.05 x	Apr/Aug 21		72° S
		Sep/Mar 21	9/3	44	0.31 y	0.15 x	Mar/Sep 21		
		Sep/Mar 21	10/2	59	0.31 y	0.15 x	Mar/Sep 21		
		Aug/Apr 21	9/3	41	0.67 y	0.33 x	Feb/Nov 21		
64° N		Oct/Feb 21	9/3	46	0.17 y	0.09 x	Apr/Aug 21		64° S
		Oct/Feb 21	10/2	60	0.23 y	0.11 x	Apr/Aug 21		
		Sep/Mar 21	9/3	42	0.47 y	0.23 x	Mar/Sep 21		
		Sep/Mar 21	10/2	58	0.47 y	0.23 x	Mar/Sep 21		
56° N		Dec 21	10/2	63	0.13 y	0.06 x	Jun 21		56° S
		Nov/Jan 21	10/2	62	0.19 y	0.10 x	May/July 21		
		Oct/Feb 21	9/3	45	0.32 y	0.16 x	Apr/Aug 21		
		Oct/Feb 21	10/2	59	0.38 y	0.19 x	Apr/Aug 21		
48° N		Dec 21	9/3	49	0.18 y	0.09 x	Jun 21		48° S
		Dec 21	10/2	62	0.27 y	0.14 x	Jun 21		
		Nov/Jan 21	9/3	48	0.25 y	0.13 x	May/July 21		
		Nov/Jan 21	10/2	61	0.34 y	0.17 x	May/July 21		
40° N		Dec 21	9/3	48	0.33 y	0.17 x	Jun 21		40° S
		Dec 21	10/2	61	0.43 y	0.21 x	Jun 21		
		Nov/Jan 21	9/3	46	0.41 y	0.21 x	May/July 21		
		Nov/Jan 21	10/2	59	0.51 y	0.25 x	May/July 21		

Ridge Heights of Solar Envelopes–Cardinal Orientation, part one

North Latitide	Plan View	Northern Hemisphere Dates	Hours	w or s Plan Angle	East/West Ridge	North/South Ridge	Southern Hemisphere Dates	Plan View	South Latitude
32° N		Dec 21	9/3	46	0.49 y	0.25 x	Jun 21		32° S
		Dec 21	10/2	59	0.60 y	0.30 x	Jun 21		
		Nov/Jan 21	9/3	44	0.59 y	0.29 x	May/July 21		
		Nov/Jan 21	10/2	57	0.70 y	0.35 x	May/July 21		
24° N		Dec 21	9/3	44/9	0.68 y	0.34 x	Jun 21		24° S
		Dec 21	10/2	56/5	0.82 y	0.41 x	Jun 21		
		Nov/Jan 21	9/3	42/9	0.79 y	0.39 x	May/July 21		
		Nov/Jan 21	10/2	54/5	0.93 y	0.46 x	May/July 21		
16° N		Dec 21	9/3	41/18	0.91 y	0.46 x	Jun 21		16° S
		Dec 21	10/2	53/20	1.08 y	0.54 x	Jun 21		
		Nov/Jan 21	9/3	38/18	1.05 y	0.52 x	May/July 21		
		Nov/Jan 21	10/2	50/20	1.23 y	0.61 x	May/July 21		
8° N		Dec 21	9/3	37/25	1.20 y	0.60 x	Jun 21		8° S
		Dec 21	10/2	48/32	1.44 y	0.72 x	Jun 21		
		Nov/Jan 21	9/3	33/25	1.39 y	0.70 x	May/July 21		
		Nov/Jan 21	10/2	44/32	1.65 y	0.83 x	May/July 21		
0°		Dec 21	9/3	32/32	1.62 y	0.81 x	Jun 21		0°
		Dec 21	10/2	41/41	1.98 y	0.99 x	Jun 21		
		Nov/Jan 21	9/3	28/32	1.85 y	0.92 x	May/July 21		
		Nov/Jan 21	10/2	37/41	2.34 y	1.17 x	May/July 21		

Ridge Heights of Solar Envelopes-Cardinal Orientation, part two

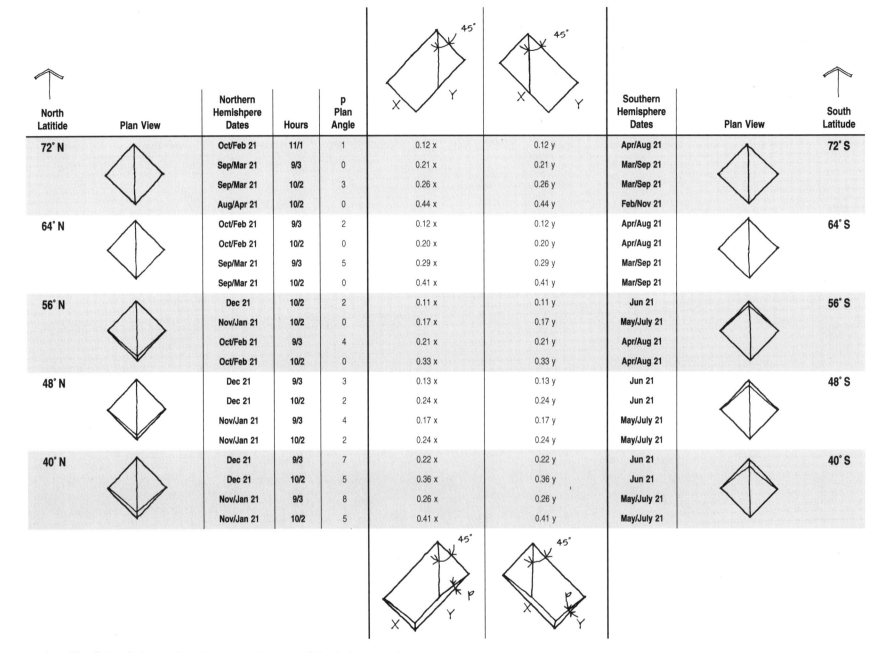

North Latitide	Plan View	Northern Hemishpere Dates	Hours	p Plan Angle			Southern Hemisphere Dates	Plan View	South Latitude
72° N		Oct/Feb 21	11/1	1	0.12 x	0.12 y	Apr/Aug 21		72° S
		Sep/Mar 21	9/3	0	0.21 x	0.21 y	Mar/Sep 21		
		Sep/Mar 21	10/2	3	0.26 x	0.26 y	Mar/Sep 21		
		Aug/Apr 21	10/2	0	0.44 x	0.44 y	Feb/Nov 21		
64° N		Oct/Feb 21	9/3	2	0.12 x	0.12 y	Apr/Aug 21		64° S
		Oct/Feb 21	10/2	0	0.20 x	0.20 y	Apr/Aug 21		
		Sep/Mar 21	9/3	5	0.29 x	0.29 y	Mar/Sep 21		
		Sep/Mar 21	10/2	0	0.41 x	0.41 y	Mar/Sep 21		
56° N		Dec 21	10/2	2	0.11 x	0.11 y	Jun 21		56° S
		Nov/Jan 21	10/2	0	0.17 x	0.17 y	May/July 21		
		Oct/Feb 21	9/3	4	0.21 x	0.21 y	Apr/Aug 21		
		Oct/Feb 21	10/2	0	0.33 x	0.33 y	Apr/Aug 21		
48° N		Dec 21	9/3	3	0.13 x	0.13 y	Jun 21		48° S
		Dec 21	10/2	2	0.24 x	0.24 y	Jun 21		
		Nov/Jan 21	9/3	4	0.17 x	0.17 y	May/July 21		
		Nov/Jan 21	10/2	2	0.24 x	0.24 y	May/July 21		
40° N		Dec 21	9/3	7	0.22 x	0.22 y	Jun 21		40° S
		Dec 21	10/2	5	0.36 x	0.36 y	Jun 21		
		Nov/Jan 21	9/3	8	0.26 x	0.26 y	May/July 21		
		Nov/Jan 21	10/2	5	0.41 x	0.41 y	May/July 21		

Ridge Heights of Solar Envelopes-45 Degree Orientation, part one

North Latitude	Plan View	Northern Hemisphere Dates	Hours	p Plan Angle			Southern Hemisphere Dates	Plan View	South Latitude
32° N		Dec 21	9/3	12	0.30 x	0.30 y	Jun 21		32° S
		Dec 21	10/2	9	0.46 x	0.46 y	Jun 21		
		Nov/Jan 21	9/3	14	0.33 x	0.33 y	May/July 21		
		Nov/Jan 21	10/2	10	0.51 x	0.51 y	May/July 21		
24° N		Dec 21	9/3	18	0.35 x	0.35 y	Jun 21		24° S
		Dec 21	10/2	15	0.54 x	0.54 y	Jun 21		
		Nov/Jan 21	9/3	20	0.38 x	0.38 y	May/July 21		
		Nov/Jan 21	10/2	17	0.58 x	0.58 y	May/July 21		
16° N		Dec 21	9/3	26	0.40 x	0.40 y	Jun 21		16° S
		Dec 21	10/2	24	0.60 x	0.60 y	Jun 21		
		Nov/Jan 21	9/3	28	0.42 x	0.42 y	May/July 21		
		Nov/Jan 21	10/2	25	0.64 x	0.64 y	May/July 21		
8° N		Dec 21	9/3	35	0.43 x	0.43 y	Jun 21		8° S
		Dec 21	10/2	34	0.64 x	0.64 y	Jun 21		
		Nov/Jan 21	9/3	37	0.44 x	0.44 y	May/July 21		
		Nov/Jan 21	10/2	36	0.67 x	0.67 y	May/July 21		
0°		Dec 21	9/3	45	0.44 x	0.44 y	Jun 21		0°
		Dec 21	10/2	45	0.65 x	0.65 y	Jun 21		
		Nov/Jan 21	9/3	47	0.45 x	0.45 y	May/July 21		
		Nov/Jan 21	10/2	47	0.68 x	0.68 y	May/July 21		

Ridge Heights of Solar Envelopes–45 Degree Orientation, part two

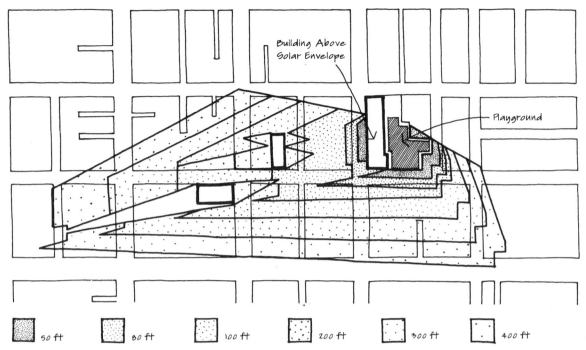

Playground

▨ 50 ft	▨ 80 ft	⬚ 100 ft
⬚ 200 ft	⬚ 300 ft	⬚ 400 ft

Solar Envelope Around Chinese Playground, San Francisco, CA

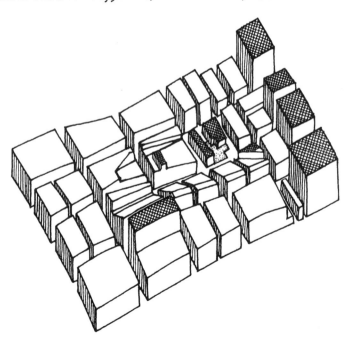

Allowable Building Volumes on Blocks Around Chinese Playground, San Francisco, CA

A variation of the solar access envelope was used to develop height controls around the **Chinese Playground in San Francisco, California.** The proposed "solar fan" was based on protecting solar access between Mar 21 and Sep 21 from 10:00 AM to 4:00 PM standard time and from 11:00 AM to 5:00 PM when daylight savings time applies (Bosselmann et al., 1983, pp. 68–69, 108–112).

The solar envelope for open space is generated by two sets of sun angles. One portion of the envelope is governed by the sun angles between 9 AM and 3 PM (or other desired criteria) on the fall date for which access is desired (angle a, lengths X and Z—see diagrams next to factor tables); the other, by the sun angle at 9 AM and 3 PM for the days between the summer solstice (angle b, length Y) and the fall day. The north (south in the Southern Hemisphere) line is determined by the azimuth angle of the sun (angle b) on Jun 21 (Dec 21 in SH) at 9 AM on the east side and at 3 PM on the west side. The points at which the contour lines intersect the diagonals can be calculated by using the altitude angle for the time and date. Using this procedure, a solar envelope for any latitude and climate can be constructed.

To create a solar envelope for any rectangular open space:

1) Select a fall or winter criteria date and times. For gardens, use the first frost date for the climate (Appendix B), or any date between the first frost and the winter solstice.

2) From the table, **Factors for Constructing Solar Envelopes for Open Space,** find the row for the site's latitude and criteria of dates and times. Then read values for angles a and b. Draw the diagonal lines in plan for Jun 21, 9 AM (Dec 21 in SH), Jun 21, 3 PM (Dec 21 in SH), Fall Date–AM criteria, and Fall Date–PM criteria.

3) Using f_x, f_y and f_z from the table, calculate the horizontal distance to the envelope edge for the desired or regulated allowable heights:

$$X = H(f_x)$$
$$Y = H(f_y)$$
$$Z = H(f_z)$$

where, X = distance along fall date line, Y = distance along summer solstice line, and H = the building height allowed. The envelope can extend infinitely from around the open space until it reaches the height of the tallest building allowed or desired in the neighborhood. Select a height that is reasonable for the site.

4) Using these dimensions, complete the envelope construction.

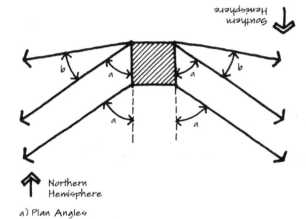

a) Plan Angles

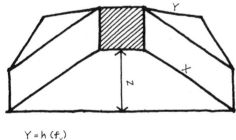

$$Y = h\,(f_Y)$$
$$X = h\,(f_X)$$
$$Z = h\,(f_Z)$$

b) Solar Envelope in Plan

Construction of Solar Envelope for Protection of Open Space

Factors for Constructing Solar Envelopes for Open Space, 40-72 degrees Latitude

Latitude	Hours	Dates	Angle a	Angle b	f_X	f_Y	f_Z	Dates	South Latitude
72° N	11/1	Oct 30/Feb 11	15	38	10.20	1.40	9.87	Apr 30/Aug 11	72° S
	9/3	Sep 30/Mar 11	46	7	6.39	1.40	4.47	Mar 30/Sep 11	
	10/2	Sep 30/Mar 11	31	0	0.00	1.40	0.00	Mar 30/Sep 11	
	9/3	Aug 30/Apr 11	48	4	2.62	1.40	1.74	Feb 28/Oct 11	
	9/3	Jul 30/May 11	51	1	1.70	1.40	1.07	Jan 30/Nov 11	
64° N	10/2	Oct 30/Feb 11	43	14	14.30	1.20	10.39	Apr 30/Aug 11	64° S
	9/3	Oct 30/Feb 11	44	14	5.79	1.20	4.16	Apr 30/Aug 11	
	10/2	Sep 30/Mar 11	32	26	2.97	1.20	2.53	Mar 30/Sep 11	
	9/3	Sep 30/Mar 11	47	11	3.87	1.20	2.65	Mar 30/Sep 11	
	9/3	Aug 30/Apr 11	51	7	2.04	1.20	1.28	Feb 28/Oct 11	
	9/3	Jul 30/May 11	55	2	1.41	1.20	0.81	Jan 30/Nov 11	
56° N	10/2	Dec 21	28	34	8.92	1.14	7.91	Jun 21	56° S
	10/2	Nov 30/Jan 11	41	21	7.30	1.14	5.50	May 30/July 11	
	10/2	Oct 30/Feb 11	30	32	3.76	1.14	3.25	Apr 30/Aug 11	
	9/3	Oct 30/Feb 11	44	18	5.79	1.14	4.16	Apr 30/Aug 11	
	9/3	Sep 30/Mar 11	49	13	2.78	1.14	1.84	Mar 30/Sep 11	
	9/3	Aug 30/Apr 11	55	7	1.67	1.14	0.97	Feb 28/Oct 11	
	9/3	Jul 30/May 11	60	1	1.21	1.14	0.60	Jan 30/Nov 11	
48° N	10/2	Dec 21	28	43	4.20	0.94	3.70	Jun 21	48° S
	9/3	Dec 21	41	31	7.40	0.94	5.59	Jun 21	
	10/2	Nov 30/Jan 11	29	43	3.76	0.94	3.30	May 30/July 11	
	9/3	Nov 30/Jan 11	42	30	6.24	0.94	4.66	May 30/July 11	
	9/3	Oct 30/Feb 11	45	26	3.61	0.94	2.54	May 30/July 11	
	9/3	Sep 30/Mar 11	51	20	2.14	0.94	1.34	Mar 30/Sep 11	
	9/3	Aug 30/Apr 11	59	13	1.41	0.94	0.73	Feb 28/Oct 11	
	9/3	Jul 30/May 11	67	5	1.07	0.94	0.42	Jan 30/Nov 11	
40° N	10/2	Dec 21	29	51	2.67	0.88	2.33	Jun 21	40° S
	9/3	Dec 21	42	0	0.00	0.88	0.00	Jun 21	
	10/2	Nov 30/Jan 11	30	0	0.00	0.88	0.00	May 30/July 11	
	9/3	Nov 30/Jan 11	43	37	3.71	0.88	2.72	May 30/July 11	
	9/3	Oct 30/Feb 11	47	33	2.59	0.88	1.76	May 30/July 11	
	9/3	Sep 30/Mar 11	55	26	1.75	0.88	1.01	Mar 30/Sep 11	
	9/3	Aug 30/Apr 11	64	16	1.23	0.88	0.53	Feb 28/Oct 11	

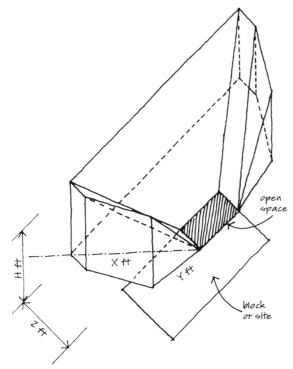

Example of a Solar Envelope Protecting Open Space

Latitude	Hours	Dates	Angle a	Angle b	f_X	f_Y	f_Z	Dates	South Latitude
32° N	10/2	Dec 21	31	54	1.93	0.89	1.65	Jun 21	32° S
	9/3	Dec 21	44	42	2.79	0.89	2.02	Jun 21	
	10/2	Nov 30/Jan 11	45	41	1.82	0.89	1.30	May 30/July 11	
	9/3	Nov 30/Jan 11	45	41	2.63	0.89	1.87	May 30/July 11	
	9/3	Oct 30/Feb 11	50	36	2.01	0.89	1.30	Apr 30/Aug 11	
	9/3	Sep 30/Mar 11	59	27	1.47	0.89	0.76	Mar 30/Sep 11	
24° N	10/2	Dec 21	34	65	1.47	0.87	1.23	Jun 21	24° S
	9/3	Dec 21	46	53	2.12	0.87	1.47	Jun 21	
	10/2	Nov 30/Jan 11	35	64	1.40	0.87	1.15	May 30/July 11	
	9/3	Nov 30/Jan 11	47	52	2.01	0.87	1.37	May 30/July 11	
	9/3	Oct 30/Feb 11	53	45	1.64	0.87	0.98	Apr 30/Aug 11	
16° N	10/2	Dec 21	49	58	1.68	0.93	1.10	Jun 21	16° S
	9/3	Dec 21	31	77	1.68	0.93	1.44	Jun 21	
	10/2	Nov 30/Jan 11	39	69	1.11	0.93	0.87	May 30/July 11	
	9/3	Nov 30/Jan 11	51	57	1.62	0.93	1.03	May 30/July 11	
	9/3	Oct 30/Feb 11	58	50	1.38	0.93	0.74	Apr 30/Aug 11	
8° N	10/2	Dec 21	42	73	0.94	1.03	0.69	Jun 21	8° S
	9/3	Dec 21	53	62	1.39	1.03	0.83	Jun 21	
	10/2	Nov 30/Jan 11	44	71	0.90	1.03	0.65	May 30/July 11	
	9/3	Nov 30/Jan 11	55	60	1.35	1.03	0.77	May 30/July 11	
	9/3	Oct 30/Feb 11	63	52	1.20	1.03	0.54	Apr 30/Aug 11	
0°	10/2	Dec 21	49	69	0.77	1.14	0.50	Jun 21	0°
	9/3	Dec 21	58	60	1.18	1.14	0.62	Jun 21	
	10/2	Nov 30/Jan 11	51	67	0.74	1.14	0.47	May 30/July 11	
	9/3	Nov 30/Jan 11	60	58	1.15	1.14	0.57	May 30/July 11	
	9/3	Oct 30/Feb 11	70	48	1.07	1.14	0.37	Apr 30/Aug 11	

Factors for Constructing Solar Envelopes for Open Space, 0-32 degrees Latitude

30 *TALL BUILDINGS* can be shaped in relationship to other buildings and to the wind to create favorable street and open-space microclimates. [heating]

Tall buildings create turbulent downward air flows toward street level, which can be either a benefit or a liability, depending on climate. In cool climates, this decreases pedestrian comfort, but in hot-humid climates it increases comfort and cooling in the streets. Tall buildings are also exposed to stronger wind flows because of their height (see Techniques 5 & 6). They create several disturbances in the urban wind pattern (Gandemer, 1978; Thurow, 1983, pp. 23–27). The **Downwash Vortex Effect** is created because faster wind speeds at the top of a building create higher pressure, while the bottom is sheltered from winds by other buildings. Wind moves toward areas of low pressure (Technique 6), so the flow is down the windward face of the building. When the wind hits the ground, it becomes turbulent and spirals, decreasing winter comfort. The speed at the street may be four times that of the streets protected by low-rise buildings. Wider, slab buildings with long sides to the wind increase the downwash effect. A rounded, convex form facing the wind, such as the design of the **Commerzbank Building,** in Frankfurt, Germany, by Norman Foster & Partners, diverts more air around the tall building, while a concave face creates stronger flows upward and downward along the face (Davies & Lambot, 1997).

The **Corner Effect** is an increase in wind velocity created by wind moving around the building; taller and wider buildings create more intense corner effects. The impact extends to an area equal to the building's width. A spiralling, erratic, upward flow **Wake Effect,** creates turbulence on the leeward side. These effects are strongest when there are large height differences between a tall building and its surroundings. Passageways under tall slab buildings create zones of higher velocity in the passage and in the open space downwind of the building. This **Gap Effect** depends on the building height.

The **DG Bank Building** in Frankfurt, Germany, by Kohn Pedersen Fox, responds to its urban context by surrounding the tower with lower buildings and a roofed

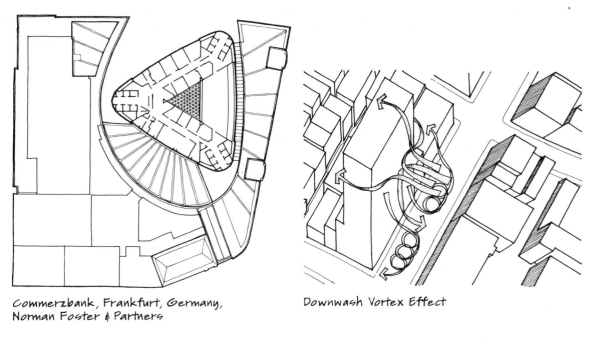

Commerzbank, Frankfurt, Germany,
Norman Foster & Partners

Downwash Vortex Effect

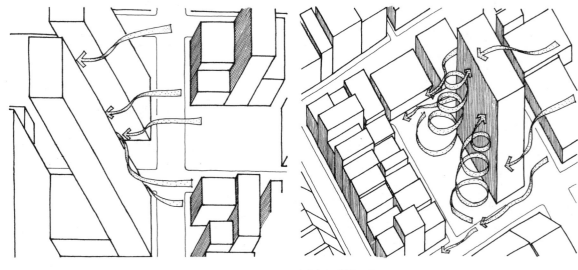

Corner Effect

Wake Effect

EFFECT (height)	Comfort Parameter (Ψ)
Corner Effect	
15 m (49 ft)	1.2
15 m (49 ft) < h < 35 m (115 ft)	1.2-1.5
35 m (115 ft) < h < 45 m (148 ft)	1.4
100 m (328 ft)	2.0
Slot Effect	
15 m (49 ft) < h	little effect
21 m (69 ft)	1.2
50 m (164 ft)	1.5
Wake Effect	
48 m (158 ft)	1.4
90 m (295 ft)	2.2
Downwash effect	
60 m (197 ft)	1.5
60 m (197 ft) with low upstream bldg.	1.8
100 m (328 ft) with low upstream bldg.	2.0

Comfort Parameters Around Tall Buildings

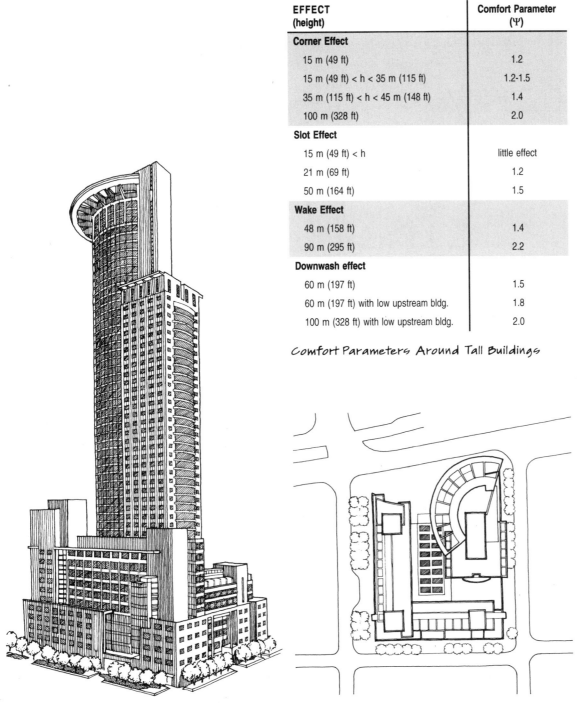

Site Plan and Perspective, DG Bank, Frankfurt, Germany, Kohn Pedersen Fox

atrium (*A+U*, 5/1994). The effect is both to moderate the scale transition and to block with the lower masses any potential downwashing from the tower to pedestrian areas. The tower face extends to street level on the eastern side only, away from the SSW and NE winter winds.

The comfort parameter (Ψ) is an indicator of comfort in relation to wind; it is a relative reference value, accounting for both wind speed and turbulence, based on the ratio of wind speed at a location near a building to the wind speed that would be present at the same point with no building (Melaragno, 1982). In winter, a higher Ψ mean less comfortable (overspeed) conditions; in summer, however, it indicates increased comfort. A 17-story building can cause a condition of Ψ = 1.5–1.8. The same building with a stepped facade can reduce Ψ to 0.5. *Sample comfort parameters are listed in the table.*

To reduce uncomfortable winds and improve the microclimate in streets and open spaces during the cool season:

• Tall buildings should have rounded aerodynamic profiles and turn their narrow face to the winter wind or be angled diagonal to winds.

• Buildings taller than their upwind neighbors should be less than twice the average height of the upwind buildings (Thurow, 1983, p. 27) (Strategy 34).

• Buildings significantly taller than their upwind neighbors should be designed with horizontal projections and stepped, setback facades starting about 6–10 m (20–33 ft) above the street (Givoni, 1998, p. 297). Setbacks from the street wall to the tower portion of a tall building should be at least 6 m (20 ft) (City of Edmonton, 1985).

The ratio of wind speed at pedestrian level to the undisturbed wind (R_h) *can be estimated for a variety of relationships between a tall building and its upwind neighbors:*

1) Find the airport wind speed *(V)* for the building's location using Techniques 4 and 5.

2) For Corner Effect and Gap Effect Flows, use the left graph, entering on the horizontal axis with the ratio *H/h* (see diagram). Move up to the appropriate curve; then from the intersection, read the wind speed ratio (R_h) on the vertical axis. Multiple R_h by *V* to get local speed.

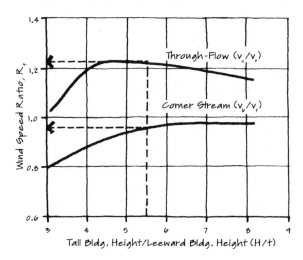

Predicting Corner and Gap Effects
Source: adapted from Penwarden & Wise (1975).

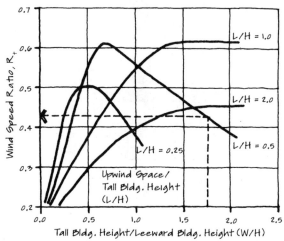

Predicting Downwash Vortex Effect
Source: adapted from Penwarden & Wise (1975).

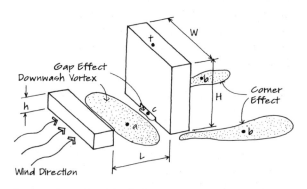

Parameters for Wind Flow Around Buildings

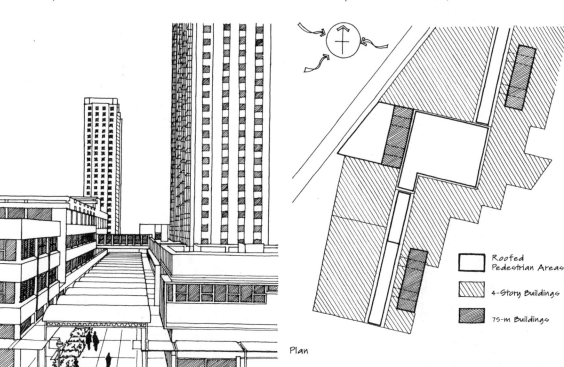

View of Roof Over Mall

Shopping District, Edmonton Green, London

Plan

Roofed Pedestrian Areas

4-Story Buildings

75-m Buildings

3) To find R_h for the Downwash Vortex between the buildings, use the right graph, entering on the horizontal axis with the ratio W/H, then moving vertically to the curve for the ratio L/H. From the intersection, move horizontally to read the speed ratio (R_h). Multiply R_h by V to get local speed.

The **Shopping District at Edmonton Green** in London illustrates the impact of tall slab buildings on pedestrian level winds and its remediation with roofs over public outdoor spaces. Apartment blocks of 75-m (246-ft) height, with open entrances underneath, created uncomfortable windy pedestrian conditions. The entire public area between buildings and in the market square was retrofitted with roofs to improve the comfort of shoppers by blocking downwash winds (Penwarden & Wise, 1975; Wise, 1970).

31 *BALANCED URBAN PATTERNS* of streets and blocks can be oriented and sized to integrate concerns for light, sun, and shade according to the priorities of the climate. [heating, cooling, and daylighting]

The orientation and layout of streets has a significant effect on the microclimate around buildings and on the access to sun and wind for use in buildings.

Wider east–west streets give better winter solar access (Strategy 38), while wider streets in the direction of prevailing wind flows promote better wind movement through the city (Strategy 36). At high latitudes in the Northern Hemisphere, the sun is more south-dominant (north-dominant in Southern Hemisphere), while at temperate latitudes, more flexibility in orientation for solar heating is permissible without severe penalties in the amount of radiation collected (Strategy 59). Narrow north–south streets can create shade from one building to the next (Strategy 27).

Depending on the climate and heat load of buildings, different combinations of strategies may be appropriate. The diagrams show potential generic solutions for a range of climates. Refer to the table of **Street Orientation and Layout by Climatic Priority** for specific recommendations by climate. Note that, because internal-load-dominated buildings have a greater requirement for cooling than skin-load-dominated buildings, the effect on the recommendations is to shift these buildings to the next hotter climate type.

The diagrams of **Summer Solstice Shadows** show the effect of different street orientations on summer solstice sun and shading patterns at different latitudes. They represent four-story buildings on 60-ft (18-m) right-of-way streets. Cardinal orientations give more sun to the south facades in winter, whereas rotated organizations tend to reduce winter gains and increase summer gains, especially on easterly and westerly facades. However, for buildings that do not require winter sun for heating, rotated organizations give more evenly distributed sun to more facades.

A cardinal orientation will generally cast more shadow on buildings facing north–south streets than a

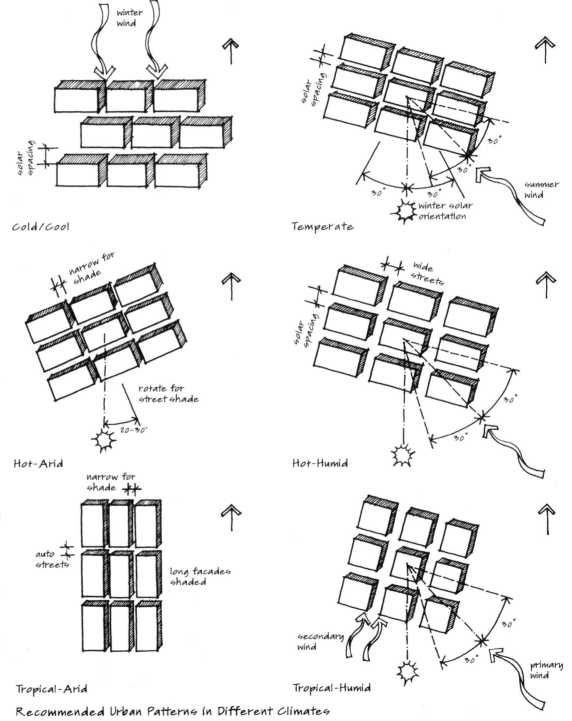

Cold/Cool

Temperate

Hot-Arid

Hot-Humid

Tropical-Arid

Tropical-Humid

Recommended Urban Patterns in Different Climates

| BUILDING TYPE | | RESPONSE | | |
Internal Loaded Buildings	Skin Loaded Buildings	1st Prioroty	2nd Prioroty	COMMMENTS
	Cold	Lee	Sun	• Strict cardinal orientation for sun. • Discontinous streets in direction of winter winds. • Space E/W streets for solar access for spring and fall.
Cold	Cool	Sun	Lee	• Cardinal orientation for sun. • Discontinous streets in direction of winter winds. • Space E/W streets for solar access at solstice.
Cool	Temperate-	Winter Sun; Summer Wind	Winter Lee; Summer Shade	• Orient +/- 30 degrees from cardinal for sun. • Adjust orientation 20-30° oblique to summer wind. • Space E/W streets for solar access. Elongate blocks E/W.
Temperate-Arid	Hot-Arid	Summer Shade	Summer Wind; Winter Sun	• Narrow N/S streets for shade. • Rotate from cardinal to increase street shading. • Space E/W streets for solar access, if needed. Elongate blocks E/W.
Temperate-Humid	Hot-Humid	Summer Wind	Summer Shade; Winter Sun	• Orient streets 20-30° oblique to summer wind. • Modify orientation by rotating from cardinal to increase street shading. • Space E/W streets for solar access if needed. Elongate blocks E/W. • Wide streets for wind flow.
Hot-Arid & Tropical-Arid	Tropical-Arid	Shade all seasons	Night Wind; Day Lee	• Narrow N/S streets for shade. • Elongate block N/S, IF E/W facades shaded. • Wider auto streets run E/W.
Hot-Humid & Tropical-Humid	Tropical-Humid	Wind all seasons	Shade	• Orient streets 20-30° oblique to predominant wind. • Respond to secondary wind direction. • Maximize street right-of-ways for wind flow, but not paving.

Street Orientation and Layout by Climatic Priority

rotated organization, and thus does a better job at shading buildings. In contrast, rotated orientations provide more shade on the streets during more of the day. A cardinal orientation will have one shady street, while cross streets will be sunny. In contrast, rotated orientations will provide shade on at least one side of the street for most of the day. Note that during midday, when the sun is high, buildings cast quite small shadows and the orientation of streets has little effect, indicating that south-facing facades (N in SH) should be shaded at the element scale (Strategies 98, 99, and 100) and that streets, open spaces, and outdoor rooms must be shaded in the overhead plane (Strategy 45).

The 22.5° rotation plans shown increase street shading while meeting solar orientation criteria and may be appropriate for a temperate climate. As rotation increases away from cardinal, shadows reach opposite buildings less and thus buildings must provide more self-shading.

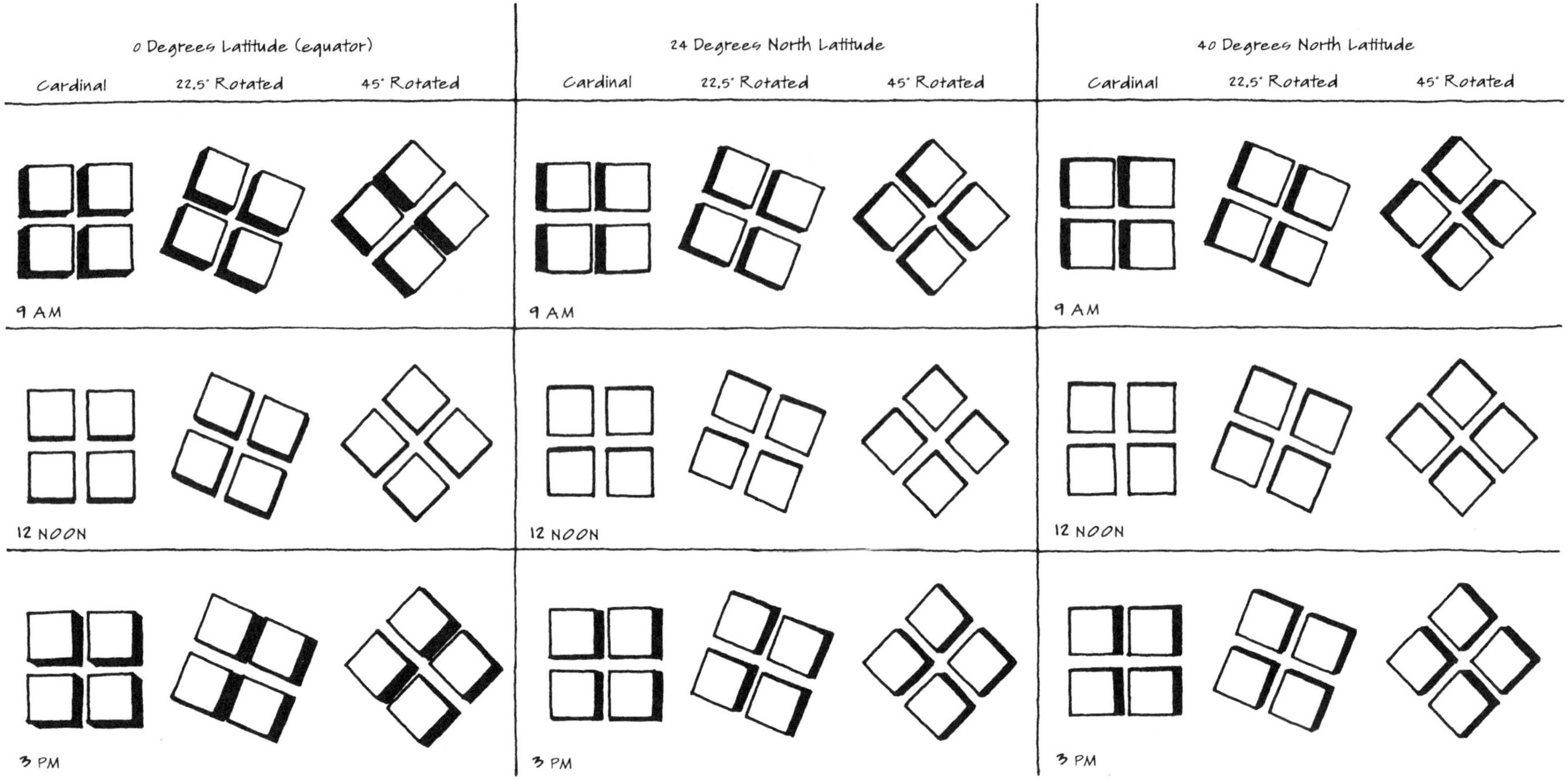

Cardinal 22.5° Rotated 45° Rotated Cardinal 22.5° Rotated 45° Rotated Cardinal 22.5° Rotated 45° Rotated

9 AM 9 AM 9 AM

12 NOON 12 NOON 12 NOON

3 PM 3 PM 3 PM

Summer Solstice Shadows as a Function of Street Orientation

32 *GLAZED STREETS* provide light to each
building organized to face them.
[daylighting]

A glazed street (linear atrium) is similar to an enclosed
atrium, except that it is enclosed by buildings on only
two sides instead of four, and may be extended indefi-
nitely. Like atria, they can be used both for lighting
adjacent rooms and for providing light to plants and activities that occur in their climate-buffered space. Potentially, glazed streets have the additional advantages
of increasing marketability, reducing conductive heat
loss and gain in the building (Strategy 57), providing
winter solar heat gain (Strategy 61), and serving as a
passive ventilation stack (Strategy 66). Glazed spaces
also offer a reduction in total life cycle cost over unglazed spaces (Hastings, 1994).

The **Galleria Vittorio Emanuele** in Milan, Italy,
shelters both building facades and pedestrians with a
glazed canopy over a cruciform plan of shopping streets
(Saxon, 1987). Henning Larsens developed the buildings for the **University of Trondheim**, Norway, along
an unheated galleria planned on a regular grid (*GA Document*, 1981, pp. 38–49; *A+U*, 1/1983, pp. 81–89). The
campus can grow by extension of the glazed street system. In summer, interior windows are shaded by fabric
blinds, and the roof is vented. In winter, the street provides a climate-buffered social and circulation space.

Design principles for glazed streets are similar to
those for atria (Strategy 70). Daylight levels in buildings adjacent to glazed streets are affected by the
height of street walls and the width of the street, the
amount of daylight available from the sky, the reflectance of facades, the size and position of windows, the
roof design, the glazing transmittance, and reflection
strategies at the window wall.

The most important factor in providing daylight via
a glazed street is the proportion of street width to
building height. Tall, narrow proportions have less
"view" of the sky than short, wide proportions. Since
less daylight is available at higher latitudes than at
lower latitudes, glazed streets at high latitudes must be
wider to provide the same level of daylight indoors.

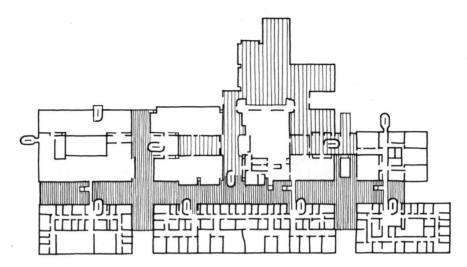

University of Trondheim, Plan

University of Trondheim, Norway, Henning Larsens

Galleria Vittorio Emanuele, Milan, Italy

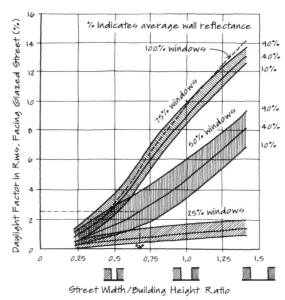

Daylighting in LOWER Rooms
Adjacent to Atrium
Source: adapted from Ashehoug (1992).

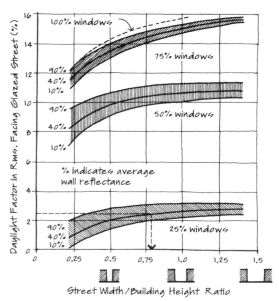

Daylighting in UPPER Rooms
Adjacent to Atrium
Source: adapted from Ashehoug (1992).

Taller buildings with more floors require wider streets than shorter buildings.

To determine the ratio of street width to building height (W/H), enter the graph for Daylighting in LOWER rooms with the desired average daylight factor for a room adjacent to the glazed street. A daylight factor appropriate to the building's climate and use can be determined from Technique 9. Move horizontally to the curve that represents the percentage of window in the facade facing the glazed street and the wall reflectivity, then down to read the minimum ratio of W/H that will provide the daylight factor target. Remember that this represents an average wall reflectance including the low (15%) reflectivity glazing.

The graph for Daylighting in UPPER Rooms can be used to check the daylight factors that can be achieved in rooms located on the upper floor adjacent to the glazed street.

Both graphs assume parallel buildings, a glazed roof with 35° pitch, overcast sky conditions, and an increasing percentage of window area in walls facing the street from 50% at the top floor to 100% glazed on the lowest floor (Ashehoug, 1992). Both the type of roof structure and the glazing type can significantly affect the illuminance level in a glazed street. Structure should be as open as possible, while glazing should have a high transmissivity (Strategy 101).

Given a W/H ratio determined for the daylighting of rooms, the daylight factor achieved on the street floor can be estimated from the graph for lighting at the Center of a Glazed Street and checked against the lighting requirements for indoor plants (Strategy 70) (Ashehoug, 1992).

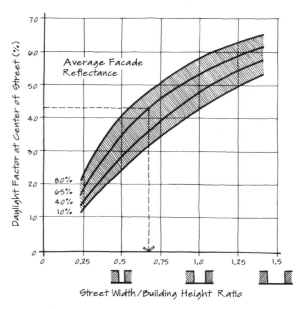

Daylighting at Center of a Glazed Street
Source: adapted from Ashehoug (1992).

33 *LOOSE URBAN PATTERNS* maximize cooling breezes in hot climates, while *DENSE URBAN PATTERNS* minimize winter winds in heating climates. [heating and cooling]

Air movement in streets can be either an asset or liability, depending on season and climate. Wind is desirable in streets of hot climates to cool people and remove excess heat from the streets; it also becomes a potential resource to cool buildings by cross-ventilation. This is important all the time in humid climates and at night in arid climates. On the other hand, wind reduces pedestrian comfort in cool seasons and increases infiltration heat losses of buildings.

For summer cooling, streets oriented 20–30° oblique to summer winds maximizes air flow through an urban area (Strategy 36). The pattern of streets and open space can also be organized to take advantage of cool air drainage and night thermal currents (Strategy 26).

To reduce wind flows in streets, windbreaks can be used to block undesirable cold winter winds or hot dusty desert winds (Strategy 43). Buildings spaced closer together will also reduce flows in the streets.

For regular organizations of buildings in an urban pattern, tall buildings on narrow streets yield the most wind protection, while shorter buildings on wider streets promote more air movement. When major streets are parallel to winds, the primary factors affecting street wind velocity are the width of streets and the frontal area (height and width) of windward building faces.

The graph shows wind speed in the streets as a function of the Blockage Ratio of a given building group organization (Wu, 1994, pp. 103–107). Blockage ratio (R_b) is defined, with variables given in the diagram, as:

$$R_b = \frac{(W \times H)}{(W + L)^2}$$

To determine the wind speed in streets oriented parallel to the wind, first find the Blockage Ratio using either the formula above or from the calculated ratios from one of the building group organizations shown in the matrix on the next page. Enter the graph on the horizontal axis with the Blockage Ratio, move vertically to intersect the curve, and then move horizontally to read on the vertical axis the predicted average wind speed in the street as a fraction of the open prevailing unobstructed wind speed. High fractions are desirable for cooling and low fractions for heating.

The graph assumes regular building layout, buildings that fill the block, forming a continuous street wall on the windward side, and wind perpendicular to the block face and parallel to the major streets. Discontinuous buildings with spaces between their ends will increase wind in secondary cross streets and decrease wind in streets oriented with the wind. Wider spacing of cross streets will increase wind to the cross streets and to buildings, but will have little effect on wind in streets oriented to the wind.

In cool climates, major streets should be oriented perpendicular to winter winds and street networks should use a discontinuous organization, with many T-intersections to slow and block wind flow in streets.

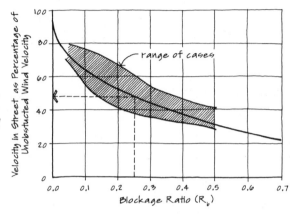

Predicting Wind Velocity in Streets

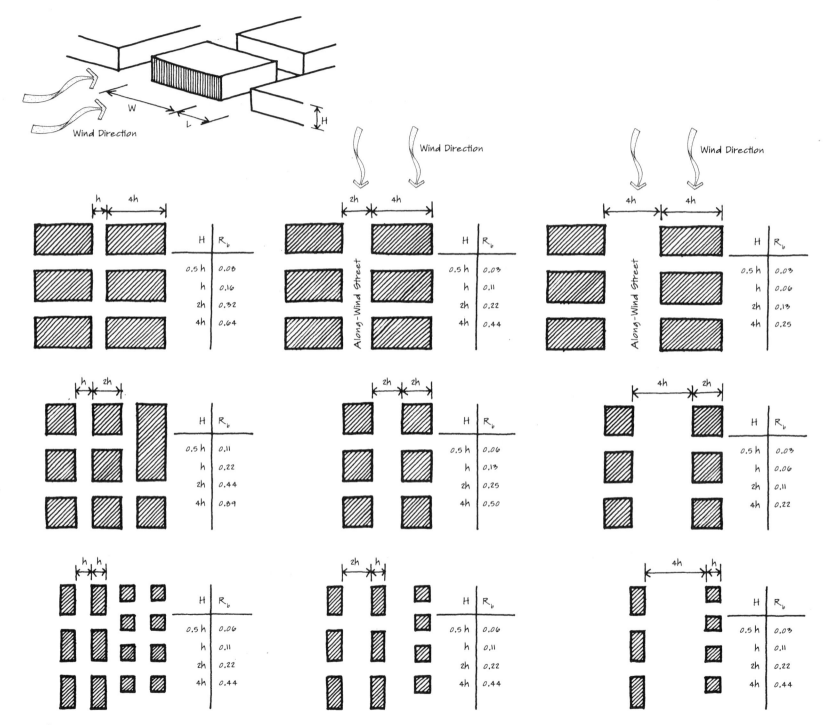

Blockage Ratios for Different Organizations of Buildings and Streets

34 *GRADUAL HEIGHT TRANSITIONS* **of building groups, sloped in the direction of prevailing winds, minimize wind movement in streets. [heating]**

Abrupt changes in building height significantly impact wind velocity in streets and open spaces. In heating climates, reducing wind speed can improve pedestrian comfort in outdoor spaces (Technique 11), and reduce heat loss from buildings. Gradual height transitions allow most of the cold wind to pass over the tops of buildings.

For urban patterns with building heights that increase in the direction of prevailing wind flow, height transitions from one building to another, or from one height district to another, should not exceed 100%. (IURD, 1984, p. 139)

For instance, if a windward height limitation is 50 ft (15 m), then the next height limitation in the leeward direction should be 100 ft (30 m) or less. Where development rules create zones of differential height, the boundary between zones should occur at the center of blocks, rather than along the center of streets. If transitions occur at streets, wind in the streets would be faster and more turbulent. Buildings in the first row of a taller height zone, along with individual buildings that rise above their surroundings, should be designed for wind mitigation (Strategy 30) and/or to block wind to downwind buildings (Strategies 43 and 41).

A study done to advise development of a new **zoning policy for San Francisco** proposed modifications to existing height restrictions to create gradual height shifts from lower buildings to tall central city structures (IURD, 1984). Prevailing wind directions in the cool San Francisco climate are from west and northwest, with some southeast winter storm winds. This approach would create an urban pattern causing wind to move over the city, being deflected upward, instead of diving into the streets; this pattern would create long wind shadows on the leeward side.

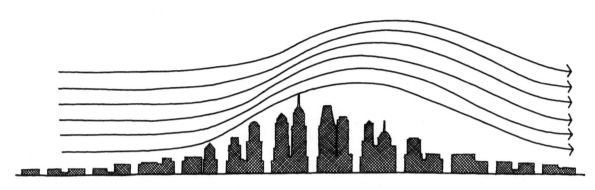

Schematic Section Diagram of City

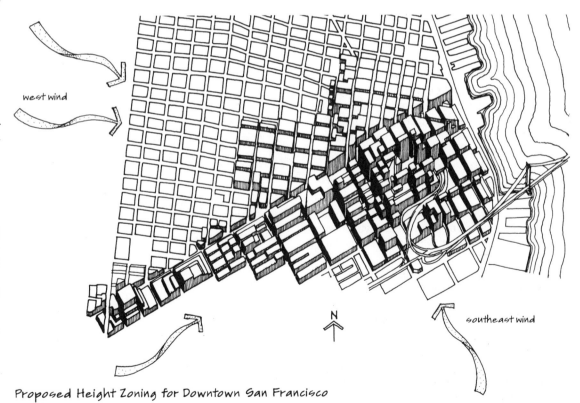

west wind

southeast wind

Proposed Height Zoning for Downtown San Francisco

35 *DAYLIGHT ENVELOPES* **can be used to shape and space buildings to assure adequate daylight access to the street and adjacent buildings. [daylighting]**

In clear sky climates, exterior illumination is often 500 times brighter than that required inside, so windows are often located such that their view of the sky dome is obstructed and light is filtered and reflected before it reaches the windows. Under overcast sky conditions, the bright sun isn't available and exterior light levels are usually lower than in clear sky conditions; therefore, exterior obstructions of the sky dome are a disadvantage, rather than an advantage, as they are in sunny, clear skies. Adjacent facades that are tall and close obstruct more of the upper sky dome than those smaller or farther away.

Daylight access is a precondition to the use of daylight in buildings. In dense contexts, limitations on building massing are necessary to insure daylight access to every building. A daylight envelope is the maximum volume that can be built on a given site while still protecting daylight access to neighboring buildings or sites. Daylight envelopes offer a prescriptive development control. As a development tool, the daylight envelope will tend to produce street-oriented buildings of high site coverage, and when a site is fully developed, stepped building forms. While solar envelopes (Strategy 29) are concerned with access to direct-beam sunlight, and thus are determined by sun angles, daylight envelopes protect access to light, which comes from the entire sky dome.

In urban situations, as street wall height increases, daylight levels are reduced. Daylight available to rooms facing the street is dependent on the ratio of building height to the width of the street, the reflectivity of exterior walls, and the amount of glazing in the walls. Taller street walls block more view of the sky from windows. Windows in lower floors are mostly lit by interreflected light, thus higher wall reflectance increases light levels near the street (Strategy 77). Ground surface reflectance will also influence the reflection of light to ceilings of lower rooms. Window size affects both the proportion of exterior light allowed to enter a

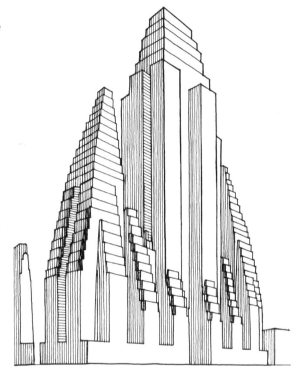

Study of the 1916 New York Zoning,
Hugh Ferriss

Look Building, New York City, 1949,
Emery Roth & Sons

room (Strategy 94) and the average reflectance of the street walls. Since glass has low reflectance, a high percentage of clear glazing in exterior walls will reduce interreflections.

The impacts of New York City's 1916 zoning law, designed to protect access to light and air, were predicted in the **drawings of Hugh Ferriss,** in his book *The Metropolis of Tomorrow* (Ferriss, 1928). The **Look Building** (Ruttenbaum, 1986, p. 200) exemplifies buildings that maximized the allowable zoning envelope in the period up to 1960, giving a stepped "setback style" form.

The table indicates rule-of-thumb Daylight Spacing Angles recommended for different latitudes.

The table assumes overcast sky conditions typical of the latitudes listed and continuous building rows. Daylight factors shown are sufficient to provide an average of 20 foot-candles (215 lux) indoors, a moderate level of ambient lighting that would require task lighting (Strategy 102) for activities such as reading or drawing. At low latitudes, higher levels of exterior illuminance are available for more of the year, while at high latitudes nearer the poles, very short winter days prevent high interior daylight levels being achieved all year round. The table shows the percentage of annual hours between 9 AM and 5 PM during which the 20 fc (215 lux) interior daylight level will be met or exceeded. Three angles are given (in degrees):

• The Low column, representing shallower spacing angles (wider streets/shorter buildings) can be generally associated with small windows and darker (low-reflectance) exterior walls.

• The Med column, the recommended values, can generally be associated with medium-sized windows and light-colored (higher reflectance) exterior walls.

• The High column, representing steeper spacing angles (narrower streets/taller buildings) can be generally associated with large windows and light-colored (high-reflectance) exterior walls.

As the comments in the table indicate, at low latitudes, large window are unnecessary for lighting and may cause excessive glare and heat gains, while at high latitudes, low-reflectance walls are not recommended (NR).

The relationships between sky condition, latitude, surface reflectivity, building spacing and continuity, and building shape and height are complex and the spacing angles in the table may be more restrictive than

Latitude N. or S.	Required Daylight Factor	H/W range	Minimum Spacing Angle			% annual hours 9 AM - 5 PM	Comments
			Low	Medium	High		
0 - 8	1.0	1.7-2.0	60	70	--	95	large windows NR
12 - 16	1.0	1.7-2.0	60	70	--	90	large windows NR
28 - 32	1.5	1.5-2.0	50	65	70	85	
34 - 38	2.0	0.8-2.0	39	60	65	85	
40 - 44	2.5	0.5-1.8	24	52	61	85	
46 - 48	3.0	0.4-1.5	22	45	56	85	
52	4.0	0.2-1.0	11	31	45	85	
56	4.0-5.5	0.3-1.0	--	23	37	80-85	low reflect walls NR
60	4.0-6.0	0.2-1.0	--	21	35	70-80	low reflect walls NR
64	4.5-6.0	0.2-0.8	--	18	32	60-70	low reflect walls NR
68	5.0-6.0	0.2-0.7	--	15	30	60-70	low reflect walls NR
70	6.0	0.2-0.5		11	24	60	low reflect walls NR

Daylight Spacing Angles for Different Latitudes
(for 20 fc interior illuminance & overcast sky)

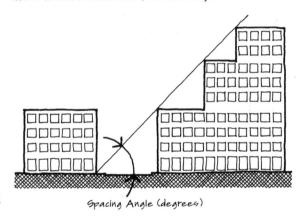

Spacing Angle (degrees)

necessary under some circumstances. Remember that many low-latitude climates may be dominated by clear skies and thus the spacing angles would generally be more restrictive than necessary. However, designers may wish to use the overcast sky as a design condition for spacing buildings and sizing windows, while providing controls at the windows to keep out excess sun and light on clear days (see Technique 9).

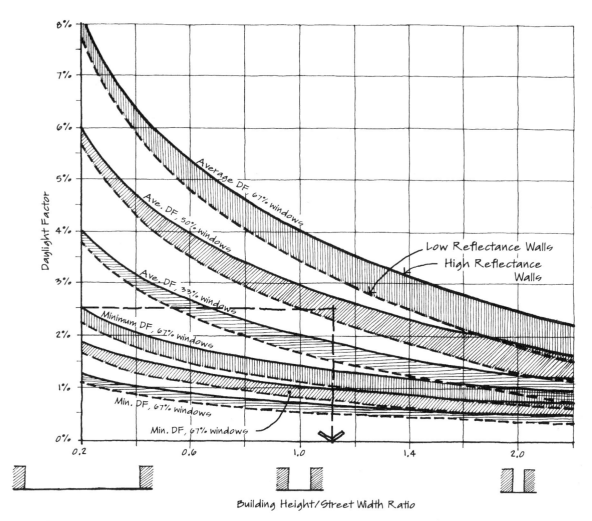

Daylight Factor as a Function of Street Canyon Proportions
rooms at street level, center of block, overcast sky

Actual site situations may be predicted more accurately using the graph of Daylight Factor as a Function of Street Canyon Proportions. To determine the minimum building height to street width ratio (H/W) to provide daylight to a ground floor room: Use Technique 9 to determine the design daylight factor (DF) for the building's use and climate. Enter the graph on the vertical axis using this design DF. Move horizontally to the average daylight factor zone representing the percentage of the facade occupied by windows. The upper side of the zone represents high-reflectance exterior walls; the lower side represents low-reflectance walls. Drop down to read the required H/W ratio. Using this H/W ratio, check the minimum daylight factor (at the back of the room) by moving vertically to the minimum DF zone representing the same window percentage. Again, the high side is for high-reflectance walls; the low side, for low reflectance. Move left to read the minimum DF.

The significant effect of urban canyon proportions on daylight levels can easily be seen from the graph. The daylight factor inside a building decreases with increasing *H/W*. Increasing window area has the effect of increasing daylight factors. Larger increases occur at lower *H/W* ratios. The practical upper limit of increasing window area is about two-thirds of the area of the exterior wall. Increasing wall reflectivity has greater impact at higher *H/W* ratios, since a larger percentage of interior illumination is derived from reflected light. At low *H/W* ratios, increasing window area has a much greater impact on raising DF than does increasing wall reflectivity.

The graph assumes overcast skies and a ground floor room 750 ft^2 (21.2 m^2), 25 ft (7.6 m) deep by 30 ft (9.1 m); sill height, 3 ft (0.9 m); and window head and ceiling height, 10 ft (3.0 m). Surfaces are assumed to have typical interior and exterior reflectances: floor, 30%; ceiling and interior walls, 70%; windows, 15%; street, 7%; sidewalks, 40%. Glazing is clear. The room represented is in the center (thus the worst case) of 400-ft (122-m)-long street wall, a common block face dimension.

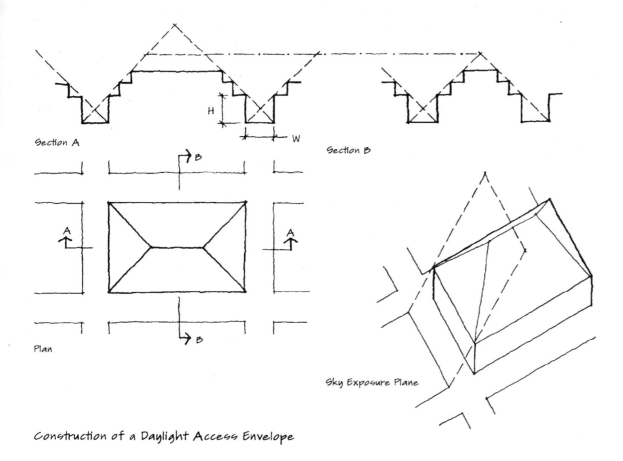

Section A

Section B

Plan

Sky Exposure Plane

Construction of a Daylight Access Envelope

After the H/W ratio is known, a daylight envelope may be constructed: Determine street width and building street wall height. Then, strike a sky exposure plane from one side of the street at ground level through the top of the street wall on the other side, as illustrated. When this is done on all four sides of a block, a hip-roof-shaped pyramid is formed above the street-wall-defined rectangular volume.

This is a daylight envelope. As long as a window cannot "see" a part of the building across the street that is above the specified street wall height, its daylight ac-

cess will not be impacted further. Because sky luminance varies with latitude, higher latitudes require using higher daylight factors to achieve the same effect as in lower latitudes (see table in Strategy 94). From the graph, one can see that DF varies with H/W, therefore lower H/W ratios, and thus smaller daylight access envelopes, are required at higher latitudes.

For additional information, refer to Hopkinson et al. (1966, Ch. 17, "Daylight and Design-Town Planning,"), Department of City Planning (New York, 1981), and Bressi (1994).

36 *BREEZY STREETS* oriented to the prevailing wind maximize wind movement in urban environments and increase the access of buildings to cross-ventilation. [cooling]

In hot climates, especially under humid conditions, good ventilation is necessary to remove excess heat from streets and open spaces and to provide cross-ventilation in buildings. For cross-ventilation in buildings, access to sufficient wind flows is a necessary precondition. Since dense urban areas create high levels of heat gain and have less ability to lose heat by radiation (due to narrow sky view factors), wind in streets and open spaces can be critical to cooling.

In most cases, wind speeds in the city are significantly reduced relative to more open locations, such as airports, where winds are often measured (Technique 5). This is due to friction and blockage of wind by obstructions, such as buildings and trees. The configuration of buildings and streets in relation to the prevailing summer breezes can maximize air movement through the city, and thus provide wind access to more buildings.

Streets parallel to the prevailing wind have the highest velocity in the streets, while streets perpendicular to the wind encourage most of the wind to blow over buildings, yielding lower velocity and more turbulent wind in the streets (Yannas, 1995). A street orientation oblique to prevailing winds will create two sides of buildings with positive pressure and two sides with negative pressures, thus maximizing cross-ventilation potential in the buildings. If the orientation is not too far from the prevailing direction, good circulation can still be promoted in the street, such that wind moves through the city.

The **city of Charleston, South Carolina,** lying on a peninsula between the Ashley and Cooper rivers, is laid out to maximize the use of cool, southwesterly, summer breezes that dependably blow every afternoon. Streets are aligned east–west, extending from river to river, thus guiding wind into the city. Blocks are elongated north/south, but in an innovative site design, one room wide houses, called *singles,* turn their short side to the street, with long sides facing south, flanked by full-

1856 City Plan, Charleston, South Carolina

"Single" House, Charleston, South Carolina

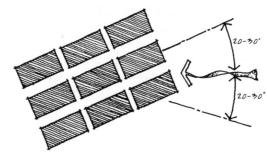

Orientation of Primary Streets for Ventilation

length, usually two-storied porches. To the south of the porches are gardens, up to the north wall of the next house, which is placed on the lot line. This arrangement allows a staggered, dispersed organization with gardens and porches benefiting from ample wind flow through their open spaces and buildings turned oblique to the southwest winds.

To maximize cross-ventilation access and air movement in streets, orient primary avenues at an angle of approximately 20–30° either direction from the line of the prevailing summer breeze (Givoni, 1992).

In general, narrow streets will slow wind, while wide streets tend to encourage faster flow due to reduced friction (Strategy 33). In temperate climates, winter heating is as important as summer cooling, thus east–west–oriented streets should be wide enough for solar access to south facades (north in the Southern Hemisphere) and orientation for wind should also place long block faces within 30° of south to insure solar access (Strategies 38 and 59). Strategy 31 discusses design of grid organizations for balancing sun, wind, and light in different climates.

37 *DISPERSED BUILDINGS* with continuous and wide open spaces preserve each building's access to breezes. [cooling]

Each building creates an area of reduced wind velocity on its leeward side; therefore, *buildings in which cross-ventilation is important should be separated by a distance of five to seven times the building height to assure adequate airflow* if they are directly behind one another (M. Evans, 1980, p. 64; Koenigsberger et al., 1973, p. 129). Compared to multistory buildings, lower one-story buildings cause smaller wind shadows and can be spaced close together.

The Texas firm of Lake/Flato architects have created a series of elegant, climatically adapted houses using variations on the theme of dispersed pavilions connected by roofs and trellises and surrounded by outdoor living areas (Guerra & Ojeda, 1996). The **South Burke Ranch** (*Texas Architect,* 1990) is organized with three block and stucco buildings arranged in a southeast oriented U-shape to catch prevailing breezes. Each building has windows on opposite sides. Deciduous mustang grape-covered arbors and screened rooms surround and connect the indoor spaces. Ted Flato designed the **La Barronena Ranch** (Flanagan, 1988), in the south Texas coastal plains of Hebbronville, as three buildings under a single roof, separated by breezeways and surrounded by large screened porches. In winter, large barn doors extend across the breezeways to block north winds. The **Carraro Residence,** in Kyle, TX (Moorhead, 1991), south of Austin, reuses an industrial structure to create a three-part compound arranged in an L-shape to form two courts. A dogtrot entry separates the bedroom from a utility core. A two-story screened room in the main building is open to southerly breezes and shielded in winter by the solid parts of the house. Finally, the **El Tule Ranch,** in Falfurrias, TX, is a series of small structures organized around two courtyards. Rooms along the south side of the court open toward the southeasterly breeze, allowing flow between them and to rooms across the court.

Three distinct flow regimes can be identified between buildings, based on their spacing. *Skimming Flow* is caused when buildings are organized in rows spaced

Indoor Rooms	
Screened Porches	
Shaded Terraces	

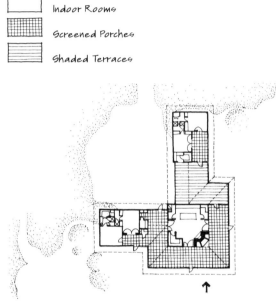

La Barronena Ranch, Hebbronville, TX, Ford, Powell & Carson

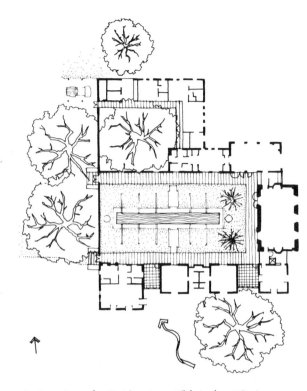

El Tule Ranch, Falfurrias, TX, Lake/Flato

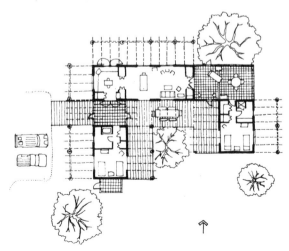

South Burke Ranch, Zavala County, TX, Lake/Flato

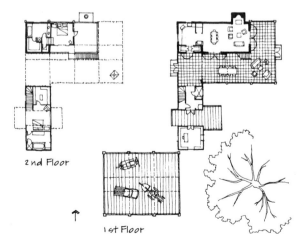

2nd Floor

1st Floor

Carraro Residence, Kyle TX, Lake/Flato

closely together and oriented perpendicular to wind. When spacing is larger than that required to create a stable vortex between buildings, but smaller than the sum of the upwind and downwind eddies, a *Wake Interference Flow* is induced. If spacing between buildings is larger than the sum of the upwind and downwind eddies, wind will drop between the buildings in a pattern of *Isolated Roughness,* which is good for ventilation (Lee et al., 1980a, b).

Larger building spacing in the direction of wind flow, space between the ends of buildings, and lower building heights minimize wind speed reduction. If the buildings are staggered, the wind flow around one building helps provide ventilation air for the adjacent building and along-wind spacing between buildings may be decreased.

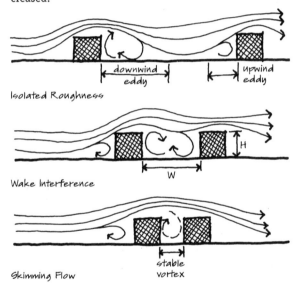

Isolated Roughness

Wake Interference

Skimming Flow

Three Flow Regimes Between Buildings

To estimate the relative effectiveness of different spacings and densities of rows of buildings, enter the graph on the horizontal axis with the building height-to-spacing ratio. Move vertically to the diagonal zone, then horizontally to read the ventilation effectiveness on the vertical axis.

Percentages on the vertical axis are relative to the ventilation of an isolated building with no wind obstructions; these values are based on the decreasing pressure differentials between the windward and lee-

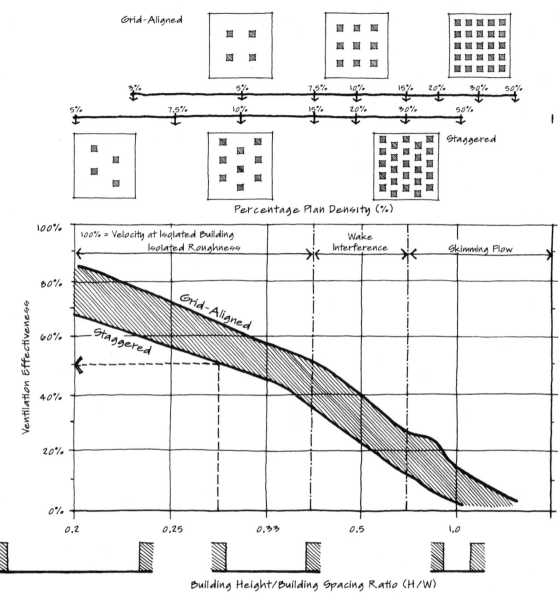

Percentage Plan Density (%)

Ventilation Effectiveness as a Function of Row Spacing and Plan Density

ward side of buildings as spacing decreases. The graph assumes wind perpendicular to buildings (Bittencourt, 1993, p. 131).

38 *EAST–WEST ELONGATED BUILDING GROUPS* spaced in the north–south direction maximize solar gain while insuring solar access to each building. [heating]

The placement of a building such that it has access to the sun without shading other buildings has important implications for the form and arrangement of groups of buildings.

Individual dwelling units at **Pueblo Acoma,** in New Mexico, are arranged in long, thin east–west-elongated clusters, each having a south-facing terrace. The clusters of dwellings are spaced far enough apart in the north–south direction that even in the winter, when sun angles are low, the higher buildings do not shade their neighbors to the north (Knowles, 1974, p. 27).

The appropriate spacing between buildings is determined by the profile angle of the low altitude winter sun. Multiply the height of the building, **H,** *by the value* **X** *from the table to determine the spacing,* **S,** *that will provide optimum winter exposure for a cluster of buildings.*

The table is based on the sun position on Dec 21 and Jan/Nov 21 for Northern Hemisphere latitudes between 0° and 52°. Corresponding Southern Hemisphere months are also given. Because at high latitudes the

Pueblo Acoma

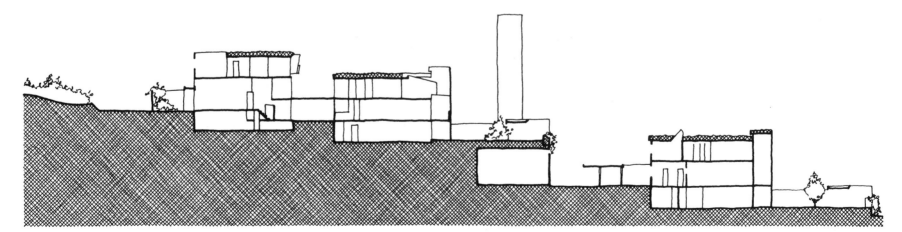

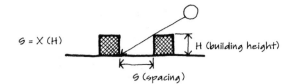

$S = X (H)$

H (building height)

S (spacing)

VALUES of "X" for BUILDING SPACING

LATITUDE	9 AM		10 AM		11 AM		12 Noon		1 PM		2 PM		3 PM	
North lat.	Dec	Jan / Nov	Dec	Jan / Nov	Dec	Jan / Nov	Dec	Jan / Nov	Dec	Jan / Nov	Dec	Jan / Nov	Dec	Jan / Nov
0°	0.6	0.5	0.5	0.4	0.4	0.4	0.4	0.4	0.4	0.4	0.5	0.4	0.6	0.5
4°	0.7	0.6	0.6	0.5	0.5	0.5	0.5	0.4	0.5	0.5	0.6	0.5	0.7	0.6
8°	0.8	0.7	0.7	0.6	0.6	0.5	0.6	0.5	0.6	0.5	0.7	0.6	0.8	0.7
12°	0.9	0.8	0.8	0.7	0.7	0.6	0.7	0.6	0.7	0.6	0.8	0.7	0.9	0.8
16°	1.1	0.9	0.9	0.8	0.8	0.7	0.8	0.7	0.8	0.7	0.9	0.8	1.1	0.9
20°	1.3	1.1	1.1	0.9	1.0	0.9	0.9	0.8	1.0	0.9	1.1	0.9	1.3	1.1
24°	1.5	1.2	1.2	1.1	1.1	1.0	1.1	1.0	1.1	1.0	1.2	1.1	1.5	1.2
28°	1.7	1.4	1.4	1.2	1.3	1.1	1.3	1.1	1.3	1.1	1.4	1.2	1.7	1.4
32°	2.0	1.7	1.6	1.4	1.5	1.3	1.5	1.3	1.5	1.3	1.6	1.4	2.0	1.7
36°	2.4	2.0	1.9	1.7	1.7	1.5	1.7	1.5	1.7	1.5	1.9	1.7	2.4	2.0
40°	3.0	2.4	2.3	1.9	2.1	1.8	2.0	1.7	2.1	1.8	2.3	1.9	3.0	2.4
44°	3.9	2.9	2.8	2.3	2.5	2.1	2.4	2.1	2.5	2.1	2.8	2.3	3.9	2.9
48°	5.4	3.8	3.6	2.9	3.1	2.6	3.0	2.5	3.1	2.6	3.6	2.9	5.4	3.8
52°	8.8	5.3	5.0	3.7	4.1	3.2	3.9	3.1	4.1	3.2	5.0	3.7	8.8	5.3
South lat.	Jun	May / Jul	Jun	May / Jul	Jun	May / Jul	Jun	May / Jul	Jun	May / Jul	Jun	May / Jul	Jun	May / Jul

North lat.	Jan / Nov	Feb / Oct	Jan / Nov	Feb / Oct	Jan / Nov	Feb / Oct	Jan / Nov	Feb / Oct	Jan / Nov	Feb / Oct	Jan / Nov	Feb / Oct	Jan / Nov	Feb / Oct
56°	8.4	2.9	5.0	2.5	4.2	2.4	4.0	2.3	4.2	2.4	5.0	2.5	8.4	2.9
60°	20.7	3.8	7.9	3.2	6.1	2.9	5.7	2.9	6.1	2.9	7.9	3.2	20.7	3.8
South lat.	May / Jul	Apr / Aug	May / Jul	Apr / Aug	May / Jul	Apr / Aug	May / Jul	Apr / Aug	May / Jul	Apr / Aug	May / Jul	Apr / Aug	May / Jul	Apr / Aug

North lat.	Feb / Oct	Mar / Sep	Feb / Oct	Mar / Sep	Feb / Oct	Mar / Sep	Feb / Oct	Mar / Sep	Feb / Oct	Mar / Sep	Feb / Oct	Mar / Sep	Feb / Oct	Mar / Sep
64°	5.2	2.1	4.1	2.1	3.8	2.1	3.7	2.1	3.8	2.1	4.1	2.1	5.2	2.1
68°	8.3	2.5	5.9	2.5	5.2	2.5	5.1	2.5	5.2	2.5	5.9	2.5	8.3	2.5
72°	19.7	3.1	10.2	3.1	8.4	3.1	7.9	3.1	8.4	3.1	10.2	3.1	19.7	3.1
South lat.	Feb / Oct	Mar / Sep	Feb / Oct	Mar / Sep	Feb / Oct	Mar / Sep	Feb / Oct	Mar / Sep	Feb / Oct	Mar / Sep	Feb / Oct	Mar / Sep	Feb / Oct	Mar / Sep

Values of X for Calculating Building Spacing

Dates are for 21 st of each month

Solar City Pilching, Linz, Austria, Norman Foster & Partners,
Section Through South Sector Housing

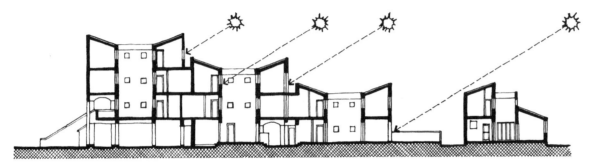

North-South Section, Public Housing Estate, Giudecca Island, Venice, Italy, Gino Valle

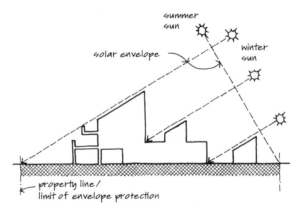

Solar Collection Within the Solar Envelope

sun in midwinter is very low or below the horizon, solar access all winter may be impossible. Therefore, for 56–60° latitude, the solstice month is omitted, and for 64–70° latitude, the three winter months with the lowest sun are omitted. The most intense solar radiation falls between the hours of 10 AM and 2 PM (solar time).

Spacing will change substantially if the site is sloped, increasing for north-facing slopes (south in SH) and decreasing for south-facing slopes (N in SH), as can be seen in Atelier 5's **Siedlung Halen,** in Bern, Switzerland. The rows are much closer together than they could be on a flat site, allowing a more compact development without sacrificing southern exposure (Futagawa, 1973).

In planning the **"Solar City Pilching"** a new district for Linz, Austria, architects Foster, Herzog, and Rogers planned two of the district's sectors as east–west-elongated, roughly parallel rows (Herzog, 1996, pp. 180–191). As shown in the section, the buildings of the south sector are spaced with an 18° angle, giving solar access on Jan/Nov 21 between 10 AM and 2 PM. Additionally, the spacing distance between the buildings has been reduced by raising the first floor with parking below, and by cutting back the north side of the upper floor on some buildings.

The ideal massing to collect sun on site can be in conflict with the ideal massing to protect solar access to neighboring sites (Strategy 29). The solar envelope will slope from a low point on the north side (south in SH) of a site toward a ridge over the site, or on its southern (northern in SH) boundary, depending on a number of variables. *To both achieve solar collection and protect solar access, the massing for on-site collection should be within the solar envelope.*

In the **Public Housing Estate at Giudecca** in Venice, by architect Gino Valle, buildings are organized in east-west-elongated rows, spaced in the north–south direction (*GA Houses*, 1988; *A + U*, 8/1988). The tallest block is four stories, located on the north side of the site. The complex steps down to the south in stages. While this allows more sun to each row than would rows of equal height, the taller north side block also casts a shadow onto the neighboring park to the north of the site. Since the park is filled with trees, the shadows are not a major issue, but in other site conditions, tall north buildings can block sun to open spaces and other buildings.

39 Organizations of *INTERWOVEN BUILDINGS & PLANTING* can be used to reduce the ambient air temperature. [cooling]

The temperature in densely built-up areas is frequently several degrees higher than in the surrounding rural areas due to heat generation from fuels, increased absorption and storage of solar radiation, poorer radiant sky cooling, and reduced wind speed due to surface roughness. Planted areas can be as much as 10–15 °F (6–8 °C) lower than built-up areas due to a combination of evapotranspiration, reflection, shading, and storage of cold. When parks are located in dense areas, localized air circulation patterns are created as heated air rising over dense areas of heat island peaks is replaced by cooler air from the vegetated areas (Chandler, 1976, p. 43).

James Oglethorpe's **plan for Savannah, Georgia** is based on a repetitive module of neighborhood wards centered around a park block. Each ward consists of eight residential blocks of housing facing on to east–west streets, with four blocks between reserved for public buildings. Open space, in the form of shaded parks, is thus democratically distributed in the cellular grid (Historic Savannah Foundation, 1968).

A very similar scheme was used by Migual Romero Sotelo in the **plan for the self-build community of Villa El Salvador** on the edge of Lima, Peru. The district is planned with repetitive pattern of 16 residential blocks surrounding a public green (Duivesteijn & van de Wal, 1994, pp. 106–114). For an illustration of the larger city plan, see Strategy 44.

Le Corbusier's **plan for Chandigarh, India,** the new town capital of Punjab, addresses a composite climate with cool winters, and hot-arid summers, shifting to hot-humid with the monsoons. Major streets are oriented with the prevailing winds, while a system of linear open spaces cuts through the center of each superblock, allowing night drainage down the gently sloping plain during the often calm evenings (also see Evenson, 1966; Futagawa, 1974).

Studies such as the one done for **LaFontaine Park in Montreal** show that the cooling effect of planting is greatest in the blocks near the open space, but extends

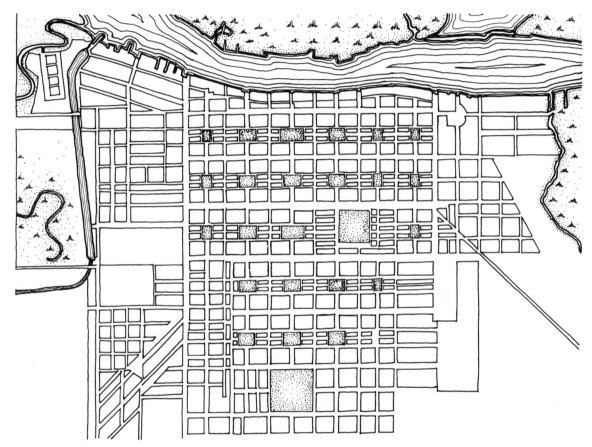

Plan of Savannah, Georgia, 1856, James Oglethorpe

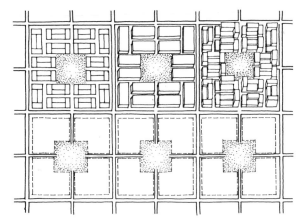

Villa El Salvador, Lima, Peru,
Migual Romero Sotelo

into built-up areas a distance of 200–400 m (360–720 ft). The pool of cool air is also carried into the surrounding area by southwest winds (Akbari et al., 1992; Thurow, 1983, p. 16).

Thus, more smaller open spaces, evenly distributed will have a greater cooling effect than a few large parks. Streets should be oriented to carry cooler air away from parks.

Hypothetical studies suggest that for a city of one million, urban temperatures do not start decreasing until the evaporating surfaces, i.e., planting, are 10–20% of the city area. The minimum air temperature decreases by 6–7 °F (3.3–3.9 °C), and the maximum temperature decreases from 9 to 10 °F (5 to 5.6 °C) as the evaporating area goes from 20 to 50% of the city (Myrup, 1969, p. 918).

The graph of Cooling Rates Due to Vegetation Cover shows temperature drop as a function of surface

area (Oke et al., 1972). It is specific to Montreal, but is likely to be representative of other temperate climate cities. The curves suggest a nonlinear performance, where 30% of the surface area covered with vegetation produces 66% of the possible cooling achieved by evapotranspiration.

Total cooling results from vegetation are due to the combined effects of shading and evapotranspiration. Trees reduce air temperature while raising humidity. The cooling effect of vegetation in hot climates comes predominantly from evaporation, while in hot-humid climates, the proportional effect of shading is more significant. The effect of shading ranges from 15 to 35% of total cooling energy savings from trees. In all climates, the combined effect of shading and evapotranspiration from trees creates savings in cooling energy, on the order of 17–57% for a 25% increase in tree cover.

The two graphs of **Cooling Due to Tree Cover** show

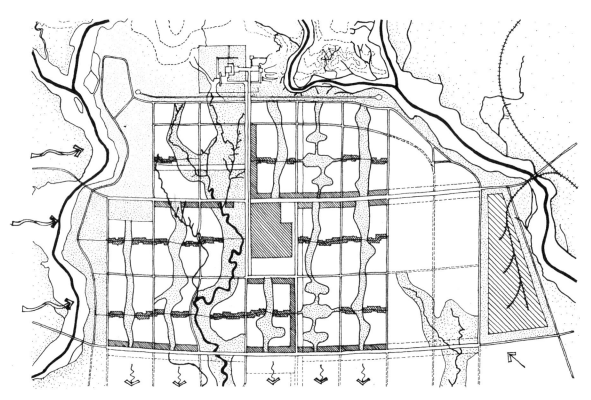

Plan of Chandigarh, Punjab, India, Le Corbusier, 1951

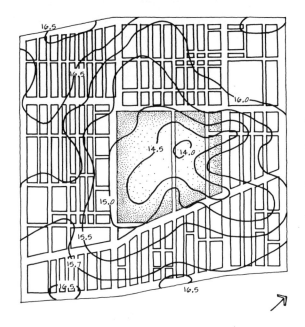

Cooling Effect From La Fontaine Park,
Montreal, Canada (degrees C)

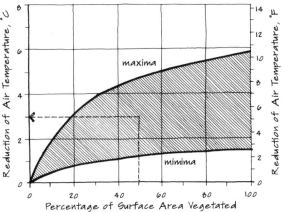

Cooling Rates Due to Vegetation Cover

the effect of increased tree cover on diurnal summer temperatures in Sacramento and Phoenix for two different levels of increased tree cover: a 10% increase (one tree per house), and a 25% increase (three trees per house) (Huang et al., 1987 in Akbari et al., 1992). The results, which agree with field studies, show that increased tree cover can significantly decrease citywide temperature.

Increased water use to irrigate landscaped areas is an issue in some cities; however, since trees use less water and provide more cooling than turf, replacing turf with trees is an improvement on both accounts (Akbari et al., 1992, p. 55).

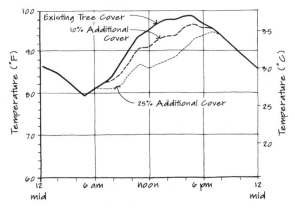

Cooling Due to Tree Cover, Sacremento
Redrawn from Akbari et al. (1992).

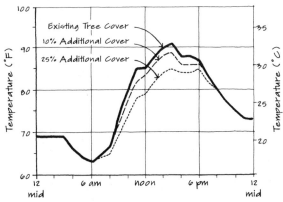

Cooling Due to Tree Cover, Phoenix
Redrawn from Akbari et al. (1992).

40 Organizations of *INTERWOVEN BUILDINGS & WATER* can be used to reduce the ambient air temperature. [cooling]

In hot-arid climates, water evaporating into the air can cool the air temperature. The evaporation rate in an enclosed open space, such as a courtyard, depends on the surface area of the water, the relative humidity of the air, and the water temperature.

The Iranian alluvial fan **villages of Muhiabad and Kousar Riz** are organized around the flow of water that has been brought to the surface though the use of *qanats*, horizontal channels cut deep, sometime miles, into the uphill alluvial soils to drain groundwater. The emerging stream passes in and out of houses and courtyards in surface and subsurface channels. Gardens and orchards, surrounded by walls to block windblown sand, are irrigated to provide cool, shaded, food-producing compounds filled with trees, vines, vegetables, herbs, and pools. The courtyard level of houses is set near the water's elevation, at times sunken 6 m (20 ft) or more below grade (English, 1966, pp. 50–55; Ardalan and Bakhtiar, 1973, p. 82).

When enclosed by walls or brought inside into open pavilions, water has the potential to cool the enclosure surfaces, particularly the ceiling, by radiation. Because radiant cooling is a function of the area and angle of heat sink "seen" by a warmer body, if the cooler water can be run down vertical or sloping surfaces, it will be much more effective at radiantly cooling occupants. A shaded pond will be cooler than an unshaded one; shaded, a pond will have an average temperature near the daily average wet-bulb temperature of the air (Givoni, 1994, p. 256). Since the reflectance of water is poor, it transmits most of the radiation that strikes it. Horizontal surfaces containing water in the sun should, therefore, be light in color (Strategy 78, 79).

For evaporation to be effective, the cooled space should be isolated from the ambient air to prevent mixing. Since the heat transfer between air and a horizontal film of water is poor (Santamouris & Asimakopolous, 1996, p. 111) the evaporating surface area of water should be increased by sprays and fountains with very fine droplets (Yannas, 1995, p 2.13).

Climatic conditions when evaporative cooling is effective can be estimated from the bioclimatic chart in Technique 18. For the effects of water edges on evaporatively cooling incoming breezes at the building scale, see Strategy 73.

Village of Kousar Riz

Village of Muhiabad

Vegetated Compounds

Buildings

Watercourse

Key

Village Plans of Muhiabad and Kousar Riz, Iran

41 *WINTER OUTDOOR ROOMS* that are sunny and wind-protected can be formed by the location and arrangement of buildings. [heating]

An outdoor space can be comfortable for a person with moderately warm clothing at temperatures as low as 40 °F (4 °C) if the wind is blocked and sufficient solar radiation is available (Technique 11). Comfort can also be achieved at lower temperatures, depending on the insulation provided by heavier clothing or on more strenuous activity levels.

Sun in open spaces and shading from the buildings that form the open space can easily be evaluated using a model and the sundial from Technique 1.

In the absence of precise information from wind tunnel simulations, one could expect, as a rule of thumb, that *the area of reduced wind velocity on the leeward side of the building group should extend to at least three to four times the building height (Melaragno, 1982, pp. 347, 377). Based on studies of windbreaks, the reduction in velocity will be at the most 75–80% near the building, decreasing to the leeward (see Strategy 43).*

Elevating temperature in outdoor spaces is difficult, since heat is quickly dissipated to the ambient environment, especially if wind is present. Heat storage outdoors has a small effect on increasing local radiant temperature, but storage outdoors is much shorter than indoors; warmed massive surfaces quickly cool as the sun goes down and temperatures drop. Therefore, promoting direct radiant gain from the sun to people, while protecting them against convective heat loss from the wind are the two main ways of improving winter outdoor comfort.

Ralph Erskine's town project in **Resolute Bay, Canada,** illustrates the potential impact of this design strategy. This new town is located halfway up a south-facing slope to maximize its exposure to the sun, while avoiding the high wind velocities characteristic of the hilltops. The complex is organized as a "sun trap," with the tallest buildings at the north, where they provide protection from the prevailing northwest wind and do not shade outdoor spaces. The dwellings, school, and circulation routes are placed within this sun trap,

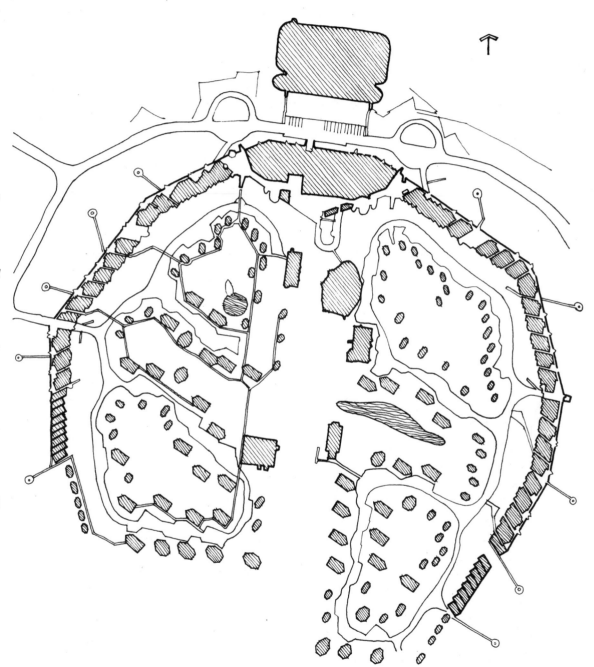

Township Plan, Resolute Bay, Northwest Territories, Canada, Ralph Erskine

maximizing the microclimatic comfort while allowing the city's inhabitants to maintain contact with the outside environment in going about their daily tasks (Egelius, 1977, pp. 846–851; Collymore, 1994, pp. 132–135).

The wind shelter patterns created by different arrangements of building groups in relation to variations in incident wind direction can be approximated using the diagrams on this and the following pages (Jensen & Franck, 1963, pp. 56–67). Outdoor rooms should be located in the areas with the greatest protection from wind. If possible, the outdoor room should also be placed in an area with good solar access.

Shelter percentages in the diagrams indicate the fraction that unobstructed incident wind velocity is reduced. The diagrams show patterns for single-story buildings arranged as two-sided L-shaped configurations, U-shaped, three-sided courtyards, and closed, four-sided courtyards. Projection distances for the sheltered zone of other building heights can be estimated from the diagrams in Technique 6.

As can be seen from the diagrams, the area of greatest wind shelter occurs in L-shaped buildings when the buildings are oriented with the outside corner toward the prevailing wind. For U-shaped building groups, shelter is maximum when the U open side faces leeward. A closed courtyard will have an area of greater shelter on one side, depending on the orientation of the court with respect to the wind. Larger dimensions of the open space will create larger areas without shelter. Increasing the height of courtyard buildings will extend the area of the sheltered zone. For more details on wind in courtyards, see Strategy 74. To check building spacing for solar access, see Strategy 38. For related wind information, see Technique 6, Air Movement Principles, and Strategy 43, Windbreaks.

North Side of Wall Building, Resolute Bay, Canada

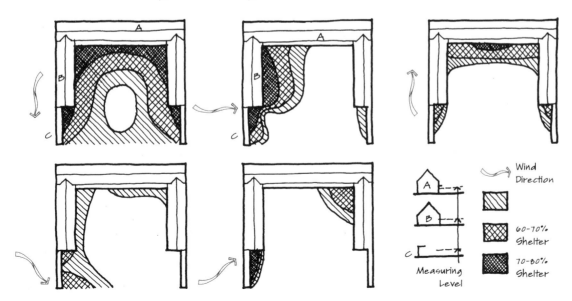

Wind Shelter Patterns in U-Shaped Organizations for Different Wind Directions

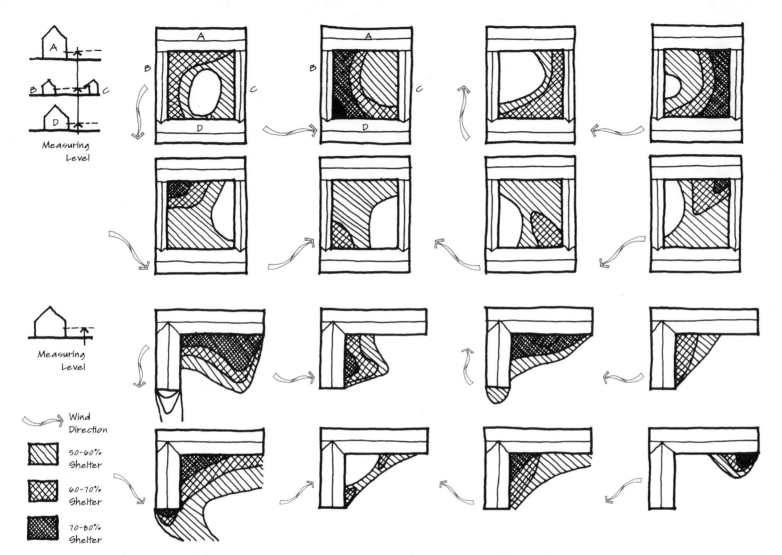

Measuring Level

Measuring Level

Wind Direction

50-60% Shelter

60-70% Shelter

70-80% Shelter

Wind Shelter Patterns in L-Shaped and Closed Courtyard Organizations for Different Wind Directions
Adapted from Jensen & Frank (1963, pp. 56-67).

42 *NEIGHBORHOOD SUNSHINE* can be insured by appropriate configurations of buildings and open space, given a street orientation. [heating]

An ideal organization of streets, open spaces, and buildings for solar access and utilization at maximum density is for building groups to be elongated in the east–west direction and spaced in the north–south direction (Strategy 38). This places buildings facing the south (north in Southern Hemisphere) to collect sun and far enough apart not to shade each other. However, because of topography or preexisting conditions, many streets do not have an east–west orientation.

The diagrams on the next page show several variations of patterns for buildings and open space, along with their implication for solar access, on streets with east–west, north–south, and rotated orientations. The sundial from Technique 1 can be used with a model of the site and buildings to study shadow patterns. Alternatively, the altitude and azimuth angles for the sun at the site's latitude at any time of the day and day of the year can be estimated from the Sun Path Diagrams in Technique 2 and used to study shadow patterns on a site plan. The shadows given are diagrammatic only; depending on latitude, solar access criteria, and building form; the actual shadow patterns on your site may vary substantially from those shown.

On east–west streets, parallel rows of buildings on deep lots, giving ample space between rows, allow full solar access to the south (north in SH) side of each building **(diagram a)**. Recommendations for building spacing by latitude and access criteria are covered in Strategy 38. Staggering setbacks will decrease solar access and increase building shading, unless buildings are spaced very far apart in the east–west direction **(diagram b)**. On shallow lots, buildings may shade each other **(diagram c)**. However, decreasing the setback on the north (south in SH) side of the block allows more space in-between buildings in the north–south direction, while providing the potential for south-facing (north-facing in SH) outdoor space for each building **(diagram d)**. Note that on the north side of blocks, sunny outdoor space will be to the rear of buildings, while on the south side of the block, it will be in front of buildings.

On north–south streets, the narrow dimension of buildings should face the street, if possible, to allow more solar exposure on their sides. Wide lots are necessary to keep solar access. Small setbacks on the north side, or zero-lot-line development will give maximum usable sunny outdoor space to the south side of build-ings **(diagram e)**. Flag lots (or alleys) allow access to an inner block parcel configured longer in the north–south dimension (diagram f). This increases density, while providing good solar access. Duplexes, and attached town houses offer similar benefits on north–south streets **(diagram g)**. For narrow lots on north–south streets, staggering setbacks allows at least one half day of solar access per building **(diagram h)**.

For streets not oriented to the cardinal directions, there are several options to provide solar access. Even though lots and streets are oriented non-cardinally, buildings may be oriented on these sites in relation to the sun **(diagram i)**. Remember that solar collection apertures should be within 30° from south (north in SH) (Strategy 59). To obtain full solar access, lots should be wide enough to prevent shadows cast from one building onto another. Angled lots offer a more direct and conventional relationship between buildings and the street, but depending on street and building orientation, may offer less than full solar access to south facing elevations **(diagram j)**. Narrow lots on angled streets provide a similar level of solar access if buildings are south oriented **(diagram k)**.

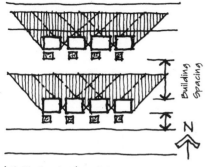

a) E-W streets, deep lots

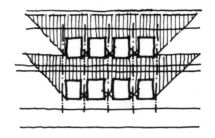

b) E-W streets, staggered setbacks

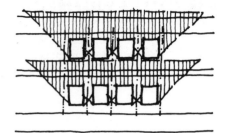

c) E-W streets, shallow lots, even setbacks

d) E-W streets, shallow lots, differentiated or narrow setbacks

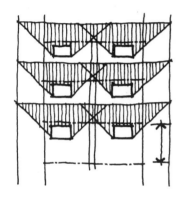

e) N-S streets, narrow face to street, wide lots

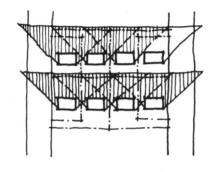

f) N-S streets, flag lots

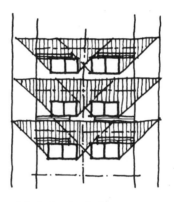

g) N-S streets, duplexes

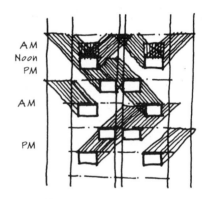

h) N-S streets, staggered setbacks

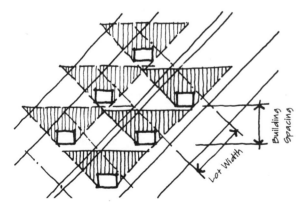

i) Noncardinal streets, south-oriented buildings, wide lots

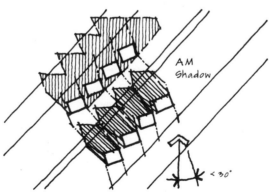

j) Noncardinal streets, southerly-oriented buldings, angled lots

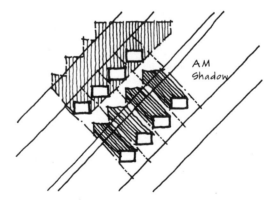

k) Noncardinal streets, south-oriented buildings, partial day sun

Patterns of Open Space and Buildings for Solar Access

43 *WINDBREAKS* **can be used to create edges that shelter buildings and open spaces. [heating and cooling]**

Windbreaks can be used to protect both buildings and outside areas from hot and cold winds. In cold climates windbreaks can reduce the heat loss in buildings by reducing wind flow over the buildings, thereby reducing convection and infiltration losses. A single-row, high-density windbreak can reduce infiltration in a residence by about 60% when planted about four tree heights from the building. This corresponds to about 15% reduction in energy costs (Stathopoulos et al., 1994, p. 141). If the wind is blocked in outside areas that have access to sun, people can be comfortable at temperatures as low as 40 °F (4 °C) or less, depending on clothing and activity level (Technique 11).

When the winds to be blocked come from a prevailing direction, partial wind screens like the L-shaped ones sheltering clusters of **farm buildings in Shimane Prefecture** in Western Japan can be used. When winds are more varied, a more completely enclosing shelter may be required. On the Italian **island of Pantellenia,** stone walls completely surround single lemon trees to protect them from the wind.

When trees are used as barriers, the velocity reduction behind the windbreak depends on their height, density, cross-sectional shape, width, and length. Height and density are the most important factors.

The section diagram for Reductions in Wind Speeds From Trees shows that a reduction of 62–78% occurs in an area five times the barrier height on the lee side of a moderately dense windbreak, 24–61% in the area five to ten barrier heights, and 13–23% in the area ten to fifteen barrier heights beyond the windbreak (R. A. Reed, 1964, p. 5).

When the wind doesn't blow perpendicular to the windbreak, the sheltered area is decreased. Since the rate of infiltration in buildings is proportional to the wind pressure, it is more important to design windbreaks for the maximum wind speed reduction than to attempt to maximize the distance over which the windbreak is effective. An extended coverage of windbreak design can be found in Heisler (1984).

In hot, dry climates, in addition to thermal comfort,

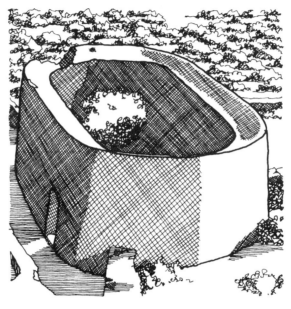

Lemon Trees, Giardino, Pantelleria Island, Italy

Vegetation Wind Breaks for Farms in Shimane Prefecture, Japan

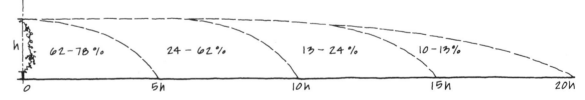

Reduction in Wind Speed From Trees

windbreaks provide important dust and sand protection. Because of their light weight, particles follow the main air stream around the building, so eddy areas of reduced velocity formed by courts and walls are less dusty.

Courts that are at most two times longer than the building height offer good dust protection. Walls on the windward side should be as high as the building and less than 20 ft (6 m) from the building. Sand, because it is heavier, can be stopped with lower walls, down to a height of 5.5 ft (1.7 m) (Sain, 1980, p. 60).

The Reduction in Wind Speed from Fences depends on their porosity and their height. The maximum reduction occurs in an area 2–7 times the barrier height on the leeward side of the barrier for a wind blowing perpendicular to the barrier. A barrier of 36% permeability shows a reduction of 90% at four times the barrier height, 70% at eight times, 30% at sixteen times, and 5% at thirty-two times the barrier height (Melaragno, 1982, p. 377).

The graph of **Average Wind Speeds at Shelterbelts of Different Permeability** shows that very dense windbreaks are more effective in reducing speeds in the area immediately behind the barrier, but are less effective than more porous barriers at greater lee side distances. This is because the low-pressure suction eddies on the leeward side pull the airflow back toward the ground (James, 1988, p. 109).

Studies have shown that an upwind "wall" building can decrease wind flows in urban setting to as low as 15% of prevailing wind speed (Givoni, 1989, pp. 3–21).

The **Byker Redevelopment,** in Newcastle upon Tyne, England, designed by Ralph Erskine, is situated on a southwest-facing slope with a view toward the Newcastle city center. Erskine surrounded the northern perimeter of the entire neighborhood with a continuous thin building, forming a wall that blocked off both North Sea winds and isolated the center of the community from rail and roadway noise (Collymore, 1994, pp. 117–121; Egelius & Futoagawa, 1980).

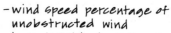

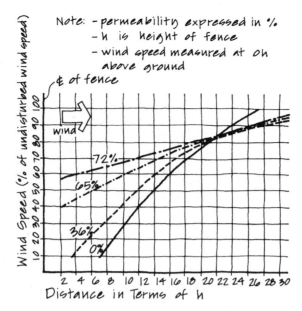

Reduction in Wind Speed From Fences

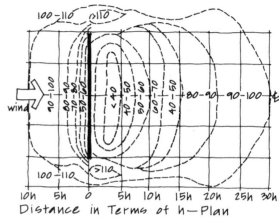

Distribution of Velocity Around a Moderately Dense Windbreak

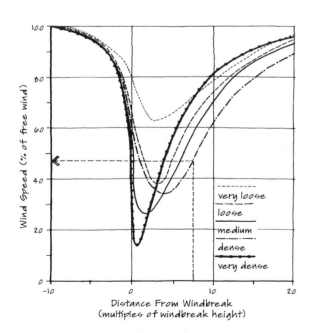

Average Wind Speeds at Shelterbelts of Different Permeability

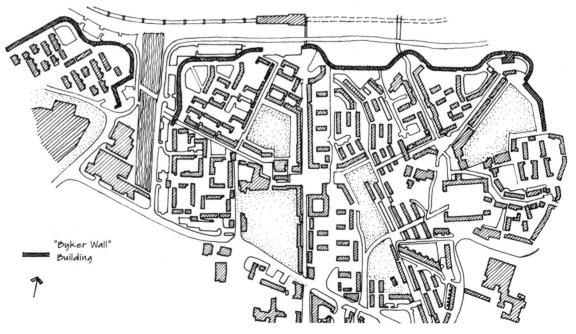

Site Plan, Housing at Byker, Newcastle-Upon-Tyne, England, Ralph Erskine

44 *GREEN EDGES* of irrigated vegetation can be formed to cool incoming breezes. [cooling]

Planted areas can be as much as 10–15 °F (5.6–8.3 °C) cooler than built-up areas due to a combination of evapotranspiration, reflection, shading, and storage of cold (Chandler, 1976, p. 43). Plants cool by both shading and evaporation of water. A tree in an arid climate can transpire up to 100 gallons (380 L) of water a day (Akbari et al., 1992, pp. 32–33). This process raises the humidity while lowering the air temperature, a desirable effect in an arid climate. The cooling effects of vegetation are increased by two factors: wind and water. Wind increases the rate of evaporation. Unless groundwater or rainfall is abundant, keeping the vegetated area irrigated is important in driving the evaporative effect of plants. In a hot-humid climate, the air is already heavy with moisture, so evaporation is a much slower process and comfort is not necessarily improved by raising the humidity.

In the plan for the self-build **community of Villa El Salvador** on the edge of arid Lima, Peru, Migual Romero Sotelo, placed a vegetated zone between the Pacific Ocean and the community. Cooler wind flows from the ocean over land irrigated with waste water from the district, and then is channeled by wide avenues deeper into the city (Duivesteijn & van de Wal, 1994, pp. 106–114). Lima is very dry, with almost no annual rainfall. Ocean breezes are more humid than land breezes; air passing over the evapotranspiring green zone is further cooled and humidified on its way to buildings and open spaces.

For more on the effects of planting in cities, see Strategy 39.

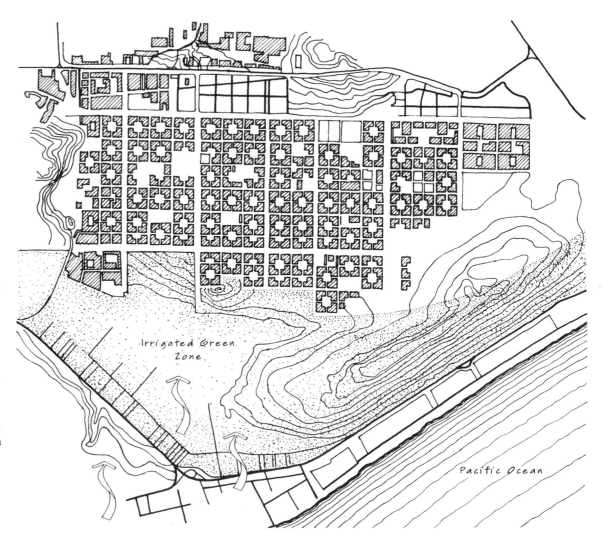

Plan of Villa El Salvador District, Lima, Peru, Migual Romero Sotelo

45

A layer of _OVERHEAD SHADES_ can protect outdoor spaces and buildings from the high sun. [cooling]

In hot climates, pedestrian streets can be quite uncomfortable unless shaded. Heat-absorbing massive elements of paving and facades, high sun angles, and intense solar radiation levels all contribute to the potential for extreme conditions.

In many hot climates, both humid and arid, groups of buildings may be linked by shaded pedestrian streets or pedestrians may be protected by arcades at the edge of streets and open spaces. In hot arid climates, daytime protection from hot, possibly dust-laden winds is also important, thus circulation can be mostly enclosed. Conversely, in hot humid climates, shading should not block ventilation.

The **Bazaar of Isfahan,** in the extreme Iranian hot-arid climate, is the main public street and commercial spine of the city. A shaded microclimate is created by rhythmically organized repetitive masonry dome-covered bays. The street and lower shops are toplit by a small oculus at the top of each dome. The Bazaar is intersected by secondary covered streets, forming a network through much of the city, connecting mosques, public buildings, fountains, places of rest, and public baths (Herdeg, 1990b, pp. 30–35).

Balkrishna Doshi, in the **Indian Institute of Management, Bangalore,** adapted the traditional bazaar form to a complex of buildings in the more humid climate of south India. Doshi referred to the complex as a "bazaar for education." The academic section of the institute is organized around a series of courts and terraces and connected with pergola-shaded pedestrian streets, often flanked by overlooking galleries. In the section of covered circulation shown, a solid opaque ribbed slab for full shade over the pedestrian street is combined with fixed vertical louvers, offering partial shade, over the planted areas on each side. The general openness of the plan and the range of semi-outdoor spaces allows ample ventilation (Curtis, 1988, pp. 98–109; A+U, 7/1997, pp. 66–73; Bhatt & Scriver, 1990, pp. 78-83).

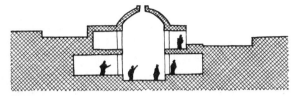

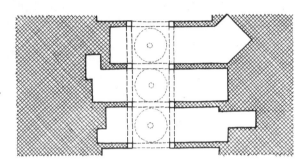

Typical Plan and Section of Bazaar

Overhead louvers for shading can shade while admitting light. They must be sized and configured to protect space below during times that shading is required. _Louvers can be set at varying angles and orientations, as long as the cutoff angle is greater than the profile angle (see diagram)._ The profile angle is the sectional angle normal to the shading device that will provide full shade. If less than 100% shade is desired, use a cutoff angle less than the profile angle. When the solar azimuth is equal to the orientation of the shading element, the profile angle is equal to the solar altitude. Profile angles can be determined for combinations of orientation, time of day, and latitude (for 24–52°) with the _LOF Sun Angle Calculator_ (Libbey-Owens-Ford, 1974). Profile angles for any latitude can be calculated using the _PEC Solar Calculator_ (Benton & Marcial, 1993).

For shading between 8 AM and 4 PM, for horizontal louvers oriented to the south (north in Southern Hemisphere), the profile angle is 90° (straight overhead) for latitudes up to 40°. In this orientation, the profile an-

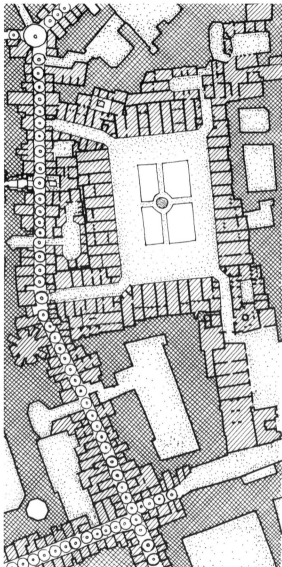

Partial Plan of Bazaar, Isfahan, Iran

gle is highest in the early morning and late afternoon. For horizontal louvers oriented east-west (elongated in the north-south direction), the maximum governing profile angle is 90° for all latitudes. Since the profile angle increases during the morning, peaks at noon, and decreases during the afternoon, shading designed with a profile angle less than 90° will not provide shading during the midday hours of maximum solar radiation.

As a general rule, assuming full sun exposure and no shading of the louvers from obstructions:

To provide shading by fixed overhead louvers, the cutoff angle of the louver design should be greater than 90° (see diagram).

Louvers oriented to the south (north in SH), elongated east-west, will provide shade all day long except near the equator, when the sun spends part of its path in the north sky (south in SH). Louvers oriented east or west will provide shade only half of the day and will admit sun half of the day. This indicates that east-west-oriented louvers are most effective when operable. Many other fixed shading designs are possible, including horizontal eggcrate, multiple layers, opaque roofing, and perforated filtering strategies. Technique 16 and Strategy 99 show examples of these techniques used to protect vertical windows .

Shaded Pedestrian Street, Indian Institute of Management, Bangalore, India, Balkrishna Doshi

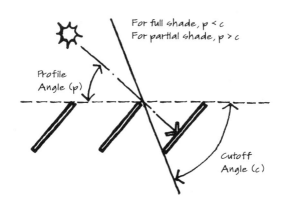

Geometry of Overhead Louvered Sunshades

IIB   Buildings

The strategies at the building scale deal with single buildings and their major components, rooms and courtyards. This section contains more strategies than the sections for either of the other two scales, which probably reflects the importance of this scale in the schematic design stage and the fact that much of the research and testing has been done at the building scale.

A few strategies deal with the orientation and location of rooms to sun and wind. Strategy 47, Locating Outdoor Rooms, gives prototypical patterns for placing outdoor rooms in relation to the building for summer and winter conditions in different types of climates. Strategy 59, Rooms Facing the Sun & Wind, gives orientation guidelines for solar heating and cross-ventilation, while Strategy 74, Breezy Courtyards and Calm Courtyards, gives suggestions for orienting courts and their openings depending on the microclimate objective of the designer. Water Edges, Strategy 73, suggests how to position evaporation sources to cool incoming breezes.

The bulk of the Buildings section concentrates on the shape and enclosure of rooms either to reduce heating and cooling loads or to meet the building's needs for heating, cooling, and lighting with site-based resources. Five strategies recommend ways that rooms can be formed to collect, store, and distribute solar heat. Strategies 60, 61, and 62 give design guidelines for three familiar passive solar configurations: Direct Gain Rooms, Sunspaces, and Thermal Storage Walls. They show how heat can be collected and stored in either distributed or centralized ways, and either within a space or at its edge. Strategy 63, Roof Ponds, gives advice for a way to perform heating in the ceiling plane. Finally, the strategy for Thermal Collector Walls and Roofs, 64, directs the designer on a way to handle collection and storage independent of each other.

A large number of strategies give design guidance for ways to cool buildings with the form and enclosure of rooms or groups of rooms. The Roof Pond, 63, is the one strategy that has the potential for both heating and cooling. Four strategies are concerned with ventilation. Cross-Ventilation, Strategy 65, uses the wind as a resource, while Stack Ventilation, Strategy 66, shows how to cool with the chimney effect in the absence of wind. The Wind Catchers strategy, 67, quantifies the effects of a historic response to wind-driven ventilation in a dense low-rise context. When it is too hot during the day to make use of natural ventilation, consider using Strategy 68, Night Cooled Mass, in which the building cycles between thermal openness and closure.

A useful cooling strategy in arid circumstances when it is too hot outside for ventilative cooling is Strategy 69, Evaporative Cooling Towers.

Another large set of strategies, in Part 2 of the Buildings section, includes design options for relating one room to another in plan or section, as either zoning strategies or organizational strategies.

A few strategies suggest how activities and their associated rooms can be zoned in response to light, temperature variations, and sources of heat and cold. These are Strategies 46, Migration; 55, Heat-Producing Zones; 56, Stratification Zones; 57, Buffer Zones; and 58, Daylight Zones.

Six strategies address building organization. Strategy 49, Clustered Rooms, shows the effect of exposed envelope on heating and cooling. Strategy 50, Permeable Buildings, offers design alternatives for combining plan and section orders to facilitate both cross-ventilation and stack-ventilation. Strategies 52, East–West Plan, and 53, Deep Sun, focus on organizing rooms to maximize winter solar gain. Building organization for lighting is covered in Strategies 51, Thin Plan, and 54, Borrowed Daylight.

Lastly, three of the strategies, 48, Layer of Shades; 57, Buffer Zones; and 72, Earth Edges, discuss the protection of rooms from the extremes of heat and cold.

46 *MIGRATION:* **Rooms and courts can be zoned so that activities can take place in cooler areas during warm periods and warmer areas during cool periods of the day or season. [heating and cooling]**

This strategy combines migration—moving from one place to another to maintain thermal comfort—with providing a variety of zones, each of which is comfortable under a different set of climatic conditions. Because each zone is tuned to a limited set of conditions, its design can be simpler. Design criteria can be selected that do no more than simply moderate climatic extremes; they may take advantage of the beneficial relationship between some materials' thermal characteristics and certain climate patterns, such as thermal lag and large diurnal temperature swings; or they may exploit the compatibility of certain climate conditions with existing social patterns, like moving from a living to a sleeping area.

Pueblo Acoma, near Albuquerque, New Mexico, is an example of a two-zone residence in which the time of day that each zone is used changes dramatically from season to season. In cool seasons, the outside terraces are used during the day and the interior spaces at night. In the warm seasons the reverse is true: The outside terraces are used at night and the shaded cool interiors during the day.

One zone, the exterior south-facing terrace, is wind-protected and sunny during the day, an advantage when the air is cool and a disadvantage when it is warm. It radiates heat to the sky at night, an advantage when it's warm and a disadvantage when it's cool. The second zone, the interior room, follows the outside climate less closely than the terrace. The heat storage characteristics of the massive construction cause the interior temperature to lag several hours behind the exterior temperature. In the cool seasons the mass absorbs the sun's heat during the day and releases it to the interior at night. In warm seasons, the mass is cooled at night by the air and by radiation to the sky, and so remains cool during the day.

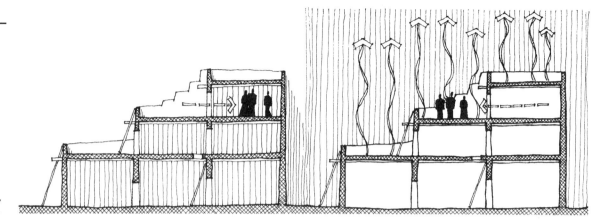

Pueblo Acoma, Warm Season Day

Pueblo Acoma, Warm Season Night

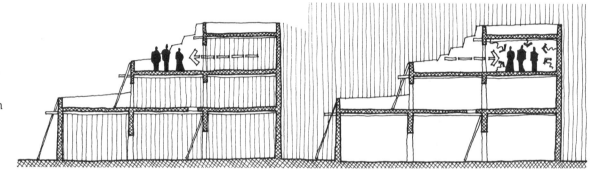

Pueblo Acoma, Cool Season Day

Pueblo Acoma, Cool Season Night

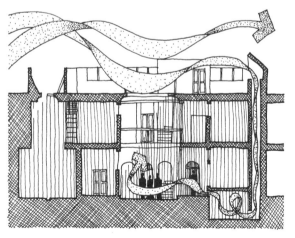

Iraq House, Summer Day

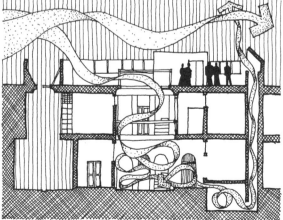

Iraq House, Summer Night

The **house in Iraq** is zoned vertically; the use of these layers changes both daily and seasonally. The court and chimneys, combined with the building's massive construction, effectively moderate the high summer temperatures. During the summer day, people live on the first level, which is cooled by several strategies. The incoming breezes are directed into the wind catchers at the top of the chimneys; the air is cooled by the mass of the chimneys and falls to rooms or to the basement, where it is further cooled by evaporation before it flows into the court. The court, which is tall enough to be partially protected from the sun, is sprinkled daily to cool its air. On summer evenings, people sleep on the roof, which is cooled by radiation to the night sky. At night, the cool air from the roof falls into the court, flows through the building, cooling the mass heated during the day, and exits up the warm chimney.

During the short mild winter, the family lives on the second level, away from the cool court floor. In the transitional periods of spring and fall when the roof is too cool and the rooms are too warm, the second level gallery is used for sleeping (Al-Azzaui, 1969, p. 91).

Charles Correa used two different climatically derived sections placed parallel to each other to facilitate seasonal and daily migration in the **Parekh House,** in Ahmedabad, India. The "winter section," intended for

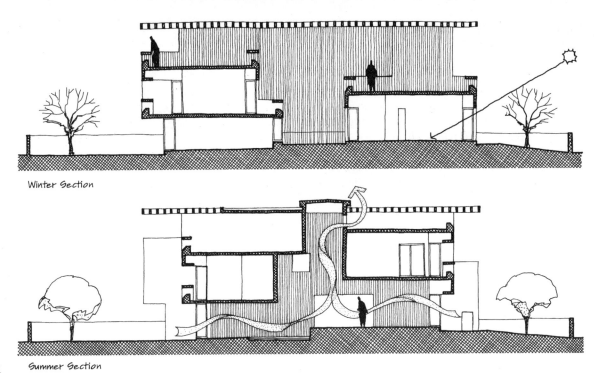

Winter Section

Summer Section

Parekh House, Ahmedabad, India, Charles Correa

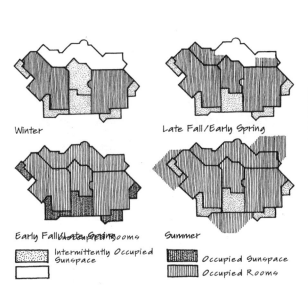

Winter

Late Fall/Early Spring

Early Fall/Late Spring

Summer

Unoccupied Rooms
Intermittently Occupied Sunspace

Occupied Sunspace
Occupied Rooms

Migrational Patterns, Primary School, Tournai, Belgium, Jean Wilfart/SCP

View from Southeast, Primary School, Tournai

use on winter days and summer evenings, is located on the eastern elevation where it can be warmed by morning sun. It has roof terraces under a partial shade pergola. The "summer section," a retreat for hot summer afternoons, is placed in the center of the house, between the winter section and the service core, minimizing exposure to the outside. It's height is used to exploit stack ventilation (Khan, 1987, pp. 42–43).

The **Primary School at Tournai,** Belgium, by Jean Wilfart/SCP D'Architectes, takes a more metabolic approach to thermal zoning. The use of the building expands and contracts according to the outdoor temperature (see plan and section in Strategy 53). From late spring to early fall, an outdoor amphitheater and several outdoor rooms are used. As the weather gets colder, the occupied space gradually contracts. The central sunspace (including the library) and the four smaller perimeter sunspaces have no auxiliary heating system and are occupied only when sufficiently warm (Buckley et al., 1991, Ch. 15; Hildon & Seager, 1989, pp. 17–22).

Thermal zones were designed for the **residence in Grants Pass, Oregon,** by Equinox Design, Inc., to organize activities and passive heating and cooling systems. The zones are graded from most thermally controlled to least. The building expands and contracts daily and seasonally with movable walls so that its heating and cooling loads remain fairly constant even when outdoor temperatures vary. System characteristics are matched with zone characteristics. For example, trombe walls, which supply even heat, are located in the most thermally stable enclaves.

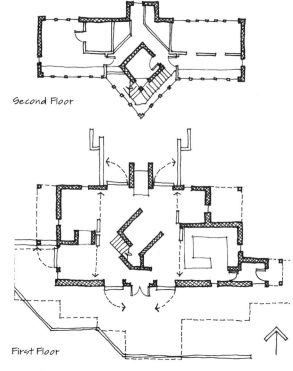

Second Floor

First Floor

McCoy House Project, Equinox Design Inc.

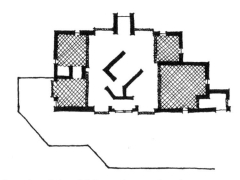

Closed - winter nights, sunless winter days

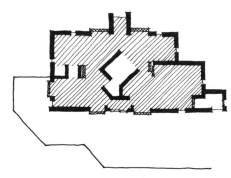

Open Inside - winter days, sunny spring and fall days and nights

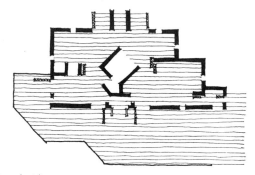

Open Inside/ Open Skin - warmest spring and fall days, summer days and nights

McCoy House Zoning

47 *LOCATING OUTDOOR ROOMS* in relation to sun and wind can extend the seasons of outdoor comfort. [heating and cooling]

Because buildings can block sun and wind, they create a series of different microclimates around them. Combinations of wind and sun directions have implications for where to locate outdoor rooms. For example, the matrix for **Locating Outdoor Rooms based on Microclimate** shows that in temperate-humid summers, when summer wind and sun directions are oblique to each other, the outdoor room can be located to the north side (south in Southern Hemisphere) of the building where there is more shade and the wind will blow through the space. However, when summer wind and sun directions are co-incident, the outdoor room should not be located on the north side of the building, because it would then not have access to wind. When cooling winds are opposed to the hot sun direction, the outdoor room may be located for best shade and the building will not block the wind.

For the temperate New England climate of Lincoln, Massachusetts, Walter Gropius and Marcel Breuer placed the screened porch of the **Gropius House** extending from the south side of the house where it could be swept by the southwesterly summer breezes. Although a location on the north would have provided some shade by the building, the screened porch would have had no access to wind. Therefore, the porch is shaded by an opaque roof and roll-down shades. The house is also provided with a sunny south-facing second-floor roof deck, screened from winter winds by an opaque west wall (*Process Architecture*, 1980, pp. 6–10).

In heating seasons, the matrix shows that outdoor rooms should be in the sun and protected from the wind. For related strategies at the Building Groups scale, see Strategies 28 and 41. In cold climates, there will be little need to cool outdoor spaces and a location on the sunny south side (north in SH) of the building is prime. When winter wind is coincident with or oblique to the sun, windbreaks should be used to shelter the space (Strategy 43).

Bernard Maybeck set the **Wallen Maybeck House** on the top of a cool, windy hill near Berkeley, California.

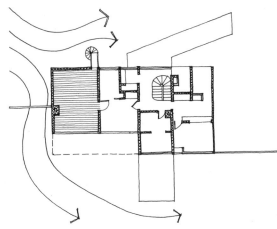

Second Floor

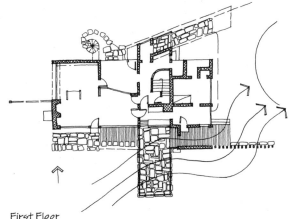

First Floor

Gropius House, Lincoln, Massachusetts,
Walter Gropius & Marcel Breuer

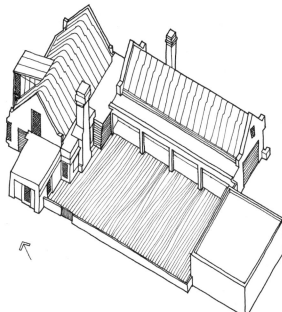

Wallen Maybeck House,
Berkeley, California, Bernard Maybeck

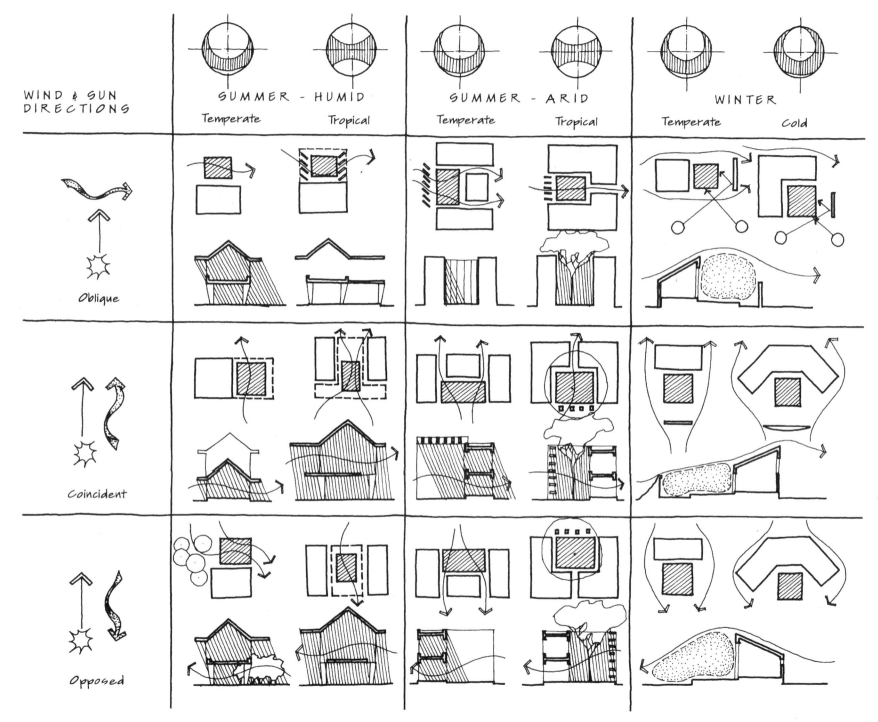

SUMMER - HUMID

Temperate   Tropical

SUMMER - ARID

Temperate   Tropical

WINTER

Temperate   Cold

Oblique

Coincident

Opposed

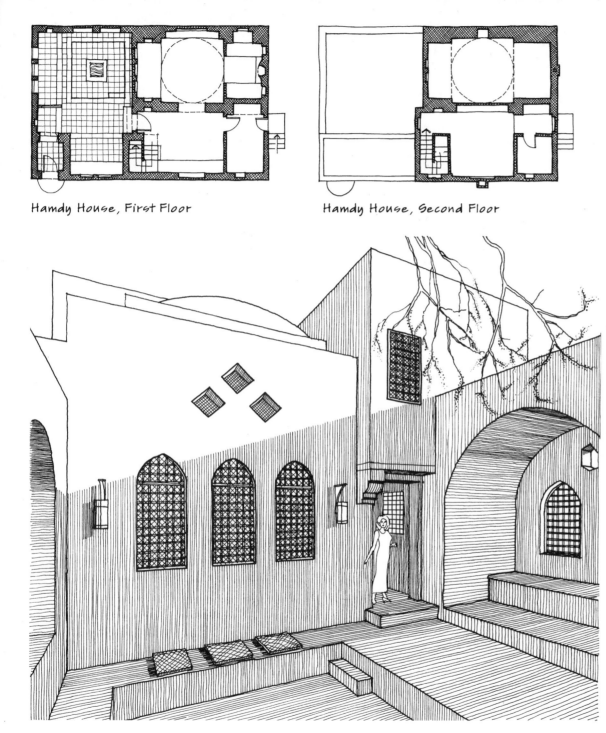

Hamdy House, First Floor

Hamdy House, Second Floor

The southwest-facing outdoor space is surrounded on two sides by the house, on a third by the garage, and on the fourth by a low wall. The organization allows the occupants to keep the view while being protected from winter winds from the north-northwest (Woodbridge, 1992, pp. 199–209).

In tropical climates, cooling is the dominant condition, whereas in temperate climates, there will be some need for outdoor rooms to be warmed by the sun in winter. Therefore, in temperate climates, outdoor rooms should be designed to work well for both heating and cooling, or more than one outdoor room should be designed, allowing users to migrate daily or seasonally, based on the comfort of each space (Strategy 46).

In humid cooling seasons, outdoor rooms should be located in places with access to breezes while also providing shade, either from the building (Strategy 27) or by means of overhead shades (Strategy 48). Because access to wind is most important, shade should be a second priority in determining location. For more detail on microclimatic design priorities in different climates, see Technique 7. In hot-arid climates, shade is a priority and wind may be too hot or dusty at times, but is desirable at night.

Abdel Wahed El-Wakil's scheme for the **Hamdy House** in hot-arid Cairo, Egypt, uses almost half of the building footprint for an outdoor room that is both entry and courtyard. Surrounded on three sides by walls with wood-screened windows and on one side by the rest of the house, the main part of the courtyard is open to sky around a sunken fountain. Along one edge is a deep vaulted seating alcove. The design offers a range of options from full shade to sun. During summer mornings and afternoons, the high walls shade the court, while at midday, occupants can escape the high sun in the alcove, or within the more protected house interior. The windows in the walls allow enough air to move through for night cooling, while the screens help to create turbulence and remove dust from the air (Jacobson et al., 1990, pp. 82–85).

Hamdy House, Cairo, Egypt, Abdel Wahed El-Wakil

48 A *LAYER OF SHADES* overhead protects the courtyard and building from the high sun, while a layer of vertical shades can protect from low sun. [cooling]

During the summer at temperate latitudes, or year-round at tropical latitudes, the sun is high enough in the sky for much of the day that horizontal overhead shading devices are more effective at shading outdoor space than vertical ones and more effective than shade from a building's massing. However, in the morning or afternoon, shading elements in the vertical plane are more effective at blocking low-angle sun.

Because the sun changes position throughout the day, an overhead shading device must be larger than the outdoor room if it is to shade continuously throughout the day. Its size must increase as the height of the shades above the outdoor room increases and as the period of desired shading increases. As the sun moves, it will also shade adjacent areas.

From the diagrams, the horizontal dimension of the overhead shading device may be determined as a function of its height above the ground. The cross-hatched area represents the continuously shaded area. Though square in the diagram, it can be any rectangular shape. The rectangle represents the shading device, drawn in plan, above the shaded area. The dimensions a and b are the distances, in plan, from the edge of the shaded area to the edge of the shading device.

The shading devices may be opaque or louvered, as they are in a **Tucson, Arizona, house** by Judith Chafee, where the shades partially cover the building as well as outside areas (Watson & Labs, 1983, p. 15). Paul Rudolph used the same strategy in the **Hiss Residence (Umbrella House)** in Sarasota, Florida, covering with louvered shades the entire house and the outdoor space, extending on all sides. While the shades over the pool are held back to give an area of partial sun, an opaque plane is suspended over part of the terrace to give an area of full shade (Olgyay & Olgyay, 1957, pp. 196–197; Moholy-Nagy & Schwab, 1970).

In hot climates, the overheated period in summer often begins near sunrise and extends into the evening. In some buildings, such as residences, the building is

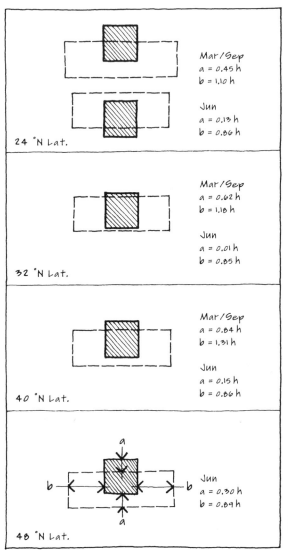

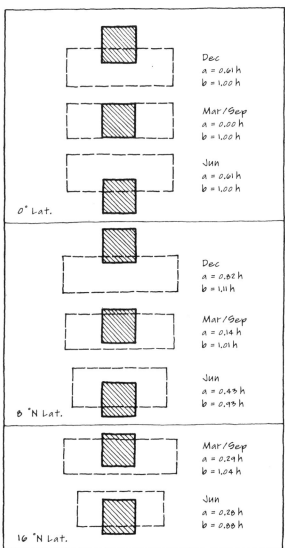

Size and Location of Overhead Shades
h = height of overhead shades

House in Tucson, Arizona, Judith Chafee

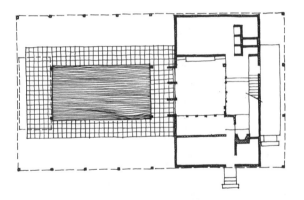

Hiss Residence, Plan

Hiss Residence (Umbrella House), Sarasota, Florida, Paul Rudolph

occupied more during the early morning and late afternoon than during the middle of the day. So, shading for outdoor rooms may be desirable when the sun is very low. To shade low sun by overhead shades would require very long extensions beyond the courtyard. William Turnbull of MLTW addressed this issue in the **Zimmerman House** in Fairfax County, Virginia, by creating a house within an encompassing layer of shades. A vertical redwood lattice envelope, pierced by large view-framing windows gives shade from low-angle sun to porches around the inner house and roof terraces above. The outer roof is glazed with translucent plastic and fully vented below to prevent heat buildup (*GA Houses*, 1976, pp. 98–103; *Architectural Review*, 6/1976, p. 381).

Shades can be movable so that the sun can be let in when it is cold and screened when it is hot. Fixed shades have the potential disadvantage of shading equally for months on either side of the summer solstice. In climates with cool springs, say March and April in the Northern Hemisphere, it is desirable to admit the sun, but in August and September, when it is hot and sun positions are identical, shade is needed.

Unlike fixed shades, selected deciduous vines follow the climate rather than the sun path's symmetry. They are in full leaf in the hottest summer months after the solstice, but still bare and relatively transparent at the spring equinox and the month after. The **Abramson House** in Sacramento, California, by Brent Smith, has leafy vines on its trellis to shade both the house and the deck (Wright & Andrejko, 1982, p. 90). As the Abramson house demonstrates, while the zone of shading is basically horizontal, the shading elements are not limited to horizontal planes. For more detail on shading with plants, see Strategy 99; for details on louver design, see Overhead Shades, Strategy 45.

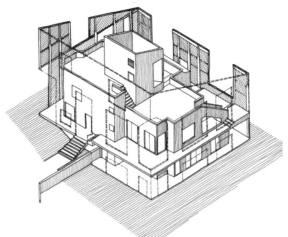
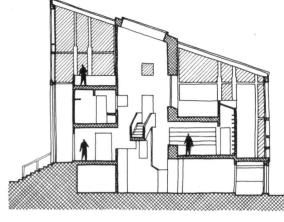

Zimmerman House, Fairfax County, Virginia, William Turnbull/MLTW   Zimmerman House

Abramson House, Sacramento, California, Brent Smith

49 *CLUSTERED ROOMS* reduce skin area, thus heat loss and gain. [heating and cooling]

The amount of exposed skin relative to the volume enclosed increases as compact forms like cubes elongate to forms like rectangles or more articulated envelopes. Therefore, the heat loss or gain through the skin by conduction and convection is greater for elongated forms than for compact forms of the same volume. Similarly, large buildings have less area of exposed skin as a ratio of floor area than do small buildings of the same massing proportions. Buildings with a higher skin/volume ratio also have more radiation falling on their walls, windows, and roof. This is an advantage in the heating season if the long side faces south (Strategy 52), but a disadvantage in the cooling season, especially if the major surfaces face east or west, or are horizontal.

When controlling heat loss or gain through the skin is a primary concern, rooms can be contracted into a compact form, as they were in the traditional **New England Salt Box,** in which the rooms also surrounded a central heat source. When this house fronts the south, it has the largest and the most windows facing south to collect the sun, and the source of constant heat, the kitchen, is on the coldest north side (Rifkind, 1980, p. 7).

Envelope transfer is a function of the insulation level (thermal resistance), the area of skin, and the temperature difference between inside and outside. The impact of the ratio of skin surface to floor area (S/F) is more important for poorly insulated buildings.

As can be seen from the graph, the rate of heat transfer through the skin increases as the *S/F* ratio increases, but for buildings with high levels of insulation, the difference is small, whereas for walls and roofs with low *R*-values, the effect of *S/F* on envelope heat transfer is great.

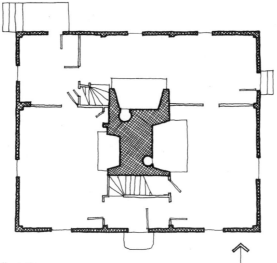
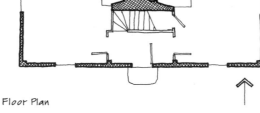

Floor Plan

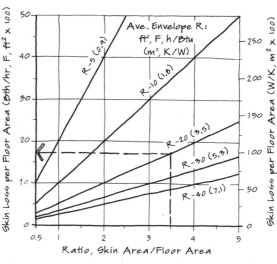

Skin Loss/Gain as a Function of Massing

East Elevation

Old Ogden House, Fairfield, Connecticut

South Elevation

50 *PERMEABLE BUILDINGS* **can combine open plans and sections for cross-ventilation, stack-ventilation, or both. [cooling]**

Cross-ventilation is a particularly valuable means of cooling during warm periods because it not only removes heat from the space but also increases the sensation of cooling by increasing people's rate of evaporation (Strategy 65). However, in hot climates and in temperate climates at night, air movement is frequently slow, in which case stack-ventilation becomes an important supplementary strategy (Strategy 66). Combined strategies may also be employed for different rooms in the same building. For example, cross-ventilation might be used in windward side and upper level rooms, while stack-ventilation might be used in lee side and lower rooms that have little access to wind.

Both cross-ventilation and stack-ventilation work better in certain configurations, yet can be facilitated with a variety of different room organizations. When designing a scheme for both types of ventilation, parts of both the plan and the section must be kept open to air movement.

The **Logan House** in Tampa, Florida, designed by Rowe Holmes Associates, bunches the rooms to use a central stack but opens the three center spaces to each other and the outside to form a cross-ventilated breezeway through the entire house (*Progressive Architecture*, 6/1981, p. 86).

Three strategies are used to promote cross-ventilation in the **Building Research Establishment Office Building** in Garston, UK, by the firm of Feilden-Clegg (Allen, 1997; Jones, 1998, pp. 178–181). First, the building is zoned so that circulation is open through one side of an open office plan, so there are no corridor walls. Second, the north side cellular offices are not continuous along the building's perimeter, but are interrupted by alcoves that are open to the larger south side offices. Third, even when the cellular offices are closed, or if a tenant did build them continuously along the north side, the hollow concrete slab allows air to be pulled by fans above the ceiling of the small offices and supplied above the circulation. The hypocaust (air core) slab can also be used as thermal storage and cooled by night ventilation (see section drawing in Strategy 66).

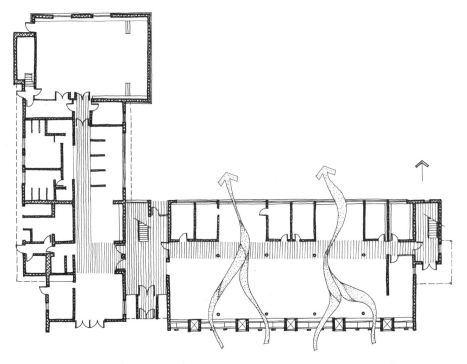

Building Research Establishment Office Building, Garston, UK, Feilden-Clegg

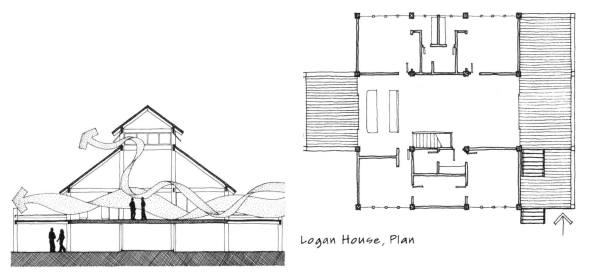

Logan House, Plan

Logan House, Section, Tampa, Florida
Rowe Holmes Associates

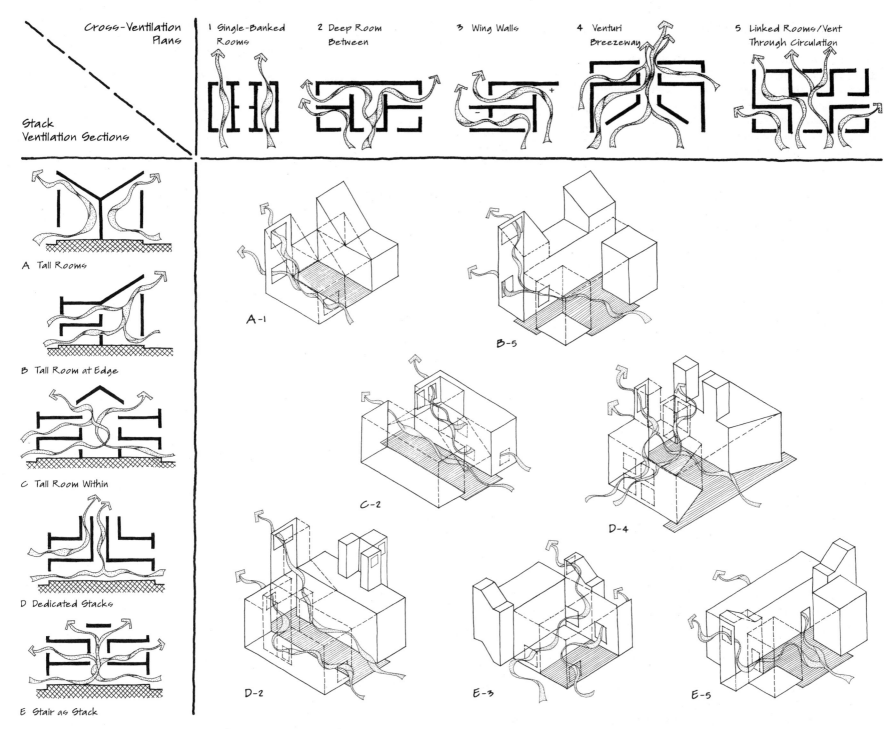

Cross-Ventilation Plans

1 Single-Banked Rooms
2 Deep Room Between
3 Wing Walls
4 Venturi Breezeway
5 Linked Rooms/Vent Through Circulation

Stack Ventilation Sections

A Tall Rooms

B Tall Room at Edge

C Tall Room Within

D Dedicated Stacks

E Stair as Stack

A-1

B-5

C-2

D-4

D-2

E-3

E-5

Room Organization Strategies That Facilitate Both Cross and Stack-Ventilation

The ideal cross-ventilated building is one room thick, thin in plan, and elongated to maximize exposure to prevailing winds. In practice, this is rarely possible in all but small buildings with few site constraints. In buildings more than one room thick and in all buildings with circulation corridors, the windward rooms can block the wind to leeward rooms. *The horizontal axis of the matrix shows several strategies of organizing rooms for cross-ventilation that bring air to all rooms.*

Stack-ventilation is dependent on the height between inlets and outlets, and so is maximized by tall rooms and chimneys. *The vertical axis of the matrix shows several strategies of organizing rooms for stack-ventilation. The body of the matrix shows a few of the possible diagrammatic combinations of organizations that facilitate both cross and stack-ventilation that brings air to all rooms.*

The combined effect of stack and cross-ventilation is due to the sum of the pressures driving both air flows. Since pressure varies as the square of velocity, the combined cooling effect is nonlinear. The combined flow rate is equal to the square root of the sum of the squares of the individual flow rates (ASHRAE, 1997, p. 25.11).

If the openings are such that the flow rates for cross and stack-ventilation can be coordinated, for typical buildings the cooling rate from the combination can be estimated from the graph. First determine the cooling rate for the window design and wind speed from Strategy 65, Cross-Ventilation. Next determine the cooling rate for the stack height and area from Strategy 66, Stack-Ventilation. Using these two individual rates, enter the graph on the vertical axis with the cooling rate for cross-ventilation and move horizontally to the curve for the cooling rate of the building by stack-ventilation. From the intersection move vertically to read on the horizontal axis the combined rate of cooling. This is the total rate of heat that can be removed by ventilation, per unit of floor area. Compare this value to the rate of heat gain for the building, from Technique 21.

Corridor buildings require particular attention to ventilation. José Luis Sert minimized the way in which

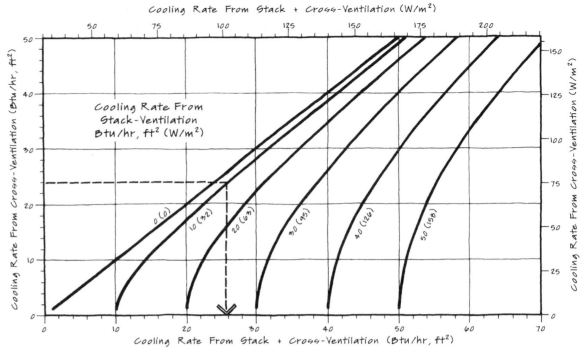

Cooling Rate From Combined Cross and Stack-Ventilation

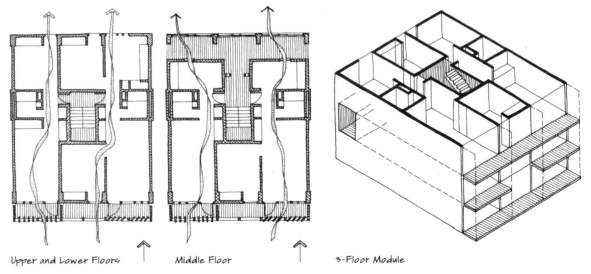

Upper and Lower Floors   Middle Floor   3-Floor Module

Peabody Terrace, Cambridge, Massachusetts, José Luis Sert

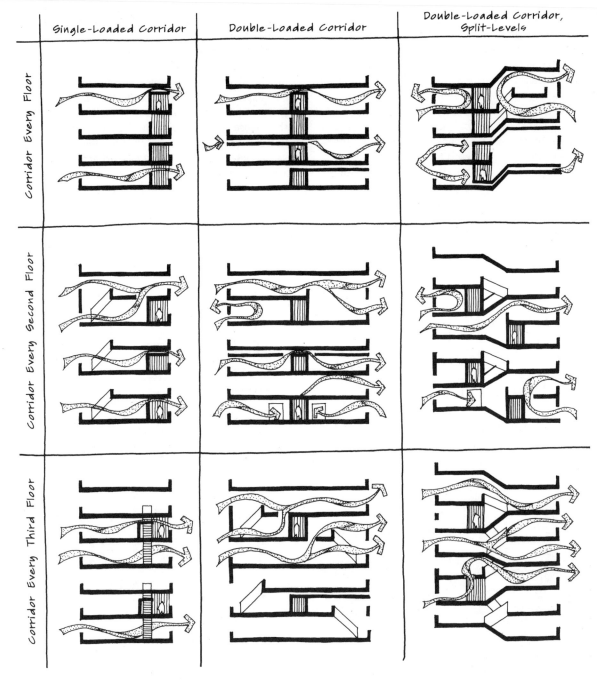

	Single-Loaded Corridor	Double-Loaded Corridor	Double-Loaded Corridor, Split-Levels
Corridor Every Floor			
Corridor Every Second Floor			
Corridor Every Third Floor			

Organizational Strategies for Cross-Ventilation in Corridor Buildings

corridors can block ventilation by using a skip-stop elevator building section with corridors every third floor in the **Peabody Terrace Married Student Housing** at Harvard University in Cambridge, Massachusetts (Bastlund, 1967, pp. 220–231). Local stairs give access to six units on three floors off of each corridor. This allows through ventilation from south to north for units on the floors above and below the corridor floor. Outside terraces provide a second egress for these floors.

The matrix on this page shows numerous strategies for providing cross-ventilation in single-loaded, double-loaded, and split-level corridor buildings. Whenever air flow is blocked by a room or corridor, there are three basic solutions: 1) use transom windows or vents overhead; 2) drop the ceiling over the smaller space to provide a plenum; or 3) use the floor or ceiling structure as a hypocaust. Corridors on every second or third floor free up some floors for through venting, but are mostly applicable to housing, because of handicapped access requirements. Split level sections often can use their height difference to aid the stack effect.

Charles Correa avoided the problem of wind-blocking corridors altogether in the **Kanchunjunga Apartments** in Bombay, India, with the use of vertical circulation cores serving two units per floor (Khan, 1987, pp. 56–61). This allows ventilation air to move from one side of the building to another by flowing around the cores. Because air must move from the windward rooms through one or two more rooms, the plans and sections are both treated in a loose, open manner, with private bedrooms on the upper levels for privacy. Double volumes provide some opportunity for stack-ventilation, while numerous level changes help create spatial definition with a minimum of internal partitions. Because the sea breezes are from the west, the main facades face east and west and are protected from storm rains and sun by a buffer zone of double-height terrace gardens. The same basic strategy of one or more vertical circulation cores serving two units of floor area works equally well for shorter buildings.

When hot-humid conditions predominate, circulation can be exposed and unconditioned, even in large buildings. Ken Yeang's **MBF Tower** in Penang, Malaysia, uses both a "loose" plan and generous floor openings to provide access to breezes for four units per floor (Yeang, 1994, pp. 86–89; Abel, 1994). The apartments are separated by air gaps, both between each other and between the apartments and the access walkways. Upper floors have open-air, two-story lobbies, and the entire circulation is open, having no exterior walls.

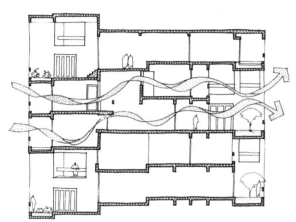

E-W Section, Kanchunjunga Apartments

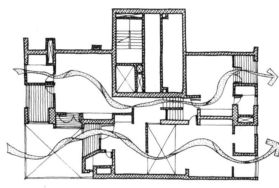

Upper Level Plan

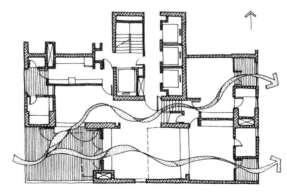

Lower Level Plan

Kanchunjunga Apartments, Bombay, India, Charles Correa

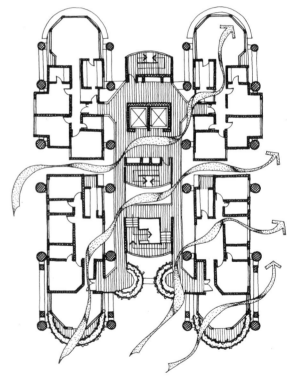

Typical Upper Level Plan, MBF Tower, Penang, Malaysia, Ken Yeang

51 *THIN PLAN* **room arrangements will have daylight available for each space. [daylighting]**

The amount of light that reaches the interior of a room lit from one side is a function of the distance from the window, the height of the window above the floor, the size of the window (Strategy 94), and the reflectivity of the room surfaces (Strategy 78). As one moves away from the window wall, the proportion of the exterior daylight available inside decreases. Therefore, the thickness of the building is an important design consideration for a daylit building.

The **Science and Technology Park** in Gelsenkirchen, Germany, by Kiessel + Partner, is organized into nine thin office pavilions, with offices facing north and south, connected by a single-loaded spine with offices facing east. Thus, the large office building gives ample natural light to every unit of floor area (Rumpf, 1995).

In a more compact plan, the basic thin building section is wrapped around shallow indentions and central courts, giving daylight to each patient room in the **Klinikum NürnBerg, Germany,** by Architektengruppe Klinikum II (von Arnim, 1993).

The **Wainwright Building** in St. Louis, Missouri, by Louis Sullivan, has side-lit offices arranged on both sides of a single corridor. The building is U-shaped to fit a corner site and to provide a continuous facade for both streets. The "light courts" traditionally formed by O-, U-, and E-shaped buildings reduce the amount of light available to the windows that face them because the court walls absorb some of the light. Sullivan addressed this problem in the Wainwright Building by giving the rooms facing the court less depth than the ones facing the more open street.

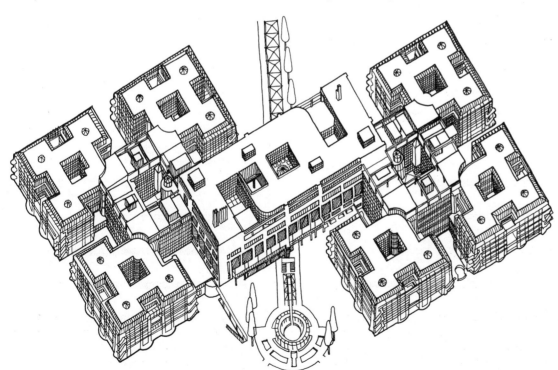

Klinikum NürnBerg, Germany, Architektengruppe Klinikum II

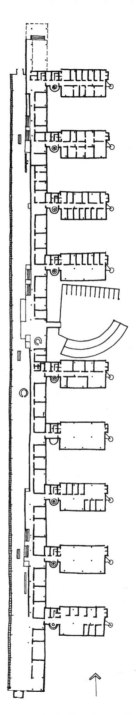

Science and Technology Park, Gelsenkirchen, Germany, Kiessel + Partner

Use the chart to determine the maximum room depth for a desired minimum daylight factor 2 ft (0.6 m) from the rear wall.

Enter the chart on the vertical axis at the desired daylight factor and proceed horizontally to the curve that corresponds to the ratio of window width to window wall width. Then move down to the horizontal axis that shows the maximum allowable room depth, in units of window height.

The graph assumes clear glazing, no external obstruction, reflectiveness of 70% in the ceiling, 50% in the walls, and 15% on the floor, a sill height of 3 ft (0.9 m), a head height 1 ft (0.3 m) below the ceiling, and evenly distributed windows (CIE, 1970, p. 22). For more information on Daylit Room Depth, see Strategy 71.

The penetration of light into spaces can be enhanced by light shelves (Strategy 96). When the sun is visible, either in the partly cloudy sky or the clear sky, the penetration of light into the space may be much greater than under overcast sky conditions. When sunlight reflectors are used (Strategy 92), the width of the building may be increased, yet effectively daylit, as it was in the **TVA Building** (Matthews & Calthorpe, 1979).

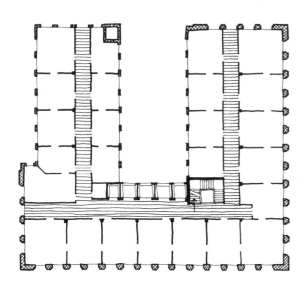

Wainwright Building
St. Louis, Missouri, Adler & Sullivan

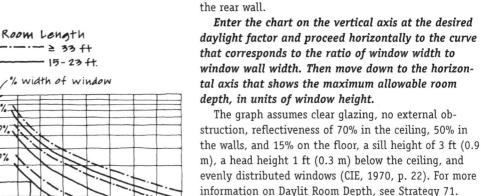

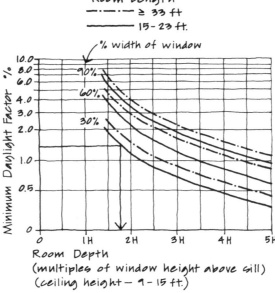

Room Length
— · — · — ≥ 33 ft
——— 15 - 23 ft.

% width of window

Minimum Daylight Factors–Unilateral Lighting

Room Depth
(multiples of window height above sill)
(ceiling height – 9 - 15 ft.)

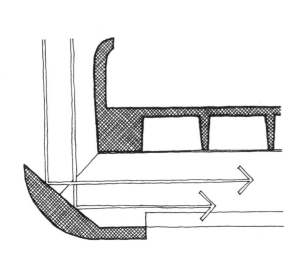

TVA Office Building,
Detail of Interior Lighting Reflector

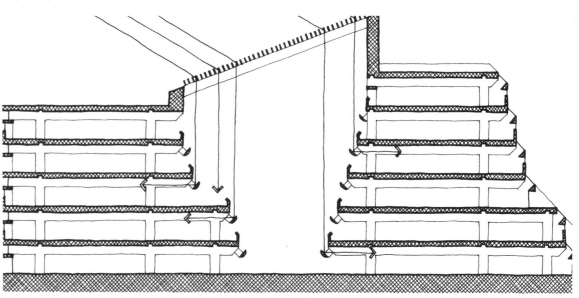

TVA Office Building, Chattanooga, Tennessee

52 Long *EAST–WEST PLAN* arrangements increase winter sun-facing skin available to collect solar radiation. [heating]

As the proportion of south-facing glazing required in individual rooms for solar heating increases, so grows the necessity for care in organizing rooms within buildings, in both plan and section (see Strategy 93 for Solar Glazing).

The amount of south-facing skin (north-facing in Southern Hemisphere), and thus the opportunity for solar collection, may be increased by organizing the rooms along a south-facing (north-facing in SH) circulation spine as it is in Frank Lloyd Wright's **Lloyd Lewis House** in Libertyville, Illinois. The house is organized on an east–west axis, with circulation on the north, giving all the rooms opening to the south sun and a view of the river. By elongating the building's proportions to face the winter sun, the size of east and west facades is usually reduced, which helps lower unwanted solar gain in summer, when the sun rises further east and sets further west than it does in winter.

In the **Prince Residence** designed by Equinox Design Inc., in Portland, Oregon, the circulation zone is a sunspace in some places and a direct gain space in others. It extends the full length of the south facade, organizing the living spaces along an east–west axis, so that each space has access to the sun's warmth and the view to the northern mountain range.

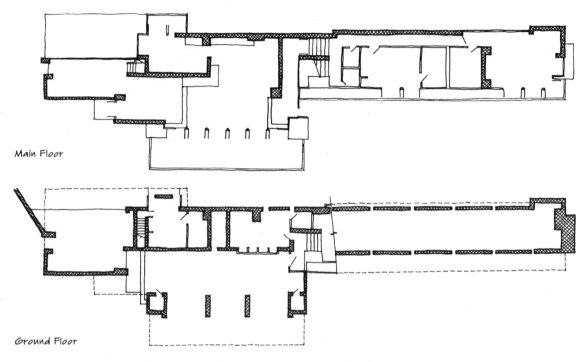

Main Floor

Ground Floor

Lloyd Lewis House, Libertyville, Illinois, Frank Lloyd Wright

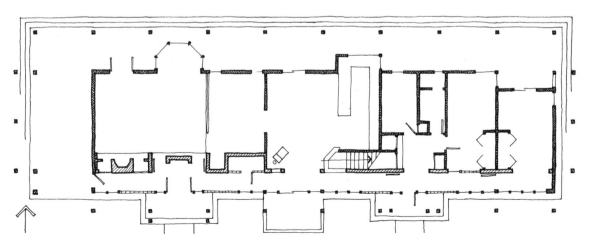

Prince House, Portland, Oregon, Equinox Design Inc.

Not all sites are configured to allow an ideal east–west elongation. Architects Reinberg-Trebersperg-Raith addressed a thin site having a long west side facing the main street in their design for the **Housing Development Brunnerstrasse-Empergasse,** in Vienna, Austria. The scheme organizes the plan into twelve fingers of three-story, south-facing rowhouses. The rowhouse blocks are linked by a thin strip of housing facing the street. The south-facing units are heated by a combination of direct gain and sunspaces. The fingers are spaced in the north–south direction to provide winter solar access. The poorer solar access of the east–west spine units is improved by canting windows in the east facade toward the southeast. Circulation for the spine units is along the street, within a west-facing, unconditioned, glazed thermal buffer space used to preheat ventilation air and block street noise (*Baumeister,* 10/1996).

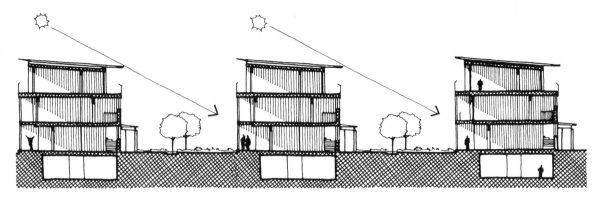

Housing Development Brunnerstrasse-Empergasse, Typical North-South Section

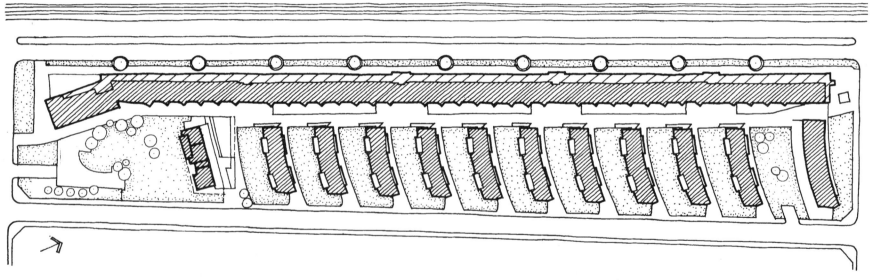

Housing Development Brunnerstrasse-Empergasse, Vienna, Austria, Reinberg-Trebersperg-Raith

53 *DEEP SUN* **in thick buildings depends on effectively organized plans and sections.** [heating]

While solar access to each room makes solar heating each space simple for thin, elongated organizations facing the sun (Strategy 52), thicker buildings of two or more rooms thick provide a challenge when solar heat is desired.

Several formal strategies are available in both plan and section to bring sun deeper into buildings, as shown in the diagrams.

Plans of two or more rooms deep may be staggered to get some sun to each room. The wall of one room or building can be used to reflect more sun to the south windows (north in Southern Hemisphere). North side (S in SH), nonsolar-zone rooms with no access to south sun can be convectively linked to solar zone rooms that have better solar access. When rooms are linked east–west by a connector room or corridor, the connector can be used to collect and store heat and each room can be opened to the collector room as heat is needed. A deep room between smaller rooms can be used to collect heat and distribute it to the surrounding rooms. A south-facing (N in SH) atrium serves the same purpose and may also have sun-capturing glass in its roof.

When a building must be oriented long in the north–south direction, it can be stepped in section so that more northern rooms capture heat above more southern ones. This works nicely on a south slope, but on a flat site, leaves space under the north rooms that is more difficult to heat. Topheating, such as a south-facing sawtooth roof, can be used to capture sun above adjacent obstructions or for large, single-story buildings. Combined with a sloped roof and mezzanine, topheat can bring sun deep to the north. A tall room can often capture south sun and distribute the heat to smaller rooms. The tall room may be on the south side, on the north, or in between smaller rooms. Finally, a big room or a large roof may encompass smaller rooms or zones. The roof may be stepped, sloped, or have clerestories or monitors to bring sun to the center and north side. Remember that sloped glazing collects dirt easily, requires greater attention to detailing for water, and is more difficult to externally shade in summer.

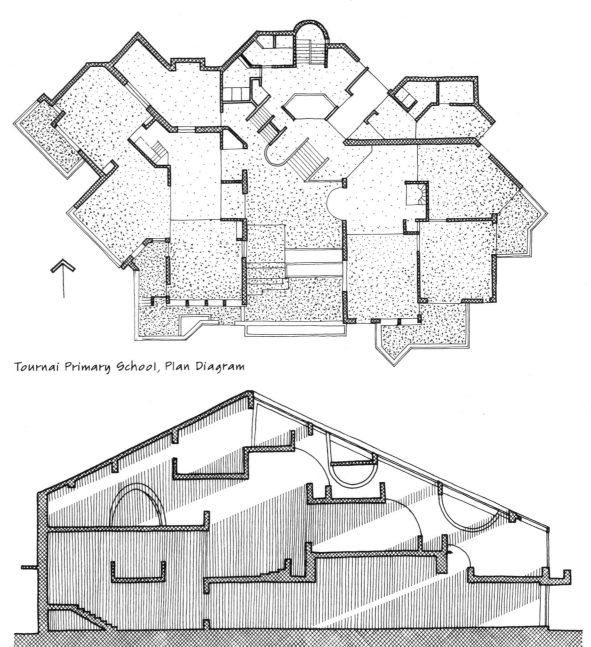

Tournai Primary School, Plan Diagram

Primary School, Tournai, Belgium, Jean Wilfart, North-South Section

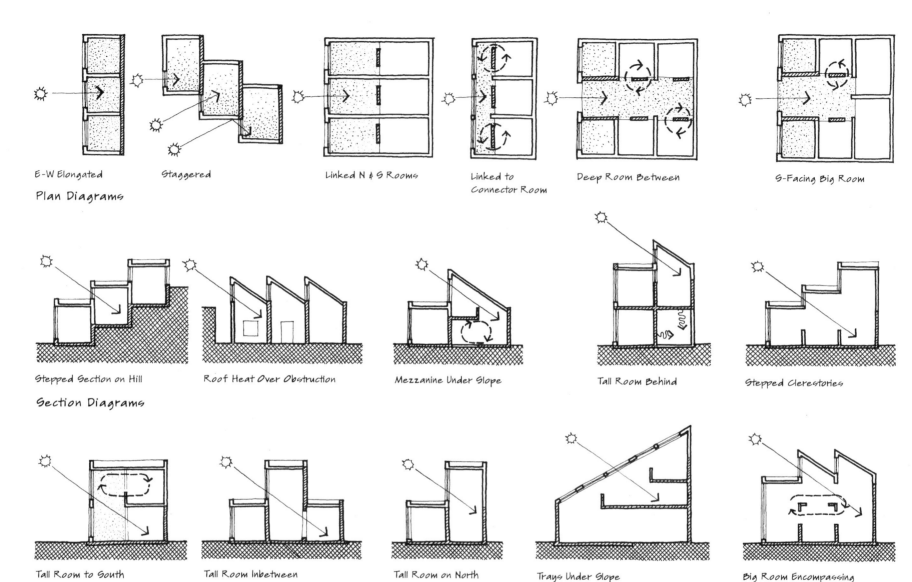

E-W Elongated

Staggered

Linked N & S Rooms

Linked to Connector Room

Deep Room Between

S-Facing Big Room

Plan Diagrams

Stepped Section on Hill

Roof Heat Over Obstruction

Mezzanine Under Slope

Tall Room Behind

Stepped Clerestories

Section Diagrams

Tall Room to South

Tall Room Inbetween

Tall Room on North

Trays Under Slope

Big Room Encompassing

Section Diagrams

Plan and Section Organizations for Solar Heating of Thick Buildings

Stepping the building section, with the high side to the north (S in SH), by placing thinner rooms above thicker rooms allows sun to penetrate deeper into the building. The roof then can be terraced, providing solar gain opportunity through south-facing monitors, or may be sloped to create a continuous ceiling over a series of semi-open floors, such as in the **Primary School in Tournai,** Belgium, by Jean Wilfart. An unconditioned central, south-facing atrium with a sloped glazed roof penetrates deep into the building, with openings to each level of the building. The north side library is heated only by the sunspace and by gains from the adjacent heated spaces (Buckley et al., 1991, Chapter 15; Hildon & Seager, 1989, pp. 17–22).

The tall heat-collecting room may be a central great room within or an inner circulation zone. The **Enerplex Prudential Office Buildings** in Princeton, New Jersey, by S.O.M. and Alan Chimacoff, uses southern toplight in a tall, thin corridor zone and in wider entrance atria to bring heat and light to most parts of the building. In a scheme with entries to both sides of a street, the south building atrium is heated entirely from above, while the north building atrium has solar heat gain from both the south side and top (Diamond, 1988; Fisher, 1984). The Princeton Professional Park, in Princeton, New Jersey, by Harrison Fraker, uses a similar strategy by bringing solar heat from a south-facing glazed roof over a linear circulation atrium (see section in Strategy 104).

Once heat has been collected in the taller room, it can be distributed to adjacent rooms, either by convection through openings in common walls, or with the aid of fans (Strategy 106), which will also help to reduce the temperature stratification and to draw warmed air down to lower rooms. If there is not enough thermal storage in the collector space, warmed air may be ducted to remote rock bed storage (Strategy 104).

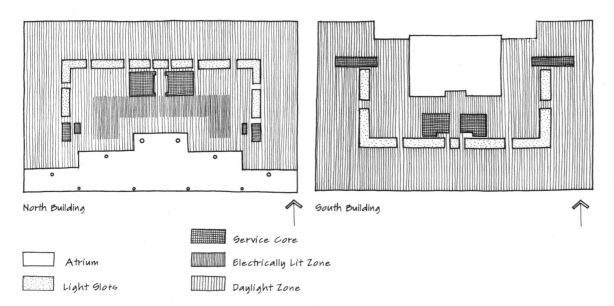

North Building · South Building

Atrium

Light Slots

Service Core

Electrically Lit Zone

Daylight Zone

Lighting Diagram of Upper Levels, Enerplex Offices

Enerplex Prudential Office Buildings, Princeton, New Jersey, Skidmore/Owings/Merrill and Alan Chimacoff

54 *BORROWED DAYLIGHT* is possible when small rooms are organized adjacent to larger or taller daylit rooms. [daylighting]

When site configuration or program limits the use of thin planning for light (Strategy 51), more rooms can be naturally lit by using atria lit from the side, which allows deep side-light penetration when the atria window wall is high (see also Strategy 70, Atrium). If the atrium faces south (north in Southern Hemisphere), it can also become a sunspace for heat collection (Strategy 61). Foster and Partners used a series of northeast-facing five-story multipurpose rooms to bring light to wedge-shaped fingers of office and meeting facilities in the **Microelectronics Center in Duisburg, Germany.** The shallow offices borrow light and ventilation air from the larger atrium. External shading partially shields the glass from high sun, while low vents feed stack ventilation for the unconditioned court, which also serves as a thermal buffer (Strategy 57) (Rossmann, 1997; Fitzgerald & Lewis, 1996, pp. 214–218).

In direct gain solar heating, there is often a conflict between the need to collect sun and the potential for glare from contrast between uncomfortably strong light and shadows. When more diffuse and indirect light is desired, solar heat can be collected in a room at the south-facing (N in SH) edge of the building and then transferred by convection to nearby spaces. Daylight can then be reflected through the collector room, which will be bright and sunny in winter, to the adjacent rooms, where the lighting pattern will be more diffuse. This strategy was used in the **Unicon Beton Headquarters,** in Roskilde, Denmark, by Jan Sondergaard of KHR A/S. The building's curved southwest wall is pierced with tall windows, admitting low-angle winter sun, enhanced by reflections off of the pond (or snow). A two-story main hall and circulation zone behind the wall stores heat in its mass floors and walls, and reflects light to the north-facing and east-facing offices. The back side of the curved wall bounces more light through a slanted skylight. Two stories of open-plan offices open onto the hall; since there is no separating wall, air can move freely. A mechanical ventilation system moves air from one end of the building to another, promoting an even distribution where morning heat is moved to

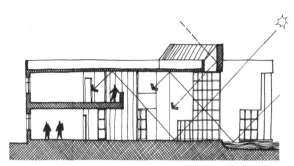

Unicon Beton Headquarters, Roskilde, Denmark, Jan Sondergaard

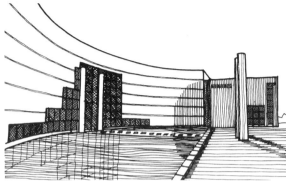

South to West Curved Wall, Unicon Beton

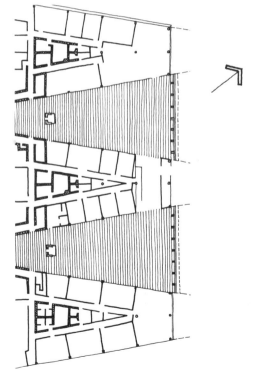

Microelectronics Center, Duisburg, Germany, Foster and Partners

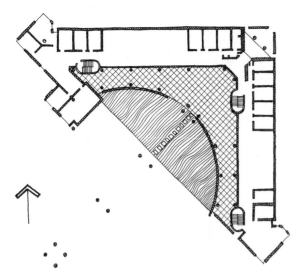

Plan, Unicon Beton Headquarters,
Roskilde, Denmark, Jan Sondergaard

the western wing and afternoon heat is recirculated to the eastern wing (Solinfo; Christiansen, 1989).

Daylight can be brought into deep plan buildings either by toplighting in single-story buildings or by the use of large, multistory, sidelit rooms. The **National Renewable Energy Laboratory (NREL) Solar Energy Research Facility** in Golden, Colorado, by Anderson De-Bartolo Plan, covers office cubicles of a deep, open plan, single story office landscape with a roof stepped toward the south and protected with fixed overhangs. Essentially, the interior cubicles are small rooms within the larger room, bounded by private offices at the edge. The roof admits reflected light bounced from internal and external light shelves, increasing reflected solar gain in winter and reflecting low-angle sun off of the ceiling (Jones, 1998, pp. 86–91; Harriman, 1992).

The daylight factor in a room is made up of a sky component (SC), which is direct light from a view of the sky, an external reflected component (ERC), which is light reflected from the ground or other surfaces, and an internal reflected component (IRC). The ERC and the IRC together make up the indirect component (IC). As the distance from a sidelit window wall increases, the sky view angle seen from the room decreases, thus reducing SC, and the IC becomes more important. IC is a function of the window size, room size, reflectance of the interior surfaces, the transmittance of the inner and outer glazings, and the exterior obstructions.

When one room borrows light from another, interior surfaces of both the inner and outer rooms should be as reflective as possible (Strategy 78). Windows in the interior wall should be as large as possible—proportionally, at least as large as the exterior windows—and placed to maximize their sky view angle.

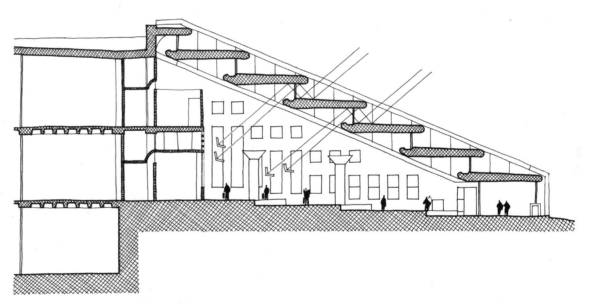

Section at Office Wing, NREL Solar Energy Research Facility

NREL Solar Energy Research Facility,
Golden, Colorado, Anderson DeBartolo Plan

To estimate the daylight factor (DF) of a room with borrowed sidelight, first determine both the sky view angle (v) and the angle of exterior obstruction (90° - θ), as shown in the diagrams.

The sky view angle can be drawn from any point in the room to the head of the external window (or internal window if more restrictive). Strike the lower line from the same point to the top of the external obstruction, the reference plane, or the external or internal sill, whichever is higher. If there are no external obstructions, the ratio *H/D* of head height above the reference plane *(H)* to depth from the window *(D)* can be substituted.

The angle of obstruction is equal to 90 minus θ, where θ is the angle between horizontal and the top of the obstruction, drawn from the center height of the inner window.

Enter the upper section of the graph on the vertical axis with the ratio of outer window area (A$_w$) to the total room surface area (A$_s$) in the outer room. Move left to the diagonal for the angle of exterior obstruction (90° - θ). From the intersection, draw a line down to the scale for the indirect component.

Enter the lower left part of the graph on the horizontal axis with the ratio W/D of the outer window width (W) to the distance from the window (D). Move up to the curve for the sky view angle (v). From the intersection, move right until intersecting the indirect component line drawn previously. Read the combined daylight factor from the diagonal lines.

The graphs are developed based on split flux methods modified from Hopkinson (1963, pp. 56, 184). An overcast sky, double glazing in the external wall, single glazing in the internal wall, and light colored interior surfaces are assumed.

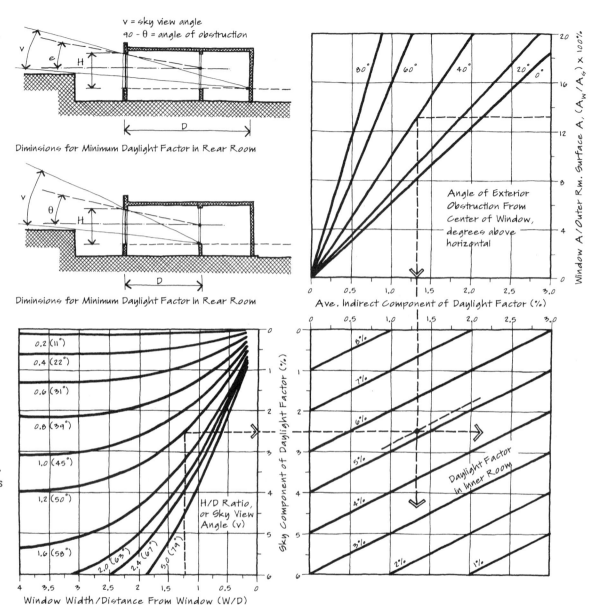

Dimensions for Minimum Daylight Factor in Rear Room

Dimensions for Minimum Daylight Factor in Rear Room

Estimating Daylight Factor in a Room With Borrowed Light

55 *HEAT PRODUCING ZONES:* **Rooms can be zoned within buildings to use or reject sources of internal heat gain. [heating and cooling]**

In many buildings, certain areas generate large quantities of heat from heavy concentrations of equipment or people. Buildings with a heating requirement can exploit these sources to supply some of the needed heat. Traditional New England houses frequently clustered their rooms around the central hearth used for cooking, in order to share its heat (see example in Strategy 49). These heat sources can be positioned to heat the north side (south in Southern Hemisphere), which compliments the sun-warmed south areas (N in SH).

In warmer climates where cooling requirements predominate, the heat-producing elements can be isolated from the other spaces. In Robert E. Lee's home, **Stratford Hall,** in warm, humid Virginia, the kitchen, which is a constant source of heat, is located in a separate dependency. To heat the main house when it is cold, fireplaces unrelated to the continuous cooking activity are used. They are placed at centralized points in the plan and are surrounded on all sides by rooms.

Two other examples of heat-producing zones are restaurant kitchens and mechanical rooms. Because they produce high rates of heat gain and require high rates of outside fresh air, restaurant kitchens are often heated, cooled, and ventilated separately from the dining areas. Mechanical rooms, which may contain heat-producers such as boilers, furnaces and hot water storage, can be located to share their excess heat with adjacent rooms, such as when placed in a central core. Alternatively, a mechanical room may be placed in a location that makes venting it separately much easier, such as on at the edge of a building's upper floor or as a penthouse.

South Elevation, Stratford Hall, Virginia

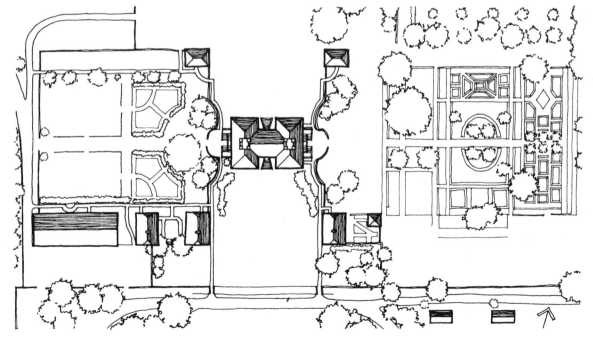

Site Plan, Stratford Hall, Virginia

56 STRATIFICATION ZONES: Rooms can be zoned vertically within buildings to take advantage of temperature stratification. [heating and cooling]

Because hot air rises, the upper levels of a building are frequently warmer than the lower levels. This temperature stratification can be used to zone uses or activities by temperature requirements. This phenomenon was recognized by the Inuit (Eskimo) **Igloo** builders of the Canadian north, who used the lower levels of the entrance as a cold air trap and for storage and the upper levels for living (Schoenauer, 1973, p. 28).

Ralph Erskine followed the same principle in his design for a **Ski Lodge at Borgfjäll,** in Sweden. The circulation spaces with the least strict temperature requirements are lowest in the section. The living/cooking quarters are on an intermediate level and the sleeping quarters, which need to be the warmest, are on the uppermost level (*Architectural Design*, 11–12/1977, p. 763; Collymore, 1994).

In hot climates, the same principle may be exploited in the opposite direction, placing daytime use rooms on lower levels where it is cooler, placing beds near the floor, and using high ceilings to allow heat to collect above the heads of occupants where it can be vented out of high windows while maintaining privacy at the view level.

In two-story, passively heated buildings that depend on natural convection as a means of heat transfer, the temperature differences between upper and lower levels have been found to be at least 4–5 °F (2.2–2.8 °C) (Balcomb & Yamaguchi, 1983, p. 289). In tall rooms, excessive heat stratification in winter is undesirable and the warm air may be recirculated to lower areas with the aid of fans and possible ducts. (See the Bateson Building example in Strategy 107.)

Inuit (Eskimo) Igloo

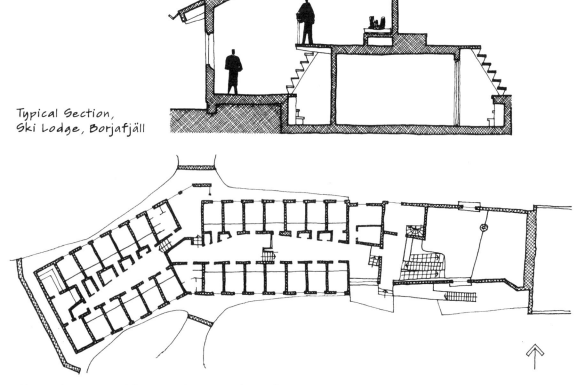

Typical Section,
Ski Lodge, Borjafjäll

Ski Lodge, Borjafjäll, Sweden, Ralph Erskine

57 *BUFFER ZONES:* **Rooms that can tolerate temperature swings can be located between protected rooms and undesired heat or cold. [heating and cooling]**

Some spaces in a building's program have less rigid temperature requirements because of the nature of their use, like storage, or the duration of their use, like circulation. Some spaces, like bedrooms, have temperature requirements only at certain times of the day. These spaces can frequently be used as thermal buffer zones between the exterior environment and spaces that need careful temperature control.

Ralph Erskine used the garage and storage areas in the **Villa Gadelius** as a buffer zone against the cold north winds in Lindingö, Sweden. The south zone of the house is extended in the east–west direction and increased in height so that the living spaces have access to the south sun (*Deustch Bauzeitung* 8/1965; Collymore, 1994)./

The opposite approach was taken by Frank Lloyd Wright in the **Pauson House** in the hot Phoenix, Arizona, climate. The virtually unglazed circulation and storage spaces are used as a buffer zone along the northwest part of the house to protect the living spaces from the low, late afternoon sun (Hitchcock, 1942, fig. 392).

Large, glazed rooms, if not heated or cooled mechanically, will usually have an average temperature in winter somewhere between the indoor and outdoor temperatures, thus reducing the heating load of the conditioned spaces. The buffer space will also reduce the daylight available to adjacent rooms, so windows facing a buffer must be larger than those in exterior facades. See also related Strategies 32, 61, 70, and 108.

If the buffer space faces south (north in Southern Hemisphere), it can provide heat for nearby spaces, in which case, its average temperature will be close to that of the interior rooms. If it faces east, west, or north (south in Southern Hemisphere), it reduces envelope losses, but will not provide net winter solar gains.

A southeast-facing buffer zone was used by Coop Himmelblau for the **High-Rise Apartment Building in Wohnpark Alte Donau**, in Vienna, Austria. The glazed buffer zone stretches from a 9th floor sky lobby to the 22nd floor. Balconies and terraces from the apartments

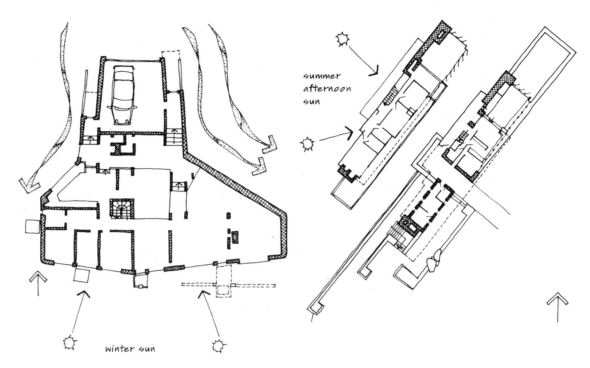

Villa Gadelius, Lindingö, Sweden, Ralph Erskine

Pauson House, Phoenix, Arizona, Frank Lloyd Wright

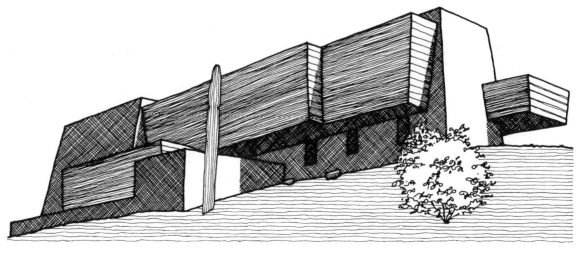

Northwest Facade, Pauson House, Phoenix, Arizona, Frank Lloyd Wright

extend into the space, while heat is stored in concrete floors and walls. Ventilation air is recirculated from the top of the open space, down through an internal shaft and returned to the bottom of the buffer zone. Minimum winter temperatures in the buffer zone never fall below 7 °C (45 °F) (*Baumeister*, 1/1999; Futagawa, 1996a).

The thermal savings from a glazed buffer space depend on the area of exterior glazing, the *R*-value of the buffer's glazing and that of the separating wall, and the strategy for ventilating the building. Increasing glazing *R*-value dramatically increases thermal savings in colder climates, but has less impact in warmer climates. Studies for a range of European climates show that recircu-

lating air from the buffer space to the building and back saves the most energy, particularly in colder climates. Natural infiltration rates will not be large enough for building ventilation if the buffer is small relative to the size of the occupied rooms. Preheating ventilation air though the buffer saves somewhat more energy than exhausting to the buffer (Strategy 108) (Goulding et al., 1992, pp. 267–278).

Heat flows between buffers and parent spaces are complex and usually calculated with a computer; however, the buffer zone's winter temperature is an indicator of its effectiveness.

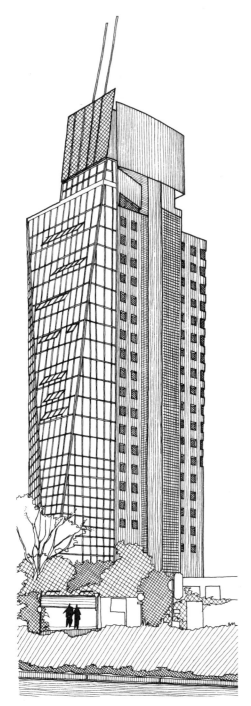

Apartment Building in Wohnpark Alte Donau, Vienna, Austria, Coop Himmelblau

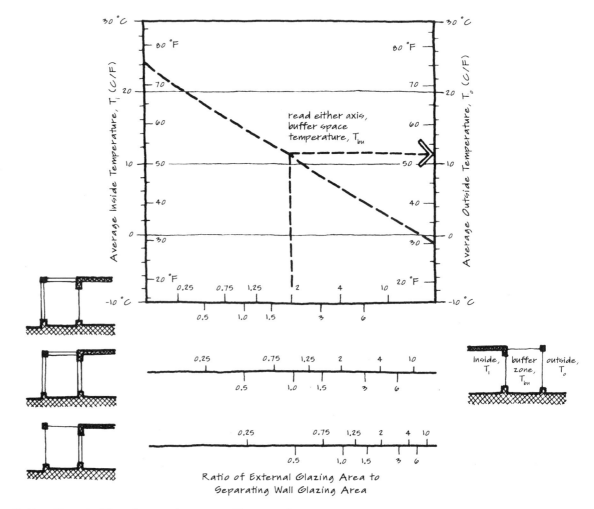

Ratio of External Glazing Area to Separating Wall Glazing Area

Estimating Buffer Space Average Temperature

Use the graph to estimate the buffer's winter average temperature, without effects of solar gain and ventilation. Draw a diagonal line between the left vertical indoor and right vertical outdoor temperature scales. Using the appropriate scale for the building's glazing conditions, enter the horizontal axis with the ratio of external buffer glazing to separating glazing; move up to the diagonal line previously drawn and then move horizontally to read either temperature scale for the average buffer indoor temperature (Goulding et al., 1992, p. 270).

Direct solar radiation, which makes up the majority of summer envelope heat load, can be kept off of walls and windows by the shade offered from porches. If the building envelope is fully shaded from the sun, then the only heat entering the building from outside is from conduction and infiltration/ventilation.

Outdoor rooms can use microclimates around the building to enhance their comfort by drawing shade from the adjacent building (Strategies 24 and 47). On the other hand, outdoor spaces that are able to create their own shade can cast this shade on the building, as in Charles Correa's design for the **British Council in New Delhi,** India. The main western entrance to the building passes through a garden and under a four-story portico. The building section is carved back underneath the partial shade pergola roof to provide a series of terraces. The resulting series of outdoor rooms are bounded on three sides by walls with large windows. The result is a relatively well-protected facade that retains both its sense of institutional scale and its openness (Correa, 1996, pp. 188–197).

At low latitudes the sun attains a high altitude for much of the day, and the roof is the major collector of heat gain. Ken Yeang located shaded outdoor rooms on the roof of his **Roof-Roof House** in Kuala Lampur, Malaysia. The living spaces are located below an overarching, white, louvered, concrete, umbrella roof. The louvers are slanted to keep the high sun from projecting though them. Across the roof curve, their angle shifts, reflecting the most sun in the afternoon (see Strategy 45 for louver details). The ground floor plan is fragmented by interwoven outdoor space, providing an option for full shade and rain shelter, while remaining open to prevailing winds (Yeang, 1987, pp. 52–55; Khan, 1995, pp. 108–109).

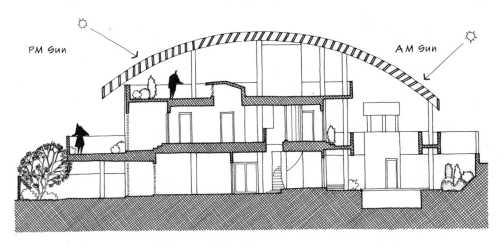

PM Sun   AM Sun

Roof-Roof House in Malaysia, Ken Yeang

British Council, New Delhi, India, Charles Correa, View of West Facade

58 *DAYLIGHT ZONES:* **Rooms can be arranged within the building so that activities that need higher lighting levels are near the windows while activities that don't need as much light are farther from daylight sources. [daylighting]**

Many buildings have a range of activities that have varying visual tasks and therefore different illumination needs. Areas nearest the skin of the building have the greatest opportunity for daylight at the highest illumination levels. If activities are zoned so that those that need the light are placed near openings in the skin and those that don't are placed in the interior, then the amount of relatively expensive skin and glazed openings can be reduced because of a smaller skin/volume ratio. The rate of electric light use, and thus heat gains are also reduced.

The **Mount Angel Library** in Oregon, by Alvar Aalto, divides activities into two main groups: reading, which requires high levels of illumination, and book storage, which requires lower levels. The reading areas are next to openings in the skin along the perimeter wall and under the skylight in the center, while the book storage occurs between the two reading areas, farthest from the pools of light.

Louis Sullivan followed a similar approach in the **Auditorium Building** in Chicago, ringing the exterior of the building with offices that need light and putting the auditorium, which needs light control, in the darker center of the building.

In dense urban areas with narrow streets or tall buildings, there is more light available on upper floors than at street level (Strategy 35). Rooms with a greater need for light can be placed on upper floors, while those requiring less light can be located nearer the ground level.

Some uses occur for only short periods, such as circulation or rest rooms, or have little human occupancy, such as storage and mechanical rooms. These may be located in areas with less access to perimeter lighting, while longer occupancy uses are located closer to daylight apertures.

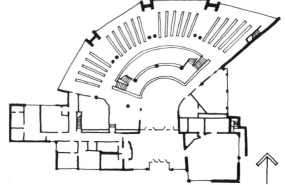

Library, Mount Angel Abbey, Oregon, Alvar Aalto

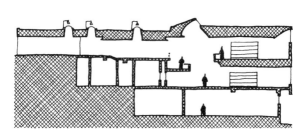

Library, Mount Angel Abbey

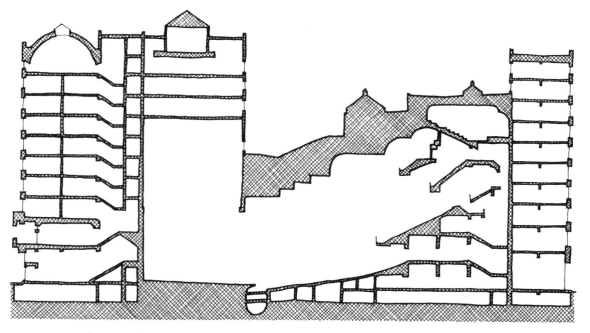

Auditorium Building, Chicago, Illinois, Adler & Sullivan

59 ***ROOMS FACING THE SUN AND WIND* increase the effectiveness of solar heating and cross-ventilation. [heating and cooling]**

As air flows around a building, it causes higher pressure zones on the windward side and lower pressure zones on the lee side. Cross-ventilation occurs when inlets are placed in higher pressure areas and outlets in lower pressure zones (Melarango, 1982, p. 321). Maximum ventilation occurs when inlets and outlets are large (Strategy 65) and the wind is relatively perpendicular to openings.

Variations in orientation up to 40° from perpendicular to the prevailing wind do not significantly reduce ventilation. (Givoni, 1976, p. 289). When buildings are more than one room thick, an orientation of 20–45° from the prevailing wind will give two sides positive pressure and two sides negative pressure. To determine wind direction, see Techniques 4 and 5.

A **church in the Philippines** completely opens its long sides with folding doors. All the ventilating openings are protected with deep overhangs or interior drains so that the building may be ventilated during rain storms (Fry & Drew, 1956, p. 181).

When openings cannot be oriented to the prevailing breeze, landscaping or wing walls (Strategy 65) can be used to alter the positive and negative pressure zones around the building and induce wind flow through windows parallel to the prevailing wind directions.

In the winter when the sky is clear and the sun low, most radiation falls on a south-facing (north-facing in the Southern Hemisphere) surface, because radiation is most intense at noon and decreases rapidly several hours before and after. Additionally, the amount of radiation reflected from the glazing increases as the angle of incidence is more acute. The effect of glazing orientation on solar heating performance depends on the ratio of solar gain to envelope loss and on the nighttime *R*-value of glazing. Buildings with large solar glazing and low night glazing *R*-values are more sensitive to orientation. Sunspaces are about half as sensitive to orientation as other solar heating systems.

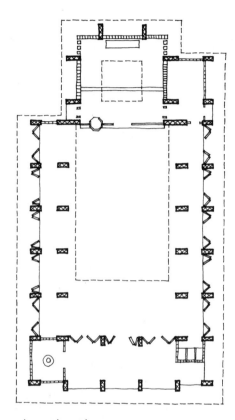

Church in the Philippines

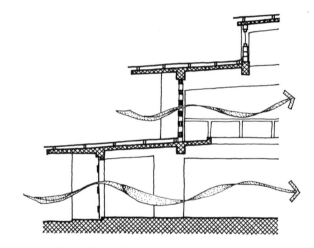

Church in the Philippines

If the glazing is within 30° east or west of south (N in SH), the decrease in performance will be less than 10% of the optimum. Performance decreases with the glazing declination from south (Balcomb et al., 1984, p. 2.10).

Frank Lloyd Wright used this flexibility in orientation to bend the rooms in the **Marting House** in an arc to form a south-facing outside terrace (*Architectural Forum, 1/1948*).

The most severe performance decreases for off-south orientation are for direct gain windows in cold, cloudy climates. Therefore, decrease the rule to ± 15° for these cases. Climates with long cloudy heating seasons, such as Seattle, are less sensitive to orientation because they have a higher proportion of diffuse radiation; therefore, the rule can be relaxed to ± 40° from south.

ROOMS: Orientation **59**

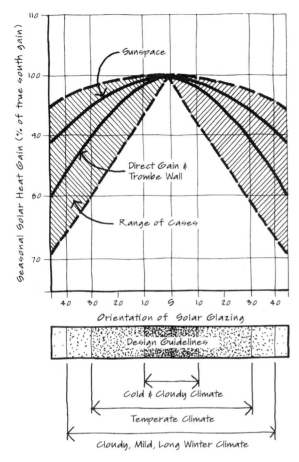

Effect of Orientation on Seasonal
Solar Heating Performance

When local climatic conditions produce morning or afternoon cloudiness, change the orientation of solar windows 10° toward the times of more clearness. Because the heat gained in the afternoon can be more effectively stored for use at night, solar-heated buildings frequently perform best if oriented a few degrees west of south. All of these guidelines assume that the winter sun is unobstructed. If site obstructions block the sun during a portion of the 10 AM–2 PM winter hours, shift the orientation toward the least obstructed direction. Site obstructions can be evaluated with Technique 1.

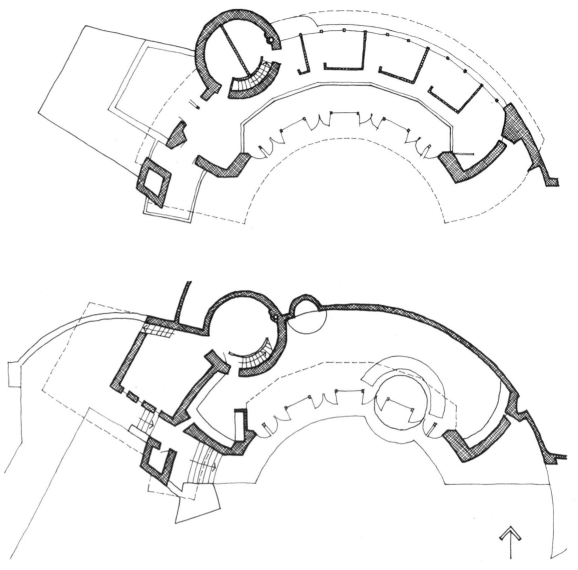

Marting House, Akron, Ohio, Frank Lloyd Wright

Tilting the glazing will also increase solar gain up to 30%. Tilted glass also increases heat gain in summer, unless well shaded. *To maximize winter solar gain, tilt the glazing at an angle above horizontal equal to the site's latitude plus 15°.*

60 *DIRECT-GAIN ROOMS* are open to collect the sun and can store heat within a space. [heating]

The proportion of the annual heating load that can be supplied by the sun results from a balance between the amount of solar radiation collected, the building's rate of heat loss, and the amount of heat that can be stored during the day for use at night. Collectible radiation is a function of the amount of south-facing (north-facing in Southern Hemisphere) glazing and the climate's available radiation; the amount of heat loss is a function of the insulating qualities of the building skin and the severity of the climate.

Direct-gain solar buildings collect radiation in south-facing (N in SH) habitable spaces to heat the air and thermal mass. The thermal mass absorbs the heat, which keeps the air temperature from rising too high during the day, and gives its stored heat back to the space at night (Mazria, 1979, p. 28).

As the amounts of sun-collecting glazing and thermal mass increase, greater demands are placed on the shape, orientation, and materials of rooms.

The **Shelton Solar Cabin,** by James Lambeth, is a diagrammatic expression of these demands. The south exposure of the cabin is enlarged in both plan and section and filled with glass, while the remaining exposures are reduced in size, almost windowless, and well insulated. The concrete floor is used for thermal storage (Lambeth & Delap, 1977, p. 56).

The **Milford Reservation Environmental Center,** by Kelbaugh and Lee, uses a section similar to Lambeth's but at a larger scale and with its largest wall facing north rather than south. This gave the architects the opportunity to puncture the roof with dormers, thereby increasing the south-facing glazing area and allowing sunlight to penetrate to the north edge of the building (*Progressive Architecture,* 4/1980, p. 16; 4/1981, p. 118).

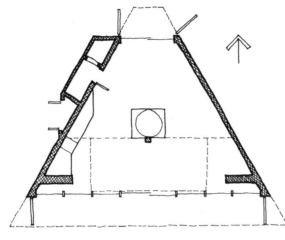

Shelton Solar Cabin, Hazel Valley, Arkansas, James Lambeth

Shelton Solar Cabin

Milford Reservation Environmental Center, Milford, Pennsylvania, Kelbaugh & Lee

The **Mere House,** a superlative design by the outstanding design group Bumpzoid, increases the southern exposure of its major room by elongating it in the east–west direction without sacrificing the room's important axial connection to the lake on the east end. The masonry stairway that runs the length of the south wall serves as a place for heat storage (*Architectural Record,* 5/1983, p. 90).

Mere House, Flint Hill, Virginia, Bumpzoid

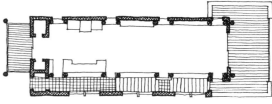

Top Level

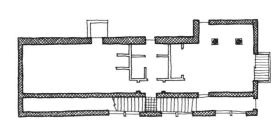

Middle Level

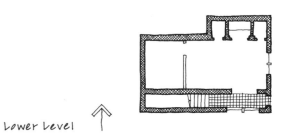

Lower Level

Mere House, Flint Hill, Virginia

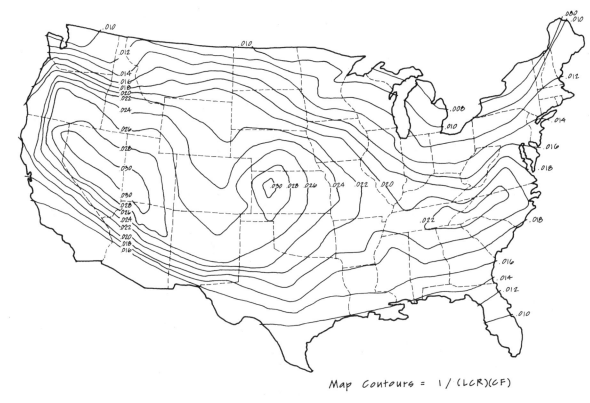

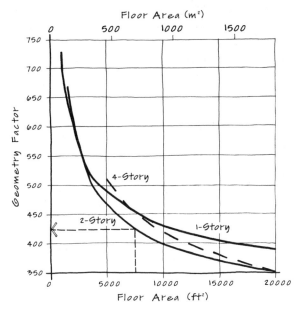

Floor Area (m²)

Floor Area (ft²)

Determining Geometry Factors

Map Contours = 1 / (LCR)(CF)

Locational Values for Sizing Direct Gain Windows

The recommended amount of south-facing glazing (N in SH), as a percentage of floor area, can be estimated by taking the value from the map for the site's location and multiplying it by the value from the Geometry Factors graph that corresponds to the floor area of the building. To find the geometry factor for the building, enter the graph on the horizontal axis with the floor area. Move vertically to the curve for the number of stories, then read left for the geometry factor. Use this number to multiply by the value from the map.

The amount of glazing chosen should be within 20% of the estimated product. For sloped glazing, use the vertical projected area. Because winter sun angles are low, glazing with a low pitch will provide little if any net heat gain. These values are based on balancing the cost of conservation strategies, like insulating, against the cost of solar gain, that is, windows and mass. They tend to predict small glazing areas. See Strategy 93, for more detailed window sizing information. The estimate applies to direct gain, trombe walls, sunspaces, and combinations of these. The values in the tables are applicable to residential or small commercial buildings with internal heat gains of 30–60 Btu/ft², day (95–189 W/m², day), that are well insulated and have low infiltration and ventilation rates. The values on the map are equal to 1/(load collector ratio) × (conservation factor) (Balcomb et al., 1983, p. 117).

For related design guidelines, see Strategies 59, Rooms Facing the Sun and Wind; Strategies 77 and 83, about Mass Surface Absorptance and Thermal Mass thickness; and Strategy 97, Movable Insulation.

61 *SUNSPACES* **can be used to collect the sun's heat, store it centrally, and distribute it to other rooms. [heating]**

A sunspace, unlike direct gain and trombe wall systems, adds a room to the building. Since the purpose of the sunspace is to provide heat to the rest of the building, it experiences large diurnal temperature swings and is therefore not always comfortable. In sunny periods it will be too warm, and at night it will be too cold. It is usually assumed that the sunspace can get as hot as 95 °F (35 °C) and as cool as 45 °F (7 °C).

More thermal mass will reduce the temperature swings in the sunspace and store more of the heat collected. *The ratio of mass area to glazing collection area should be at least 3:1. If water is the primary storage material, the ratio should be about 3.8 gal/ft² of glass (155 L/m²).* For additional details on thermal mass sizing and color, see Strategies 77 and 83.

The sunspace may be attached to the main space, sharing one common wall, or encompassed by the building, sharing three common walls. Enclosed sunspaces are more efficient than attached sunspaces because they lose heat at night through only one exposed wall. Heat is usually transferred to the main space through a common masonry thermal storage wall and by convection through openings in the common wall. The common wall may also be an insulated wall with all the mass located in the sunspace and the heat transfer completely dependent on either passive thermocirculation or the aid of fans. To get enough thermal storage, sunspaces with insulated common walls usually need additional mass, either in the form of water or a rock bed under the sunspace floor.

The primary heat transfer between the sunspace and spaces it serves is by convection. *Use one of the following recommendations for sizing common wall vents: doors, 10% of glazing area; windows, 15%; or paired high and low vents through the wall, 6% (Balcomb et al., 1984, pp. 2–16).*

Insulated masonry end walls of attached sunspaces will improve both performance and thermal comfort in the sunspace, as compared to glazed end walls, which have a lower *R*-value and collect little winter heat. Like all passive solar approaches, sunspaces should be well

South Facade, Solarhaus Lützowstrasse, Berlin, Germany, IBUS

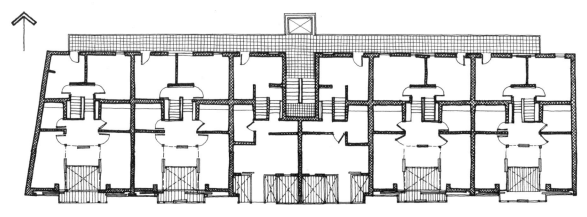

Level 4 Plan, Solarhaus Lützowstrasse, Berlin, Germany, IBUS

shaded and well ventilated in summer to prevent excessive heat gain.

The **Solarhaus Lützowstrasse** in Berlin by the Institute for Building, Environment, and Solar Research (IBUS: Institut für Bau-, Umwelt-, Solarforschung), uses one- and two-story semi-enclosed sunspaces for levels 3–6. Moveable sliding insulation panels insulate these at night. Attached sunspaces, with blown-in polystyrene bead night insulation between the glazing layers, heat penthouse split level units. North-facing bedrooms are one-half level lower to promote better sun and light penetration from the south (see section in Strategy 64) (*A+W,* 12/1991; Kok & Holtz, 1990, pp. 33–42).

In the **International Meeting Center** in Berlin by Otto Steidle and Partner, the sunspaces are used as a buffer zone between inside and out, extending the living area and providing heat on sunny days. The projecting sunspaces visually break down the mass of the 80-unit apartment building, allowing it to be read as five separate houses, more to scale with other buildings in the neighborhood (*Progressive Architecture,* 4/1981).

The area of sunspace glazing as a percentage of the building floor area can be estimated using the method in Strategy 60, Direct Gain Rooms. For a typical sunspace, the annual solar savings fraction (SSF) for heating, using the method in Strategy 60, can be estimated from the map on this page.

For sloped glazing, use the vertical projected area. Because winter sun angles are low, glazed sunspace roofs with a low pitch will provide little if any net heat gain. See Strategy 93, for more detailed glazing sizing information. The SSF values on the map represent performance of a semi-enclosed sunspace with 50° sloped glazing, opaque end walls, double glazing, a masonry common wall, and no night insulation (Balcomb, et al., 1984, p. 2-9). Sunspace performance can be dramatically improved in many climates by the use of night insulation (Strategy 97).

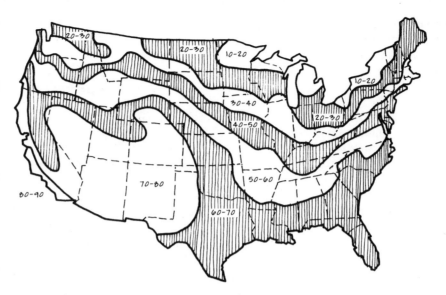

SSF (%) for a Typical Sunspace Without Night Insulation

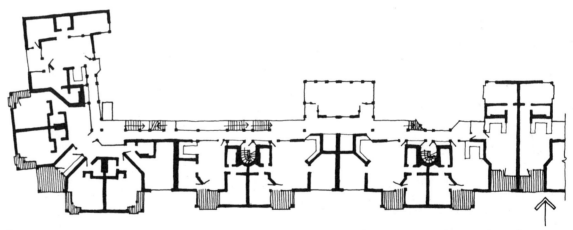

International Meeting Center, Berlin, Germany, Otto Steidle & Partner (partial plan)

62 *THERMAL STORAGE WALLS* collect and store solar heat at the edge of a room. [heating]

Indirect-gain solar systems, such as trombe walls or water walls, place the thermal storage mass between the space to be heated and the south-facing glazing (north in Southern Hemisphere). Consequently, unlike direct-gain systems, they do not allow sunlight into the heated space if built in their pure form. The sun passes through the glazing and heats the thermal storage wall, which in turn heats the space. The rate of heat flow through the wall depends on the materials and thickness of the wall. Masonry storage walls delay the transfer of heat from the sunny side of the wall to the room by several hours. Water storage walls transfer the heat much more rapidly because they work by convection as well as conduction.

Unlike water walls, masonry storage walls can be used as bearing walls, and because of their mass they make good acoustical barriers. However, water can provide in much less volume the same thermal storage capacity as masonry.

Two characteristics of trombe walls, their opaque, separating thickness and their creation of ambiguous areas of external glazing, are used effectively by Kelbaugh and Lee in the **Sisko House** in Metuchen, New Jersey. The trombe walls, which are punctured by windows, provide an enclosing, well-defined, but nonoppressive edge for all the major rooms in the house. The south elevation makes a clear distinction between windows that are not in the trombe wall, by articulating them on the facade, and those that *are* part of the trombe wall, by hiding them within the trombe wall glazing (Dixon, 4/1982).

The optimum thickness of trombe walls is 12–16 in (300–400 mm) with vents and 10–14 in (250–350 mm) without vents, depending on the density of the wall material. For additional details on thermal mass sizing and color, see Strategies 77 and 83.

The most common thermal transfer between the trombe wall and the served space is by radiation and conduction through the wall. If the trombe wall is designed to primarily offset daytime loads, high and low vents may be provided to create a convective loop between the room and the wall's air space. Excessive vent

South Facade, Sisko House

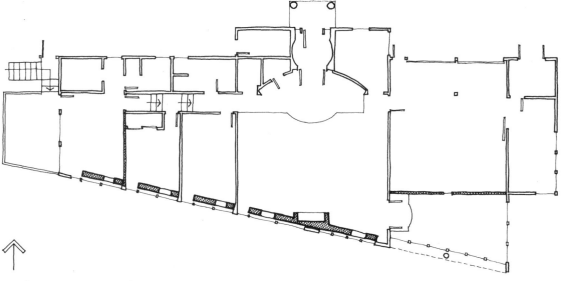

Sisko House, Metuchen, New Jersey, Kelbaugh & Lee

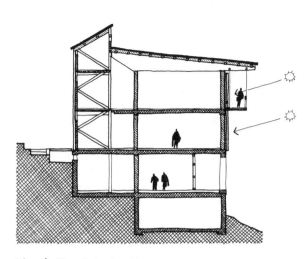

Youth Hostel, Section

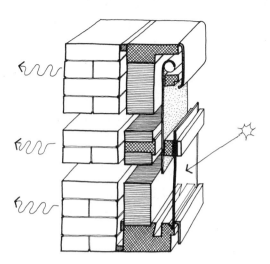

Schematic Section of Thermal Storage Wall
With Fixed Translucent Insulation

size can lead to large interior temperature swings.

The follow recommendations apply to vent sizing: For a solar savings fraction percentage (SSF) = 0–25, make vent areas 3% of glazing area; for SSF = 25–50, 2%; for SSF = 50–90, 1%; and for SSF = 90–100, use no vents (Balcomb et al., 1984, p. 2.17).

The required area of thermal storage wall glazing as a percentage of the building floor area can be estimated using the map in Strategy 60, Direct-Gain Rooms. The annual SSF obtained using this sizing method can be approximated from the map in Strategy 61, Sunspaces. See Strategy 93, for more detailed sizing information.

Thermal storage wall performance can be dramatically improved in many climates by the use of night insulation (Strategy 97). The air space between the mass and glass provides a good place for this insulating layer. As an alternative to night insulation, Thomas Herzog used a recently developed translucent thermal insulation (TI) fixed behind the glass in the **Hostel for Youth Education Institute** in Windberg, Germany (Cofaigh et al., 1996, pp. 135–138; *Deutsche Bauzeitung,* 8/1992; *Deutsche Bauzeitschrift,* 1/1992). The TI material has high sunlight transmission, low emittance, and a U-value of less than 0.18 Btu/hr, °F, ft^2 (1.0 W/m^2, K). Like all passive solar approaches, thermal storage walls should be well shaded and well ventilated in summer to prevent excessive heat gain. The hostel building uses a roll-down blind between the glazing and TI and is partially shaded by a large roof overhang.

Hostel for Youth Education Institute, Windberg, Germany, Thomas Herzog

63 *ROOF PONDS* **collect and store heat and cold in the ceiling plane of a room. [heating and cooling]**

Roof ponds have the capacity for both heating and cooling and are particularly useful at lower latitudes in climates with clear skies. They usually consist of water bags 4–10 in (100–250 mm) deep, placed on a flat metal deck, the underside of which forms the ceiling surface, while its top surface is covered by movable insulation (Mazria, 1979, p. 194).

In the heating mode, the insulating panels slide open in the daytime, allowing the bags to collect and store solar heat. At night the insulating panels are closed, and the warm water and metal deck radiate their warmth to the room. In the cooling mode, the insulated panels are opened at night so that the pond radiates to the night sky the heat it has stored from the day. During the day they are closed to protect the bags from the sun. Excess heat inside radiates and convects to the ceiling and is stored for release to the sky at night.

Because winter sun angles are low, the horizontal surface of the pond collects less heat than an equally sized vertical collection surface. Heat absorption can be enhanced by reflectors, which become necessary above 32° latitude (see Strategy 82). The cooling mode can be enhanced by wetting the bags so that night radiation is assisted by evaporative cooling. Heat transfer down from the ceiling can be significantly assisted by ceiling fans (Fleischnaker et al., 1983, p. 835).

In climates with substantial cooling requirements, the necessary pond area usually approaches 100% of the floor area. As a result, storage of the movable insulation panels becomes an important consideration. This problem was solved in the **Sunstone house** in Phoenix, Arizona, designed by Daniel Aiello, who put terraces on the east and north ends of the house, where their roofs form storage areas for the sliding insulating panels (Wright & Andrejko, 1982, p. 127).

Roof ponds used for both heating and cooling should be sized for the larger load. For winter conditions, recommendations for the ratio of pond area to floor area are given in the graph for Roof Pond Sizing for Winter Solar Heating. Options for four types of roof pond strategies are given (Mazria, 1979, p.

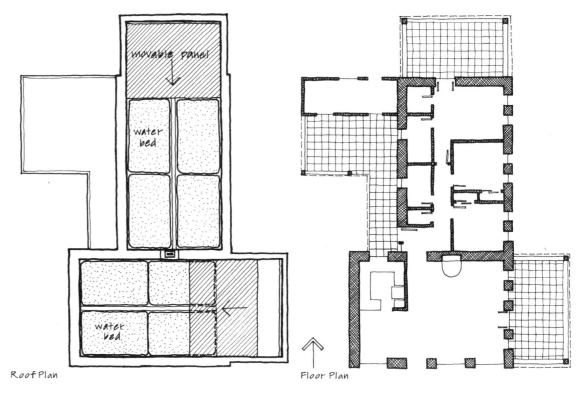

Roof Plan   Floor Plan

Sunstone House, Phoenix, Arizona, Daniel Aiello

187). In selecting design details, remember that a single-glazed roof pond is twice as effective at summer cooling than a double-glazed design.

Cooling by radiant loss to the night sky is more effective in climates with higher diurnal variations and clear conditions at night. *For cooling, use the following recommendations for the ratio of roof pond area to floor area, for buildings that generate internal heat gains similar to residences (Mazria, 1979, p. 188): For hot-humid climates,* $A_{pond}/A_{floor} = 1.0$, *or 0.75–1.0, if augmented by evaporation. For hot-arid climates,* $A_{pond}/A_{floor} = 0.75–1.0$, *or 0.33–0.50 if augmented by evaporation (Mazria, 1979, p. 188).*

To size the depth and area of the roof pond for cooling with no evaporation and any rate of heat gain:

1) Find the pond minimum temperature (T_{pmin}), which is approximately equal to the low night air temperature, for the summer design conditions. Design conditions for the building's climate can be found in ASHRAE (1997), Reynolds & Stein (2000), and Appendix A.

2) Find the daily temperature range (ΔT) of the pond:

pond ΔT = 80 °F max. – $T_{p\text{-}min}$ °F

pond ΔT = 27 °C max. – $T_{p\text{-}min}$ °C

One may also substitute a different upper bound for the comfort zone, other than 80 °F (27 °C).

3) Enter the **Sizing Roof Ponds for Summer Cooling** graph on the left side horizontal axis with the value for the pond ΔT, from step 2, moving vertically to the diagonal for a trial pond depth. From the intersection, strike a horizontal line to the right side of the graph to read the Pond Cooling Capacity on the right vertical axis in Btu/day, ft² (W/day, m²). From the point where the line drawn crosses the curve for the building's daily heat gain rate (from Technique 21), drop a line to the right side horizontal axis to find the required ratio of pond area to floor area (pond area/ floor area). If less roof coverage for the pond is desired, try increasing the pond depth. If more area is available, the depth can be less. The recommended maximum pond depth is 8 in (200 mm).

Remember, a roof pond creates a thermally closed building, so infiltration or ventilation is included in the heat gain total. A roof pond building may stay closed for the entire 24-hr cycle, or may be ventilated at night (Strategy 68). If closed at night, nighttime internal gains must be included in the total.

This method assumes that 70% of the heat stored in the pond is from the rooms below, while 30% is gained through the insulation (Reynolds & Stein, 2000, p. 244). For a more detailed method for designing roof ponds, see Reynolds & Stein (2000, pp. 313–322) or Fleischnacker et al. (1982).

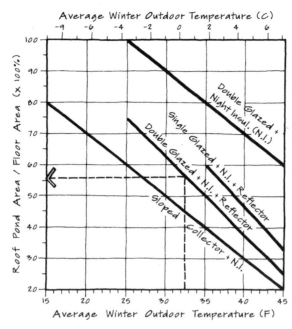

Roof Pond Sizing for Winter Solar Heating

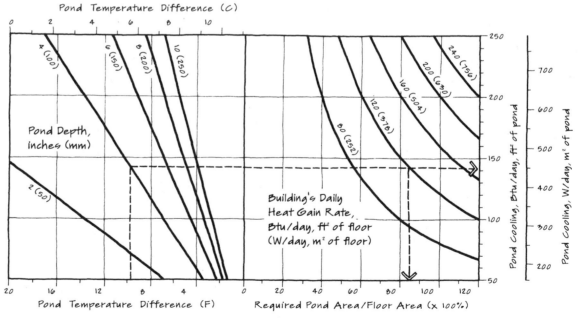

Sizing Roof Ponds for Summer Cooling

ROOMS: Shape and Enclosure   63

177

64 *THERMAL COLLECTOR WALLS and ROOFS* capture solar heat at the edge of a room in a layer of air, which carries the heat to storage in the building's structure. [heating]

In many buildings, it is not possible to get each room to have access to winter sun. For buildings two or more rooms thick, solar heat must be collected on the south side (north in Southern Hemisphere) and moved to storage or use on the north side of the building. Air circulated through the assembly of a glazed solar wall or roof can be distributed to spaces within a building and stored within the building's structure, or in accessory storage, such as a rock bed (Strategy 104). Unlike strategies that collect and store heat at the edge of a room, such as trombe walls, in this strategy, the exterior wall may be of insulated, lightweight construction. This is an advantage in colder climates where a significant amount heat can be lost to the environment at night.

Air collectors may be manufactured products or may be site-built and integrated with the architectural design. If the building's section is designed in an open scheme between levels, distribution can be by natural convection, similar to the function of vented thermal storage walls. However, because the performance of thermosiphoning systems are so hard to predict, a fully-sized back-up mechanical ventilation system should be designed. When rooms must be closed to each other, when manufactured collectors are used, or when storage is within voids of the structure, distribution *must* be assisted by fans (Strategy 105) and may use ducts or plenums (Strategy 107). Warm air collectors are especially well suited to buildings with high daytime heat loads or those that require high levels of fresh ventilation air (Strategy 87, Technique 17).

In the **Housing Development in Passau,** architects Schröder and Widmann used as warm air collectors glazed, unconditioned airlock entries connected to thin glazed shafts above, covering portions of the exterior wall and windows. Doors and windows are used as the primary means of regulating air flow from the collector to rooms behind. A central internal stair promotes a convective loop within the section of each dwelling. Thermal storage is in the massive floors and ceilings. In summer, fabric shading is used to reduce heat gain, low-

Housing Development, Passau, Germany, Schröder & Widmann

er glass panels are removed to make an outdoor room, and ventilation flaps at the top of the collector can be opened to release excess heat by stack effect.

Heat from air collectors can be transferred to mass using the room air, or, as in the **Lützstrasse Apartments** in Berlin, warmed air can be blown, using fans, through hollow cores in a massive floor, called a *hypocaust* (Hastings, 1999, pp. 92–95). Architects from the Institute for Building, Environment, and Solar Research designed the building with a closed loop from collectors in the south facade (see images in Strategy 61) though tubes embedded in the concrete floor, and back to the collector. Discharge is by radiant transfer through the slab. This has the advantage of keeping the indoor air temperature from rising rapidly when the collector is heated by the sun.

In a dense urban context, full solar access to walls may not be possible, but the roof often retains solar access all winter. Warm air collectors allow the heat to be captured high on the roof, as it is in the retrofit of the **Apartment Block in Gothenburg,** Sweden, by Christer Nordström (Hastings, 1999, pp. 113–117). Air warmed from rooftop collectors is ducted by mechanical ventilation to a *murocaust* cavity in the external walls, formed by adding an insulated layer outside the existing uninsulated masonry wall. The detail sketch of the site-built air collector shows typical features: a clear layer of double glazing over a thin air space, backed up by a black-painted corrugated sheet metal absorber plate that captures heat and transfers it to air circulated behind the plate and over an insulating layer.

The area of glazed collector must be sized to meet the heat load of the building. This size varies with climate, tilt of the collector, the efficiency of the collector itself, and the seasonal heat load of the building. ASHRAE (1988) has determined seasonal performance levels based on a range of collector efficiencies and locations.

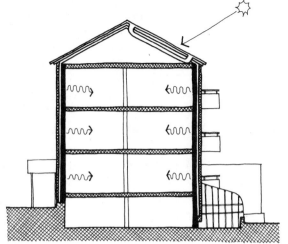

Rooftop Air Collector and Murocaust Wall, Retrofit of Apartments in Gothenberg

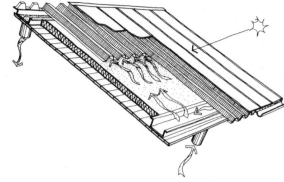

Collector Detail, Apartments in Gothenberg

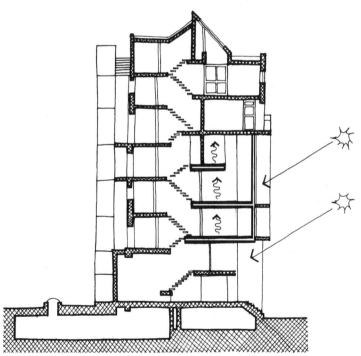

Vertical Air Collector and Hypocaust Floor, Lützstrasse Apartments, Berlin, Germany

Murocaust Wall, Apartments in Gothenberg

The Air Collector Sizing Recommendations table estimates minimum collector size as a fraction of conditioned floor area (A_f/A_g) for building balance points (T_b) of 55 °F (13 °C) and 45 °F (7 °C) and recommended solar savings fraction targets. The table follows a general rule:

A solar collection area of (Low A_f/A_g)% to (High A_f/A_g)% of the floor area can be expected to reduce the annual heating load of a building in (Location) by (Low SSF)% to (High SSF)% if tilted at the latitude, or if vertical collectors are used, a solar collection area of (Low A_f/A_g)% to (High A_f/A_g)% is required to produce the same performance.

For example, in St. Louis, Missouri, for a building with T_b = 55 °F, a solar collection area of 11 to 18% of the floor area can be expected to reduce the annual heating load by 41 to 65%, or for vertical collectors, a solar collection area of 13 to 20% of the floor area is needed.

Exceeding the larger end of the recommendations may result in clear day winter overheating. If a high SSF is desired, more mass must be used (Strategy 83) to dampen extreme interior thermal swings.

To determine the minimum warm air collector size for the building:

1) From the map of U.S. climate zones, select the city that most closely matches the site's climate. A close match for both degree days and solar radiation is important (Technique 3).

2) Select the appropriate balance point for the building (Techniques 22 and 23). For newer, well insulated buildings with low internal loads, use T_b = 55; for buildings with high internal loads, such as office buildings, use T_b = 45. If the building's average balance point is known, interpolate between values as necessary.

3) Select a target solar fraction. For each city, the recommended solar savings fraction values (SSF) are given as a range from low (lo) to high (hi). The SSF is the percentage of energy saved by using solar energy to heat a building, compared to a non-solar building with similar thermal characteristics.

City	Lat.	Annual Degree Days 65 F	18.3 C	SSF Rule of Thumb low	high	Collector Slope = Latitude° T_b = 55 F low	high	T_b = 45 F low	high	Collector Slope = Vertical T_b = 55 F low	high	T_b = 45 F low	high
AK, Annette	55	6987	3882	35	55	0.10	0.16	0.04	0.07	0.12	0.19	0.05	0.08
AK, Bethel	61	13098	7277	40	60	0.23	0.35	0.16	0.24	0.28	0.41	0.19	0.29
AK, Fairbanks	65	13940	7744	40	60	0.39	0.59	0.30	0.45	0.46	0.69	0.35	0.53
AR, Little Rock	34	3155	1753	37	62	0.07	0.11	0.03	0.04	0.08	0.13	0.03	0.05
AZ, Phoenix	33	1556	864	48	75	0.01	0.02	0.00	0.00	0.01	0.02	0.00	0.00
CA, Fesno	37	2556	1420	41	65	0.04	0.06	0.01	0.01	0.04	0.07	0.01	0.01
CA, Los Angeles	34	1458	810	44	72	0.00	0.01	0.00	0.00	0.00	0.01	0.00	0.00
CT, Hartford	42	6354	3530	40	64	0.11	0.17	0.06	0.10	0.13	0.21	0.07	0.11
DC, Washington	38	4047	2248	37	61	0.09	0.14	0.04	0.06	0.10	0.16	0.04	0.07
FL, Jacksonville	30	1327	737	35	62	0.01	0.03	0.00	0.00	0.02	0.03	0.00	0.00
FL, Miami	26	206	114	31	54	0.00	0.00	0.00	0.00	0.00	0.00	0.00	0.00
IA, Des Moines	41	6718	3732	50	75	0.17	0.26	0.10	0.15	0.20	0.31	0.12	0.18
ID, Boise	43	5861	3256	48	71	0.10	0.15	0.05	0.08	0.12	0.17	0.06	0.09
IN, Indianapolis	39	5615	3119	37	60	0.14	0.22	0.08	0.12	0.16	0.26	0.09	0.14
KS, Dodge City	38	5001	2778	46	73	0.06	0.09	0.03	0.05	0.07	0.10	0.03	0.05
LA, New Orleans	30	1465	814	35	61	0.02	0.04	0.00	0.01	0.03	0.05	0.01	0.01
ME, Caribou	47	9651	5362	53	74	0.19	0.27	0.13	0.18	0.23	0.32	0.15	0.21
MN, Minneapolis	45	7981	4434	55	76	0.21	0.30	0.14	0.19	0.25	0.35	0.16	0.23
MO, St Louis	39	4758	2643	41	65	0.11	0.18	0.06	0.09	0.13	0.20	0.07	0.11
MS, Jackson	32	2300	1278	34	59	0.04	0.07	0.01	0.02	0.05	0.08	0.02	0.03
MT, Billings	46	7279	4044	53	76	0.10	0.15	0.09	0.12	0.12	0.18	0.10	0.15
MT, Glasgow	48	8986	4992	55	75	0.14	0.19	0.02	0.03	0.18	0.25	0.03	0.04
NM, Albuquerque	35	4425	2458	46	73	0.05	0.07	0.02	0.03	0.05	0.08	0.02	0.03
NV, Ely	39	7818	4343	50	77	0.06	0.10	0.04	0.06	0.08	0.13	0.05	0.07
NY, Rochester	43	6722	3734	37	58	0.15	0.23	0.08	0.13	0.18	0.28	0.10	0.16
OR, Corvallis	44	4854	2697	37	59	0.22	0.36	0.10	0.17	0.30	0.48	0.14	0.22
OR, Medford	42	4611	2562	27	43	0.06	0.10	0.02	0.03	0.07	0.12	0.02	0.04
PA, Philadelphia	40	4875	2708	38	62	0.10	0.16	0.05	0.08	0.12	0.19	0.06	0.10
SC, Charleston	33	2013	1118	34	59	0.03	0.04	0.01	0.01	0.03	0.05	0.01	0.01
SD, Rapid City	44	7301	4056	51	76	0.08	0.12	0.05	0.07	0.09	0.14	0.06	0.08
TN, Chattanooga	35	3515	1953	33	56	0.06	0.09	0.02	0.04	0.07	0.11	0.03	0.04
TX, Ft. Worth	33	2405	1336	38	64	0.03	0.05	0.01	0.01	0.04	0.06	0.01	0.02
TX, Houston	30	1434	797	34	59	0.02	0.03	0.01	0.01	0.02	0.04	0.01	0.01
TX, Midland	32	2627	1459	44	72	0.04	0.06	0.01	0.02	0.04	0.07	0.01	0.02
UT, Salt Lake C	41	5765	3203	48	72	0.10	0.15	0.05	0.08	0.11	0.17	0.06	0.09
WA, Seattle	47	4908	2727	39	59	0.16	0.24	0.05	0.08	0.18	0.28	0.06	0.09
WI, Madison	43	7673	4263	51	74	0.16	0.24	0.10	0.15	0.19	0.27	0.12	0.17
WY, Lander	43	7889	4383	54	79	0.08	0.11	0.05	0.07	0.09	0.12	0.05	0.08

Air Collector Sizing Recommendations (area of glazing / area of floor)

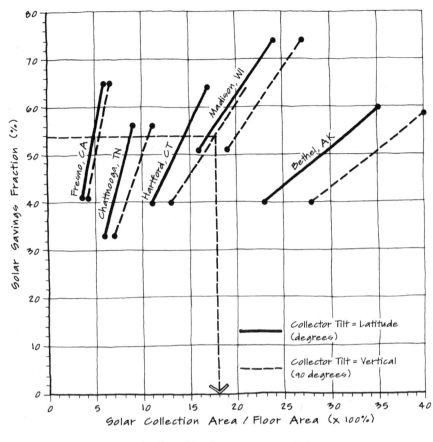

Sizing Solar Air Collector Glazing
data plotted from table

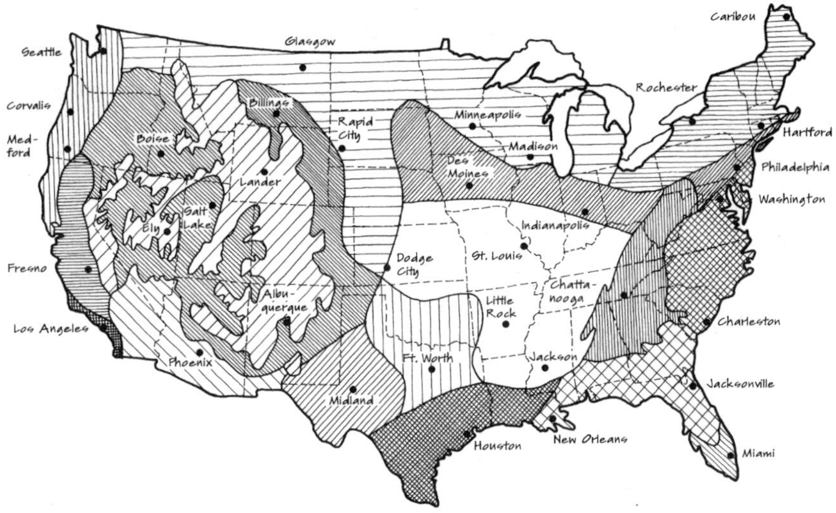

Regional Climate Zones

4) From the columns for the building's balance point and desired SSF, read on the city row the collector sizing ratio. This value is the ratio of solar glazing area to conditioned floor area. Multiply this ratio by the building's heated floor area to determine the minimum collector size.

The table assumes average efficiency, well built, manufactured collectors that are single glazed with selective absorbing surfaces and engineered rates of air flow. Higher efficiency products are available; site-built collectors may perform less efficiently. Tilted collectors are assumed to be set at an angle above the horizon equal to the site's latitude. A steeper tilt of latitude +15° will optimize winter performance. The rate of envelope loss is assumed to decrease as climate severity increases (see Technique 21).

Graphic interpolation is simple if the recommendations for the building's climate are first plotted on the graph. Plot low SSF with the low glazing ratio and the high SSF with the high glazing ratio. The graph shows recommendations for Hartford, which is cold and cloudy; Madison, very cold and cloudy; Medford, cool and very cloudy; Chattanooga, cool and cloudy, Fresno, mild and sunny, and Bethel, which has 10 months of heating required and little winter sun.

65 *CROSS-VENTILATION* through rooms is increased by large openings on both the windward and leeward sides. [cooling]

The rate at which air flows through a room, carrying away heat with it, is a function of the area of the inlets and outlets, the wind speed, and the direction of the wind relative to the openings. The amount of heat removed by a given rate of air flow depends on the temperature difference between inside and outside the building. As air flows around a building, it causes higher pressure zones on the windward side and lower pressure zones in the lee of the building. The most effective cross-ventilation occurs when the inlets are placed in the higher pressure area and the outlets in the lower pressure zones. The rate of air flow depends on the pressure difference between inlet and outlet (Melarango, 1982, p. 321). The maximum rate of ventilation occurs when the area of the inlets and outlets is large and the wind is relatively perpendicular to the window openings (Strategy 59).

The maximum ventilating area may be achieved, as in Paul Rudolph's **Cacoon House,** in Sarasota, Florida, by treating almost the entire house as a single room and opening its opposite walls completely with operable louvers (Fry & Drew, 1956, p. 75).

The **Rectorate of the Academy of the Antilles and Guiana,** in Fort-de-France, Martinique, adopts a similar strategy, completely opening its long sides with operable louvers. In the constantly hot humid Caribbean climate, the design uses very large openings to allow high-volume, low-velocity air flow under varying wind speeds to cool the offices without blowing papers. Architects Christian Hauvette and Jérôme Nouel provided all the ventilating openings with protected, deep, louvered sunshades to reduce the cooling load from the sun (Hauvette & Contal, 1997, pp. 60–69; Hauvette et al., 1995; Jones, 1998, pp. 104–106).

The size of the opening required to remove heat from a building, as a percentage of floor area, assuming a temperature difference of 3 °F (1.7 °C) between inside and out, may be determined from the graph. Enter the graph on the vertical axis with the design wind speed, move horizontally until the curve for the building's heat gain rate is intersected; then

Cacoon House, Sarasota, Florida, Paul Rudolph

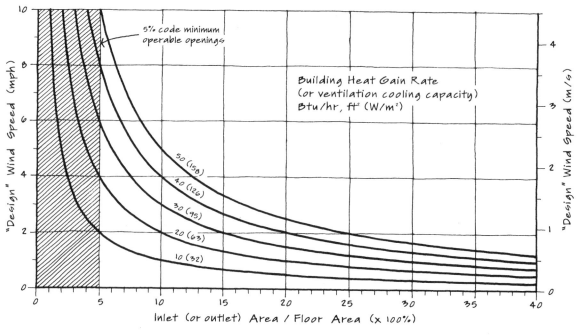

Sizing Openings for Cross-Ventilation

Rectorate of the Academy of the Antilles and Guiana, Fort-de-France, Martinique,
Christiane Hauvette & Jérôme Nouel

windows in one wall, landscaping or wing walls can be used to alter the positive and negative pressure zones around the building and induce wind flow through windows parallel to the prevailing wind directions (R. H. Reed, 1953, p. 56; Robinette, 1977, p. 29).

If located correctly, vertical fin projections can create a positive pressure at one window and a negative pressure at another. Outward opening casement win-

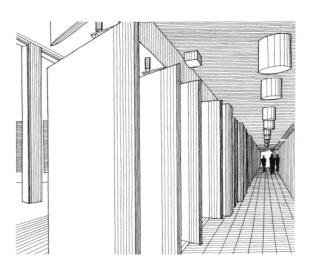

Interior View of Alierons
Academy of the Antilles and Guiana

drop down to the horizontal axis to read the size of the inlet (and outlet) as a percentage of the floor area.

See Techniques 4 and 5 for wind analysis and Technique 21 for heat gain analysis. Remember to adjust the airport wind speed for local terrain conditions. If using mean wind speeds from climate data, be sure to include a further reduction factor so that openings will be sized to work well in a slower than average wind. A reduction factor of 0.5 should cover most conditions. To estimate the impact of building spacing and density on wind speed, see Strategy 37, Dispersed Buildings.

If the temperature difference between inside and out is less than 3 °F (1.7 °C), the openings need to be proportionally larger, and if the temperature difference is greater, the openings may be smaller [multiply the size from the graph by the ratio of 3 °F / the actual T °F

(1.7 °C / actual T °C)]. Because occupant cooling is a function of air movement as well as heat removal, when the temperature is above the comfort zone, openings may need to be sized on the basis of maintaining a certain wind velocity through the building (Strategy 90).

The graph assumes an wind incidence angle of 0–40°. For wind incidence angles 40–60° from perpendicular to the window, multiply the inlet area recommended on the graph by 1.4, and multiply by 2.5 for a 60–80° incidence angle (Chandra et al., 1986, p. 66).

Effective ventilation may be achieved when the wind does not come from a direction perpendicular to the window (Givoni, 1976, p. 289; Chandra et al., 1986, p. 66). **Variations in orientation up to 40° from perpendicular to the prevailing wind do not significantly reduce ventilation (Strategy 59).** When openings cannot be oriented to the prevailing breeze and for rooms with

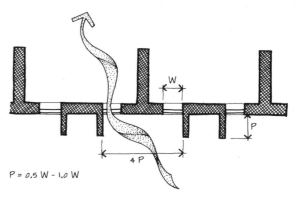

$P = 0.5 W - 1.0 W$

Recommended Wing Wall Dimensions
Adapted from Chandra et al. (1986, p. 37).

183

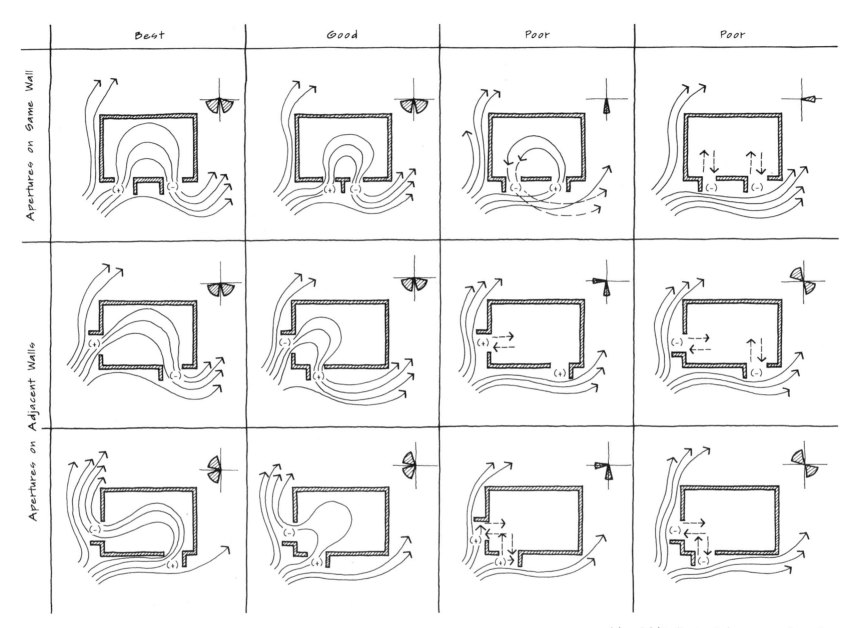

	Best	Good	Poor	Poor
Apertures on Same Wall				
Apertures on Adjacent Walls				
Apertures on Adjacent Walls				

Wing Wall Design Strategies

(+) and (-) indicate wind pressure at openings

dows can create a similar effect. The effect of wing walls is limited to windows on the windward side of a building and has no effect on leeward openings. The **Rectorate of the Academy of the Antilles and Guiana** uses on the windward side of the building wide vertical aileron fins that are constantly adjusted in response to

variations in wind direction. The fins also help with shading the openings, which are sheltered from rain by a large projection of the upper floor.

Use the plan diagrams as a guide to locating wing walls. The wind roses indicate the prevailing wind directions for which room airspeed is improved by the ***addition of wing walls. The depth of wing wall protrusions should be at least 0.5-1 times the width of the window. The spacing between wing walls should be at least 2 times the window width.***

56 *STACK-VENTILATION* through rooms is increased by greater distance between high and low openings. [cooling]

When the wind is blowing and the outside temperature is below the inside temperature, cross-ventilation can be an effective cooling strategy (Strategy 65). However, wind may not be available during some times, such as at night, or it may be very calm in some climates, or the site or urban condition may block a building's access to wind. In such conditions, stack-ventilation, which does not require wind to move the air through a building, can provide a similar cooling effect. It also has the advantage of orientation independence.

In a room cooled by stack-ventilation, warm air rises, exits though openings at the top of the room, and is replaced by cooler air entering low in the room. The rate at which the air moves through the room, carrying heat away with it, is a function of the vertical distance between the inlets and outlets, their size, and the difference between the outside temperature and the average inside temperature over the height of the room. Several strategies may be used to enhance this gravity ventilation system; all deal with the design of a building's section.

The effective height of the room can be increased by a stack chimney at the top, as it is in the **Building Research Establishment Office Building** in Garston, UK, by the firm of Feilden-Clegg. Five stacks, serving the lower two floors, are located on the south side of the building and extend the distance between inlets and outlets by two stories. Their south face is glazed to further heat the outgoing air and increase the temperature difference with the incoming air. Fans in the stacks assist ventilation when natural flow is insufficient (Allen, 1997; Jones, 1998, pp. 178–181).

The performance of the outlet may be enhanced by placing it in a negative pressure or suction zone created by wind flowing over the building, as in the upper floor of the BRE building, which is stack cooled by clerestory windows on the leeward side.

The room providing stack-ventilation can be a large atrium, as it is in the **National Building Museum** in Washington, DC. Outside air is drawn in through the small offices surrounding the atrium and exhausted through its top (Smith, 1981, p. 63).

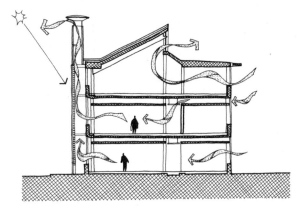

BRE Office, Typical Section

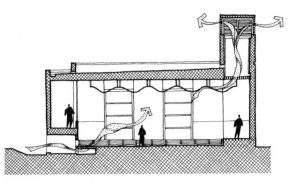

BRE Office, Section at Seminar Room

BRE Office Building, Garston, UK, Feilden-Clegg

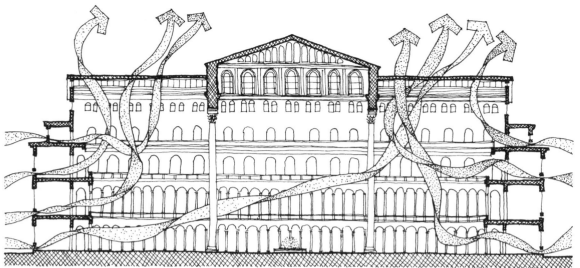

Pension Building, Washington, DC, Montgomery C. Meigs

Natural ventilation, in addition to admitting cooler fresh air, can create lighting and acoustic issues by admitting outdoor sounds and daylight or preventing acoustic isolation between rooms. This problem was addressed in the BRE building's seminar room by bringing inlet air from a service space under the corridor, through a floor plenum, to low wall inlets. The **Queen's Building of the deMonfort University Engineering School** in Leicester, England, by Short + Ford architects, addresses acoustic isolation by ventilating separate acoustic zones with individual stacks. In the auditorium, where ventilation must keep flowing even when the room is darkened, sound-baffled inlets are located in the wall beneath the seats. Air enters the room from registers under the seats and exits through two dedicated stacks with outlets above roof level, allowing daylight to be controlled separately from the ventilation (Davies, 1995; Thomas, 1996, pp. 171–188).

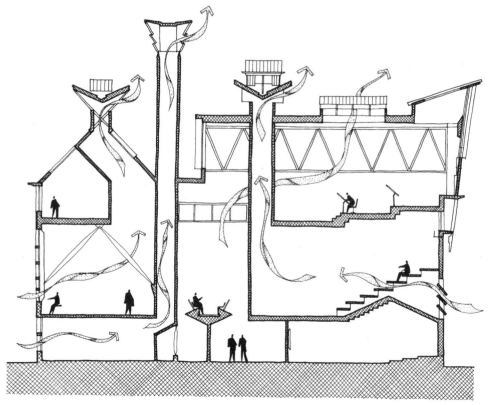

Queen's Building, deMonfort University, Leicester, England, Short + Ford

Queen's Building, Stack Ventilators

Given the ventilation rate (in cfm or L/s) or the heat gain to be removed (in Btu/hr, ft² or W/m²), use the graph to determine the height of the stack or room and the area of the stack cross section. Enter the graph on the vertical axis with the height of the stack, measured from center of inlets to center of outlets. Move horizontally to the curve for the building's rate of heat gain (Technique 21). From the intersection, drop to the horizontal axis to find the stack area as a percentage of the floor area to be cooled. The stack area must be equaled or exceeded by the area of outlets and also by the area of inlets: the smallest area of constraint on air movement will govern the rate of flow.

This graph assumes a temperature difference of 3 °F (1.7 °C) between inside and outside. For a temperature difference greater than 3 °F, such as for night ventilation of mass, the stack area can be reduced by multiplying the fractional area from the graph by the ratio of the square root of (3 °F / the actual *T* °F) or [SQRT (1.7 °C / actual *T* °C)]. Approximate the building's rate of heat gain using Technique 21.

Stack-ventilation flow rates are maximum when the area of inlets is equal to the area of outlets. In practice, it is often difficult to design the outlets as big as inlets. Increasing the inlet area over the outlet area (or vice versa) increases air flow, but not proportionally to the area added.

The graph at right gives the percentage increase in cooling capacity (heat removed), and in air flow rate, due to differential sizes of inlets and outlets. *To find the increased cooling due to differential openings, enter the graph on the horizontal axis with the ratio of inlets to outlets (A_{in} / A_{out}), or vice versa if outlets are larger. Move vertically to the curve, then horizontally and read the percentage increase on the vertical axis. Add this percentage to 100% and multiply by the cooling rate (or cfm) obtained from the Stack Ventialtion Sizing graph above (ASHRAE, 1997, p. 25.13).*

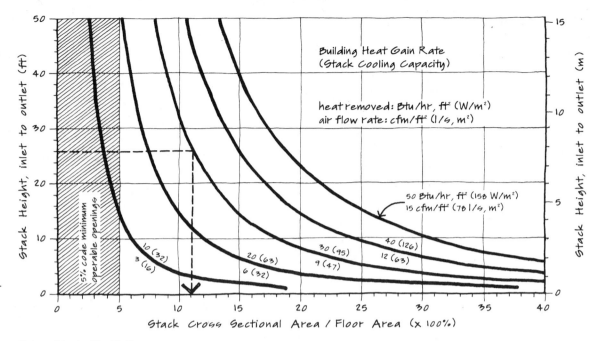

Sizing Stack-Ventilation

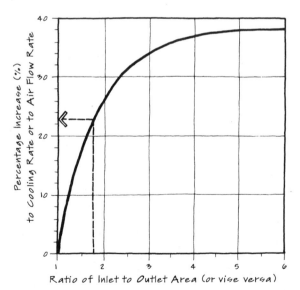

Increase in Stack Flow Rate From
Differential Opening Sizes

67 *WIND CATCHERS* **can capture breezes above roof level for buildings whose windows have little access to breezes. [cooling]**

In low-rise, high-density settlement patterns, it is difficult to get good wind access to each building because the upwind buildings block breezes from flowing to the leeward buildings. In such cases, it is possible to capture wind above the buildings, where it is cooler and less dusty, and direct it down to rooms below.

In orienting a building, there is sometimes a conflict between orientation for sun or shade and orientation for wind. Another benefit of wind catchers is that they may be oriented in any direction to catch the wind, while the primary building form responds to other forces, such as collecting sun in winter.

Mean wind velocity increases with height above the ground (Technique 5), so wind towers can admit winds of significantly higher speeds and therefore, their openings can be smaller than windows at ground level. Since there are fewer obstructions, wind towers can potentially admit wind from any direction.

Buildings at **Qatar University,** in Doha, Qatar, are based on an octagonal module topped with a rotated square, four-sided wind catcher known as a *badgir* (Taylor, 1985). With rooms arranged in a compact organization around a series of internal courtyards, openings from above are the only way to bring in wind for cross-ventilation. Vertical panels direct wind down from opposing inlets. Ventilation air can then exit though smaller adjacent rooms and porches.

For the **Souk (marketplace) at New Bariz, Egypt,** Hassan Fathy created a series of tall unidirectional *malkaf*, or wind catchers. The section of the *souk* shows that the shops on the windward side of the courtyard can be cross-ventilated, but they would block much of the wind to shops on the leeward side of the courtyard. To solve this, wind is captured high and directed down to two levels, one below ground for storage of perishable food. Air can then exit out an updraft stack-ventilation tower that is capped with slanted metal louvers to help create a Venturi effect and increase suction (Steele, 1988, pp. 92–95; Richards et al., 1985, pp. 126–132).

Wind catchers should be designed to match the degree of directional variability of local winds. The

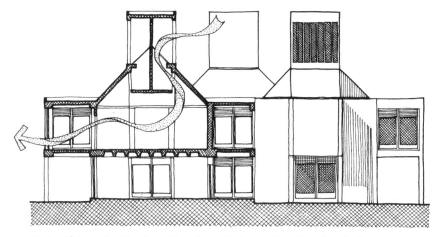

Qatar University, Section/Elevation of Humanities Faculty Modules

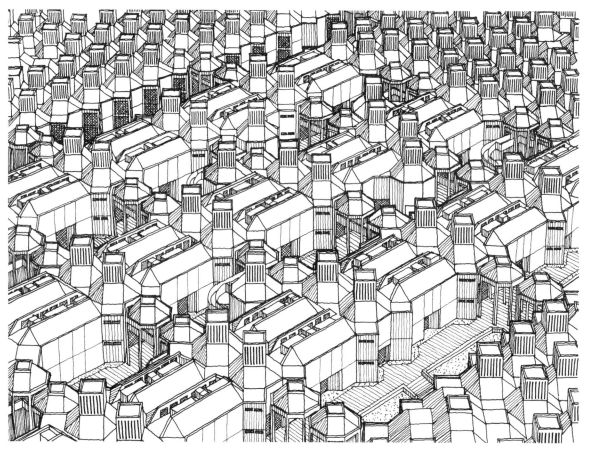

Qatar University (phase I), Doha, Qatar, Kamal El-Kafrawi

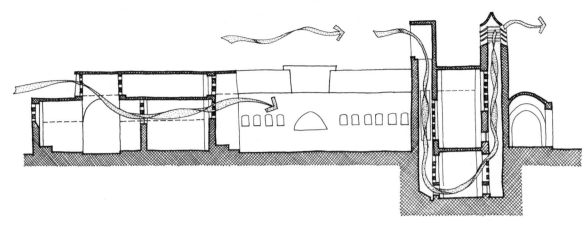

Section Through Souk, New Bariz, Egypt, Hassan Fathy

Souk, New Bariz, Egypt

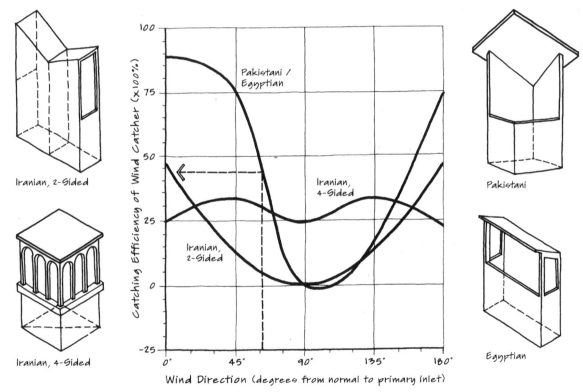

Iranian, 2-Sided

Iranian, 4-Sided

Pakistani

Egyptian

Catching Efficiency for Different Wind Catcher Designs

choice of a wind catcher open to wind on one, two, or more sides should be made based on a wind rose analysis for the months the building requires cooling.

If cooling winds blow consistently from one direction, then an Egyptian wind catcher might be appropriate. If the variability is mostly within a 90° sector of the compass, then a Pakistani-type catcher will respond well to such a wind regime. If winds fluctuate between two opposing directions, as is the case in some climates, choose an Iranian-type, 2-sided catcher. If the wind rose shows great variability of winds in a roughly equal distribution blowing from many directions, the Iranian 4-sided wind catcher can capture wind from any direction.

Both of the Iranian types require vertical panels inside the head to keep wind from blowing through the top of the catcher. The vertical separations should extend into the tower shaft to the point of outlet, in order to keep the air flow path from short circuiting to the other side of the tower.

The graph shows the catching device efficiency (CE) of these four types of wind catchers at a range of incident wind angles (Al-Megren, 1987, p. 191). The catching efficiency is defined as the ratio of the flow rate inside the tower to the product of the wind velocity and the cross sectional area of the tower. Higher CE values mean higher ventilation velocity with smaller tower cross sections. The graph shows that the Pakistani and Egyptian types are much more efficient than either of the Iranian types, so long as the wind comes from the direction to which they are oriented. The Iranian 4-sided catcher, although not highly efficient, shows little fluctuation with changes in wind direction. ***To rise above the layer of turbulence and drag, the inlets should be at least 8 ft (2.4 m) above the height of surrounding buildings and obstructions, if possible.***

The size of the wind catcher opening required to remove building heat gain, as a percentage of floor area, assuming a temperature difference of 3 °F (1.7 °C) between inside and out, may be determined from the graph. Enter the graph on the vertical axis with the design wind speed, move horizontally until the curve for the building's rate of heat gain is intersected; then drop to the horizontal axis to read the size of the inlet as a percentage of the floor area.

If the temperature difference between inside and out is less than 3 °F (1.7 °C), the openings need to be proportionally larger, and if the temperature difference is greater, the openings may be smaller [multiply the size from the graph by the ratio of 3 °F / the actual T °F (1.7 °C / actual T °C)]. The graph is based on an incident wind angle of between 0° (normal) and 40° to the wind catcher opening.

For wind catcher designs with openings in multiple directions, the openings in each direction should be sized to meet the building's heat load. The inlet from a single direction should be no larger than the cross-sectional area of the tower, while operable windows used for outlets should be about twice as large as the inlets.

Remember to adjust the airport wind speed for local terrain conditions. If using mean wind speeds from climate data, be sure to include a further reduction factor so that openings will be sized to work well in a slower than average wind. A reduction factor of 0.5 should cover most conditions. See Techniques 4 and 5 for wind analysis, and Technique 21 for heat gain analysis.

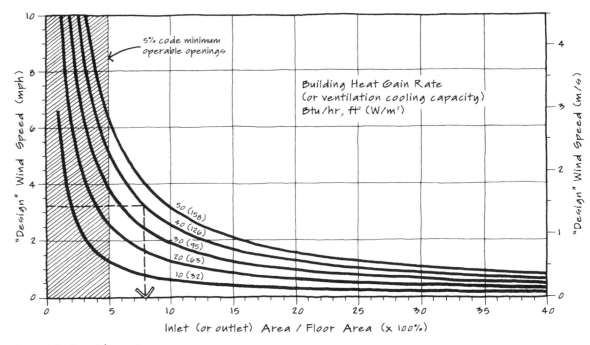

Sizing Wind Catchers for Cooling

68

NIGHT-COOLED MASS: **Thermal mass can be used to absorb heat from a room during the day and then be cooled at night with ventilation. [cooling]**

Cooling a building nighttime ventilation of the thermal mass depends on a twofold process. First, during the day, when the outside temperature is too warm for ventilation, the building envelope is closed and excess heat gains are stored in the building's mass. Second, at night, when the outside temperature is lower, outdoor air is allowed to ventilate through the building to remove the stored heat from the mass. The mass is thus cooled, so that it can absorb excess heat again the next day. For this to work, there must be enough mass in the building to absorb the heat gains, and the mass must be distributed over enough surface area so that it will absorb the heat quickly and keep the interior air temperature comfortably low. The openings must be large to allow enough cool outside air to flow past the mass to remove the heat accumulated during the day and carry it outside the building.

Pearce Partnership, with Ove Arup engineers, designed the high-mass, night-ventilated **Eastgate Building in Harare,** for Zimbawe's tropical high-altitude climate. Only the lower two shopping floors are mechanically conditioned. For the narrow office blocks above, air is drawn in with the aid of large fans from a central atrium and up through 32 vertical supply ducts, then distributed horizontally through a plenum under the floor, where the air can cool the mass. The major mass is in the ceiling, which is vaulted to increase the exposed surface area. Air enters rooms low near the windows and moves diagonally back to the interior, where it is collected at high bulkheads and discharged through stack towers to outlets above the roof level. During the day, the flow is reduced to a rate sufficient for fresh air supply, and the massive structure can absorb heat from internal and envelope gains. At night, air flow increases to 7 air changes per hour (Slessor, 1996).

In night ventilation schemes, the area of the mass that can be incorporated into a structure is a major limitation on the cooling potential. The ratio of mass surface area to floor area is usually between 1:1 and 1:3; it

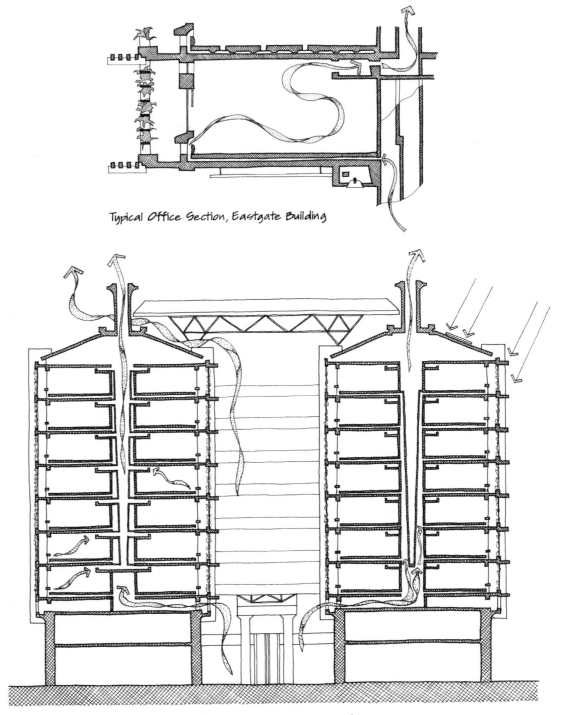

Typical Office Section, Eastgate Building

Section, Eastgate Building, Harare, Zimbabwe, Pearce Partnership

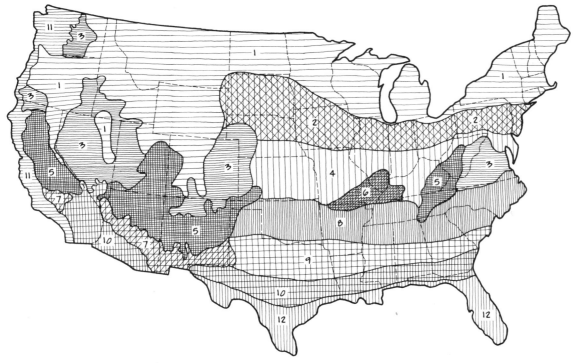

Climate Zones to Assess the Potential for Night-Cooled Mass

| Zone | SLD Buildings | | ILD Buildings | All Buildings |
	NVM Possible	Cooling Unnecessary	NVM Possible	Too Hot for NVM
1	July & Aug	Sep to Jun	ALL	NONE
2	Jun to Aug	Sept to May	ALL	NONE
3	Jun to Sep	Oct to May	ALL	NONE
4	June & Sep	Oct to May	Sep to May	Jul & Aug
5	May to Sep	Oct to Apr	ALL	NONE
6	May & Jun; Aug & Sep	Oct to Apr	Aug to Jun	July
7	April to Jun; Aug & Sep	Nov to Mar	Sep to Jun	July & Aug
8	May & Sep	Oct to Apr	Sep to May	Jun to Aug
9	May; Sep & Oct	Nov to Apr	Sep to May	Jun to Aug
10	April & May; Oct	Nov to Mar	Oct to May	Jun to Sep
11	ALL	ALL	ALL	NONE
12	NONE		NONE	ALL

is difficult to develop more mass surface area within the building. For details on mass sizing for solar heating, see Strategy 83.

Night ventilation is most effective in climates with a high diurnal range and night temperatures below the comfort zone. The effectiveness of night ventilation in a particular climate can be estimated by plotting temperature and humidity data for the overheated months on the Building Bioclimatic Chart, Technique 18.

The map of Night Ventilation Zones shows the months for which night ventilation of mass (NVM) is likely to provide cooling (Iwersen, 1992). Find the zone for the building's climate from the map and then refer to the that zone's row in the table. Use the SLD columns for skin-load-dominated buildings with balance points above 60 °F (15.6 °C). Use the ILD column for internal-load-dominated buildings with a balance point below 60 °F (15.6 °C).

The ability to cool with outside air at night depends on having a low enough minimum temperature. Since the low mass temperature will be about 5 °F (3 °C) above the minimum outdoor air temperature, estimate the potential for night ventilation for a given month by adding 5 °F to the minimum temperature. If this low mass temperature is below 72 °F (22 °C), then there is good potential for night cooled mass.

The thermal storage capacity of mass depends on the amount of exposed area, its thickness, and the density and specific heat of the material. Since warmed air rises, ceilings and walls are better than floors for storing heat. If the mass is located where people can see it, they will be able to benefit from radiant loss to the cool surfaces. Also, make sure that the mass is well shaded and never in direct radiation from the summer sun.

To determine the amount of mass necessary to cool a building, enter the nomograph on the left side horizontal axis with the value of the diurnal temperature difference of the mass (Mass T), which is equal to 80 °F (27 °C) minus the low mass temperature. Move vertically to the diagonal line for the building's mass type. From the intersection, move right to the line for the ratio of exposed mass area to floor area, then vertically to find the mass storage capacity. The mass storage capacity is the total amount of heat, per unit of floor area, that can be stored on a daily basis, in units of Btu/day, ft² (W/

day, m²). Compare this amount to the rate of total daily heat gain for the building from Technique 21.

The graph assumes a maximum indoor temperature of 80 °F (27 °C). To find cooling for other indoor maxima, substitute the desired maximum temperature for 80 °F / 27 °C in the calculation of the mass ΔT. For a given material, increasing the thickness beyond the values shown will not significantly increase the daily heat stored.

Once heat has been stored in the mass, it must be removed at night by ventilation. *To determine the area of inlet needed, which must be equalled by the outlet area and the cross-section of the stack, enter the graph on the vertical axis with wind speed for cross-ventilation or stack height for stack ventilation. Move horizontally until the appropriate curve is intersected; then drop down to determine the area of the inlet as a percentage of the mass area.*

The graph assumes that the wind blows from between perpendicular and diagonal to the openings for cross-ventilation and that the difference between the outside temperature and inside temperature (ΔT) is 3 °F (1.7 °C). In many climates, the ΔT during the hours of the most cooling will be 8–14 °F (4–8 °C). To adjust inlet size for ΔT greater than 3 °F (1.7 °C), see Strategies 65 and 66.

If the same openings are to be used for daytime ventilation in other months, check sizing in Strategy 65, 66, or 67. Since winds are usually slower and often calm at night, fans may be used to assist the passive flow (Strategy 105).

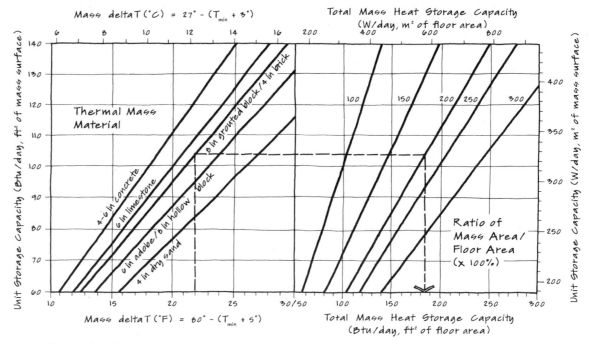

Sizing Night Cooled Mass

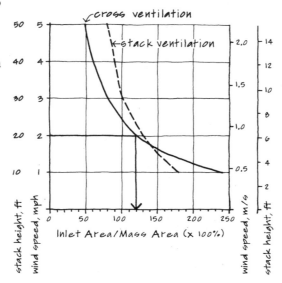

Sizing Ventilation Inlets for Night-Cooled Mass

69 *EVAPORATIVE COOLING TOWERS* can supply cool air to rooms without the use of fans or wind. [cooling]

In climates where evaporative cooling is effective, downdraft evaporative cooling towers (cool towers) can be used to supply cool air to rooms, without the use of fans or the need for wind. If designed with outlets at the top, they can also be used for stack-ventilation during periods when the outside air is below the indoor temperature.

The cool tower provides cool air by taking in hot, dry outdoor air through high inlets covered with a wetted evaporative pad. The trickle flow in the pad is fed by a small electric water pump, which may be photovoltaic powered. As the air passes through the pad, it picks up moisture, raising its humidity, while lowering its temperature. The cooler, more dense air then falls

by gravity down the tower shaft, creating a positive pressure that pushes air through the occupied space and out of operable windows at the rooms' perimeter. A negative pressure is also created at the inlets, drawing in more outside air through the pads.

Since cool towers supply air at a single point at the bottom of the tower, rooms can be bunched around two or more sides of the tower. For air to flow through the building, there must be an open path from the supply tower, through adjacent rooms to outlet windows.

Small buildings may be served by a single tower, but in larger buildings with multiple towers, each tower will cool one zone of the building. Because cool towers take in air above the roof level, they are a good match with

the compact, courtyard organizations typical of hot-arid climates, which have less opportunity for cross-ventilation than dispersed organizations. Exiting air can also be used to temper adjacent courtyards.

Pliny Fisk's **Laredo Blueprint Demonstration Farm**, in Laredo, Texas, uses two downdraft evaporative cooling towers to cool sheds housing offices, classrooms, and packing areas. Air from the cooler drops into one shed from above, cools the space below, passes into an adjacent shed, and exits out an updraft stack-ventilation tower (Tilley, 1991).

Evaporative cooling requires no air recirculation and provides a positive pressure pushing air out of openings, thus the relationship between inside and outside can be

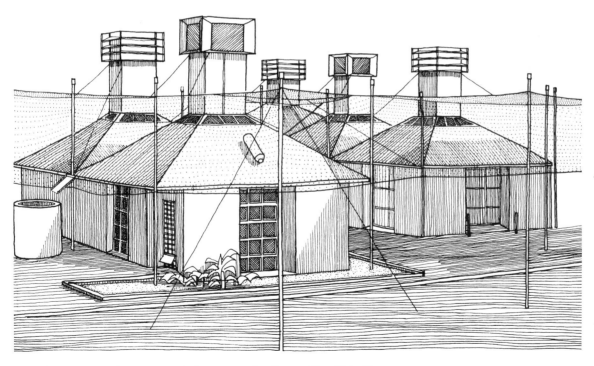

Laredo Demonstration Blueprint Farm, Laredo Texas, Pliny Fisk, III

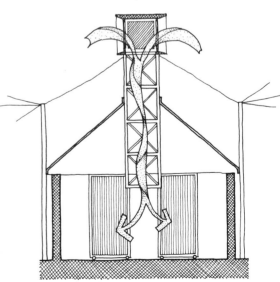

Section Through Evaporative Tower, Laredo Demonstration Blueprint Farm

Courtyard, University of Arizona Residence Hall, Moule & Polyzoides

Presidential Rest House, Kalabash, Egypt, Hassan Fathy

more freely open. It can even be used to condition partially enclosed outdoor rooms, such as in the courtyards of the **Residence Halls at the University of Arizona,** by Moule and Polyzoides (Steele, 1997, pp. 85–99).

Hassan Fathy's design for the **Presidential Rest House in Kalabsha, Egypt** also uses both downdraft evaporation and a high stack outlet. In this case, Fathy designed a water spray system in which air passes through and around a series of metal mesh baffles with trays of moistened charcoal. Exiting the downdraft tower, air passes through the main entertaining rooms and out either the high windows in the tall, vaulted *ka'a* or across the long vaulted space and out the updraft stack (Richards et al., 1985, pp. 78–81).

The greater the temperature drop across the evaporative pads, the higher is the pressure created to drive the system. The cooling effectiveness of a cool tower is a function of two variables: the temperature of air exiting the evaporative cooler pads and the rate of air flow generated by the tower. The temperature out of the

cooler is determined by the effectiveness of the evaporative pads, which varies by manufacturer, and the difference between outdoor dry-bulb and wet-bulb temperature conditions. The flow rate in the tower is determined by the outdoor air conditions, the tower height, the size of the inlets, and the air pressure drop through the building (Givoni, 1994, pp. 138–143 and 168–173; Argiriou & Santamouris, 1995, pp. 19–22).

Increasing the tower height and the inlet size creates a higher volume of air passing through the pads and down the tower. A larger difference between the dry-bulb and wet-bulb temperatures, indicating lower relative humidity of outdoor air, increases the temperature drop across the pads.

The four-part nomograph shows the effect of these variables on the Sizing of Passive Downdraft Cooling Towers. To size a cool tower:

1) Find the summer outdoor design dry bulb temperature (T_{db}) and coincident wet bulb temperature (T_{wb}) for the site from Appendix A or from ASHRAE (1997) or

Reynolds & Stein (2000). Subtract T_{wb} from T_{db} to get the outdoor web bulb depression, $T_{db} - T_{wb}$.

2) Enter the graph on the left side horizontal axis using this $T_{db} - T_{wb}$, in either °F or °C.

3) In the upper left quadrant, move vertically to the curve for the height of the tower. Tower height should be measured from the center of inlets (pads) to the center or the outlets at the bottom of the tower. Then move right, horizontally, into the upper right quadrant until intersecting the diagonal line for the total area of tower inlets. Inlet area is expressed as a percentage of the floor area intended to be cooled.

4) Drop a line vertically to the lower right quadrant, crossing the curves for the cooling rate produced by the tower.

5) On the same line for $T_{db} - T_{wb}$ as in Step 2, move vertically to the lower left quadrant, intersecting the diagonal line for the site's outdoor design dry bulb temperature. Then move horizontally until intersecting the vertical line dropped in Step 4.

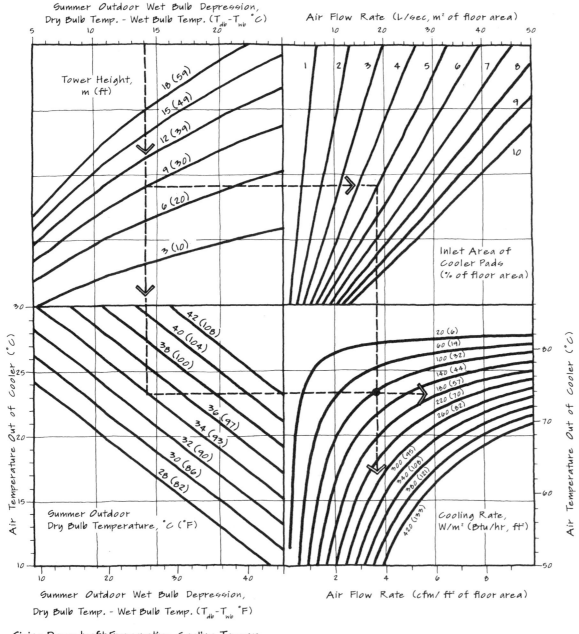

Summer Outdoor Wet Bulb Depression,
Dry Bulb Temp. - Wet Bulb Temp. (T$_{db}$-T$_{wb}$ °C)

Air Flow Rate (L/sec, m² of floor area)

Tower Height, m (ft)

18 (59)
15 (49)
12 (39)
9 (30)
6 (20)
3 (10)

Inlet Area of Cooler Pads (% of floor area)

Air Temperature Out of Cooler (°C)

42 (108)
40 (104)
38 (100)
36 (97)
34 (93)
32 (90)
30 (86)
28 (82)

20 (6)
60 (19)
100 (32)
140 (44)
180 (57)
220 (70)
260 (82)
300 (95)
340 (108)
380 (121)
420 (133)

Cooling Rate, W/m² (Btu/hr, ft²)

Air Temperature Out of Cooler (°C)

Summer Outdoor Dry Bulb Temperature, °C (°F)

Summer Outdoor Wet Bulb Depression,
Dry Bulb Temp. - Wet Bulb Temp. (T$_{db}$-T$_{wb}$ °F)

Air Flow Rate (cfm/ ft² of floor area)

Sizing Downdraft Evaporative Cooling Towers

6) From this intersection point, read from the curves the cooling rate produced by the cool tower. Compare this to the rate of total heat gain expected in the building (Technique 21).

Using the graph, the designer may experiemnt with different combinations of tower height and inlet area to meet the building's cooling load. The graph assumes a pad effectiveness of 75% and an insulated tower. It is developed based on a model by Givoni (1994, pp.168–173). If the tower is uninsulated, heat flow through the tower wall will warm the air inside it, decreasing the cooling effectiveness of the system.

The presence of wind will increase the flow rate across the pads, but the temperature drop will not be as great as for still air, so the effect of wind on the design of the tower can be ignored (Givoni, 1991, pp. 370–371).

The cross-sectional area of the tower affects the velocity of the air exiting the tower, but has little effect on the rate of cooling produced. A larger cross section will yield a slower velocity of air movement. *Tower cross section should generally be about one-half the area of the inlets. Outlets at the bottom of the tower can be horizontal or vertical; their size should be at least as large as the tower cross section.*

70 An *ATRIUM* or light court within a building can provide light to surrounding rooms. [daylighting]

When buildings are thicker than the dimensions that can support sidelighting, unglazed light courts or glazed atria may be used to bring light into the interior. Atria are used both for lighting adjacent rooms and for providing light to plants and activities that occur in their climate-buffered space. Potentially, they have the additional advantages of increasing marketability, reducing conductive heat loss and gain in the building (Strategy 57), providing winter solar heat gain as sunspaces (Strategy 61), and serving as a passive ventilation stack (Strategy 66).

The **Reiterstrasse Building,** in Bern, Switzerland, by Bureau D' Architecture, uses a combination of toplit circulation and regularly spaced light courts to bring daylight to every occupied room. Perimeter rooms are conventionally sidelit, but since the two-story building is very thick in plan, light from the edge can not penetrate beyond the corridor. The addition of unglazed light courts allows internal rooms to have windows on at least one side. Many rooms also have a second source of light borrowed form the skylit corridor. The primary corridor is essentially a two-story linear atrium, with second floor circulation on either side of the floor opening. Secondary corridors have floor openings on either side of the circulation that serve as light slots to admit toplight to the lower floor. Interior clerestories facing the corridor project from the wall and are angled to face upward toward the source of daylight.

Frank Lloyd Wright designed the offices of the **Larkin Administration Building** around a tall toplit atrium. Openings into the atrium were unglazed, and the atrium floor was also used for office work. Wide, light-colored sills with filing storage underneath were used as light shelves (Strategy 96) to reflect light into the office galleries. The atrium is roofed with a double layer consisting of a gridded horizontal ceiling covered by a gabled upper glass layer (Quinan, 1987).

Sidelighting can be usable to a depth of 2–2.5 times the head height *(H)* of exterior windows, (Strategy 71), thus the width of effective sidelit buildings is limited to 5*H*, if all spaces are to be daylit. The thickness of rooms between an atrium and the exterior wall is simi-

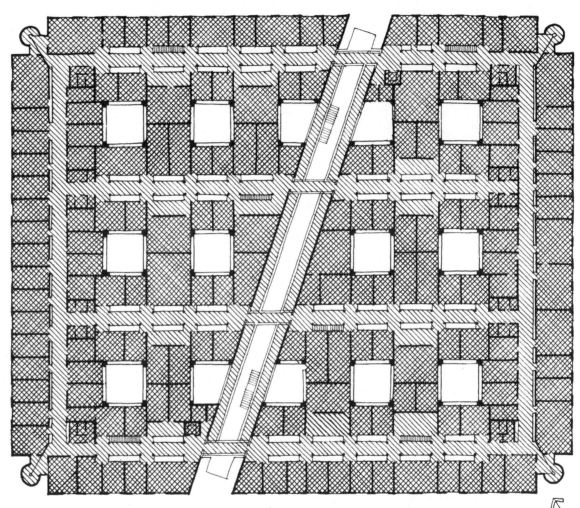

Second Floor Plan, Reiterstrasse Building, Bern, Switzerland, Bureau D'Architecture

Atrium, Larkin Administration Building, Frank Lloyd Wright

or sidelighting, room lighting is affected by room geometry, window glazing transmission, and interior room reflectances.

The most important of these factors in providing daylight via an atrium is the proportion of the atrium. Tall, narrow atria have less "view" of the sky than short, wide atria. Since less daylight is available at higher latitudes than at lower latitudes, atria at high latitudes must be larger to provide the same level of daylight indoors. Taller buildings with more floors require larger atria than shorter buildings. At low height to width ratios (1:1) atrium plan geometry is not very significant. Square and rectangular atria perform similarly. At higher ratios (2:1) square atria provide 7–10% more light to the atrium floor than rectangular atria with a 1:2 plan aspect (Goulding et al., 1992; Willbold-Lohr, 1989).

To determine atrium size, first determine the required design daylight factor from Technique 9. Then enter the Sizing Atria for Daylight in Adjacent Rooms graph on the vertical axis using the design daylight factor. Since lower rooms have the most restrictive daylight conditions, move horizontally to the curved zone for lower rooms. For most buildings, use the bottom of the zone (50% glazing). From the intersection, move down to read the minimum atrium volumetric aspect ratio.

Roof construction should provide the minimum of daylight blockage. Framing will reduce daylight by at least 10%. Glazing will also reduce transmission. Therefore, increase the required daylight factor as follows:

$$DF_{design} = DF_{target} \div T_{roof}$$

larly limited to about 5*H*, for full daylight. While this is not undesirable from a daylighting or aesthetic point of view, it may reduce the site's development potential more than necessary and produce plans with high proportions of circulation. If, however, an internal electrically lit zone is used for circulation, services, and storage, the building thickness can be increased. Building thickness affects the fraction of a building's floor area that can be daylit.

*Use a thickness dimension between outside wall and atria of 6*H *to achieve 90–100% rentable area daylit, and use 7*H *to achieve 80–90% rentable area daylit (DeKay, 1992).*

This principle holds true for all latitudes and atrium sizes. The rule of thumb assumes a gross to net ratio of 1.35, excluding atrium area, and a 2.5*H* maximum penetration of daylight.

Daylight levels in rooms adjacent to atria are affected by the height and width of the atria, the amount of daylight available in the building's climate, the reflectivity of interior facades, the size and position of windows facing the atrium, the atrium roofing design, the transmittance of the glazing system, and reflection strategies at the interior window wall. Just as in exteri-

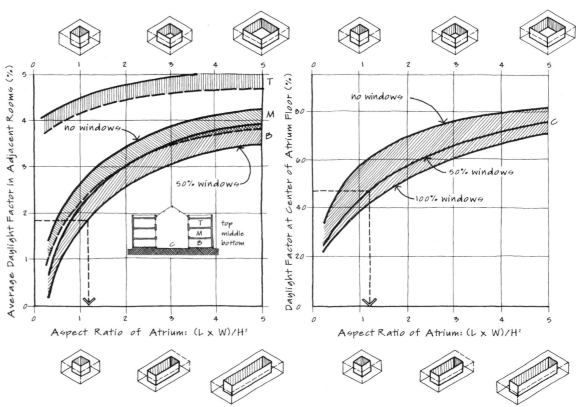

Sizing Atria for Daylight in Adjacent Rooms

Sizing Atria for Daylighting at the Center of Atrium Floor

where DF_{design} is the daylight factor for atrium design; DF_{target} is the recommended daylight factor from Technique 9; and T_{roof} is the transmission of the roof and glazing construction, in % (Strategy 101).

The graph is based on model tests using a square atrium with white walls in two configurations: 1) no windows (ave. reflectance, $R = 70\%$); and 2) 50% glass/50% white walls (ave. $R = 40\%$). A medium-sized office of $9 \times 9 \times 3$ m ($30 \times 30 \times 10$ ft) with a window opening of 1.5×9 m (5×10 ft) and a sill height of 0.85 m (2.8 ft) was assumed. Interior reflectances assumed are walls, 60%; floor, 25%; ceiling, 70%. Overcast sky condition and courtyards without glazing and roofing are assumed (Baker, et al., 1993).

Atria may also be designed to provide sufficient light to any plants growing in the atrium. Minimum daylight level is at the floor. Interior plants require between 250 lux (23 fc) for small plants and 2000 or more lux (186 fc) for trees and tropical plants, with most plants requiring a minimum of 700–1000 lux (65–93 fc) for 10–12 hr per day. Based on available exterior daylight, the required daylight factor inside the atrium to support plant growth can be determined from Strategy 9. For a 500 fc (5400 lux) overcast sky, this means required daylight factors in the atrium of 5–40% (Baker et al., 1993). Toplighting is preferable to sidelight for plant growth; clear glazing is better than tinted.

The graph for Sizing Atria for Daylighting at the Center of Atrium Floor can be used to check atrium sizing for plant light levels. Enter the chart on the horizontal axis using the design daylight factor for planting. Move horizontally to the curve that approximates the average glazing percentage of the atrium walls, then move down to read the minimum atrium volumetric aspect ratio. Be sure to compare this to the aspect ratio required for daylighting of adjacent rooms. Use the larger of the two sizes.

Another common type of atria building uses a linear atrium with rooms facing the atrium only on two sides, and the two ends of the atrium made of glazed walls facing the outdoors. The regional **Government Headquarters in Marseille, France,** uses a linear atrium to link two parallel office blocks. It is covered by a ventilated glass roof with interior automated sun shading (Davies, 1994).

Direct sunlight admitted to the atrium can cause glare or undesirable strong patterns of shadow and

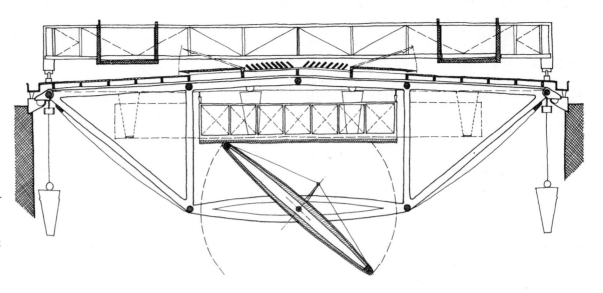

Atrium Roof Detail, Regional Govenrment Headquarters

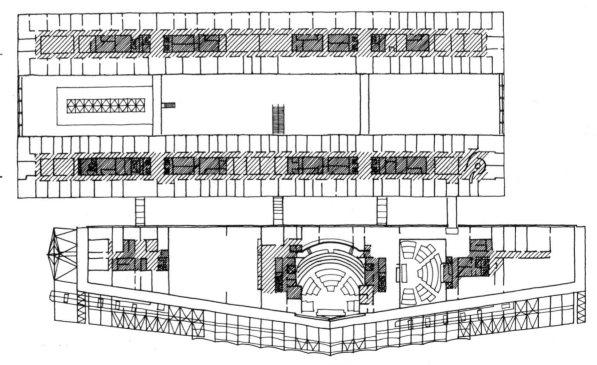

Regional Govenrment Headquarters, Marseille, France, William Alsop

Atrium Interior, Regional Government
Headquarters, Marseille, France

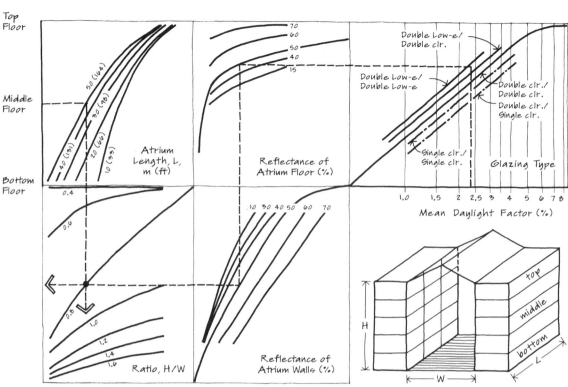

Sizing Linear Atria for Daylight in Adjacent Rooms

light. Sunlight can be intercepted at the window wall facing the atrium (see University of Trondheim example in Strategy 32) or at the atrium roof as it is in the Marseille Government Headquarters. The rotating translucent fabric sunshades diffuse the direct sun by filtering and reflecting. A second horizontal sun shade move from one side of the atrium to the other with the aid of counterweights.

Szerman (1992; Hastings, 1994) has developed a thorough nomograph relating the multiple design factors of linear atria. The chart may be used to determine the daylight factors of a proposed design or, given a daylight goal, to size the atrium dimensions.

To determine the height to width ratio of a linear atrium, enter the Sizing Linear Atria for Daylighting in Adjacent Rooms graph on the daylight factor scale with the target daylight factor for a room adjacent to the atrium. Move vertically to the curve for the glazing type, then horizontally until intersecting the curve for floor reflectance, then down to the curve for atrium wall reflectance (average including glazing). From the wall reflectance curve draw a horizontal line left across the height/width ratio (H/W) lines. From the intersection of the ground floor line and the curve for atrium width, drop a vertical line until it intersects the horizontal construction line drawn previously. From this point, read the required minimum H/W ratio.

Note that several combinations of atrium length and H/W ratio are possible. The method assumes a window/facade ratio of 60%, interior room reflectances of 50% walls, 15% floor, 70% ceiling, illuminance measured at 85 cm (2.8 ft) above floor, room 4.8 m (16 ft) deep, ceiling height 2.7 m (9 ft), and window head 2.7 m (9 ft).

71 *DAYLIT ROOM DEPTH* **should be less than 2½ times the height of the window head to maintain a minimum level of illumination and an even distribution of light. [daylighting]**

In a sidelit room the illumination is high near the window and falls off rapidly farther away from the window wall. The deeper the room, the greater the contrast between the area near the window and the wall farthest from the window. Under overcast conditions, assuming nearly continuous windows, when the room depth is greater than 2½ times the height of the window's head, the ratio between the brightest and darkest part of the room will exceed 5:1 (Flynn & Segil, 1970, p. 111). Excessive gradients tend to make the lighting seem uneven; and if the eye is adapted to the lightest parts of the room, especially the window, then the darker parts of the room will seem darker than they actually are (Hopkinson et al., 1966, p. 306).

The **Temple of Dendur wing at the Metropolitan Museum of Art,** in New York, New York, designed by Roche and Dinkeloo, is one large sidelit room whose light interior surfaces evenly distribute the light from the north-facing window, which runs from floor to ceiling and maximizes the amount of light entering the space.

As the room depth increases beyond 3 times the window wall height, the light levels in the darkest parts of the room approach 1% or less of the illumination available outside on an overcast day, which may be inadequate for some tasks. The light levels at the rear of the space can be greatly affected by reflectors or light shelves at the window wall (Strategies 92 and 96), the reflectivity of the interior surfaces (Strategy 78) and shading devices (Strategy 98), and nonovercast sky conditions (Strategy 92).

Temple of Dendur Wing, Metropolitan Museum of Art, New York City, Roche & Dinkeloo

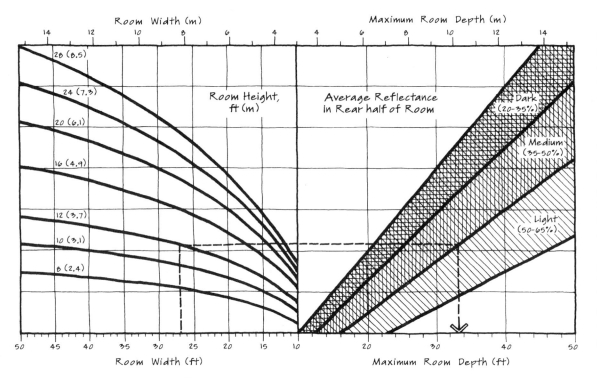

Estimating Maximum Room Depth for Daylight Uniformity

If more specific room characteristics are known, the graph for **Estimating Maximum Room Depth for Daylight Uniformity** can be used. If the room depth exceeds the maximum recommendation from the graph, the rear half of the room will look dark and supplementary electric lighting will be necessary most of the time (developed from a model in Littlefair, 1996, p. 33).

To find the maximum room depth, enter the graph on the left-side horizontal axis with the room width. Move vertically to intersect the curve for the room's ceiling height, then right to the right side of the graph and over to the diagonal zone for the average reflectance in the back half of the room. Finally, move vertically to read the maximum allowable room depth on one of the horizontal scales.

The average reflectance is a weighted average of all surfaces in the back half of the room. Remember that floors and furnishings tend to be dark and glazing has low reflectance, so even with light-colored walls and ceiling, the average reflectance of most rooms does not exceed 50%. For more on surface reflectance, see Strategy 78.

2 *EARTH EDGES* can be used to shelter buildings from extremes of heat and cold and to meet a portion of the building's cooling load. [heating and cooling]

Earth sheltering reduces heat loss and heat gain in two ways: by increasing the resistance to heat flow of the walls, roof, and floor, and by reducing the temperature difference between inside and outside. At a depth greater than 2 ft (0.6 m) below the earth's surface, daily temperature fluctuations are negligible. The effectiveness of earth contact for heating and cooling in a particular climate can be evaluated in Technique 19.

Earth sheltering takes three basic forms: either sinking the building into the excavated earth, berming the earth up around the building, or building the structure into an existing hillside. In all of these forms, earth sheltering may range from partially covered walls to totally covered walls to completely covered walls and roof. The energy and other effects of earth-sheltered roofs should be carefully weighed against the costs of structure, waterproofing, and maintenance.

Light may be admitted through skylights, by providing a courtyard or atrium, or by sidelit windows on one or more sides. It is important in designing earth-sheltered buildings to provide adequate ventilation to remove both moisture and heat. The matrix shows various design strategies for providing both light and ventilation. If direct access to the wind is not available, wind catchers (Strategy 67) or stack ventilation (Strategy 66) may be employed.

In the **Cooperative Homesteads** project, and the **Jacobs II house,** Frank Lloyd Wright used berms formed with earth from sunken gardens to protect the buildings from winter winds and provide insulation (Sergeant, 1975, pp. 76, 82). The Jacobs house is an example of a house tuned to the cold Wisconsin climate, reducing the loss of heat on the north with the berm, while opening the south wall and garden to the warming sun. The **Winston House** in New Hampshire by Don Metz (*Architectural Record*, 5/1974, p. 52) is similar to the Jacobs

Jacobs II House, Middleton, Wisconsin, Frank Lloyd Wright

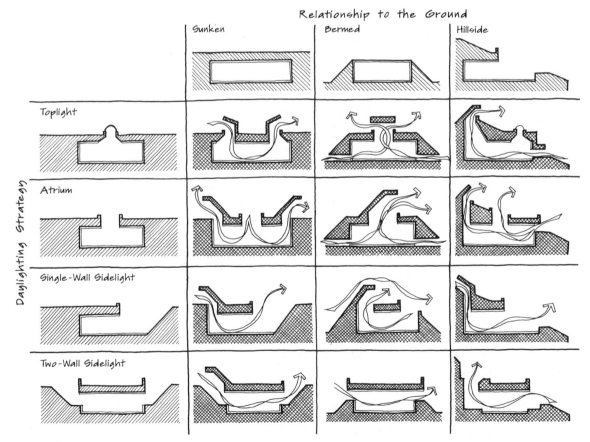

Strategies for Light and Ventilation in Different Types of Earth Sheltering

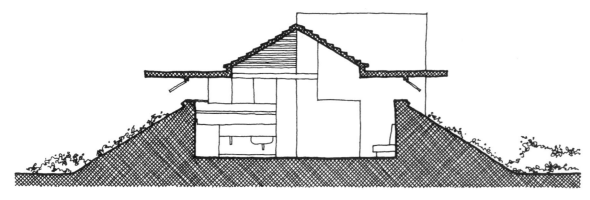

Cooperative Homesteads Project, Detroit Michigan, Frank Lloyd Wright

Winston House, Lyme, New Hampshire, Don Metz

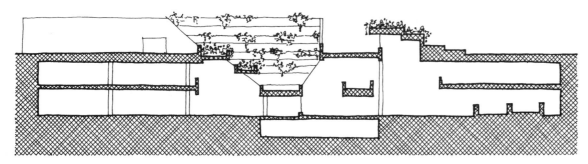

East Bank Bookstore, University of Minnesota, Minneapolis, Minnesota, Myers & Bennett

II house with its closed north and open south. However, it is built into a hillside, and the earth completely covers the roof.

The **Bookstore at the University of Minnesota** by Meyers and Bennett (*Progressive Architecture*, 1/1975, p. 52) was completely buried in the earth to increase its energy efficiency and maintain the openness of that section of the campus.

Winter heat loss can be calculated to the outside air temperature using *R*-values for the below-grade walls. Winter heat loss to the floor is usually ignored because of the small temperature difference between indoor air and the ground.

The resistance of an earth-sheltered wall (not including the wall itself) at a given depth may be estimated from the graph. Enter the graph on the left side horizontal axis with the depth below the top of the berm or grade. Then move vertically to the family of diagonal lines representing berm types, then horizontally until intersecting the soil type diagonal line. Finally, move vertically to the horizontal axis to determine the R-value of the wall at that depth. Calculate the average of the R-values at the top and bottom of the wall, or find the R at some representative

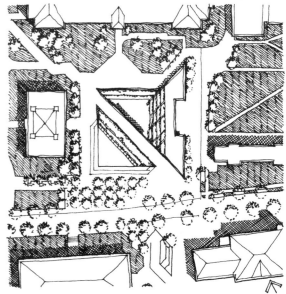

Site Plan, East Bank Bookstore

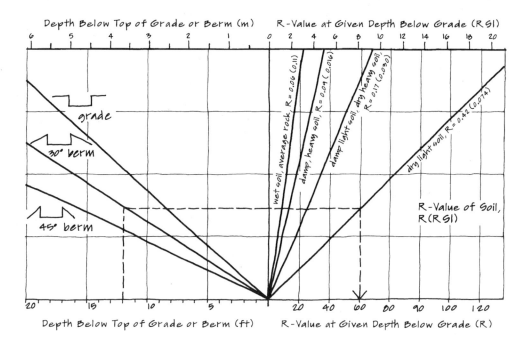

R-Values for Bermed Walls

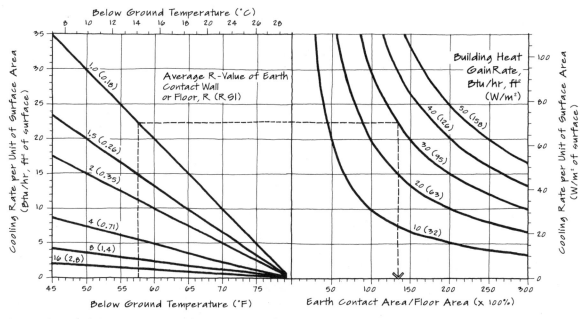

Sizing Walls and Floors for Ground Contact Cooling

intermediate depth to determine the berm's average R-value. Add this to the R of the wall itself.

The summer cooling effect from heat loss through walls and floors requires knowing the ground temperature. The mean earth temperature ranges from 45 °F (7 °C) in the northern United States to 75 °F (24 °C) in south Florida. Because the ground temperature peak lags behind surface earth temperature by 10–13 weeks, it can be used as a heat sink in some climates (Labs, 1980, p. 129). Be sure to check the appropriateness of earth sheltering in the building's climate using Technique 19. Particularly in cooling applications for humid climates, condensation on cool mass surfaces may be an issue.

To estimate the total area of ground contact surface required to meet the building's cooling load, first find the summer ground temperature for the building's site and average depth of ground contact surface from Appendix B. Enter the nomograph on the left side horizontal axis with this ground temperature. Move vertically to the line for the average R-value of the floor or wall. From the intersection, move right to the right half of the graph until intersecting the curve for the building's rate of heat gain. Then drop to the right horizontal axis to read the required ratio of earth contact area to floor area. Finally, multiply this value by the floor area to get the size of the earth contact surfaces.

The graph may also be used in reverse to evaluate the cooling of a given design; different floor and wall surfaces may be evaluated separately and their cooling rates added. The graph assumes an indoor temperature of 80 °F (26.7 °C). A relatively high indoor air temperature may feel comfortable during summer in earth sheltered buildings because the lower surface temperatures of floors and walls reduce the indoor mean radiant temperature.

73 *WATER EDGES* can be formed to cool incoming breezes. [cooling]

In hot-arid climates, water evaporating into the air can substantially reduce the air temperature. The evaporation rate and, therefore, the cooling rate depends on the surface area of the water, the velocity of the wind, the relative humidity of the air, and the water temperature. Of these, the designer has the most control over the surface area of water and its location relative to the wind direction and spaces to be cooled.

Under average wind, humidity, and temperature conditions, the cooling from 1 m² (11 ft²) of exposed water surface is about 200 W (682 Btu/hr), indicating the heat transfer between air and a horizontal film of water is poor (Santamouris & Asimakopolous, 1996, p. 111). In addition to increasing the surface area of the pond, the effective area can be increased by sprays and fountains with very fine droplets, in pools or on other surfaces (Yannas, 1995, p. 2.13). This greatly increases the heat exchange between water and air, while increasing evaporation and thus humidity. Climatic conditions when evaporative cooling is effective can be estimated from the Building Bioclimatic Chart in Technique 18.

The cooling effect can be localized in courts that trap the cool air or used to cool the air flowing through the building. The **Baha'i Temple in New Delhi,** India, by the Iranian architect Fariburz Sahba, uses nine sunken reflecting pools to cool air taken in at the basement level. The air is then drawn into the central hall and exhausted through a vent in the top of the structure, using fan assistance when required (Bahga et al., 1993; *A + U,* 11/1987; Sabinkhi, 1987).

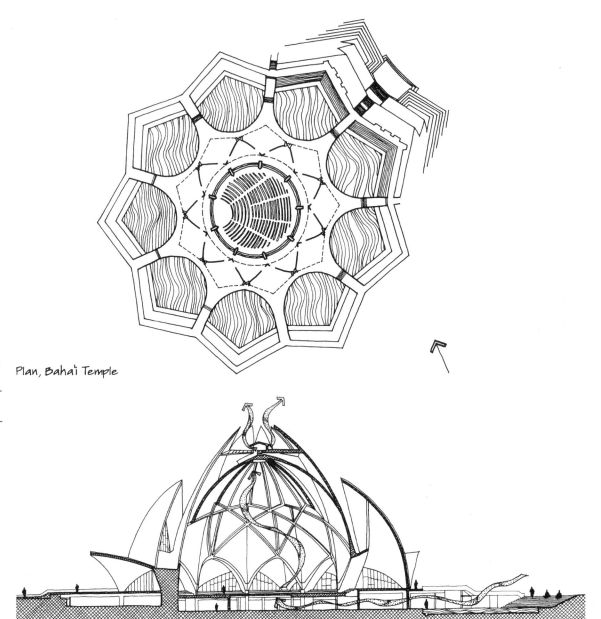

Plan, Baha'i Temple

Section, Baha'i Temple, New Delhi, India, Fariburz Sahba

COURTYARDS:
Size, Shape, and Orientation

BREEZY COURTYARDS should be low, wide, and permeable, while **CALM COURTYARDS** should be closed and tall enough for wind shelter, but wide enough to admit sun. [heating and cooling]

Inside a courtyard, wind conditions are primarily dependent on the proportion between building height and courtyard width in the section along the wind flow line. Conditions are secondarily affected by the proportions in the crosswind direction. As shown in Strategies 41 and 43, buildings create a protected zone of reduced velocity and increased turbulence, the size of which is a function of their height and width. Wind hitting the windward building of a courtyard separates from the roof and gradually returns to the ground on the leeward side of the building. Wind speed in the courtyard, therefore, generally increases with the along-wind dimensions of the courtyard and decreases with the height of the windward building. Wind speed in the courtyard will also increase for larger crosswind dimensions of the courtyard.

For the **Entrepreneurship Development Institute** in Ahmedabad, India, architect Bimal Patel sited the facility above a gradual rise and oriented the major open space to the southwest humid season wind. Even though Ahmedabad has a long spring and early summer arid season, accommodation for the monsoon-induced 3-month hot-humid season is very important. The complex is organized as a series of permeable courtyards, sized wide in relation to their height to allow more wind to flow into them. The courtyard buildings are oriented at a 45° angle to the wind, maximizing the exposure of rooms and providing opposite positive and negative pressures for each room. The single-banked rooms are open to shaded circulation arcades, and many informal shaded outdoor seating areas are provided at the edges of each court (*Architectural Review*, 10/1992, pp. 54–55; Bhatia, 1995, p. 76).

As a guide to sizing courtyards for wind conditions, the matrix shows average wind speeds in courtyards of different proportions for three incident wind angles.

Remember that to make a court big enough for summer wind, the court will provide little summer shade,

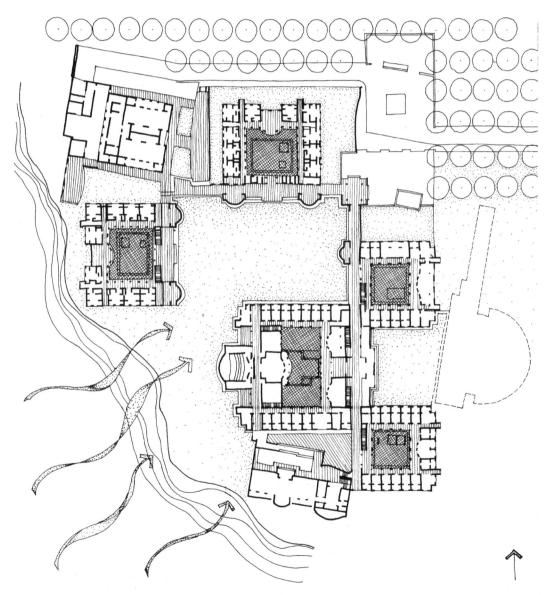

Entrepreneurship Development Institute, Ahmedabad, India, Bimal Patel

Interior of Training Center Courtyard, Entrepreneurship Development Institute

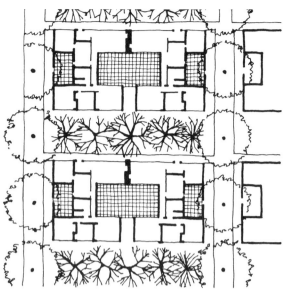

Site Plan, Housing in Alice Springs

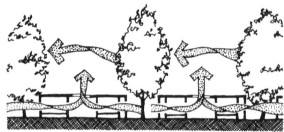

Housing in Alice Springs, Australia,
Mareuil Aitchison

so other element scale shading strategies (98, 99, 100), such as vegetation, loggia, or shading layers at the building envelope, must be employed.

In hot climates where ventilation is desired, a courtyard orientation 45° from the prevailing wind maximizes both wind in the courtyard and cross-ventilation in the buildings.

Openings between buildings into the courtyard will increase wind speeds through the opening, but will have little overall effect on the average wind in the courtyard unless the opening is located to face the prevailing wind and one or more openings are provided to allow air to exit the courtyard. In this case, wind speeds in a narrow courtyard can be greatly increased, relative to a closed court.

In cooler climates, small courts will create better wind protection, but they should be wide enough in the north–south direction to admit winter sun (Strategy 38).

When heating is a priority and solar access is not desired, courtyards with a width to height ratio less than 1.0 will afford maximum wind protection.

Remember that solar access may be desired either in the courtyard itself or for buildings facing the courtyard. Opening the courtyard to the south (north in Southern Hemisphere) or making south buildings shorter will admit more sun. Tall, narrow courts may also be appropriate in hot-arid climates where self-shading is desired, buildings are kept closed during the day, and

potentially hot and dusty winds may be undesirable (Strategy 75).

Combinations of shaded and open courts can be used to induce air flow from one to the other. In a project by Mareuil Aitchison in **Alice Springs, Australia**, courts in the center of a two-house group are heated by the sun, causing the hot air to rise and be replaced by cold air, which is then drawn through the house from the cooler shaded entrance courts (Sain, 1980, p. 90).

More details on wind in courtyards can be found in Wu (1994).

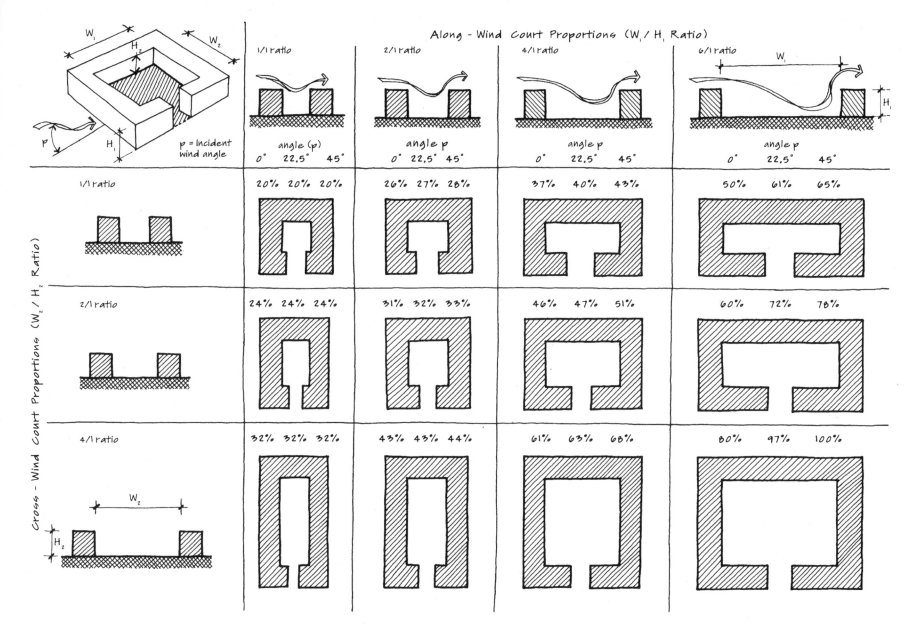

Along - Wind Court Proportions (W₁ / H₁ Ratio)

p = incident wind angle

Cross-Wind Court Proportions (W₂ / H₂ Ratio)	1/1 ratio angle (p) 0° 22.5° 45°	2/1 ratio angle p 0° 22.5° 45°	4/1 ratio angle p 0° 22.5° 45°	6/1 ratio angle p 0° 22.5° 45°
1/1 ratio	20% 20% 20%	26% 27% 28%	37% 40% 43%	50% 61% 65%
2/1 ratio	24% 24% 24%	31% 32% 33%	46% 47% 51%	60% 72% 78%
4/1 ratio	32% 32% 32%	43% 43% 44%	61% 63% 68%	80% 97% 100%

Sizing Courtyards for Ventilation
Average Wind Speeds as a Percentage of Free, Unobstructed Incident Wind (%).

75 *SHADY COURTYARDS* are tall and narrow and can be used as cold air sinks. [cooling]

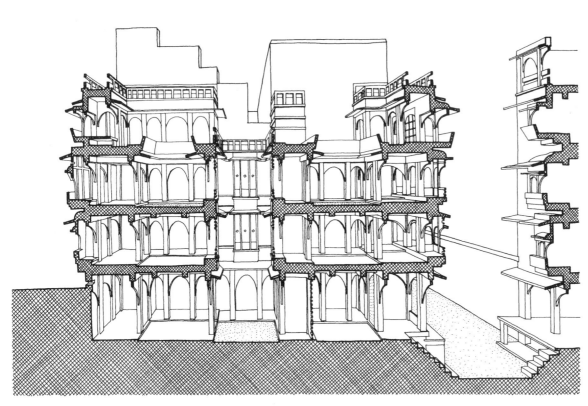

Perspective Section, City Mansion, Jaisalmer, India, 15th century

Interior Court, Ministry of Foreign Affairs

The courtyard building is a traditional and effective configuration for cooling in hot-arid climates where there is a large diurnal temperature swing. Tall courts provide shade from morning and afternoon low-angle sun, particularly if they are narrow in the east–west direction. One part of the building can cast a shadow on the court floor and opposite walls. Since the sun is high when it comes from the south (north in Southern Hemisphere), the court may be elongated in the north–south direction with little effect on the degree of shading. During the middle of the day, the court will be in the sun unless overhead shading is provided (Strategy 48).

In tall courts, wind blowing over the building won't disturb the air in the court, and dust, which is primarily held in air near the ground, will be kept out of the inner parts of the building.

At night, the building's roof and the court, especially its floor, radiate heat to the cold night sky directly overhead. Air that is next to these surfaces cools and settles to the bottom of the court. The cold air in the court cools the surrounding surfaces, which have stored heat from the daytime. During the day the court remains more comfortable than exposed outdoor areas, because its surfaces and the ambient air are relatively

cool (Koenigsberger et al., 1973, p. 205).

A beautiful example of sophisticated courtyard planning from 15th century India can be seen in the **City Mansion in Jaisalmer.** Located on a tall narrow street that provides shade to the street facade, the building is organized around three internal courtyards. The central courtyard extends four floors to the ground, while the other two courts are two stories deep, with the upper level part of a large roof terrace. Except for the stairs, kitchen, and bath, every space changes its use with the rhythms of climate. Upper rooms are used in the morning and cooler shaded lower rooms are used during the

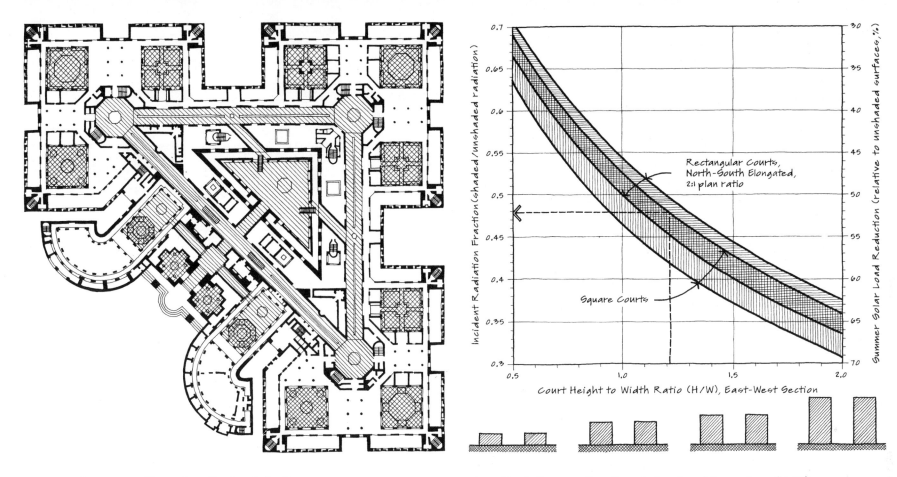

Ministry of Foreign Affairs, Riyadh, Saudi Arabia, Henning Larsens

Solar Radiation as a Function of Courtyard Proportions (H/W)
Developed using data from SHADOWPACK software (Peckham, 1990). Results are for cumulative solar radiation, Jun 1 to Aug 31, under clear sky.

day, while warmed roof terraces open to the night sky provide sleeping space (Herdeg, 1990a, pp. 17–21).

Henning Larsens merged the spareness of Danish modernism with numerous climatic strategies of desert Islamic architecture in the **Saudi Arabian Ministry of Foreign Affairs** in Riyadh. The office building for 1000 workers is organized around nine three- and four-story open-to-sky courts linked by internal *souks* (shaded pedestrian streets) surrounding a covered triangular interior court. Five of the courts have walls covered with a lattice for vegetation, offering further shade to the interior walls, while all the windows are further shaded with wooden *mashrabiyya*, grilles that filter light while

allowing ventilation. Some courts, such as the one shown, are provided with trellised pavilions. Building interiors are mostly white, while the court walls are blue, reducing glare from bright sun. Windows facing the courts are large relative to the small windows on the building exterior (*Arkitektur DK*, 1985; Abel, 1985).

Use the graph to estimate the effect of a courtyard's height to width ratio (H/W) on decreasing summer radiation falling on the court walls and floor. The overlapping curve zones indicate two court proportions: a square plan and a 1:2 rectangle, elongated north–south. Use the bottom of each zone for temperate latitudes and the upper part for tropical

latitudes. The curve for sites above 40° lat. will be lower.

East–west elongated courts have less shade and more sun on the walls and floor, as can be seen from the matrix of **Summer Season Radiation for Courtyards at 24° N. Lat.** on the next page. Each diagram shows radiation contours for the court floor and its east and west walls, which are the primary walls shaded by the court.

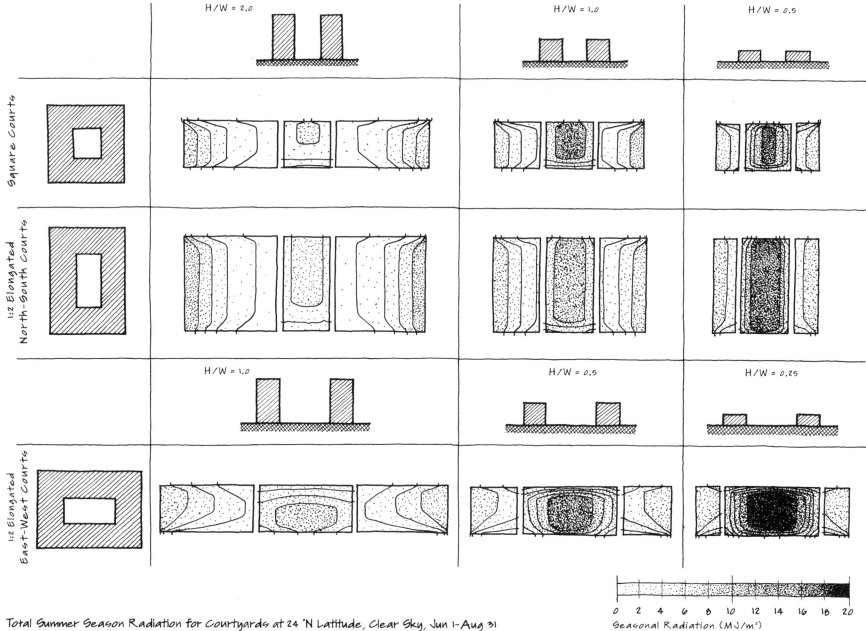

Total Summer Season Radiation for Courtyards at 24 °N Latitude, Clear Sky, Jun 1–Aug 31
Developed using SHADOWPACK software (Peckham, 1990).

Seasonal Radiation (MJ/m²)

0 2 4 6 8 10 12 14 16 18 20

IIC   Building Parts

Design strategies at this scale deal with the parts used to make rooms, courtyards, and buildings. They are the skin elements—walls, roofs, and floors—and openings in the skin, windows, doors, and skylights. Because their scale is smaller and their design may seem more detailed than larger scale formal elements, designers are often tempted to wait until very late in the design process to consider these elements. The scale of building parts, however, has an important role in supporting the systemic energy and lighting processes of the building and should not be left until the end when it may be too late to change the design. For instance, while the site and massing of building groups may be designed to insure solar access, and the shape and enclosure of a room at the building scale formed to collect solar heat, if the element scale strategies of thermal mass sizing and color, and insulation placement and thickness are not handled appropriately, the building may either overheat on a clear day or loose too much heat during the day to retain a reserve for use at night. So, the element scale strategies, which often have an affect on the characteristics of building scale patterns, should also be worked with relatively early in the design process.

Four strategies address the color and absorptance characteristics of materials. Strategy 77, Mass Surface Absorptance, considers the use of color—when to use dark colors that absorb radiation and when to use light colors that reflect radiation to mass. Strategy 79, Exterior Surface Color, addresses the role of color in helping to keep the building either cool or warm. Two strategies give design guidance on colors and finishes that reflect either light or sun. Strategy 82, Solar Reflectors, tells the designer how to increase winter solar gain to openings that do not face true south (true north in Southern Hemisphere). Strategy 78 recommends light colors to reduce contrast and evenly distribute daylight.

Three strategies discuss the placement of insulation and its impact on the design of walls and windows. Strategy 76, Skin Thickness, gives design recommendations for the envelope to accommodate sufficient insulation, while Insulation Outside, Strategy 88, suggests placing insulation outside mass, so the mass can exchange heat with the interior and support passive heating and cooling. Third, Strategy 97, Movable Insulation, shows how to keep heat from being lost through windows at night.

Four strategies address the issue of transmitting or enhancing the capture of light or sun. Strategies 84, Low Contrast; 85, Skylight Wells; and 96, Light Shelves; all give design options for reducing glare and distributing light. Strategy 101, Window and Glass Types, helps the designer select windows based on balancing concerns for blocking or admitting heat, reducing conductive heat loss/gain, and admitting light.

Two of the parts scale strategies give guidance on the size of elements related to solar heating. Strategy 83, Thermal Mass, proportions thermal storage area and thickness to sun-collecting glazing. Strategy 87, Tran-spiring Walls, shows how to preheat ventilation air with the sun. Using the sun to reduce the building's need for power to supply building services is the topic of Strategy 80, Photovoltaic Walls and Roofs, and Strategy 86, Solar Hot Water.

The nature and placement of openings in the envelope is addressed in Strategy 89, Separated or Combined Openings, and Strategy 90, Ventilation Openings Arrangement.

Five strategies at this scale give design guidelines for sizing windows. Strategy 91, Limited Nonsolar Windows, concerns reducing winter heat loss. Reflected Sunlight, Strategy 92, and Daylight Glazing, Strategy 94, guide the designer on window sizing for two common types of lighting situations. Solar Glazing, Strategy 93, establishes the relationship between sun-collecting window size and the percentage of annual heating the building gets from the sun. Air Flow Windows, Strategy 95, is a way to use windows as heat exchangers for ventilation air.

The remaining four strategies address reducing the solar heat gain to a building by various means of shading. Strategy 81, Double Skin, is intended for very hot climates on roofs and east or west walls. Strategy 98, Daylight Enhancing Shades, highlights the complex relationships between daylight and shading, while Strategies 99, External Shading, and 100, Internal and In-between Shading, help estimate sizing and performance of a variety of shading design options.

76 **The building's *SKIN THICKNESS* should be enough to accommodate the required insulation. [heating and cooling]**

There are three basic strategies for placing thermal insulation. First, the insulation may be contained within the skin cavity; second, the insulation can be applied to the surface of the skin; and in the third strategy, the insulation and structure are integrated, with no framing. At moderate, thin insulation levels, when insulation is placed within the hollow between the framing members, the overall thickness of the wall can be less than with masonry walls, which must have the insulation on their surface.

When the insulation is placed on the surface of the wall, such as on the surface of an exterior masonry wall, one side of the skin material can be left exposed, and the structure does not need to be enlarged to accommodate thicker layers of insulation. Two strategies can be combined, with some insulation placed on the skin's surface and some between the framing members. In frame structures, a continuous layer of insulation reduces thermal bridging, especially in metal stud walls. Some insulating materials also have structural characteristics: straw bales and stress skin insulated core panels (SSIC) are two examples.

Recommended insulation levels for residential buildings can be determined by finding the site's insulation zone on one of the three maps (USA, Alaska, or Canada) and then referring to the Residential Insulation Recommendations table. Hawaii and the Caribbean are considered Zone R-2.

Where a range of recommendations is given, use the low end recommendation for residences heated with natural gas, a middle value for fuel oil and LP gas, and the high end for electric heat. Recommendations in the 48 contiguous United States are based are based on life-cycle cost analyses, including assumptions about mechanical system efficiencies, economic return, and local fuel and construction costs. For site locations with fuel costs significantly above those in the building's region, insulation should be increased to the next higher zone. For recommendations based on specific locations and user-set parameters, see the www-based ZIP CODE computer program (ORNL, 1997).

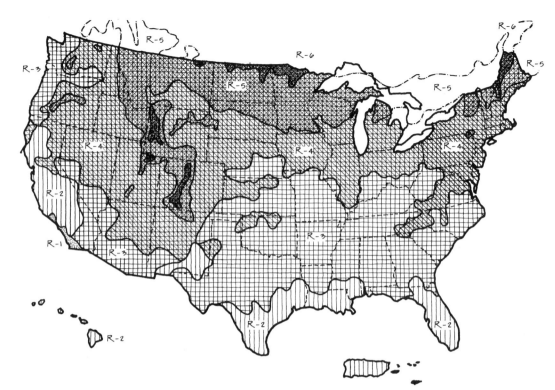

Residential Insulation Zones, Contiguous USA

Zone	Attic/Roof		Floor		Wall		Basement/Slab	
	R (RSI)	in (mm)	R (RSI)	in (mm)	R (RSI)	in (mm)	R (RSI)	in* (mm)*
R-1	22-49 (3.9-8.6)	**8-16"** **(150-350)**	11-25 (1.9-4.4)	**4-8"** **(100-200)**	13-20 (2.3-3.5)	**4-6"** **(100-150)**	0 (0)	**0"** **(0)**
R-2	38-49 (6.7-8.6)	**12-16"** **(300-350)**	13-25 (2.3-4.4)	**4-8"** **(100-200)**	15-20 (2.6-3.5)	**6"** **(100-150)**	0 (0)	**0"** **(0)**
R-3	49 (8.6)	**16"** **(350)**	25 (4.4)	**8"** **(200)**	15-22 (2.6-3.9)	**6-8"** **(100-150)**	10 (1.8)	**2"** **(50)**
R-4	49 (8.6)	**16"** **(350)**	25 (4.4)	**8"** **(200)**	15-28 (2.6-4.9)	**6-10"** **(100-200)**	16 (2.8)	**3"** **(100)**
R-5	49 (8.6)	**16"** **(350)**	25 (4.4)	**8"** **(200)**	21-28 (3.7-4.9)	**8-10"** **(150-200)**	20 (3.5)	**4"** **(100)**
R-6	49 (8.6)	**16"** **(350)**	30 (5.3)	**10"** **(250)**	25-28 (4.4-4.9)	**8-10"** **(200)**	20 (3.5)	**4"** **(100)**
R-7	49 (8.6)	**16"** **(350)**	38 (6.7)	**12"** **(300)**	30 (5.3)	**10"** **(250)**	25 (4.4)	**5"** **(150)**
R-8	52 (9.5)	**18"** **(400)**	43 (7.6)	**14"** **(350)**	35 (6.2)	**12"** **(300)**	N/A	N/A

* basement/slab thickness assumes rigid insulation, all other thicknesses assume batt insulation

Residential Insulation Recommendations

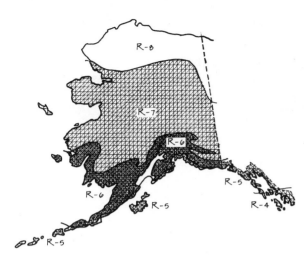

Residential Insulation Zones, Alaska

For Canadian residences, the recommendations exceed the *R*-2000 energy efficiency standards (CHBA, 1994, p. 320) and are based on extending the ORNL system, based on the number of heating degree days. Recommendations for Alaska are similar to those of the 1991 Building Energy Efficiency Standard (AHFC, 1999, App. A).

Recommended insulation levels for skin-load-dominated, passively cooled buildings are based on maintaining a temperature difference between inside and out and on reducing solar gain. If cooling strategies like cross-ventilation and stack-ventilation are used, the inside temperature is slightly higher than the outside, so insulation isn't needed to reduce the heat flow due to the temperature difference. It is needed only to reduce the heat flow due to solar radiation. If walls and roofs are protected from solar gain by full shading and/or radiant barriers, insulation levels can be significantly reduced.

In nonresidential buildings, winter heat losses are partially or totally offset by internal gains, so they tend to need more cooling than heating. The temperature difference between inside and outside during the cooling season is typically much smaller than during the heating season. Consequently, the proportion of the building's heat flow due to conductive transfer through the skin can be relatively small. In fact, in buildings with higher internal loads (low balance point

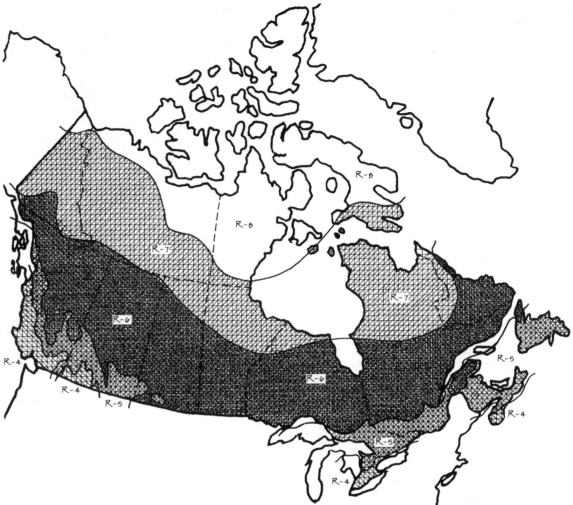

Residential Insulation Zones, Canada

temperature) set in moderate climates, insulation can reduce the building's ability to lose heat. Thus, recommended insulation levels in nonresidential buildings are usually lower than those for residential buildings.

Recommended insulation levels for non-residential buildings can be determined by finding the site's insulation zone on the nonresidential zone map (at right) and then referring to the table, Recommended Minimum Nonresidential Buildings Insulation Recommendations.

The *Model Energy Code (MEC)* gives minimum prescriptive requirements for commercial buildings in different climates, based on the ASHRAE 90.1 standard (ASHRAE, 1989a). Values shown in the table meet or exceed the values given by the *MEC* prescriptive requirements. Many states and some cities have their own energy codes with requirements more stringent than the *MEC*. The table assumes steel frame walls, continuous roof insulation, cavity floor insulation, and windows 10–25% of the wall area. For other options, see U.S. Department of Energy (1997b, 1998).

Depending on the type of insulation used, walls, roofs, and floors may be relatively thin, as in the section from the **Cascadia Prototype House,** which uses stressed skin insulated core panels that have *R*-4/in (RSI-0.28/cm) rigid expanded polystyrene (ESBL, 1997). When the material used is less resistive, the envelope needs to become thicker to provide sufficient insulation, such as in Bill Cook's **Guest House in Sonoita, AZ** which uses *R*-1.5/in (RSI-0.10/cm) straw bales (Steen et al., 1994, p. 162).

Insulation thickness in inches can be approximated by dividing the recommended insulation levels by 3 for fiberglass batt insulation and by 5 for rigid insulation. Insulation thickness in centimeters can be approximated by dividing the recommended RSI insulation levels by 0.2 for fiberglass batt insulation and by 0.4 for rigid insulation. R-values per unit thickness for several insulating materials are given in the table on the next page. A detailed listing of R-values can be found in ASHRAE (1997) or Hoke (1996).

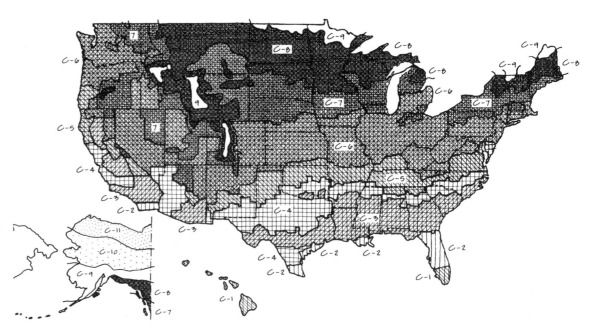

Zone	Attic / Roof R (RSI)	Attic / Roof in (mm)	Floor R (RSI)	Floor in (mm)	Wall R (RSI)	Wall in (mm)	Basement / Slab R (RSI)	Basement / Slab in* (mm)*
C-1	12-18 (2.1-3.2)	**4-6"** **(100-150)**	0-6 (0-1.1)	**0-2"** **(0-50)**	0 (0)	**0"** **(0)**	0 (0)	**0"** **(0)**
C-2	12-18 (2.1-3.2)	**4-6"** **(100-150)**	6-12 (1.1-2.1)	**2-4"** **(50-100)**	0-6 (0-1.1)	**0-2"** **(0-50)**	0 (0)	**0"** **(0)**
C-3	12-18 (2.1-3.2)	**2-3"** **(100-150)**	6-12 (1.1-2.1)	**2-4"** **(50-100)**	6-12 (1.1-2.1)	**2-4"** **(50-100)**	0 (0)	**0"** **(0)**
C-4	18-24 (3.2-4.2)	**6-8"** **(150-200)**	6-12 (1.1-2.1)	**2-4"** **(50-100)**	6-12 (1.1-2.1)	**2-4"** **(50-100)**	0 (0)	**0"** **(0)**
C-5	18-24 (3.2-4.2)	**6-8"** **(150-200)**	12-18 (2.1-3.2)	**4-6"** **(100-150)**	12-18 (2.1-3.2)	**4-6"** **(100-150)**	0-6 (0-1.1)	**0-1"** **(0-50)**
C-6	18-24 (3.2-4.2)	**6-8"** **(150-200)**	24-30 (4.2-5.3)	**8-10"** **(200-250)**	12-18 (2.1-3.2)	**4-6"** **(100-150)**	6-12 (1.1-2.1)	**1-2"** **(50)**
C-7	24-30 (4.2-5.3)	**8-10"** **(200-250)**	24-30 (4.2-5.3)	**8-10"** **(200-250)**	18-24 (3.2-4.2)	**6-8"** **(150-200)**	12-18 (2.1-3.2)	**2-3"** **(50-75)**
C-8	30-36 (5.3-6.4)	**10-12"** **(250-300)**	24-30 (4.2-5.3)	**8-10"** **(200-250)**	18-24 (3.2-4.2)	**6-8"** **(150-200)**	18-22 (3.2-3.9)	**3-4"** **(75-100)**
C-9	36-42 (6.4-7.4)	**12-14"** **(300-350)**	30-36 (5.3-6.4)	**10-12"** **(250-300)**	24-30 (4.2-5.3)	**8-10"** **(200-250)**	18-22 (3.2-3.9)	**3-4"** **(75-100)**
C-10	42-48 (7.4-8.5)	**14-16"** **(350-400)**	30-36 (5.3-6.4)	**10-12"** **(250-300)**	30-36 (5.3-6.4)	**10-12"** **(250-300)**	22-26 (3.9-4.6)	**4-5"** **(100-125)**
C-11	54 (9.5)	**18"** **(450)**	42 (7.4)	**14"** **(350)**	36 (6.4)	**12"** **(300)**	N/A	**N/A**

* basement/slab thickness assumes rigid insulation, all other thicknesses assume batt insulation

Recommended Minimum Nonresidential Insulation

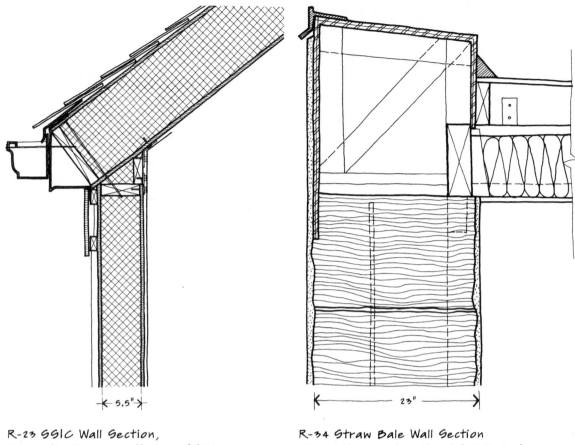

INSULATION TYPE	R-per inch (RSI-per cm)	
Cavity Insulations		
Straw bale	1.5	(0.10)
Cotton batt or loose fill	3.0-3.7	(0.21-0.26)
Fiberglass blanket or batt	2.9-3.8	(0.20-0.26)
High performance fiberglass blanket/batt	3.7-4.3	(0.26-0.30)
Loose-fill fiberglass	2.3-2.7	(0.16-0.19)
Loose-fill rock wool	2.7-3.0	(0.19-0.21)
Loose-fill cellulose	3.4-3.7	(0.24-0.26)
Perlite or vermiculite	2.4-3.7	(0.17-0.26)
Cavity Insulations, spray		
Spray cellulose	2.9-3.5	(0.20-0.24)
Spray fiberglass	3.7-3.9	(0.26-0.27)
Cementitious foam	3.9	(0.27)
Spray polyurethane foam	5.6-6.3	(0.39-0.44)
Surface Insulations, rigid		
Mineral fiberboard	2.9	(0.20)
Expanded polystyrene board	3.6-4.0	(0.25-0.28)
Fiberglass board	4	(0.28)
Icynene	4.3	(0.27)
Extruded polystyrene board, unfaced	4.5-5.0	(0.31-0.35)
Polyisocyanurate board, foil-faced	7.0	(0.49)

R-23 SSIC Wall Section,
Cascadia Prototype House, ESBL

R-34 Straw Bale Wall Section
Guest House, Sonoita, AZ, Bill Cook

Resistance Values of Insulation Materials

77 *MASS SURFACE ABSORPTANCE* for interior thermal storage should be high to absorb radiation, while nonmassive surfaces should be reflective to redirect radiation to mass. [heating]

When solar radiation strikes a surface, a portion of the energy is absorbed and the rest is reflected. If too little is absorbed by massive surfaces, the room air can become hot. Absorptance of a material depends on the color, finish, and type of material. Massive floors in direct-gain spaces should generally be dark to absorb solar radiation. As the mass surface area in a room increases beyond three times the area of solar glazing, absorptance is less important.

If a mass surface is the first to be struck by the sun but is a small part of the total mass area, then that surface should be moderately reflective so that radiation is spread to other absorbing surfaces. If more than half the walls in a room are massive, they can be light in color. If only one wall is massive, it should be dark. In sunspaces, light-colored surfaces can reflect sun back out of the sunspace.

When the ratio of mass surface area to solar glazing area is 3:1 or less, materials used to absorb and store solar radiation should be at least 50% absorbent (Balcomb et al., 1984, pp. 12.8–12.10). The surfaces of lightweight, nonmassive materials should be light in color, at least 50% reflectance, so that they will reflect solar radiation to the massive surfaces.

These principles are evident in Fernau and Hartman's **Broadhead House,** in La Honda, California. The quarry tile covering the entire main floor is dark red-brown to absorb direct gain from south-facing windows in the living room, dining area, and the hallway connecting them. Nonmassive walls and the ceiling are white, reflecting light to other surfaces. A masonry core wall containing a fireplace wraps around the two-story entrance hall and extends up to catch sun from the upper hall. Mostly not in the sun, the wall is composed of layers of a medium tan concrete block slump stone alternated with smooth gray block (*GA Houses*, 1982; Woodbridge, 1981).

Thermal storage wall mass should have high absorptance, such as flat black paint, on the outside or a "se-

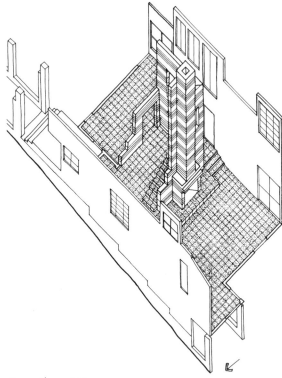

Broadhead House,
La Honda, CA, Fernau & Hartman

lective surface," such as a dark metallic foil, with high absorptance and low emittance. The influence of a low-emittance exterior surface is much less significant for glazing beyond a single layer. In relative terms, absorptance is about five times more influential on the SSF performance of thermal storage walls than is emittance (Balcomb et al., 1984, pp. 2.13–2.18, 14.8–14.12).

Solar Absorptance/Reflectance of Finishes are given in the table. Both factors, absorptance and emittance, can be compared, for selected materials, in the graph, Surface Properties of Materials, in Strategy 81.

Color/Material	Absorptance	Reflectance
optical flat black paint	**0.98**	0.02
flat black paint	**0.95**	0.05
black lacquer	**0.92**	0.08
dark grey paint	**0.91**	0.09
black concrete	**0.91**	0.09
dark blue lacquer	**0.91**	0.09
black oil paint	**0.90**	0.10
stafford blue bricks	**0.89**	0.11
dark olive drab paint	**0.89**	0.11
dark brown paint	**0.88**	0.12
dark blue-gray paint	**0.88**	0.12
azure blue / dark green lacquer	**0.88**	0.12
brown concrete	**0.85**	0.15
medium brown paint	**0.84**	0.16
medium light brown paint	**0.80**	0.20
brown or green lacquer	**0.79**	0.21
medium rust paint	**0.78**	0.22
light grey oil paint	**0.75**	0.25
red oil paint	**0.74**	0.26
red bricks	**0.70**	0.30
uncolored concrete	**0.65**	0.35
moderately light buff bricks	**0.60**	0.40
medium dull green paint	**0.59**	0.41
medium orange paint	**0.58**	0.42
medium yellow paint	**0.57**	0.43
medium blue paint	**0.51**	0.49
medium kelly green paint	**0.51**	0.49
light green paint	0.47	0.53
white semi-gloss paint	0.30	0.70
white gloss paint	0.25	0.75
silver paint	0.25	0.75
white lacquer	0.21	0.79
polished aluminum reflector	0.12	0.88
aluminized mylar film	0.10	0.90
lab vapor-deposited coatings	0.02	0.98

Solar Absorptance/Reflectance of Finishes

78 *DAYLIGHT REFLECTING SURFACES* **that are light colored increase the lighting level in the space. [daylighting]**

As one moves away from a daylight source, whether window or skylight, the amount of light provided directly from the sky decreases, and the proportion provided by reflection from interior surfaces increases. For example, consider a sidelit room, with the depth approximately equal to twice the height and the glazing area equal to about 20% of the floor area. The illumination 10 ft (3 m) from the window is 62% from the sky and 38% from internal reflections, while at 20 ft (6 m) from the window, 44% of the illumination is from the sky and 66% from internal reflections. The reflectivity of the interior surfaces is extremely important in enhancing the daylight factor's internally reflected component, which is a substantial part of the illumination level away from the window. For example, the internally reflected light in our sidelit room changes from a daylight factor of 0.1% to 1.1% to 3.4% as the reflectance of interior surfaces varies from 10% to 40% to 80% (Hopkinson et al., 1966, pp. 441–442).

It is important that the surface that first reflects the daylight be light in color to increase the amount of light reflected into the space. This surface may be the floor when light is coming directly from the sky, or the ceiling if the light is being reflected from exterior ground surfaces. For approximate reflectances, consult the table, Daylight Reflectance of Colors.

In the main auditorium at the **Institute of Technology, at Otaniemi,** Finland, Aalto used light-colored baffles and upper ceiling surfaces to reflect and completely diffuse the south sunlight throughout the auditorium space (Fleig, 1975, p. 88).

Light colors on surfaces near the daylight glazing and on window mullions can also reduce glare. See details in Strategy 84, Low Contrast.

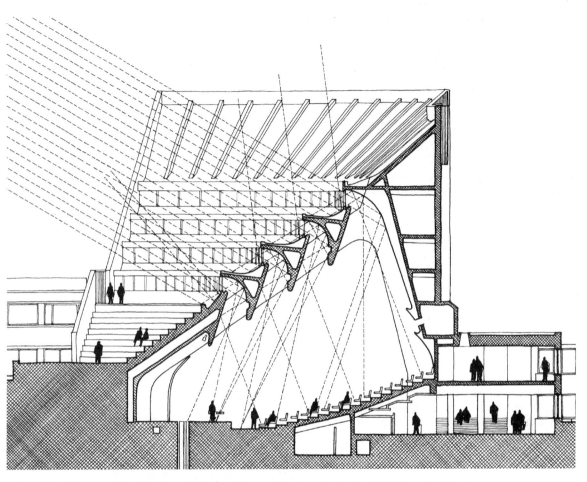

Main Auditorium, Institute of Technology, Otaniemi, Finland, Alvar Aalto

Surface	Recommended Reflectance (%)
Ceilings	70-80
Walls	40-80
Floors	20-40

Recommended Finish Reflectances

Color	Reflectance (%)
white	80-90
pale yellow & rose	80
pale beige & lilac	70
pale blue & green	70-75
mustard yellow	35
medium brown	25
medium blue & green	20-30
black	10

Daylight Reflectance of Colors

79 *EXTERIOR SURFACE COLOR* **should be dark in cold climates to absorb radiation and light in hot climates to reflect radiation. [heating and cooling]**

In cold climates, the surface temperature of exterior walls and roofs can be increased with the use of dark exterior materials. Since heat flow through the building's envelope is proportional to the temperature difference between inside and outside, raising the external surface temperature by increasing the solar radiation absorbed reduces envelope heat loss. For reflectance and absorptance values of materials, see Strategy 81 and, for roofing materials, the table on the next page.

The Tegnestuen Vandkunsten has designed several housing developments in Denmark using black exteriors, such as these **Rowhouses in Ballerup** (*A + W*, 9/1997; Schneider, 1996).

In hot climates, dark surfaces absorb heat and raise the air temperature around them. Increasing a building's reflectance, and therefore reducing its solar load, can reduce cooling energy use by 7–12% in newer, well insulated houses and 13–22% in older, poorly insulated houses, for buildings in U. S. cities with hot summers. The combined cooling energy savings from the effects of increased reflectance on reducing solar gain and outdoor temperature are estimated at up to 50% during average conditions and 30% during peak cooling hours (Akbari et al., 1992).

Surfaces that reflect more sun in summer will also reflect more sun in winter and can increase the heating load. In hot climates the summertime benefit greatly outweighs the wintertime penalty. Because the summer sun is high, reflective roofs work best then and have little effect on reducing heat gains in winter, when the sun mainly shines low and from the south side (north in Southern Hemisphere). At temperate latitudes, the same holds for east and west walls, which intercept only low levels of radiation in winter, but if light in color can reflect intense summer sun. High reflectance walls can cause glare in sunny clear sky climates, particularly if specular reflections hit windows in nearby buildings. To reduce this possibility, use materials and surfaces that diffuse the sunlight.

The surface temperature of a material is dependent

Rowhouses, Ballerup, Denmark, Tegnestuen Vandkunsten

Sangath, Ahmedabad, India, Balkrishna Doshi

on both its ability to reject solar radiation (its solar reflectance) and its ability to release back to the environment heat that it absorbs (its infrared emittance). Balkrishna Doshi used both of these factors in developing the vaulted roofs of **Sangath,** his studio in Ahmedabad, India. The vaults are made of two layers of ferrocement with hollow clay tile between. The surface of the vaults and much of the outdoor surfaces and pools are finished with broken white-glazed ceramic tiles. The white ceramic has a high reflectance and a high emittance, so it absorbs only a small fraction of the insolation, and freely releases what it does absorb (*A + U,* 7/1997b; *Architecture d'aujourd'hui,* 9/1983; Steele, 1998; *Architecture,* 8/1993).

The Solar Reflectance Index (SRI) is a measure of a material's ability to reject solar heat, as shown by its temperature rise under full sun. It is defined so that a standard black (reflectance 0.05, emittance 0.90) has an SRI of 0 and a standard white (reflectance 0.80, emittance 0.90) has an SRI of 100. Materials with higher SRI values are cooler.

Note from the table of **Solar Reflectance Index of Roofing Materials** that some materials, such as aluminum and galvanized steel, are highly reflective, but have a low emittance. These materials will heat up over the course of the day. If exposed underneath, they radiate this absorbed heat to occupants and interior surfaces. White materials have both high reflectance and high emittance. Look for SRI ratings on manufacturers' product labeling. ***For internal-load-dominated buildings in temperate climates, and all buildings in hot climates, select materials with an SRI above 50 (LBL, 1999).***

Roofing Material	Solar Reflectance	Infrared Emittance	Temperature Rise	Solar Reflectance Index (SRI)
Asphalt				
Premium white	0.36	0.91	59 F (33 C)	41
Generic white	0.25	0.91	70 F (39 C)	27
Grey	0.22	0.91	73 F (41 C)	23
Light brown	0.19	0.91	76 F (42 C)	19
Medium brown	0.12	0.91	83 F (46 C)	9
Dark brown	0.08	0.91	87 F (48 C)	4
Black	0.05	0.91	90 F (50 C)	0
Metal				
Steel, galvanized	0.61	0.04	55 F (31 C)	46
Aluminum	0.61	0.25	48 F (27 C)	56
Siliconized polyester, white	0.59	0.85	37 F (21 C)	71
Tiles				
Metal, white	0.67	0.85	28 F (16 C)	82
Clay, red	0.33	0.9	62 F (34 C)	41
Concrete, red	0.18	0.91	77 F (43 C)	23
Cement, unpainted	0.25	0.9	70 F (39 C)	31
Concrete, light brown	0.42	0.9	53 F (29 C)	49
Fiber cement, earth brown	0.26	0.9	69 F (38 C)	28
Coatings				
White polymer	0.7-0.85	0.86-0.91	9-24 F (5-13 C)	88-107
Light yellow	0.79	0.91	16 F (9 C)	99
Gray	0.40	0.91	55 F (31 C)	47
Dark blue	0.12	0.91	83 F (46 C)	9
Aluminized	0.61	0.25	48 F (27 C)	56

Solar Reflectance Index of Roofing Materials

80 *PHOTOVOLTAIC ROOFS AND WALLS* should be oriented to collect sun and large enough to meet the building's electric load. [power]

Photovoltaic cells (PVs) convert sunlight to direct current electricity. Like any solar collection surface, photovoltaics collect more sun when oriented properly. A true south-facing (true north in Southern Hemisphere) orientation maximizes yield. *Solar collection surfaces should be oriented within 30° of south (N in SH).* At higher latitudes, winter yield will be significantly reduced for non-south orientation (non-N in SH). At tropical latitudes, because the sun is high, tilt can be more important than orientation. See Strategy 59 for more detail on the effects of orientation on collected solar radiation.

Maximize winter production by setting collector tilt at an angle above horizontal equal to the latitude (in degrees) plus 15°. Summer production is maximized by setting collector tilt at latitude minus 15°. Overall annual production is maximized by setting collector tilt to match the site's latitude.

Collectors may be mounted on flat or sloping roofs, or on south-facing walls. Vertical mounting will reduce output substantially, especially at lower latitudes and in summer, when the sun is at a higher altitude angle.

PV arrays may be integrated with the building's design in various ways. They may be 1) mounted on racks and attached to the building's structure; 2) affixed to short stand-off mounts above the weather envelope; 3) integrally mounted to the structure, with PV's serving as the building skin; or 4) integrated as a part of other materials, such as roofing tiles, spandrel panels, shading devices, or glazing.

Roof design strategies that support the use of photovoltaics include 1) roof ridges oriented east–west; 2) larger roofs sloped toward the south (N in SH), with smaller roofs sloped to the north (S in SH); and 3) chimneys, plumbing vents, and other roof penetrations located on non-south (non-N in SH) oriented roofs.

In the **Children's Day Home** (*Kindertagesstätte*), in Frankfurt, Germany, architects Funk and Schröder used photovoltaics attached on short stand-off mounts above the 45° sloped glazing of the large south-facing "glass house." The glass house connects a service building to

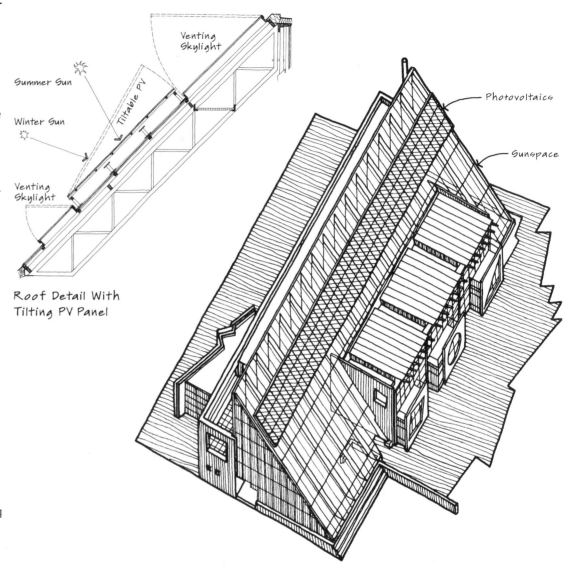

Roof Detail With Tilting PV Panel

Children's Day Home, Frankfurt, Germany, Funk and Schröder

the north with two floors of children's houses on the south side. The PVs are hinged to pivot to a steeper angle for maximized winter collection (Humm & Toggweiler, 1993; *A + W*, 3/1991).

Photovoltaics can perform a second function as architectural shading. PVs mounted on frames above the roof were used by Nicholas Grimshaw & Partners to power the lighting and evaporative wall water pumps while shading the roof and skylights of the **U. K. Pavilion at Expo 92** in Seville, Spain (Davies, 1992; Haryott, 1992).

Photovoltaics can be sized to match the building's electric load (or some fraction of it) or to reduce peak electric loads during expensive summer rate periods. To look up electric loads, see Technique 24. The amount of

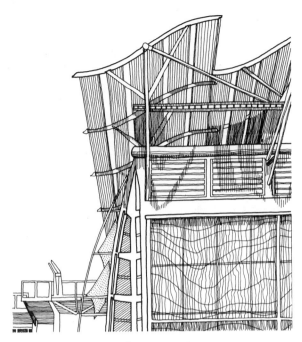

UK Pavillion, Expo '92, Seville, Spain, Nicholas Grimschaw & Partners

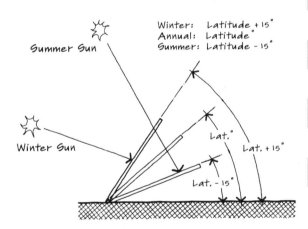

Summer Sun

Winter: Latitude + 15°
Annual: Latitude°
Summer: Latitude - 15°

Winter Sun

Lat.°
Lat. + 15°
Lat. - 15°

Recommended PV Tilts

	DECEMBER		ANNUAL			
	Tilt = Lat + 15		Tilt = Lat		Tilt = 90	
U.S. CITIES	Wh/m² d	Wh/ft² d	Wh/m² d	Wh/ft² d	Wh/m² d	Wh/ft² d
AK, Anchorage	139	12.9	341	31.7	283	26.3
AK, Annette	166	15.4	333	31.0	256	23.8
AK, Barrow	247	23.0	299	27.8	264	24.5
AK, Fairbanks	126	11.7	378	35.1	322	30.0
AK, Kotzebue	182	17.0	373	34.7	326	30.3
AR, Little Rock	387	36.0	525	48.8	330	30.7
AZ, Phoenix	511	47.5	654	60.8	413	38.4
CA, Fresno	330	30.7	596	55.5	360	33.5
CA, Los Angeles	442	41.1	581	54.0	372	34.6
CT, Hartford	325	30.2	478	44.4	331	30.8
DC, Washington	271	25.2	504	46.9	336	31.3
FL, Jacksonville	415	38.6	518	48.2	318	29.5
FL, Miami	454	42.2	527	49.0	312	29.0
IA, Des Moines	380	35.3	517	48.1	360	33.5
IA, Sioux City	387	36.0	519	48.2	372	34.6
ID, Boise	329	30.6	547	50.9	382	35.5
IN, Indianapolis	321	29.8	495	46.0	329	30.6
KS, Dodge City	477	44.3	591	55.0	398	37.0
LA, New Orleans	390	36.3	518	48.1	306	28.5
ME, Caribou	353	32.8	466	43.3	359	33.4
MN, Minneapolis	363	33.7	503	46.8	364	33.8
MO, St. Louis	359	33.4	510	47.4	346	32.2
MS, Jackson	397	36.9	531	49.4	320	29.8
MT, Billings	397	36.9	543	50.5	394	36.6
MT, Cut Bank	360	33.5	527	49.0	399	37.1
NE, North Platte	465	43.3	570	53.0	405	37.6
NM, Tucumcari	514	47.8	628	58.4	424	39.5
NV, Ely	506	47.0	628	58.4	440	40.9
NY, Buffalo	271	25.2	448	41.7	300	27.9
OR, Medford	237	22.1	523	48.7	336	31.2
OR, Salem	220	20.5	444	41.3	305	28.4
PA, Philadelphia	335	31.2	493	45.8	336	31.2
PI, Guam	468	43.5	513	47.7	258	24.0
PR, San Juan	466	43.3	550	51.1	287	26.7
SC, Charleston	419	38.9	515	47.9	339	31.5
TN, Knoxville	361	33.6	500	46.5	325	30.2

	DECEMBER		ANNUAL			
	Tilt = Lat + 15		Tilt = Lat		Tilt = 90	
U.S. CITIES	Wh/m² d	Wh/ft² d	Wh/m² d	Wh/ft² d	Wh/m² d	Wh/ft² d
TX, Brownsville	375	34.9	511	47.5	283	26.3
TX, Fort Worth	448	41.7	559	52.0	347	32.3
TX, Houston	430	40.0	496	46.2	295	27.4
TX, Midland	515	47.9	621	57.7	380	35.3
UT, Salt Lake C.	358	33.3	565	52.6	381	35.4
VA, Roanoke	383	35.6	510	47.5	346	32.2
WA, Seattle	174	16.2	417	38.8	296	27.6
WI, Madison	355	33.0	491	45.7	355	33.0
WV, Charleston	313	29.1	472	43.9	304	28.2
WY, Rock Spr.	454	42.2	600	55.8	421	39.2
CANADA						
AB, Edmonton	375	34.8	528	49.1	442	41.1
AB, Suffield	367	34.1	536	49.9	426	39.6
BC, Vancouver	153	14.2	392	36.4	278	25.8
BC, Prince Geo.	182	16.9	395	36.8	306	28.4
MB, Winnipeg	349	32.5	504	46.8	403	37.5
NB, Fredericton	289	26.8	437	40.6	334	31.0
NF, St. John's	191	17.8	370	34.4	278	25.8
NS, Halifax	273	25.4	427	39.7	321	29.8
NT, Norman W.	231	21.5	422	39.3	373	34.7
NT, Yellowknife	170	15.8	467	43.4	409	38.0
NT, Resolute	364	33.9	430	40.0	404	37.6
NT, Baker Lake	191	17.8	486	45.2	442	41.1
ON, Moosonee	283	26.3	439	40.8	358	33.3
ON, Ottawa	262	24.4	448	41.6	336	31.2
ON, Toronto	199	18.5	425	39.5	302	28.1
ON, Thunder Bay	404	37.6	518	48.2	412	38.3
QC, Inukjuak	244	22.7	476	44.3	415	38.6
QC, Quebec City	358	33.3	480	44.7	374	34.8
QC, Schefferville	352	32.7	455	42.3	396	36.9
SK, Swift Current	379	35.2	533	49.6	428	39.8
YT, Whitehorse	132	12.3	393	36.6	327	30.4

Developed using RETScreen software (CANMET, 1998).

Yield from Photovoltaics, Wh/m², day (Wh/ft², day)

electricity produced by photovoltaic surfaces depends on the energy incident on the surface, the efficiency of the PV cells, and the ambient outdoor temperature.

Buildings producing their own electricity with PVs either can be connected to the utility grid or may be completely self-sufficient. Grid-connected systems buy power from the utility at night and sell power when the PVs produce more power than the building needs during the day. Stand-alone systems must be appropriately sized to account for cloudy day storage and battery storage losses. For stand-alone PV system design, see CANMET (1991) or Sandia (1991).

To determine the minimum roof or wall area for grid-connected nonresidential photovoltaics:

1) Look up the building's electric load in Technique 24. Reduce the total load to the load that is the desired design target. For instance, if the design target is 40% of your total electric load, multiply the total load by 0.4. For grid-integrated buildings, 100% of the load will rarely be economically practical.

2) Find the rate of PV Yield, in Watt-hours (Wh) per

unit of PV area, from the table. Select a city that most closely matches the building's site. A map of climate zones is given in Appendix A for reference. If winter peak load sizing is critical (usually off-grid buildings), use the values for December; otherwise, use the average annual performance values (usually grid-connected buildings).

3) Enter the graph, **Nonresidential PV Sizing,** on the horizontal axis with the load from Step 1. Move vertically to the diagonal line for the PV system yield (from Step 2). From the intersection, move left to

read the PV array area as a fraction of the building floor area. Finally, multiply this value by the floor area to get PV array area.

To determine the minimum roof or wall area for grid-connected residential photovoltaics, use the graph, Residential PV Sizing.

The methods assume a 12% cell efficiency, and losses totaling 10% for power conditioning, wiring, dirt and snow, and downtime. For efficiencies other than 12%, multiply the PV array area from Step 3 by the ratio of 0.12/actual efficiency of the cells. PV cell efficiencies

vary from 4 to 28%. Efficiency is a function of the cell technology and the outdoor temperature. Efficiency decreases as the temperature increases, thus good air circulation behind modules is advisable.

Typical module efficiencies are amorphous silicon, 4-6%; mono-crystalline silicon, 12-16%; and polycrystalline silicon, 9-12% (Hamm & Toggweiler, 1993; Sick & Erge, 1996). Crystalline silicon is the most common PV cell type, but amorphous silicon has advantages of lower embodied energy, lower cost, and application on curved surfaces.

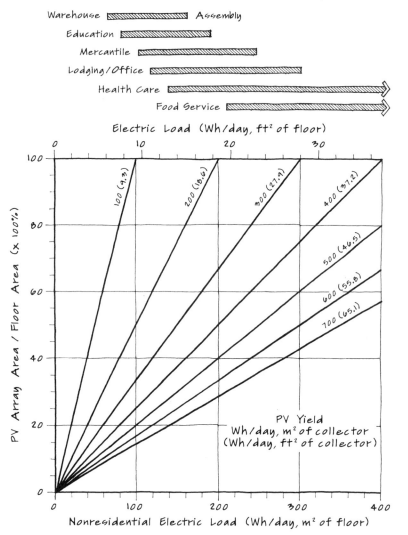

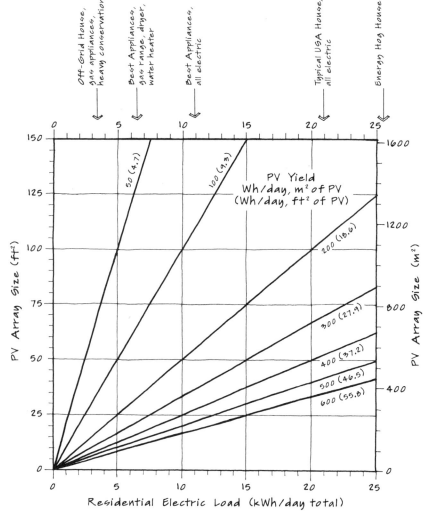

Residential PV Sizing

81 *DOUBLE-SKIN MATERIALS* should be selected to reflect solar heat gain and avoid transmitting heat to the inner layer. [cooling]

In summer, when sun strikes the exterior of a building, part of it is reflected and part is absorbed by the exterior materials. Of the portion that is absorbed, some of that heat will migrate inward via conduction. The effect can be to raise the surface temperature of the envelope well above the ambient air temperature, thus increasing heat gain to the building. Double-skin systems are a cooling load reduction strategy applicable in hot climates on exposures with the highest summer solar radiation, usually roofs and east and west facades. The outer secondary skin provides shade for inner opaque walls, roof, and/or windows, while ventilation in the cavity between the skins removes excess heat that passes through the outer skin.

The efficiency of a double-skin cavity at reducing radiant solar gain is a function of the absorptivity of the outer skin, the emissivity of the cavity, and the rate of ventilation in the cavity. The ideal system has an outer skin with a highly reflective, low-absorptance outer surface and a low-emittance *(low-e)* inner surface. Since heat builds up within the cavity as the outer skin temperature increases, maximizing ventilation of the cavity is very important (Shabban, 1981).

José Luis Sert used a double roof for the **U.S. Embassy to Iraq** in Bhagdad. The roof is made of a thin folded concrete plate topped with flat precast planks. The ceiling inside is flat plaster, suspended from the bottom of the folded slab. Thus there are two 3-ft (0.9-m) deep triangular air cavities. The cavities are open on each end to allow warm air to escape. The exterior surface is painted white, giving low absorptance and high emissivity (Bastlund, 1967, pp. 98–109).

Continuous ventilation openings around the entire perimeter of a double-skin cavity will maximize cavity ventilation and allow the efficiency of the system to approach 1.0. Horizontal cavities on double roofs are at the most risk for poor ventilation Although the width of the cavity has little effect on its thermal efficiency, a deeper horizontal cavity allows more cross-ventilation inlet and outlet area. Orient inlets toward the prevailing breeze. Wall and sloping roof cavities can be vented by

U.S. Embassy to Iraq, Bhagdad, José Luis Sert

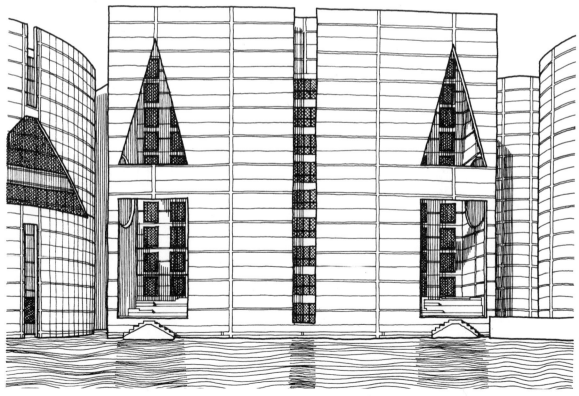

Office Block, National Assembly Building, Dhaka, Bangladesh, Louis I. Kahn

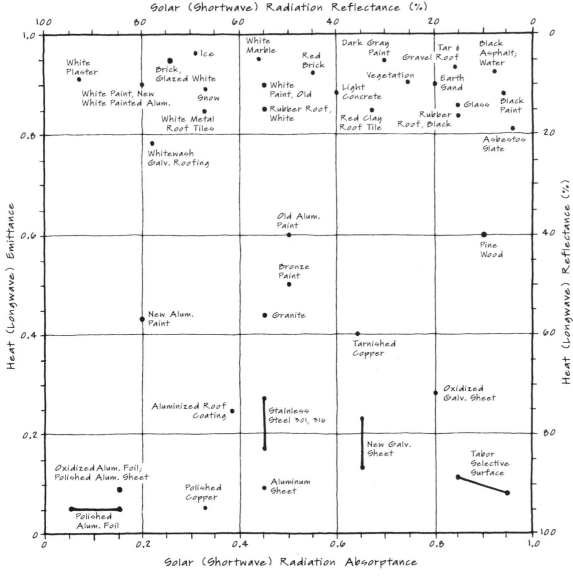

Surface Properties of Materials

stack effect if they are provided with low inlets and high outlets.

In **Sher-e-Bangla, the National Assembly Building of Bangladesh** in Dhaka, Louis Kahn used a double-wall design to shield walls and windows from solar gain. In the office wings, a void is subtracted from one corner of each cubic mass, leaving a glass block-roofed court with an external shade wall. The outer wall has large openings for view, while the inner, more protected wall has smaller windows that make use of reflected light. The prayer hall is lighted entirely by reflected light from the top of four cylindrical corner towers, which surround and protect most of the hall's exterior (Futagawa, 1994; Büttiker, 1994, pp. 160–177).

A translucent outer skin reduces system efficiency because it transmits some of the incident radiation. Lightweight outer-skin materials generally increase efficiency because they do not store heat well. A low average emissivity of the two surfaces facing the cavity is desirable to keep them from radiating heat to each other, yet only one of the surfaces needs to be low-e. In double-roof systems, dust can build up on the upward-facing surface, so the low-e surface should be on the bottom side of the outer skin.

Use the Surface Properties of Materials graph to select materials for the outer and inner shells. Choose outer skin materials with low solar absorptance (high solar reflectance) and high heat emittance characteristics. For outer skins, a low absorptance material with high-e is better than a similarly absorbing material with low-e, because high-emittance materials can readily reradiate the heat that they do absorb.

One exception to the above principle is a vegetated sun screen, such as ivy growing on a pergola (Strategies 98 and 99). Although leaves absorb a high percentage of solar radiation, the cavity will be well-ventilated because of space between the leaves, and excess heat is dissipated by evapotranspiration. Solar absorptance is the inverse of shortwave reflectance, while long-wave emittance is the inverse of long-wave reflectance. For most surfaces, emittance and absorptance vary with the wavelength of the radiation. Only for polished metals and nonmetallic black surfaces are these properties independent of wavelength (Yellot, 1983, p. 250).

DOUBLE SKIN TYPE	Efficiency
Roof	
Typical poorly vented attic	0.2
Typical well-vented attic	0.45
Canvas Louvers, horizontal, white outer, gray inner, fully vented	0.8-0.98
Walls	
Canvas Sheet, continuous, white, vented top & bottom	0.65
Canvas Sheet, continuous, dark brown, vented top & bottom	0.30
Canvas Sheets, staggered, vertical on east–west, gray, 50% vented	0.89
Canvas Sheets, staggered, vertical on east–west, gray, fully vented	0.95-1.0
Sheet Metal Louvers, galvanized, vertical on east–west, fully vented	0.88-0.98

Tested Double-Skin Constructions

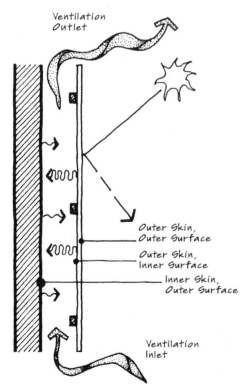

Diagrammatic Section of Double-Skin Wall

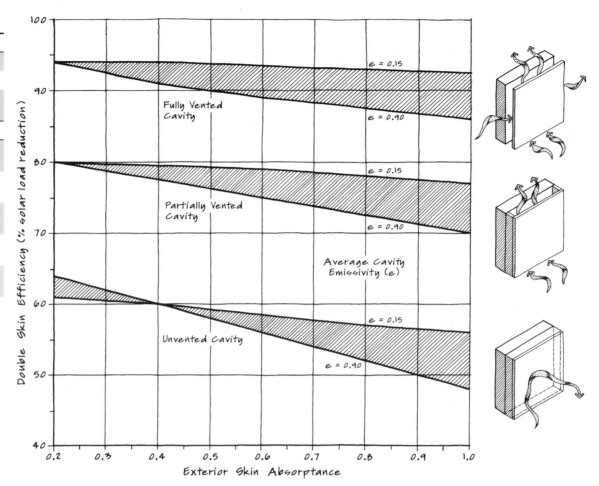

Double-Skin Efficiencies by Design Characteristics

Use the graph of Double-Skin Efficiencies by Design Characteristics to estimate the solar reduction.

Predicted efficiency can be found for any combination of 1) average emissivity of the two surfaces facing the cavity, 2) the exterior skin's absorptivity, and 3) the degree of cavity ventilation. Note that cavity emissivity is more important if exterior shell absorptivity is high. An efficiency of 1.0 means that all incident solar radiation is intercepted and dissipated, with none being passed on to the inner shell. The graph was developed based on a model in Shabban (1981). The table, **Tested Double-Skin Constructions** gives performance values for some monitored design variations (Shabban, 1981).

82 **Roofs and walls can be used as *SOLAR REFLECTORS* to increase the solar radiation entering sun-collecting glazing. [heating]**

Reflective exterior surfaces can augment the amount of radiation entering openings intended to collect sun. The amount of radiation reflected into the opening depends on the angles between the sun, reflector, and the opening, the size and reflectivity of the reflector, and the latitude of the building site. Any reflective surface, including the ground, with the correct relationship to the south-facing (north-facing in Southern Hemisphere) opening, can be used. Reflection can also be used to enhance daylighting (Strategy 92).

For vertical south-facing (north in Southern Hemisphere) openings, the reflector length should be 1–2 times the height of the opening, and the reflector width should be approximately the same as the opening width. The angle between them should be 90 ± 5°. A reflector with 80% reflectance sized this way will enhance the radiation entering a vertical south-facing (N in SH) window by 30–40% (Mazria, 1979, p. 241).

The **Lane Energy Center** in Cottage Grove, Oregon, by Equinox Design, Inc., uses an aluminized roofing material to reflect winter sunlight into the building clerestory. The sunlight is reflected from the building's ceiling down to the concrete floor and the water barrels on the rear wall for heat storage.

The reflector surface should be specular, which makes the angle of incidence equal to the angle of reflection, rather than textured or matte, which gives a diffuse reflection in many directions. **The table gives solar reflectances of common reflector materials.** Water is a relatively poor reflector; varying from 2% reflectance at 90° incidence to a maximum of 35% at very low angle sun (Bansal, 1994, p. 85-6). For more solar reflectances, see Strategy 77. Dirt can significantly reduce reflector effectiveness.

Reflectors oriented in a vertical position can be used to increase the solar gain for windows oriented beyond 30° from south (N in SH), such as a southeast window, but are ineffective at increasing gain to a south oriented window.

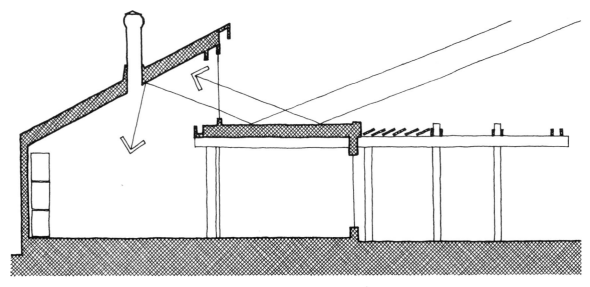

Lane Energy Center, Cottage Grove, Oregon, Equinox Design

Reflector Finish	Reflectance (%)
Concrete	30-50
Old snow	40-70
New snow	80-90
Polished aluminum	75-95
Aliminized mylar	60-80
Polished stainless steel	60-80
White porcelain enamel	70-77
Acrylic with aluminized backing	85
Aluminum foil	86
Electroplated Silver, new	96

Solar Reflectance of Finishes

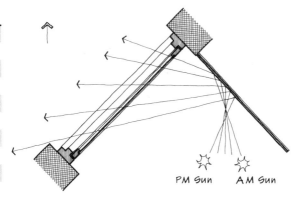

Plan View, Vertical Reflector for a Southeast-Facing Window
(northeast-facing in the Southern Hemisphere)

View of West Facade, Cafeteria, St. Göran Hospital, Ralph Erskine

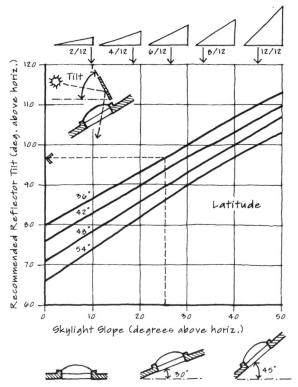

Reflector Tilts for South-Facing Skylights
(north-facing in the Southern Hemisphere)

Reflectors for south-sloped skylights in a roof should be located above the skylight. The graph can be used to determine the reflector's optimum slope depending on the roof slope and latitude. The graph is developed based on a model in Mazria (1979, p. 245).

To increase penetration from the low-angle Swedish winter sun, Ralph Erskine used three roof-mounted, metal reflectors supported on space frame brackets to reflect sun down through a south-facing linear skylight in the **Cafeteria of the St. Göran Hospital** in Stockholm. The reflectors are of a compound, faceted design with nine different planes to catch sun from a variety of directions. They are painted gloss white and are slotted to reduce wind drag (Lundahl, 1988; Collymore, 1994, pp. 174–175, 188–191).

83 *THERMAL MASS* surfaces should be large enough and thick enough to store adequate heat and cold. [heating and cooling]

There are three basic approaches to sizing the area and thickness of thermal mass. The first is appropriate for storage systems like trombe walls, roof ponds, and sunspaces where the collection area equals the surface area of the mass storage and thickness is the primary consideration. The second is more appropriate for direct gain, where both mass surface area and thickness are variable. Because the storage mass is in the inhabited space in direct-gain schemes, air and mass temperatures can't be allowed to get too high or too low, so this system depends on the large transfer areas afforded by relatively thin masonry masses. The third approach is when water is used for storage, where sizing is based on volume and the surface areas can be smaller, because heat is transferred, by convection, more readily between the surface and the bulk of the mass in water than it is in masonry. To size thermal storage for cooling by night ventilation of mass, see Strategy 68.

In direct-gain systems, assuming that the mass is in the same zone as the south (north in Southern Hemisphere) aperture so that the mass can exchange long-wave infrared radiation with surfaces struck by the sun, the masonry mass thickness should be 4–6 in (100–150 mm) thick, and the surface area should be 3–6 ft² of mass per ft² of south-facing (N in SH) glazing. If water is the storage medium, use 3.5–6.5 gal/ft² of solar collection glazing (145–265 L/m²) (Balcomb et al., 1980, p. 26). The greater amount of mass area within this range the better the performance, especially in buildings in which a large percentage of the heat is supplied by solar energy.

Water stores much more heat per unit of volume than masonry. It is also a good solution for thermal storage in buildings with light frame structure, such as in the **Bart Prince House** in Albuquerque, New Mexico. Prince stored the water in tall translucent cylinders along the south wall, allowing all other room surfaces to be carpeted over lightweight construction (*GA Houses*, 1985, pp. 48–59). Because the containers are translucent, they transmit some of the radiation and have relatively low absorptance (see Strategy 77 for a discus-

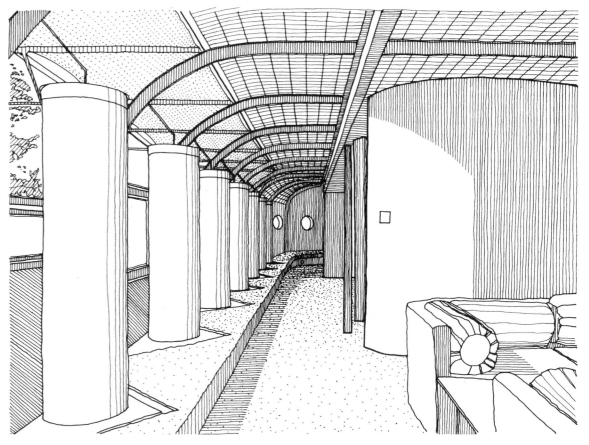

Interior of Bart Prince House, Albuquerque, New Mexico, Bart Prince

sion of mass absorptance). For more details on direct gain solar heating, see Strategy 60.

Higher solar savings fractions (SSFs) require more thermal storage. When SSF is less than 30%, solar heat mostly offsets daytime heat losses and little thermal storage is required. Between 30 and 70% SSF, more mass provides for storage into the night. An SSF beyond 70% is difficult to achieve in most climates without daytime overheating, thus remote multi-day storage is usually required (see Strategy 104).

To size the mass for passive solar heating, enter the graph, Sizing Thermal Mass for Direct-Gain Rooms and Sunspaces, on the horizontal axis with the estimated solar savings fraction for the design. The SSF can be estimated from Strategy 93. Move vertically to intersect the diagonal line for the mass type and thickness, then horizontally to read the recommended ratio of mass area to solar glazing area.

For a given material, daily heat storage will not increase significantly for thicknesses in excess of those shown on the graph. Remember that for interior mass walls or floors exposed on both sides, the area can be counted twice at one-half the total thickness–once for each side.

By definition, the mass surface area of trombe walls and roof ponds is equal to the area of glazing. The thickness of the walls and roofs determines the amount of heat they can store and when the heat can be released. *Water walls should be 9–12 in (230–305 mm) thick. Beyond 12 in (305 mm) thick, SSF increases continuously with volume. Masonry trombe walls should be 10–14 in (255–355 mm) thick if vented and 12–16 in (305–405 mm) if unvented.* Use the lower end of the recommended range for less dense materials, like adobe, and the higher end for more dense materials, like concrete. The optimum recommendations are based on balancing increased performance from more storage mass with decreasing performance from the inability for heat to pass all the way through the wall on a daily cycle. The annual SSF will drop significantly if a thinner mass is used, while increasing thickness will cause a much smaller drop in SSF (Balcomb et al., 1984, p. 2.17, 14.5).

Unvented trombe wall thickness also affects the time required for heat to pass through the wall and be delivered to the interior. Thicker walls also have lower amplitude temperature swings, generally increasing comfort. Because unvented trombe walls deliver heat late in the day, they are a good strategy to combine with direct gain, which delivers heat with morning sun. For more details on trombe wall design, see Strategy 62.

Sunspaces are assumed to have a masonry wall between the sunspace and the room; this should be 9–12 in (230–305 mm) thick. The floor and side walls of the sunspace should also be massive, with a minimum of 3 ft² of exposed mass per 1 ft² of south-facing (N in SH) sunspace glazing. Sunspaces with an insulated wall between the sunspace and the room they heat by convection should have 0.5–1.0 ft³ (3.5–7.5 gal) or more of water per 1 ft² of south collector glass (N in SH).

The water should be in containers with high absorptance (Strategies 77 and 81) (Balcomb, et al., 1980, p. 95; 1984, pp. 2–16). For more details on sunspace design, see Strategy 61.

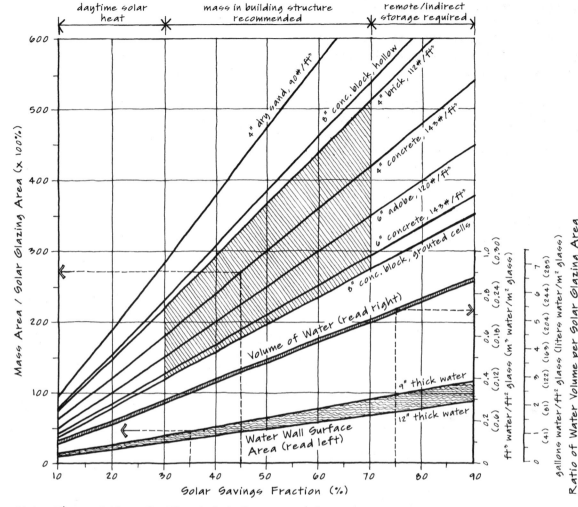

Sizing Thermal Mass for Direct-Gain Rooms and Sunspaces

Roof ponds used for cooling usually cover the entire roof area of a single-story building and therefore have a one-to-one ratio of mass area to floor area. Pond depths are usually 4–8 in (100–200 mm) (Fleischnacker et al., 1983, p. 835; Mazria, 1979, p. 187).

For more details on roof pond design, see Strategy 63.

84 *LOW CONTRAST* **between the window frame and adjacent walls will reduce glare and improve vision. [daylighting]**

One cause of glare is a sharp contrast between the window and its surround (Hopkinson et al., 1966, p. 330). This is because the window, with light coming through it, appears very bright in relationship to the reflected light coming from surrounding surfaces. This effect is exacerbated if the window is small and located in the middle of a thin wall. Discomfort glare from the window will be worse if the sky is bright and the room has a low level of ambient illumination, because the occupants' eyes will be adapted to the lower interior light level.

The glare-inducing contrast can be reduced by minimizing the size of mullions within the window, splaying them and the adjacent wall so that they are illuminated by the window, and painting them a light color.

If the walls are thick, as they are in Thomas Jeffer-son's **Rotunda at the University of Virginia,** in Charlottesville, (B. H. Evans, 1981, p. 72), it is relatively easy to achieve the light gradations between the wall and the window. If the wall is thin, additional reflecting surfaces at the edge of the window may be achieved by projecting the window out from the wall.

The area of gradation around the window in the window wall is valuable up to a distance of 10 times the window dimensions. Effective window edge reveals are 9–12 in (230–305 mm) deep, at an angle of 60° to the plane of the window, and are 60–90% reflective. The window wall itself should be a light color (Strategy 78).

Splayed jambs, sills, and heads also spread light from an aperture over a larger region of the room, especially when the skin is thick. This is especially true of skylights penetrating deep roofs (see Skylight Wells, Strategy 85).

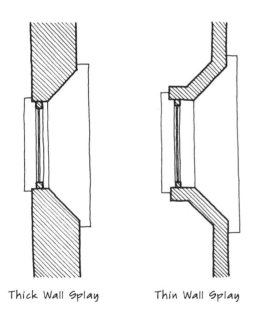

Thick Wall Splay   Thin Wall Splay

Splayed Window Jamb Options

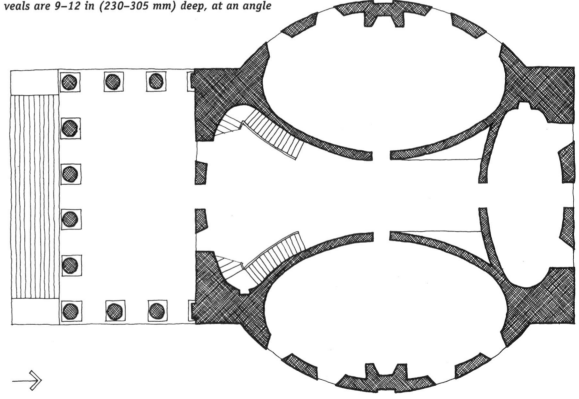

Rotunda, University of Virginia, Charlottesville, Virginia, Thomas Jefferson

85 *SKYLIGHT WELLS* **should be shaped to distribute daylight to rooms. [daylighting]**

Daylight captured from skylights at roof level must be channeled down through the roof section to the ceiling. Interreflections between the side walls of a skylight well absorb light and decrease the overall daylight transmission to the space. The efficiency with which the well transmits daylight is a function of the well wall reflectance and the shape of the well. Tall narrow wells are less efficient.

The graph shows the magnitude of these relationships based on a well index (WI) that accounts for the depth and aspect ratio of the well. The well index is defined as:

$$WI = \frac{H(W + L)}{(2W \times L)}$$

To find the daylight efficiency of a skylight well, enter the graph on the horizontal axis with the well's index, move up to the diagonal line for the well wall reflectance, and then horizontally to find the efficiency on the vertical scale.

Daylight factors calculated based on skylight size must be reduced by this fraction. For instance, if the daylight factor (DF) determined from Strategy 94 is 4% and the skylight has a well efficiency of 60%, then multiply the 4% original DF by 0.6 to get a revised DF of 2.4%. Similarly, the lower the efficiency of the well, the larger the skylight must be to provide the same light level. Finish reflectance values are given in Strategy 82.

Moshe Safdie used tall, thin, long wells to bring skylight to the lower floor galleries of the **National Gallery of Canada** in Ottawa, Ontario. The well runs continuously along the ceiling vault's top. The well index in this scheme is quite high, about 3.0, so a very high reflectance, specular, silver Mylar was used to line the well walls. The design is reported to give acceptable lighting under overcast sky with no electric lights (Kohn, 1996; Campbell, 1988).

Remember that horizontal glazing is difficult to shade and captures the high levels of unwanted summer radiation. Consider vertical glazing and shading devices.

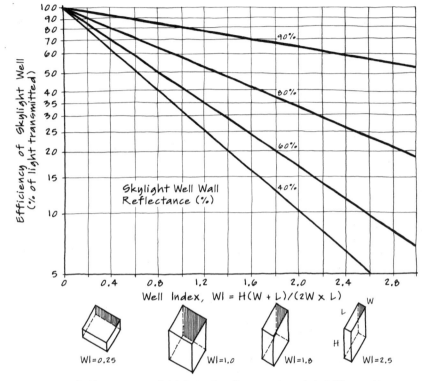

Sizing and Shaping Light Wells to Transmit Light Efficiently

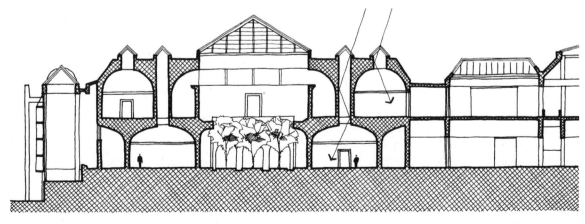

National Gallery of Canada, Ottawa, Ontario, Moshe Safdie

86 **Roofs should be large enough as well as sloped and oriented to collect sun for *SOLAR HOT WATER* systems. [power]**

Solar hot water systems have many benefits, including substantial reduction of fuel consumption, reduced pollution and attractive economics. In a solar hot water system, water, or in cool climates, a nonfreezing solution, is circulated through a solar collector, most often with the aid of a pump. The water is heated by the sun as it passes through the collector and then is circulated to a storage tank. In the case of a nonfreezing solution, the warmed solution heats water from storage by means of a heat exchanger. From storage (or the heat exchanger), the fluid is circulated back to the collector. Usually, an auxiliary hot water heater provides heat when the solar resource is insufficient, such as in midwinter.

In the **Solar Village 3** neighborhood in Athens, Greece, Alexandros N. Tombazis and Associates used solar water collectors mounted on racks to provide heated water while also shading roof terraces of multistory housing (Cofaigh et al., 1996, pp. 147–154; *Architecture in Greece,* 1986, pp. 196–199). Collectors are tilted, facing south. The complex uses both active and passive solar heating and cooling systems in a variety of types. Heated water is for domestic use and in some cases, for some of the space heating requirements. Banks of collectors alternate with open rails, to give both a shady and a sunny side to the roof terraces, expanding options for seasonal use and views.

The size of a building's collectors are based on the amount of energy that can be collected at the building site, the temperature of incoming city water, the temperature of hot water provided to occupants, and the rate of water use in the building.

Collectors should face the south (north in Southern Hemisphere) whenever possible. Deviations from a true south (N in SH) orientation result in less heat being collected from the sun, especially at high latitudes in winter. However, on an annual basis, performance at Alaskan latitudes decreases less than 10% for orientations up to 50° from south (Siefert, 1981, p. 47).

For a winter bias, use a collector tilt above horizontal of latitude plus 15°. For maximizing summer production, use a tilt of latitude° minus 15°. For

South Side of Two-Story Residences, Solar Village 3, Athens, Greece, Alexandros N. Tombazis & Associates

maximizing annual production, use a tilt equal to the site's latitude°.

For temperate, overcast-dominated sky conditions, a tilt lower than the latitude° is recommended, since under overcast conditions, the top of the sky dome is three times brighter than the horizon. At high latitudes, such as Alaska, winter radiation is very low, so annual performance is maximized by a tilt of latitude° minus 10-20° (Siefert, 1981, p. 47).

In sunny locations, collectors for residences should be about 20 ft² (2 m²) of collector area for each of the first two occupants and 8 ft² (0.7 m²) for each additional occupant. In cloudy climates, or latitudes above 40°, allow 12–14 additional ft² (1.1–1.3 m²) per person (EREN).

To size roofs for solar hot water collectors:

1) Determine the annual rate of demand for hot water in the building from Technique 25.

2) Determine the temperature rise of the water by subtracting the building's hot water temperature from the well water temperature found on the upper map (NREL, 1998, p. 4.) or from local water temperature data for surface water sources such as rivers or lakes (see ASHRAE, 1988).

3) Determine the annual collector performance from the lower map. A true south (true N in SH) orientation is assumed, with collector tilt equal to latitude. Evacuated collectors yield 5–25% more heat than flat plate collectors, depending on the climate (NREL, 1998, p. 5). They are more effective in cold climates because they are insulated with a vacuum and so lose less heat to the cold ambient air.

4) Enter the **Solar Hot Water Collector Sizing** nomograph on the upper vertical axis with the annual hot water demand (from Step 1). Move horizontally to the diagonal for the water temperature rise (Step 2). From the intersection, move down to the bottom left chart, intersecting the line for annual collector performance (from Step 3). Finally, from the intersection, move horizontally to read collector size on the vertical axis. Sizing represents a 100% solar fraction, meaning provision of all the building's hot water energy. In practice, this is rarely economical and may be reduced proportionally to provide 50–80% of the annual load.

Mechanical rooms should be large enough to accommodate tanks for water heated by solar collectors and stored for later use. When the pattern of energy use is

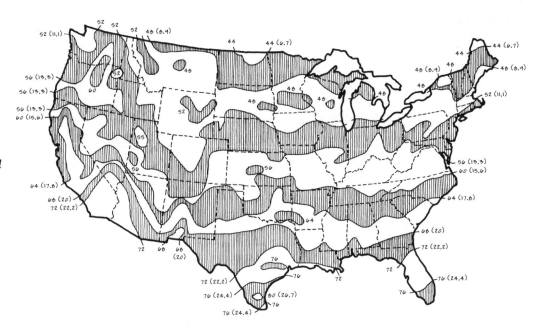

Ground Water Temperature, °F (°C), in 50-150 ft (15-46 m) Deep Wells

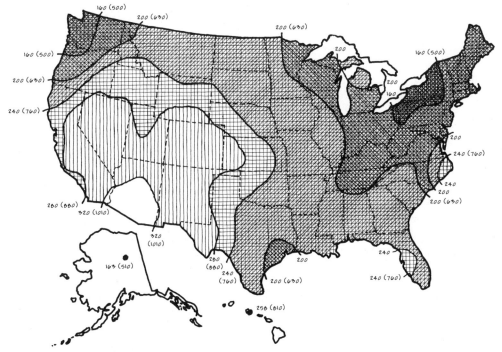

Annual Energy Production of Flat Plate Solar Water Heating Collectors, South-Facing (N in SH), kBtu/ft², yr (kWh/m², yr)

closely matched to energy generation, such as regular daytime demand, storage may be minimal. When the match is poor, such as nighttime loads, storage volume must increase. For a given collector size and load, a larger storage size will improve thermal efficiency. Storage in mechanical rooms or other locations within the building is recommended over outdoor or underground locations.

To determine storage tank size for service hot water, use the graph, Water Storage Sizing. Enter the graph on the vertical axis with the size of collectors (from Step 4). Move horizontally to the diagonal line for the building's load profile, then vertically to read storage tank volume on either horizontal scale. In very warm, sunny climates, storage size should be increased by 25%. To convert to liquid measure: multiply ft³ by 7.48 to get gallons, or multiply m³ by 1000 to get liters.

To accommodate pumps, heat exchangers, and other associated components, the floor area of mechanical rooms for solar hot water storage tanks should be about twice the size of the required tank floor area (ASHRAE, 1988, p. 1-27).

Ideally, collectors, storage, and end uses are located as near to each other as possible. Tall, small-diameter tanks are preferable to short, large-diameter tanks, because height increases temperature stratification between hot water input at the top and cold water outlet (return to the collector) at the tank's bottom.

A small, 50 to 60 gal (190 to 230 L) system is sufficient for 1–3 people; a medium, 80-gal (300-L) system is adequate for a 3 or 4-person household; and a large, 120-gal (450-L) system is appropriate for 4–6 people (EREN). For space heating thermal storage, where water is the primary storage medium from collectors, use a preliminary volume of 1.0 gal/ft² of collector (40.8 L/m²) (ASHRAE, 1988). For more information on design of solar hot water systems, see ASHRAE (1988, p. 3-61).

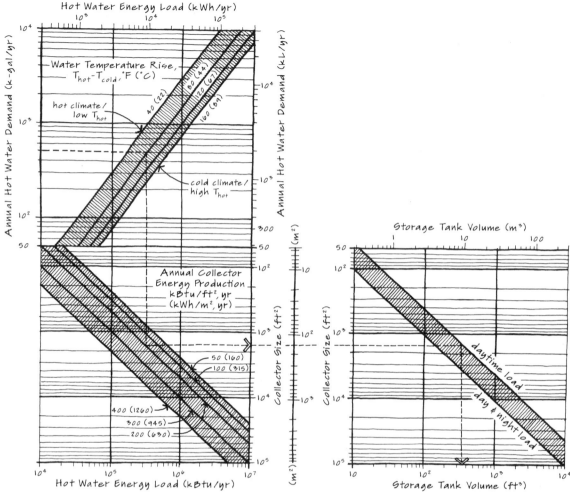

Solar Hot Water Collector Sizing

Water Storage Sizing

.7 Sunny *BREATHING WALLS* can preheat fresh air for ventilation. [heating]

Fresh air supplied to buildings prevents the buildup of indoor pollutants and provides clean air to breathe. When it is warmer outside than inside, fresh air ventilation produces a cooling load because the air must be cooled to comfort conditions; when colder outside, a heating load is produced (Technique 17). During the winter, solar preheating of outdoor ventilation air can reduce the heating load.

A transpiring wall both preheats fresh air for ventilation and reduces conductive heat losses through the solar wall. In the system, a south-facing (north-facing in Southern Hemisphere) dark, perforated metal wall is installed over a 6-in (15-cm) air space with a structural wall behind. Solar radiation is absorbed by the metal surface. Fans at the top of the wall pull air through the perforations, into the air gap, and up, to be ducted into the building (NREL, 4/1998). In the process, heat from the absorber plate is transferred to the air, raising its temperature by 10–40 °F (6–22 °C) (Conserval, 1998). During summer, the air gap is vented naturally to the outdoors and an intake bypass damper is employed to bring in untempered outdoor air.

The amount of heat collected is dependent on the solar radiation available, the absorptance of the metal plate, the area of the wall, and the air flow rate through the wall. Typical air flow rates are 4–7 cubic feet per minute per square foot (cfm/ft^2) of transpired wall (20–36 L/s, m^2). A higher flow rate will collect more heat, but will deliver the air at a lower temperature. The approximate equivalent *R*-value of the transpired wall during a sunny winter day is *R*-50 (RSI-9).

To size a transpired wall, find from the table the minimum rate of outdoor air required, in cfm/ft^2 of floor area (or L/s, m^2) With this value, enter the nomograph (next page), Sizing Transpired Walls, on the left-side horizontal axis, moving vertically to the diagonal zone for air flow rate, then horizontally to read transpired wall area as a percentage of the floor area.

The table was developed based on occupant densities from Technique 12 and ventilation rates from ASHRAE (1989b).

BUILDING TYPE / ROOM		OUTDOOR AIR REQUIRED					
		cfm/ft^2 of Floor			Liters/sec/m^2 of Floor		
	cfm/person	Average (perform.)	Maximum (peak size)	L/s/person	Average (perform.)	Maximum (peak size)
Assembly	15	0.30		7	1.52	
Auditorium spaces	15	1.88	2.10	7	9.52	10.67
Conference rooms	20		1.00	9		5.08
Recreational Facilities						
Spectator areas	15		2.25	7		11.43
Gymnasium	20		0.60	9		3.05
Ball room	25		2.50	12		12.70
Restaurant	20	0.14		9	0.71	
Dining rooms	20		1.40	9		7.11
Fast food, bars	30		3.00	14		15.24
Kitchens	15		0.30	7		1.52
Auto Repair Shop			1.5			7.62
Education	15	0.15	0.45	7	0.76	2.29
Classroom	15		0.75	7		3.81
Laboratory	20		0.60	9		3.05
Libraries	15		0.30	7		1.52
Grocery Store	15	0.12	0.30	7	0.61	1.52
Retail	10	0.07	0.30	5	0.36	1.52
Mall	10		0.20	5		1.02
Office	20	0.08	0.14	9	0.41	0.71
Lodging	15	0.06	0.08	7	0.30	0.38
Hospital patient rms.	25		0.25	12		1.27
Residential, multifamily	15	0.05	0.05	7	0.23	0.23
Dormitory sleeping rms.	15		0.30	7		1.52
Warehouse	10	0.01	0.05	5	0.05	0.25

Rate of Fresh Outdoor Air Required for Ventilation

To find the ventilation heating energy saved, move right on the line of transpired wall area/floor area ratio to the diagonal for annual energy produced by the transpired wall. Values for energy delivered can be estimated from the map (NREL, April, 1998, p. 12). From the intersection, move vertically to read the amount of annual energy saved on either horizontal axis.

More detailed sizing and economic estimates can be made with the *RETScreen* software (CANMET, 1998).

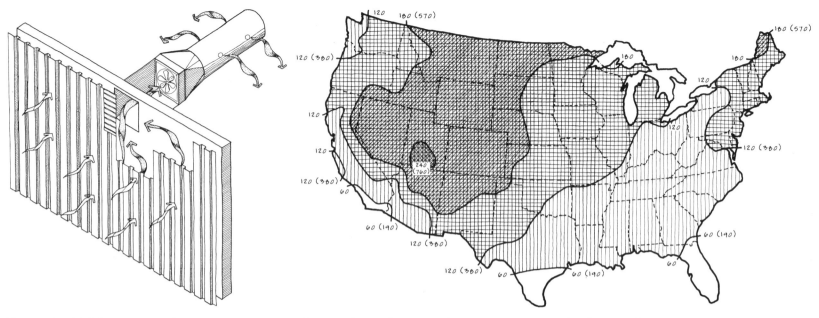

Transpired Wall Components

Energy From Transpired Wall, kBtu/ft², yr (kWh/m², yr)

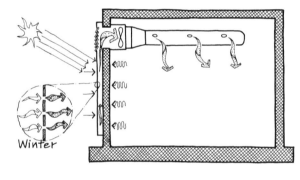

Winter

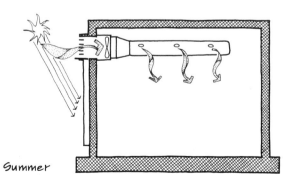

Summer

Transpired Wall Operation

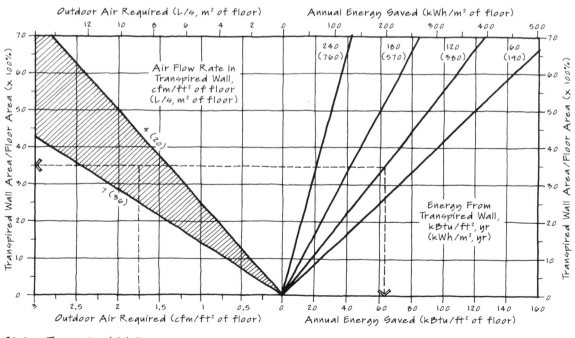

Sizing Transpired Walls

WALLS: Size and Materials   87

INSULATION OUTSIDE the mass of walls allows the mass to store heat from the room and stabilize the interior air temperature. [heating and cooling]

Masonry materials are often regarded as exterior finish materials. However, to be effective thermal masses for storing heat or cold, they must have exposed surfaces inside the space. Therefore, the insulation must be between the mass and the outside air. To achieve a masonry exterior finish, an additional layer of masonry must be added, usually as a veneer layer.

In the **Stockebrand House,** in Albuquerque, New Mexico, by Edward Mazria & Associates, urethane insulation was sprayed on the outside of filled concrete block. It was then covered with stucco colored to match the surrounding ground and detailed to recall the New Mexico adobe traditions (*Progressive Architecture*, 4/1981b).

In the **Roberts Residence** in Reston, Virginia, a masonry inner house is surrounded by a highly insulated wood frame wrapper (Viladas, 1982; Wright & Andrejko, 1982, p. 115). The south wall is a hybrid of trombe wall, direct gain, and air collector. Some solar gain is stored in the south wall mass, some passes trough openings in the mass wall to the rooms behind, and some is ducted with the aid of fans from the top of the trombe wall cavity, through an attic greenhouse, to the hollow cores of the interior mass wall, and then back through a crawl space to the bottom of the trombe wall. From the interior mass, stored heat can move through the wall and radiate to both the south and north-facing rooms. At night, an insulating curtain can be lowered in the cavity between the south glass and the masonry wall to retain the heat collected during the day (see Strategy 97, Movable Insulation).

Batt and fill insulations have an R-value of 3–4 per inch (RSI 0.23–0.28 per cm); rigid insulation, 4–6 per inch (RSI 0.28–0.42 per cm).

See Strategy 76 for recommended insulation levels and Strategies 68, 77, and 83 for more on the design implications of thermal mass.

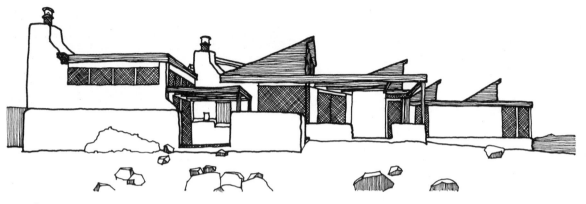

Stockebrand Residence, Albuquerque, New Mexico, Edward Mazria

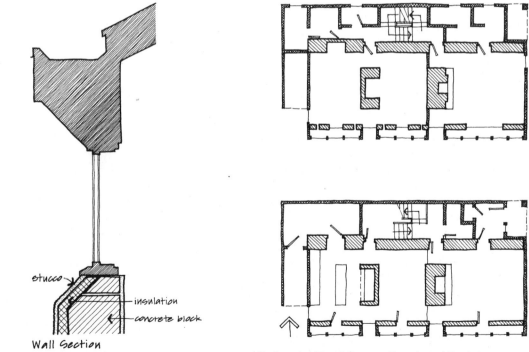

stucco

insulation

concrete block

Wall Section

Stockebrand Residence

Roberts Residence, Reston, Virginia, Walter Roberts

89 Ventilation, light, and solar gain may be accommodated with *SEPARATED OR COMBINED OPENINGS.* [heating, cooling, and daylighting]

When building components such as windows are designed to perform a single function, like ventilation, solar gain, or lighting, their design may be very specific to that function, and they have a better chance of performing it well. Combining various functions in a single component allows the cost of the component to be justified in terms of several attributes. Depending on the climate and building type, the functions of ventilating, solar gain, and lighting may be strongly related over the entire year, may be related for some time periods but unrelated for others, or may be completely unrelated for the entire year.

The roof monitors in the **One University Plaza** office building in Fairfax, Virginia, combine the tasks of solar heating, daylighting, and ventilating. The 10 x 10-ft (3.1 x 3.1-m) monitors occur in each 30 x 30-ft (9.2 x 9.2-m) bay of this largely underground building. The monitors change their role seasonally: They provide solar heating and daylighting in the winter and daylighting and stack ventilation in the summer (Viladas, 1982).

Louis Kahn separated the wooden shuttered ventilation panels of the **Esherick House** from the simple fixed glass windows. The ventilation shutters are located in niches along the thickened north and south walls, allowing good cross-ventilation. Separated into several sections, combinations of opened and closed shutters high and low in the wall allow a variety of ventilation, daylight, view, and privacy relationships with the outdoors (Futagawa, 1996b; Büttiker, 1994, pp. 90–96).

Separate ventilation openings, if sun-protected with dark louvers, allow ventilation during the times when occupants need to darken a room. They are also useful in hot climates when openings for ventilation need to be larger than openings for light. Finally, separate ventilation openings permit view windows to be unobstructed by the insect screens and the thicker frames of operable windows.

In the **Pension Building** in Washington, DC, which has a ring of offices around a central atrium, architect

One University Plaza, Fairfax, Virginia, Alternative Design

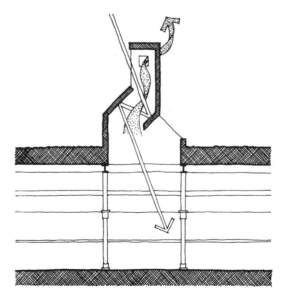

One University Plaza, Roof Monitor

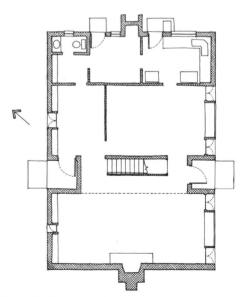

Esherick House, Chestnut Hill, Pennsylvania, Louis I. Kahn

Esherick House, Chestnut Hill, Pennsylvania, Louis I. Kahn

Pension Building, Washington, M. C. Meigs

Social Security Administration, Northeast Program Service Center,
Gruzen Partnership, The Ehrenkrantz Group, and Syska & Hennessy

Montgomery C. Meigs separated the functions of fresh air ventilation and daylighting by putting vents below each window (see section drawing in Strategy 66). Air can flow through the offices, be warmed, rise, and finally be exhausted through the clerestories in the atrium (Smith, 1981, p. 63; *Architecture,* 2/1985).

In the **Social Security Administration, Northeast Program Service Center** by the Gruzen partnership, The Ehrenkrantz Group, and Syska & Hennessy, windows for daylighting and windows for view are treated as separate components. The windows for daylighting form a continuous strip high in the wall. The windows for view are spaced periodically below the daylighting strip. They are all glazed as one unit, of which the top is primarily for light and the bottom is for view (Vonier, et al., 1984, p. 155).

90 *VENTILATION OPENINGS ARRANGEMENT* can be **optimized to increase the rate of cross-ventilation in a room and to move air across occupants to increase their rate of cooling.** [cooling]

In addition to removing hot air from a room, ventilation can also affect occupant cooling, if the air is moving fast enough, by increasing the rate of evaporation from their skin. *When the outside ambient air temperature is above the comfort zone, vents should be designed for occupant cooling as well as for heat removal. Use the Bioclimatic Chart from Technique 11 to determine the wind speed that will create comfort for given air temperatures. Interior air velocity in a room can be estimated by modifying the wind speed from Techniques 5 & 6 by the percentages in the table. Choose from the table the size and arangement of windows that best approximates the proposed room design.* The table is based on the work of Melaragno and Givoni and assumes that the window height is one-third of the wall height.

The average interior air velocity is a function of the exterior free wind velocity, the angle at which the wind strikes the inlet, and the location and size of the opening. For openings two-thirds of the wall width, rooms that have only one opening in one wall have average velocities of 13–17% of the outside air velocity, depending on the wind direction. The difference in this velocity is small between openings that vary from 33–100% of the wall area. For two openings placed in the same wall, average velocities are higher, about 22% of the outside air velocity, because one opening acts as an inlet and the other as an outlet. If perpendicular wings are added to the wall between the openings, this average velocity can be increased to 35% when the wind blows obliquely to the wall (Givoni, 1976, p. 289; Melaragno, 1982, p. 321). For more on wing walls for ventilation, see Strategy 65.

When openings in a room are located in two walls, the average interior velocity is much higher, 35–65% of outside air velocity, because one opening will always be in a higher pressure zone than the other. The volume of air flow, and thus the heat removed, is greatly influenced by the size of the openings; see Strategy 65 for

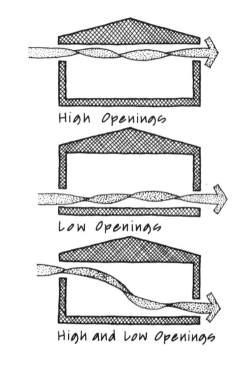

High Openings

Low Openings

High and Low Openings

window height as a fraction of wall height	1/3	1/3	1/3
window width as a fraction of wall width	1/3	2/3	3/3
single opening	12-14%	13-17%	16-23%
two openings in the same wall	----	22%	23%
two openings in adjacent walls	37-45%	37-45%	40-51%
two openings in opposite walls	35-42%	37-51%	47-65%

Average Interior Air Velocity as a Percentage of the Exterior Wind Velocity
range = wind 45° to perpendicular to opening

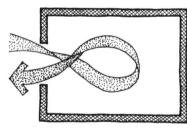

Single Opening

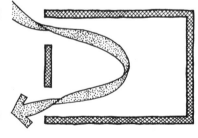

Two Openings-Same Wall

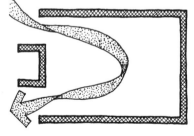

Two Openings With Wings

TwoOpenings-Adjacent Walls

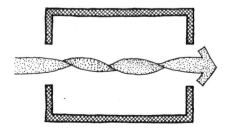
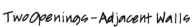

Two Openings-Opposite Walls

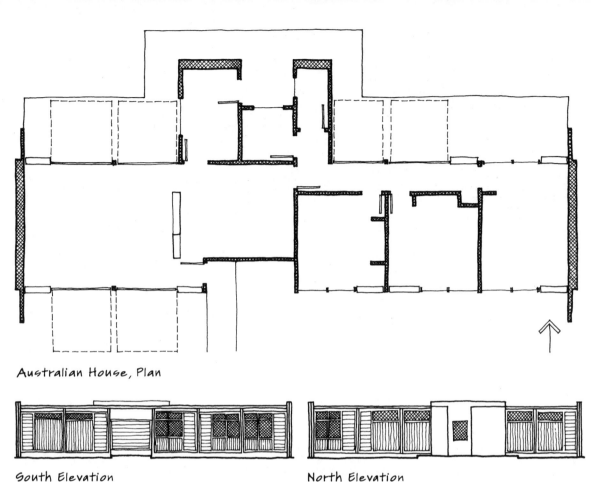

Australian House, Plan

South Elevation

North Elevation

cross-ventilation opening sizing and Strategy 66 for stack-ventilation opening sizing. Orientations where the wind is more than 40° from perpendicular to the window cause a significant reduction on interior velocity (Strategy 59).

The location of the openings and interior partitions in both plan and section influence the route of the air flow through the room. Therefore, air velocity varies within the room (Melaragno, 1982, p. 326). Although openings in opposite walls create rapid movement, openings in adjacent walls and wind directions oblique to the window encourage both turbulence and air mixing, and thus a more even velocity distribution and cooling effect throughout the room. It is important that openings are located so that air moves past the occupants to be cooled. If the openings are all near the ceiling or all near the floor, the maximum velocity won't occur in the occupied zone, usually 1–6 ft (0.3–1.8 m) above the floor. If the openings are midheight in the wall or if some are high and some are low, then higher velocities will occur in the occupied zone.

In the **house designed for the hot/humid regions of Australia,** the major rooms have openings on both sides, and the interior partitions run parallel to the prevailing wind flow. The walls have several types of openings to accommodate different ventilation rates, wind speeds, privacy and security needs, and rain control (Saini, 1970, p. 27).

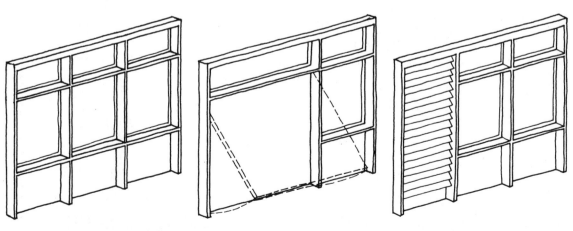

Australian House, Wall Types

91 WELL-PLACED WINDOWS can reduce winter heat loss. [heating]

Within well-insulated, skin-load-dominated buildings, the primary causes of heat loss are infiltration and windows. The size, number, and orientation of windows greatly affect the building's energy use for heating. In the daytime during the heating season, windows are simultaneously losing heat because it's warmer inside than out and gaining heat because direct or diffuse solar radiation is passing through the glass and heating the interior. At night, of course, the windows only lose heat. If a window gains more heat than it loses over the course of the heating season, it reduces the heating requirements of the building. Windows that don't face south (north in the Southern Hemisphere) usually lose more energy than they gain and therefore increase the building's heating requirements. The amenities of non-south-facing (non-N in SH) windows, such as view, daylight (Strategies 92 and 94), and ventilation (Strategies 65 and 66), should be carefully weighed against their thermal liability in the heating season.

In the Chicago, Illinois, **Glessner House,** H. H. Richardson concentrated the major living spaces and most of the glazing on the south side of the building, overlooking a sun-filled court. The service spaces and circulation, which require little glazing, are located along the north edge of the building (Hitchcock, 1936, p. 128). This maximizes the window area that gains heat from the sun and minimizes that which does not.

Assuming a well-insulated solar-heated building, the nonsouth windows on each orientation should be limited to 10–15% of the total window area, but should be large enough for effective daylight (Strategies 92 and 94) (Goulding et al., 1992, p. 160).

This may present the designer with a conflict between daylighting and heat loss. For example, a daylight factor of 4% might require windows equal to 20% of the floor area, distributed in proportion to the area of the rooms they daylight. In temperate and colder climates, the *U*-value of windows should be reduced to compensate for the heat loss potential from increased daylight glazing area (see Strategy 101, Glass Types).

J. J. Glessner House, View From the Northeast

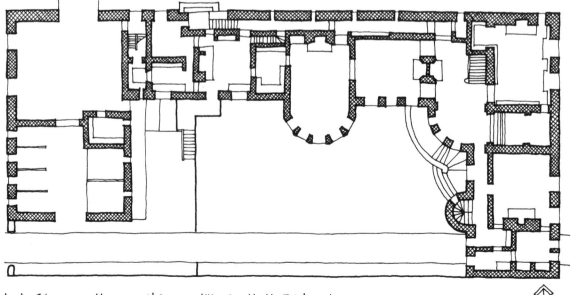

J. J. Glessner House, Chicago, Illinois, H. H. Richardson

92

REFLECTED SUNLIGHT can be used for daylighting in clear sky climates. [daylighting]

Buildings that use daylighting to reduce their level of electric lighting and thus their cooling requirements are common in clear sky climates. The dominant source of illumination in a clear sky is the sun and the area immediately around it (Technique 8). Because the sun is an extremely powerful light source, providing up to 10,000 foot-candles (108 lux), but also a source of heat gain of up to 300 Btu/hr, ft² (945 W/m²), it is important to balance the lighting benefits against heat gain liabilities. The desirable illumination levels inside a building are up to 1000 times less than they are outside, so a small amount of sunlight can be distributed over a large area and still provide adequate illumina-

tion. The design goal should be to meet minimum illumination levels through as much of the day as possible without significantly exceeding the minimum, because excess light also means excess heat gain.

There are two basic strategies for using the sun for lighting while minimizing heat gain. The first is to use a very small window opening (10–20% of the wall area) to illuminate a surface inside the space that then spreads the light out over a large area. The second is to use a moderately sized window that "sees" an exterior reflective surface but is shaded from the direct sun.

In the hot, sunny Fort Worth, Texas climate, Louis Kahn used small openings in the top of the vaults of the **Kimbell Art Museum** to let in sunlight. The light is reflected from an internal reflector onto the ceiling, which in turn reflects it onto the walls and floor (Brawne, 1992; Kahn, 1978, B. H. Evans, 1981, pp. 158–162; Büttiker, 1994, pp. 134–139). On average, a hori-

zontal skylight will have the most illumination throughout the year and therefore, the openings can be quite small. The graphs show clear sky illuminance for Fort Worth.

To estimate window sizes for small windows with internal reflection, first find the clear sky daylight factor required, using Technique 9. For skylights, the design daylight factor should be increased to account for light lost in the well: multiply DF by 1 + (1 - well efficiency). See Strategy 85. If all of the collected light is bounced off of a reflector, the DF target should also be increased proportionally to the reflectance of the surface: multiply DF by 1 + (1 − reflectance). Use this DF, along with the sky view angle, for sizing openings with the graph in Strategy 94 for window sizing. For interior reflectances, see Strategies 77 and 78.

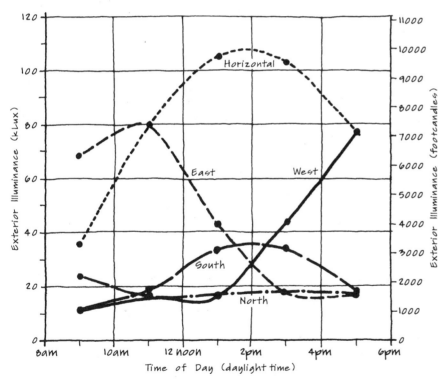

June "Mostly Clear" Illuminance, Fort Worth, TX (<50% clouds)

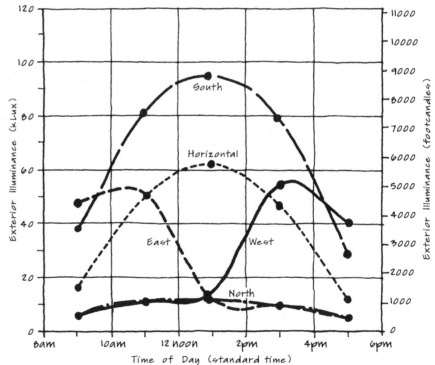

December "Mostly Clear" Illuminance, Fort Worth, TX (<50% clouds)

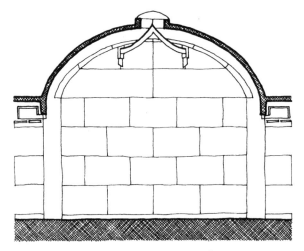

Kimbell Art Museum, Fort Worth, Texas, Louis I. Kahn

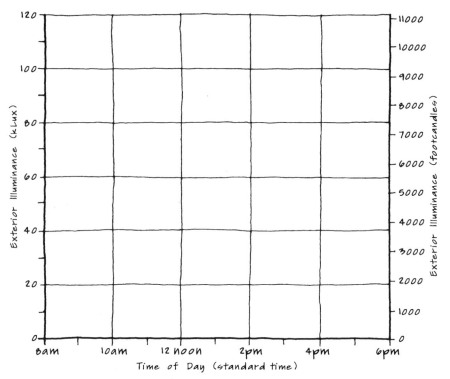

"Mostly Clear" Illuminance   City: Month:

Kahn made use of exterior reflecting surfaces in the **Chancellery for Luanda**, Angola, by creating a court outside each office so that the windows receive only sunlight reflected from the court walls and ground (Scully, 1962, p. 35).

The amount of illumination available to a window from the sun changes dramatically with the sun position, but the exterior illumination available from the clear sky, ground reflectance, and light reflected from vertical walls remains relatively constant throughout the day, with the exception of the hours just after sunrise and before sunset. As a consequence, shaded windows that face courts or streets with buildings on the other side have a relatively constant source of illumination.

Building users can be protected from glare by locating the openings out of their direct line of sight, if the windows are admitting direct sunlight, or by reducing the luminance of the first reflecting surface. In no case should the designer allow direct sun on a task surface.

When an obstruction is located outside of a vertical window, the window receives light from the sky (and possibly the sun) above the obstruction. Neglecting direct sun, the light received is proportional to the sky view angle above the obstruction, as seen from the center of the window (angle *v* in the diagram on the next page). The window also receives light reflected off of the obstruction, the amount being proportional to the

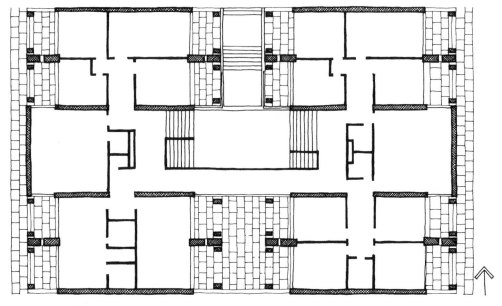

Chancellery, U.S. Consulate, Luanda, Louis, I. Kahn

angle of the reflector obstruction above the horizon, as seen from the center of the window (angle *e* in the diagram) (Robbins, 1986, p. 183).

To size apertures for a design with an external reflecting wall, first find the illuminance on the aperture from the four-part nomograph. Use this value to calculate the room's required design daylight factor (DF). Begin by finding from Technique 9 the clear sky unobstructed illuminance on both the window wall and the reflecting wall. Remember that the reflecting wall is oriented differently (usually opposite) from the facade onto which it reflects.

Enter the upper left graph on the vertical axis with the illuminance on the reflector plane, moving horizontally to the diagonal line for the angle of obstruction (e). Then drop vertically to the diagonal line in the lower left graph corresponding to the reflectance of the exterior reflector plane. From the intersection, move horizontally to find the light level on the aperture from the reflector plane.

Next, enter the upper right graph with the illuminance on the window wall; move horizontally to the diagonal line for the opening's sky view angle (v). From the intersection, move vertically to find the light level on the aperture from above the reflector plane.

The total exterior illuminance on the aperture is the sum of the light from above the reflector and the light reflected from the reflector plane. Use the lower right graph to find this total illuminance. To find the design daylight factor, divide the required indoor illuminance (Technique 13) by the total illuminance on the aperture found on the lower right graph. Then use this DF in the window sizing graph of Strategy 94. Since the obstruction and reflection have already been accounted for here, be sure to use an obstruction angle of 90° (unobstructed) in the Strategy 94 graph.

This method is quick, but quite rough. It should be used only for preliminary sizing and should be developed at a later stage with more sophisticated tools. Lighting from the clear sky is complex and dynamic; it is best studied with physical models as described in Moore (1991) and B. H. Evans (1981) or with computer simulation.

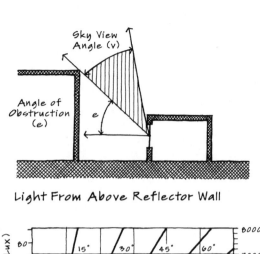

Light From Above Reflector Wall

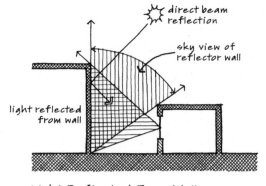

Light Reflected From Wall

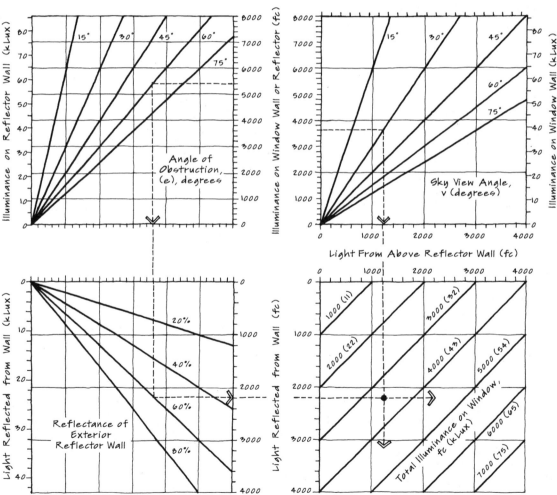

Combined Illuminance From Sky and External Reflector Wall of Infininte Length

93 *SOLAR APERTURES* can be enlarged to increase the percentage of the annual heating requirement supplied by solar energy. [heating]

The percentage of the annual heating load that can be supplied by the sun is determined by a balance between the amount of solar radiation that can be collected, the amount of heat loss, and the amount of heat that can be stored during the day for use at night. Collectible radiation is a function of the amount of south-facing (north in Southern Hemisphere) glazing and the radiation available in the climate. Heat loss is a function of the insulating qualities of the building skin and the severity of the climate. The amount of solar radiation collected that is usable for heating the interior depends on how the heat is stored and distributed.

The **Brookhaven House,** a prototype designed by Total Environmental Action, uses three systems—direct gain, sunspace, and trombe walls—to meet its heating requirements. See Strategies 60, 61, and 62 for a more complete explanation of these systems. The trombe wall, which is punctured by a direct gain window, is located at the end of the dining room; the sunspace, which is separated from the kitchen and family room by a mass storage wall, completes the south side of the lower floor. Direct-gain windows are used on the second-floor bedrooms. The second floor also has a balcony that opens to the sunspace. The house is designed so that the entry can be located in either the sunspace or the porch, so the house can be built with either side facing the street and still have the solar-collecting surfaces facing south. It is estimated that the sun will supply this house with 65% of its heating requirements in Boston, 65% in New York, 57% in Chicago, 77% in Baltimore, 56% in Madison, Wisconsin, and 69% in Louisville, Kentucky (Peri et al., 1988; Total Environmental Action, 1979).

The solar savings fraction (SSF) is the percentage of annual energy saved by using solar energy for space heating, compared to heating a nonsolar building with similar thermal characteristics (Balcomb et al., 1983, p. 5).

The **Passive Solar Glazing Area Design Recommendations** table gives estimated SSF for buildings in representative U.S. and Canadian cities. Consult the maps

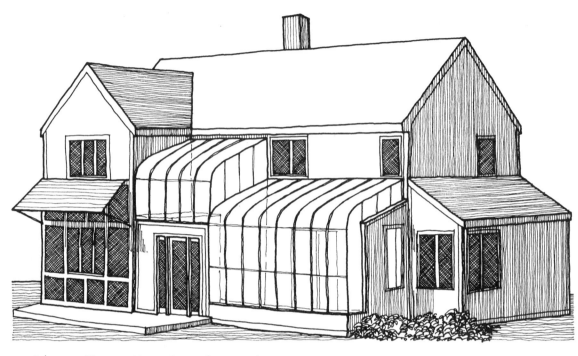

Brookhaven House, View From the Southeast, Total Environmental Action

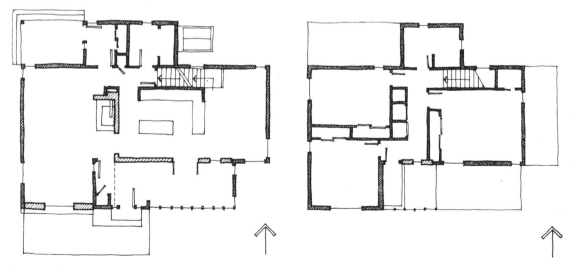

Ground Floor Plan   Second Floor Plan

of climate zones in Appendix A to find the city most representative of the building site. For a full listing of glazing area recommendations, see Reynolds & Stein (2000, pp. 212-216) and Balcomb et al. (1980). Simplified design guidelines have not been developed for Alaska. For passive solar design in Alaska, see Siefert (1981).

The variables are south-facing (N in SH) collection area (A_g) as a fraction of floor area (A_f) and whether or not night insulation is used. The design recommendation takes the general form of:

A solar collection area of (Low A_g / A_f)% to (High A_g / A_f)% of the floor area can be expected to reduce the annual heating load of a building in (Location) by (Low SSF)% to (High SSF)%, or if R-9 (RSI-1.6) night insulation is used, by (Low SSF)% to (High SSF)% (Balcomb et al., 1980, pp. 20–23).

For example, a solar collection area of 15 to 29% of the floor area can be expected to reduce the annual heating load of a building in St. Louis, MO by 21 to 33%, or if *R-9* night insulation is used, by 41 to 65%.

Exceeding the larger end of the recommendations may result in clear day winter overheating. If a high SSF is desired, more mass must be used to dampen extreme interior thermal swings (Strategy 83). If additional mass cannot be stored in the building's structure, accessory storage in a rock bed may be appropriate (see Strategy 104).

The recommendations assume that buildings are well insulated with low infiltration rates, with a better overall thermal loss rate required in more extreme winter climates as follows: <1000 degree days (DD) base 65 °F: 7.6 Btu/DD, ft^2 of floor area; 1000–3000 DD: 6.6; 3000–5000 DD: 5.6; 5000–7000 DD: 4.6; >7000 DD: 3.6. These thermal loss values are exclusive of south wall (N in SH). Metric values are: >556 degree days base 18.3 °C: 24 W/DD, m^2; 556–1667 DD: 20.8; 1667–2778 DD: 17.7; 2778–3889 DD: 14.5; >3889 DD: 11.3.

Upper SSF is based on a limit of 75 °F (24 °C) interior maximum temperature on an average January clear day without night insulation. Internal heat sources are assumed to warm the building by 5 °F (3 °C), representing a skin-load-dominated building such as a residence or light commercial building with low internal loads. Buildings with high internal loads from lights, people, and equipment, generating an internal temperature rise greater than 5 °F (3 °C), such as office buildings, will

USA CITIES	A_{glass}/A_{floor} ratio of solar glazing area to floor area		Approximate SSF No Night Insulation		Approximate SSF R9 (RSI1.6) Night Insulation	
	Low	High	Low	High	Low	High
AR, Little Rock	0.10	0.19	23	38	37	62
AZ, Phoenix	0.06	0.12	37	60	48	75
AZ, Winslow	0.12	0.24	30	47	48	74
CA, Fresno	0.09	0.17	29	46	41	65
CA, Los Angeles	0.05	0.09	36	58	44	72
CA, Santa Maria	0.05	0.11	31	53	42	69
CO, Eagle	0.14	0.29	25	35	53	77
CT, Hartford	0.17	.035	14	19	40	64
DC, Washington	0.12	0.23	18	28	37	61
FL, Jacksonville	0.05	0.09	27	47	35	62
FL, Miami	0.01	0.02	27	48	31	54
ID, Boise	0.14	0.28	27	38	48	71
IN, Indianapolis	0.14	0.28	15	21	37	60
IA, Sioux City	0.23	0.46	20	24	53	76
KS, Dodge City	0.12	0.23	27	42	46	73
LA, New Orleans	0.05	0.11	27	46	35	61
ME, Caribou	0.25	0.50	NR	NR	53	74
MN, Miinneapolis	0.25	0.50	NR	NR	55	76
MS, Jackson	0.08	0.15	24	40	34	59
MO, St. Louis	0.15	0.29	21	33	41	65
MT, Billings	0.16	0.32	24	31	53	76
MT, Cut Bank	0.24	0.49	22	23	62	81
NE, N. Platte	0.17	0.34	25	36	50	76
NV, Ely	0.12	0.23	27	41	50	77
NV, Las Vegas	0.09	0.18	35	56	48	75
NM, Tucumcari	0.10	0.20	30	48	45	73
NY, Buffalo	0.19	0.37	NR	NR	36	57

USA CITIES	A_{glass}/A_{floor} ratio of solar glazing area to floor area		Approximate SSF No Night Insulation		Approximate SSF R9 (RSI1.6) Night Insulation	
	Low	High	Low	High	Low	High
OR, Medford	0.12	0.24	21	32	38	60
OR, Salem	0.12	0.24	21	32	37	59
PA, Philadelphia	0.15	0.29	19	29	38	62
SC, Charleston	0.07	0.14	ZS	41	34	59
TN, Knoxville	0.09	0.18	20	33	33	56
TX, Brownsville	0.03	0.06	27	46	32	57
TX, Fort Worth	0.09	0.17	26	44	38	64
TX, Houston	0.06	0.11	25	43	34	59
TX, Midland	0.09	0.18	32	52	44	72
UT, Salt Lake C.	0.13	0.26	27	39	48	72
WA, Seattle	0.11	0.22	21	30	39	59
WV, Charleston	0.13	0.25	16	24	32	54
WI, Madison	0.20	0.40	IS	17	S1	74
WY, Rock Spr.	0.14	0.28	26	38	54	79
CANADA						
AB, Edmonton	0.25	0.50	NR	NR	54	72
AB, Suffield	0.25	0.50	2B	30	67	85
BC, Nanaimo	0.13	0.26	26	35	45	66
BC, Vancouver	0.13	0.26	20	28	40	60
MB, Winnipeg	0.25	0.50	NR	NR	54	74
NS, Dartmouth	0.14	0.28	17	24	45	70
ON, Moosonee	0.25	0.50	NR	NR	48	67
ON, Ottawa	0.25	0.50	NR	NR	59	80
ON, Toronto	0.18	0.36	17	23	44	68
QC, Normandin	0.25	0.50	NR	NR	54	74

Passive Solar Glazing Area Design Recommendations

have higher SSF performance than those given.

Performance does not significantly depend on the type of passive solar system used, except in the case of direct gain from south windows without night insulation, which will be lower than the SSF values indicated. Performance is significantly improved by the use of night insulation, especially in colder climates. Increased performance with night insulation is a nonlinear function. Much of the value of *R-9* (RSI-1.6) night insulation can be achieved with *R-4* to *R-5* (RSI-0.7 to RSI-0.9). For the effect of night insulation other than *R-9*, see Strategy 97.

Interpolation and limited extrapolation between the recommended values are allowed. Graphic interpolation is simple if the SSF recommendations for the building's climate are first plotted on the on the graph at right, Sizing Glazing for Passive Solar Heating.

The graph shows recommendations for Albuquerque, which is cool and very sunny; Boston, cold and cloudy; Madison, very cold and cloudy; Medford, cool and very cloudy; Nashville, cool and cloudy, and Santa Maria, which is mild and sunny.

To estimate the performance of a passive solar heating design, taking into account design variables such as the system type, amount of mass, and glazing type, refer to the load collector ratio (LCR) method found in Reynolds and Stein (2000, pp. 263-272), Moore (1993, pp. 157-164), or Balcomb et al. (1984, pp. 5.1-5.5). The LCR method is the basis of the *BuilderGuide* software available from the Sustainable Buildings Industry Council (PSIC, 1990). LCR methods for Alaska, are covered in Siefert (1981).

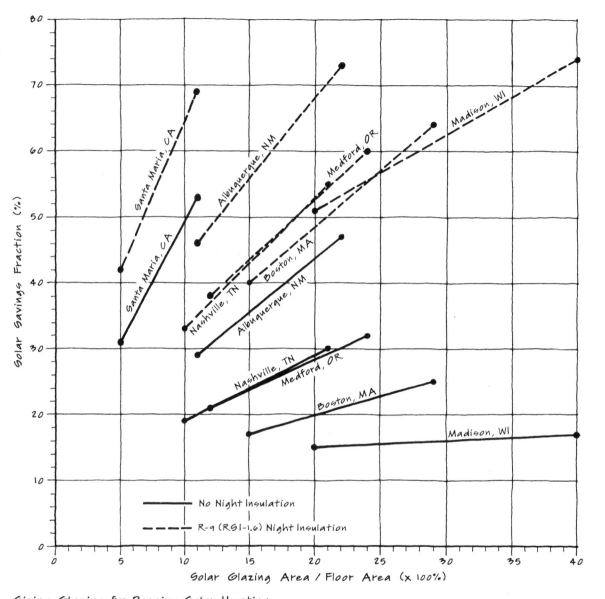

Sizing Glazing for Passive Solar Heating
Plot values from table. Solar glazing should be +/- 30 degrees from south (north in southern hemisphere)

4 *DAYLIGHT APERTURES* **can be enlarged to increase interior illumination levels.** **[daylighting]**

The amount of light that reaches the interior of a room is a function of the apertures' transmissivity, wall and ceiling reflectance, aperture placement and size, room proportion and size, and external obstructions. For a room with average proportions and surface reflectances of approximately 40%, the average amount of light in the space is directly proportional to the area of the glazing (Hopkinson et al., 1966, p. 432). Daylight at locations within the room will vary considerably from the average as a function of their proximity to the apertures. For apertures that are large relative to the wall area, the average reflected value of the interior surfaces falls below 40%, and the glazing area becomes a less accurate indicator of average illumination.

Obstructions outside the glazing, such as fences, trees, and other buildings, block the aperture's view of the sky and reduce the amount of light that falls on the glazing. The sky view angle *(v)* is the angle subtended, in the vertical plane perpendicular to the window, by sky visible from the center of the aperture. See the diagrams on the next page (CIBSE, 1987; Littlefair, 1991, pp. 58–59).

The graph, Sizing Windows for Daylighting, may be used to determine the glazing area needed to achieve a certain average daylight factor for a given floor area or to determine the average daylight factor for a combination of given floor and glazing areas. To find the required size of a vertical unobstructed daylight aperture, begin on the upper graph on the vertical axis with the room's floor area, move horizontally to the diagonal for the design daylight factor (see table at the end of this strategy). From the intersection, move horizontally to read the required glazing area on the horizontal scale.

For sloped or obstructed glazing, continue to the lower graph, dropping along the line of unobstructed vertical glazing area to the diagonal for the aperture's sky view angle (v), (see diagram). From the intersection, move horizontally to read the revised glazing area.

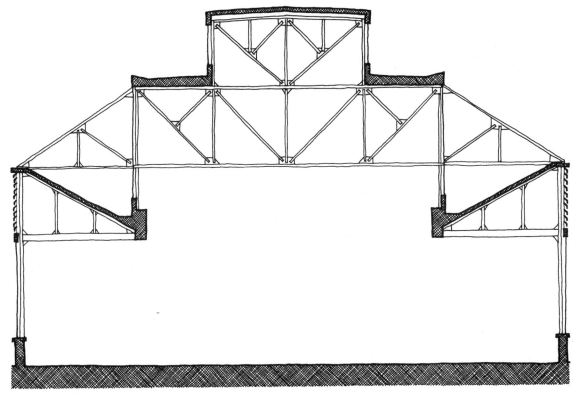

Packard Forge Shop, Detroit, Michigan, Albert Kahn

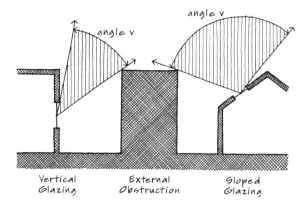

Sky View Angle (v) From Glazing

The graph assumes a 60% transmissivity for clear double glazing plus frame effects, a maintenance factor of 80%, an average room reflectance of 40%, and a fairly large room, about the size of a classroom. It was developed using a model from Littlefair (1988). If other glazing and frame types with poorer visible light transmission are used (Strategy 101), the glazing area will need to be increased proportionally. Because room size and proportions affect the pattern of internal reflections, light in small rooms is reflected more times before reaching the work plane than light in large rooms. *For small rooms, such as bedrooms and private offices, increase the glazing size from the graph by up to 60%. For very large rooms, such as a gymnasium, reduce the glazing size by up to 30%.*

For sidelighting, the daylight factors apply to a floor zone with a maximum depth into the room of 2.5 times the height of the window wall (Strategy 71). For toplighting, the floor area associated with the glazing can be estimated by projecting 45° lines from the opening to the floor. If more than one opening type is used for the same area, the daylight factors may be added. An example of using more than one opening type is Albert Kahn's use of sidelighting and monitors in the **Packard Forge Shop** in Detroit, Michigan (Hildebrand, 1974, p. 57).

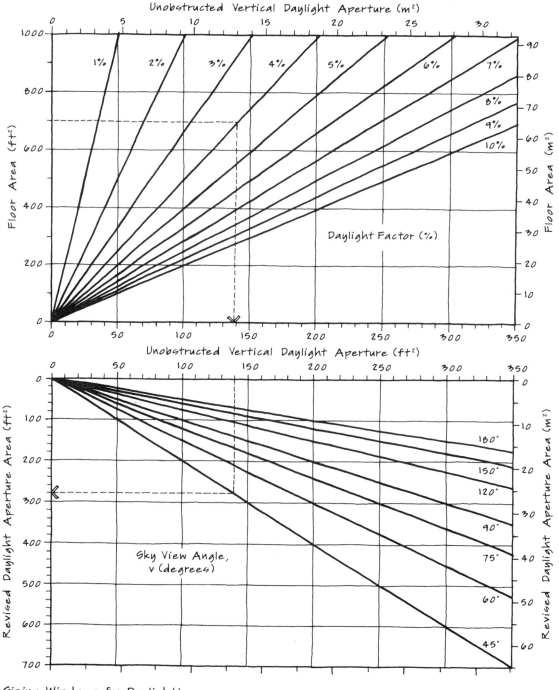

Sizing Windows for Daylighting

TASK/USE	fc (Lux)	10°–20°	30°	40°	50°	60–70°
				Latitude		
Assembly Tasks, simple	20-50 (215-538)	1.5-3	1.5-4	2-6	3.5-9	4-10
moderatly difficult	50-100 (538-1076)	3-6.5	4-8	5.5-14.5	9-17.5	10-20
Air Terminals	10-20 (108-215)	0.5-1	1-1.5	1-2.5	2-3.5	2-4
Bank, lobby	10-20 (108-215)	0.5-1	1-1.5	1-2.5	2-3.5	2-4
teller	50-100 (538-1076)	3-6.5	4-8	5.5-14.5	9-17.5	10-20
Calssroom, general	20-50 (215-538)	1.5-3	1.5-4	2-6	3.5-9	4-10
reading	50-100 (538-1076)	3-6.5	4-8	5.5-14.5	9-17.5	10-20
Conference Room	20-50 (215-538)	1.5-3	1.5-4	2-6	3.5-9	4-10
Corridor, stairs	5-10 (54-108)	0.5-1	0.5-1	0.5-1	1-2	1-2
Dining Hall	5-10 (54-108)	0.5-1	0.5-1	0.5-1	1-2	1-2
Drafting	50-100 (538-1076)	3-6.5	4-8	5.5-14.5	9-17.5	10-20
Exhibition, general	10-20 (108-215)	0.5-1	1-1.5	1-2.5	2-3.5	2-4
display	20-50 (215-538)	1.5-3	1.5-4	2-6	3.5-9	4-10
Hotel Rooms	20-50 (215-538)	1.5-3	1.5-4	2-6	3.5-9	4-10
Lobby, lounge, reception	10-20 (108-215)	0.5-1	1-1.5	1-2.5	2-3.5	2-4
Library stacks, active	20-50 (215-538)	1.5-3	1.5-4	2-6	3.5-9	4-10
inactive	5-10 (54-108)	0.5-1	0.5-1	0.5-1	1-2	1-2
Locker Rooms	10-20 (108-215)	0.5-1	1-1.5	1-2.5	2-3.5	2-4
Museum Display	20-50 (215-538)	1.5-3	1.5-4	2-6	3.5-9	4-10
Offices, general	10-20 (108-215)	0.5-1	1-1.5	1-2.5	2-3.5	2-4
Reading, normal	20-50 (215-538)	1.5-3	1.5-4	2-6	3.5-9	4-10
Restaurant Kitchen	50-100 (538-1076)	3-6.5	4-8	5.5-14.5	9-17.5	10-20
Residences, kitchens	20-50 (215-538)	1.5-3	1.5-4	2-6	3.5-9	4-10
living	10-20 (108-215)	0.5-1	1-1.5	1-2.5	2-3.5	2-4
bedrooms	5-10 (54-108)	0.5-1	0.5-1	0.5-1	1-2	1-2
Sewing	50-100 (538-1076)	3-6.5	4-8	5.5-14.5	9-17.5	10-20
Science Lab	50-100 (538-1076)	3-6.5	4-8	5.5-14.5	9-17.5	10-20
Sports, indoor	50-100 (538-1076)	3-6.5	4-8	5.5-14.5	9-17.5	10-20
Toilet Rooms	10-20 (108-215)	0.5-1	1-1.5	1-2.5	2-3.5	2-4

Recommended Daylight Factors by Room Use and Site Latitude

Preliminary design target daylight factors are shown in the table, Recommended Daylight Factors by Room Use and Site Latitude. The table is based on IES illuminance recommendations for each use (Technique 13) and the outside illuminance available during 9 AM–5 PM (Technique 9). For 10–20° latitude, the indoor illuminance targets will be met over 90% of the time; for latitudes 30–50°, 85% of hours; for 60°, 75%; and at 70°, less than 60%. A more specific design daylight factor for the building's exact latitude and interior illuminance target can be determined using Technique 9.

95 **The area of *AIR FLOW WINDOWS* used to temper fresh air for ventilation supply or reclaim heat from ventilation exhaust can be sized to match the ventilation load. [heating and cooling]**

One way to reduce the energy used to heat or cool incoming air without reducing its flow (volume per unit time) below safe limits is to use the heat or cold escaping from the building to heat or cool the incoming air. Fan-powered air-to-air heat exchangers are frequently used for this purpose in ducted systems (Strategy 108). Although not as efficient, ventilation air can also be heated or cooled by bringing it past exterior building surfaces, such as windows. This has the advantage of reducing or eliminating fresh air duct work and supplying fresh air at the point of need. Aalto used this approach at the **Tuberculosis Sanatorium in Paimio,** Finland, where air is brought in-between layers of glass to individual rooms. Heat being lost through the glass is used to heat the incoming air (Fleig, 1975, p. 78).

"Supply air ventilation windows" take in ventilation air between the panes of a multilayer assembly, bringing outside air temperature nearer to the interior temperature. "Exhaust air ventilation windows" remove stale air from the room, passing it between the glazing layers on its way either to the outside or through ducts to a central heat exchanger (Hastings, 1994, pp. 93–111). Exhaust air windows decrease conductive heat transfer, but have no effect on ventilation heat load.

In air flow windows, the effective R-value is approximately doubled. For a supply air window, the ventilation heat exchange efficiency is about 20–50% (Traver et al., 1991; Bakarat, 1987). The air temperature change and heat exchange efficiency depend on the *R*-values of the glass layers, the ΔT between inside and outside, the amount of solar radiation incident on the window, the rate of air flow through the window, and whether or not a layer of blinds is used to absorb solar gain in the cavity.

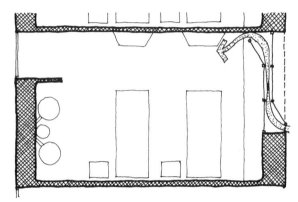

Typical Patient's Room, Tuberculosis Sanitorium, Paimio, Finland, Alvar Aalto

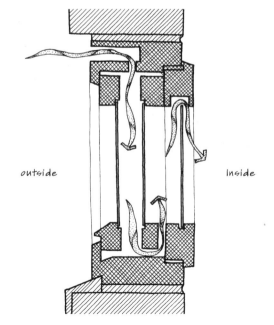

outside   inside

Supply Air Ventilation Window

Preliminary air flow window sizing can be determined from the graph. Rates of fresh air ventilation for different building types can be determined from Strategy 87. Use the rate of required outdoor air to enter the graph on the horizontal axis. Move vertically to the diagonal for the rate of air flow through the window, then horizontally to read the air flow window area as a percentage of ventilated floor area.

Use the upper part of the flow rate zone for buildings with lower outdoor air requirements, such as residences. Use the lower part of the zone for buildings with higher fresh air requirements and for south-facing (north-facing in the Southern Hemisphere) air flow windows with collector blinds that capture solar radiation.

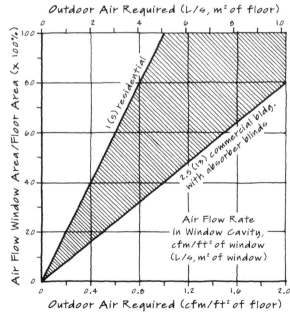

Approximate Sizing of Air Flow Windows

96 *LIGHT SHELVES* **can be used to shade view glazing, evenly distribute light and reduce glare. [cooling and daylighting]**

Compared to an ordinary window of equal size and height, a window divided into upper and lower sections by a horizontal light shelf performs better in several ways. If the light shelf extends beyond the exterior surface of the glazing on sunny exposures, it can be used to shade the view glazing. At the same time, it can reflect light off its top surface through the upper glazing to the ceiling, where it is then reflected deeper into the space. The light shelf section that extends into the space also reflects light from the upper part of the window deeper into the space, while decreasing the light levels immediately adjacent to the window, thereby evening the distribution of light throughout the space. The interior portion of the light shelf also blocks the occupants' view of the sky, which is a potential source of glare.

The **Lockheed Building 157** in Sunnyvale, California, designed by Leo Daly, uses light shelves on both its north and south edges. The building is rectangular in plan, glazed on the north and south sides, with service functions located on the windowless east and west ends. A central atrium extends through all five floors, supplying light to the center of the building. The light shelves on the south side project out and are angled to reflect the high summer sun through the clear glazing, deep into the space. The lower winter sun passes directly through the glazing and reflects off the interior light shelves. The clear upper glazing can be shaded by an exterior translucent roll-down shade. The light shelf shades the lower glazing, which is tinted and has a reflective coating. On the north side an exterior light shelf isn't needed for sun protection and the lower glazing doesn't require a reflective coating. The light shelf also houses ducts and indirect fluorescent lighting (Vonier et al., 1984, p. 144; Benton & Fountain, 1990).

The section and elevation of Michael Hopkins & Partners' **Inland Revenue Offices** in Nottingham, England, shows light shelves on the lower three floors. The upper floor has a central ridge skylight that provides higher internal light levels, and thus more even distribution, so a light shelf is not required. Light reflected from the

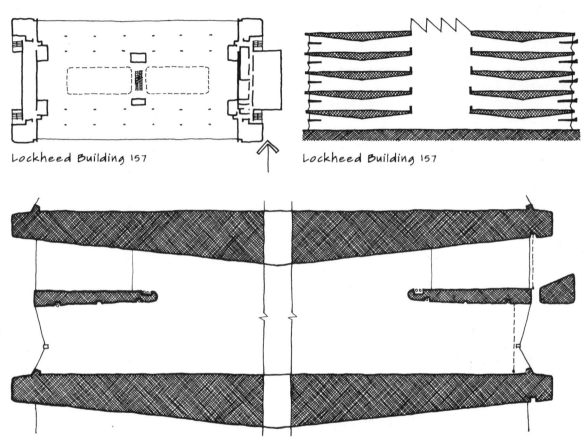

Lockheed Building 157

Lockheed Building 157

Lockheed Building 157, Sunnyvale, California, Leo Daly

shelf bounces onto a vaulted concrete ceiling that helps to spread it. The glass shelves have a partially reflective upper surface and a fritted lower surface, transmitting less than 20% of the light and thus preventing glare that can be caused from a dark shelf bottom. The venetian blinds between the glazing layers are fixed for shading at 45° in the section above the light shelf and are adjustable in the view glass section below. Because the upper blinds always block the view of the sky, an internal shelf to reduce glare is not needed (*Architectural Review*, 1995; Buchanan, 1995).

The optimum size of light shelves is governed by several considerations. They should be as low as possible, without interfering with view through the lower part of the window, so that as much light as possible reflects off their tops and penetrates deep into the space. If reducing solar gain is an important concern, the light shelves should extend beyond the building far enough to shade the view glazing during the cooling season. They should extend inside the building enough to block the view of the bright sky, thus reducing glare.

The length of the external light shelf should vary with orientation. For 20° either side of south (north in the Southern Hemisphere), make the shelf 1.25–1.5 times the height of the clerestory. Beyond 20° east or west of south (N in SH), extend the length to 1.5–2.0 times the clerestory glass height (Place & Howard, 1990, p. 50).

To prevent excess heat gain, the upper glazing above a light shelf should be shaded on south exposures (N in SH) during the cooling season. This can be accomplished with reflective louvers or by recessing the upper glazing to the back of the shelf. Smaller overhangs above the glazing improve light capture.

Under clear skies, reflected-beam daylighting on the south side (N in SH) from curved mirrors can increase the daylit zone from about 15–20 ft (4.5–6 m) to about 30–35 ft (9–11 m) and up to 45 ft (14 m) with sun-tracking mirrors (Place & Howard, 1990, pp. 17–18). Any beam-reflecting design should be evaluated for its potential increase to solar heat gains and glare.

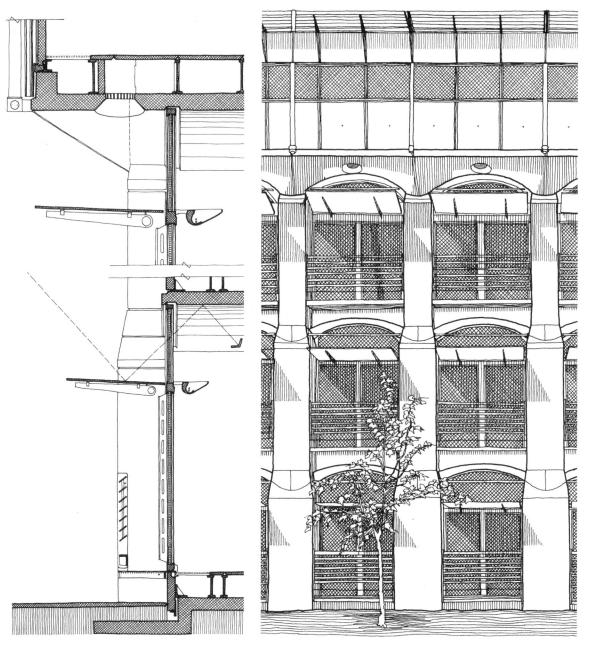

Inland Revenue Offices, Nottingham, England, Michael Hopkins & Partners

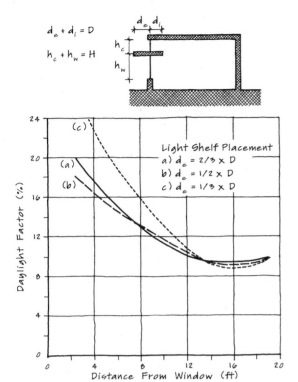

Clear Sky Daylight Distribution From Light Shelf, $h_c = 1/3\ H$

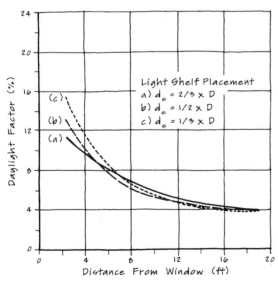

Overcast Sky Daylight Distribution From Light Shelf, $h_c = 1/3\ H$

The upper surface of the light shelf should be white or, if heat gain is not an issue, mirrored. Ceiling reflectance should be high (Strategy 78). The top surface of the light shelf should never be seen by occupants, because of its glare potential. A mirrored light shelf with a white ceiling performs better for lighting than a white light shelf with a mirrored ceiling (Baker et al., 1993, p. 5.52).

Light shelves can be used on any orientation if skies are mostly overcast, and on south orientations (N in SH) for reflecting sunlight. Under clear sky conditions, light shelves on east and west orientations should be designed to control glare from low-angle sun.

Both the vertical position in the wall and the length of the shelf outside the glass impact the amount of light reflected to the ceiling. The two graphs of Daylight Distribution From Light Shelves show the effect of these design variables on daylight factor levels in a large room (Bourbekri, 1992, p. 98).

The graphs assume diffuse lighting conditions without sun under both clear and overcast skies. With diffuse sky, light shelves mainly control glare, increasing the daylight at the back of a room very little. A lower position will increase light to the center of the room. By contrast, curved mirrored specular light shelves receiving direct sunlight and reflecting through relatively small openings can significantly increase daylight levels in the rear of the space (Beltran et al., 1994).

Tilting the external part of a light shelf above horizontal can increase the light reflected onto the ceiling. **For white shelves facing south (N in SH), make shelf tilt = 40° – (0.5 x latitude°). For east, west, and north (S in SH) exposures, make shelf tilt = 15° (Moore, 1991, pp. 88–89). Decrease tilt from the recommendation for diffusing glazing or if an overhang shades the glass. Increase rear wall reflectance with tilt. The optimum tilt is less for shallow rooms than for deep rooms, as can be seen in the graph, Optimum Tilt of Light Shelves (Baker et al., 1993, p. 5.55).** Remember that sloping the shelf reduces it effectiveness at shading the lower glazing, so it should be lengthened or thickened.

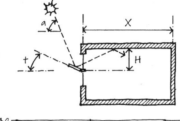

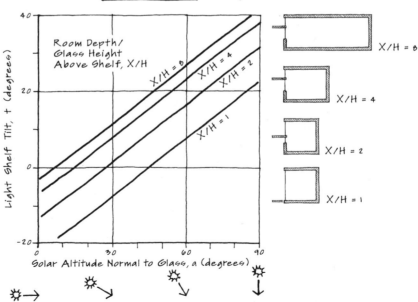

Optimum Tilt of Light Shelves, Clear Sky

97 A *MOVABLE INSULATION* layer can be placed over windows to reduce heat loss at night. [heating]

Windows are usually the weakest link in the building envelope in terms of heat loss during cold weather. Heat flows out through a double-glazed window 10 times faster, or more, than it does through a well-insulated wall. But because it is desirable to have large windows for admitting solar radiation during the day and because the most effective window-insulating systems are opaque, the question of how to store the window insulation during the day becomes an important design consideration. While there seems to be an almost infinite variety of movable insulation schemes (Shurcliff, 1980), there are only a few conceptual design decisions that must be made at the schematic level. The two most important are whether the insulation should be in large rigid panels or flexible coverings made of small rigid pieces or membranes, and whether the insulation should be located outside, inside, or within the plane of the glazing.

Rigid panels, which require the most storage space, can be completely removed and stored in racks, hinged at the top or bottom, or mounted on sliding rails. The economic benefit of window insulation can be increased if it is usable not only when it is in the closed position, but also when it is open. An example of this is the **Reflecting Insulating Trombe Wall Shutter,** which serves as a reflecting surface to increase the solar radiation collected. Rigid panels may be used in the plane of the windows like sliding pocket doors or broken into **Insulated Louvers** as they are for the glazing in this sloped ceiling. The louvers may be adjusted to reflect light to the thermal mass without causing glare (Wright & Andrejko, 1982, p. 55).

Flexible covers take much less storage area than rigid covers and may be motorized and automatically closed at night and opened during the day. The trombe wall example uses a **Self-Inflating Curtain** made of several radiant reflective layers that are rolled to storage in a recessed ceiling cavity. It is frequently simpler and less expensive to insulate several sections of glazing together than to treat each window separately.

The average R-value of a window over a 24-hr period can be determined from the graph. Find the

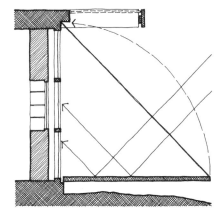

Reflecting Insulating Shutter

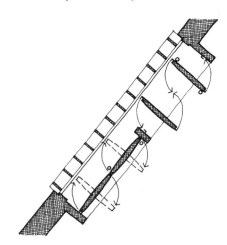

Insulated Louvers

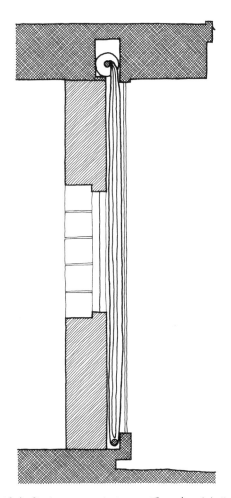

Self-Inflating Curtain on Trombe Wall

R-value of the glass on the vertical axis and move horizontally to intersect the diagonal line corresponding to the R-value of the movable insulation and the period of operation. Then move vertically to the horizontal axis to determine the average R-value of the window over 24 hr.

The example *R*-values of glazing on the vertical scale represent the total average *R* of the window, including glass and frame (ASHRAE, 1997, p. 29.8). Triple and quadruple glazing assemblies can be made with glass or clear films for the inner layers.

Movable insulation varies in thickness depending on R-value and varies from about 1/4 in (7 mm) for roll-down curtains with an R-4 (RSI–0.7), to 2–3 in (50–75 mm) for multilayer curtains with R-9 (RSI-1.6), to rigid boards with an R of 4–6/in of thickness (RSI-0.3/cm).

The use of night insulation increases solar heating performance significantly in most climates because it allows heat gain when the sun is out and minimizes heat loss when the sun isn't out (Strategy 93). This is especially true in cool or cold winter climates where uninsulated solar apertures may lose as much heat as they gain. An alternative to the use of movable insulation is to use glazing with a much higher R-value, but to capture solar heat and admit sufficient daylight, it must have a high shading coefficient or solar heat gain coefficient (Strategy 101).

In a cold climate like Grand Rapids, Michigan, doubling the south glass from 18 to 38% of the floor area improves the annual solar savings fraction (SSF) by only 1%. Adding *R*-9 night insulation, however, improves the annual SSF by a factor of 3–4, allowing an SSF of 39–61%. Even in climates with relatively mild winters, night insulation can dramatically improve performance. In Meridian, Mississippi, *R*-9 night insulation improves performance by about 48%.

The design guidelines for solar aperture sizing (Strategy 93) relate solar savings fraction values to glazing size and floor area for conditions with no night insulation and for *R*-9 night insulation. While *R*-9 can be achieved in practice, it may not be cost-effective or practical in all applications. Much of the value of *R*-9 (RSI-1.6) night insulation can be achieved with an *R*-value of 4–5 (an RSI-value of 0.7–0.9).

To estimate the effect on SSF of adding less than R-9 (RSI-1.6) night insulation to solar collection apertures:

1) Find from Strategy 93 the approximate SSF for the building, assuming *R*-9 (RSI-1.6) night insulation.

2) Enter the **graph, Effect of Adding Night Insulation on Solar Heating Performance**, on the horizontal axis with the *R*-value of the insulation to be used. Move vertically to the curve for the solar system type being insulated. From the intersection, move left to read the percentage performance change to the building's SSF. The graph was developed based on models in Balcomb et al. (1980, 1983, 1984).

3) Multiply the *R*-9 SSF from Step 1 by the percentage from the chart (from Step 2).

If this procedure is done for the upper and lower recommended glazing areas, one can plot a new line for SSF performance on the graph in Strategy 93.

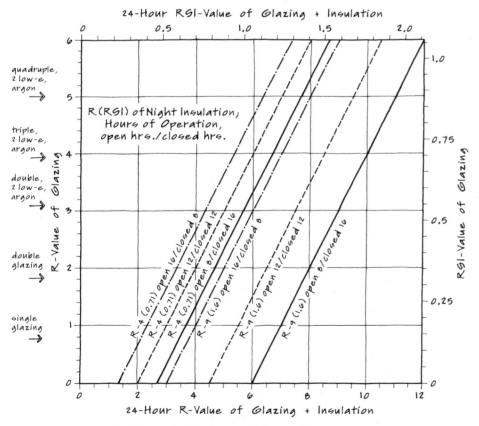

24-hr Average R-Value of Glazing and Insulation

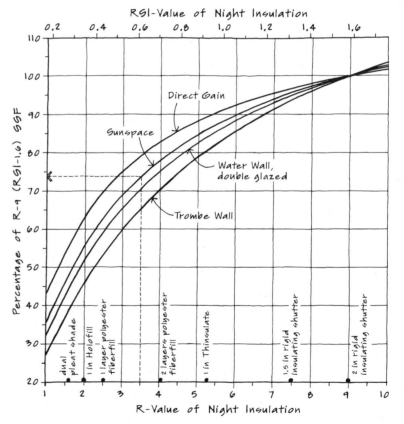

Effect of Adding Night Insulation on Solar Savings Fraction

98 *DAYLIGHT-ENHANCING SHADES* can protect windows from solar gain while preserving sky view, reflecting daylight, and reducing glare. [cooling and daylighting]

Buildings that require shaded glazing frequently also need to reduce the internal heat generated by electric lighting. However, because they cut off the windows' view of the sky dome, shading devices also reduce interior daylight levels. For example, a 6-ft (1.8-m) horizontal overhang outside a 24-ft (7.3-m) deep room produces a reduction in illumination of 39% near the window and 22% near the rear wall (B. H. Evans, 1981, p. 62). Other studies predict reductions in illumination of 50% from exterior vertical fins at 45° to the building surface (Ander & Navvab, 1983, p. 180). Carefully designed perforations or louvers in overhangs and fins allow them to maintain the same shading characteristics but still reflect light into the space (Millet et al., 1981, p. 333). A window also "sees" more of the sky dome through well-designed louvers, thereby increasing the daylight in the room.

Horn & Mortland used a series of louvers to form the overhang in their **Sunshine School** in Fresno, California The louvers are tightly spaced near the building to shade the high sun and loosely spaced farther away from the building to shade the low sun. In addition to admitting diffuse radiation, the open overhang also allows the circulation of air within the shading device itself, reducing heat transfers from it to the interior spaces (Olgyay & Olgyay, 1957, p. 105).

For daylight reflection, louvers should be light in color, as they are in Aalto's **Library at Seinäjoki,** in Finland, to reflect a large proportion of the diffuse light into the space (Dunster, 1978, p. 51). *Because light reflected from shading devices is a potential source of glare, they should be carefully located to avoid the occupants' field of view.* In selecting materials and finishes for shading devices, it is important to distinguish those which reflect light but not heat, such as white paint, from those which reflect both light and heat, such as polished metals.

Reflectances of colors can be found in Strategy 78, Daylight Reflecting Surfaces. *Designers should avoid using for shading devices materials and finishes that*

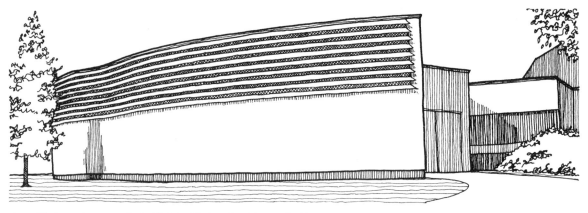

Seinäjoki Library, Seinäjoki, Finland, Alvar Aalto

Sunshine School, Fresno, California, Horn & Mortland

make good solar reflectors (see strategy 79, *Exterior Surface Color* and 82, *Solar Reflectors*). *Heat reflectance of materials is also shown on the graph in Strategy 81, Double Skin Materials. The best options for shading devices are in the upper left quadrant of that chart.*

Opaque shading devices on sunny facades can appear dark on the side in shade, such as underneath an overhang. This apparent darkness, in contrast to the more well lit surfaces can cause the perception of glare. *Therefore, shady sides of shading devices should be very light in color.* A perforated shade allows a small amount of light to penetrate the shading surface, lightening the appearance of the underside while still blocking most of the solar radiation.

This strategy was used by the Hampshire County Architect's Department for the **Queen's Inclosure Middle School** in Cowplain, England. Perforated curved metal louvers are used to block sun on both of the building's long facades: on the south side to shade the window wall and on the north, to reflect low-angle winter sun and light into the north side rooms. The north facade faces a forest, so the windows' small sky view is increased by reflection from the louvers. To ensure effective shading and reflecting, the angle of the louvers can be adjusted seasonally with a system of hand cranks.

This allows the building to benefit from the high heat reflectance of the metal in winter when heat is needed and outdoor illuminance is lower, but avoid the liability of heat gain in summer (because reflections can be adjusted away from the glass) when the extra light is less needed because of the much brighter skies (Davey, 1990; Williams, 1991).

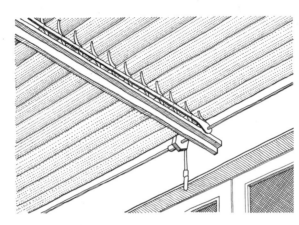

Perforated Louver Detail,
Middle School in Cowplain

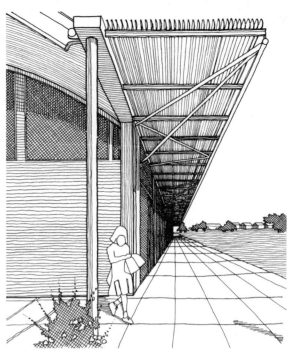

South Facade Louvers,
Middle School in Cowplain

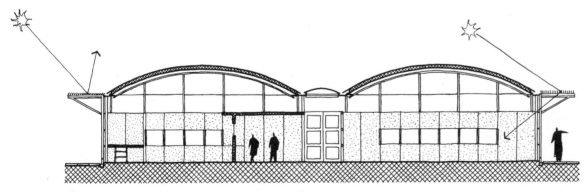

Queen's Inclosure, Middle School, Cowplain, England,
Hampshire County Architect's Department

99 An *EXTERNAL SHADING* layer outside the window can shade the glazing and reduce solar heat gain. [cooling]

Exterior shading devices can be either horizontal, vertical, or a combination of horizontal and vertical called "egg crates." Horizontal shades, like the overhangs on the **Radbill Building,** by Louis Kahn, provide effective shading on the south facade (north in the Southern Hemisphere) when the sun altitude is high. The depth of the device determines the length of the shadow on the window wall. In the Radbill building, the depth of the overhangs varies with the height of the glazing. They are deep on the ground floor, where the glass extends from just above the floor to the ceiling; and they are short on the top floor, where the sill heights are rel-

atively high. The overhangs are punctured by flue tiles to let reflected light penetrate the glazing and to dissipate heat absorbed by the shades (Olgyay & Olgyay, 1957, p. 100).

The sun is higher in the summer than in the winter, so horizontal shades can be proportioned to shade in the summer but admit sun in the winter to help heat the building. Because the summer sun's movement is symmetrical around Jun 21 (Dec 21 in the Southern Hemisphere), south-facing (N in SH) horizontal shades that shade the glazing in hot months (August and September; February & March in SH) will also shade in cooler months (March and April; September & October in SH) when the sun might be welcome. This problem can be solved by making the shades seasonally adjustable, like canvas awnings. Deciduous vines make effective shades since they are bare in the cool spring but have dense foliage throughout the hot summer and early fall.

The **Price Tower,** in Bartlesville, Oklahoma, by Frank Lloyd Wright, uses both horizontal and adjustable vertical shades, depending on orientation. Vertical shades are effective when the sun is low and the broad side of the vertical elements faces the sun (Wright, 1956; *Architectural Forum*, 2/1956). Vertical shades perpendicular to the window are most effective on the north side (S in SH), where no horizontal element is needed, except at tropical latitudes where the sun is much higher.

Egg crates combine the advantages of both horizontal and vertical shades and are particularly effective on facades that do not face south. On the west facade of the **Millowners' Building,** in Ahmedabad, India, by Le Corbusier, the horizontal elements shade in the early afternoon when the sun is high and the angled vertical elements shade in the late afternoon when the sun is low and in the west (Futagawa, 1975).

S. Radbill Building, Philadelphia, Pennsylvania, Louis I. Kahn

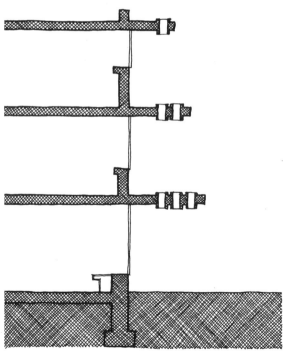

S. Radbill Building, South Wall Section

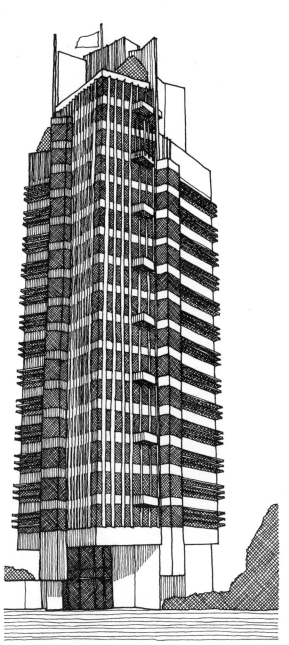

Price Tower, Bartlesville, Oklahoma,
Frank Lloyd Wright

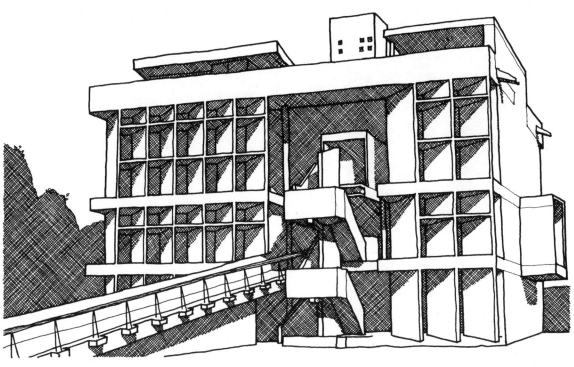

Millowner's Association Building, West Facade

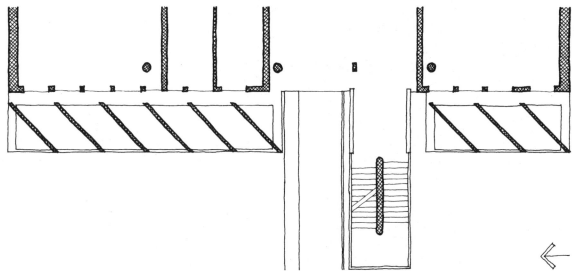

Millowner's Association Building, Ahmedabad, India, Le Corbusier

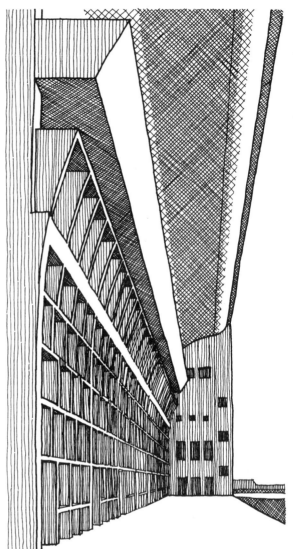

**Palace of Justice,
Chandigarh, India, Le Corbusier**

Shading devices can vary in size without changing their shading characteristics, as long as the *ratio* between the depth and the spacing of the elements remains constant. An example is the **Palace of Justice**, in Chandigarh, India, by Le Corbusier, where the depth and spacing of the screen varies with height (Futagawa, 1974).

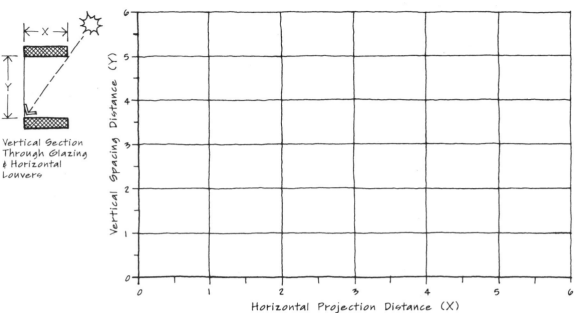

Vertical Section
Through Glazing
& Horizontal
Louvers

Sizing Horizontal Shading for a Building's Latitude
(Plot line slopes using data from tables for horizontal louvers)

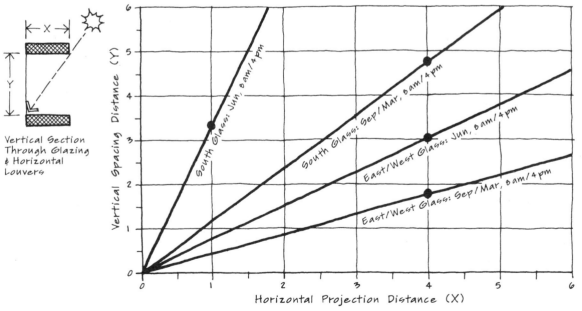

Vertical Section
Through Glazing
& Horizontal
Louvers

Sizing Horizontal Shading for 40 degrees N Latitude
(Line slopes were plotted using data from tables for horizontal louvers)

Because shading devices are in the direct sun, special care must be taken so that they do not cause glare or transfer the heat they absorb into the interior of the building. The proper size and spacing of shading elements is a function of the orientation of the windows and the time of day and year when shading is needed. The times when shading is needed can be determined by using Technique 20.

Even when the glazing is totally shaded, diffused light from the sky, ground, and reflection and radiation from the shading elements will contribute 20% of the total exterior solar radiation to the space in the form of light and heat (Olgyay & Olgyay, 1957, p. 71).

The size and spacing of some simple shading elements may be estimated from the three tables which follow, or values from the tables may be used to create a customized horizontal louver sizing graph for the building's latitude. First, determine the period of required shade (Technique 20).

To determine the length of a horizontal louver, use the first table for windows facing south (N in SH) and the second for windows facing east or west. Using times and dates that match shading criteria (Technique 20) find the value of P from the row for the building site's latitude. Multiply the vertical spacing, Y, of louvers by the value P to determine louver length, X.

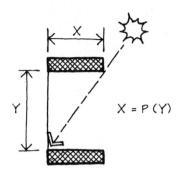

$X = P(Y)$

Vertical Section Through Glazing & Horizontal Louvers

Latitude North lat.	8 AM / 4 PM							9 AM / 3 PM						
	Dec	Nov/Jan	Oct/Feb	Sep/Mar	Aug/Apr	May/Jul	Jun	Dec	Nov/Jan	Oct/Feb	Sep/Mar	Aug/Apr	May/Jul	Jun
0°	0.87	0.73	0.38	0.00	N.S.	N.S.	N.S.	0.61	0.51	0.27	0.00	N.S.	N.S.	N.S.
4°	1.00	0.84	0.46	0.07	N.S.	N.S.	N.S.	0.71	0.61	0.35	0.07	N.S.	N.S.	N.S.
8°	1.15	0.97	0.55	0.14	N.S.	N.S.	N.S.	0.83	0.71	0.43	0.14	N.S.	N.S.	N.S.
12°	1.32	1.11	0.65	0.21	0.01	N.S.	N.S.	0.95	0.82	0.51	0.21	0.01	N.S.	N.S.
16°	1.54	1.28	0.75	0.29	0.08	N.S.	N.S.	1.09	0.94	0.60	0.29	0.08	N.S.	N.S.
20°	1.80	1.49	0.87	0.36	0.15	0.00	N.S.	1.26	1.08	0.70	0.36	0.15	0.00	N.S.
24°	2.14	1.74	1.00	0.45	0.22	0.07	0.01	1.46	1.25	0.81	0.45	0.22	0.07	0.01
28°	2.60	2.06	1.15	0.53	0.29	0.14	0.08	1.70	1.44	0.94	0.53	0.29	0.14	0.08
32°	3.26	2.48	1.32	0.62	0.37	0.21	0.15	2.01	1.68	1.08	0.62	0.37	0.21	0.15
36°	4.31	3.09	1.53	0.73	0.45	0.29	0.22	2.42	1.98	1.24	0.73	0.45	0.29	0.22
40°	6.27	4.03	1.80	0.84	0.54	0.36	0.30	2.99	2.38	1.43	0.84	0.54	0.36	0.30
44°	11.30	5.70	2.13	0.97	0.63	0.45	0.37	3.87	2.94	1.67	0.97	0.63	0.45	0.37
48°	54.21	9.60	2.59	1.11	0.74	0.53	0.46	5.41	3.79	1.97	1.11	0.74	0.53	0.46
52°	B.H.	29.41	3.25	1.28	0.85	0.62	0.54	8.81	5.26	2.37	1.28	0.85	0.62	0.54
56°	B.H.	B.H.	4.29	1.48	0.98	0.73	0.64	23.15	8.43	2.92	1.48	0.98	0.73	0.64
60°	B.H.	B.H.	6.23	1.73	1.13	0.84	0.74	B.H.	20.72	3.76	1.73	1.13	0.84	0.74
64°	B.H.	B.H.	11.17	2.05	1.30	0.97	0.86	B.H.	B.H.	5.19	2.05	1.30	0.97	0.86
68°	B.H.	B.H.	51.28	2.48	1.51	1.11	0.98	B.H.	B.H.	8.26	2.48	1.51	1.11	0.98
72°	B.H.	B.H.	B.H.	3.08	1.76	1.28	1.13	B.H.	B.H.	19.72	3.08	1.76	1.28	1.13
South lat.	Jun	May/Jul	Aug/Apr	Sep/Mar	Oct/Feb	Nov/Jan	Dec	Jun	May/Jul	Aug/Apr	Sep/Mar	Oct/Feb	Nov/Jan	Dec

Values of P for South-Facing (N in SH) Horizontal Louvers
B.H. = Sun Below Horizon; N.S. = No Sun on facade.

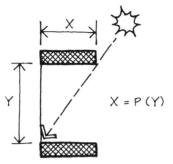

Vertical Section Through Glazing
& Horizontal Louvers

$X = P (Y)$

The sizing of louvers and overhangs is a function of the profile angle, the angle of the sun normal to the plane of the window. Profile angles for any date and time can be determined using the *LOF Sun Angle Calculator* for latitudes 24–52° (Libbey-Owens-Ford, 1974) or in a spreadsheet using the *PEC Solar Calculator* (Benton & Marcial, 1993).

To create a custom horizontal louver sizing graph for a given latitude, select the months and times for which shading is desired. Calculate the Y projection for one assumed X distance. Plot the X and Y lengths on the graph and draw a line from the zero point through the plotted point to establish the slope of the line. Repeat for as many conditions as dersired.

The last table gives solar azimuth angles useful for sizing vertical fins on easterly or westerly facades. Slanted vertical fins are more effective at shading than fins perpendicular to an east or west-facing window, which will allow full sun penetration when the sun is shining from due east or west (perpendicular to the glass). The azimuth angles given in the table are measured from south (N in SH). *Use the azimuth east of south for morning shade on an easterly facade and measure west from south for afternoon shade on a*

Latitude	9 AM / 3 PM							9 AM / 3 PM						
North lat.	Dec	Nov/Jan	Oct/Feb	Sep/Mar	Aug/Apr	May/Jul	Jun	Dec	Nov/Jan	Oct/Feb	Sep/Mar	Aug/Apr	May/Jul	Jun
0°	1.73	1.73	1.73	1.73	1.73	1.73	1.73	1.00	1.00	1.00	1.00	1.00	1.00	1.00
4°	4.24	4.15	3.94	3.74	3.54	3.41	3.35	1.85	1.83	1.78	1.74	1.69	1.65	1.64
8°	1.99	1.95	1.85	1.75	1.65	1.59	1.56	1.11	1.09	1.05	1.01	0.97	0.94	0.93
12°	2.17	2.09	1.93	1.77	1.63	1.53	1.50	1.18	1.15	1.08	1.02	0.96	0.92	0.90
16°	2.40	2.28	2.02	1.80	1.61	1.49	1.44	1.26	1.22	1.13	1.04	0.96	0.91	0.88
20°	2.69	2.51	2.14	1.84	1.60	1.46	1.40	1.37	1.31	1.18	1.06	0.96	0.90	0.87
24°	3.09	2.81	2.28	1.90	1.60	1.43	1.37	1.51	1.42	1.24	1.09	0.97	0.89	0.86
28°	3.64	3.20	2.46	1.96	1.61	1.41	1.34	1.68	1.56	1.32	1.13	0.98	0.89	0.85
32°	4.46	3.75	2.68	2.04	1.63	1.40	1.32	1.91	1.74	1.42	1.18	1.00	0.89	0.85
36°	5.79	4.54	2.96	2.14	1.65	1.40	1.31	2.23	1.97	1.54	1.24	1.02	0.90	0.85
40°	8.31	5.81	3.33	2.26	1.68	1.40	1.31	2.69	2.30	1.69	1.31	1.05	0.91	0.86
44°	14.84	8.11	3.81	2.41	1.72	1.41	1.31	3.41	2.76	1.88	1.39	1.09	0.93	0.87
48°	70.94	13.51	4.49	2.59	1.78	1.43	1.32	4.69	3.49	2.13	1.49	1.13	0.95	0.89
52°	B.H.	41.20	5.50	2.81	1.84	1.46	1.33	7.56	4.76	2.48	1.62	1.18	0.98	0.91
56°	B.H.	B.H.	7.13	3.10	1.93	1.49	1.35	19.76	7.55	2.98	1.79	1.25	1.01	0.94
60°	B.H.	B.H.	10.21	3.46	2.02	1.53	1.38	B.H.	18.44	3.75	2.00	1.33	1.06	0.97
64°	B.H.	B.H.	18.14	3.95	2.15	1.59	1.42	B.H.	B.H.	5.10	2.28	1.43	1.11	1.01
68°	B.H.	B.H.	83.00	4.62	2.29	1.65	1.47	B.H.	B.H.	8.03	2.67	1.55	1.17	1.06
72°	B.H.	B.H.	B.H.	5.61	2.48	1.73	1.53	B.H.	B.H.	19.07	3.24	1.71	1.25	1.12
South lat.	Jun	May/Jul	Aug/Apr	Sep/Mar	Oct/Feb	Nov/Jan	Dec	Jun	May/Jul	Aug/Apr	Sep/Mar	Oct/Feb	Nov/Jan	Dec

Values of P for East or West-Facing Horizontal Louvers
B.H. = Sun Below Horizon; N.S. = No Sun on facade.

westerly facade. The azimuth angle determines the combination of fin spacing, fin length, and fin slant angle, as shown in the diagram. Azimuth angles for times and dates not shown can be determined from Libbey-Owens-Ford (1974) or Benton & Marcial (1993).

Vegetation placed between the sun and building's surfaces reduces a building's heat gain in three ways: by reducing radiation transmitted though windows, by reducing the solar load on opaque surfaces, and by lowering via evapotranspiration the outdoor air temperature near building surfaces. Leaves typically absorb 60–90% of incident sunlight, most of which is converted into lo-

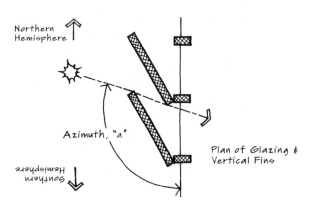

Latitude	8 AM / 4 PM							9 AM / 3 PM						
North lat.	Dec	Nov/Jan	Oct/Feb	Sep/Mar	Aug/Apr	May/Jul	Jun	Dec	Nov/Jan	Oct/Feb	Sep/Mar	Aug/Apr	May/Jul	Jun
0°	63	67	78	90	103	113	117	58	63	75	90	106	117	122
4°	62	65	75	88	101	111	115	56	60	71	86	102	114	118
8°	60	64	73	85	99	109	113	53	57	68	82	98	110	115
12°	59	62	71	83	96	106	110	51	55	65	78	94	106	111
16°	57	61	70	81	94	104	108	49	52	62	75	90	102	107
20°	56	59	68	79	91	101	105	47	50	59	71	86	98	103
24°	55	58	66	77	89	98	103	46	49	57	68	82	94	99
28°	54	57	65	75	86	96	100	45	47	55	65	78	89	94
32°	54	56	64	73	84	93	97	44	46	53	62	74	85	89
36°	53	56	63	71	82	90	94	43	45	51	60	71	80	85
40°	53	55	62	70	79	87	91	42	44	50	57	67	76	80
44°	53	55	61	68	77	84	88	41	43	48	55	64	72	76
48°	53	55	60	67	75	82	85	41	43	47	53	61	68	72
52°	B.H.	54	59	66	73	79	82	41	42	46	52	59	65	68
56°	B.H.	B.H.	59	64	71	76	79	40	42	46	50	56	62	64
60°	B.H.	B.H.	59	63	69	74	76	B.H.	42	45	49	54	59	61
64°	B.H.	B.H.	58	63	67	71	73	B.H.	B.H.	45	48	52	56	58
68°	B.H.	B.H.	58	62	66	69	71	B.H.	B.H.	44	47	51	54	55
72°	B.H.	B.H.	B.H.	61	65	67	68	B.H.	B.H.	44	46	49	52	53
South lat.	Jun	May/Jul	Aug/Apr	Sep/Mar	Oct/Feb	Nov/Jan	Dec	Jun	May/Jul	Aug/Apr	Sep/Mar	Oct/Feb	Nov/Jan	Dec

Solar Azimuth Angle (a) for Sizing East- or West-Facing Slanted Vertical Louvers,
* degrees east or west from south (N in SH). B.H. = Sun Below Horizon; N.S. = No Sun on facade.

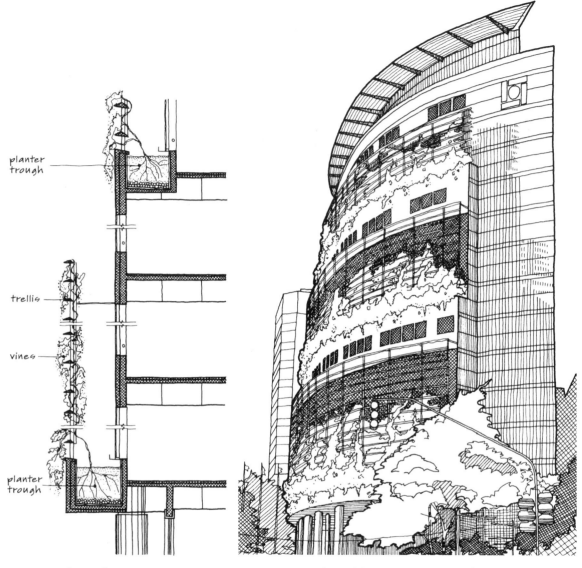

planter
trough

trellis

vines

planter
trough

Section through West Elevation,
Consorcio-Vida Offices

Consorcio-Vida Offices, Santiago, Chile,
Enrique Browne & Borja Huidobro

half of the trellis. This illustrates the need to begin plantings as early as possible and have an interim shading strategy while the vegetation matures. In this scheme, shorter trellises of two stories with more planter troughs would have allowed the entire facade to be covered in the same number of years. Vines can generally produce a dense leaf structure much faster than trees; shade plants can begin growing before the building is constructed.

The shading coefficient (SC) of plants depends on the density of the canopy, the plant's age, the seasonal growth of the plant, and the angle between the receiving surface and the sun. In winter, deciduous plants lose their leaves and provide less shade. However, the bare branches of most trees still block about 30–60% of the sunlight (SC = 0.70–0.40).

Evergreen plants maintain their shading throughout the year, and so should not be used where sunlight penetration is desirable. Deciduous plants vary in their dates of foliation and defoliation. They have the advantage of foliation that is triggered by outdoor temperature, rather than sun position. Therefore, vegetation can often outperform fixed shading. Deciduous plants also respond to seasonal conditions that are colder or warmer than average. In a cool spring, leaves appear later; in a warm fall, they drop later. In contrast, criteria for the design of fixed shading must be based on long-term average temperatures. Ideally, the plant would begin foliation when the building switched from a need for heating to a need for cooling, and end its defoliation when the building needed heating again.

Choose perennial plants with a dense canopy and a foliation period matched to the overheated times of the building (Technique 20). When winter heat is required, choose plants with a branching structure as open as possible, because branches reduce the amount of radiation reaching the building. However, do not use plants to shade solar collection apertures, unless they can be seasonally removed.

The table of **Shade Tree Selection Criteria** gives winter and summer shading coefficients for selected trees, along with approximate dates of foliation and defoliation for temperate latitudes. Data in the table is compiled from McPhereson (1984, pp. 144-146), Montgomery (1987, p. 88), Hightshoe (1988), Cathey (1998b), and CMHC (1998). Plants in warmer microclimates, such as on slopes facing the sun, and sites at

cal heat and then lost from the plant by convection or reradiation, or is consumed in evapotranspiration.

Architects Enrique Browne & Borja Huidobro used a vertical screen of vines grown on a planting trellis to shield the **Consorcio-Vida Offices** in Santiago, Chile from harsh western sun (Slessor, 1999). The trellis

frames, which vary in height between two and four stories, are set 1.5 m (5 ft) outside the window wall. The vines provide a filtered animated light, blocking approximately 60% of the solar gain on the wall. The perspective shows the building four years after construction, the vines having grown to cover approximately

SPECIES	Mature Ht. ft (m)	Winter SC	Summer SC	Foliate/Defoliate	Heat Zones[1]	Hardi. Zones
Ash, Green	50-75 (15-23)	0.70-0.71	0.13-0.20/0.34-0.62	Late/Early	8-2	2
Mountain	20-40 (6-12)	-----	0.50-0.60	-----	-----	-----
Aspen, Quaking	40-90 (12-28)	-----	0.20-0.31	Early/Ave	9-3	4-9
Beech, European	50-70 (15-21)	0.83	0.12	Late/Late (p)	9-4	4-8
Birch, European	40-70 (12-21)	0.48-0.88	0.15-0.20	Ave/Early	9-3	4-9
Paper	80-100 (25-30)	-----	0.40-0.80	-----	-----	-----
Weeping	30-40 (10-12)	0.34-0.46	-----	-----	-----	-----
Catalpa, Western	75-100 (23-30)	0.52-0.83	0.24	-----/Late	-----	-----
Cottonwood	90 (28)	0.68	0.15	Early/Ave	-----	2
Dogwood, Flowering	35-50 (10-15)	0.53	0.43	Late/Early	9-1	5-9
Elm, American	75-100 (23-30)	0.63-0.89	0.13/0.58-0.72	Ave/Ave	8-2	2
Manchurian	40-50 (12-15)	-----	0.38	-----	-----	-----
Hackberry, Common	75-100 (23-30)	-----	0.12	Ave/Ave	-----	3a
Hawthorn, Washington	25-30 (8-9)	-----	0.24	Late/Early	5-8	5-8
Hickory, Shagbark	120 (37)	0.66	0.23	Ave/Early	-----	4a
Horsechestnut	35-50 (10-15)	0.73	0.08-0.15	Ave/Late	8-4	5a
Larch	40-60 (12-18)	-----	0.60-0.80	-----	-----	-----
Linden, Little-leaf	70 (21)	0.46-0.70	0.07-0.35/0.65	Late/Early	-----	4-8
Locust, Honey	50-75 (15-23)	0.48-0.85	0.30-0.38	Late/Ave	9-4	5-9
Black	70 (21)	0.40	0.38	Late/Early	9-4	1-3
London Plane	90 (27)	0.46-0.64	0.11-0.17	Late/Late (p)	-----	5-9
Maple, Norway	50 (15)	0.61-0.75	0.10-0.14	Ave/ Ave	10-3	3-8
Red	75-100 (23-30)	0.63-0.82	0.17	Ave/Ave	10-3	3-8
Silver	75-100+ (23-30+)	0.59-0.87	0.11-0.21	Ave/Ave	10-3	3-8
Sugar	75-100 (23-30)	0.56-0.82	0.16	Ave/Early	10-3	3-8
Manitoba	40-60 (12-18)	-----	0.13	-----	-----	-----
Oak, Pin	50-75 (15-23)	0.63-0.88	0.15-0.30	Late/Late (p)	9-2	5-10
White	75-100 (23-30)	-----	0.25	Ave/V. Late (p)	9-2	4a
Red	50-75 (15-23)	0.70-0.81	0.19	-----/Ave	9-2	3
Olive, Russian	15-20 (5-6)	-----	0.13	Ave/Late	-----	-----
Pear, Common	30-40 (9-12)	0.60	0.20	-----	9-3	5-9
RedBud, Eastern	20-35 (6-10)	0.74	0.62	Ave/Late	12-9	5-9
Sycamore, Calif.	80-100 (24-30)	0.45-0.60	0.09	Early/Late	-----	5-10
Sweetgum	75-100 (23-30)	0.65-0.84	0.18	Ave/Late	8-1	6-9
Tuliptree	75-100 (23-30)	0.69-0.78	0.10	Late/Ave	8-2	5a
Walnut, Black	75-100 (23-30)	0.55-0.72	0.09	Late/Early	-----	4b

o Foliation Periods: Early = April 15-30; Average = May 1-15; Late = After May 15.

o Defoliation Periods: Early = Oct 15 - Nov 15; Average = Nov 16-30; Late = After Dec 1.

1. Heat Zones refer to genus; individual species adn cultivars may vary.

(p) = persisitent foliage, significant percentage remains into winter or early spring, typical of many oaks.

Shade Tree Selection Criteria

lower latitudes may foliate earlier, while the same tree at high elevations will leaf out later than in surrounding valleys. Within a given hardiness range, foliation occurs earlier in the warmer regions and later in cooler regions. For instance, sugar maple foliation varies by six weeks across its range from south to north (Hightshoe, 1988, p. 61). Some plants are deciduous in cooler climates but do not lose their leaves in warm winter climates. For more species and a full discussion of shading with plants, see McPherson (1984, pp. 141–164).

Numerous strategies for using plants to shade and recommended plants for passive cooling in Eastern U.S. temperate climates, including trees, shrubs, and vines, can be found in Spirn & Santos (1981). For plant suggestions by climate, see Moffat & Schiller (1994). Hightshoe (1988) is the authoritative guide for selecting North American native plants, and includes a calendar of flower, leaf, and fruit timing for 122 species (pp. 61–68), plus a categorization of branching and foliage complexity (pp. 20–21), which can be used to approximate the shading coefficient of species for which measured data are unavailable. Rapid plant growth and mature shape are both important for plants used to shade. Hudak (1980) contains tree silhouettes at 10-year and 25-year growth stages, showing height and branching structure.

Select species that grow well in the site's climate. The USDA Map of Hardiness Zones for North America is based on the average minimum winter temperature (ARS, 1990; Cathey, 1998a). In hot climates, plant survival may also be limited by hot weather. The AHS Heat Zones are based on the average number of days each year that a region experiences temperatures over 86° F (30 °C), the point at which many plants begin suffering physiological damage from heat (Cathey, 1998b; AHS, 1997). Species are typically rated for one or both zone systems. The heat zone system is relatively new, so not all species have been rated. Native plants will usually be the best adapted to local climates.

The spacing method in Strategy 38 can also be used to ensure solar access above trees. Be sure to locate trees so that wind for cross-ventilation is not blocked; a high canopy with higher branching can shade higher altitude summer sun, while allowing air to move beneath.

100 An *INTERNAL SHADING* layer behind the window or an *IN-BETWEEN SHADING* layer separating two glazing panes can reduce solar heat gain. [cooling]

While external operable shades can be very effective at stopping solar gain, they are also subject to degradation by the elements, collect dirt easily, and can be difficult to maintain. Controllable shading placed inside the glass or between layers in double- and triple-glazed window and envelope systems can reduce solar heat gain in summer, reflect daylight to the interior, reduce glare, protect the shading from pollution and weather, and reduce maintenance time and effort.

If blinds are placed between the glazing, the shading coefficient (SC) will be relatively low, because solar gain is removed at the window before entering the space (ASHRAE, 1997, p. 29.24). A lower SC blocks more solar heat gain. The shading coefficient for shading between glazing layers will be somewhere between the low SC of external shading and the higher SC of internal shades. For example, a double-glazed window will have an SC of about 0.14 with light-colored adjustable external venetian blinds, 0.33 with the blinds between the glazing, and 0.58 with the blinds located inside the window. The table gives typical **Shading Coefficients for Double Glazing With Internal and Between-Glass Shading.**

CONSTRUCTION TYPE	Shading Coefficient
1/8" Clear Glass, in & out	
Venetian Blinds Between (light/medium)	0.33/0.36
Venetian Blinds Inside (light/medium)	0.58/0.62
Louvered Sun Screen Between	0.43
Special Shaped Mirrored Louvers Between	0.25-0.59[1]
Opaque Roller Shade Inside (white/translucent/dark)	0.35/0.40/0.71
Draperies Inside	
open weave/dark color	0.62
semi-open weave/medium color	0.52
closed weave/light color	0.42
1/4" Heat Absorb. Glass Out, Clear Glass In	
Venetian Blinds Between (light/medium)	0.28/0.30
Venetian Blinds Inside (light/medium)	0.36/0.39
Louvered Sun Screen Between	0.37
Opaque Roller Shade Inside (white/translucent/dark)	0.22/0.30/0.40
Draperies Inside	
open weave/dark color	0.47
semi-open weave/medium color	0.41
closed weave/light color	0.35

(1) Varies with sun angle, Compagno, 1995, p. 74.

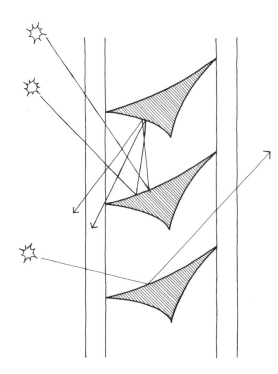

Shading Coefficients for Double Glazing With Internal and Between-Glass Shading

Glazing Section, Haas Offices

Haas Offices, Tilburg, The Netherlands, Jo Coenen

SC values as low as 0.12 are possible with some combinations of shading and glazings (ASHRAE, 1997, pp. 29.38-40).

In-between the glazing layers of the window walls of the **Haas Offices** in Tilburg, The Netherlands, by Jo Coenen, are special profile mirrored louvers. They are designed to reject high-angle summer sun and reflect lower winter sun into the room. The elevation of each floor is broken into three bands. The shading/reflection louvers are used in all areas where a clear view is not preferable (*Bauwelt*, 5/1992; Compagno, 1995, pp. 74–75).

A similar system was used by Thomas Herzog in the **Design Center Linz** in Linz, Austria. The vaulted exhibition hall is skinned with double-glazed panels containing parallel light-deflecting, high-reflectance, aluminum-coated plastic elements. Double parabolic reflectors form a cross grid for a third reflection. The geometry of the grid bars is set to admit diffuse north light while rejecting all direct sunlight. Because the roof is vaulted, each row of glazing panels are fitted with louvers of differently cut geometry. The overall light transmission is 33% and the solar heat gain coefficient (SHGC) is 0.29. (Herzog, 1994, pp. 100–104; Fitzgerald & Lewis, 1996, pp. 126–133).

Options for shading include vertical or horizontal louvers, roller blinds, and draperies on the interior. Depending on color, coatings, angle, and finishes, the assembly's SC and SHGC will vary substantially.

The cavity between glazing layers may also be ventilated to remove excess heat captured by between-glazing blinds in summer or to move captured heat to rooms for space heating. Solar heat absorbed in the cavity is emitted, driving a stack effect that convects heat away.

Webler + Geisler used a double skin with two kinds of blinds for the **Gröz GmbH Head Offices**, in Würzburg, Germany. Each floor has an independently computer-controlled upper and lower blind. The upper blind is reflective, to direct daylight to the ceiling, while the lower blind is dark and absorptive, to capture solar heat in a part of the glazing that provides little light to the room. The lower blind is perforated to reduce glare and provide some view when blinds are closed. The cavity is vented with low inlets and high outlets, while fans can move excess heat to other facades or into the building. Occupants can open sliding glass doors into the cavity

for fresh air (*A+U*, 5/1997; Krewinkel, 1998, pp. 74–79).

To keep air temperature in the cavity from becoming too high, the cavity height should generally to be limited to 2–3 floors. Acoustic and fire safety issues may also limit cavity height. In summer, ventilation air inlets should be separated from the glazing cavity.

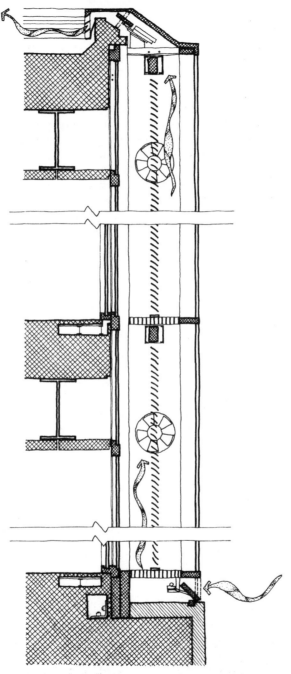

Gröz GmbH Head Offices, Würzburg, Germany, Webler + Geisler

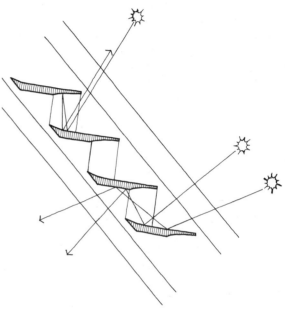

Glazing Detail, Design Center Linz

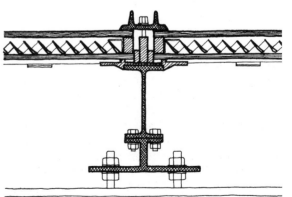

Roof Section, Design Center Linz, Linz, Austria, Thomas Herzog

101 WINDOW AND GLASS TYPES can be selected to balance concerns for daylighting, winter solar gain, and summer shading. [heating, cooling, and daylighting]

Several types of energy flows occur through windows: 1) conductive and radiative flows through the window assembly; 2) solar radiant heat gain; and 3) infiltration gains and losses through air leakage.

Conduction transfers through the window are controlled by the window's U-factor, which indicates the rate of heat flow through a material. Lower U-factors (or higher R-values) indicate better insulation. Glass has a much lower resistance to heat than most other building materials. In skin-load-dominated (SLD) buildings, windows can dominate the building's heating or cooling loads. Therefore, window U-factors should generally decrease as the severity of the outdoor climate increases. In passively solar-heated buildings, low U-factors are important in reducing winter heat loss from large solar-collecting glazing areas and in retaining heat collected during the day for use at night.

For buildings in cool climates with high internal loads (ILD buildings) that require cooling most of the time, low U-factor windows are not necessarily helpful. "Poorly" insulated windows increase the rate of heat loss to the outside, but this must be balanced against indoor comfort. Keeping inside surface temperatures from becoming too hot or cold improves the comfort of occupants within the window's radiant field. This is also important in hot climates, where the glass itself can absorb solar heat. Lower glazing U-factors accomplish this. Local energy codes may specify maximum U-factors for the building's climate zone, and such requirements may be tied to the area of glazing.

To find the recommended R-value for windows in solar heated residential and light commercial buildings with low internal loads (SLD), find the climate zone for the building's site from the map. Then use the table of Recommended Insulation Values for Windows in Passive Solar Heated Buildings (Balcomb et al., 1984, pp. 2.1–2.11). Window insulation levels can be decreased by one or two zones if night insulation is used (Strategy 97).

The recommendations are based on life-cycle cost analysis that balances the incremental cost/benifit of conservation and solar strategies. Low and high fuel costs in the table are relative to other locations within a zone. In most cases, use the high fuel cost recommendations as a starting point. If expensive electricity is used, such as in New England, use recommendations from the next lower zone number. If local cost for windows is high and fuel is cheap, use one zone number higher. If window costs are low and fuel cost high, use the next lower zone number.

The window's insulating performance also controls its interior surface temperature, which determines whether or not condensation will form on the interior surface in the building's climate. *The graph of Condensation Conditions for Glazing Types shows condensation potential on glazing at various combinations of indoor relative humidity and outdoor temperature conditions. Condensation can occur at points on or above the curves.* Windows with lower U-factors reduce the chance of condensation; windows with thermally broken edge seals will prevent edge fogging from conductive spacers (U. S. Dept. of Energy, 1997a, p. 4).

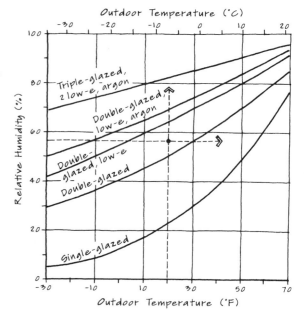

Condensation Conditions for Glazing Types

Zone	Low Fuel Cost				High Fuel Cost			
	R	(RSI)	U	(USI)	R	(RSI)	U	(USI)
1	3.7	0.66	0.27	1.52	4.1	0.72	0.25	1.39
2	3.4	0.60	0.29	1.67	3.7	0.66	0.27	1.52
3	3.1	0.54	0.33	1.85	3.4	0.60	0.29	1.67
4	2.7	0.48	0.37	2.09	3.1	0.54	0.33	1.85
5	2.4	0.42	0.42	2.38	2.7	0.48	0.37	2.09
6	2.0	0.36	0.49	2.78	2.4	0.42	0.42	2.38
7	1.7	0.30	0.59	3.34	2.0	0.36	0.49	2.78
8	1.4	0.24	0.74	4.17	1.7	0.30	0.59	3.34
9	1.0	0.18	0.98	5.56	1.4	0.24	0.74	4.17

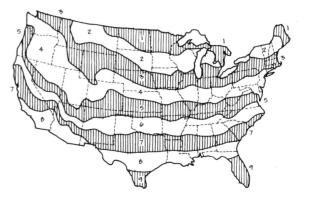

Recommended Insulation Values for Windows in Passive Solar-Heated Buildings

Use the graph to help select glazing types. First find the winter outdoor extreme temperature condition and estimate the indoor winter humidity. Enter the graph on the horizontal axis with the outdoor temperature, and draw a construction line vertically across the chart. Then enter the vertical axis with the expected relative humidity and draw a horizontal line until it crosses the vertical construction line. From the intersection, choose any of the glazing types above the point. Any glazing types below the point have a high likelihood of condensation.

Extreme "design day" figures can be found in Appendix A for selected cities, or in Reynolds & Stein (2000, pp. 1623-1633) for North America, or in ASHRAE (1997, pp. 26.6-26.53) for cities throughout the world. Indoor humidities are normally kept in the range of 30–50% for mechanically conditioned buildings with humidity control. Passively heated and cooled buildings have little or no control over humidity and will tend to have higher humidity in both summer and winter than mechanically cooled buildings. Kitchens, showers areas, and areas with many plants will have higher humidities, often over 60%. Although condensation is mostly a problem in cool conditions, it can also occur on the outside of glass in hot-climate air-conditioned buildings with high U-factors.

The table of Generalized Recommendations for Window Type Selection gives suggestions by glazing orientation, climate type (cooling dominated, mixed, or heating dominated), and whether the building is internal-load-dominated (ILD) or skin-load-dominated (SLD). SHGC and U-factors in the table refer to the total window, including glass and frame.

Windows admit daylight at different levels, based on their *visible transmittance* (VT), an optical property measuring the fraction of visible light striking the glazing that is passed through, expressed as a ratio between 0 and 1 (O'Connor, 1997, p. 4.1). It can be applied to both the glazing alone and the window as a whole, including its frame and mullions. A high VT maximizes daylight. *Daylit buildings should generally use clear glass, with a VT of 0.70 or above for the glass, which translates to VT = 0.50 or above for the total window.* Low VT glazings do not provide enough light for most daylighting situations, unless illuminance targets are low, or very large glazing areas are provided. Care must be taken with high VT glazings to prevent glare:

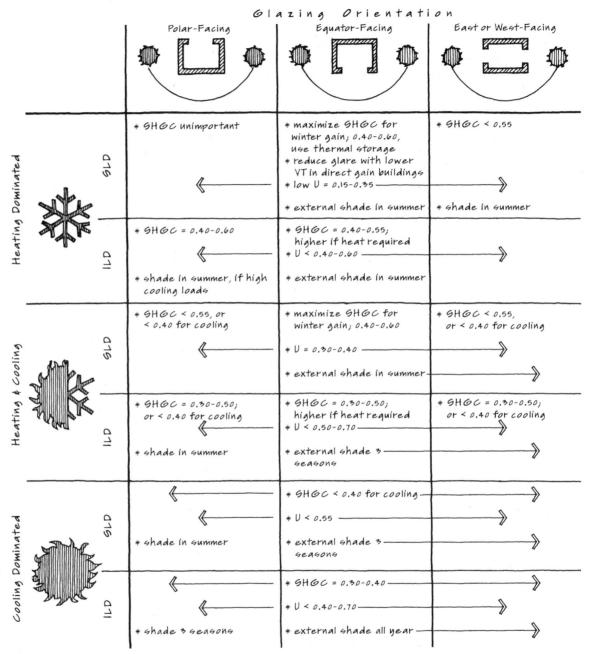

Generalized Recommendations for Glazing + Window Selection at Temperate Latitudes
Values are for glass + frames; Recommended values for glazing alone differ. See text.

		Polar-Facing	Equator-Facing	East or West-Facing
Heating Dominated	SLD	* SHGC unimportant	* maximize SHGC for winter gain; 0.40-0.60, use thermal storage * reduce glare with lower VT in direct gain buildings * low U = 0.15-0.35 * external shade in summer	* SHGC < 0.55 * shade in summer
	ILD	* SHGC = 0.40-0.60 * shade in summer, if high cooling loads	* SHGC = 0.40-0.55; higher if heat required * U < 0.40-0.60 * external shade in summer	
Heating & Cooling	SLD	* SHGC < 0.55, or < 0.40 for cooling	* maximize SHGC for winter gain; 0.40-0.60 * U = 0.30-0.40 * external shade in summer	* SHGC < 0.55, or < 0.40 for cooling
	ILD	* SHGC = 0.30-0.50; or < 0.40 for cooling * shade in summer	* SHGC = 0.30-0.50; higher if heat required * U < 0.50-0.70 * external shade 3 seasons	* SHGC = 0.30-0.50; or < 0.40 for cooling
Cooling Dominated	SLD	* shade in summer	* SHGC < 0.40 for cooling * U < 0.55 * external shade 3 seasons	
	ILD	* shade 3 seasons	* SHGC = 0.30-0.40 * U < 0.40-0.70 * external shade all year	

the larger the windows, the more critical is glare control.

Windows also admit solar heat, which can be a benefit or a liability, depending on the building's needs for heating or cooling at a given time. A window's *solar heat gain coefficient (SHGC)* and *shading coefficient (SC)* are indicators of the window's transmittance of total solar heat gain. SHGC is the fraction of incident radiation transmitted by the glazing or window. SC is the fraction of heat transmitted by glazing, in comparison to clear single glass. SC   1.15 x SHGC (O'Conn or, 1997, p. 4.1).

Select a high (0.40–0.60) SHGC for south-facing (N in SH) windows in passively solar heated buildings, to capture as much heat as possible. South windows in lLD buildings can have high SHGCs also, so long as the potential for overheating is controlled by appropriate window sizing or thermal storage. This glass should then be shaded, with external shades if possible, during the summer. East and west windows in SLD buildings, which do not provide significant winter gains and are harder to shade in summer, should generally have lower SHGCs, than windows on south orientations. North-facing (S in SH) windows can actually admit significant heat gain in summer, if unshaded and provided with a full sky view, because all light, including diffuse sky light, carries heat with it. Use a low SHGC for north orientations in buildings with significant cooling loads. ILD buildings, particularly those in hot climates that require cooling most of the year, can use a low SHGC on all orientations.

Windows can be selected to balance the need for admitting daylight with the need for either admitting or blocking solar heat. The *light-to-solar-gain ratio (LSG)* is an indicator of the spectral selectivity of the glazing and the "coolness" of the light." The LSG is defined as the window's visible transmittance divided by the solar heat gain coefficient (LSG = VT/SHGC) (ASHRAE, 1997, p. 29.48).

Use the graph of Light-to-Solar-Gain Ratio for Different Glazing Types to select glazing that meets the building's criteria for lighting, heating, and cooling. Remember that tinted or colored glazings will also change the color of daylight in a room. The graph is based on a range of values for each category of glass and assumes operable windows with non-aluminum frames (ASHRAE, 1997, pp. 29.35–29.26). It should only

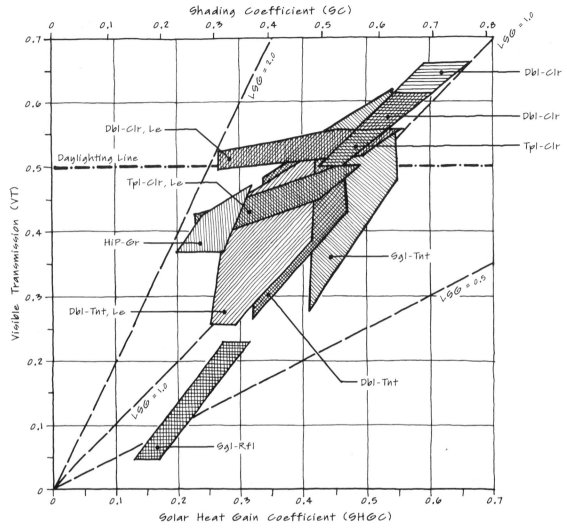

HiP-Gr[1] = double glazed, low-e, hi-performance green or triple glazed, uncoated, hi-performance green
Tpl-Clr = triple glazed, clear
Tpl-Clr, Le[1,2] = triple glazed, clear, low-e

Sgl-Rfl = single glazed, reflective coating
Sgl-Clr = single glazed, clear
Sgl-Tnt = single glazed, tinted
Dbl-Clr = double glazed, clear
Dbl-Clr, Le[1] = double glazed, clear, low-e
Dbl-Tnt, Le[1] = double glazed, tinted, low-e

1) includes a range of low-e coatings from e=0.2 to e=0.05
2) includes a range of windows with low-e coatings on one surface and on two surfaces.

Light-to-Solar-Gain Ratio (LSG) for Different Glazing Types in an Operable Window

be used for preliminary selection of glass type; be sure to check manufacturer's specifications and the National Fenestration Rating Council (NFRC) rating for each window. Actual performance for particular products can vary significantly from those shown, and glazing technology is changing rapidly.

The addition to the **Princeton University Firestone Library,** by Koetter, Kim, and Associates, includes a toplit reading room infilled between the old and new structures. The north-sloping shed roof is glazed with $U = 0.32$ (USI = 1.8) low-emissivity *(low-e)* double glazing, to reduce winter heat loss. The low-*e* coating lowers the space's annual heating bill by 16% compared to ordinary double glazing. The glazing's VT = 0.64, and the SHGC = 0.41. Winter gain is shaded by the adjacent building, and the relatively low SHGC reduces summer solar gains. Interior shading is provided by rows of white metal tubing below the glass, reducing glare and adding a shading coefficient of 0.5, while transmitting 75% of the visible light. This combination still provides enough light to daylight the adjacent perimeter spaces of the new addition (Freeman, 1990; Johnson, 1991, pp. 20-21).

For more guidance on glass type selection, see EWC (n. d.) and U. S. Dept.of Energy (1997a).

Princeton University Firestone Library, Princeton, New Jersey, Koetter, Kim, & Assoc.

Part III   STRATEGIES FOR SUPPLEMENTING PASSIVE SYSTEMS

As the size of buildings increases, the opportunity for total daylighting or passive solar heating and cooling decreases. Because large buildings are more complex, it is more difficult to predict and guarantee their performance, and the criteria used to judge their performance become more restrictive. For example, the large temperature swings that might be tolerated by a few people in a small residential or commercial building might be unacceptable to the many people who occupy a large office building. A totally passive system uses no auxiliary energy for fans, pumps, or to produce heating or cooling. Passive systems typically use the building's architectural elements to modify the climate, as covered in Part 2, Design Strategies, while active systems are typically more mechanical in nature.

While a few solar buildings are totally passive, most use auxiliary backup systems for peak loads. This is the case even in very efficient small buildings in relatively mild climates, because the passive solar system designed to perform under the worst conditions is significantly larger than one that performs under typical conditions.

As a result, in most design situations, an important question to answer at the preliminary design stage is, "How much of the heating, cooling, and lighting requirements should be satisfied by passive architectural systems, and how much should be relegated to active mechanical systems?"

There is also a related question about the degree to which the passive and active systems should replicate each other. The diagram illustrates that a building may have a range of dependence on active mechanical systems from complete to partial, and a range of dependence on passive systems from partial to complete. The combination of the two ranges results in a broad range of useful permutations. These can be simplified into three generic categories: (A) both active and passive systems are designed to perform at peak loads; (B) passive systems predominate, with an active backup; and (C) active systems predominate, but there are passive components.

The safest design approach is (A), an active system capable of meeting the entire heating, cooling, and lighting load with a complete passive system to carry those loads whenever it can. While safest, it is also the most expensive in terms of initial construction costs. Therefore, the designer usually tries to reduce the redundancy in the systems by tending toward options (B) or (C). Since this book is mostly concerned with passive systems, the emphasis of Part Three is shown in the dotted zone—using ac-

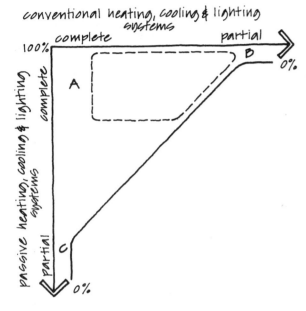

conventional heating, cooling & lighting systems

tive systems to supplement substantially complete passive systems.

Part Three doesn't describe in any detail the active systems used to supplement the passive systems. Instead, it outlines some strategies for solving problems that passive systems frequently pose. These problems include achieving high illumination levels away from windows and under changing exterior lighting conditions, enhancing the building's ability to store heat and cold, and moving heat and cold from one area to another. The strategies in Part Three are more general in nature than those in Part Two and are meant to be a general introduction to how passive systems can be supplemented, at a level that is appropriate for the scheming phase in the design process. If completely active systems are anticipated, especially for large buildings, their influence on the form and organization of the building

might be extremely important at this design stage.

In any case, passive systems have an impact on the role of active heating, cooling, and lighting systems in buildings. Daylighting strategies tend to call for more external skin area, so large buildings may be less strongly dominated by internal loads. Because of the more extensive glass areas, the thermal loads at the skin, which are usually offset by active heating and cooling systems, can be greater. The need to get windows high in the wall can result in greater floor-to-floor heights, resulting in more air to condition and the loss of the dropped ceiling in which to place mechanical equipment.

A night ventilation of mass strategy calls for storing heat in the building during the day and removing it at night. As a consequence, the peak electrical loads that frequently occur in the afternoons on hot days, when internal gains and skin gain coincide, can be reduced, thus mechanical refrigeration loads can be smaller. Because air is used as a heat transfer medium at night in passive ventilation systems, mechanical air systems, rather than water-cooling systems, frequently are more compatible with night ventilation. The need to expose the thermal mass may result in the loss of a dropped ceiling and exposure of mechanical equipment.

Daytime natural ventilation schemes may eliminate the fresh air ventilation requirements normally met by active systems. Spaces in naturally ventilated buildings are generally open and connected to each other, so when the active system is moving air, all or part of the return air ductwork may be eliminated.

Since solar-heating strategies frequently result in more hot air in one location than can be used, and the excess heat is transferred by ducts to cooler areas, active systems that use air to transfer heat may be more compatible with solar systems than those that use water.

The strategies in Part Three fall into two groups: those that affect the electric lighting systems and those that affect the heating, ventilation, and air conditioning systems.

The lighting strategies (102, Task Lighting, and 103, Electric Lighting Zones) address the questions of how electric lights should be arranged to facilitate switching so that they won't be used unnecessarily and how daylight can be used to meet most lighting requirements, with electric lights used only for special jobs.

Two of the strategies (104, Rock Beds, and 105, Mechanical Mass Ventilation) suggest methods for extending the thermal storage capacity of buildings and improving the performance of the building's existing thermal storage. Strategy 106, Mechanical Space Ventilation, addresses the supplementing of natural ventilation when the forces that drive it are weak.

Strategies 107, Ducts and Plenums, and 108, Passive Buffer Zones and Heat Exchangers, suggest how heat and cold can be transferred from where they aren't needed to where they are, while the last two strategies, 108 and 109, Earth–Air Heat Exchangers, show how waste heat and cold can be recycled from ventilation air and how ventilation air can be pretempered.

These supplemental system strategies shouldn't be seen as the final step in design. Rather, they should be regarded as just one more item on the schematic design checklist, to be accounted for before proceeding to the next level of detail in passive considerations.

102 Electric *TASK LIGHTING* can be used for localized, high-illumination requirements and daylight for ambient lighting. [daylighting]

The farther one moves from the window, the more difficult it becomes to maintain the daylight illumination levels required for some tasks. When those tasks are localized, like desk work, the daylight can be supplemented with electric lighting located near the task and under the control of the user. This is an effective combination because daylight can still be used in large sections of the building that are distant from the window, where ambient light level requirements for talking or moving about may be lower. For instance, in an office, ambient daylight can be supplied at 10–20 foot-candles (108–215 lux) over the whole office, while detailed reading at a desk may require 50 fc (538 lux) on a very small area. ***To prevent glare, the task/background luminance ratio should be less than 3:1 locally and less than 9:1 within the room*** (Robbins, 1986, p. 285).

If the entire area is daylit to the higher task levels, windows have to be large, resulting in too much heat gain and loss. If electrically lit to the task level, lights consume too much energy, producing too much heat gain. At night, when there is no daylight available, the lower illuminance of ambient general lighting can be provided by high efficiency types of electric lights. In considering the design of electric lighting, both the day and night distribution patterns should be considered.

People can also adjust their light levels to suit their tasks and their proximity to the window, sometimes using daylight only and sometimes using a combination of daylight and electric light. Aalto took this approach in the **Mt. Angel Library** in Oregon. He put the major reading area in the center of the building directly under the skylight, where the illumination is highest, but also provided individually controlled desk lamps along the counter for use when the reading tasks are particularly difficult or when sky conditions reduce the available daylight.

Library, Mt. Angel Abbey, Oregon, Alvar Aalto

03 *ELECTRIC LIGHT ZONES* **can be layered parallel to the window plane so that individual rows can be switched on as needed. [daylighting]**

Whether daylighting is used to meet task lighting conditions or ambient lighting within the daylit zone, there is a decrease in illumination as one moves away from the opening. As sky conditions change and less light is available from the sky, conditions within the zone change, with the areas farthest from the windows becoming darker sooner. If the electric lighting is layered parallel to the window plane, then lights can be turned on in the areas that need additional light and left off in areas that do not. The lighting can be controlled by a photosensitive cell so that it is automatically switched on or off when daylighting reaches a certain level or continuously dimmed so that electric lighting supplies just the supplemental light required to meet the overall illumination requirements (Sain, 1983, p. 365). If the lights are not automatically controlled, little electric lighting energy will be saved. The use of automated daylight controls can save 30–50% of the electric lighting energy in office buildings, often during a building's peak load times (Eley Assoc., 1993, pp. 9–19). Reduced lighting use also reduces internal heat gains and can reduce the use and size of cooling equipment.

The **Central Lincoln PUD** office building in Newport, Oregon, designed by Moreland/Unruh/Smith, is daylit from the exterior sides and through a central atrium covered by a south-facing clerestory. The electric lighting system includes user-controlled task lights at each desk and indirect fluorescent lights suspended from the ceiling in rows running parallel to the windows and the atrium. The fluorescent lights are dimmer-controlled, so that they automatically adjust to available exterior illumination and maintain the minimum desirable ambient light level of 30 foot-candles (323 lux).

The most important architectural impact of daylight controls is the organization of electric lights into zones that match room activities and the patterns of daylight distribution. *All floor areas that receive at least half their illuminance from daylight for several hours per day should have daylight controls (Reynolds & Stein, 2000, p. 1290).* Establishing a map of daylight factor distribution patterns using model studies (Moore, 1991;

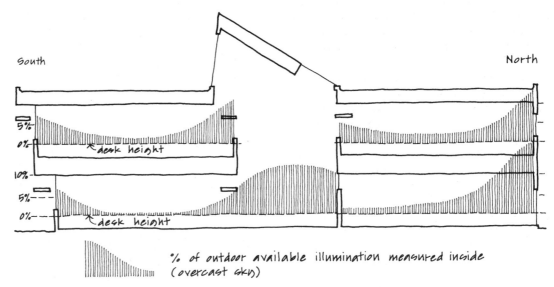

% of outdoor available illumination measured inside (overcast sky)

Central Lincoln P.U.D., Newport, Oregon, Moreland/Unruh/Smith

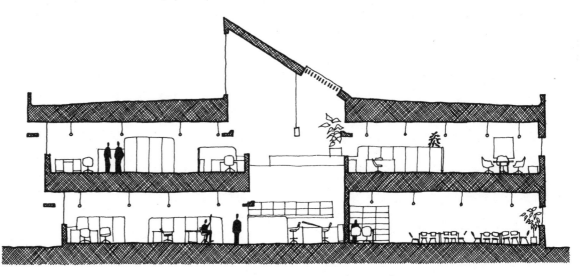

Central Lincoln P.U.D., Newport, Oregon, Moreland/Unruh/Smith

B. H. Evans, 1981) or computer simulation is the best way to optimize the control of zones. More zones means greater control of lighting and better opportunities for energy savings, but higher installation costs. The size and placement of windows and the type of shading devices can affect the lighting zones. For instance, open plans and strip windows may be able to use large linear zones, whereas zones for small rooms, punched windows, and locally controlled operable shading will need to be smaller.

Although they do not indicate precise energy savings, the Power Adjustment Factors (PAF) from ASHRAE 90.1 (1989a) are an indicator of the relative energy savings from different lighting control system options.

PAFs are used in calculating light power budgets for energy code compliance. Higher factors indicate that a higher connected lighting power density would be allowed by code, thus more lighting energy savings from the controls is assumed. Lighting energy savings can also be improved by combining daylight controls with occupancy sensors and lumen maintenance strategies. Occupancy controls turn lights off when a zone is unoccupied, while lumen maintenance controls dim lights when lamps are new and turn them up as their light output falls off with age.

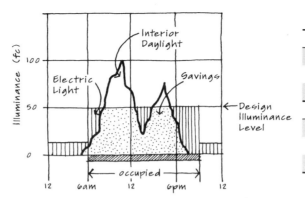

Potential Energy Savings From Daylighting

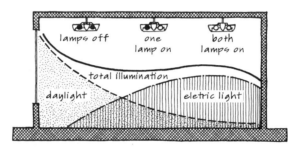

Maintaining Design Illuminance With Electric Light Switching In Layered Zones

LIGHTING CONTROL SYSTEM	PAF
Daylight Sensing Controls	
continuous dimming	0.30
multiple step dimming	0.20
single step- on/off	0.10
Daylight Sensing Controls with Programmable Timing	
continuous dimming	0.35
multiple step dimming	0.25
single step- on/off	0.15
Daylight Sensing Controls with Programmable Timing & Lumen Maintenance	
continuous dimming	0.40
multiple step dimming	0.30
single step- on/off	0.20
Daylight Sensing Controls with Occupancy Sensors	
continuous dimming	0.40
multiple step dimming	0.35
single step- on/off	0.35
Daylight Sensing Controls with Occupancy Sensors & Lumen Maintenance	
continuous dimming	0.45
multiple step dimming	0.40
single step- on/off	0.35

Power Adjustment Factors (PAF)

04 ROCK BEDS located remote from the occupied space can be used to increase the amount of heat and cold that can be effectively stored. [heating and cooling]

In passive heating and cooling systems, it is frequently advantageous to increase the thermal storage beyond what is available in the building's structure. Rock beds are a means of enlarging the thermal mass of the building and thereby increasing its ability to store energy. In a heating system, air is drawn in by fans (Strategy 105) and ducts (Strategy 107) from a location where it is hot, like the top of a sunspace or in front of a trombe wall, and through a bed of rocks. Heat is given off to the rocks and the air is recirculated to a location in the hot space to collect more heat. At night, when heat is needed, air from the occupied space is drawn through the rock bed, where it picks up heat and is distributed back to the occupied space. The rock bed can be located under a concrete floor that will be heated by the bed. The floor then heats the space by radiation after a lag time of several hours required for the heat to move through the mass. The fans required to charge and discharge the rock bed are frequently part of the conventional HVAC system. The size of the rock bed is a function of the input air temperature, heat storage requirements, rock size, and the flow rate (Balcomb et al., 1983, p. 192).

Rock beds for cooling are similar to those for heating except that the source of cool air is frequently outside the building. In climates that experience a large diurnal temperature swing, cool outside air can be drawn through the bed at night (Strategy 68). In hot-arid climates, the rock bed may be cooled by evaporatively cooled air that has been conditioned with a mechanical evaporative cooler (Yellott, 1981, p. 767).

In the **Princeton Professional Park** in Princeton, New Jersey, designed by Harrison Fraker, an under-floor rock bed is used to store both heat and cold. During the winter day, hot air is drawn from the top of the solar-heated atrium into the rock bed, where the air gives off its heat to the rocks and is returned to the atrium to be reheated. At night, the heat is transferred from the rock bed to the space by two modes: by heating the floor slab directly via conduction, which then radiates

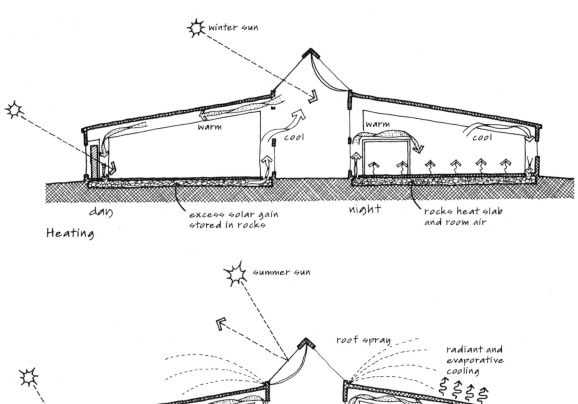

Heating

Cooling

Princeton Professional Park, Princeton, New Jersey, Princeton Energy Group

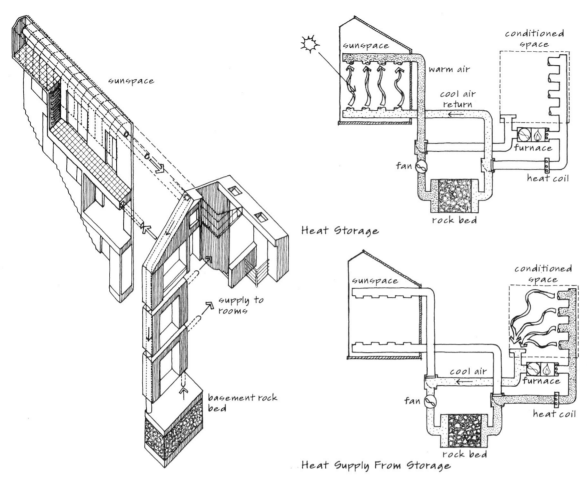

Solar Heating System,
San Francisco Residence, William Leedy

Heat Storage

Heat Supply From Storage

Rock Bed Storage Schematics,
San Francisco Residence, William Leedy

to the space, and by warming the air via an active forced system.

In the summer at night the metal roof is cooled by radiation to the night sky and by evaporation of a water spray. Air from the rock bed is blown under the metal roof, losing its heat to the roof, and then recirculated through the rock bed, cooling the rocks. During the day air from the space is circulated through the rock bed to cool the air (*Progressive Architecture*, 4/1983a, p. 96).

Remote storage such as a rock bed is also useful when mass cannot be located near collection and when collection cannot be located near rooms that need heat. For a **San Francisco Residence and Remodel,** William

Leedy was faced with a very steep site and rowhouse ends facing east and west. The ingenious solution uses a long south-facing sunspace on the top floor, set to the north of a south side outdoor zone between the buildings. Because of seismic structural requirements, the mass could not be located on the top floor, so a rock bed is located at the lowest level, built into the hill behind the garage. The sunspace and rock bed are linked by a system of ducts, fans, and dampers (*Passive Solar Journal,* Winter/1983).

Rock bed design is quite flexible. The bed must be sized to meet the heat storage capacity required, yet a variety of configurations is possible. Although vertical

flow rock beds maximize thermal efficiency due to their good thermal stratification, this arrangement is not always possible and may not allow any conductive/radiative heat transfer to the occupied space. Rock beds should be located at the ground level and must be insulated to prevent condensation and heat loss. All surfaces, except those intended for heat transfer (such as a floor slab), should be insulated.

Overall flow path through the bed should be limited to 8 ft (2.4 m) to keep pressure losses down. Maximum bed depth should be 4 ft (1.2 m) with pebbles of 0.75–1.5 in (19–38 mm) in diameter (ASHRAE, 1988).

The volume of a rock bed for heat collected passively at low temperatures can be determined from the graph, Sizing Rock Beds for Sunspaces and Trombe Walls. Enter the graph on the horizontal axis with the spring season radiation transmitted through the south-facing glass (north-facing in the Southern Hemisphere). Move vertically to the diagonal for the air's ΔT, then horizontally to read the storage volume of the rock bed per unit area of solar aperture. Multiply the solar glass area by the storage volume ratio to get the minimum storage volume required.

Transmitted solar radiation can be found for double glazing and U.S. cities in Marion and Wilcox (1995); and, for latitudes 16–64° and single glazing, in Reynolds & Stein (2000, pp. 1635-1643) or ASHRAE (1997, pp. 29.29–29.35). Rock bed size is based on the day for which maximum storage is required, usually in spring when radiation is high but temperatures are still low, unless the system is designed for a very high solar fraction during winter. Air ΔT is the temperature difference between hot air going into the rock bed and cooler air exiting it. An air ΔT of 15–20 °F (8.5–11 °C) is equivalent to warm air temperatures out of a passive heat source of 80–90 °F (27–32 °C). The graph assumes storage of one-third of the heat collected (with two-thirds being stored in the building's structure). If more or less than one-third of the collected radiation is to be stored, the rock bed volume may be adjusted proportionally. Packing is assumed to produce an overall density of 100 lb/ft³ (1600 kg/m³) (Balcomb et al., 1980, pp. 192-206).

The volume of a rock bed for heat collected remotely in higher temperature systems, such as from an air collector, can be determined from the graph,

Sizing Rock Beds for Air Collectors. *Using the radiation level incident on the collector for a sunny spring day (Appendix A; Marion & Wilcox, 1994), enter the graph on the horizontal axis and move vertically to the diagonal zone for the collector efficiency (average or good). Use the top of each range for higher solar savings fraction (SSF) targets and the bottom of the zone for lower SSFs. Then move horizontally to read the storage volume as a fraction of collection area. Finally, multiply the collector area by the storage volume ratio from the graph to get the minimum storage volume required.*

The graph assumes storage of two-thirds of the heat collected, a temperature increase in the thermal storage of 70 °F (39 °C), and an overall density of 100 lb/ft³ (1600 kg/m³) (ASHRAE, 1988). If more or less than two-thirds of the collected radiation is to be stored, the rock bed volume may be adjusted proportionally.

Use the last graph for Sizing Rock Beds for Night Ventilation Cooling. To determine the amount of heat that needs to be stored in the rock bed, subtract the daily heat stored in the building's structure (Strategy 68) from the building's total daily heat gain (Technique 21). Using this difference, enter the graph on the horizontal axis. Move vertically to the diagonal for the daily minimum outdoor temperature during

the month for which cooling is being designed (Appendix A; NCDC, 1996; NOAA, 1995). From the intersection, move horizontally to read the storage volume as a fraction of floor area. Finally, multiply the building floor area by the storage volume ratio from the graph to get the minimum storage volume required.

The graph assumes a maximum indoor air temperature of 80 °F (21 °C) and an overall density of 100 lb/ft³ (1600 kg/m³).

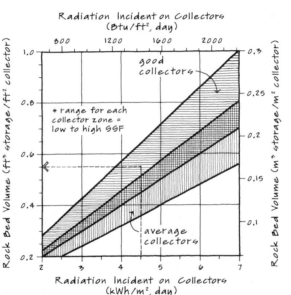

Sizing Rock Beds for Sunspaces and Trombe Walls
(low temperature source)

Sizing Rock Beds for Air Collectors
(high temperature source)

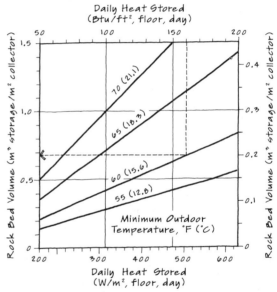

Sizing Rock Beds for Night Cooled Mass
1) 83 °F (28.3 °C) maximum indoor temperature

105 *MECHANICAL MASS VENTILATION* can be used to ensure adequate air movement past the building's thermal storage, thereby improving its cooling potential. [cooling]

Schemes for night ventilation of mass are designed to store heat during the day in the mass of the building and lose heat to the cool ventilating air at night. Because night wind speeds are frequently low and the interior flow of natural ventilation is often poorly distributed, the cooling potential of totally passive night ventilation is limited. Using fans to increase the rate of air movement past the mass increases the amount of heat that can be removed during the night.

Mechanical night ventilation of thermal mass is an important cooling strategy in the **Bateson Building** in Sacramento, California, designed by the Office of the State Architect (see section drawing in Strategy 107). Night cooled mass satisfies about 65% of the building's cooling load. The building uses extensive shading and daylighting and an interior atrium to reduce the magnitude of the cooling load. The night ventilation system works by pulling cool outside air down the ventilation shaft at night and distributing it to each space using the HVAC system. The air then picks up stored heat from the concrete structure and is exhausted to the outside. The major mass area is in the ceiling, where the precast concrete double T's are left exposed. The thermal mass of the building is supplemented with a rock bed storage system (*Progressive Architecture*, 9/1981; Lechner, 1991, pp. 450–455; Reynolds & Stein, 1992, pp. 259–265).

Night ventilation can begin as soon as the outdoor temperature drops below the indoor mass temperature, so the ΔT used for cooling begins at about 3 °F (1.7 °C) and increases as the outdoor temperature drops. Fans should be sized to provide enough air movement during the maximum hour of night cooling. The ΔT at this hour is 8–18 °F (4.5–10 °C), depending on climate conditions. For humid climates, use a low ΔT; for arid climates, use a higher ΔT. The heat to be removed from mass during the maximum hour of cooling is about 14–22% of the total daily heat stored in the mass, depending on climate conditions (Reynolds & Stein, 2000, p. 236).

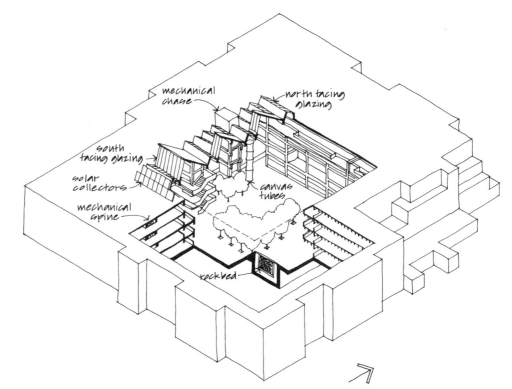

Bateson Building, Sacramento, California, Office of the State Architect

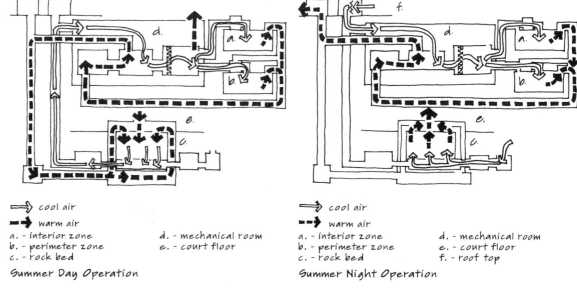

⇒ cool air
⇢ warm air
a. - interior zone   d. - mechanical room
b. - perimeter zone   e. - court floor
c. - rock bed

Summer Day Operation

⇒ cool air
⇢ warm air
a. - interior zone   d. - court floor
b. - perimeter zone   e. - court floor
c. - rock bed   f. - roof top

Summer Night Operation

Bateson Building Night Ventilation Schematics

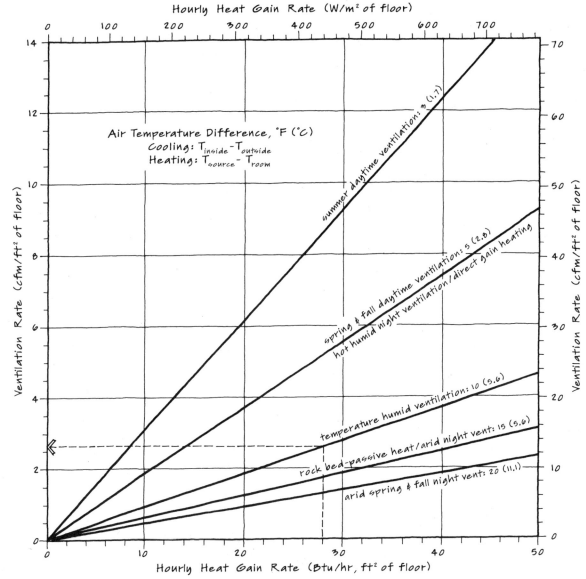

Hourly Heat Gain Rate (W/m² of floor)

Air Temperature Difference, °F (°C)
Cooling: T$_{inside}$ - T$_{outside}$
Heating: T$_{source}$ - T$_{room}$

Ventilation Rate (cfm/ft² of floor)

summer daytime ventilation: 3 (1.7)

spring & fall daytime ventilation: 5 (2.8)

hot humid night ventilation/direct gain heating

temperature humid ventilation: 10 (5.6)

rock bed-passive heat/arid night vent: 15 (5.6)

arid spring & fall night vent: 20 (11.1)

Hourly Heat Gain Rate (Btu/hr, ft² of floor)

Sizing Air Flow of Fans for Mechanical Ventilation

To size fans for night ventilation, enter the graph with an hourly cooling load about 1/5 of the daily heat stored (Strategy 68). Move vertically to the diagonal for the mass-to-air ΔT, then horizontally to read the forced ventilation rate per unit of floor area. Finally, multiply this air flow rate (cfm/ft² or L/sec, m²) by the floor area to get the total ventilation rating of the fan(s).

To approximate the fan capacity and/or fan room size required, see Strategy 106.

If the same fans are to be used for daytime space cooling ventilation, check fan size using the maximum *hourly* heat gain rate from Technique 21 and use a ΔT of 3 °F (1.7 °C) in the graph. For more on design for mechanical ventilation, see Strategy 106.

106 *MECHANICAL SPACE VENTILATION* **can be used to cool the building and people during times when natural ventilation forces are weak. [cooling]**

There are two basic types of mechanical ventilation: space cooling, which uses fans to move cooler outdoor air to the inside, removing heat from rooms, and people cooling, which uses fans to move air across occupants and remove heat from their bodies.

Mechanical ventilation may be used as a supplement to natural ventilation for space cooling in a variety of circumstances. Examples include when cross-ventilation is limited by lack of access to sufficient wind speeds (Strategy 65) and when stack-ventilation is limited by low room height or small areas available for high outlets (Strategy 66).

In areas with low wind speeds, during calm hours, and when cooling mass with night ventilation, there may not be enough wind velocity to provide the required rate of cooling. At night, winds speeds are typically lower than during the day (Technique 5). On urban sites, winds speeds may be half of airport speeds and other buildings may totally block wind access. Additionally, ground-level pollution and traffic noise may make direct natural ventilation through windows undesirable. In many buildings, open sections, communicating levels, or ventilation chimneys to create stack-driven ventilation may not be possible.

Mechanical ventilation makes sense as an assist to natural ventilation in many of these cases. It is a way to dependably introduce a high rate of outdoor air into buildings at a relatively low rate of energy consumption, compared to conventional air conditioning. Mechanical ventilation inlets can be at the roof level, where air is may be cooler (depending on roof surface) and cleaner. Air can also be filtered to remove pollutants and a mechanical heat exchanger (Strategy 108) can be more easily applied than with natural ventilation alone.

To size fans for forced ventilation, find the building's heat gain rate from Technique 21; then use the graph in Strategy 105 to find the ventilation rate per unit of floor area that would remove this rate of heat gain. Using this value, along with the total floor area, the total fan air volume, and the area of inlets,

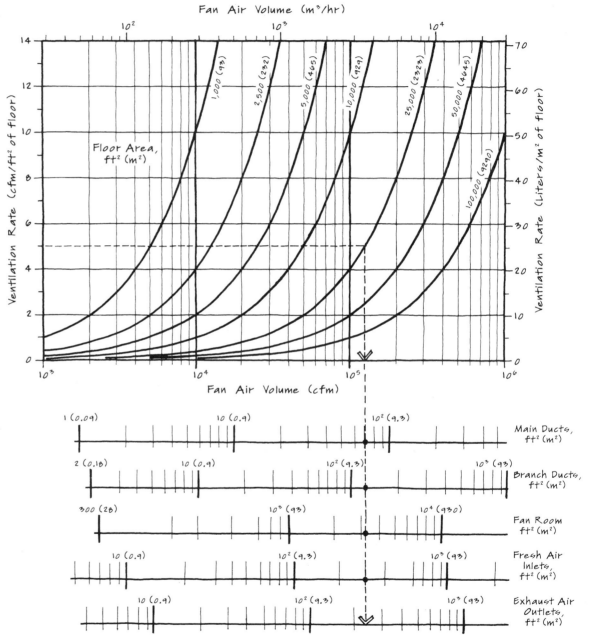

Sizing Mechanical Ventilation Components

outlets, ducts, and fan rooms can be approximated from the graph for Sizing Mechanical Ventilation Elements. Enter the graph on the vertical axis with the ventilation rate from the graph in Strategy 105. Move horizontally to the curve for the building's or zone's floor area; from the intersection, move vertically to read the fan air volume on either horizontal axis. Drop a line through all of the lower horizontal scales to read the size of other system elements. For more details on ducts, see Strategy 107.

Surface mount fans in walls or ceilings, used without ductwork, have about a 12–16 in (305–405 mm) diameter for 500–2500 cfm (14–70 m³/hr); and a 20–30 in (510–760 mm) diameter for 3000–5000 cfm (85–140 m³/hr).

Whole-house fans, which are large volume, low velocity fans used to space cool a small building by exhaust, can be used to supplement natural ventilation, especially at night when winds are calmer. Whole-house fans draw air from windows and exhaust from a central high point to the outside or an attic. Because fans can create higher pressures than natural ventilation, inlets can be small, allowing security control by locking windows open only a few inches.

Total inlet area should be a minimum of twice the fan area, or three times its area if insect screens are used. Attic outlet area must be at least one square foot per 750 cfm (0.1 m² per 20 m³/hr). As a rule, whole-house fans in hot-humid climates are usually sized to provide 20 air changes per hour (ACH) (Chandra et al., 1986, p. 55; U. S. Dept. of Energy, 1989).

To convert ACH to a fan air flow rate in cubic feet per minute (cfm), multiply building volume (ft³) by ACH and divide by 60 min/hr. A more accurate sizing estimate can be determined by using the graph in Strategy 105, along with a maximum hourly heat gain rate from Technique 21.

Localized room fans, such as ceiling fans and oscillating fans, do not remove heat from a space, but provide convective cooling to people and increase the evaporation rate of their perspiration. Fans that create an air movement of 150–200 ft/min (0.75–1.0 m/sec) can create a cooling effect of up to 4 °F (2.2 °C), effectively raising the top of the comfort zone (Technique 11). This can greatly increase the times and dates when passive cooling strategies will be effective and can reduce the running hours of a mechanical cooling system (Chandra et al., 1986, p. 23).

Ceiling fan size should be matched to room size, as shown in the table for Recommended Ceiling Fan Size. Fans should be mounted at least 10 in (250 mm) from the ceiling; in tall rooms, mount fans 7.5–8 ft (2.4 m) above the floor to be closer to the occupants. Air speed drops off with distance from the fan, so fans should be located in a room close to where occupants spend the most time. *The diagram shows that the most cooling effect is within a circular zone of diameter twice that of the fan diameter* (Chandra et al., 1986, p. 24). Ceiling fans provide cooling only when the room is occupied, so they should be controlled by timers or occupancy sensors to avoid constant running and energy consumption.

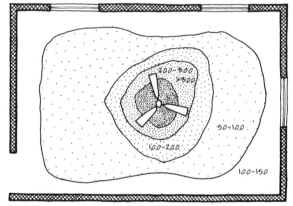

Air Flow Pattern From a Ceiling Fan
Maximum speed, ceiling = 8 ft (2.4m), fan dia. = 48 in (1.2m).

Largest Room Dimension ft (m)	Minimum Fan Diameter in (mm)
< 12 (3.7)	36 (915)
12-16 (3.7-4.9)	48 (1220)
16-17.5 (4.9-5.3)	52 (1320)
17.5-18.5 (5.3-5.6)	56 (1420)
>18.5 (5.6)	2 fans

Recommended Ceiling Fan Size

107 *DUCTS AND PLENUMS* can be used to move heat to cool parts of the building and cold to hot parts of the building. [heating and cooling]

Heat sources like the sun and heat sinks like the night sky are not equally accessible to all parts of the building. Thus, some buildings need to have heat transported to cooler areas in the heating season and cold transported to hot areas during the cooling season. Internal-load-dominated buildings typically have some zones with constant cooling loads and excess heat. This heat may be moved to zones that require heat, such as a north perimeter in winter.

The central atrium in the **Bateson California State Office Building** in Sacramento, California, is used primarily to supply light to the building interior (see axonometric in Strategy 105). Because it is not conditioned but is used as a circulation and meeting space, it must supply its own heating, which it does by capturing solar radiation through its south-facing clerestories. Because the space is tall, the hot air tends to collect at the top of the space. The hot air is circulated from the top of the space to the bottom, where the people are, through canvas ducts hung from the ceiling. Each duct has a fan at its lower end. In the summer, cool night air is drawn down ventilating shafts located above the roof to cool the mass of the atrium, and then the warmed air is released through skylight vents (*Progressive Architecture,* 9/1981, p. 76; Lechner, 1991, pp. 450–455; Reynolds & Stein, 1992, pp. 259–265).

In the **Conservation Center, Society for the Protection of New Hampshire Forests,** in Concord, New Hampshire, designed by Banwel, White and Arnold, sunlight is collected through south-facing windows and clerestories. Solar energy that is not immediately stored in the building's mass, water tubes, or ceiling phase change materials heats the air that rises to the top of the clerestory. The hot air is drawn, by a fan located below the clerestory, through a roof plenum, down the rear masonry wall and through the hollow concrete floor, losing its heat to the mass. In the summer, overheated air is vented from the clerestory to the outside (*Progressive Architecture,* 4/1983b).

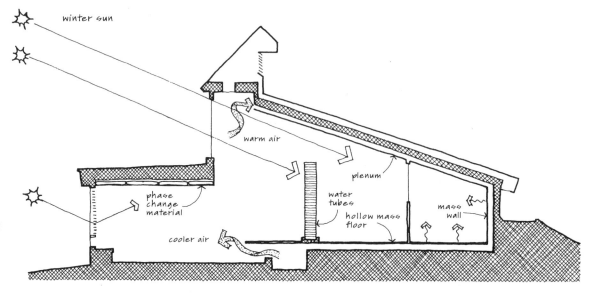

Conservation Center, Concord, New Hampshire, Banwell/White/Arnold

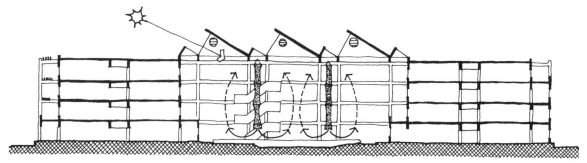

Bateson Building, Sacramento, California, Office of the State Architect

Duct size is a function of the velocity of the air and the volume of air being moved through the duct per unit of time. The volumetric air flow rate is a function of the amount of heat to be moved and the temperature difference between supply and return. For mechanical ventilation, the volume is proportional to the rate of hourly heat gain; for night ventilation, volume is proportional to the heat to be removed from mass at the maximum hour of cooling. For solar heating, the volume of air moved is based on the amount of excess heat in the collector space on a sunny spring day, which can be estimated by subtracting the rate of heat loss from the rate of heat gain (Technique 21).

To estimate minimum duct size, enter the graph on the horizontal axis with the volumetric air flow, per unit of floor area, to be moved through the duct. The air volume moved by a fan, and thus through one or more ducts can be estimated from the graph in Strategy 105. Move vertically to the diagonal for the desired velocity in the duct, and then horizontally to read the duct's cross sectional area per unit of floor area. Multiply this value by the floor area generating the heat resource (heating season) or cooling load (cooling season) to get the total duct area.

The total area may be carried in one or multiple ducts. The graph assumes a rectangular duct of 1:5 proportion. A square duct will be about 5–10% smaller; a round duct, about 20% smaller. Use higher air velocity for main ducts and buildings where noise is less of an issue, such as industrial buildings. Use lower velocity for branch ducts, residences, and occupancies where noise from air friction would be intrusive. To avoid perceptible air noise at diffusers, registers, and openings into plenums use velocities of 500–700 ft/min (2.5–3.5 m/sec).

If cooling predominates, a high supply to the space being cooled and a low return are preferred. If heating dominates, reverse this principle: low supply, high return.

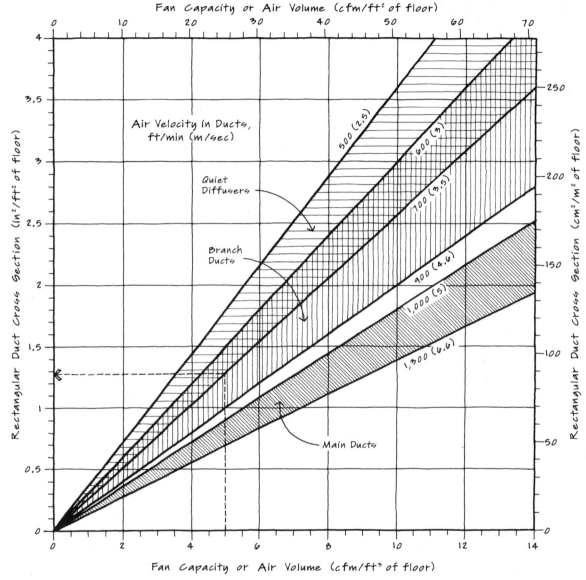

Estimating Duct Sizes

108 *PASSIVE BUFFER ZONES* can temper fresh ventilation air before it enters the occupied space, and *AIR–AIR HEAT EXCHANGERS* can be used to reclaim heat and cold from the ventilation air. [heating and cooling]

In closed building design strategies in which heat loss and gain through the building skin are carefully controlled, heating or cooling incoming fresh air becomes a major energy user in the building. With ventilation rates below one air change per hour, there is a danger of air pollution within the building as a result of chemicals emitted by building materials and the accumulation of naturally occurring radioactive radon gas. One way to reduce the energy used to heat or cool incoming air without reducing its volume below safe limits is to use the heat or cold escaping from the building to heat or cool the incoming air.

Fan powered air-to-heat exchangers are frequently used in ducted systems. Air exhausted from the building is passed by or through a series of thin metal planes, giving off its heat or cold, and incoming air is passed by or though the same planes, picking up heat or cold. *Air-to-air heat exchangers can recapture 70–90% of the outgoing heat or cold (Shurcliff, 1981, p. 12.02).* Air flow windows (Strategy 95) and earth–air heat exchangers (Strategy 109) can also temper fresh air for ventilation.

In buildings with sunspaces (Strategy 61), atria (Strategy 70), or unconditioned buffer zones (Strategy 57), the air in these spaces is typically warmer that the outside air during winter. Ventilation air can be moved, often with the aid of fans, ducts, and heat exchangers, from these spaces to occupied conditioned rooms.

Atelier Z used mechanical heat exchangers in each dwelling unit of the **Urban Villa, "Licht en Groen,"** in Amstelveen, The Netherlands. In winter, preheated ventilation air is taken from a large atrium with a south-sloping roof. Incoming air is passed through cross-flow air-to-air heat exchangers to recover 80% of the heat from outgoing stale air. Sunlight is admitted to the atrium during the day and roof shading is closed at night to hold heat. In summer, the heat exchanger fans are used to exhaust ventilation that enters through vents in the south facade. A signal light in each room indicates when windows can be opened for natural ventilation; the exhaust ventilator stays on all the time to insure the Dutch standard minimum ventilation rate of 250 m³/hr per apartment (8830 cfm). A timer control system sets ventilation rates lower during unoccupied periods (Hestnes et al., 1997, pp. 133–138; Hastings, 1995, pp. 33–34).

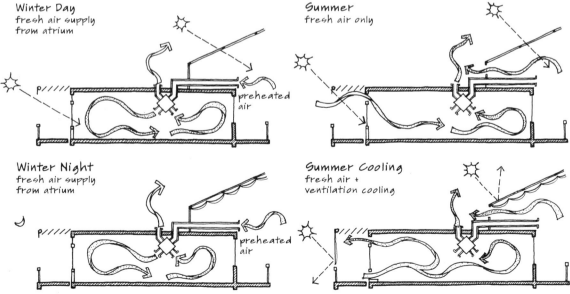

View From Southwest, Urban Villa, Amstelveen   Ventilation Modes, Urban Villa, Amstelveen, The Netherlands, Atelier Z Zarvel

.09 *EARTH–AIR HEAT EXCHANGERS* **can temper incoming ventilation air in all seasons and help cool the building in summer. [heating and cooling]**

The temperature of the ground several feet below the surface does not fluctuate on a daily basis. Its temperature lags behind the average air temperature by about a month, making it warmer in winter and cooler in summer than the air temperature above.

When air is fan-forced through underground ducts, also known as "cool pipes" or "earth tubes," it can exchange heat with the ground. The system can be used to preheat or precool ventilation air or to provide a part of a building's space cooling. In winter, depending on climate, the air will generally require further warming. In summer, it may be cool enough to use without additional tempering. Only a portion of a building's cooling load can typically be met economically with this strategy.

The amount of heat transfer is based on the temperature difference between the ground and air, the soil type and dampness, the volume of air mass moving through the duct, and on the length and diameter of the duct.

The main design impact of earth tubes is finding enough site area to accommodate them. *Duct length should be 10–90 m (33–295 ft) long and 0.2–0.3 m (8–12 in) in diameter.* More ducts of shorter length improve thermal performance, but may increase cost. Smaller diameter ducts have more surface area relative to their cross section. *Recommended placement depth is 1.5–3 m (5–10 ft); since ground-to-air ΔT increases with depth, place ducts as deep as is practical. The air velocity though the duct should be 2.5–8 m/ sec (500–1600 ft/min).* A higher velocity increases total cooling (or heating), but decreases the temperature change in the air. Ducts should be surrounded with at least 5 cm (2 in) of sand to insure good thermal contact and prevent damage. They can be made of any material—plastic, metal, ceramic, concrete—with little impact on performance. (Santamouris & Asimakopolous, 1996, pp. 389–90; Argiriou & Santamouris, 1995, pp. 95–96; Labs, 1989, pp. 318–323; Abrams, 1986, pp. 264–278).

To estimate the length of earth tubes requires

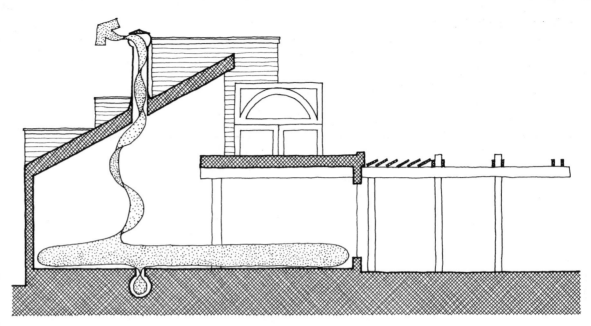

Lane Energy Center, Cottage Grove, Oregon, Equinox Design

three pieces of information. First, find the building's heat transfer rate, either heat gain (Technique 21) or net heat loss (Technique 21, subtract gain from loss). If designing the underground ducts only for ventilation air, include only gains or losses from ventilation. Second, find the earth temperature at the depth the ducts will be placed (Strategy 72). Third, find the outdoor air temperature during the month being considered, usually the summer design temperature for a totally passive building, or the average high temperature for a building with backup mechanical cooling. For winter, use the lowest temperature likely to occur during occupied hours (Appendix A).

Enter the graph on the horizontal axis with the air-to-ground temperature difference, ΔT. Move vertically to the curve for the building's heat transfer rate; from the intersection, move horizontally to read the total length of ducts per unit floor area. Finally, multiply this value by the occupied floor area of the building to get the length of buried ducts required.

The total length can be broken up between several ducts as required. Space them 3 m (10 ft) or more apart, using as few turns as possible, in a configuration that fits on the site. The graph assumes a velocity of 2.5

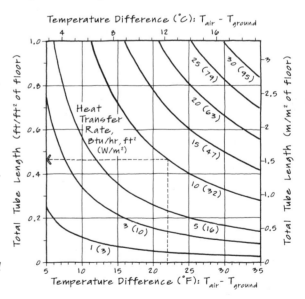

Sizing Earth-Air Heat Exchangers

m/sec (500 ft/min) and duct runs of 30 m (100 ft) each. It was developed based on methods found in Reynolds & Stein (2000, pp. 320–325) and Abrams (1986, p. 272).

APPENDIXES

Appendix A
Climate Data by Latitude/City

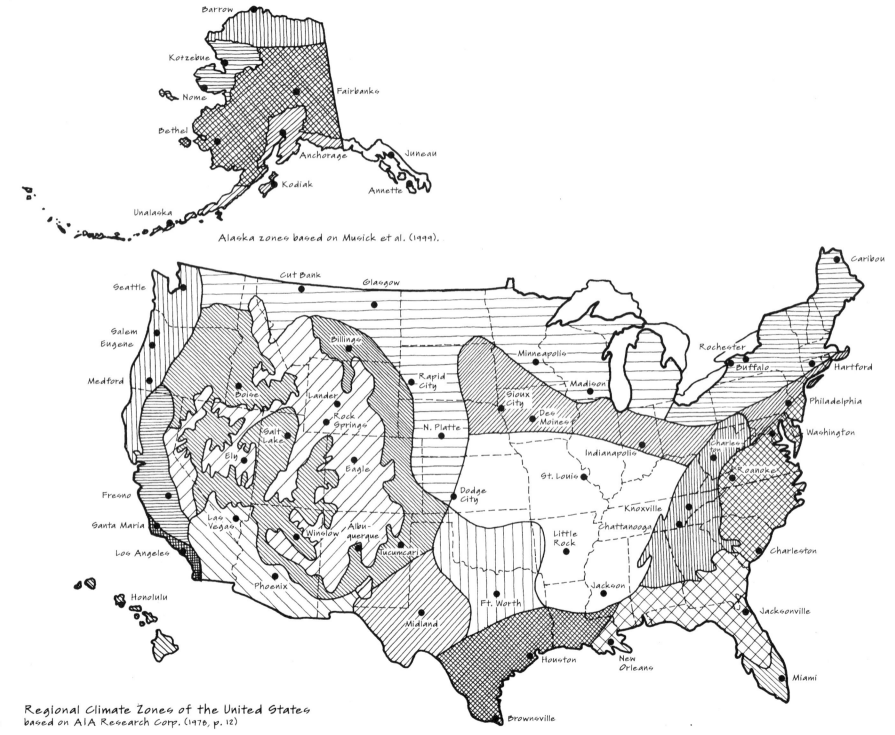

Alaska zones based on Musick et al. (1999).

Regional Climate Zones of the United States
based on AIA Research Corp. (1978, p. 12)

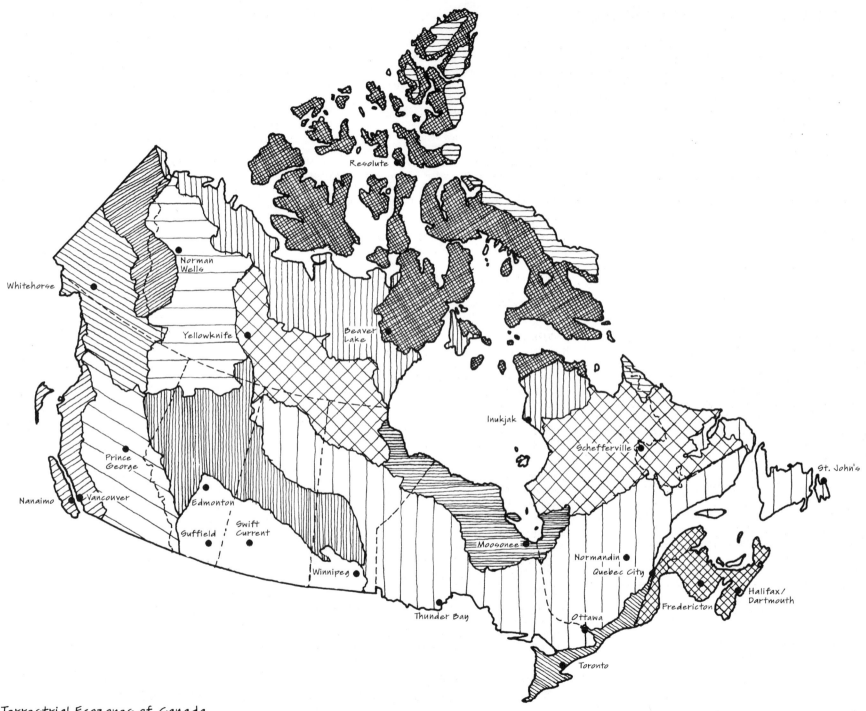

Terrestrial Ecozones of Canada
based on Environment Canada (1995).

DATA SOURCES BY ANALYSIS TECHNIQUE

* References marked with an asterisk were used as sources for the climate data given in the appendix for specific cities.

Normals, Means, and Extremes Data

International Station Meteorological Climate Summary, Version 4.0 (NCDC, 1996).
Canadian Climate Normals, 1961–1990 (Environment Canada, 1993).
Canadian Monthly Climate Data on CD-ROM (Environment Canada, 1994).
Comparative Climatic Data for the United States Through 1994. (NOAA, 1995).
Climates of the States (NOAA, 1985).

1 Sundials

Climate Consultant software (Milne, 1991).

2 Sun Path Diagrams

Passive Solar Energy Book (Mazria, 1979).
Climate Consultant (Milne, 1991).
Manual of Tropical Housing and Building (Koenigberger et al., 1973).
SUN-CHART software (Crawford, 1995).
SolrPath sotfware (TEES, 1999).

3 Solar Radiation

Average Hourly Solar Radiation by City

*Mean Hourly Global Horizontal Radiation for cities in the appendix is derived from TMY2 data (Marion & Urban, 1995).
Hourly Solar Radiation Data for Vertical and Horizontal Surfaces on Average Days in the U.S. and Canada (Kusuda & Ishii, 1977).
National Solar Radiation Data Base (1961-1990) (NREL, 1993a).
Solar and Meteorological Surface Observation Network, 1961–1990 (NREL, 1993b).
Solar Radiation Data Analysis for Canada (Environment Canada).

Hourly Clear Day Radiation by Latitude

Mechanical and Electrical Equipment for Buildings, 9th ed. (Reynolds & Stein, 2000).
Solar Thermal Engineering (Lunde, 1980).

Average Daily Solar Radiation on a Horizontal Surface

Solar Radiation Data Manual for Buildings (Marion & Wilcox, 1995).
Solar Radiation Data Manual for Flat-Plate and Concentrating Collectors (Marion & Wilcox, 1994).
See also radiation maps in Appendix B.

Degree Days

Mechanical and Electrical Equipment for Buildings, 9th ed. (Reynolds & Stein, 2000).
Solar Radiation Data Manual for Buildings (Marion & Wilcox, 1995).

Solar Radiation Data Manual for Flat-Plate and Concentrating Collectors (Marion & Wilcox, 1994).
See sources above for "Normals, Means, and Extremes." See also degree days maps in Appendix B.

Radiation on Solar Collectors

Solar Radiation Data Manual for Flat-Plate and Concentrating Collectors (Marion & Wilcox, 1994).
Photovoltaic Systems Design Manual (CANMET, 1991). Canadian locations.
An Analysis of Solar Radiation Data for Selected Locations in Canada (Hay, 1977).
METORNORM software (Meteotest, 1997). Radiation for sites anywhere in the world, at any tilt and orientation.
Water Pumping: The Solar Alternative (Thomas, 1992) World Maps of radiation for 4 seasons at 3 tilts.

4 Wind Rose

Airport Climatological Summary (U.S. Dept. of Commerce)
International Station Meteorological Summary CD-ROM (NCDC, 1996).
Climatic Atlas of the United States (NOAA, 1993; ESSA, 1975) Pre-drawn, simplified wind roses.
The Climatic Atlas Canada (Environment Canada, 1988). Pre-drawn, simplified wind roses.

5 Wind Square

*Mean Hourly Wind for cities in the appendix is derived from TMY2 data (Marion & Urban, 1995).
Airport Climatological Summary (U.S. Dept. of Commerce).
International Station Meteorological Summary CD-ROM (NCDC, 1996).

8 Sky Cover

*Mean Hourly Sky Cover for cities in the appendix is derived from TMY2 data (Marion & Urban, 1995).

Sky Cover Monthly Normals

Comparative Climatic Data for the United States Through 1994 (NOAA, 1995).
See also, sources above for "Normals, Means, and Extremes."

Maps of Mean Sky Cover

Climatic Atlas of the United States (NOAA, 1993; ESSA, 1975).
The Climatic Atlas Canada (Environment Canada, 1988).
See also sky cover maps in Appendix B.

Three-Hour Interval Sky Cover Data

Revised Uniform Summary of Surface Weather Observations (U.S. Dept. of Commerce)
Airport Climatological Summary (U.S. Dept. of Commerce)
International Station Meteorological Summary CD-ROM (NCDC, 1996).

9 Daylight Availability

*Mean Hourly Global Horizontal Illuminance for cities in the appendix is derived from TMY2 data (Marion & Urban, 1995).

Solar Radiation Data Manual for Buildings (Marion and Wilcox, 1995).
239 US cities; given in kilolux for five times dai;y/four seasons.
Daylighting, Design and Analysis (Robbins, 1986).
Hourly clear and cloudy sky illuminance data for 77 U.S. locations.
IES Lighting Handbook (Kaufman, 1984).
Hourly data typical of latitude, rather than city.
See also clear sky data by latitude in Appendix B.

10 Daylight Obstructions

See daylight obstruction dot charts in Appendix B.

11 Bioclimatic Chart

International Station Meteorological Climate Summary, Version 4.0 (NCDC, 1996).
Climate Consultant (Milne, 1991).
Plots climate data on a psychrometric version of the bioclimatic chart.
See also sources above for "Normals, Means, and Extremes." Temperature and humidity data are required for this technique.

16 Window Solar Gain

Percentage of Possible Sunshine

Comparative Climatic Data for the United States Through 1994. (NOAA, 1995)
Climatic Atlas of the United States (NOAA, 1983; ESSA, 1975).
The Climatic Atlas Canada (Environment Canada, 1988).

Solar Heat Gain Factor (SHGF), gain through glazing

ASHRAE Hanbook, Fundamentals (ASHRAE (1997).
Passive Solar Energy Book (Mazria, 1979).
Mechanical and Electrical Equipment for Buildings, 9th ed. (Reynolds & Stein, 2000).
PEC Solar Calculator (Benton & Marcial, 1993).

18 Building Bioclimatic Chart

See sources above for Technique 11, Bioclimatic Chart.

20 Shading Calandar

*Mean Hourly Temperature for cities in the appendix is derived from TMY2 data (Marion & Urban, 1995).
SolrPath sotfware (TEES, 1999).
Climate Consultant (Milne, 1991).

21 Total Heat Gains and Losses

Design Temperatures

ASHRAE Handbook, Fundamentals (ASHRAE, 1997).

Degree Days

See sources above for degree days under Technique 3, Solar Radiation.

23 Balance Point Profiles

BPgraph spreadsheet (Utzinger & Wasley, 1997a).
See also sources above for "Normals, Means, and Extremes."

0° LATITUDE (equator)

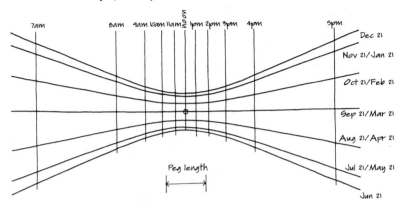

Sundial, 0° Latitude (equator)

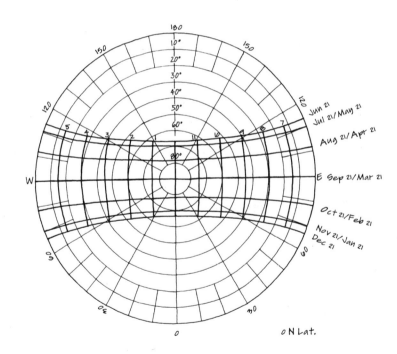

Sun Path Diagram, 0° Latitude (equator)

4° LATITUDE

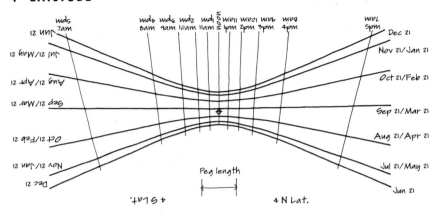

Sundial, 4° Latitude

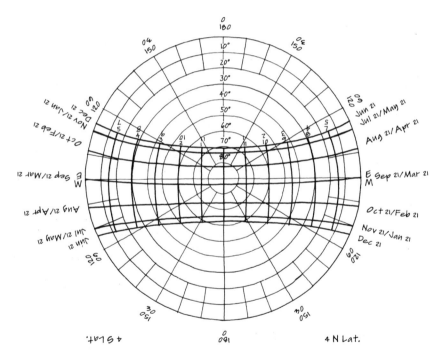

Sun Path Diagram, 4° Latitude

8° LATITUDE

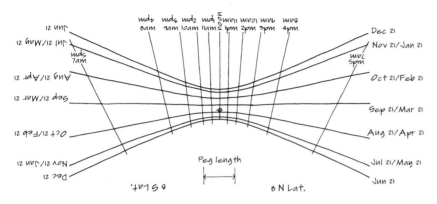

Sundial, 8° Latitude

12° LATITUDE

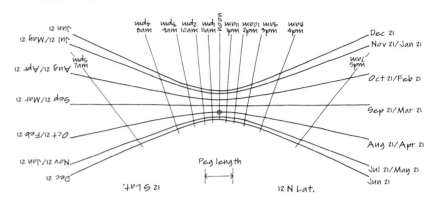

Sundial, 12° Latitude

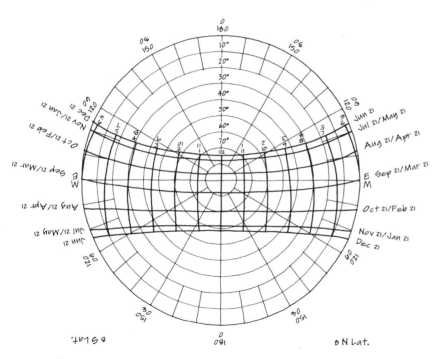

Sun Path Diagram, 8° Latitude

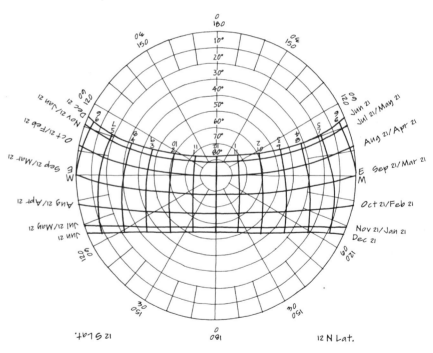

Sun Path Diagram, 12° Latitude

16° LATITUDE

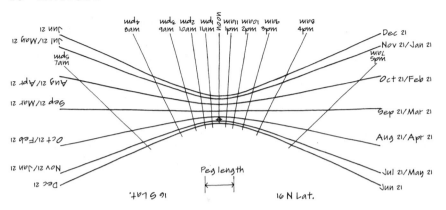

Sundial, 16° Latitude

20° LATITUDE

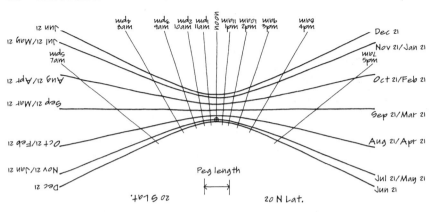

Sundial, 20° Latitude

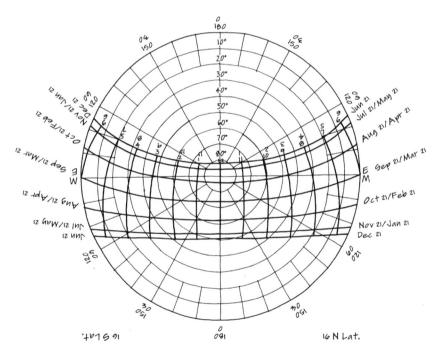

Sun Path Diagram, 16° Latitude

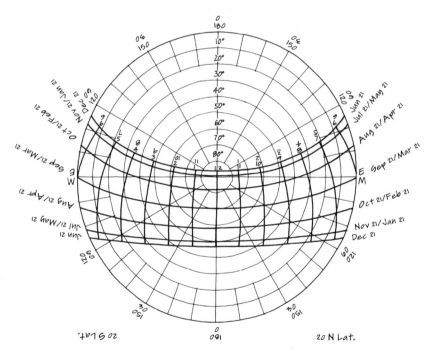

Sun Path Diagram, 20° Latitude

24° LATITUDE

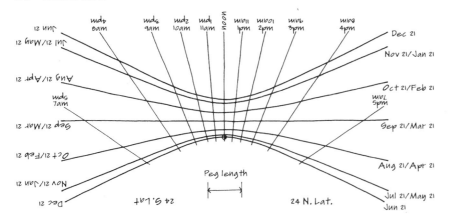

Sundial, 24° Latitude

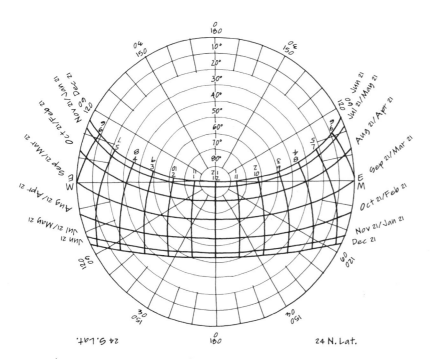

Sun Path Diagram, 24° Latitude

28° LATITUDE

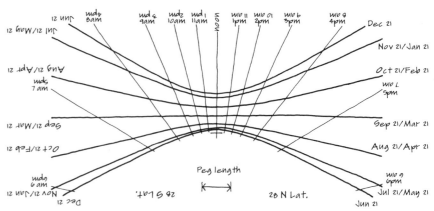

Sundial, 28° Latitude

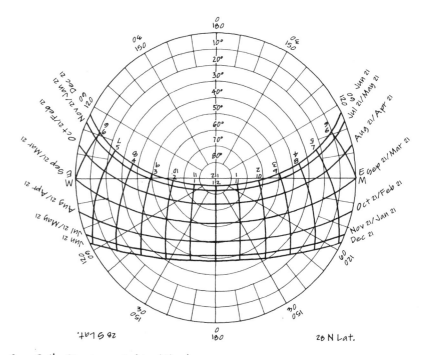

Sun Path Diagram, 28° Latitude

HOT-HUMID CLIMATE: New Orleans, Louisiana

Lat 29° 59' N; Long 90° 15' W
Elev 10 ft (3 m)
Jan Vertical Rad = 1030 Btu/ft², d
HDD/CDD65 °F = 1513/2655
HDD/CDD18 °C = 841/1475

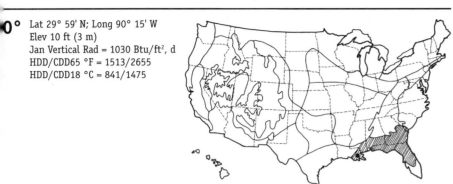

2 SUN PATH DIAGRAM

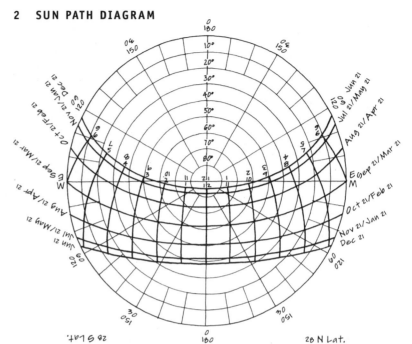

Sun Path Diagram, 28° Latitude

1 SUNDIAL

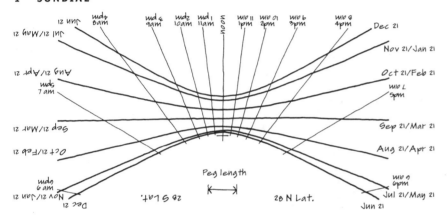

Sundial, 28° Latitude

3 SOLAR RADIATION

ELEMENT		Jan	Feb	Mar	Apr	May	Jun	Jul	Aug	Sep	Oct	Nov	Dec	Year
HDD	18.3C	250	176	90	16	0	0	0	0	0	17	99	194	**841**
CDD	18.3C	14	9	31	74	169	250	291	284	218	87	34	13	1475
HDD	65F	450	316	162	28	0	0	0	0	0	30	178	349	**1513**
CDD	65F	25	17	56	133	304	450	524	512	393	157	61	23	2655
AVERAGE INCIDENT SOLAR RADIATION (Btu/sq. ft./day)														
HORIZ.	Global	860	1130	1410	1750	1920	1940	1820	1730	1550	1370	990	820	1440
SOUTH 90° (VS)	Global	**1030**	1120	1010	850	660	580	600	740	970	1240	1170	1070	920
SOLAR RADIATION FOR FLAT-PLATE COLLECTORS FACING SOUTH AT A FIXED-TILT (kWh/sq. m./day)														
0°	Ave.	2.7	3.6	4.5	5.5	6.1	6.1	5.7	5.5	4.9	4.3	3.1	2.6	4.6
Lat – 15°	Ave.	3.3	4.2	4.9	5.7	6	6	5.7	5.6	5.3	5	3.8	3.2	4.9
Lat	Ave.	3.7	4.5	5	5.6	5.7	5.5	5.3	5.4	5.3	5.3	4.3	3.7	5
Lat + 15°	Ave.	3.9	4.6	4.9	5.3	5.1	4.8	4.7	4.9	5.1	5.4	4.5	3.9	4.8
90°	Ave.	3.3	3.5	3.2	2.7	2.1	1.8	1.9	2.3	3	3.9	3.7	3.4	2.9

Degree Days and Incident Solar Radiation

	J	F	M	A	M	J	J	A	S	O	N	D
1 am	0	0	0	0	0	0	0	0	0	0	0	0
2	0	0	0	0	0	0	0	0	0	0	0	0
3	0	0	0	0	0	0	0	0	0	0	0	0
4	0	0	0	0	0	0	0	0	0	0	0	0
5	0	0	0	0	0	0	0	0	0	0	0	0
6	0	0	0	4	10	11	8	4	0	0	0	0
7	0	3	11	30	49	53	43	29	22	13	6	1
8	13	25	48	79	103	111	94	81	69	57	35	18
9	47	69	98	133	154	171	139	132	119	109	79	59
10	80	115	141	186	189	213	190	182	158	158	122	98
11 am	106	157	176	220	231	238	224	211	195	190	156	123
12 noon	128	177	189	237	257	259	230	221	205	206	161	138
1 pm	132	182	197	222	236	241	242	229	211	202	156	132
2	127	170	193	209	225	212	231	211	189	176	135	121
3	96	132	167	171	200	184	188	166	160	136	103	89
4	65	100	126	137	148	137	148	129	111	90	60	51
5	24	49	72	81	97	93	99	82	59	36	17	14
6	4	12	21	31	43	45	47	32	15	6	0	0
7	0	0	1	5	8	10	11	6	1	0	0	0
8	0	0	0	0	0	0	0	0	0	0	0	0
9	0	0	0	0	0	0	0	0	0	0	0	0
10	0	0	0	0	0	0	0	0	0	0	0	0
11 pm	0	0	0	0	0	0	0	0	0	0	0	0
12 mid	0	0	0	0	0	0	0	0	0	0	0	0

0	1-100	101-250	>250

Mean Global Horizontal Radiation, Btu/h, ft²

4 WIND ROSE

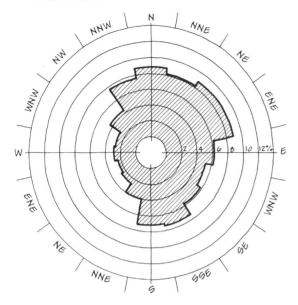

December Wind Rose, New Orleans

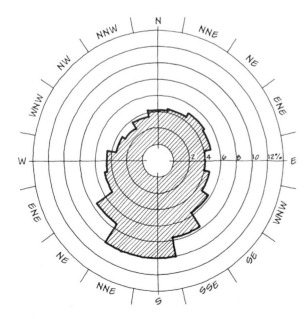

June Wind Rose, New Orleans

5 WIND SQUARE

Mean Airport Wind Conditions, direction/mph

	J	F	M	A	M	J	J	A	S	O	N	D
1 am	NE 9.4	ENE 9.0	N 7.8	N 7.6	N 6.5	S 3.6	S 3.9	NNE 4.7	NNE 5.1	N 5.3	ENE 7.5	E 8.0
2	SSE 8.6	ESE 8.7	NNW 7.4	N 7.6	ESE 6.4	S 3.6	N 3.9	NE 4.3	E 4.7	E 5.3	SE 8.1	SE 7.7
3	SSE 8.9	W 8.4	W 7.0	S 8.2	S 5.7	S 3.2	N 3.8	N 3.9	N 4.9	SE 5.4	SSE 8.3	NNW 8.3
4	N 8.7	NE 8.5	NE 6.6	NNE 7.0	N 5.5	N 2.7	NNE 3.8	NNW 3.9	N 4.6	N 5.4	N 8.2	N 8.5
5	N 8.6	N 8.7	SE 6.0	SE 6.9	NNW 4.3	WNW 2.8	SSW 4.0	S 5.2	SE 5.5	S 8.3	NNW 8.3	NNW 8.2
6	S 7.9	SSE 8.8	S 5.6	S 7.3	SE 5.0	NNW 2.5	NNW 3.7	N 4.0	NE 5.5	NNW 5.6	W 8.7	SE 7.8
7	SE 7.9	N 9.8	SSW 7.0	NNW 8.9	NNW 7.1	N 5.4	WNW 5.2	WNW 6.0	NW 6.4	S 9.0	N 8.6	N 8.6
8	S 8.9	NW 10.8	SSW 8.5	S 10.0	S 8.7	S 6.9	SSW 7.3	N 6.5	NE 8.3	E 7.2	E 10.9	SSW 8.8
9	N 10.9	NNE 11.8	ESE 9.9	SSE 10.6	SSW 9.8	N 7.2	N 9.0	S 7.8	SE 8.9	S 8.9	N 11.5	NNW 10.4
10	N 11.5	N 12.1	S 10.1	SW 11.4	SW 10.1	N 7.8	N 8.9	N 8.2	N 8.8	SSW 8.3	SSW 13.1	SSW 10.2
11 am	N 11.4	N 12.4	N 10.2	SSE 11.8	N 11.4	SSW 8.1	SSW 8.8	N 8.7	W 9.2	N 9.9	SE 12.3	N 9.8
12 noon	N 11.5	E 12.7	NNE 10.3	NE 11.9	ESE 11.4	SE 7.5	S 8.7	SW 9.2	N 9.1	S 8.7	N 12.4	N 9.9
1 pm	SSW 11.9	ENE 12.3	S 10.5	WSW 11.6	WSW 11.6	WSW 8.6	N 8.7	ENE 9.3	ESE 9.5	W 8.6	W 12.8	SSW 10.3
2	SW 11.8	SW 11.9	SW 10.7	NW 11.0	ESE 11.0	NE 8.7	NE 8.7	E 9.3	SW 8.9	SW 8.5	W 12.1	S 9.6
3	SSW 11.5	SSW 11.5	WSW 10.9	SSW 11.4	SW 10.2	S 8.5	S 8.7	S 9.4	SSE 8.4	ESE 8.4	S 11.8	W 9.3
4	N 11.1	S 10.7	S 10.2	ESE 11.5	W 10.3	N 8.6	N 8.1	N 8.6	N 8.6	NE 7.5	ENE 10.4	NNE 8.8
5	ENE 10.1	N 10.0	N 9.5	N 10.5	SW 10.1	N 7.6	SW 7.5	SSW 7.9	N 7.1	ENE 6.7	ENE 8.6	ENE 7.8
6	ENE 8.7	ENE 9.2	N 8.8	N 9.5	N 9.4	NE 7.1	ENE 6.9	NE 7.1	NE 6.2	N 5.9	NNE 7.2	N 7.6
7	SSW 8.9	NNE 9.4	N 8.4	ENE 8.8	SSE 8.2	SSW 5.8	NNE 6.2	N 6.5	N 5.1	NNE 5.8	W 7.4	NNW 7.5
8	N 9.5	W 9.7	W 8.0	E 8.9	E 8.2	ENE 4.5	NNW 5.5	NW 5.9	N 5.6	N 5.8	N 8.3	E 7.9
9	N 9.9	ENE 9.9	N 7.6	N 8.8	N 8.0	ESE 5.2	ESE 4.9	N 5.3	N 5.7	N 5.8	ESE 8.7	ESE 8.0
10	WNW 9.2	NE 9.7	N 7.7	N 9.8	N 7.3	ESE 4.4	ESE 4.6	SE 5.2	E 5.4	NW 5.6	N 8.2	W 7.7
11 pm	NW 9.8	NW 9.5	N 7.9	N 8.7	E 6.7	NE 4.3	NE 4.4	ESE 5.1	E 5.7	ENE 5.5	N 7.9	N 8.1
12 mid	N 9.0	N 9.3	E 8.1	SE 8.4	S 6.4	NNE 4.1	N 4.1	N 5.0	NE 5.3	N 5.3	NE 7.8	E 7.8

Legend: 0-5 | 5.1-9 | 9.1-12 | >12

Mean City Center Wind Conditions, direction/mph

	J	F	M	A	M	J	J	A	S	O	N	D
1 am	NE 4.4	ENE 4.2	N 3.7	N 3.6	N 3.0	S 1.7	S 1.8	NNE 2.2	NNE 2.4	N 2.5	ENE 3.5	E 3.8
2	SSE 4.1	ESE 4.1	NNW 3.5	N 3.6	ESE 3.0	S 1.7	N 1.8	NE 2.0	E 2.2	E 2.5	SE 3.8	SE 3.6
3	SSE 4.2	W 3.9	W 3.3	S 3.9	S 2.7	S 1.5	N 1.8	N 1.8	N 2.3	SE 2.5	SSE 3.9	NNW 3.9
4	N 4.1	NE 4.0	NE 3.1	NNE 3.3	N 2.6	N 1.2	NNE 1.8	NNW 1.8	N 2.2	N 2.6	N 3.8	N 4.0
5	N 4.0	N 4.1	SE 2.8	SE 3.2	NNW 2.0	WNW 1.3	SSW 1.8	S 1.9	SE 2.4	S 2.6	NNW 3.9	NNW 3.8
6	S 3.7	SSE 4.1	S 2.6	S 3.5	SE 2.3	NNW 1.2	NNW 1.8	N 1.9	NE 2.6	NNW 2.6	W 4.1	SE 3.6
7	SE 3.7	N 4.6	SSW 3.3	NNW 4.2	NNW 3.4	N 2.5	WNW 2.6	WNW 2.5	NW 2.8	S 3.0	S 4.2	N 4.0
8	S 4.2	NW 5.1	SSW 4.0	S 4.7	S 4.1	S 3.2	SSW 3.4	N 3.1	NE 3.9	E 3.4	E 5.1	SSW 4.1
9	N 5.1	NNE 5.5	ESE 4.7	SSE 5.0	SSW 4.6	N 3.4	N 4.2	S 3.6	SE 4.2	S 3.8	N 5.4	NNW 4.9
10	N 5.4	N 5.7	S 4.7	SW 5.4	SW 4.7	N 3.7	N 4.2	N 3.9	N 4.1	SSW 3.9	SSW 6.2	SSW 4.8
11 am	N 5.4	N 5.8	N 4.8	SSE 5.5	N 5.3	SSW 3.8	SSW 4.1	N 4.1	W 4.3	N 4.6	SE 5.8	N 4.6
12 noon	N 5.4	E 6.0	NNE 4.8	NE 5.6	ESE 5.3	SE 3.5	S 4.1	SW 4.3	N 4.3	S 4.1	N 5.8	N 4.6
1 pm	SSW 5.6	ENE 5.8	S 4.9	WSW 5.5	WSW 5.5	WSW 4.0	N 4.1	ENE 4.4	ESE 4.5	W 4.0	W 6.0	SSW 4.8
2	SW 5.5	SW 5.6	SW 5.0	NW 5.1	ESE 5.2	NE 4.1	NE 4.1	E 4.4	SW 4.2	SW 4.0	W 5.7	S 4.5
3	SSW 5.4	SSW 5.4	WSW 5.1	SSW 5.4	SW 4.8	S 4.0	S 4.1	S 4.4	SSE 4.0	ESE 3.9	S 5.5	W 4.4
4	N 5.2	S 5.0	S 4.8	ESE 5.4	W 4.8	N 4.0	N 3.8	N 4.1	N 4.1	NE 3.5	ENE 4.9	NNE 4.1
5	ENE 4.8	N 4.7	N 4.5	N 4.9	SW 4.7	N 3.6	SW 3.5	SSW 3.7	N 3.3	ENE 3.1	ENE 4.1	ENE 3.7
6	ENE 4.1	ENE 4.3	N 4.2	N 4.5	N 4.4	NE 3.3	ENE 3.3	NE 3.4	NE 2.9	N 2.8	NNE 3.4	N 3.6
7	SSW 4.2	NNE 4.4	N 4.0	ENE 4.1	SSE 3.8	SSW 2.7	NNE 2.9	N 3.0	N 2.6	NNE 2.7	W 3.5	NNW 3.5
8	N 4.5	W 4.5	W 3.8	E 4.2	E 3.9	ENE 2.1	NNW 2.6	NW 2.8	N 2.6	N 2.7	N 3.9	E 3.7
9	N 4.5	ENE 4.6	N 3.6	N 4.1	N 3.8	ESE 2.4	ESE 2.3	N 2.5	N 2.7	N 2.7	ESE 4.1	ESE 3.7
10	WNW 4.3	NE 4.6	N 3.6	N 4.6	N 3.4	ESE 2.1	ESE 2.2	SE 2.4	E 2.5	NW 2.6	N 3.9	W 3.6
11 pm	NW 4.6	NW 4.5	N 3.7	N 4.1	E 3.1	NE 2.0	NE 2.1	ESE 2.4	E 2.7	ENE 2.6	N 3.7	N 3.8
12 mid	N 4.2	N 4.4	E 3.8	SE 4.0	S 3.0	NNE 1.9	N 2.0	N 2.3	NE 2.5	N 2.5	NE 3.7	E 3.7

Legend: 0-5 | 5.1-9 | 9.1-12 | >12

6 AIR MOVEMENT PRINCIPLES
Technique 6 uses data from Techniques 4 and 5.

7 SITE MICROCLIMATES
Technique 7 uses data from Techniques 1, 2, 4, and 5.

8 SKY COVER

	J	F	M	A	M	J	J	A	S	O	N	D
1 am	6.4	5.5	5.6	5.3	3.1	2.5	4.5	4.3	3.3	4.3	4.6	5.8
2	7.0	5.4	5.6	5.6	2.9	2.9	4.5	4.0	3.4	4.3	4.1	5.9
3	7.2	5.3	5.6	5.6	3.3	3.0	4.6	3.8	3.6	4.4	4.0	5.5
4	6.9	5.6	6.1	5.4	3.7	3.0	5.0	4.3	3.7	4.5	4.4	5.7
5	7.0	5.8	6.6	5.7	5.3	3.5	5.5	4.6	4.0	4.6	4.0	5.9
6	7.0	6.1	7.2	6.3	5.7	4.1	5.9	5.1	5.0	4.6	4.4	5.7
7	7.7	6.1	7.3	5.7	5.2	3.9	5.9	5.1	4.5	4.5	5.2	6.0
8	8.1	6.2	7.3	5.5	5.7	3.9	6.0	5.3	5.1	4.5	4.9	6.2
9	7.9	6.1	7.4	5.4	6.4	3.9	6.0	5.1	5.0	4.5	5.1	5.8
10	7.8	5.9	7.3	4.7	6.4	3.8	5.9	5.3	5.2	4.5	5.0	5.5
11 am	8.0	5.9	7.2	6.3	6.3	4.5	5.8	5.6	5.4	4.6	5.2	5.6
12 noon	7.7	5.2	7.2	6.0	6.1	4.6	5.7	5.8	5.3	4.6	5.5	6.1
1 pm	7.8	5.5	7.0	6.1	5.8	5.5	5.5	6.3	5.3	4.7	5.6	6.0
2	7.3	5.7	6.7	6.4	5.6	5.4	6.2	6.8	5.5	4.6	5.5	6.0
3	7.3	6.0	6.5	6.3	5.6	5.4	6.4	7.3	5.8	4.7	5.5	5.9
4	7.5	6.0	6.4	5.8	5.9	6.0	6.6	7.4	5.8	4.6	5.5	6.0
5	7.6	5.9	6.3	5.9	5.4	5.9	6.9	7.6	6.3	4.5	5.5	6.1
6	6.8	5.9	6.3	5.6	5.0	5.5	7.1	7.6	6.3	4.5	5.4	5.8
7	5.9	5.6	5.8	5.1		6.4	6.6	7.1	6.1	4.4	4.6	5.3
8	5.8	5.3	5.2	5.0	4.2	5.7	5.9	6.6	5.8	4.5	4.9	5.7
9	6.1	5.0	4.7	4.4	3.6	4.2	5.3	6.1	4.3	4.5	5.2	5.6
10	6.5	5.1	5.0	4.6	2.8	3.5	5.0	4.6	4.6	4.3	5.4	5.5
11 pm	6.6	5.3	5.2	4.5	2.7	2.5	4.5	4.9	4.2	4.4	4.4	5.5
12 mid	6.2	5.4	5.5	4.6	3.1	2.5	4.2	4.4	3.9	4.5	5.3	5.6

0-2	2.1-5	5.1-8	8.1-10
clear	scattered	broken	overcast

Mean Hourly Sky Cover, tenths of sky covered

9 DAYLIGHT AVAILABILITY

	J	F	M	A	M	J	J	A	S	O	N	D
1 am	0	0	0	0	0	0	0	0	0	0	0	0
2	0	0	0	0	0	0	0	0	0	0	0	0
3	0	0	0	0	0	0	0	0	0	0	0	0
4	0	0	0	0	0	0	0	0	0	0	0	0
5	0	0	0	0	0	0	0	0	0	0	0	0
6	0	0	0	84	302	363	251	109	0	0	0	0
7	0	35	331	956	1565	1720	1394	949	708	401	140	0
8	419	792	1533	2536	3341	3625	3063	2639	2245	1815	1107	568
9	1497	2214	3159	4289	4992	5592	4567	4336	3906	3498	2514	1868
10	2549	3693	4535	6007	6151	7028	6282	6007	5195	5047	3913	3110
11 am	3416	5034	5678	7097	7496	7874	7425	7000	6431	6097	4970	3904
12 noon	4142	5681	6099	7659	8383	8551	7667	7338	6762	6587	5120	4388
1 pm	4266	5830	6354	7167	7671	7972	8024	7576	6953	6466	4974	4205
2	4093	5438	6197	6747	7304	7051	7632	6950	6224	5640	4305	3855
3	3093	4245	5338	5527	6466	6077	6224	5454	5220	4340	3281	2830
4	2070	3183	4014	4423	4784	4491	4868	4217	3613	2854	1906	1628
5	772	1556	2284	2611	3137	3050	3230	2647	1888	1126	516	452
6	73	343	662	1004	1400	1459	1524	1037	490	145	0	0
7	0	0	0	118	264	336	348	199	0	0	0	0
8	0	0	0	0	0	0	0	0	0	0	0	0
9	0	0	0	0	0	0	0	0	0	0	0	0
10	0	0	0	0	0	0	0	0	0	0	0	0
11 pm	0	0	0	0	0	0	0	0	0	0	0	0
12 mid	0	0	0	0	0	0	0	0	0	0	0	0

>250	251-1000	1001-2000	>2000

Mean Hourly Global Horizontal Illuminance, foot-candles

HOUR	J	F	M	A	M	J	J	A	S	O	N	D	Ann
CLR DAYS 0/8-2/8	7	8	8	8	9	8	5	7	10	14	10	8	101
PT CD DAYS 3/8-6/8	7	6	8	10	11	13	15	14	11	8	8	7	118
OVR DAYS 7/8-8/8	17	14	15	12	11	9	12	10	10	9	12	16	146
% CLR	23	29	26	27	29	27	16	23	32	45	33	26	28
% PT CD	23	21	26	33	35	43	47	45	35	26	27	23	32
% OVR	55	50	48	40	35	30	38	32	32	29	40	52	40

Sky Cover Monthly Normals
Eighths of sky covered; % of days for sky condition

		June					December				
		9 am	11 am	1 pm	3 pm	5 pm	9 am	11 am	1 pm	3 pm	5 pm
HORIZ	M. Clear	43	83	103	97	65	26	57	63	42	6
	M. Cloudy	31	62	74	69	45	14	33	37	24	4
NORTH	M. Clear	24	18	17	18	21	8	12	13	10	3
	M. Cloudy	17	19	19	19	18	6	13	14	10	2
EAST	M. Clear	67	71	31	18	16	56	43	13	10	3
	M. Cloudy	39	50	27	19	16	15	22	14	10	2
SOUTH	M. Clear	13	20	30	27	16	49	83	88	67	15
	M. Cloudy	12	20	26	24	16	14	33	38	25	5
WEST	M. Clear	13	18	17	54	75	8	12	26	57	23
	M. Cloudy	12	19	19	40	44	6	13	18	22	6
M. Clear	(% hrs)	45	40	40	37	35	33	32	33	36	35

Average Incident Illuminance (klux-h)

10 DAYLIGHT OBSTRUCTIONS

Overcast Dot Charts are in Technique 10. For Clear Sky Dot Charts, see Appendix B.

11 BIOCLIMATIC CHART

	Temperature (°F) means			Temperature (°F) extreme		Rel Humidity (percent)		Wind (kts) prevail		Wind (kts) max	Sky Cvr	Mean # days w/ temp (°F) max 90	max 70	min 32	min 10
	max	min	ave	max	min	6 am	3 pm	dir	spd	gst		90	70	32	10
Jan	62	43	53	83	14	85	63	N	10	55	OVR	0	1	19	5
Feb	65	46	56	85	19	84	59	N	10	58	OVR	0	1	14	3
Mar	71	52	62	89	25	85	57	S	10	54	OVR	0	6	9	#
Apr	78	58	69	92	32	88	57	S	10	54	OVR	#	15	2	#
May	85	66	75	96	41	58	0.64	9	60		SCT	8	27	#	0
Jun	89	71	81	100	50	90	61	S	8	58	SCT	16	30	0	0
Jul	91	73	82	101	60	92	66	SW	6	69	SCT	21	31	0	0
Aug	90	73	82	102	60	92	65	NE	7	57	SCT	20	31	0	0
Sep	87	70	79	101	42	89	63	NE	8	97	SCT	9	28	#	0
Oct	80	60	70	92	35	88	56	NE	8	52	CLR	1	17	2	0
Nov	71	50	61	87	24	59	0.39	9	48		CLR	7	5	10	1
Dec	65	45	55	84	11	86	62	N	9	60	OVR	0	2	16	4
Ann	78	59	69	102	11	60	0.51	9	97		OVR	114	192	71	13

Climatic Normals, 1945-1990

16 WINDOW SOLAR GAIN

For insolation data used in this technique, see radiation data for Technique 3.

	Jan	Feb	Mar	Apr	May	Jun	Jul	Aug	Sep	Oct	Nov	Dec	Ann
% Poss Sun	46	50	56	62	62	63	58	61	61	64	54	48	57

Average Percentage of Possible Sunshine, %

18 BUILDING BIOCLIMATIC CHART

See temperature and humidity data for Technique 11.

20 SHADING CALENDAR

	J	F	M	A	M	J	J	A	S	O	N	D
1 am	49.9	49.0	55.8	63.7	69.8	74.3	76.3	75.5	73.1	64.0	57.4	51.7
2	49.7	48.6	55.3	62.8	68.9	73.5	75.8	75.0	72.4	63.3	57.1	51.3
3	49.7	48.1	54.7	62.0	68.1	73.0	75.3	74.4	71.9	62.6	56.4	51.2
4	49.6	47.8	54.2	61.8	67.5	72.3	75.2	74.1	71.7	62.3	56.0	51.1
5	49.1	47.4	53.6	61.4	67.4	72.1	75.2	73.8	71.5	62.0	55.7	51.1
6	48.8	47.1	53.0	61.2	68.3	73.8	75.1	73.4	71.2	61.7	55.8	50.6
7	48.8	48.6	55.3	64.6	73.3	80.2	78.5	76.7	74.0	64.6	56.5	49.8
8	50.1	50.2	57.6	68.0	75.8	82.9	81.8	79.8	77.5	67.3	60.0	51.5
9	53.3	51.8	59.8	70.1	77.6	84.5	85.2	83.2	79.7	70.1	62.7	54.5
10	56.1	53.8	61.6	72.0	79.1	85.8	85.9	84.2	81.4	71.8	65.3	56.8
11	58.2	55.9	63.4	73.7	80.3	86.5	86.7	85.2	82.1	71.7	67.1	58.6
12 noon	59.7	57.9	65.2	75.0	81.5	87.1	87.5	86.2	83.2	75.0	68.2	60.0
1 pm	60.8	58.5	66.0	75.6	82.0	87.4	87.9	86.2	83.8	75.4	69.2	60.1
2	61.1	59.2	66.9	76.3	82.2	86.0	88.1	86.2	84.4	75.8	69.4	60.9
3	61.0	59.8	67.7	76.3	81.7	86.6	88.4	86.2	84.2	76.2	69.7	61.0
4	60.4	58.4	66.5	76.1	81.4	85.4	87.4	85.1	83.3	73.9	68.6	59.9
5	58.0	56.9	65.3	75.0	80.9	84.5	86.4	83.9	81.5	71.6	65.5	57.3
6	55.7	55.5	64.2	72.4	79.2	82.8	85.3	82.8	78.4	69.3	61.9	55.1
7	53.9	54.1	62.2	69.7	76.2	79.9	83.2	81.0	75.9	68.1	60.9	53.8
8	53.1	52.7	60.3	68.0	74.2	78.0	81.2	79.3	75.1	66.8	60.1	53.1
9	52.6	51.3	58.4	67.0	73.1	77.0	79.2	77.6	74.3	65.5	59.3	52.8
10	52.4	50.5	57.7	65.9	72.2	76.4	78.5	77.1	73.7	65.1	59.2	52.3
11 pm	51.5	49.8	57.2	64.9	71.1	75.7	77.7	76.5	73.2	64.8	58.4	52.4
12 mid	51.1	49.1	56.5	64.6	70.3	75.2	77.0	76.0	73.4	64.4	57.8	52.1

Cold <32 | Cool 32-64.9 | Comfort 65-79.9 | Hot ≥80

Mean Hourly Temperature, °F
Shading for Outdoor Rooms, Balance Point = 65°F (18.3°C)

	J	F	M	A	M	J	J	A	S	O	N	D
1 am	49.9	49.0	55.8	63.7	69.8	74.3	76.3	75.5	73.1	64.0	57.4	51.7
2	49.7	48.6	55.3	62.8	68.9	73.5	75.8	75.0	72.4	63.3	57.1	51.3
3	49.7	48.1	54.7	62.0	68.1	73.0	75.3	74.4	71.9	62.6	56.4	51.2
4	49.6	47.8	54.2	61.8	67.5	72.3	75.2	74.1	71.7	62.3	56.0	51.1
5	49.1	47.4	53.6	61.4	67.4	72.1	75.2	73.8	71.5	62.0	55.7	51.1
6	48.8	47.1	53.0	61.2	68.3	73.8	75.1	73.4	71.2	61.7	55.8	50.6
7	48.8	48.6	55.3	64.6	73.3	80.2	78.5	76.7	74.0	64.6	56.5	49.8
8	50.1	50.2	57.6	68.0	75.8	82.9	81.8	79.8	77.5	67.3	60.0	51.5
9	53.3	51.8	59.8	70.1	77.6	84.5	85.2	83.2	79.7	70.1	62.7	54.5
10	56.1	53.8	61.6	72.0	79.1	85.8	85.9	84.2	81.4	71.8	65.3	56.8
11	58.2	55.9	63.4	73.7	80.3	86.5	86.7	85.2	82.1	71.7	67.1	58.6
12 noon	59.7	57.9	65.2	75.0	81.5	87.1	87.5	86.2	83.2	75.0	68.2	60.0
1 pm	60.8	58.5	66.0	75.6	82.0	87.4	87.9	86.2	83.8	75.4	69.2	60.1
2	61.1	59.2	66.9	76.3	82.2	86.0	88.1	86.2	84.4	75.8	69.4	60.9
3	61.0	59.8	67.7	76.3	81.7	86.6	88.4	86.2	84.2	76.2	69.7	61.0
4	60.4	58.4	66.5	76.1	81.4	85.4	87.4	85.1	83.3	73.9	68.6	59.9
5	58.0	56.9	65.3	75.0	80.9	84.5	86.4	83.9	81.5	71.6	65.5	57.3
6	55.7	55.5	64.2	72.4	79.2	82.8	85.3	82.8	78.4	69.3	61.9	55.1
7	53.9	54.1	62.2	69.7	76.2	79.9	83.2	81.0	75.9	68.1	60.9	53.8
8	53.1	52.7	60.3	68.0	74.2	78.0	81.2	79.3	75.1	66.8	60.1	53.1
9	52.6	51.3	58.4	67.0	73.1	77.0	79.2	77.6	74.3	65.5	59.3	52.8
10	52.4	50.5	57.7	65.9	72.2	76.4	78.5	77.1	73.7	65.1	59.2	52.3
11 pm	51.5	49.8	57.2	64.9	71.1	75.7	77.7	76.5	73.2	64.8	58.4	52.4
12 mid	51.1	49.1	56.5	64.6	70.3	75.2	77.0	76.0	73.4	64.4	57.8	52.1

Cold <32 | Cool 32-55 | Comfort 55-69.9 | Hot ≥70

Mean Hourly Temperature, °F
Shading for Balance Point = 55°F (12.8°C)

	J	F	M	A	M	J	J	A	S	O	N	D
1 am	49.9	49.0	55.8	63.7	69.8	74.3	76.3	75.5	73.1	64.0	57.4	51.7
2	49.7	48.6	55.3	62.8	68.9	73.5	75.8	75.0	72.4	63.3	57.1	51.3
3	49.7	48.1	54.7	62.0	68.1	73.0	75.3	74.4	71.9	62.6	56.4	51.2
4	49.6	47.8	54.2	61.8	67.5	72.3	75.2	74.1	71.7	62.3	56.0	51.1
5	49.1	47.4	53.6	61.4	67.4	72.1	75.2	73.8	71.5	62.0	55.7	51.1
6	48.8	47.1	53.0	61.2	68.3	73.8	75.1	73.4	71.2	61.7	55.8	50.6
7	48.8	48.6	55.3	64.6	73.3	80.2	78.5	76.7	74.0	64.6	56.5	49.8
8	50.1	50.2	57.6	68.0	75.8	82.9	81.8	79.8	77.5	67.3	60.0	51.5
9	53.3	51.8	59.8	70.1	77.6	84.5	85.2	83.2	79.7	70.1	62.7	54.5
10	56.1	53.8	61.6	72.0	79.1	85.8	85.9	84.2	81.4	71.8	65.3	56.8
11	58.2	55.9	63.4	73.7	80.3	86.5	86.7	85.2	82.1	71.7	67.1	58.6
12 noon	59.7	57.9	65.2	75.0	81.5	87.1	87.5	86.2	83.2	75.0	68.2	60.0
1 pm	60.8	58.5	66.0	75.6	82.0	87.4	87.9	86.2	83.8	75.4	69.2	60.1
2	61.1	59.2	66.9	76.3	82.2	86.0	88.1	86.2	84.4	75.8	69.4	60.9
3	61.0	59.8	67.7	76.3	81.7	86.6	88.4	86.2	84.2	76.2	69.7	61.0
4	60.4	58.4	66.5	76.1	81.4	85.4	87.4	85.1	83.3	73.9	68.6	59.9
5	58.0	56.9	65.3	75.0	80.9	84.5	86.4	83.9	81.5	71.6	65.5	57.3
6	55.7	55.5	64.2	72.4	79.2	82.8	85.3	82.8	78.4	69.3	61.9	55.1
7	53.9	54.1	62.2	69.7	76.2	79.9	83.2	81.0	75.9	68.1	60.9	53.8
8	53.1	52.7	60.3	68.0	74.2	78.0	81.2	79.3	75.1	66.8	60.1	53.1
9	52.6	51.3	58.4	67.0	73.1	77.0	79.2	77.6	74.3	65.5	59.3	52.8
10	52.4	50.5	57.7	65.9	72.2	76.4	78.5	77.1	73.7	65.1	59.2	52.3
11 pm	51.5	49.8	57.2	64.9	71.1	75.7	77.7	76.5	73.2	64.8	58.4	52.4
12 mid	51.1	49.1	56.5	64.6	70.3	75.2	77.0	76.0	73.4	64.4	57.8	52.1

Cold <32 | Cool 32-44.9 | Comfort 45-59.9 | Hot ≥60

Mean Hourly Temperature, °F
Shading for Balance Point = 45°F (7.2°C)

21 TOTAL HEAT GAINS AND TOTAL HEAT LOSSES

- Latitude = 30 °N
- Summer Design Temp/Coincident Wet-Bulb Temp, °F (°C)

    1.0%   92/78 (33/26)

    2.0%   90/78 (32/26)

- Winter Design Temperature, °F (°C)

    99.6%   30 (-1)

    99%   34 (1)

- Annual Heating Degree Days 65 °F (18 °C)   4758 (2643)
- Annual Cooling Degree Days 65 °F (18 °C)   1534 (852)

23 BALANCE POINT PROFILES

For temperature data used in Step 2, see data for Technique 11.

32° LATITUDE

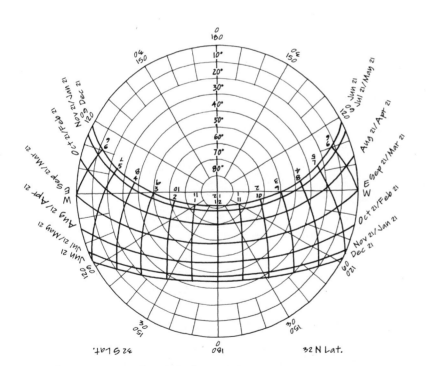

Sundial, 32° Latitude

36° LATITUDE

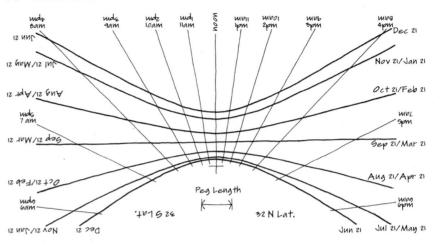

Sundial, 36° Latitude

Sun Path Diagram, 32° Latitude

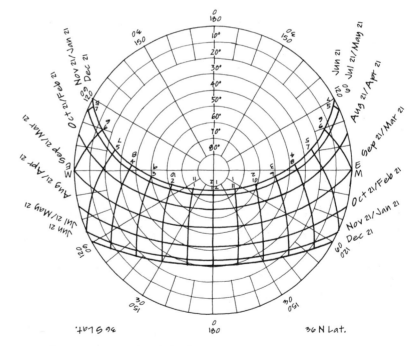

Sun Path Diagram, 36° Latitude

33° Lat 33° 26' N; Long 112° 1' W
Elev 773 ft (339 m)
Jan Vertical Rad = 1550 Btu/ft², d
HDD/CDD65 °F = 1350/4162
HDD/CDD18 °C = 750/2312

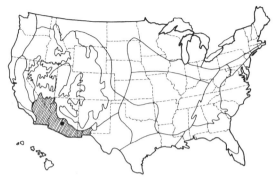

2 SUN PATH DIAGRAM

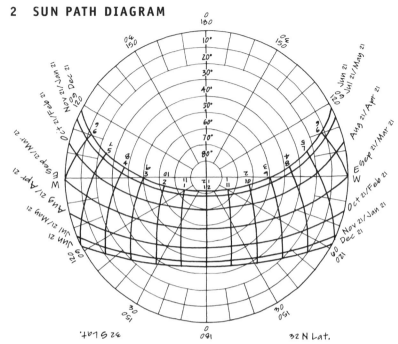

Sun Path Diagram, 32° Latitude

1 SUNDIAL

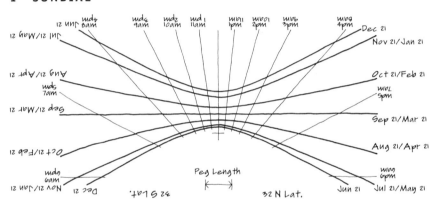

32° Latitude Sundial

3 SOLAR RADIATION

ELEMENT		Jan	Feb	Mar	Apr	May	Jun	Jul	Aug	Sep	Oct	Nov	Dec	Year
HDD	18.3C	201	126	101	42	4	0	0	0	0	9	74	192	**750**
CDD		4	12	53	123	242	387	491	457	343	173	23	4	**2312**
HDD	65F	362	227	182	75	8	0	0	0	0	17	134	345	**1350**
CDD		8	22	95	222	436	696	884	822	618	311	41	7	**4162**
AVERAGE INCIDENT SOLAR RADIATION (Btu/sq. ft./day)														
HORIZ.	Global	1020	1350	1750	2240	2540	2650	2410	2240	1930	1550	1140	930	1810
SOUTH 90° (VS)	Global	1550	1590	1420	1160	860	720	760	990	1320	1610	1620	1540	1260
SOLAR RADIATION FOR FLAT-PLATE COLLECTORS FACING SOUTH AT A FIXED-TILT (kWh/sq. m./day)														
0°	Ave.	3.2	4.3	5.5	7.1	8	8.4	7.6	7.1	6.1	4.9	3.6	3	5.7
Lat − 15°	Ave.	4.4	5.4	6.4	7.5	8	8.1	7.5	7.3	6.8	6.1	4.9	4.2	6.4
Lat	Ave.	5.1	6	6.7	7.4	7.5	7.3	6.9	7.1	7	6.5	5.6	4.9	6.5
Lat + 15°	Ave.	5.5	6.2	6.6	6.9	6.6	6.3	6	6.4	6.7	6.7	5.9	5.3	6.3
90°	Ave.	4.9	5	4.5	3.7	2.7	2.3	2.4	3.1	4.2	5.1	5.1	4.8	4

APPENDIX A/ HOT-ARID: Phoenix, AZ   33°

	J	F	M	A	M	J	J	A	S	O	N	D
1 am	0	0	0	0	0	0	0	0	0	0	0	0
2	0	0	0	0	0	0	0	0	0	0	0	0
3	0	0	0	0	0	0	0	0	0	0	0	0
4	0	0	0	0	0	0	0	0	0	0	0	0
5	0	0	0	0	0	0	0	0	0	0	0	0
6	0	0	0	1	6	8	4	1	0	0	0	0
7	0	0	4	20	41	45	30	20	12	5	0	0
8	4	12	32	78	106	112	86	73	60	39	17	6
9	34	57	91	152	177	180	152	143	131	100	63	39
10	82	116	145	213	235	238	218	199	191	156	112	84
11 am	127	162	199	263	284	275	263	247	237	199	156	125
12 noon	161	193	230	292	310	303	287	283	267	228	181	150
1 pm	175	214	245	304	321	317	306	300	274	235	190	156
2	167	202	245	291	306	311	302	289	261	218	173	143
3	139	173	216	255	273	279	281	253	230	185	136	119
4	94	132	166	200	226	232	234	212	170	132	91	76
5	42	78	112	132	162	172	172	150	107	68	36	26
6	7	24	49	69	94	105	101	82	45	16	6	3
7	0	2	9	16	31	42	38	23	8	0	0	0
8	0	0	0	1	4	7	6	1	0	0	0	0
9	0	0	0	0	0	0	0	0	0	0	0	0
10	0	0	0	0	0	0	0	0	0	0	0	0
11 pm	0	0	0	0	0	0	0	0	0	0	0	0
12 mid	0	0	0	0	0	0	0	0	0	0	0	0

0 | 1-100 | 101-250 | >250

Mean Global Horizontal Radiation, Btu/h, ft²

4 WIND ROSE

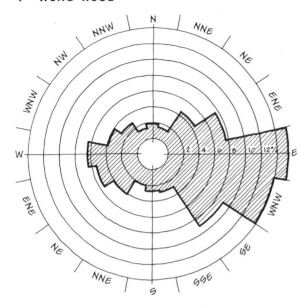

December Wind Rose, Phoenix

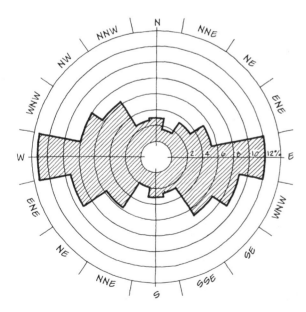

June Wind Rose, Phoenix

5 WIND SQUARE

Mean Airport Wind Conditions, direction/mph

	J	F	M	A	M	J	J	A	S	O	N	D
1 am	WSW 4.5	N 6.3	N 5.7	E 6.2	N 6.0	E 5.9	E 7.1	ESE 7.3	E 7.4	N 5.3	N 5.5	E 5.0
2	E 5.2	SE 6.8	W 5.7	N 6.2	NNE 6.0	N 4.8	E 6.9	N 7.2	E 6.9	E 5.3	E 5.5	E 5.0
3	ESE 4.7	W 6.8	ESE 5.9	E 6.1	N 5.9	N 5.7	ESE 6.6	E 7.0	E 6.6	W 5.7	ESE 5.7	E 3.9
4	E 5.3	W 6.6	E 6.6	E 6.0	E 5.9	NNW 5.4	N 6.3	ESE 6.9	ESE 6.0	ESE 6.1	ESE 5.9	E 3.6
5	WSW 6.2	SE 7.1	E 6.7	WNW 5.9	E 5.9	E 6.1	N 5.7	WSW 6.8	ESE 6.4	ESE 6.5	E 6.0	E 3.6
6	ESE 5.8	E 7.1	N 7.1	ESE 6.5	ESE 6.3	SE 5.7	ESE 5.6	W 6.7	E 6.6	E 6.6	W 6.1	ESE 3.5
7	ESE 5.9	E 6.3	E 7.4	E 7.2	ESE 6.7	SE 7.0	WSW 5.8	E 6.6	WSW 6.0	E 6.8	E 6.2	ESE 3.7
8	WSW 5.2	WSW 6.8	WSW 7.1	E 7.8	E 7.1	E 7.2	E 6.3	E 6.6	W 6.7	E 6.9	E 6.3	ESE 4.5
9	W 6.0	W 7.5	E 7.4	ESE 7.4	E 6.9	E 8.0	E 6.6	E 6.5	SE 8.6	SE 6.9	W 6.5	WSW 5.1
10	E 6.7	ESE 7.4	W 7.1	W 7.0	W 6.6	E 8.0	ESE 7.0	E 6.4	E 8.0	E 6.8	E 6.7	E 5.6
11 am	E 6.2	W 7.5	W 7.7	N 6.6	ESE 6.3	E 8.9	E 7.5	E 6.3	W 7.6	SE 7.0	SW 7.0	E 6.7
12 noon	W 6.1	W 7.8	N 6.3	E 7.1	E 7.0	W 8.7	E 8.0	E 7.1	W 7.3	W 6.8	W 6.6	W 7.2
1 pm	N 5.8	ESE 6.9	NW 6.5	ESE 7.7	N 7.6	W 9.1	ESE 7.9	W 8.0	WNW 7.2	ESE 6.8	W 6.3	W 6.8
2	W 6.0	E 6.7	WSW 7.8	NW 8.3	WNW 8.3	W 10.2	W 9.7	N 8.8	ESE 7.9	W 6.9	WSW 6.0	E 6.1
3	NE 6.0	N 7.2	W 8.1	W 8.6	SE 9.4	E 10.5	S 8.9	W 7.7	WNW 7.1	S 5.7	E 5.7	E 6.7
4	E 5.8	SSE 7.6	W 8.6	W 9.0	W 9.6	NNW 10.0	S 10.5	ESE 8.9	N 7.3	ESE 7.3	W 5.3	ESE 6.3
5	ESE 5.7	ESE 7.7	E 9.4	ESE 10.3	N 10.8	SE 10.8	ENE 9.0	ENE 7.2	E 7.4	ESE 6.5	E 4.6	ESE 2.7
6	ESE 4.2	S 7.5	W 9.6	SW 8.3	NW 9.3	SE 11.1	ESE 11.1	W 8.8	E 7.5	ESE 6.5	ESE 4.6	E 4.8
7	SE 4.7	E 6.8	ESE 7.1	ESE 7.2	SE 8.2	E 9.6	E 11.6	ESE 8.5	E 6.6	E 5.5	W 4.2	WNW 3.6
8	NE 4.4	ESE 5.4	W 5.7	E 6.1	ESE 7.1	E 8.2	E 9.4	E 8.3	E 5.9	E 4.6	ESE 3.9	E 3.7
9	ESE 3.5	ESE 4.6	E 5.2	E 6.2	E 6.8	E 6.3	E 8.3	ESE 8.0	SE 5.1	E 4.8	E 4.4	E 3.7
10	E 3.9	ESE 4.8	E 5.4	E 6.2	E 6.4	E 6.3	SE 8.0	E 7.8	E 6.4	W 5.0	E 5.0	E 4.6
11 pm	N 4.5	N 6.3	N 5.4	N 6.2	E 6.1	N 6.0	N 7.2	E 7.6	E 6.5	ESE 5.2	E 5.5	ESE 5.0
12 mid	E 5.4	E 6.6	W 6.0	W 6.3	W 6.0	ENE 6.0	N 7.4	N 7.5	N 7.6	N 5.2	WSW 5.5	W 5.5

Legend: 0-5 | 5.1-9 | 9.1-12 | >12

Mean City Center Wind Conditions, direction/mph

	J	F	M	A	M	J	J	A	S	O	N	D
1 am	WSW 2.1	N 3.0	N 2.7	E 2.9	N 2.8	E 2.8	E 3.3	ESE 3.4	E 3.5	N 2.5	N 2.6	E 2.3
2	E 2.4	SE 3.2	W 2.7	N 2.9	NNE 2.8	N 2.2	E 3.2	N 3.4	E 3.2	E 2.5	E 2.6	E 2.3
3	ESE 2.2	W 3.2	ESE 2.8	E 2.9	N 2.8	N 2.7	ESE 3.1	E 3.3	E 3.1	W 2.7	ESE 2.7	E 1.8
4	E 2.5	W 3.1	E 3.1	E 2.8	E 2.8	NNW 2.6	N 3.0	ESE 3.2	ESE 2.8	ESE 2.9	ESE 2.8	E 1.7
5	WSW 2.9	SE 3.3	E 3.1	WNW 2.8	E 2.8	E 2.9	N 2.7	WSW 3.2	ESE 3.0	ESE 3.0	E 2.8	E 1.7
6	ESE 2.7	E 3.3	N 3.3	ESE 3.1	ESE 3.0	SE 2.7	ESE 2.6	W 3.1	E 2.6	E 3.1	W 2.9	ESE 1.6
7	ESE 2.8	E 3.0	E 3.5	E 3.4	ESE 3.1	SE 3.3	WSW 2.7	E 3.1	WSW 2.8	E 3.2	E 2.9	ESE 1.7
8	WSW 2.5	WSW 3.2	WSW 3.3	E 3.7	E 3.4	E 3.4	E 2.9	E 3.1	W 3.2	E 3.2	E 2.9	ESE 2.1
9	W 2.9	W 3.5	ESE 3.5	ESE 3.2	E 3.8	E 3.1	E 3.0	E 4.0	SE 3.2	SE 3.0	W 3.0	WSW 2.4
10	E 3.1	ESE 3.5	W 3.3	W 3.3	W 3.1	E 3.8	ESE 3.3	E 3.0	E 3.8	E 3.2	E 3.2	E 2.6
11 am	E 2.9	W 3.5	W 3.6	N 3.1	ESE 3.0	E 4.2	E 3.5	E 2.9	W 3.6	SE 3.3	SW 3.3	E 3.2
12 noon	W 2.9	W 3.7	N 3.0	E 3.4	E 3.3	W 4.1	E 3.7	E 3.3	W 3.5	W 3.2	W 3.1	W 3.4
1 pm	N 2.7	ESE 3.2	NW 3.0	ESE 3.6	N 3.6	W 4.3	ESE 3.7	W 3.7	WNW 3.4	ESE 3.2	W 3.0	W 3.2
2	W 2.8	E 3.2	WSW 3.7	NW 3.9	WNW 3.9	W 4.8	W 4.6	N 4.1	ESE 3.7	W 3.2	WSW 2.8	E 2.9
3	NE 2.8	N 3.4	W 3.8	W 4.1	SE 4.2	E 4.4	S 4.9	W 4.2	WNW 3.6	S 3.3	E 2.7	E 3.2
4	E 2.7	SSE 3.6	W 4.1	W 4.2	W 4.5	NNW 4.7	S 5.0	ESE 4.2	N 3.4	ESE 3.4	W 2.5	ESE 3.0
5	ESE 2.7	ESE 4.4	E 4.4	ESE 4.8	N 5.1	SE 5.1	ENE 4.2	ENE 3.4	E 3.5	ESE 2.4	E 2.7	ESE 1.4
6	ESE 2.0	S 3.5	W 4.5	SW 3.9	NW 4.3	SE 5.2	ESE 5.2	W 4.1	E 3.5	ESE 3.1	ESE 2.2	E 2.2
7	SE 2.2	E 3.2	ESE 3.3	ESE 3.4	SE 3.4	E 4.5	E 5.5	ESE 4.0	E 3.1	E 2.6	W 2.0	WNW 1.7
8	NE 2.1	ESE 2.6	W 2.7	E 2.9	ESE 3.4	E 3.8	E 4.4	E 3.9	E 2.8	E 2.2	ESE 1.8	E 1.7
9	ESE 1.6	ESE 2.2	E 2.5	E 2.9	E 3.2	E 2.9	E 3.9	ESE 3.8	SE 2.4	E 2.2	E 2.1	E 1.8
10	ESE 1.8	ESE 2.2	E 2.6	E 2.9	E 3.0	E 2.9	SE 3.7	E 3.7	E 3.0	W 2.3	E 2.3	E 2.1
11 pm	N 2.1	N 2.9	N 2.6	N 2.9	E 2.8	N 2.8	N 3.4	E 3.6	E 3.0	ESE 2.4	E 2.6	ESE 2.4
12 mid	E 2.5	E 3.1	W 2.8	W 2.9	W 2.8	ENE 2.8	N 3.5	N 3.5	N 3.6	N 2.5	WSW 2.6	W 2.6

Legend: 0-5 | 5.1-9 | 9.1-12 | >12

6 AIR MOVEMENT PRINCIPLES

Technique 6 uses data from Techniques 4 and 5.

7 SITE MICROCLIMATES

Technique 7 uses data from Techniques 1, 2, 4 and 5.

8 SKY COVER

	J	F	M	A	M	J	J	A	S	O	N	D
1 am	3.8	2.8	3.7	2.0	1.9	1.8	3.5	3.5	2.0	1.5	3.1	3.1
2	3.6	2.7	3.8	1.8	2.1	1.6	3.6	3.3	2.1	1.2	3.2	3.1
3	3.7	2.6	3.5	1.7	2.2	1.5	3.1	3.2	2.0	1.4	3.3	3.1
4	3.7	2.4	3.4	1.5	2.2	1.4	2.7	3.0	1.9	1.5	3.5	3.3
5	4.4	3.0	3.1	1.4	2.3	1.7	3.6	2.8	1.6	1.7	3.6	3.1
6	4.8	2.6	3.6	1.7	2.5	1.9	4.2	2.8	2.2	2.0	3.9	3.1
7	4.7	3.5	4.7	2.1	2.6	1.5	4.1	2.9	2.3	2.4	4.0	3.5
8	4.9	4.8	4.7	2.5	2.8	1.1	3.5	3.1	2.1	2.7	4.3	4.0
9	4.6	4.4	4.7	2.9	2.7	1.2	3.4	2.9	2.0	2.7	4.2	4.0
10	4.4	3.9	4.7	3.2	2.7	1.1	2.4	2.6	2.0	2.7	4.0	3.9
11 am	4.2	4.4	4.4	3.6	2.7	1.3	2.5	2.6	2.1	2.7	3.9	3.7
12 noon	4.0	4.8	4.8	3.9	2.5	1.3	2.5	2.4	2.0	2.4	3.8	4.1
1 pm	4.1	4.1	4.9	4.1	2.4	1.3	2.3	2.1	2.0	2.3	3.9	4.4
2	4.6	4.1	5.1	4.4	2.2	1.4	1.6	1.8	2.2	2.0	3.8	4.1
3	4.9	3.8	4.7	4.4	2.2	1.7	1.3	2.1	2.6	2.0	3.9	4.0
4	5.7	4.0	5.0	4.4	2.2	1.8	1.5	2.5	2.7	2.0	4.0	4.2
5	6.2	4.3	5.4	4.4	2.3	2.1	2.6	2.7	2.6	2.0	4.1	4.1
6	5.8	4.9	5.2	4.2	2.3	2.2	3.5	3.1	2.6	2.2	3.9	3.9
7	5.5	4.5	4.3	4.0	2.3	2.4	4.0	3.5	2.7	2.4	3.7	3.5
8	4.8	3.9	3.7	3.8	2.4	2.4	4.4	3.8	2.5	2.6	3.5	3.0
9	4.2	3.7	3.1	3.3	2.1	2.1	3.7	3.7	2.0	2.5	3.4	2.9
10	3.8	3.4	3.1	2.9	1.9	1.8	3.1	3.8	2.1	2.4	3.3	2.4
11 pm	3.6	3.2	3.4	2.3	1.5	1.5	3.2	3.7	1.9	2.3	3.2	2.9
12 mid	3.8	2.9	3.3	2.2	1.7	1.5	3.7	3.6	1.8	2.1	3.3	3.0

0-2	2.1-5	5.1-8	8.1-10
clear	scattered	broken	overcast

Mean Hourly Sky Cover, tenths of sky covered

9 DAYLIGHT AVAILABILITY

	J	F	M	A	M	J	J	A	S	O	N	D
1 am	0	0	0	0	0	0	0	0	0	0	0	0
2	0	0	0	0	0	0	0	0	0	0	0	0
3	0	0	0	0	0	0	0	0	0	0	0	0
4	0	0	0	0	0	0	0	0	0	0	0	0
5	0	0	0	0	0	0	0	0	0	0	0	0
6	0	0	0	0	129	223	88	0	0	0	0	0
7	0	0	82	578	1255	1398	969	621	356	89	0	0
8	45	352	1019	2462	3305	3530	2760	2338	1897	1191	507	138
9	1051	1760	2884	4740	5536	5649	4904	4558	4119	3121	1969	1218
10	2562	3628	4580	6635	7333	7471	6993	6357	6029	4904	3500	2615
11 am	3981	5068	6276	8161	8855	8612	8428	7871	7465	6242	4892	3905
12 noon	5022	6027	7214	9035	9657	9485	9253	9023	8409	7127	5661	4699
1 pm	5469	6699	7699	9395	9947	9905	9769	9526	8603	7343	5925	4874
2	5205	6335	7671	9013	9523	9716	9606	9157	8205	6816	5386	4492
3	4332	5414	6756	7946	8536	8720	8860	8021	7200	5770	4242	3725
4	2949	4147	5210	6247	7073	7274	7380	6743	5330	4109	2798	2364
5	1300	2416	3501	4217	5050	5381	5421	4731	3363	2093	1087	821
6	191	731	1521	2159	2939	3303	3160	2572	1400	456	92	16
7	0	0	244	481	968	1313	1197	713	196	0	0	0
8	0	0	0	36	203	180	9	0	0	0	0	0
9	0	0	0	0	0	0	0	0	0	0	0	0
10	0	0	0	0	0	0	0	0	0	0	0	0
11 pm	0	0	0	0	0	0	0	0	0	0	0	0
12 mid	0	0	0	0	0	0	0	0	0	0	0	0

>250	251-1000	1001-2000	>2000

Mean Hourly Global Horizontal Illuminance, foot-candles

HOUR	J	F	M	A	M	J	J	A	S	O	N	D	Ann
CLR DAYS 0/8-2/8	14	13	14	17	21	23	17	18	22	20	18	15	211
PT CD DAYS 3/8-6/8	7	7	8	7	7	5	10	10	5	6	6	6	85
OVR DAYS 7/8-8/8	10	9	8	6	3	2	4	4	3	4	6	9	70
% CLR	45	45	47	57	68	77	55	56	73	67	60	50	58
% PT CD	23	24	27	23	23	17	32	31	17	20	20	20	23
% OVR	32	31	27	20	10	7	13	13	10	13	20	30	19

Sky Cover Monthly Normals
Eighths of sky covered; % of days for sky condition

		June					December				
		9 am	11 am	1 pm	3 pm	5 pm	9 am	11 am	1 pm	3 pm	5 pm
HORIZ	M. Clear	62	97	110	97	60	15	48	61	46	10
	M. Cloudy	50	81	95	84	50	10	34	45	33	8
NORTH	M. Clear	19	16	16	16	20	5	11	12	10	4
	M. Cloudy	19	19	18	19	19	4	11	14	11	4
EAST	M. Clear	86	65	16	16	13	44	50	12	10	4
	M. Cloudy	62	55	19	19	14	18	30	14	11	4
SOUTH	M. Clear	13	28	37	28	13	34	80	95	78	25
	M. Cloudy	14	28	36	29	14	15	44	57	44	11
WEST	M. Clear	13	16	17	67	85	5	11	15	54	34
	M. Cloudy	14	19	19	58	62	4	11	15	32	14
M. Clear (% hrs)		82	83	84	83	83	55	57	54	54	53

Average Incident Illuminance (klux-h)

10 DAYLIGHT OBSTRUCTIONS

Overcast Dot Charts are in Technique 10. For Clear Sky Dot Charts, see Appendix B.

11 BIOCLIMATIC CHART

	Temperature (°F)					Rel Humidity (percent)		Wind (kts)			Sky Cvr	Mean # days w/ temp (°F)			
	means			extreme				prevail		max		max	max	min	min
	max	min	ave	max	min	6 am	3 pm	dir	spd	gst		90	70	32	10
Jan	66	41	54	88	17	68	34	E	5	52	CLR	0	9	4	0
Feb	70	44	58	92	22	63	28	E	6	47	CLR	#	15	2	0
Mar	75	49	62	100	25	57	25	E	6	45	CLR	1	23	#	0
Apr	84	55	70	105	37	45	17	E	6	43	CLR	9	28	0	0
May	93	64	79	113	40	37	14	E	6	51	CLR	22	31	0	0
Jun	103	72	88	122	51	33	12	W	8	63	CLR	29	30	0	0
Jul	105	80	93	121	66	46	21	W	7	75	CLR	31	31	0	0
Aug	103	79	91	116	61	53	24	E	6	68	CLR	31	31	0	0
Sep	99	72	86	118	47	50	23	E	6	53	CLR	28	30	0	0
Oct	88	61	75	107	34	52	23	E	6	53	CLR	15	30	0	0
Nov	75	48	62	93	27	59	28	E	5	52	CLR	#	22	#	0
Dec	66	42	54	88	22	66	35	E	5	59	CLR	0	11	3	0
Ann	86	59	73	122	17	52	24	E	6	75	CLR	167	293	9	0

Climatic Normals, 1945-1990

16 WINDOW SOLAR GAIN

For insolation data used in this technique, see radiation data for Technique 3.

	Jan	Feb	Mar	Apr	May	Jun	Jul	Aug	Sep	Oct	Nov	Dec	Ann
% Poss Sun	78	80	84	89	93	94	85	85	89	88	83	77	85

Average Percentage of Possible Sunshine, %

18 BUILDING BIOCLIMATIC CHART

See temperature and humidity data for Technique 11.

20 SHADING CALENDAR

	J	F	M	A	M	J	J	A	S	O	N	D
1 am	49.1	47.6	59.4	62.3	70.4	82.4	86.1	85.3	78.0	64.9	56.0	48.4
2	48.3	46.3	58.4	59.8	68.0	79.9	84.3	83.9	76.9	63.1	54.7	47.2
3	47.1	45.4	57.1	58.2	66.1	77.9	83.1	82.4	75.1	61.8	54.0	46.1
4	46.4	44.2	55.9	56.5	64.1	76.2	81.6	80.9	74.6	60.4	53.3	44.9
5	46.0	43.5	54.5	54.8	62.1	74.1	80.3	79.4	73.6	59.1	52.6	44.3
6	45.7	42.8	53.6	57.7	65.6	74.4	79.9	80.8	72.8	60.3	52.8	44.0
7	45.6	41.7	52.8	60.6	69.1	79.5	82.2	82.3	73.5	61.7	53.1	44.1
8	45.7	42.8	55.9	63.6	72.7	84.4	86.1	83.6	79.2	63.0	53.4	44.7
9	48.1	48.6	61.0	68.3	76.6	89.2	89.6	86.7	84.4	68.4	58.7	48.1
10	51.8	53.6	65.1	72.9	80.5	93.1	92.5	89.7	88.1	73.8	63.9	52.0
11	55.5	57.7	68.3	77.5	84.4	95.3	95.5	92.7	90.9	73.8	69.1	55.4
12 noon	58.6	61.1	71.2	80.2	86.5	98.0	97.6	94.9	93.5	81.7	71.5	57.8
1 pm	61.5	63.4	73.5	82.9	88.7	99.5	99.3	97.0	95.1	84.3	74.0	60.1
2	63.3	65.0	75.2	85.7	90.8	100.7	101.3	99.2	96.7	86.8	76.4	61.6
3	64.5	66.4	76.6	85.7	91.2	102.1	102.6	99.6	97.3	87.0	76.2	62.9
4	64.7	67.0	76.8	85.6	91.5	102.8	103.6	100.0	97.5	87.1	76.1	63.0
5	63.6	66.5	76.5	85.6	91.8	101.7	103.3	100.5	96.7	87.2	75.9	61.5
6	61.0	65.2	75.4	82.3	89.3	101.5	102.2	98.8	95.4	83.5	72.3	58.5
7	58.0	62.4	73.0	78.9	86.8	99.5	99.7	97.0	92.0	79.7	68.6	56.4
8	55.6	59.9	70.9	75.5	84.2	95.2	96.2	95.2	88.5	75.9	64.9	54.3
9	54.1	56.7	67.6	72.8	81.2	92.8	93.4	92.7	85.4	73.3	62.6	52.8
10	53.1	54.3	64.8	70.1	78.3	89.5	91.1	90.3	83.0	70.7	60.3	51.6
11 pm	52.0	51.9	62.9	67.3	75.4	87.5	89.2	87.8	80.7	68.1	58.0	50.7
12 mid	50.5	50.5	60.8	64.9	73.0	84.7	87.8	86.5	79.1	66.3	56.8	49.6

Cold	Cool	Comfort	Hot
<32	32-64.9	65-79.9	≥ 80

Mean Hourly Temperature, °F
Shading for Outdoor Rooms, Balance Point = 65°F (18.3°C)

	J	F	M	A	M	J	J	A	S	O	N	D
1 am	49.1	47.6	59.4	62.3	70.4	82.4	86.1	85.3	78.0	64.9	56.0	48.4
2	48.3	46.3	58.4	59.8	68.0	79.9	84.3	83.9	76.9	63.1	54.7	47.2
3	47.1	45.4	57.1	58.2	66.1	77.9	83.1	82.4	75.1	61.8	54.0	46.1
4	46.4	44.2	55.9	56.5	64.1	76.2	81.6	80.9	74.6	60.4	53.3	44.9
5	46.0	43.5	54.5	54.8	62.1	74.1	80.3	79.4	73.6	59.1	52.6	44.3
6	45.7	42.8	53.6	57.7	65.6	74.4	79.9	80.8	72.8	60.3	52.8	44.0
7	45.6	41.7	52.8	60.6	69.1	79.5	82.2	82.3	73.5	61.7	53.1	44.1
8	45.7	42.8	55.9	63.6	72.7	84.4	86.1	83.6	79.2	63.0	53.4	44.7
9	48.1	48.6	61.0	68.3	76.6	89.2	89.6	86.7	84.4	68.4	58.7	48.1
10	51.8	53.6	65.1	72.9	80.5	93.1	92.5	89.7	88.1	73.8	63.9	52.0
11	55.5	57.7	68.3	77.5	84.4	95.3	95.5	92.7	90.9	73.8	69.1	55.4
12 noon	58.6	61.1	71.2	80.2	86.5	98.0	97.6	94.9	93.5	81.7	71.5	57.8
1 pm	61.5	63.4	73.5	82.9	88.7	99.5	99.3	97.0	95.1	84.3	74.0	60.1
2	63.3	65.0	75.2	85.7	90.8	100.7	101.3	99.2	96.7	86.8	76.4	61.6
3	64.5	66.4	76.6	85.7	91.2	102.1	102.6	99.6	97.3	87.0	76.2	62.9
4	64.7	67.0	76.8	85.6	91.5	102.8	103.6	100.0	97.5	87.1	76.1	63.0
5	63.6	66.5	76.5	85.6	91.8	101.7	103.3	100.5	96.7	87.2	75.9	61.5
6	61.0	65.2	75.4	82.3	89.3	101.5	102.2	98.8	95.4	83.5	72.3	58.5
7	58.0	62.4	73.0	78.9	86.8	99.5	99.7	97.0	92.0	79.7	68.6	56.4
8	55.6	59.9	70.9	75.5	84.2	95.2	96.2	95.2	88.5	75.9	64.9	54.3
9	54.1	56.7	67.6	72.8	81.2	92.8	93.4	92.7	85.4	73.3	62.6	52.8
10	53.1	54.3	64.8	70.1	78.3	89.5	91.1	90.3	83.0	70.7	60.3	51.6
11 pm	52.0	51.9	62.9	67.3	75.4	87.5	89.2	87.8	80.7	68.1	58.0	50.7
12 mid	50.5	50.5	60.8	64.9	73.0	84.7	87.8	86.5	79.1	66.3	56.8	49.6

Cold	Cool	Comfort	Hot
<32	32-55	55-69.9	≥ 70

Mean Hourly Temperature, °F
Shading for Balance Point = 55°F (12.8°C)

	J	F	M	A	M	J	J	A	S	O	N	D
1 am	49.1	47.6	59.4	62.3	70.4	82.4	86.1	85.3	78.0	64.9	56.0	48.4
2	48.3	46.3	58.4	59.8	68.0	79.9	84.3	83.9	76.9	63.1	54.7	47.2
3	47.1	45.4	57.1	58.2	66.1	77.9	83.1	82.4	75.1	61.8	54.0	46.1
4	46.4	44.2	55.9	56.5	64.1	76.2	81.6	80.9	74.6	60.4	53.3	44.9
5	46.0	43.5	54.5	54.8	62.1	74.1	80.3	79.4	73.6	59.1	52.6	44.3
6	45.7	42.8	53.6	57.7	65.6	74.4	79.9	80.8	72.8	60.3	52.8	44.0
7	45.6	41.7	52.8	60.6	69.1	79.5	82.2	82.3	73.5	61.7	53.1	44.1
8	45.7	42.8	55.9	63.6	72.7	84.4	86.1	83.6	79.2	63.0	53.4	44.7
9	48.1	48.6	61.0	68.3	76.6	89.2	89.6	86.7	84.4	68.4	58.7	48.1
10	51.8	53.6	65.1	72.9	80.5	93.1	92.5	89.7	88.1	73.8	63.9	52.0
11	55.5	57.7	68.3	77.5	84.4	95.3	95.5	92.7	90.9	73.8	69.1	55.4
12 noon	58.6	61.1	71.2	80.2	86.5	98.0	97.6	94.9	93.5	81.7	71.5	57.8
1 pm	61.5	63.4	73.5	82.9	88.7	99.5	99.3	97.0	95.1	84.3	74.0	60.1
2	63.3	65.0	75.2	85.7	90.8	100.7	101.3	99.2	96.7	86.8	76.4	61.6
3	64.5	66.4	76.6	85.7	91.2	102.1	102.6	99.6	97.3	87.0	76.2	62.9
4	64.7	67.0	76.8	85.6	91.5	102.8	103.6	100.0	97.5	87.1	76.1	63.0
5	63.6	66.5	76.5	85.6	91.8	101.7	103.3	100.5	96.7	87.2	75.9	61.5
6	61.0	65.2	75.4	82.3	89.3	101.5	102.2	98.8	95.4	83.5	72.3	58.5
7	58.0	62.4	73.0	78.9	86.8	99.5	99.7	97.0	92.0	79.7	68.6	56.4
8	55.6	59.9	70.9	75.5	84.2	95.2	96.2	95.2	88.5	75.9	64.9	54.3
9	54.1	56.7	67.6	72.8	81.2	92.8	93.4	92.7	85.4	73.3	62.6	52.8
10	53.1	54.3	64.8	70.1	78.3	89.5	91.1	90.3	83.0	70.7	60.3	51.6
11 pm	52.0	51.9	62.9	67.3	75.4	87.5	89.2	87.8	80.7	68.1	58.0	50.7
12 mid	50.5	50.5	60.8	64.9	73.0	84.7	87.8	86.5	79.1	66.3	56.8	49.6

Cold	Cool	Comfort	Hot
<32	32-44.9	45-59.9	≥ 60

Mean Hourly Temperature, °F
Shading for Balance Point = 45°F (7.2°C)

21 TOTAL HEAT GAINS AND TOTAL HEAT LOSSES

- Latitude = 33 °N
- Summer Design Temp/Coincident Wet Bulb Temp, °F (°C)

  1.0%   107/ 71 (42/22)
  2.0%   105/ 71 (41/22)

- Winter Design Temperature, °F (°C)

  99.6%   35 (2)
  99%   38 (3)

- Annual Heating Degree Days 65 °F (18 °C)   4758 (2643)
- Annual Cooling Degree Days 65 °F (18 °C)   1534 (852)

23 BALANCE POINT PROFILES

For temperature data used in Step 2, see data for Technique 11.

APPENDIX A/ HOT-ARID: Phoenix, AZ   33°

309

39° Lat 38° 45' N; Long 90° 22' W
Elev 535 ft (163 m)
Jan Vertical Rad = 1080 Btu/ft², d
HDD/CDD65 °F = 4758/1534
HDD/CDD18 °C = 2643/852

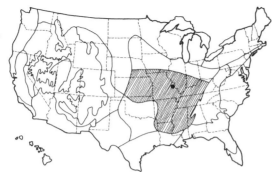

2 SUN PATH DIAGRAM

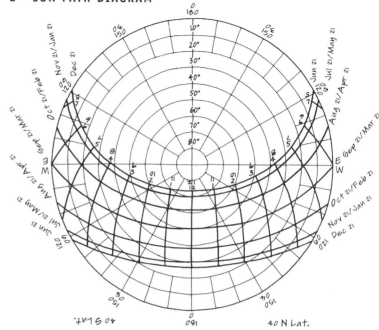

Sun Path Diagram, 40° Latitude

1 SUNDIAL

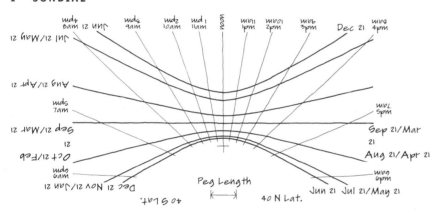

Sundial, 40° Latitude

3 SOLAR RADIATION

ELEMENT		Jan	Feb	Mar	Apr	May	Jun	Jul	Aug	Sep	Oct	Nov	Dec	Year
HDD	18.3C	615	484	343	148	62	0	0	0	12	132	313	536	**2643**
CDD		0	0	0	9	81	173	255	217	98	18	0	0	**852**
HDD	65F	1107	871	617	266	111	0	0	0	21	237	564	964	**4758**
CDD		0	0	0	17	145	312	459	391	177	33	0	0	1534
AVERAGE INCIDENT SOLAR RADIATION (Btu/sq. ft./day)														
HORIZ.	Global	690	930	1230	1590	1860	2030	2020	1800	1460	1100	720	580	1340
SOUTH 90° (VS)	Global	**1080**	1110	1060	970	830	780	820	950	1110	1220	1020	940	990
SOLAR RADIATION FOR FLAT-PLATE COLLECTORS FACING SOUTH AT A FIXED-TILT (kWh/sq. m./day)														
0°	Ave.	2.2	2.9	3.9	5	5.9	6.4	6.4	5.7	4.6	3.5	2.3	1.8	4.2
Lat – 15°	Ave.	3.2	3.8	4.6	5.4	5.9	6.3	6.3	6	5.3	4.5	3.2	2.7	4.8
Lat	Ave.	3.6	4.2	4.7	5.3	5.6	5.8	5.9	5.7	5.3	4.8	3.5	3.1	4.8
Lat + 15°	Ave.	3.8	4.3	4.6	4.9	4.9	5	5.1	5.2	5.1	4.8	3.7	3.3	4.6
90°	Ave.	3.5	3.7	3.4	3.1	2.6	2.4	2.6	3	3.5	3.8	3.2	3	3.2

	J	F	M	A	M	J	J	A	S	O	N	D
1 am	0	0	0	0	0	0	0	0	0	0	0	0
2	0	0	0	0	0	0	0	0	0	0	0	0
3	0	0	0	0	0	0	0	0	0	0	0	0
4	0	0	0	0	0	0	0	0	0	0	0	0
5	0	0	0	0	4	15	5	0	0	0	0	0
6	0	0	0	4	15	19	15	7	0	0	0	0
7	0	1	9	30	53	60	58	38	22	9	2	0
8	8	17	41	78	95	110	109	85	66	41	19	8
9	34	57	86	121	146	158	153	134	109	87	54	34
10	70	95	130	167	181	199	196	171	151	125	87	67
11 am	99	126	162	193	223	234	220	205	177	154	110	85
12 noon	115	138	179	205	233	249	225	209	192	168	122	102
1 pm	119	143	189	210	242	247	242	209	198	164	119	100
2	104	136	177	199	217	226	228	193	181	141	100	85
3	79	111	146	163	188	194	200	176	150	110	71	59
4	47	76	107	126	143	155	168	140	111	70	36	33
5	14	34	61	77	95	115	117	95	63	26	9	7
6	1	7	18	32	50	61	69	51	19	4	0	0
7	0	0	1	6	13	22	23	12	0	0	0	0
8	0	0	0	0	3	8	0	0	0	0	0	0
9	0	0	0	0	0	0	0	0	0	0	0	0
10	0	0	0	0	0	0	0	0	0	0	0	0
11 pm	0	0	0	0	0	0	0	0	0	0	0	0
12 mid	0	0	0	0	0	0	0	0	0	0	0	0

0	1-100	101-250	>250

Mean Global Horizontal Radiation, Btu/h, ft²

4 WIND ROSE

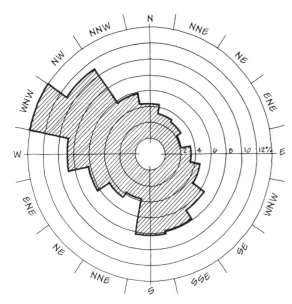

January Wind Rose, St. Louis

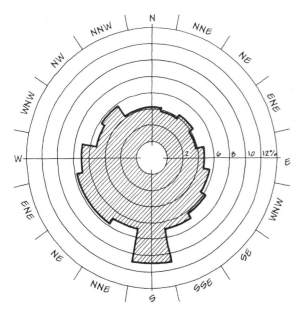

July Wind Rose, St. Louis

5 WIND SQUARE

Mean Airport Wind Conditions, direction/mph

	J	F	M	A	M	J	J	A	S	O	N	D
1 am	W 10.8	NE 9.9	W 9.1	WNW 9.2	WNW 6.3	SE 8.0	SSE 6.8	ESE 6.5	NNE 7.2	N 6.8	NW 8.9	WNW 12.4
2	NW 10.1	N 10.2	NW 8.5	S 9.5	W 6.9	W 7.3	W 6.4	SE 5.8	WNW 6.6	W 7.5	WSW 8.9	NW 12.7
3	SSE 9.5	WNW 10.4	WNW 9.2	S 9.7	SE 6.5	SW 8.2	W 6.0	SW 6.6	W 6.1	N 7.5	ENE 9.0	NW 12.4
4	WNW 9.4	SE 10.3	WNW 9.2	WNW 9.7	WSW 6.4	SW 8.0	SW 6.1	NNW 5.8	WSW 6.3	ENE 7.3	E 9.0	E 11.8
5	SSE 9.3	NW 10.3	N 8.7	NNE 9.6	E 6.0	ESE 7.8	SE 6.2	ENE 5.6	ENE 6.5	W 7.0	SSE 10.0	S 11.5
6	N 9.3	E 10.2	N 9.6	E 9.8	E 6.4	ESE 8.3	ESE 6.4	S 6.3	S 6.7	NW 7.8	NW 10.8	ENE 12.1
7	WNW 9.8	NNW 10.9	SW 9.9	WNW 10.6	SSE 7.3	WNW 9.3	N 7.4	S 7.5	SE 7.3	SE 8.4	ESE 10.4	N 11.8
8	E 10.4	NE 11.5	WSW 10.7	E 11.3	E 8.4	WNW 10.6	SE 8.4	SE 8.0	SSE 7.8	SSE 9.1	NE 10.7	N 12.3
9	N 11.0	W 12.2	W 10.6	WNW 12.0	NNW 9.9	W 10.4	SSE 8.6	NE 8.3	WSW 10.4	N 12.7	E 12.7	ESE 12.8
10	W 11.2	WNW 12.3	N 11.1	N 12.2	E 9.7	W 10.7	E 9.5	ESE 7.8	S 8.7	W 10.7	W 13.8	W 13.6
11 am	W 11.5	S 12.4	S 11.9	S 12.3	SE 10.8	SSW 11.9	W 9.6	ESE 9.0	S 10.0	S 10.9	SW 13.6	SE 12.8
12 noon	S 11.7	S 12.5	SSW 11.3	S 12.4	W 10.5	WNW 11.6	ESE 9.7	N 9.7	E 9.3	E 10.9	SSE 13.3	WSW 13.0
1 pm	WSW 11.7	NW 11.9	N 12.0	S 12.2	NW 13.3	S 13.0	E 9.6	ESE 8.8	SSW 9.4	WNW 11.4	N 13.6	N 13.8
2	S 11.6	S 11.9	N 12.0	ENE 12.2	NE 10.1	S 12.7	S 9.6	S 9.4	S 9.6	SSW 11.6	SW 14.0	S 13.9
3	SSE 11.6	S 11.9	NW 12.1	N 12.1	N 10.6	S 12.2	S 10.2	W 9.7	N 11.2	NE 13.0	ESE 14.3	S 14.3
4	SW 10.9	S 11.4	SSE 12.4	WNW 12.1	SW 11.7	ESE 12.8	SE 9.6	SSE 9.4	SW 9.2	WSW 11.3	N 13.1	SSE 13.1
5	N 10.3	ENE 10.5	ESE 12.5	S 12.1	N 11.0	N 9.7	N 9.7	W 9.7	SE 8.6	SSE 9.6	S 11.9	SE 13.6
6	NNE 9.6	ENE 10.0	NE 11.6	E 12.1	E 10.7	NW 9.7	NW 9.8	WSW 9.9	SSE 8.1	N 9.0	S 10.5	SE 12.1
7	N 9.6	N 9.6	S 10.1	N 11.4	ESE 9.7	WNW 10.0	S 9.2	W 9.0	WNW 8.1	SE 8.2	NW 10.3	WNW 13.2
8	WNW 9.5	W 9.1	N 10.1	SSE 10.7	SW 8.8	SE 8.8	SSE 8.5	NW 8.0	SSE 8.2	S 7.5	ESE 10.6	S 12.9
9	W 9.5	WNW 8.7	SE 10.0	S 8.0	NW 8.2	S 7.8	NW 7.9	NW 8.0	N 7.8	WNW 10.1	S 9.6	W 12.2
10	WSW 10.1	S 9.0	S 9.6	SE 9.8	W 8.2	WSW 8.5	S 7.6	W 7.4	W 7.9	WNW 8.2	WNW 9.3	W 12.3
11 pm	W 10.8	NNE 9.3	E 9.6	WNW 9.3	WNW 7.0	SE 8.0	WNW 7.4	SE 6.9	S 7.9	S 8.3	SE 9.2	SSE 12.5
12 mid	WSW 11.4	W 9.6	WNW 9.3	W 9.2	S 6.9	WNW 7.7	W 7.3	NW 6.9	WSW 7.8	S 7.7	S 8.9	E 13.0

0-5	5.1-9	9.1-12	>12

Mean City Center Wind Conditions, direction/mph

	J	F	M	A	M	J	J	A	S	O	N	D
1 am	W 5.1	NE 4.7	W 4.3	WNW 4.3	WNW 3.0	SE 3.7	SSE 3.2	ESE 3.0	NNE 3.4	N 3.2	NW 4.2	WNW 5.8
2	NW 4.8	N 4.8	NW 4.0	S 4.4	W 3.2	W 3.4	W 3.0	SE 2.7	WNW 3.1	W 3.5	WSW 4.2	NW 6.0
3	SSE 4.4	WNW 4.9	WNW 4.3	S 4.6	SE 3.1	SW 3.8	W 2.8	SW 3.1	W 2.9	N 3.5	ENE 4.2	NW 5.8
4	WNW 4.4	SE 4.8	WNW 4.3	WNW 4.6	WSW 3.0	SW 3.8	SW 2.9	NNW 2.7	WSW 3.0	ENE 3.4	E 4.2	E 5.5
5	SSE 4.4	NW 4.8	N 4.1	NNE 4.6	E 2.8	ESE 3.7	SE 2.9	ENE 2.6	ENE 3.1	W 3.3	SSE 4.7	S 5.4
6	N 4.3	E 4.8	N 4.5	E 4.6	E 3.0	ESE 3.9	ESE 3.0	S 3.0	S 3.2	NW 3.7	NW 5.1	ENE 5.7
7	WNW 4.6	NNW 5.1	SW 4.7	WNW 5.0	SSE 3.4	WNW 4.4	N 3.5	S 3.5	SE 3.4	SE 4.0	ESE 4.9	N 5.5
8	E 4.9	NE 5.4	WSW 5.1	E 5.3	E 3.9	WNW 5.0	SE 3.9	SE 3.8	SSE 3.7	SSE 4.3	NE 5.0	N 5.8
9	N 5.2	W 5.7	W 5.0	WNW 5.7	NNW 4.7	W 5.2	SSE 4.4	NE 4.0	WSW 3.9	N 4.9	E 6.0	ESE 6.0
10	W 5.3	WNW 5.8	N 5.2	N 5.7	E 4.5	W 5.0	E 4.5	ESE 3.7	S 4.1	W 5.0	W 6.5	W 6.4
11	W 5.4	S 5.8	S 5.6	S 5.8	SE 5.1	SSW 5.6	W 4.5	ESE 4.2	S 4.2	S 5.1	SW 6.4	SE 6.0
12 noon	S 5.5	S 5.9	SSW 5.3	S 5.8	W 4.9	WNW 5.4	ESE 4.5	N 4.6	E 4.4	E 5.1	SSE 6.3	WSW 6.1
1 pm	WSW 5.5	NW 5.7	N 5.3	S 5.8	NW 4.9	S 6.2	E 4.5	ESE 4.2	SSW 4.4	WNW 5.3	N 6.4	N 6.5
2	S 5.5	S 5.6	N 5.6	ENE 5.8	NE 4.7	S 6.0	S 4.5	S 4.4	S 4.5	SSW 5.4	SW 6.6	S 6.6
3	SSE 5.5	S 5.5	NW 5.8	N 5.7	N 5.0	S 5.7	S 4.5	W 4.8	N 4.6	NE 6.1	ESE 6.3	S 6.7
4	SW 5.1	S 5.2	SSE 5.8	WNW 5.7	SW 5.5	ESE 6.0	SE 4.5	SSE 4.4	SW 4.3	WSW 5.3	N 6.1	SSE 6.2
5	N 4.8	ENE 5.0	ESE 5.9	S 5.7	N 5.3	N 5.4	N 4.6	W 4.6	SE 4.1	SSE 4.5	S 5.6	SE 6.4
6	NNE 4.5	ENE 4.7	NE 5.5	E 5.7	E 5.0	NW 6.0	NW 4.6	WSW 4.7	SSE 3.8	N 4.2	S 4.9	SE 5.7
7	N 4.5	N 4.5	S 4.7	N 5.4	ESE 4.6	WNW 5.0	S 4.2	W 3.8	WNW 3.9	SE 3.9	NW 4.9	WNW 6.2
8	WNW 4.5	W 4.3	N 4.7	SSE 5.0	SW 4.1	SE 4.1	SSE 4.0	NW 3.8	SSE 3.8	S 3.5	ESE 5.0	S 6.1
9	W 4.5	WNW 4.1	SE 5.1	S 4.7	NW 3.8	S 3.9	NW 3.7	NW 3.7	N 3.8	WNW 3.7	S 4.8	W 5.7
10	WSW 4.8	S 4.2	S 4.5	SE 4.6	W 3.9	WSW 4.0	S 3.6	W 3.5	W 3.7	WNW 3.9	WNW 4.4	W 5.8
11 pm	W 5.1	NNE 4.4	E 4.6	WNW 4.4	WNW 3.3	SE 3.8	WNW 3.5	SE 3.2	S 3.7	S 3.9	SE 4.3	SSE 5.8
12 mid	WSW 5.4	W 4.5	WNW 4.4	W 4.3	S 3.2	WNW 3.6	W 3.4	NW 3.2	WSW 3.7	S 3.6	S 4.2	E 6.1

0-5	5.1-9	9.1-12	>12

6 AIR MOVEMENT PRINCIPLES
Technique 6 uses data from Techniques 4 and 5.

7 SITE MICROCLIMATES
Technique 7 uses data from Techniques 1, 2, 4, and 5.

8 SKY COVER

	J	F	M	A	M	J	J	A	S	O	N	D
1 am	6.6	5.4	6.8	5.7	3.3	3.7	3.1	3.2	3.7	4.4	4.7	6.0
2	6.2	5.3	6.5	5.5	3.0	3.8	3.2	3.7	3.8	4.4	4.3	6.5
3	6.0	5.1	6.5	5.5	3.3	4.5	3.3	4.8	3.7	4.4	4.3	6.4
4	5.9	5.4	6.7	5.7	4.0	4.2	3.5	4.9	4.1	4.3	4.5	6.2
5	5.9	5.9	6.6	6.1	5.6	4.9	3.8	5.4	4.4	5.2	4.9	6.2
6	5.7	6.2	7.3	6.3	6.5	5.2	4.0	6.4	4.9	5.1	5.5	6.1
7	6.1	6.1	7.5	7.0	6.6	5.3	4.1	5.9	5.2	5.9	6.2	6.0
8	6.5	6.0	7.3	6.3	6.5	5.4	4.2	5.4	5.3	5.6	6.1	6.0
9	6.9	6.0	6.9	6.2	6.3	5.1	4.2	5.5	5.6	5.0	6.2	6.1
10	6.6	6.1	6.6	6.1	6.4	4.8	4.9	5.9	5.8	4.9	6.0	6.5
11 am	6.5	6.3	7.0	6.1	5.9	4.9	5.6	6.0	6.1	4.6	6.7	6.8
12 noon	6.3	6.4	6.7	6.0	6.4	5.0	6.3	6.2	6.3	5.1	6.7	7.0
1 pm	6.4	6.3	6.6	6.1	6.5	4.8	6.3	6.7	6.1	4.9	6.5	6.8
2	6.5	6.1	6.8	6.5	6.8	5.2	6.3	6.7	5.9	4.8	6.6	6.7
3	6.6	6.0	6.8	6.6	6.5	5.7	6.3	6.3	5.7	4.8	6.9	7.2
4	6.5	6.1	6.5	6.7	6.9	5.7	5.7	5.9	5.3	4.8	7.1	6.6
5	6.2	6.3	6.1	6.7	6.8	4.9	5.1	5.5	4.8	4.9	6.6	6.7
6	6.1	6.3	6.4	6.7	4.8	4.8	4.5	4.5	4.4	4.4	6.3	6.6
7	5.7	6.0	5.5	6.6	5.7	4.5	4.1	4.7	4.2	4.4	6.3	6.8
8	5.4	5.7	5.1	6.5	4.7	3.9	3.4	4.3	3.9	4.0	5.6	6.3
9	5.0	5.4	5.3	6.3	4.3	3.8	2.9	3.7	3.9	4.4	5.5	6.6
10	5.4	5.6	5.5	6.1	4.2	3.9	3.1	3.3	3.9	4.6	5.6	6.2
11 pm	6.0	5.7	6.0	5.8	3.8	3.3	3.2	3.2	3.7	5.2	4.6	6.4
12 mid	6.5	5.8	6.1	5.7	3.6	3.5	3.4	3.4	3.7	4.6	4.7	6.0

0-2	2.1-5	5.1-8	8.1-10
clear	scattered	broken	overcast

Mean Hourly Sky Cover, tenths of sky covered

9 DAYLIGHT AVAILABILITY

	J	F	M	A	M	J	J	A	S	O	N	D
1 am	0	0	0	0	0	0	0	0	0	0	0	0
2	0	0	0	0	0	0	0	0	0	0	0	0
3	0	0	0	0	0	0	0	0	0	0	0	0
4	0	0	0	0	0	0	0	0	0	0	0	0
5	0	0	0	0	0	0	0	0	0	0	0	0
6	0	0	0	111	466	601	485	227	2	0	0	0
7	0	0	267	972	1675	1920	1857	1216	679	273	11	0
8	220	526	1310	2505	3054	3542	3533	2738	2095	1296	608	231
9	1051	1795	2733	3887	4699	5124	4997	4358	3487	2741	1696	1076
10	2207	3008	4149	5372	5821	6486	6406	5572	4868	3949	2752	2090
11 am	3099	3997	5172	6226	7153	7605	7174	6693	5693	4874	3481	2691
12 noon	3622	4383	5714	6591	7470	8117	7401	6840	6176	5312	3875	3231
1 pm	3776	4576	6039	6745	7779	8076	7915	6844	6379	5174	3772	3172
2	3278	4332	5620	6382	6991	7396	7445	6304	5804	4465	3150	2688
3	2499	3520	4629	5238	6030	6311	6536	5729	4804	3474	2237	1861
4	1487	2421	3397	4021	4587	5046	5446	4531	3516	2189	1141	1024
5	432	1083	1937	2473	3039	3719	3788	3045	1972	814	277	212
6	0	173	558	1012	1604	1967	2207	1605	583	77	0	0
7	0	0	0	176	422	710	746	355	13	0	0	0
8	0	0	0	0	25	7	0	0	0	0	0	0
9	0	0	0	0	0	0	0	0	0	0	0	0
10	0	0	0	0	0	0	0	0	0	0	0	0
11 pm	0	0	0	0	0	0	0	0	0	0	0	0
12 mid	0	0	0	0	0	0	0	0	0	0	0	0

>250	251-1000	1001-2000	>2000

Mean Hourly Global Horizontal Illuminance, foot-candles

HOUR	J	F	M	A	M	J	J	A	S	O	N	D	Ann
CLR DAYS 0/8-2/8	7	7	6	7	7	7	9	10	11	12	9	7	101
PT CD DAYS 3/8-6/8	7	6	8	8	9	11	11	11	8	7	7	7	101
OVR DAYS 7/8-8/8	17	15	16	15	14	12	10	10	10	11	15	17	164
% CLR	23	25	20	23	23	23	30	32	38	40	29	23	28
% PT CD	23	21	27	27	30	37	37	35	28	23	23	23	28
% OVR	55	54	53	50	47	40	33	32	34	37	48	55	45

Sky Cover Monthly Normals
Eighths of sky covered; % of days for sky condition

		June					December				
		9 am	11 am	1 pm	3 pm	5 pm	9 am	11 am	1 pm	3 pm	5 pm
HORIZ	M. Clear	48	84	101	96	67	16	42	48	30	2
	M. Cloudy	32	61	76	71	49	9	25	28	17	2
NORTH	M. Clear	19	16	17	17	15	6	10	11	8	1
	M. Cloudy	15	18	19	19	16	4	10	11	7	1
EAST	M. Clear	78	72	31	17	15	42	39	11	8	1
	M. Cloudy	40	49	27	19	16	11	18	11	7	1
SOUTH	M. Clear	12	31	45	41	19	39	82	88	63	6
	M. Cloudy	12	26	37	33	18	10	29	32	20	2
WEST	M. Clear	12	16	17	53	78	6	10	22	50	9
	M. Cloudy	12	18	19	41	50	4	10	14	17	2
M. Clear	(% hrs)	43	39	32	29	34	31	30	30	30	32

Average Incident Illuminance (klux-h)

10 DAYLIGHT OBSTRUCTIONS

Overcast Dot Charts are in Technique 10. For Clear Sky Dot Charts, see Appendix B.

11 BIOCLIMATIC CHART

	Temperature (°F)					Rel Humidity (percent)		Wind (kts)			Sky Cvr	Mean # days w/ temp (°F)			
	means			extreme				prevail		max		max	max	min	min
	max	min	ave	max	min	6 am	3 pm	dir	spd	gst		90	70	32	10
Jan	39	21	30	77	-18	80	62	WNW	11	54	OVR	0	#	26	6
Feb	43	25	34	83	-10	81	59	WNW	11	47	OVR	0	1	21	3
Mar	54	34	44	89	-5	80	54	WNW	12	57	OVR	#	5	14	#
Apr	67	46	56	93	22	78	49	WNW	12	72	OVR	#	13	2	0
May	76	55	66	98	31	81	51	S	9	51	OVR	1	24	#	0
Jun	85	65	75	105	43	82	51	S	9	66	OVR	9	29	0	0
Jul	89	69	79	115	51	84	51	S	8	54	SCT	15	31	0	0
Aug	87	67	78	107	47	86	52	S	7	61	CLR	12	31	0	0
Sep	80	59	70	104	36	87	50	S	8	49	CLR	5	26	0	0
Oct	69	48	59	94	23	83	50	S	9	68	CLR	#	16	1	0
Nov	54	36	45	85	1	81	56	WNW	11	56	OVR	0	4	12	#
Dec	42	26	34	76	-16	81	63	WNW	11	49	OVR	0	1	23	3
Ann	66	46	56	115	-18	82	54	S	10	72	OVR	43	180	100	13

Climatic Normals, 1945-1990

16 WINDOW SOLAR GAIN

For insolation data used in this technique, see radiation data for Technique 3.

	Jan	Feb	Mar	Apr	May	Jun	Jul	Aug	Sep	Oct	Nov	Dec	Ann
% Poss Sun	50	52	54	56	59	66	68	65	63	60	46	43	57

Average Percentage of Possible Sunshine, %

18 BUILDING BIOCLIMATIC CHART

See temperature and humidity data for Technique 11.

20 SHADING CALENDAR

	J	F	M	A	M	J	J	A	S	O	N	D
1 am	25.2	29.3	41.1	52.3	61.8	69.8	72.1	73.3	63.9	50.1	42.0	27.8
2	24.2	28.8	40.4	51.3	60.9	68.8	71.2	72.5	63.1	49.7	41.1	27.3
3	23.2	28.3	39.7	50.3	60.0	68.0	70.3	71.9	62.3	49.2	40.5	26.8
4	22.8	27.9	39.5	49.9	58.8	66.9	70.3	71.2	61.9	48.5	40.1	26.9
5	22.3	27.5	39.1	49.4	58.1	66.3	70.2	70.5	61.5	47.8	39.4	26.6
6	21.8	27.1	38.8	48.9	58.8	67.7	70.2	70.3	61.1	47.6	39.1	26.4
7	22.5	28.2	39.1	51.7	61.7	69.5	73.2	72.0	63.9	48.4	39.2	26.4
8	23.1	29.3	40.3	54.6	64.2	72.7	76.3	75.2	66.8	51.5	40.3	26.9
9	23.7	30.4	42.7	57.4	66.9	75.4	79.3	77.6	69.7	54.3	42.5	28.5
10	26.3	32.6	44.8	59.7	68.7	77.2	80.9	79.6	71.9	57.1	44.9	30.5
11	28.8	34.8	46.9	62.0	70.6	79.1	82.6	81.1	74.0	57.3	47.1	32.4
12 noon	31.4	37.0	48.3	64.3	72.4	81.5	84.3	82.6	76.2	61.9	49.0	34.3
1 pm	32.4	38.3	50.3	65.3	74.1	82.4	85.3	83.8	76.9	63.1	50.5	36.0
2	33.5	39.5	51.4	66.3	75.3	83.1	86.2	84.4	77.7	63.7	51.4	36.7
3	34.6	40.7	52.1	67.3	76.0	83.2	87.3	84.9	78.4	64.3	51.5	36.8
4	32.9	39.1	52.3	65.9	76.2	83.2	86.2	84.4	76.7	63.5	50.9	35.6
5	31.2	37.4	51.4	64.4	75.4	82.1	85.2	83.4	74.9	61.4	49.4	33.4
6	29.6	35.8	49.8	63.0	73.8	81.1	84.1	82.4	73.2	58.3	47.5	32.3
7	28.8	34.7	47.9	60.8	71.4	78.0	81.7	80.4	71.2	55.9	46.8	31.4
8	28.1	33.6	46.7	58.6	68.7	75.4	79.3	78.8	69.6	54.2	45.9	30.8
9	27.4	32.6	45.6	56.4	66.7	74.0	77.0	77.3	67.2	53.4	44.5	29.6
10	26.8	31.8	44.4	55.5	65.8	72.5	75.6	76.0	66.3	52.5	43.5	29.1
11 pm	26.3	31.0	43.3	54.3	64.3	71.6	74.2	75.1	65.5	51.6	42.9	28.6
12 mid	25.7	30.3	42.3	53.8	62.9	71.0	72.9	74.2	64.7	50.6	42.0	28.4

Cold	Cool	Comfort	Hot
<32	32-64.9	65-79.9	≥ 80

Mean Hourly Temperature, °F
Shading for Outdoor Rooms, Balance Point = 65°F (18.3°C)

	J	F	M	A	M	J	J	A	S	O	N	D
1 am	25.2	29.3	41.1	52.3	61.8	69.8	72.1	73.3	63.9	50.1	42.0	27.8
2	24.2	28.8	40.4	51.3	60.9	68.8	71.2	72.5	63.1	49.7	41.1	27.3
3	23.2	28.3	39.7	50.3	60.0	68.0	70.3	71.9	62.3	49.2	40.5	26.8
4	22.8	27.9	39.5	49.9	58.8	66.9	70.3	71.2	61.9	48.5	40.1	26.9
5	22.3	27.5	39.1	49.4	58.1	66.3	70.2	70.5	61.5	47.8	39.4	26.6
6	21.8	27.1	38.8	48.9	58.8	67.7	70.2	70.3	61.1	47.6	39.1	26.4
7	22.5	28.2	39.1	51.7	61.7	69.5	73.2	72.0	63.9	48.4	39.2	26.4
8	23.1	29.3	40.3	54.6	64.2	72.7	76.3	75.2	66.8	51.5	40.3	26.9
9	23.7	30.4	42.7	57.4	66.9	75.4	79.3	77.6	69.7	54.3	42.5	28.5
10	26.3	32.6	44.8	59.7	68.7	77.2	80.9	79.6	71.9	57.1	44.9	30.5
11	28.8	34.8	46.9	62.0	70.6	79.1	82.6	81.1	74.0	57.3	47.1	32.4
12 noon	31.4	37.0	48.3	64.3	72.4	81.5	84.3	82.6	76.2	61.9	49.0	34.3
1 pm	32.4	38.3	50.3	65.3	74.1	82.4	85.3	83.8	76.9	63.1	50.5	36.7
2	33.5	39.5	51.4	66.3	75.3	83.1	86.2	84.4	77.7	63.7	51.4	36.7
3	34.6	40.7	52.1	67.3	76.0	83.2	87.3	84.9	78.4	64.3	51.5	36.8
4	32.9	39.1	52.3	65.9	76.2	83.2	86.2	84.4	76.7	63.5	50.9	35.6
5	31.2	37.4	51.4	64.4	75.4	82.1	85.2	83.4	74.9	61.4	49.4	33.4
6	29.6	35.8	49.8	63.0	73.8	81.1	84.1	82.4	73.2	58.3	47.5	32.3
7	28.8	34.7	47.9	60.8	71.4	78.0	81.7	80.4	71.2	55.9	46.8	31.4
8	28.1	33.6	46.7	58.6	68.7	75.4	79.3	78.8	69.6	54.2	45.9	30.8
9	27.4	32.6	45.6	56.4	66.7	74.0	77.0	77.3	67.2	53.4	44.5	29.6
10	26.8	31.8	44.4	55.5	65.8	72.5	75.6	76.0	66.3	52.5	43.5	29.1
11 pm	26.3	31.0	43.3	54.3	64.3	71.6	74.2	75.1	65.5	51.6	42.9	28.6
12 mid	25.7	30.3	42.3	53.8	62.9	71.0	72.9	74.2	64.7	50.6	42.0	28.4

Cold	Cool	Comfort	Hot
< 32	32-55	55-69.9	≥ 70

Mean Hourly Temperature, °F
Shading for Balance Point = 55°F (12.8°C)

	J	F	M	A	M	J	J	A	S	O	N	D
1 am	25.2	29.3	41.1	52.3	61.8	69.8	72.1	73.3	63.9	50.1	42.0	27.8
2	24.2	28.8	40.4	51.3	60.9	68.8	71.2	72.5	63.1	49.7	41.1	27.3
3	23.2	28.3	39.7	50.3	60.0	68.0	70.3	71.9	62.3	49.2	40.5	26.8
4	22.8	27.9	39.5	49.9	58.8	66.9	70.3	71.2	61.9	48.5	40.1	26.9
5	22.3	27.5	39.1	49.4	58.1	66.3	70.2	70.5	61.5	47.8	39.4	26.6
6	21.8	27.1	38.8	48.9	58.8	67.7	70.2	70.3	61.1	47.6	39.1	26.4
7	22.5	28.2	39.1	51.7	61.7	69.5	73.2	72.0	63.9	48.4	39.2	26.4
8	23.1	29.3	40.3	54.6	64.2	72.7	76.3	75.2	66.8	51.5	40.3	26.9
9	23.7	30.4	42.7	57.4	66.9	75.4	79.3	77.6	69.7	54.3	42.5	28.5
10	26.3	32.6	44.8	59.7	68.7	77.2	80.9	79.6	71.9	57.1	44.9	30.5
11	28.8	34.8	46.9	62.0	70.6	79.1	82.6	81.1	74.0	57.3	47.1	32.4
12 noon	31.4	37.0	48.3	64.3	72.4	81.5	84.3	82.6	76.2	61.9	49.0	34.3
1 pm	32.4	38.3	50.3	65.3	74.1	82.4	85.3	83.8	76.9	63.7	51.4	36.7
2	33.5	39.5	51.4	66.3	75.3	83.1	86.2	84.4	77.7	63.7	51.4	36.7
3	34.6	40.7	52.1	67.3	76.0	83.2	87.3	84.9	78.4	64.3	51.5	36.8
4	32.9	39.1	52.3	65.9	76.2	83.2	86.2	84.4	76.7	63.5	50.9	35.6
5	31.2	37.4	51.4	64.4	75.4	82.1	85.2	83.4	74.9	61.4	49.4	33.4
6	29.6	35.8	49.8	63.0	73.8	81.1	84.1	82.4	73.2	58.3	47.5	32.3
7	28.8	34.7	47.9	60.8	71.4	78.0	81.7	80.4	71.2	55.9	46.8	31.4
8	28.1	33.6	46.7	58.6	68.7	75.4	79.3	78.8	69.6	54.2	45.9	30.8
9	27.4	32.6	45.6	56.4	66.7	74.0	77.0	77.3	67.2	53.4	44.5	29.6
10	26.8	31.8	44.4	55.5	65.8	72.5	75.6	76.0	66.3	52.5	43.5	29.1
11 pm	26.3	31.0	43.3	54.3	64.3	71.6	74.2	75.1	65.5	51.6	42.9	28.6
12 mid	25.7	30.3	42.3	53.8	62.9	71.0	72.9	74.2	64.7	50.6	42.0	28.4

Cold	Cool	Comfort	Hot
< 32	32-44.9	45-59.9	≥ 60

Mean Hourly Temperature, °F
Shading for Balance Point = 45°F (7.2°C)

21 TOTAL HEAT GAINS AND TOTAL HEAT LOSSES

- Latitude = 39 °N
- Summer Design Temp/Coincident Wet-Bulb Temp, °F (°C)

  0.4%   95/76 (35/24)
  1.0%   93/75 (34/24)

- Winter Design Temperature, °F (°C)

  99.6%   2 (-17)
  99%   8 (-13)

- Annual Heating Degree Days 65 °F (18 °C)   4758 (2643)
- Annual Cooling Degree Days 65 °F (18 °C)   1534 (852)

23 BALANCE POINT PROFILES

For temperature data used in Step 2, see data for Technique 11.

40° LATITUDE

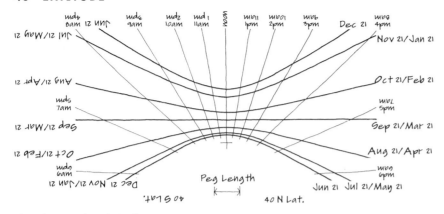

Sundial, 40° Latitude

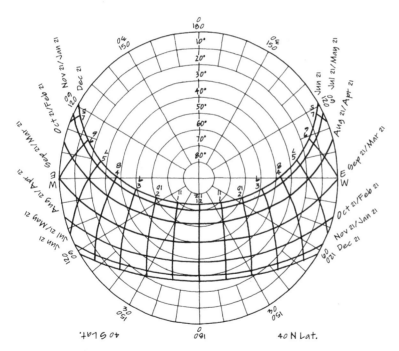

Sun Path Diagram, 40° Latitude

44° LATITUDE

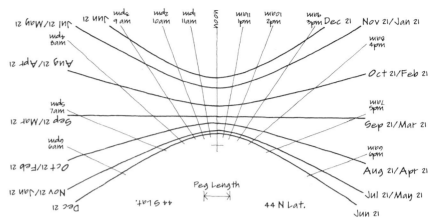

Sundial, 44° Latitude

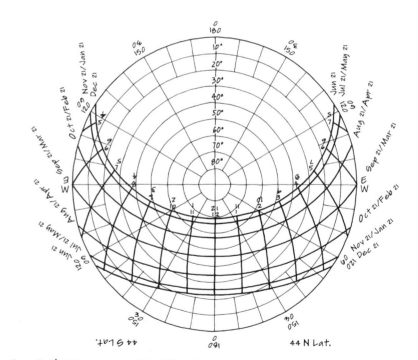

Sun Path Diagram, 44° Latitude

TEMPERATE COASTAL CLIMATE: Eugene, Oregon

4°

Lat 44° 07' N; Long 123° 13' W
Elev 249 ft (109 m)
Jan Vertical Rad = 570 Btu/ft², d
HDD/CDD65 °F = 4546/300
HDD/CDD18 °C = 2526/167

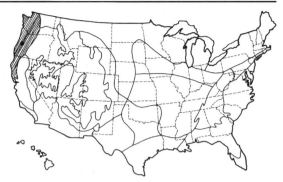

1 SUNDIAL

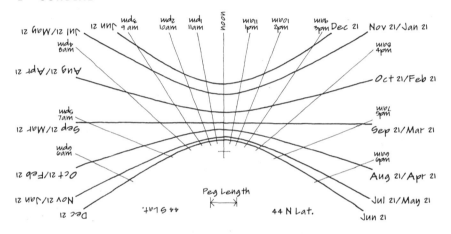

44° Latitude Sundial

2 SUN PATH DIAGRAM

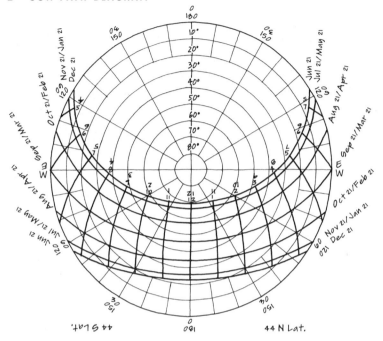

Sun Path Diagram, 44° Latitude

3 SOLAR RADIATION

ELEMENT		Jan	Feb	Mar	Apr	May	Jun	Jul	Aug	Sep	Oct	Nov	Dec	Year
HDD	18.3C	417	323	303	240	158	67	21	17	64	188	315	412	2526
CDD		0	0	0	0	0	17	61	61	28	0	0	0	167
HDD	65F	750	582	546	432	285	121	38	30	116	338	567	741	4546
CDD		0	0	0	0	0	31	109	110	50	0	0	0	300
AVERAGE INCIDENT SOLAR RADIATION (Btu/sq. ft./day)														
HORIZ.	Global	400	620	990	1390	1760	1970	2130	1850	1400	850	450	330	1180
SOUTH 90° (VS)	Global	570	740	910	940	900	860	970	1100	1220	1000	580	460	860
SOLAR RADIATION FOR FLAT-PLATE COLLECTORS FACING SOUTH AT A FIXED-TILT (kWh/sq. m./day)														
0°	Ave.	1.3	2	3.1	4.4	5.5	6.2	6.7	5.8	4.4	2.7	1.4	1	3.7
Lat – 15°	Ave.	1.8	2.6	3.8	4.8	5.6	6	6.7	6.3	5.4	3.6	1.9	1.4	4.2
Lat	Ave.	2	2.7	3.8	4.7	5.3	5.5	6.2	6	5.5	3.8	2.1	1.6	4.1
Lat + 15°	Ave.	2	2.8	3.7	4.3	4.6	4.8	5.4	5.5	5.2	3.8	2.1	1.6	3.8
90°	Ave.	1.8	2.3	2.9	3	2.8	2.7	3.1	3.5	3.9	3.2	1.8	1.5	2.7

Degree Days and Incident Solar Radiation

	J	F	M	A	M	J	J	A	S	O	N	D
1 am	0	0	0	0	0	0	0	0	0	0	0	0
2	0	0	0	0	0	0	0	0	0	0	0	0
3	0	0	0	0	0	0	0	0	0	0	0	0
4	0	0	0	0	0	0	0	0	0	0	0	0
5	0	0	0	1	2	1	0	0	0	0	0	0
6	0	0	3	13	20	16	8	1	0	0	0	0
7	0	0	4	21	41	54	52	39	14	4	0	0
8	1	7	24	57	82	95	96	87	49	23	8	1
9	15	26	57	93	124	142	144	140	89	57	27	13
10	34	56	88	122	151	162	180	179	131	88	48	31
11 am	61	71	125	153	188	198	213	208	164	119	69	49
12 noon	72	92	141	168	212	223	242	232	193	136	80	59
1 pm	76	100	150	174	205	216	252	225	199	133	77	60
2	74	90	136	160	204	216	248	229	187	129	70	55
3	57	81	118	140	190	202	232	201	158	99	50	39
4	31	53	89	115	149	167	190	167	116	66	23	18
5	11	25	51	78	111	132	149	122	72	27	7	3
6	0	6	17	39	66	84	94	68	24	4	0	0
7	0	0	1	9	26	42	44	22	2	0	0	0
8	0	0	0	0	4	9	9	2	0	0	0	0
9	0	0	0	0	0	0	0	0	0	0	0	0
10	0	0	0	0	0	0	0	0	0	0	0	0
11 pm	0	0	0	0	0	0	0	0	0	0	0	0
12 mid	0	0	0	0	0	0	0	0	0	0	0	0

0	1-100	101-250	>250

Mean Global Horizontal Radiation, Btu/hr, ft²

4   WIND ROSE

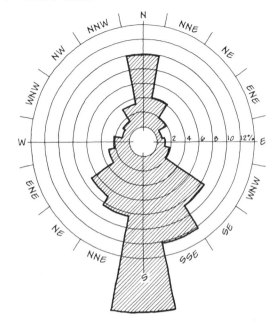

December Wind Rose, Eugene

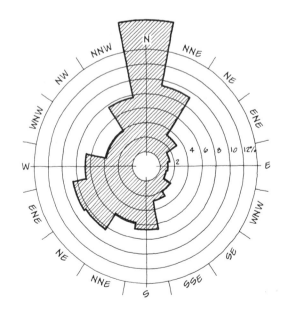

June Wind Rose, Eugene

5   WIND SQUARE

Mean Airport Wind Conditions, direction/mph

	J	F	M	A	M	J	J	A	S	O	N	D
1 am	NNW	N	N	N	N	SE	S	S	S	S	SSE	S
	7.5	6.9	6.7	7.5	5.9	4.0	4.2	5.5	5.6	3.9	7.5	5.6
2	S	SE	SE	S	SSE	S	S	S	N	N	S	SSW
	7.7	6.5	6.5	7.5	5.7	4.1	4.2	5.5	5.4	3.9	7.3	5.6
3	SSW	S	S	S	N	N	N	N	SSE	S	S	S
	7.9	6.3	6.2	7.8	5.5	4.2	4.1	5.5	5.2	4.0	7.2	5.7
4	S	S	S	S	S	N	N	SSE	S	S	SSW	S
	8.1	7.4	6.0	7.6	5.3	4.3	4.2	5.6	5.0	3.8	7.0	5.7
5	S	S	S	N	N	N	N	N	WSW	WSW	W	SSW
	8.5	6.9	5.8	7.0	5.6	4.8	4.8	5.8	5.0	4.0	7.1	6.1
6	N	N	WSW	N	S	S	S	S	SW	SW	SW	
	9.0	6.6	5.7	7.0	5.9	5.3	5.5	6.0	5.0	4.3	7.2	6.4
7	S	S	N	N	SW	N	N	SSE	W	NW	S	S
	9.4	6.8	5.5	6.9	6.3	5.8	6.2	6.2	4.9	4.2	7.3	6.8
8	N	N	N	N	N	S	N	S	S	S	S	S
	9.5	7.3	6.4	7.7	6.8	6.6	6.9	7.4	6.2	4.1	7.6	7.1
9	SSW	S	S	N	SW	N	N	SW	S	NNW	SSW	SE
	9.6	8.2	7.2	9.2	7.3	7.4	7.7	8.6	7.5	5.4	8.0	7.5
10	S	W	N	SSW	NNW	WSW	WSW	W	WSW	W	N	SE
	9.7	9.3	8.0	8.9	7.8	8.3	8.4	9.8	8.7	5.9	8.2	7.7
11 am	N	N	SSW	SW	S	N	WSW	WSW	S	N	N	N
	9.9	10.2	8.4	10.3	8.3	8.6	8.5	10.1	9.3	8.4	8.7	7.9
12 noon	N	N	N	N	S	N	N	N	NW	N	N	SW
	10.1	9.9	8.7	10.4	8.8	8.9	8.5	10.6	9.9	7.4	9.2	8.0
1 pm	SW	N	N	NNW	N	N	WSW	W	N	N	N	N
	10.3	10.8	9.0	11.6	9.3	9.2	8.6	10.9	10.5	7.6	9.6	8.2
2	N	N	N	N	N	N	N	N	N	N	SW	N
	10.2	11.1	9.1	11.8	9.5	9.7	8.7	11.3	11.0	7.2	9.2	8.0
3	N	SSW	N	N	N	N	N	N	NNE	N	N	N
	10.0	10.5	9.2	11.9	9.6	10.2	8.8	11.6	11.5	8.2	8.8	7.8
4	N	N	WSW	S	SSW	SW	S	WNW	SSW	N	N	
	9.8	9.7	8.7	12.5	9.8	10.7	8.9	12.0	12.1	8.2	8.4	7.6
5	W	N	N	SSW	SW	N	N	N	WSW	N		
	9.2	9.2	8.5	12.1	9.7	10.1	8.9	11.1	11.0	6.3	7.7	7.1
6	SW	S	S	W	N	N	N	S	WSW	N	N	
	8.6	8.8	7.6	11.8	9.6	9.6	8.3	10.3	9.9	4.8	7.1	6.5
7	N	N	N	N	S	N	N	N	N	N	N	
	8.0	7.2	6.8	9.9	9.5	8.9	8.0	9.4	8.9	5.3	6.4	6.0
8	N	N	N	N	N	N	N	N	N	N	S	N
	7.8	7.1	6.8	8.5	8.8	7.7	7.1	8.4	8.1	4.8	6.8	6.3
9	S	NNE	S	S	SSW	WSW	S	SSW	SSW	S	S	S
	7.6	7.0	6.8	7.5	8.1	6.5	6.3	7.5	7.4	4.6	7.2	6.6
10	NNW	SW	N	N	N	S	SSE	S	S	S	S	SE
	7.4	7.2	6.8	6.7	7.4	5.3	5.4	6.5	6.7	3.9	7.6	6.9
11 pm	S	S	S	SSW	N	N	SSW	S	SSW	W	N	
	7.5	7.4	6.9	6.5	6.9	4.8	5.0	6.2	6.3	4.1	7.6	6.5
12 mid	N	NNE	NNE	S	S	S	S	S	S	SW	S	N
	7.6	6.6	6.9	6.5	6.4	4.3	4.6	5.8	5.9	3.5	7.2	6.1

Legend: 0-5 | 5.1-9 | 9.1-12 | >12

Mean City Center Wind Conditions, direction/mph

	J	F	M	A	M	J	J	A	S	O	N	D
1 am	NNW	N	N	N	N	SE	S	S	S	S	SSE	S
	3.5	3.2	3.1	3.5	2.8	1.9	2.0	2.6	2.6	1.8	3.5	2.6
2	S	SE	SE	S	SSE	S	S	S	N	N	S	SSW
	3.6	3.0	3.0	3.5	2.7	1.9	2.0	2.6	2.5	1.9	3.4	2.6
3	SSW	S	S	S	N	N	N	N	SSE	S	S	S
	3.7	2.9	2.9	3.6	2.6	2.0	2.0	2.6	2.5	1.9	3.4	2.7
4	S	S	S	S	S	N	N	SSE	S	S	SSW	S
	3.8	3.5	2.8	3.6	2.5	2.0	2.0	2.6	2.4	1.8	3.3	2.7
5	S	S	S	N	N	N	N	N	WSW	WSW	W	SSW
	4.0	3.3	2.7	3.3	2.6	2.3	2.3	2.7	2.3	1.9	3.3	2.9
6	N	N	WSW	N	S	S	S	S	SW	SW	SW	
	4.2	3.1	2.7	3.3	2.8	2.5	2.6	2.8	2.3	2.0	3.4	3.0
7	S	S	N	N	SW	N	N	SSE	W	NW	S	S
	4.4	3.2	2.6	3.2	2.9	2.7	2.9	2.9	2.3	2.0	3.5	3.2
8	N	N	N	N	N	S	N	S	S	S	S	S
	4.5	3.4	3.0	3.6	3.2	3.1	3.2	3.5	2.9	1.9	3.6	3.3
9	SSW	S	N	N	SW	N	N	SW	S	NNW	SSW	SE
	4.5	3.8	3.4	4.3	3.4	3.5	3.6	4.0	3.5	2.6	3.7	3.5
10	S	W	N	SSW	NNW	WSW	W	W	WSW	W	N	SE
	4.5	4.4	3.8	4.2	3.7	3.9	4.0	4.6	4.1	2.8	3.9	3.6
11 am	N	N	SSW	SW	S	N	WSW	WSW	S	N	N	N
	4.7	4.4	3.9	4.8	3.9	4.0	4.0	4.4	3.9	4.1	3.7	
12 noon	N	N	N	N	S	N	N	W	NW	N	N	SW
	4.7	4.7	4.1	4.9	4.1	4.2	4.0	5.0	4.6	3.5	4.3	3.8
1 pm	SW	N	N	NNW	N	N	WSW	W	N	N	N	N
	4.9	5.1	4.2	5.4	4.4	4.3	4.0	5.1	4.9	3.6	4.5	3.9
2	N	N	N	N	N	N	N	N	N	N	SW	N
	4.8	5.2	4.3	5.6	4.5	4.6	4.1	5.3	5.2	3.4	4.3	3.8
3	N	SSW	N	N	N	N	N	N	NNE	N	N	N
	4.7	4.9	4.3	5.6	4.5	4.8	4.1	5.5	5.4	3.9	4.2	3.7
4	N	N	WSW	S	SSW	SW	S	WNW	SSW	N	N	
	4.6	4.6	4.4	5.9	4.6	5.0	4.2	5.6	5.7	3.9	4.0	3.6
5	W	N	N	SSW	SW	N	N	N	SW	N	WSW	N
	4.3	4.3	4.0	5.7	4.6	4.8	4.2	5.2	5.2	3.0	3.6	3.3
6	SW	S	S	W	N	N	N	S	WSW	N	N	
	4.0	4.1	3.6	5.5	4.5	4.5	3.9	4.8	4.7	2.3	3.3	3.1
7	N	N	N	N	S	N	N	N	N	N	N	
	3.8	3.4	3.2	4.7	4.5	4.2	3.8	4.4	4.2	2.5	3.0	2.8
8	N	N	N	N	N	N	N	N	N	N	S	N
	3.6	3.3	3.2	4.0	4.1	3.6	3.3	3.9	3.8	2.2	3.2	3.0
9	S	NNE	S	S	SSW	WSW	S	SSW	SSW	S	S	S
	3.6	3.3	3.2	3.5	3.8	3.0	2.9	3.5	3.5	2.1	3.4	3.1
10	NNW	SW	N	N	N	S	SSE	S	S	S	S	SE
	3.5	3.4	3.2	3.2	3.5	2.5	2.5	3.1	3.1	1.8	3.6	3.2
11 pm	S	S	S	SSW	N	N	SSW	S	SSW	W	N	
	3.5	3.5	3.2	3.0	3.2	2.3	2.4	2.9	3.0	1.9	3.6	3.0
12 mid	N	NNE	NNE	S	S	S	S	S	S	SW	S	N
	3.6	3.2	3.2	3.1	3.0	2.0	2.2	2.7	2.8	1.7	3.5	2.9

Legend: 0-5 | 5.1-9 | 9.1-12 | >12

6   AIR MOVEMENT PRINCIPLES

Technique 6 uses data from Techniques 4 and 5.

7   SITE MICROCLIMATES

Technique 7 uses data from Techniques 1, 2, 4 and 5.

8 SKY COVER

	J	F	M	A	M	J	J	A	S	O	N	D
1 am	7.6	7.7	6.5	6.0	6.9	4.8	2.3	2.6	3.7	5.0	8.2	8.5
2	7.8	8.2	6.5	6.4	7.1	5.0	2.7	2.7	3.8	4.8	8.0	8.5
3	8.0	8.3	6.6	6.5	7.3	5.3	3.2	3.0	4.0	5.1	8.0	8.5
4	8.2	8.9	6.6	6.6	7.5	5.4	3.6	3.1	4.2	5.8	7.8	8.5
5	8.7	8.8	6.9	6.7	7.8	5.7	4.1	3.4	4.5	6.0	8.2	8.5
6	9.0	8.8	7.1	7.6	8.1	6.0	4.6	3.6	4.9	6.5	8.6	8.4
7	9.5	9.2	7.4	7.6	8.5	6.3	5.0	3.9	5.2	7.1	9.1	8.4
8	9.5	9.3	7.5	7.5	8.3	6.5	5.1	4.2	5.3	6.8	9.2	8.7
9	9.6	9.2	8.0	7.7	7.9	6.4	5.1	3.9	5.3	6.7	9.3	9.1
10	9.6	9.2	8.3	7.8	7.7	6.4	5.2	4.0	5.3	6.9	9.5	9.4
11 am	9.3	9.1	7.9	7.9	7.4	6.3	5.2	4.5	5.1	5.7	9.4	9.3
12 noon	9.0	8.9	7.6	7.9	7.1	6.0	5.0	5.0	4.9	5.7	9.3	9.1
1 pm	8.7	8.9	7.3	7.7	6.8	5.9	5.0	5.5	4.7	5.6	9.3	8.9
2	8.8	9.0	7.3	7.6	6.6	5.9	4.7	5.3	4.5	5.3	9.1	8.8
3	8.6	8.8	7.2	7.7	6.4	5.8	4.3	5.1	4.4	5.2	9.1	8.8
4	8.9	8.6	7.2	7.4	6.1	5.8	4.0	4.9	4.2	5.5	9.0	8.6
5	8.7	8.6	7.3	7.0	6.3	5.3	4.2	4.5	4.1	5.3	9.0	8.6
6	8.5	8.9	7.4	7.0	6.4	5.0	4.3	4.2	4.0	5.5	8.8	8.6
7	8.3	8.4	7.4	6.8	6.6	4.5	4.6	3.8	3.9	5.4	8.9	8.6
8	8.1	8.3	7.1	6.3	6.4	4.5	4.2	3.4	3.8	5.4	8.8	8.5
9	7.9	8.5	7.0	6.5	6.1	4.3	3.6	3.0	3.8	4.9	8.7	8.5
10	7.7	8.1	6.7	6.3	5.9	4.4	3.2	2.6	3.7	5.0	8.6	8.5
11 pm	7.7	7.8	6.7	6.1	6.3	4.5	2.9	2.6	3.8	5.1	8.4	8.4
12 mid	7.7	7.6	6.6	5.7	6.5	4.4	2.5	2.5	3.7	5.1	8.4	8.5

0-2	2.1-5	5.1-8	8.1-10
clear	scattered	broken	overcast

Mean Hourly Sky Cover, tenths of sky covered

9 DAYLIGHT AVAILABILITY

	J	F	M	A	M	J	J	A	S	O	N	D
1 am	0	0	0	0	0	0	0	0	0	0	0	0
2	0	0	0	0	0	0	0	0	0	0	0	0
3	0	0	0	0	0	0	0	0	0	0	0	0
4	0	0	0	0	0	0	0	0	0	0	0	0
5	0	0	0	0	0	0	0	0	0	0	0	0
6	0	0	0	66	409	645	505	196	0	0	0	0
7	0	0	109	689	1320	1734	1661	1212	453	85	0	0
8	0	198	766	1822	2656	3070	3065	2752	1546	736	238	0
9	492	834	1831	3019	3988	4558	4614	4456	2861	1814	857	432
10	1091	1790	2844	3969	4901	5238	5789	5710	4189	2800	1546	959
11 am	1942	2298	4014	4960	6065	6375	6833	6650	5228	3794	2224	1592
12 noon	2294	2979	4527	5443	6848	7202	7727	7383	6143	4334	2545	1897
1 pm	2422	3233	4842	5627	6620	6969	8019	7178	6305	4250	2459	1923
2	2359	2918	4394	5177	6572	6948	7911	7265	5921	4112	2231	1772
3	1822	2601	3789	4537	6086	6499	7406	6382	5012	3135	1614	1255
4	981	1711	2846	3720	4799	5361	6067	5289	3686	2089	755	586
5	347	813	1613	2523	3563	4222	4721	3836	2243	840	215	82
6	0	145	540	1257	2104	2680	2959	2127	752	107	0	0
7	0	0	20	278	815	1318	1370	681	51	0	0*	0
8	0	0	0	0	86	275	275	30	0	0	0	0
9	0	0	0	0	0	0	0	0	0	0	0	0
10	0	0	0	0	0	0	0	0	0	0	0	0
11 pm	0	0	0	0	0	0	0	0	0	0	0	0
12 mid	0	0	0	0	0	0	0	0	0	0	0	0

>250	251-1000	1001-2000	>2000

Mean Hourly Global Horizontal Illuminance, foot-candles

HOUR	J	F	M	A	M	J	J	A	S	O	N	D	Ann
CLR DAYS 0/8-2/8	2	3	3	4	6	8	16	14	12	5	2	1	75
PT CD DAYS 3/8-6/8	4	4	6	7	9	8	8	9	8	9	6	4	82
OVR DAYS 7/8-8/8	25	21	22	19	17	14	7	8	9	17	23	26	209
% CLR	6	11	10	13	19	27	52	45	41	16	6	3	20
% PT CD	13	14	19	23	28	27	26	29	28	29	19	13	22
% OVR	81	75	71	63	53	47	23	26	31	55	74	84	57

Sky Cover Monthly Normals
Eighths of sky covered; % of days for sky condition

		June					December				
		9 am	11 am	1 pm	3 pm	5 pm	9 am	11 am	1 pm	3 pm	5 pm
HORIZ	M. Clear	46	81	100	96	73	7	30	36	22	0
	M. Cloudy	27	48	65	64	48	4	16	19	12	0
NORTH	M. Clear	17	15	16	16	14	3	8	9	7	0
	M. Cloudy	12	17	19	19	16	2	7	8	6	0
EAST	M. Clear	81	74	34	16	14	21	36	9	7	0
	M. Cloudy	29	37	28	19	14	5	12	8	6	0
SOUTH	M. Clear	11	35	53	50	27	19	70	79	54	1
	M. Cloudy	11	24	36	35	21	5	18	21	14	0
WEST	M. Clear	11	15	16	48	81	3	8	15	38	1
	M. Cloudy	11	17	19	34	44	2	7	9	11	0
M. Clear	(% hrs)	31	31	34	38	42	8	7	8	11	13

Average Incident Illuminance (klux-hr)

10 DAYLIGHT OBSTRUCTIONS

Overcast Dot Charts are in Technique 10. For Clear Sky Dot Charts, see Appendix B.

11 BIOCLIMATIC CHART

	Temperature (°F)					Rel Humidity (percent)		Wind (kts)			Sky Cvr	Mean # days w/ temp (°F)			
	means			extreme				prevail		max		max 90	max 70	min 32	min 10
	max	min	ave	max	min	6 am	3 pm	dir	spd	gst					
Jan	46	33	40	67	-4	91	80	S	9	57	OVR	0	#	14	#
Feb	51	35	43	72	-3	92	72	S	9	46	OVR	0	1	10	#
Mar	56	37	46	77	20	91	64	S	9	52	OVR	0	3	7	0
Apr	61	39	50	86	27	88	58	S	8	50	OVR	0	9	3	0
May	67	43	56	93	28	84	54	N	8	44	OVR	#	18	#	0
Jun	74	48	61	102	32	81	49	N	9	36	OVR	1	26	#	0
Jul	82	51	67	105	39	78	38	N	9	44	CLR	6	31	0	0
Aug	82	51	67	108	38	82	39	N	9	34	CLR	5	31	0	0
Sep	77	48	62	103	32	89	44	N	9	31	CLR	2	28	#	0
Oct	64	42	53	94	19	94	61	S	7	37	OVR	#	15	2	0
Nov	53	38	45	76	12	93	79	S	9	50	OVR	0	1	7	0
Dec	47	35	41	68	-12	92	84	S	9	53	OVR	0	#	11	#
Ann	63	42	53	108	-12	88	60	N	9	57	OVR	15	162	54	#

Climatic Normals, 1945-1990

16 WINDOW SOLAR GAIN

For insolation data used in this technique, see radiation data for Technique 3.

	Jan	Feb	Mar	Apr	May	Jun	Jul	Aug	Sep	Oct	Nov	Dec	Ann
% Poss Sun	28	38	48	52	57	56	69	66	62	44	28	23	48

Average Percentage of Possible Sunshine, %

18 BUILDING BIOCLIMATIC CHART

See temperature and humidity data for Technique 11.

20 SHADING CALENDAR

	J	F	M	A	M	J	J	A	S	O	N	D
1 am	37.8	40.6	43.8	43.6	47.9	53.1	56.8	56.5	53.0	47.7	41.6	39.8
2	37.8	40.6	43.0	42.8	47.3	52.3	55.8	55.4	52.1	46.5	41.2	39.9
3	37.8	40.3	42.2	42.2	46.8	51.5	54.7	54.3	51.3	45.9	40.9	40.0
4	37.8	40.1	41.4	41.6	46.2	50.8	53.7	53.3	50.4	45.3	40.5	40.0
5	37.8	39.6	41.2	41.5	47.2	52.7	55.2	54.5	50.9	45.4	40.3	39.9
6	37.9	39.4	41.1	41.3	48.2	54.7	56.7	55.7	51.4	45.1	40.1	39.8
7	37.9	39.2	40.9	43.3	49.3	56.7	58.3	57.0	51.9	44.9	39.9	39.7
8	38.5	39.4	43.5	46.0	51.4	59.2	61.4	61.0	55.7	47.4	41.5	40.6
9	38.9	40.7	46.0	48.2	53.5	62.5	64.5	65.2	59.6	51.1	43.1	41.5
10	39.4	42.5	48.6	50.1	55.5	65.4	67.6	69.4	63.4	54.6	44.8	42.4
11	40.4	44.3	50.8	52.0	57.7	67.3	70.2	72.4	66.8	54.2	46.1	44.0
12 noon	41.4	45.7	53.2	54.1	59.9	69.2	72.8	75.4	70.1	61.3	47.4	45.6
1 pm	42.4	47.1	55.4	55.4	62.1	71.2	75.3	78.4	73.5	63.7	48.8	47.2
2	42.7	47.8	56.1	56.1	62.5	71.7	76.6	79.8	74.4	65.8	48.6	47.2
3	43.0	48.6	56.8	56.9	63.0	72.3	78.0	81.2	75.2	67.1	48.4	47.2
4	43.3	48.4	57.4	56.9	63.5	72.9	79.3	82.6	76.0	66.6	48.3	47.3
5	42.2	47.6	55.1	55.9	61.2	71.0	77.6	79.7	72.0	63.7	47.0	45.6
6	41.2	45.7	52.8	54.0	59.0	69.1	75.9	76.9	68.0	58.9	45.7	43.9
7	40.2	44.4	50.5	51.0	56.7	67.1	74.2	74.0	63.9	55.9	44.3	42.2
8	39.9	43.4	49.1	48.4	54.5	63.6	70.1	70.0	61.5	53.8	43.8	42.0
9	39.6	42.7	47.9	46.9	52.3	60.2	66.0	66.1	59.2	52.0	43.2	41.7
10	39.3	42.3	46.6	45.8	50.1	56.8	62.0	62.3	56.9	50.8	42.7	41.4
11 pm	39.0	41.4	45.7	45.0	49.4	55.5	60.2	60.3	55.6	49.7	42.2	41.0
12 mid	38.6	40.8	44.9	44.1	48.7	54.3	58.5	58.2	54.3	48.8	41.8	40.5

Cold <32	Cool 32-64.9	Comfort 65-79.9	Hot ≥ 80

Mean Hourly Temperature, °F
Shading for Outdoor Rooms, Balance Point = 65°F (18.3°C)

	J	F	M	A	M	J	J	A	S	O	N	D
1 am	37.8	40.6	43.8	43.6	47.9	53.1	56.8	56.5	53.0	47.7	41.6	39.8
2	37.8	40.6	43.0	42.8	47.3	52.3	55.8	55.4	52.1	46.5	41.2	39.9
3	37.8	40.3	42.2	42.2	46.8	51.5	54.7	54.3	51.3	45.9	40.9	40.0
4	37.8	40.1	41.4	41.6	46.2	50.8	53.7	53.3	50.4	45.3	40.5	40.0
5	37.8	39.6	41.2	41.5	47.2	52.7	55.2	54.5	50.9	45.4	40.3	39.9
6	37.9	39.4	41.1	41.3	48.2	54.7	56.7	55.7	51.4	45.1	40.1	39.8
7	37.9	39.2	40.9	43.3	49.3	56.7	58.3	57.0	51.9	44.9	39.9	39.7
8	38.5	39.4	43.5	46.0	51.4	59.2	61.4	61.0	55.7	47.4	41.5	40.6
9	38.9	40.7	46.0	48.2	53.5	62.5	64.5	65.2	59.6	51.1	43.1	41.5
10	39.4	42.5	48.6	50.1	55.5	65.4	67.6	69.4	63.4	54.6	44.8	42.4
11	40.4	44.3	50.8	52.0	57.7	67.3	70.2	72.4	66.8	54.2	46.1	44.0
12 noon	41.4	45.7	53.2	54.1	59.9	69.2	72.8	75.4	70.1	61.3	47.4	45.6
1 pm	42.4	47.1	55.4	55.4	62.1	71.2	75.3	78.4	73.5	63.7	48.8	47.2
2	42.7	47.8	56.1	56.1	62.5	71.7	76.6	79.8	74.4	65.8	48.6	47.2
3	43.0	48.6	56.8	56.9	63.0	72.3	78.0	81.2	75.2	67.1	48.4	47.2
4	43.3	48.4	57.4	56.9	63.5	72.9	79.3	82.6	76.0	66.6	48.3	47.3
5	42.2	47.6	55.1	55.9	61.2	71.0	77.6	79.7	72.0	63.7	47.0	45.6
6	41.2	45.7	52.8	54.0	59.0	69.1	75.9	76.9	68.0	58.9	45.7	43.9
7	40.2	44.4	50.5	51.0	56.7	67.1	74.2	74.0	63.9	55.9	44.3	42.2
8	39.9	43.4	49.1	48.4	54.5	63.6	70.1	70.0	61.5	53.8	43.8	42.0
9	39.6	42.7	47.9	46.9	52.3	60.2	66.0	66.1	59.2	52.0	43.2	41.7
10	39.3	42.3	46.6	45.8	50.1	56.8	62.0	62.3	56.9	50.8	42.7	41.4
11 pm	39.0	41.4	45.7	45.0	49.4	55.5	60.2	60.3	55.6	49.7	42.2	41.0
12 mid	38.6	40.8	44.9	44.1	48.7	54.3	58.5	58.2	54.3	48.8	41.8	40.5

Cold < 32	Cool 32-55	Comfort 55-69.9	Hot ≥ 70

Mean Hourly Temperature, °F
Shading for Balance Point = 55°F (12.8°C)

	J	F	M	A	M	J	J	A	S	O	N	D
1 am	37.8	40.6	43.8	43.6	47.9	53.1	56.8	56.5	53.0	47.7	41.6	39.8
2	37.8	40.6	43.0	42.8	47.3	52.3	55.8	55.4	52.1	46.5	41.2	39.9
3	37.8	40.3	42.2	42.2	46.8	51.5	54.7	54.3	51.3	45.9	40.9	40.0
4	37.8	40.1	41.4	41.6	46.2	50.8	53.7	53.3	50.4	45.3	40.5	40.0
5	37.8	39.6	41.2	41.5	47.2	52.7	55.2	54.5	50.9	45.4	40.3	39.9
6	37.9	39.4	41.1	41.3	48.2	54.7	56.7	55.7	51.4	45.1	40.1	39.8
7	37.9	39.2	40.9	43.3	49.3	56.7	58.3	57.0	51.9	44.9	39.9	39.7
8	38.5	39.4	43.5	46.0	51.4	59.2	61.4	61.0	55.7	47.4	41.5	40.6
9	38.9	40.7	46.0	48.2	53.5	62.5	64.5	65.2	59.6	51.1	43.1	41.5
10	39.4	42.5	48.6	50.1	55.5	65.4	67.6	69.4	63.4	54.6	44.8	42.4
11	40.4	44.3	50.8	52.0	57.7	67.3	70.2	72.4	66.8	54.2	46.1	44.0
12 noon	41.4	45.7	53.2	54.1	59.9	69.2	72.8	75.4	70.1	61.3	47.4	45.6
1 pm	42.4	47.1	55.4	55.4	62.1	71.2	75.3	78.4	73.5	63.7	48.8	47.2
2	42.7	47.8	56.1	56.1	62.5	71.7	76.6	79.8	74.4	65.8	48.6	47.2
3	43.0	48.6	56.8	56.9	63.0	72.3	78.0	81.2	75.2	67.1	48.4	47.2
4	43.3	48.4	57.4	56.9	63.5	72.9	79.3	82.6	76.0	66.6	48.3	47.2
5	42.2	47.6	55.1	55.9	61.2	71.0	77.6	79.7	72.0	63.7	47.0	45.6
6	41.2	45.7	52.8	54.0	59.0	69.1	75.9	76.9	68.0	58.9	45.7	43.9
7	40.2	44.4	50.5	51.0	56.7	67.1	74.2	74.0	63.9	55.9	44.3	42.2
8	39.9	43.4	49.1	48.4	54.5	63.6	70.1	70.0	61.5	53.8	43.8	42.0
9	39.6	42.7	47.9	46.9	52.3	60.2	66.0	66.1	59.2	52.0	43.2	41.7
10	39.3	42.3	46.6	45.8	50.1	56.8	62.0	62.3	56.9	50.8	42.7	41.4
11 pm	39.0	41.4	45.7	45.0	49.4	55.5	60.2	60.3	55.6	49.7	42.2	41.0
12 mid	38.6	40.8	44.9	44.1	48.7	54.3	58.5	58.2	54.3	48.8	41.8	40.5

Cold < 32	Cool 32-44.9	Comfort 45-59.9	Hot ≥ 60

Mean Hourly Temperature, °F
Shading for Balance Point = 45°F (7.2°C)

21 TOTAL HEAT GAINS AND TOTAL HEAT LOSSES

- Latitude = 44 °N
- Summer Design Temp/Coincident Wet-Bulb Temp, °F (°C)
  - 1.0%   87/65 (31/18)
  - 2.0%   83/64 (23/18)
- Winter Design Temperature, °F (°C)
  - 99.6%   21 (-6)
  - 99%   26 (-3)
- Annual Heating Degree Days 65 °F (18 °C)   4758 (2643)
- Annual Cooling Degree Days 65 °F (18 °C)   1534 (852)

23 BALANCE POINT PROFILES

For temperature data used in Step 2, see data for Technique 11.

COOL CLIMATE: Minneapolis, Minnesota

5° Lat 44° 53' N; Long 93° 13' W
Elev 581 ft (255 m)
Jan Vertical Rad = 1020 Btu/ft², d
HDD/CDD65 °F = 7981/682
HDD/CDD18 °C = 4434/379

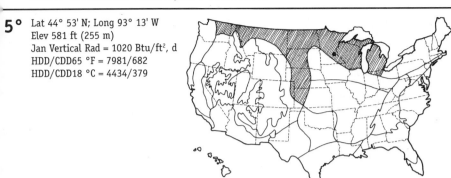

2 SUN PATH DIAGRAM

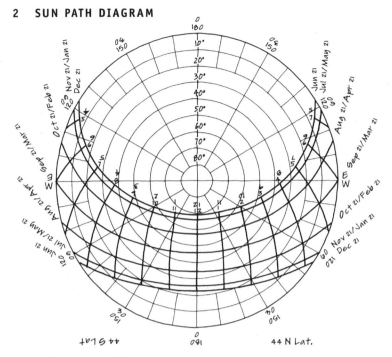

Sun Path Diagram, 44° Latitude

1 SUNDIAL

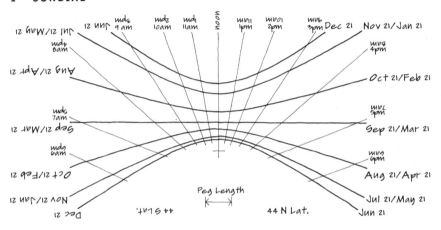

44° Latitude Sundial

3 SOLAR RADIATION

ELEMENT		Jan	Feb	Mar	Apr	May	Jun	Jul	Aug	Sep	Oct	Nov	Dec	Year
HDD	18.3C	916	733	586	310	136	23	6	12	93	279	530	811	4434
CDD		0	0	0	0	24	76	154	107	18	0	0	0	379
HDD	65F	1649	1319	1054	558	244	41	11	22	167	502	954	1460	7981
CDD		0	0	0	0	43	137	278	192	32	0	0	0	682
AVERAGE INCIDENT SOLAR RADIATION (Btu/sq. ft./day)														
HORIZ.	Global	560	860	1190	1490	1810	1980	2010	1710	1290	880	540	430	1230
SOUTH 90° (VS)	Global	1060	1230	1180	1040	940	890	960	1050	1120	1110	860	820	1020
SOLAR RADIATION FOR FLAT-PLATE COLLECTORS FACING SOUTH AT A FIXED-TILT (kWh/sq. m./day)														
0°	Ave.	1.8	2.7	3.8	4.7	5.7	6.3	6.3	5.4	4.1	2.8	1.7	1.4	3.9
Lat − 15°	Ave.	3.1	4.1	4.8	5.3	5.8	6.1	6.4	5.8	4.9	3.9	2.6	2.3	4.6
Lat	Ave.	3.5	4.5	5	5.1	5.5	5.6	5.9	5.6	5	4.1	2.9	2.7	4.6
Lat + 15°	Ave.	3.8	4.7	4.9	4.8	4.8	4.9	5.1	5.1	4.7	4.2	3	2.9	4.4
90°	Ave.	3.7	4.4	4.1	3.3	3	2.8	3	3.3	3.5	3.5	2.8	2.8	3.3

Degree Days and Incident Solar Radiation

	J	F	M	A	M	J	J	A	S	O	N	D
1 am	0	0	0	0	0	0	0	0	0	0	0	0
2	0	0	0	0	0	0	0	0	0	0	0	0
3	0	0	0	0	0	0	0	0	0	0	0	0
4	0	0	0	0	0	0	0	0	0	0	0	0
5	0	0	0	1	3	1	0	0	0	0	0	0
6	0	0	0	4	15	22	15	6	1	0	0	0
7	0	0	5	25	50	59	53	34	15	5	0	0
8	2	8	32	62	100	105	101	80	52	27	8	2
9	18	37	72	108	140	148	143	123	87	60	31	17
10	51	78	109	144	187	189	189	164	133	98	62	44
11 am	84	117	147	166	204	232	220	194	163	125	84	70
12 noon	100	137	166	177	226	241	217	205	178	139	95	81
1 pm	110	147	173	182	224	252	231	215	180	142	93	82
2	100	140	161	169	213	238	217	200	176	126	83	74
3	74	115	135	150	182	176	192	177	147	93	56	53
4	44	79	102	121	146	160	174	147	112	63	32	27
5	13	37	57	80	110	122	130	102	67	27	7	5
6	1	7	21	38	63	78	85	58	23	4	0	0
7	0	0	2	10	25	38	38	20	3	0	0	0
8	0	0	0	4	8	7	2	0	0	0	0	0
9	0	0	0	0	0	0	0	0	0	0	0	0
10	0	0	0	0	0	0	0	0	0	0	0	0
11 pm	0	0	0	0	0	0	0	0	0	0	0	0
12 mid	0	0	0	0	0	0	0	0	0	0	0	0

0   1-100   101-250   >250

Mean Global Horizontal Radiation, Btu/hr, ft²

4 WIND ROSE

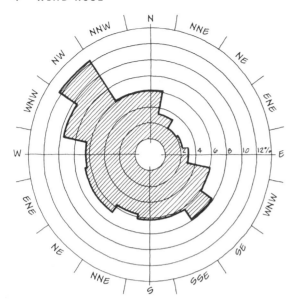

December Wind Rose, Minneapolis

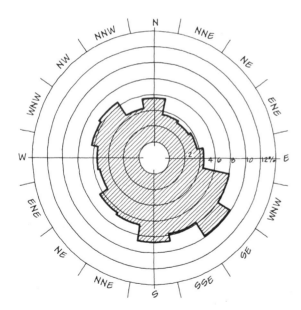

June Wind Rose, Minneapolis

5 WIND SQUARE

Time	J	F	M	A	M	J	J	A	S	O	N	D
1 am	WSW 9.1	SW 8.1	W 8.6	WNW 8.8	SSW 8.2	SSE 7.2	WNW 7.6	N 6.9	ESE 7.0	N 9.8	SSE 9.3	SE 10.4
2	N 8.8	N 7.7	ENE 8.8	N 9.0	SSW 8.1	NW 6.8	N 7.7	NW 7.5	ESE 6.8	SSE 9.9	SSE 9.0	WNW 9.4
3	ENE 9.2	E 7.5	WNW 9.2	ESE 9.3	ENE 8.0	N 6.5	SSW 8.0	SSW 8.0	WSW 6.7	N 10.1	NNE 8.6	ESE 9.7
4	WSW 8.8	ESE 7.5	NW 9.3	ESE 9.6	ENE 8.4	N 6.8	N 8.0	WNW 7.2	SSE 6.9	ESE 9.8	WNW 8.8	E 10.1
5	NW 9.1	NNE 8.9	W 9.6	N 9.3	S 8.8	ESE 7.1	SE 8.2	S 7.2	SW 7.0	NW 9.6	NW 9.0	S 9.6
6	S 8.7	WSW 8.8	NW 10.3	SSE 8.9	SSW 8.8	WNW 7.5	NW 8.3	NW 9.2	SSE 7.1	N 9.4	NNW 9.1	ESE 9.8
7	NNW 9.2	NNW 9.7	SSW 10.9	SE 10.1	ESE 9.7	N 8.7	ENE 9.3	SE 9.3	NW 8.1	S 10.3	S 9.4	WSW 9.8
8	SE 9.7	SE 9.4	NW 11.8	NNE 11.7	NNW 10.0	S 10.2	S 10.0	ESE 9.1	SE 11.1	NNE 9.6	S 10.1	S 10.4
9	E 9.5	N 10.9	WSW 12.9	NW 12.8	N 10.8	NNW 11.0	NW 11.2	WNW 10.1	N 10.1	N 12.0	SSW 9.9	N 10.5
10	S 10.4	N 10.9	N 13.6	E 13.6	SW 12.0	NE 11.4	SSE 11.5	SSW 11.1	SSW 10.9	SE 12.6	E 10.3	S 10.9
11 am	S 11.1	N 10.9	ENE 14.9	WNW 13.7	NW 12.3	S 11.8	NE 11.8	SSE 11.5	S 11.7	SW 11.6	E 10.6	NNW 11.2
12 noon	S 11.8	SSW 11.5	S 15.3	S 14.1	S 13.1	SSE 12.2	E 12.2	SE 11.8	S 12.5	S 13.8	S 10.9	W 10.9
1 pm	WSW 12.5	N 12.0	S 15.3	SSW 15.7	SSW 12.9	N 12.3	SSE 12.1	S 11.1	S 12.5	S 14.1	S 11.1	SE 11.7
2	NNW 13.0	N 12.2	S 16.6	WNW 15.4	S 12.9	NNE 12.5	SE 12.0	NW 11.0	WNW 12.5	S 14.4	S 11.3	S 12.0
3	S 13.4	SSE 12.7	N 15.9	N 15.3	NNW 12.5	SSW 12.7	N 12.0	N 10.6	NNW 12.6	N 14.8	S 11.5	SW 11.5
4	SSE 13.5	ENE 12.8	ENE 16.2	E 13.1	SSE 13.4	SSE 12.0	S 11.8	ESE 10.9	N 11.6	SSE 13.0	S 11.3	SW 11.3
5	NW 11.9	ENE 11.8	NNW 14.6	NW 13.9	S 12.4	NNE 11.3	N 11.7	S 11.4	S 10.5	S 11.3	S 11.0	S 10.4
6	SSE 11.6	N 9.6	E 13.1	SE 13.2	SE 12.4	WSW 10.7	N 11.5	WNW 10.7	WNW 9.5	W 9.5	SSW 10.7	SW 10.0
7	S 11.9	S 9.5	NW 11.5	S 11.0	SSW 11.5	S 9.6	NW 11.5	NW 9.6	E 9.0	ESE 9.2	N 10.7	N 10.0
8	S 11.8	NNW 9.2	S 10.5	S 11.0	W 10.7	S 8.6	S 9.2	S 9.6	NW 8.4	S 9.0	S 10.6	NNW 9.9
9	SSW 11.3	S 9.0	S 9.8	WSW 10.3	NNE 9.8	N 7.5	N 8.0	E 9.0	SE 8.0	NNW 8.7	S 10.6	S 9.7
10	NW 10.7	S 8.8	SSE 9.4	SSE 9.8	ESE 9.4	ESE 7.4	SE 7.8	E 8.6	WNW 7.7	WNW 9.1	NNW 10.2	SSW 9.5
11 pm	SSE 10.4	NW 8.7	N 9.6	NNW 9.4	SSE 9.1	SSE 7.3	NW 7.5	SE 8.0	ESE 7.5	N 9.6	ENE 9.8	N 10.0
12 mid	SE 9.9	E 7.9	WNW 9.3	SSE 9.4	S 8.7	E 7.3	ENE 7.2	WSW 7.2	WNW 7.1	WNW 10.0	W 9.4	W 10.0

| 0-5 | 5.1-9 | 9.1-12 | >12 |

Mean Airport Wind Conditions, direction/mph

Time	J	F	M	A	M	J	J	A	S	O	N	D
1 am	WSW 4.3	SW 3.8	W 4.0	WNW 4.1	SSW 3.9	SSE 3.4	WNW 3.6	N 3.3	ESE 3.3	N 4.6	SSE 4.4	SE 4.9
2	N 4.1	N 3.6	ENE 4.1	N 4.2	SSW 3.8	NW 3.2	N 3.6	NW 3.5	ESE 3.2	SSE 4.7	SSE 4.2	WNW 4.4
3	ENE 4.3	E 3.5	WNW 4.3	ESE 4.3	ENE 3.8	N 3.0	SSW 3.7	SSW 3.8	WSW 3.2	N 4.7	NNE 4.1	ESE 4.6
4	WSW 4.1	ESE 3.5	NW 4.4	ESE 4.5	ENE 3.9	N 3.2	N 3.8	WNW 3.4	SSE 3.2	ESE 4.6	WNW 4.1	E 4.8
5	NW 4.3	NNE 4.2	W 4.5	N 4.4	S 4.1	ESE 3.4	SE 3.8	S 3.4	SW 3.3	NW 4.5	NW 4.2	S 4.5
6	S 4.1	WSW 4.1	NW 4.8	SSE 4.2	SSW 4.3	WNW 3.5	NW 3.9	NW 4.3	SSE 3.4	N 4.4	NNW 4.3	ESE 4.6
7	NNW 4.3	NNW 4.5	SSW 5.1	SE 4.8	ESE 4.6	N 4.1	ENE 4.4	SE 4.4	NW 3.8	S 4.8	S 4.4	WSW 4.6
8	SE 4.6	SE 4.4	NW 5.5	NNE 5.5	NNW 4.8	S 4.7	S 4.8	ESE 4.7	SE 4.3	NNE 5.2	S 4.5	S 4.8
9	E 4.4	N 5.1	WSW 6.0	NW 6.0	N 5.1	NNW 5.2	NW 5.2	WNW 4.7	N 4.7	N 5.6	SSW 4.7	N 4.9
10	S 4.9	N 5.1	N 6.4	E 6.4	SW 5.4	NE 5.3	SSE 5.4	SSW 5.2	SSW 5.1	SE 5.9	E 4.8	S 5.1
11 am	S 5.2	N 5.1	ENE 7.0	WNW 6.4	NW 5.8	S 5.7	NE 5.6	SSE 5.4	S 5.5	SW 5.4	E 5.0	NNW 5.3
12 noon	S 5.6	SSW 5.4	S 7.2	S 6.6	S 6.1	SSE 5.7	E 5.7	SE 5.6	S 5.9	S 6.5	S 5.1	W 5.1
1 pm	WSW 5.9	N 5.7	S 7.2	SSW 7.4	SSW 6.1	N 5.8	SSE 5.7	S 5.2	S 5.9	S 6.6	S 5.2	SE 5.5
2	NNW 6.1	N 5.7	S 7.8	WNW 7.2	S 6.0	NNE 5.9	SE 5.7	NW 5.2	WNW 5.9	S 6.8	S 5.3	S 5.6
3	S 6.4	SSE 6.0	N 7.5	N 7.2	NNW 5.9	SSW 5.6	N 5.0	N 5.9	NNW 7.0	N 5.4	S 5.4	SW 5.4
4	SSE 6.4	ENE 6.0	ENE 7.6	E 6.2	SSE 5.9	SSE 5.6	S 5.5	ESE 5.1	N 5.4	SSE 6.1	S 5.3	SW 5.3
5	NW 5.6	ENE 5.6	NNW 6.9	NW 6.5	S 5.8	NNE 5.3	N 5.5	S 5.4	S 4.9	S 5.3	S 5.2	S 4.9
6	SSE 5.4	N 4.5	E 6.2	SE 6.2	SE 5.8	WSW 5.0	N 5.4	WNW 5.0	WNW 4.5	W 4.5	SSW 5.0	SW 4.7
7	S 5.6	S 4.4	NW 5.4	S 5.2	SSW 5.4	S 4.5	NW 4.9	NW 4.2	E 4.3	ESE 4.3	N 5.0	N 4.7
8	S 5.5	NNW 4.3	S 4.9	S 5.2	W 5.0	S 4.0	S 4.3	S 4.5	NW 4.0	S 4.2	S 5.0	NNW 4.7
9	SSW 5.3	S 4.2	S 4.9	WSW 5.0	NNE 4.9	N 3.8	N 4.2	E 4.4	SE 3.8	NNW 4.1	S 5.0	S 4.5
10	NW 5.0	S 4.1	SSE 4.4	SSE 4.6	ESE 4.4	ESE 3.5	SE 3.6	E 4.1	WNW 3.6	WNW 4.3	NNW 4.8	SSW 4.5
11 pm	SSE 4.9	NW 4.1	N 4.7	NNW 4.4	SSE 4.3	SSE 3.5	NW 3.5	SE 3.7	ESE 3.5	N 4.5	ENE 4.6	N 4.7
12 mid	SE 4.6	E 3.7	WNW 4.4	SSE 4.4	S 4.1	E 3.4	ENE 3.4	WSW 3.4	WNW 3.4	WNW 4.7	W 4.4	W 4.7

| 0-5 | 5.1-9 | 9.1-12 | >12 |

Mean City Center Wind Conditions, direction/mph

6 AIR MOVEMENT PRINCIPLES

Technique 6 uses data from Techniques 4 and 5.

7 SITE MICROCLIMATES

Technique 7 uses data from Techniques 1, 2, 4, and 5.

8 SKY COVER

	J	F	M	A	M	J	J	A	S	O	N	D
1 am	4.9	5.3	6.5	5.9	5.8	5.9	4.8	5.0	4.3	3.7	6.0	7.0
2	5.3	5.1	6.9	5.6	5.9	4.8	4.7	4.8	4.5	4.0	5.7	7.4
3	5.8	5.0	7.4	5.5	5.7	5.1	4.8	4.6	4.7	4.2	5.3	7.1
4	6.3	5.4	7.2	5.2	6.2	5.6	4.7	4.4	5.1	4.2	5.4	7.0
5	6.2	5.1	6.6	5.8	6.5	5.9	4.8	4.3	5.4	4.1	5.5	6.3
6	6.0	5.5	6.8	6.0	6.9	6.5	4.7	4.6	5.7	4.2	5.7	6.5
7	5.8	5.9	7.4	6.1	6.8	6.4	5.0	4.9	5.9	4.7	6.1	6.5
8	5.6	6.4	6.5	6.1	6.6	6.2	5.1	4.7	5.8	5.3	6.3	7.0
9	5.7	5.8	6.4	6.4	6.1	5.1	5.4	5.1	6.0	5.8	6.7	6.8
10	6.0	5.9	6.5	6.6	6.4	6.0	5.5	4.9	6.0	5.8	7.0	6.8
11 am	6.1	6.1	6.8	6.8	6.4	5.9	5.5	5.1	6.1	5.9	7.2	6.9
12 noon	6.4	5.9	6.7	6.7	6.3	5.8	5.6	6.0	6.1	5.9	7.5	6.9
1 pm	5.9	6.5	7.0	7.1	6.5	6.2	5.7	5.6	6.1	6.0	7.4	6.8
2	6.1	6.6	6.9	7.3	6.6	6.4	5.7	5.7	5.9	6.1	7.4	6.6
3	5.6	6.2	6.9	7.3	6.7	6.8	5.9	5.7	5.7	6.2	7.3	6.6
4	5.6	6.0	6.7	7.0	6.6	6.6	5.4	5.7	5.7	5.7	7.2	6.4
5	5.8	6.0	7.4	7.3	6.4	4.7	5.6	5.8	5.8	5.3	7.1	6.1
6	5.1	5.8	7.4	7.4	6.4	6.2	4.2	5.2	5.8	4.8	7.1	6.3
7	5.1	5.5	7.0	6.7	6.2	5.9	4.3	5.0	5.3	4.7	6.8	6.3
8	4.8	5.4	7.0	6.3	5.9	5.4	4.5	4.7	4.8	4.7	6.5	6.2
9	4.7	6.1	6.4	5.9	5.6	5.0	4.5	4.8	4.5	4.6	6.2	6.3
10	4.8	6.1	6.2	5.9	5.7	4.8	4.6	4.8	4.4	4.4	6.3	6.7
11 pm	4.6	6.6	5.9	5.5	5.9	4.5	4.6	4.9	4.2	4.0	6.3	7.2
12 mid	4.7	5.8	6.5	5.1	6.0	4.2	4.7	5.1	4.1	3.8	6.4	6.9

0-2	2.1-5	5.1-8	8.1-10
clear	scattered	broken	overcast

Mean Hourly Sky Cover, tenths of sky covered

9 DAYLIGHT AVAILABILITY

	J	F	M	A	M	J	J	A	S	O	N	D
1 am	0	0	0	0	0	0	0	0	0	0	0	0
2	0	0	0	0	0	0	0	0	0	0	0	0
3	0	0	0	0	0	0	0	0	0	0	0	0
4	0	0	0	0	0	0	0	0	0	0	0	0
5	0	0	0	0	0	0	0	0	0	0	0	0
6	0	0	0	89	471	697	477	179	0	0	0	0
7	0	0	145	787	1607	1889	1691	1087	453	100	0	0
8	0	221	999	1975	3186	3368	3234	2572	1635	834	211	0
9	551	1165	2282	3429	4489	4780	4601	3976	2777	1897	961	532
10	1577	2423	3465	4588	5970	6113	6111	5263	4244	3088	1939	1375
11 am	2598	3658	4644	5313	6573	7480	7094	6271	5194	3950	2645	2160
12 noon	3106	4272	5305	5687	7261	7783	7052	6623	5698	4364	2970	2524
1 pm	3394	4590	5468	5836	7187	8146	7509	6946	5778	4479	2930	2551
2	3101	4362	5083	5449	6840	7366	7060	6474	5631	3956	2610	2297
3	2309	3583	4274	4812	5834	5748	6251	5704	4665	2912	1766	1657
4	1352	2418	3224	3866	4697	5167	5592	4724	3554	1974	988	828
5	386	1139	1807	2532	3522	3939	4179	3248	2127	832	211	49
6	0	192	651	1225	2013	2493	2713	1841	724	102	0	0
7	0	0	37	293	806	1224	1209	608	73	0	0	0
8	0	0	0	0	97	269	233	24	0	0	0	0
9	0	0	0	0	0	0	0	0	0	0	0	0
10	0	0	0	0	0	0	0	0	0	0	0	0
11 pm	0	0	0	0	0	0	0	0	0	0	0	0
12 mid	0	0	0	0	0	0	0	0	0	0	0	0

>250	251-1000	1001-2000	>2000

Mean Hourly Global Horizontal Illuminance, foot-candles

HOUR	J	F	M	A	M	J	J	A	S	O	N	D	Ann
CLR DAYS 0/8-2/8	8	8	7	7	7	7	10	10	10	10	5	6	95
PT CD DAYS 3/8-6/8	7	7	7	8	9	10	12	11	8	7	6	6	101
OVR DAYS 7/8-8/8	15	14	17	15	15	12	9	10	12	14	18	18	169
% CLR	27	28	23	23	23	24	32	32	33	32	17	20	26
% PT CD	23	24	23	27	29	34	39	35	27	23	21	20	28
% OVR	50	48	55	50	48	41	29	32	40	45	62	60	46

Sky Cover Monthly Normals
Eighths of Sky covered; % days for each sky condition.

		June					December				
		9 am	11 am	1 pm	3 pm	5 pm	9 am	11 am	1 pm	3 pm	5 pm
HORIZ	M. Clear	46	80	97	94	70	7	30	38	23	0
	M. Cloudy	29	53	67	66	48	5	19	24	15	0
NORTH	M. Clear	16	15	16	17	15	3	8	9	7	0
	M. Cloudy	13	17	18	18	16	2	8	10	6	0
EAST	M. Clear	79	74	35	17	15	25	37	9	7	0
	M. Cloudy	35	43	28	18	15	7	16	10	6	0
SOUTH	M. Clear	11	36	54	51	28	22	73	87	60	0
	M. Cloudy	11	26	39	37	22	6	25	30	18	0
WEST	M. Clear	11	15	16	48	78	3	8	16	42	0
	M. Cloudy	11	17	18	36	46	2	8	12	14	0
M. Clear	(% hrs)	39	38	33	31	34	26	27	27	29	33

Average Incident Illuminance (klux-hr)

10 DAYLIGHT OBSTRUCTIONS

Overcast Dot Charts are in Technique 10. For Clear Sky Dot Charts, see Appendix B.

11 BIOCLIMATIC CHART

	Temperature (°F)					Rel Humidity (percent)		Wind (kts)			Sky Cvr	Mean # days w/ temp (°F)			
	means			extreme				prevail		max		max	max	min	min
	max	min	ave	max	min	6 am	3 pm	dir	spd	gst		90	70	32	10
Jan	21	4	13	57	-34	75	65	NW	12	58	OVR	0	0	31	17
Feb	27	9	18	60	-28	76	62	NW	12	48	OVR	0	0	27	12
Mar	39	22	31	83	-32	77	58	NW	11	52	OVR	0	1	25	3
Apr	56	36	46	95	2	75	48	NW	12	53	OVR	#	7	11	#
May	69	48	59	96	18	75	47	SE	9	58	OVR	1	20	1	0
Jun	78	58	68	102	34	79	50	SE	9	57	OVR	3	28	0	0
Jul	83	63	73	105	43	82	50	S	9	55	SCT	6	31	0	0
Aug	81	61	71	102	39	84	52	SE	8	62	CLR	4	30	0	0
Sep	71	50	61	98	26	85	53	S	10	47	OVR	1	22	#	0
Oct	59	40	50	89	15	81	52	NW	12	46	OVR	0	10	7	0
Nov	40	25	33	74	-17	80	63	NW	12	57	OVR	0	1	23	2
Dec	26	11	19	63	-29	79	68	NW	11	42	OVR	0	0	30	11
Ann	54	36	45	105	-34	79	56	NW	11	62	OVR	15	151	156	44

Climatic Normals, 1945-1990

16 WINDOW SOLAR GAIN

For insolation data used in this technique, see radiation data for Technique 3.

	Jan	Feb	Mar	Apr	May	Jun	Jul	Aug	Sep	Oct	Nov	Dec	Ann
% Poss Sun	53	59	57	58	61	66	72	69	62	55	39	42	58

Average Percentage of Possible Sunshine, %

18 BUILDING BIOCLIMATIC CHART

See temperature and humidity data for Technique 11.

20 SHADING CALENDAR

	J	F	M	A	M	J	J	A	S	O	N	D
1 am	8.1	15.3	28.9	42.8	54.6	61.9	66.5	65.7	56.3	43.8	31.0	16.8
2	8.1	14.5	28.2	42.3	53.9	61.1	65.7	64.9	55.7	43.2	30.5	16.5
3	7.9	13.7	28.2	41.8	53.2	60.3	64.9	63.9	55.0	42.5	30.1	15.9
4	7.6	13.4	28.0	40.9	53.0	60.6	64.8	63.2	54.5	41.8	29.9	15.6
5	7.5	13.5	27.1	40.0	52.8	61.1	64.7	62.8	54.1	41.1	29.7	14.9
6	7.2	12.8	27.1	40.2	52.6	61.4	64.7	63.2	53.6	40.4	29.5	14.6
7	7.3	12.1	27.4	42.1	55.7	64.2	66.9	65.8	55.9	42.5	30.3	14.5
8	7.3	12.1	29.3	44.7	58.7	67.3	69.3	68.5	58.2	44.6	31.1	14.2
9	8.0	13.2	31.1	47.7	61.7	69.9	71.6	71.3	60.5	46.7	32.0	15.1
10	9.7	15.3	33.3	49.9	63.7	71.8	73.3	73.8	62.6	49.1	33.6	16.5
11	11.9	17.7	35.3	51.4	65.7	73.8	75.1	75.6	64.7	47.5	35.3	18.2
12 noon	13.7	19.8	36.8	52.9	67.6	75.8	76.8	76.7	66.8	54.0	36.9	19.7
1 pm	15.4	21.5	37.6	54.2	68.3	76.3	77.6	77.9	67.8	54.9	37.6	20.8
2	16.2	22.6	38.4	54.9	68.9	76.7	78.3	78.2	68.7	55.8	38.2	21.4
3	16.3	23.2	38.5	55.7	69.5	77.2	79.1	78.2	69.7	56.8	38.9	21.4
4	15.8	23.2	38.5	55.6	68.7	76.6	78.6	78.0	68.5	54.9	37.6	20.6
5	14.5	22.5	37.9	54.7	67.8	76.1	78.2	77.4	67.2	52.9	36.3	19.3
6	13.0	21.1	36.5	53.3	67.0	75.5	77.8	76.1	65.9	51.1	35.0	18.6
7	12.1	20.2	34.6	50.9	64.5	73.0	75.4	73.9	63.8	49.5	34.3	17.8
8	11.6	19.5	33.6	48.4	62.1	70.6	73.1	71.7	62.0	48.0	33.5	17.3
9	10.9	18.8	32.6	46.9	59.7	68.2	70.7	70.2	59.6	46.5	32.7	17.0
10	10.0	18.5	31.6	45.5	58.3	66.5	69.5	68.9	58.6	45.6	32.2	16.8
11 pm	9.5	17.6	30.8	44.4	57.0	64.8	68.3	67.7	57.5	44.8	31.7	16.2
12 mid	9.2	16.9	30.4	43.7	55.7	63.1	67.1	66.4	56.5	43.9	31.2	15.6

Legend: Cold <32 | Cool 32-64.9 | Comfort 65-79.9 | Hot ≥80

Mean Hourly Temperature, °F
Shading for Outdoor Rooms, Balance Point = 65°F (18.3°C)

	J	F	M	A	M	J	J	A	S	O	N	D
1 am	8.1	15.3	28.9	42.8	54.6	61.9	66.5	65.7	56.3	43.8	31.0	16.8
2	8.1	14.5	28.2	42.3	53.9	61.1	65.7	64.9	55.7	43.2	30.5	16.5
3	7.9	13.7	28.2	41.8	53.2	60.3	64.9	63.9	55.0	42.5	30.1	15.9
4	7.6	13.4	28.0	40.9	53.0	60.6	64.8	63.2	54.5	41.8	29.9	15.6
5	7.5	13.5	27.1	40.0	52.8	61.1	64.7	62.8	54.1	41.1	29.7	14.9
6	7.2	12.8	27.1	40.2	52.6	61.4	64.7	63.2	53.6	40.4	29.5	14.6
7	7.3	12.1	27.4	42.1	55.7	64.2	66.9	65.8	55.9	42.5	30.3	14.5
8	7.3	12.1	29.3	44.7	58.7	67.3	69.3	68.5	58.2	44.6	31.1	14.2
9	8.0	13.2	31.1	47.7	61.7	69.9	71.6	71.3	60.5	46.7	32.0	15.1
10	9.7	15.3	33.3	49.9	63.7	71.8	73.3	73.8	62.6	49.1	33.6	16.5
11	11.9	17.7	35.3	51.4	65.7	73.8	75.1	75.6	64.7	47.5	35.3	18.2
12 noon	13.7	19.8	36.8	52.9	67.6	75.8	76.8	76.7	66.8	54.0	36.9	19.7
1 pm	15.4	21.5	37.6	54.2	68.3	76.3	77.6	77.9	67.8	54.9	37.6	20.8
2	16.2	22.6	38.4	54.9	68.9	76.7	78.3	78.2	68.7	55.8	38.2	21.4
3	16.3	23.2	38.5	55.7	69.5	77.2	79.1	78.2	69.7	56.8	38.9	21.4
4	15.8	23.2	38.5	55.6	68.7	76.6	78.6	78.0	68.5	54.9	37.6	20.6
5	14.5	22.5	37.9	54.7	67.8	76.1	78.2	77.4	67.2	52.9	36.3	19.3
6	13.0	21.1	36.5	53.3	67.0	75.5	77.8	76.1	65.9	51.1	35.0	18.6
7	12.1	20.2	34.6	50.9	64.5	73.0	75.4	73.9	63.8	49.5	34.3	17.8
8	11.6	19.5	33.6	48.4	62.1	70.6	73.1	71.7	62.0	48.0	33.5	17.3
9	10.9	18.8	32.6	46.9	59.7	68.2	70.7	70.2	59.6	46.5	32.7	17.0
10	10.0	18.5	31.6	45.5	58.3	66.5	69.5	68.9	58.6	45.6	32.2	16.8
11 pm	9.5	17.6	30.8	44.4	57.0	64.8	68.3	67.7	57.5	44.8	31.7	16.2
12 mid	9.2	16.9	30.4	43.7	55.7	63.1	67.1	66.4	56.5	43.9	31.2	15.6

Legend: Cold <32 | Cool 32-55 | Comfort 55-69.9 | Hot ≥70

Mean Hourly Temperature, °F
Shading for Balance Point = 55°F (12.8°C)

	J	F	M	A	M	J	J	A	S	O	N	D
1 am	8.1	15.3	28.9	42.8	54.6	61.9	66.5	65.7	56.3	43.8	31.0	16.8
2	8.1	14.5	28.2	42.3	53.9	61.1	65.7	64.9	55.7	43.2	30.5	16.5
3	7.9	13.7	28.2	41.8	53.2	60.3	64.9	63.9	55.0	42.5	30.1	15.9
4	7.6	13.4	28.0	40.9	53.0	60.6	64.8	63.2	54.5	41.8	29.9	15.6
5	7.5	13.5	27.1	40.0	52.8	61.1	64.7	62.8	54.1	41.1	29.7	14.9
6	7.2	12.8	27.1	40.2	52.6	61.4	64.7	63.2	53.6	40.4	29.5	14.6
7	7.3	12.1	27.4	42.1	55.7	64.2	66.9	65.8	55.9	42.5	30.3	14.5
8	7.3	12.1	29.3	44.7	58.7	67.3	69.3	68.5	58.2	44.6	31.1	14.2
9	8.0	13.2	31.1	47.7	61.7	69.9	71.6	71.3	60.5	46.7	32.0	15.1
10	9.7	15.3	33.3	49.9	63.7	71.8	73.3	73.8	62.6	49.1	33.6	16.5
11	11.9	17.7	35.3	51.4	65.7	73.8	75.1	75.6	64.7	47.5	35.3	18.2
12 noon	13.7	19.8	36.8	52.9	67.6	75.8	76.8	76.7	66.8	54.0	36.9	19.7
1 pm	15.4	21.5	37.6	54.2	68.3	76.3	77.6	77.9	67.8	54.9	37.6	20.8
2	16.2	22.6	38.4	54.9	68.9	76.7	78.3	78.2	68.7	55.8	38.2	21.4
3	16.3	23.2	38.5	55.7	69.5	77.2	79.1	78.2	69.7	56.8	38.9	21.4
4	15.8	23.2	38.5	55.6	68.7	76.6	78.6	78.0	68.5	54.9	37.6	20.6
5	14.5	22.5	37.9	54.7	67.8	76.1	78.2	77.4	67.2	52.9	36.3	19.3
6	13.0	21.1	36.5	53.3	67.0	75.5	77.8	76.1	65.9	51.1	35.0	18.6
7	12.1	20.2	34.6	50.9	64.5	73.0	75.4	73.9	63.8	49.5	34.3	17.8
8	11.6	19.5	33.6	48.4	62.1	70.6	73.1	71.7	62.0	48.0	33.5	17.3
9	10.9	18.8	32.6	46.9	59.7	68.2	70.7	70.2	59.6	46.5	32.7	17.0
10	10.0	18.5	31.6	45.5	58.3	66.5	69.5	68.9	58.6	45.6	32.2	16.8
11 pm	9.5	17.6	30.8	44.4	57.0	64.8	68.3	67.7	57.5	44.8	31.7	16.2
12 mid	9.2	16.9	30.4	43.7	55.7	63.1	67.1	66.4	56.5	43.9	31.2	15.6

Legend: Cold <32 | Cool 32-44.9 | Comfort 45-59.9 | Hot ≥60

Mean Hourly Temperature, °F
Shading for Balance Point = 45°F (7.2°C)

21 TOTAL HEAT GAINS AND TOTAL HEAT LOSSES

• Latitude = 45 °N
• Summer Design Temp/Coincident Wet-Bulb Temp, °F (°C)

1.0%	88/71 (31/22)
2.0%	85/70 (29/21)

• Winter Design Temperature, °F (°C)

99.6%	-16 (-23)
99%	-11 (-24)

• Annual Heating Degree Days 65 °F (18 °C)   4758 (2643)
• Annual Cooling Degree Days 65 °F (18 °C)   1534 (852)

23 BALANCE POINT PROFILES

For temperature data used in Step 2, see data for Technique 11.

48° LATITUDE

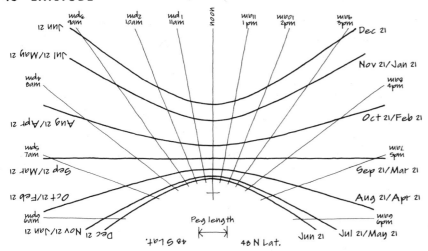

Sundial, 48° Latitude

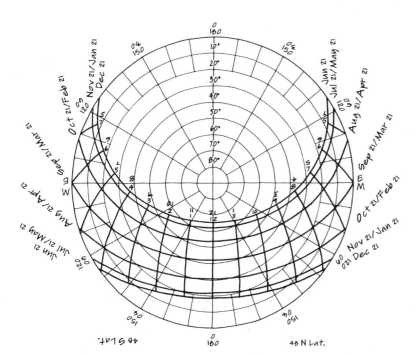

Sun Path Diagram, 48° Latitude

52° LATITUDE

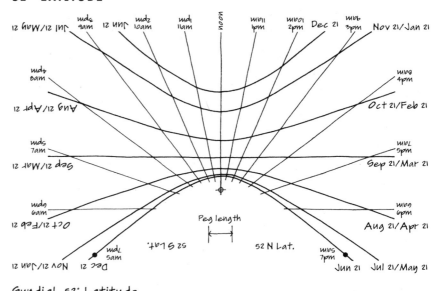

Sundial, 52° Latitude

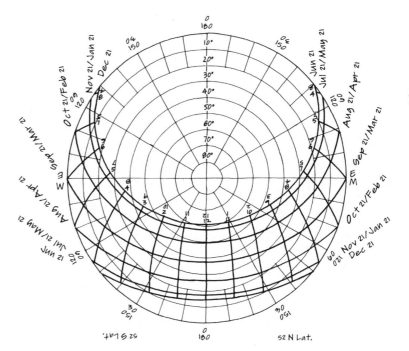

Sun Path Diagram, 52° Latitude

56° LATITUDE

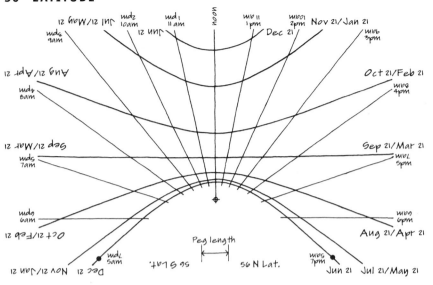

Sundial, 56° Latitude

60° LATITUDE

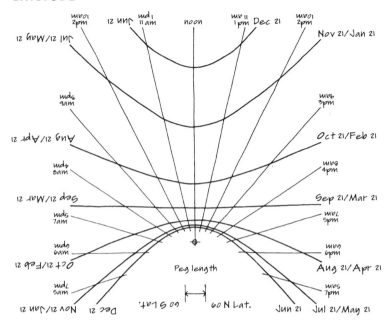

Sundial, 60° Latitude

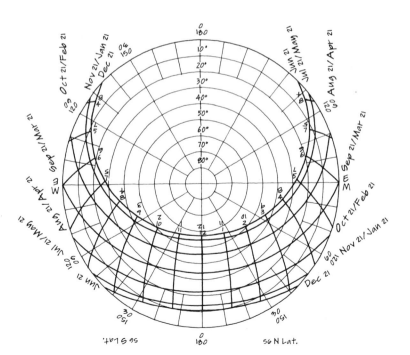

Sun Path Diagram, 56° Latitude

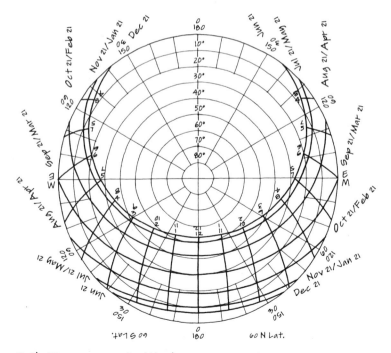

Sun Path Diagram, 60° Latitude

64° LATITUDE

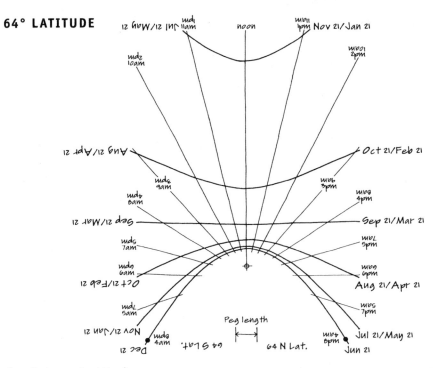

Sundial, 64° Latitude

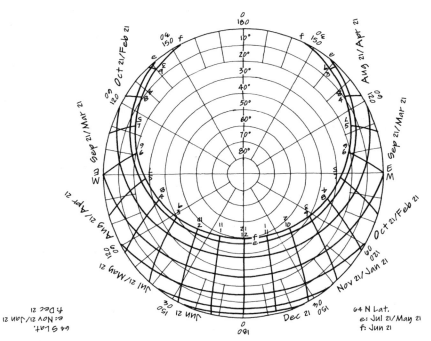

Sun Path Diagram, 64° Latitude

68° LATITUDE

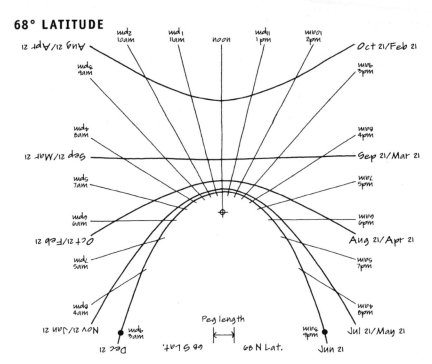

Sundial, 68° Latitude

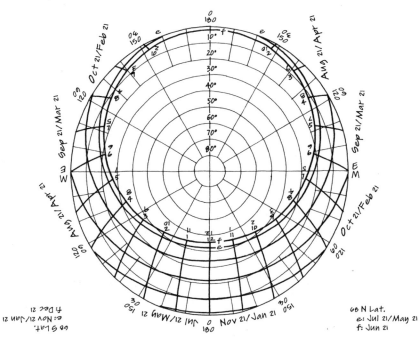

Sun Path Diagram, 68° Latitude

72° LATITUDE

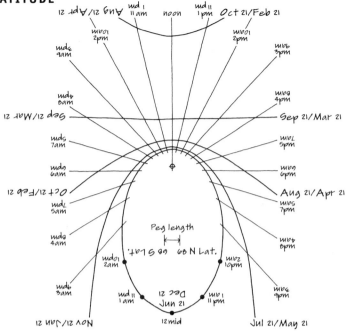

Sundial, 72° Latitude

76° LATITUDE

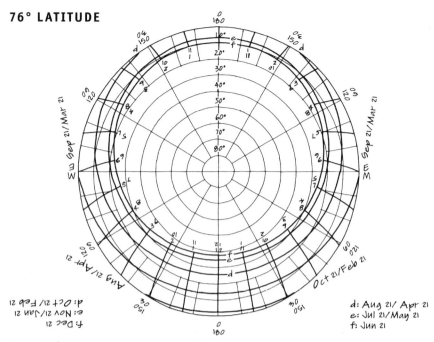

d: Aug 21/ Apr 21
e: Jul 21/May 21
f: Jun 21

f: Dec 21
e: Nov 21/Jan 21
d: Oct 21/ Feb 21

Sun Path Diagram, 76° Latitude

80° LATITUDE

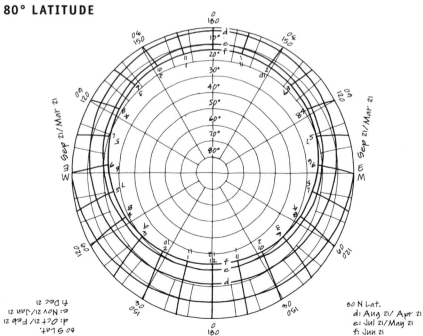

80 N Lat.
d: Aug 21/ Apr 21
e: Jul 21/May 21
f: Jun 21

f: Dec 21
e: Nov 21/Jan 21
d: Oct 21/ Feb 21

Sun Path Diagram, 80° Latitude

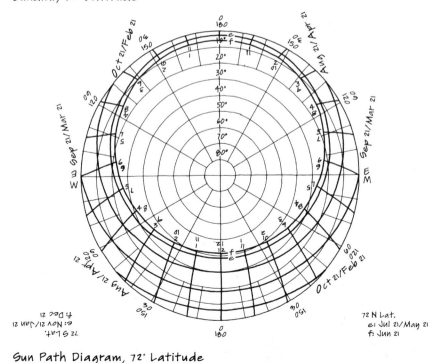

72 N Lat.
e: Jul 21/May 21
f: Jun 21

72 S Lat.
e: Nov 21/Jan 21
f: Dec 21

Sun Path Diagram, 72° Latitude

84° LATITUDE

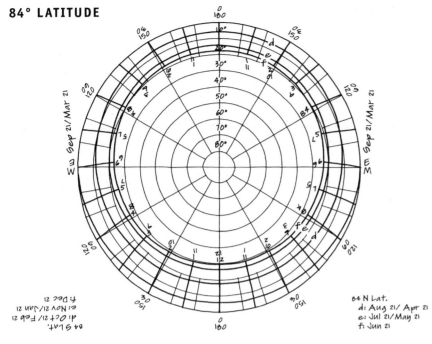

84 N Lat.
d: Oct 21/ Feb 21
e: Nov 21/Jan 21
f: Dec 21

Sun Path Diagram, 84° Latitude

90° LATITUDE

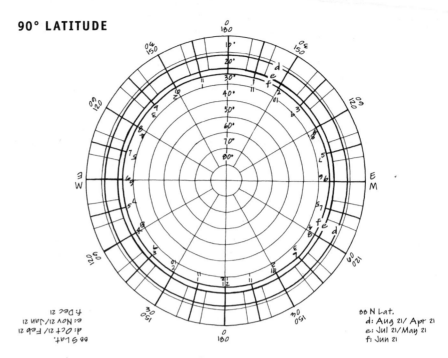

88 N Lat.
d: Oct 21/ Feb 21
e: Nov 21/Jan 21
f: Dec 21

Sun Path Diagram, 90° Latitude

88° LATITUDE

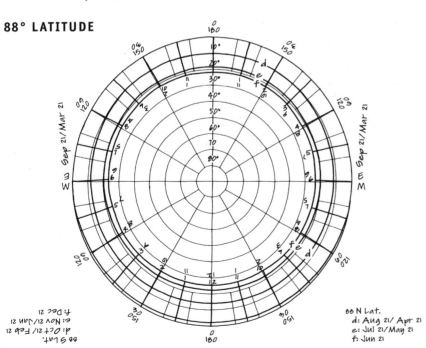

88 N Lat.
d: Oct 21/ Feb 21
e: Nov 21/Jan 21
f: Dec 21

Sun Path Diagram, 88° Latitude

Appendix B
Additional Climate Data

3 SOLAR RADIATION: Heating Degree Days Maps

Annual Heating Degree Days for United States, base 65 °F
Source: based on NOAA (1983).

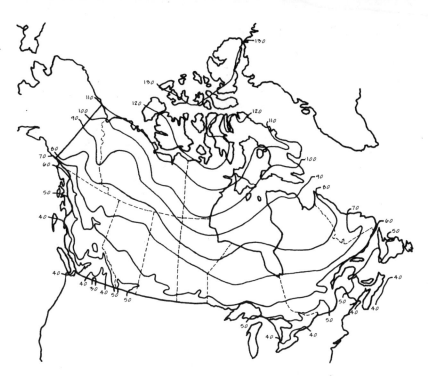

Annual Heating Degree Days for Canada, base 18 °C
Source: based on Environment Canada (1988).

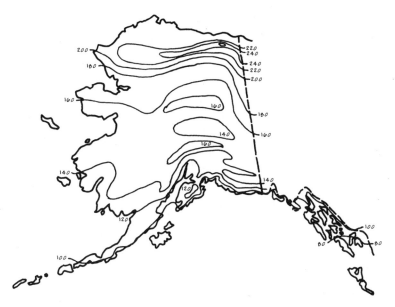

Annual Heating Degree Days for Alsaka, base 65 °F
Source: based on NOAA (1983).

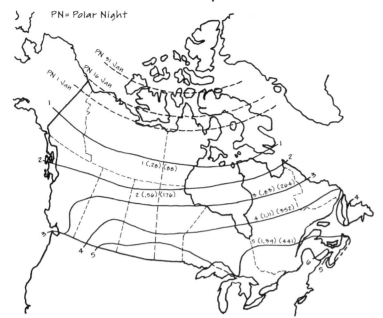

PN = Polar Night

Canada, January: Mean Daily Solar Radiation, Horizontal Surface
megajoules/m², day (kWh/m², day) (Btu/ft², day)

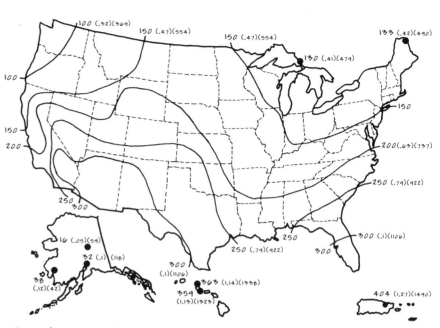

United States, Jan: Mean Daily Solar Radiation, Horiz. Surface
Langleys (kWh/m², day) (Btu/ft², day)

CANADA, March: Mean Daily Solar Radiation, Horizontal Surface
megajoules/m², day (kWh/m², day) (Btu/ft², day)

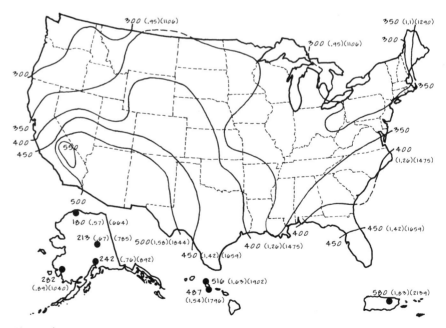

United States, Mar: Mean Daily Solar Radiation, Horiz. Surface
Langleys (kWh/m², day) (Btu/ft², day)

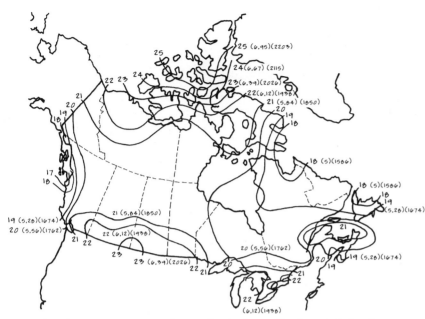

Canada, Jun: Mean Daily Solar Radiation, Horizontal Surface
megajoules/m², day (kWh/m², day) (Btu/ft², day)

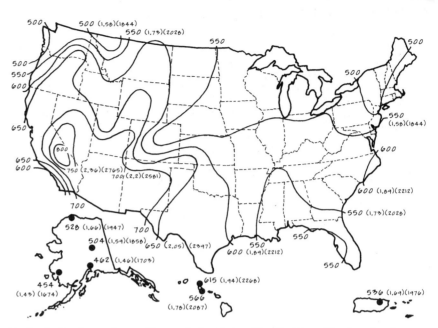

United States, Jun: Mean Daily Solar Radiation, Horiz. Surface
Langleys (kWh/m², day) (Btu/ft², day)

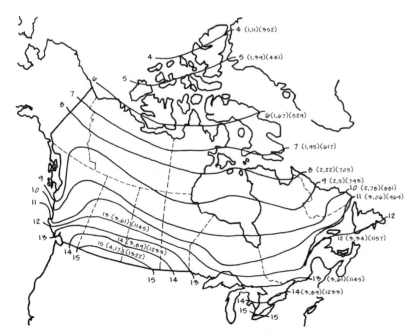

Canada, Sep: Mean Daily Solar Radiation, Horizontal Surface
megajoules/m², day (kWh/m², day) (Btu/ft², day)

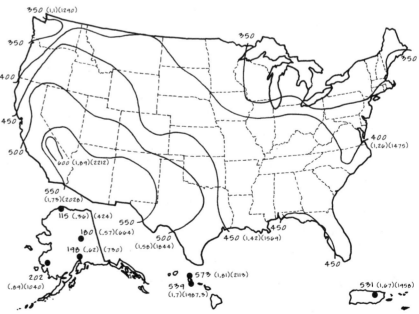

United States, Sep: Mean Daily Solar Radiation, Horiz. Surface
Langleys (kWh/m², day) (Btu/ft², day)

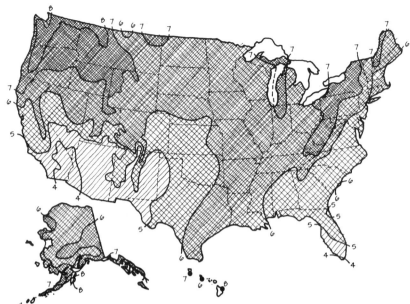

Mean Sky Cover for the United States, March

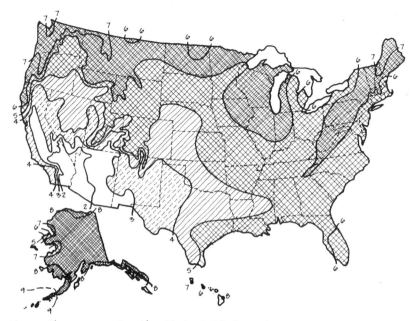

Mean Sky Cover for the United States, June

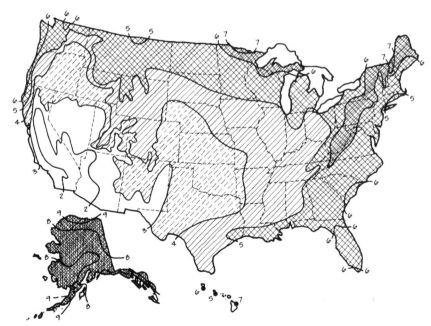

Mean Sky Cover for the United States, September
Adapted from NOAA (1983).

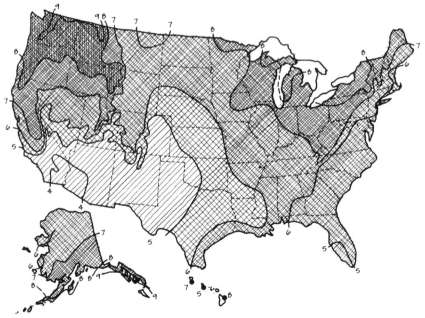

Mean Sky Cover for the United States, December

9 DAYLIGHT AVAILABILITY: Clear Sky Data

The tabled values for clear sky luminance exclude the direct sun, so in some cases they will be lower than the total illuminance of the localized data from Marion and Wilcox (1995). Values in the tables are excerpted from Kaufman (1984, pp. 7-7 to 7-9). Multiply klux by 92.9 to get foot-candles.

Latitude	Winter Solstice					Spring and Fall Equinox					Summer Solstice				
	8am	10am	12	2pm	4pm	8am	10am	12	2pm	4pm	8am	10am	12	2pm	4pm
North															
30	7	8	8	8	7	11	11	11	11	11	16	14	13	14	16
34	6	8	8	8	6	11	11	10	11	11	16	14	13	14	16
38	5	7	7	7	5	11	10	10	10	11	15	13	12	13	15
42	5	7	7	7	5	10	10	10	10	10	15	13	12	13	15
46	3	6	6	6	3	10	9	9	9	10	14	12	12	12	14
50	0	5	5	5	0	9	9	9	9	9	14	12	11	12	14
South															
30	16	25	28	25	16	16	21	22	21	16	14	15	15	15	14
34	15	25	28	25	15	17	22	24	22	17	14	16	16	16	14
38	14	24	28	24	14	17	23	25	23	17	14	17	17	17	14
42	12	23	27	23	12	17	23	26	23	17	15	18	19	18	15
46	9	22	26	22	9	17	24	27	24	17	15	19	20	19	15
50	0	21	25	21	0	17	24	27	24	17	16	20	21	20	16
East															
30	19	20	15	10	5	27	22	15	11	7	27	22	14	11	8
34	18	19	14	10	5	26	22	15	11	7	28	22	14	11	8
38	16	19	14	9	4	26	22	15	11	7	28	22	14	11	8
42	14	18	14	9	4	25	22	15	10	7	28	22	14	11	8
46	11	17	13	8	2	25	22	15	10	6	28	22	14	11	8
50	0	15	12	7	0	24	21	15	10	6	27	22	15	11	8
West															
30	5	10	15	20	19	7	11	15	22	27	8	11	14	22	27
34	5	10	14	19	18	7	11	15	22	26	8	11	14	22	28
38	4	9	14	19	16	7	11	15	22	26	8	11	14	22	28
42	4	9	14	18	14	7	10	15	22	25	8	11	14	22	28
46	3	8	13	17	11	6	10	15	22	25	8	11	14	22	28
50	0	7	12	15	0	6	10	15	21	24	8	11	15	22	27

Clear Sky Illuminance Data: Equivalent Sky Exitance (klux)
Clear days (average values, direct sun excluded).

Latitude	Winter Solstice			Spring and Fall Equinox			Summer Solstice		
	8am/4pm	10am/2pm	12	8am/4pm	10am/2pm	12	8am/4pm	10am/2pm	12
Horizontal: Diffuse/Total									
30	8/17	12/54	13/68	11/45	14/86	15/102	13/65	15/101	16/115
34	7/12	11/46	12/60	11/43	14/82	15/97	13/65	15/101	16/114
38	6/9	10/39	12/53	11/40	14/78	15/92	13/66	15/99	16/112
42	5/6	10/32	11/44	10/37	13/72	14/85	13/66	15/98	16/110
46	4/4	9/25	10/35	10/34	13/67	14/79	13/66	15/95	16/107
50	0/0	8/18	9/27	10/31	12/61	13/72	13/65	15/93	15/102

Clear Sky Illuminance Data: External Horizontal Sky Illuminance (klux)
Clear days (average values, left value is diffuse, right value is total of direct + diffuse).

10 DAYLIGHT OBSTRUCTIONS: Dot Charts

Charts are redrawn from Moore (1991, *Concepts and Practice of Architectural Daylighting,* New York: Van Nostrand Reinhold, pp. 194–196 and 234–241), by permission. Moore also covers detailed instructions on use and theory.

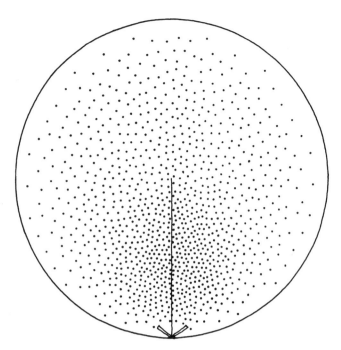

Clear Sky, 15° Solar Altitude, Sky Component

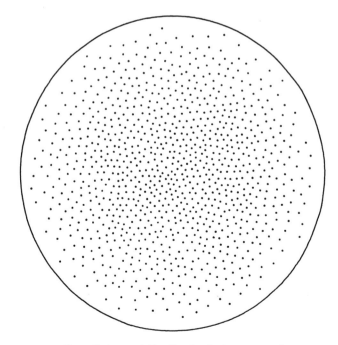

Clear Sky, External Reflected Component

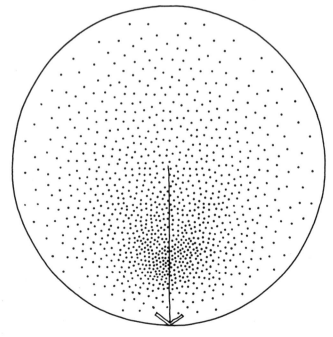

Clear Sky, 30° Solar Altitude, Sky Component

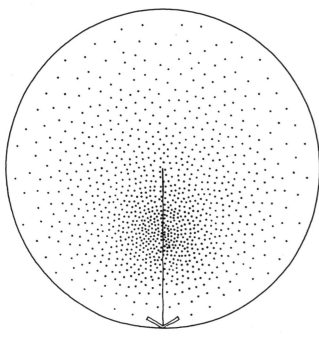

Clear Sky, 45° Solar Altitude, Sky Component

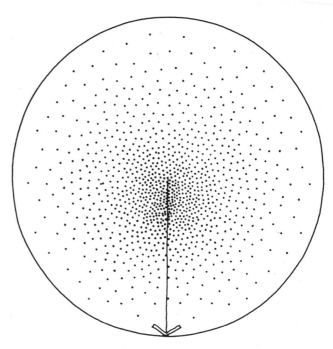

Clear Sky, 75° Solar Altitude, Sky Component

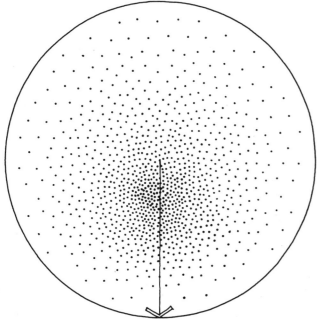

Clear Sky, 60° Solar Altitude, Sky Component

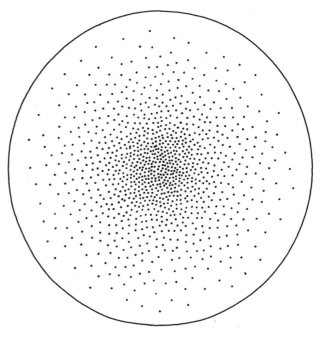

Clear Sky, 90° Solar Altitude, Sky Component

Contours are shown in 30-day increments for the United States and 15-day increments for Canada. Local microclimates may vary significantly, and the map should be used only as a general guide. More accurate information can be obtained from the local agricultural extension office in the building's county or from local gardeners. For detailed maps, see NOAA (1988) for sites in the United States or Department of the Interior (1974, p. 53) for sites in Canada. Maps shown are based on these sources.

Dates of First Frost in the Fall, 50% chance of earlier frost

Dates of First Frost in the Fall, 10% chance of earlier frost

To estimate the ground temperature at a given depth on the typical hottest day of summer:

1) Find the Mean Earth Temperature for the building's climate from the map for the contiguous United States or the Alaska map. The mean earth temperature for a given location is approximately equal to the mean annual air temperature.

2) Find the annual Surface Temperature Amplitude from one of the maps of amplitude. This is how much the air temperature varies above and below the mean annual temperature.

3) Plot curves for the climate's temperature amplitude and the site's soil type on the chart for **Ground Temperature Amplitude for Summer Extreme.** An example with a 20 °F (11 °C) amplitude is given. Mark the amplitude in the positive and negative directions along the ground surface line (zero depth). Then sketch a curve from those two points to the point of zero amplitude. The depth of zero amplitude in midsummer varies with the amount of soil moisture because damp soil is more heat conductive than dry soil. The graph shows zero amplitude points for wet soil at 14 ft (4.3 m), medium soil at 12 ft (3.7 m) and dry soil at 10 ft (3.1 m).

4) For the depth of the building floor below grade or for the depth of the walls (measured from grade to the midpoint between floor and ceiling), find on the graph the amplitude from the curve already sketched.

5) Add that amplitude to the annual mean earth temperature from the map in Step 1 to get the *summer ground temperature.*

6) The temperature difference, ΔT, between the inside air and the ground can then be calculated. In summer, if the ground temperature is not below the top of the comfort zone, then no cooling can occur.

For more on earth shelter design, see Carmody & Sterling (1985), Sterling et al. (1981), and Labs (1991, 1989, 1981, 1980).

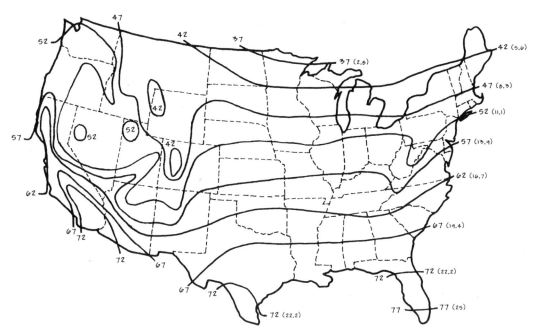

Contiguous United States Mean Earth Temperature, °F (°C) based on PNL (1998, p. 9).

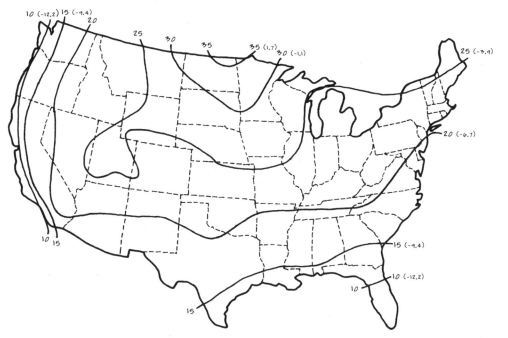

Contiguous United States Earth Surface Temperature Amplitude, °F (°C) based on PNL (1998, p. 9).

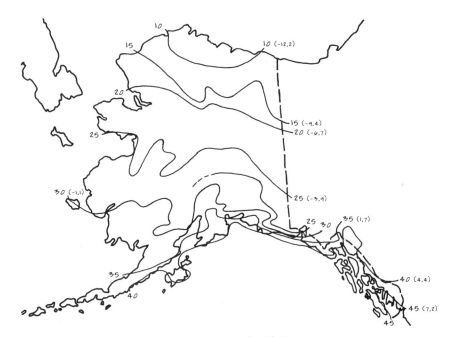

Alaska Mean Annual Temperature, °F (°C)
adapted from Hartman & Johnson (1984, p. 77).

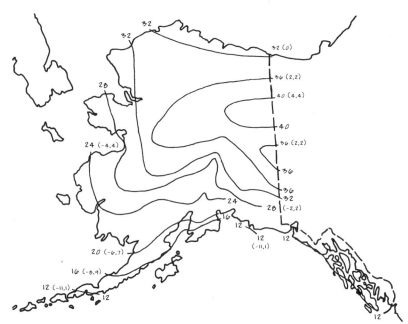

Alaska Earth Surface Temperature Amplitude, °F (°C)
adapted from Hartman & Johnson (1984, p. 77).

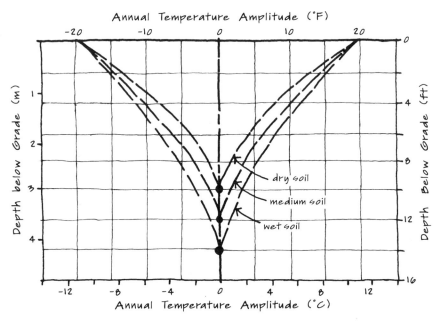

Ground Temperature Amplitude for Summer Extreme
Method: based on formulas from Watson & Labs (1983, pp. 72-74).

Appendix C
Abbreviations and Unit Conversions

ABBREVIATIONS USED IN TEXT

(°)	degrees	*ISMCS*	*International Station Meteorological Summary, CD-ROM*	RSI	m², K/W (SI units of thermal resistance)
ACH	air changes per hour			s	second
ASHRAE	American Society of Heating, Refrigeration and Air-conditioning Engineers	k	1000	SC	shading coefficient
		K	degrees Kelvin	SkC	sky component of daylight factor
Btu	British thermal units (energy)	kg	kilograms	SH	Southern Hemisphere
Btu/h	British thermal units/hour (power)	klux	kilolux (illuminance)	SHGC	solar heat gain coefficient
°C	degrees Celsius	kWh	kilowatt-hours	SHGF	solar heat gain factor
CE	catching efficiency (wind catchers)	L	liters	SI	standard international units
cfm	cubic feet per minute (air flow)	L/s	liters per second (air flow)	SLD	skin-load-dominated
cm	centimeters	lb	pounds	SRI	solar reflectance index
d	day	LCR	load collector ratio	SSIC	stress skin insulated core panels
DD	degree days	LSG	light-to-solar-gain ratio (of glazing)	SSF	solar savings fraction
DD65	degree days, base 65 °F	m	meters	T	temperature
DD18	degree days base 18 °C	min	minutes	ΔT	change in temperature
DF	daylight factor	mm	millimeters	TI	translucent insulation
ERC	external reflected component of DF	mph	miles per hour	TMY	typical meteorological year
°F	degrees Fahrenheit	m/s	meters per second	*U*	Btu/hr, F, ft² (I-P units of thermal conductance)
fc	foot-candles	MRT	mean radiant temperature		
fpm	feet per minute	*MEC*	*Model Energy Code*	*USI*	W/K, m² (SI units of thermal conductance)
ft	feet	MJ	megajoules (energy)	*v*	sky view angle or factor
gal	gallons	NCDC	National Climatic Data Center	VS	vertical surface
hr	hours	NFRC	National Fenestration Rating Council	VT	visible transmittance
HDD	heating degree days	NH	Northern Hemisphere	W	Watts
IC	indirect component of DF	NREL	National Renewable Energy Laboratory	Wh	Watt-hours
ILD	internal-load-dominated	PAF	power adjustment factor	WI	skylight well index
in	inches	PV	photovoltaic cells	yr	year
IRC	internal reflected component of DF	*R*	ft², F, hr/Btu (I-P units of thermal resistance)		
I-P	inch-pound units	RH	relative humidity		

UNIT CONVERSIONS FOR MEASURES USED IN TEXT

Variable	Multiply	By	To Get	Multiply	By	To Get
temperature	°F – 32	0.555	°C	°C	1.8	+ 32 = °F
temperature change,	°F	0.5556	°C	°C	1.8	°F
degree days	DD65 °F	0.5556	DD18.3 °C	DD18.3 °C	1.8	DD65 °F
wind speed	mph	0.447	m/s	m/s	2.237	mph
air velocity	fpm	0.00503	m/s	m/s	199	fpm
	ft/s	0.305	m/s	m/s	3.279	ft/s
air flow rate	cfm	0.02832	m3/h	m3/h	35.317	cfm
	cfm	0.472	l/s	l/s	2.119	cfm
air flow rate per floor area	cfm/ft^2	5.081	L/s per m^2	L/s per m^2	0.197	cfm/ft^2
length	ft	0.305	m	m	3.281	ft
	in	25.4	mm	mm	0.039	in
area	in^2	645.2	mm^2	mm^2	0.00155	in^2
	in^2	6.452	cm^2	cm^2	0.155	in^2
	ft^2	0.0929	m^2	m^2	10.76	ft^2
area x 1000	k-ft^2	0.0929	k-m^2	k-m^2	10.76	k-ft^2
element area/unit floor area	in^2/ft^2	69.45	mm^2/m^2	mm^2/m^2	0.0144	in2/ft^2
volume-solid	in^3	16.39	cm^3	cm^3	0.061	in^3
	ft^3	0.028	m^3	m^3	35.32	ft^3
volume-liquid	gal (gallons)	3.785	L(liters)	L(liters)	0.2642	gal (gallons)
	ft^3	28.32	L(liters)	L(liters)	0.03532	ft^3
density	lb/ft^3	16.02	kg/m^3	kg/m^3	0.06242	lb/ft^3
power	Btu/hr	0.0928	W	W	3.412	Btu/hr
energy	Btu	0.000293	kWh	kWh	3413	Btu
energy transfer	Btu/hr, ft^2	3.512	W/m^2	W/m^2	0.3172	Btu/hr, ft^2
solar radiation	Btu/ft^2	0.003152	kWh/m^2	kWh/m^2	317.2	Btu/ft^2
	Btu/ft^2	0.01135	MJ/m^2	MJ/m^2	88.11	Btu/ft^2
	Btu/ft^2	0.271	langleys	langleys	3.69	Btu/ft^2
	kWh/m^2	3.60	MJ/m^2	MJ/m^2	0.278	kWh/m^2
	kWh/m^2	86.04	langleys	langleys	0.01162	kWh/m^2
electric loads	Wh/ft^2	0.0929	Wh/m^2	Wh/m^2	10.76	Wh/ft^2
illuminance	fc	10.76	lux	lux	0.0929	fc
	fc	0.01076	klux	klux	92.9	fc
R-value (resistance)	ft^2, F, hr/Btu	0.1763	m^2, K/W	m^2, K/W	5.673	ft^2, F, h/Btu
R-value/unit thickness	R/in	0.0693	RSI/cm	RSI/cm	14.43	R/in
U-factor (conductance)	Btu/hr, F, ft^2	5.673	W/K, m^2	W/K, m^2	0.1763	Btu/hr, F, ft^2
solar mass ratio (masonry)	ft^3 mass/ft^2 floor	0.3014	m^3 mass/m^2 floor	m^3 mass/m^2 floor	3.318	ft^3 mass/ft^2 floor
solar mass ratio (water) and water consumption	gal/ft^2 floor	40.74	L/ft^2 floor	L/ft^2 floor	0.02455	gal/ft^2 floor

GLOSSARY

ABSORPTANCE/ABSORPTIVITY
The fraction of the incident radiation striking a surface that is absorbed by the surface. The term can refer to either the full solar radiation spectrum or a portion such as the visible spectrum or the infrared spectrum. Range is 0–1.0. *See also Emittance.*

ACTIVE SYSTEM
A heating or cooling system that uses mechanical devices such as fans and pumps to distribute heat, or an electric lighting system.

AIR CHANGES
A measure of the air exchange in a building due to infiltration or ventilation. One air change occurs when the building's entire volume of air has been replaced.

AIR COLLECTOR
A glazed facade or roof-integrated panel that collects solar radiation to heat air circulated behind the glass, which is then moved to thermal storage remote from the collector. The air is usually circulated next to an absorber plate.

ALTITUDE, Solar
The angle of the sun above the horizon, as seen in a section view parallel to the sun's azimuth.

AMBIENT LIGHT
General illumination in a room, usually diffuse and often at lower illuminance than lighting for specific activities. *See also Task Lighting.*

AMBIENT TEMPERATURE
Surrounding air temperature, as in a room or around a building, in contrast to a local or modified temperature.

ANGLE OF INCIDENCE
The angle between the sun and the perpendicular of the receiving surface, or depending on the system used, the angle between the sun and the receiving surface.

APERTURE
An opening in a wall or roof that admits sun, wind, or light. *See also Solar Aperture.*

ASHRAE
American Society of Heating, Refrigerating, and Air-conditioning Engineers.

ASPECT RATIO
Ratio between two sides of a rectangular object, such as the height:width of a duct or an atrium.

ASPECT, Solar
The geometric relationship between the sun and a surface, often the ground, including both the orientation (declination) and tilt (slope) of the surface.

ATRIUM
A usually large and multistoried, glass-roofed room used to bring daylight to the interior of thick buildings where sidelight alone cannot penetrate. The atrium may be enclosed on two, three, or four sides by the rooms it helps light.

ATTACHED SUNSPACE
A room that doubles as a solar collector. The term *attached* also implies a space that shares one common wall with the associated building. *See also Sunspace and Semi-Enclosed Sunspace.*

AUXILIARY HEAT
Heat delivered to a building by active systems to supplement solar heat.

AZIMUTH, Solar
The angle of the sun, as seen in plan, measured in degrees from south (or from north in the Southern Hemisphere); also, the orientation of a building. Used in this book, an azimuth of zero describes a glazing or wall that faces due south, so north orientation = 180°, west orientation = 90° west, and east orientation = 90° east. *See also Altitude.*

BALANCE POINT TEMPERATURE
The outside temperature at which a building shifts from a need for cooling to a need for heating, or vice versa. It is the temperature at which the sum of solar heat gains and internal heat gains balances envelope heat transfer from the skin and infiltration/ventilation, to maintain a desired indoor temperature.

BRIGHTNESS
The subjective human perception of luminance. *See also Luminance.*

Btu (British Thermal Unit)
A unit of heat; specifically, the heat needed to raise the temperature of one pound of water by 1 °F. *See also Joule.*

Btu/hr (British Thermal Units Per Hour)
A measure of the rate of energy flow (power) commonly used to express heat loss or heat gain or the size of heating and cooling equipment. 1 Btu/hr = 0.2929 W. *See also Watt.*

Btu/hr, ft², °F
British Thermal Units per hour, per square foot, per degree Fahrenheit of temperature difference. A measure of heat flow (thermal conductance). The (I-P) units of *U*-factor.

CANDELA (cd)
An SI unit of luminous intensity. An ordinary candle has a luminous intensity of one candela. *See also Candlepower.*

CANDLEPOWER (cp)
An I-P unit of luminous intensity. An ordinary candle has a luminous intensity of one candlepower. *See also Candela.*

CLEAR SKY
A sky condition with few or no clouds, usually taken as 0–2 tenths covered in clouds. Clear skies have high luminance and high radiation, and create strong shadows relative to more cloudy conditions. The sky is brightest nearest the sun, and away from the sun it is about three times brighter at the hori-

zon than at the zenith. *See also Overcast Sky and Partly Cloudy Sky.*

CLO

Clothing factor, a measure of the insulating value of clothing. For example, 0.3 Clo is typical for light summer clothing; 0.8 is typical for heavy winter clothing.

COMFORT PARAMETER (Ψ)

An indicator of human comfort in relation to wind; it is a relative reference value, accounting for both wind speed and turbulence, based on the ratio of wind speed at a location near a building to the wind speed that would be present at the same point with no building. In winter, a higher Ψ means less comfortable (overspeed) conditions; in summer, however, it indicates increased comfort. Range is 0–2.0.

COMFORT ZONE

On the bioclimatic chart, the area of combined temperatures and humidities that 80% of people find comfortable. People are assumed to be in the shade, fully protected from wind, engaged in light activity, and wearing moderate levels of clothing that increases slightly in winter.

CONDENSATION

The process of vapor changing into liquid. In the process, it releases heat.

CONDITIONED & UNCONDITIONED SPACES

Conditioned spaces need air treatment such as heat addition, heat removal, moisture removal, or pollution removal. Unconditioned spaces do not need such air conditioning, and no effort is made to control infiltration.

CONDITIONED FLOOR AREA

See Floor Area, Conditioned.

CONDUCTANCE

See Thermal Conductance.

CONDUCTION

The transfer of heat through a static medium, usually a solid such as concrete. *See also, Radiation, Evaporation, and Convection.*

CONDUCTIVITY

See Thermal Conductivity.

CONTRAST

A qualitative perception of the difference between two elements in the visual field, especially of their luminance. The subjective assessment of the difference in appearance of two parts of a field of view seen simultaneously or successively.

CONSERVATION FACTOR

A relative factor, based on regional climate and fuel costs, used to recommend insulation and air tightness levels (Balcomb et al., 1984, pp. 2-1 to 2-7).

CONVECTION

Heat transferred between a surface and an adjacent fluid (usually air or water) by the circulation of that fluid, induced by a temperature differential.

COOLING DEGREE DAYS (CDD)

See Degree Days.

COOLING LOAD

A total load with net cooling required. *See also Total Load and Heating Load.*

COOL TOWER

See Downdraft Evaporative Cooling Tower.

CROSS-VENTILATION

Ventilative cooling of people and spaces driven by the force of wind. When outside air is cooler than inside air, heat can be transferred from the space to the ventilation air. Cross-ventilation also removes heat from people by convection and by increasing the rate of perspiration evaporation. The cooling rate from cross-ventilation is determined by wind speed, opening sizes, and the temperature difference between inside and outside. *See also, Stack Ventilation.*

DAYLIGHT

Illuminance from radiation in the visible spectrum from the diffuse sky, reflected light, and direct sun that lights a room.

DAYLIGHT ENVELOPE

The maximum buildable volume on a site that will not unduly restrict daylight available to adjacent buildings.

DAYLIGHT FACTOR (DF)

The proportion of interior horizontal illuminance (usually taken on a work plane) to exterior horizontal illuminance under an unobstructed sky. It is the sum of the *Sky Component, External Reflected Component,* and the *Internal Reflected Component.* Range is 0–100%, but for most rooms is usually limited to 1–10%.

DELTA T (ΔT)

A difference in temperature, usually referring to the difference between indoor and outdoor temperatures.

DEGREE DAY (DD)

The difference, measured in degrees F or C, between a base temperature and the average outdoor temperature for a single day. For heating degree days, outdoor temperature is always below the base. For cooling degree days, outdoor temperature is always above the base. Heating degree days are often calculated from the building's balance point temperature: 45, 55, 65 °F (7.2, 12.8, 18.3 °C). Cooling degree days can be calculated from a base at the balance point (usually 65 °F/18.3 °C) or from the top of the comfort zone (usually 80 or 83 °F/26.7 or 28.3 °C).

DEGREE DAYS, Annual

The sum of degree days, for either heating (HDD) or cooling (CDD), for the entire year in a given location. It is determined by adding together the degree days for each individual day.

DIFFUSE RADIATION

The component of solar radiation that has been scattered by atmospheric particles. Diffuse radiation is assumed to be evenly distributed throughout the sky dome. *See also Sky Light.*

DIRECT GAIN

The transmission of sunlight through glazing directly into the space to be heated, where it is converted to heat by absorption on interior mass surfaces. *See also Indirect Gain and Isolated Gain.*

DIRECT RADIATION

The component of solar radiation that comes directly from the sun without being diffused or reflected.

DIRECT SUN LIGHT

The component of visible spectrum radiation that comes directly from the sun without being diffused or reflected.

DIFFUSE REFLECTANCE

Reflectance is the ratio of reflected radiation to incident radiation. Diffuse reflectance spreads incident flux over a range of reflected angles/directions. *See also Specular Reflectance.*

DIURNAL

Relating to a 24-hr cycle. A diurnal temperature swing is the cycle of temperature over the course of one 24-hr period.

DOWNDRAFT EVAPORATIVE COOLING TOWER

A cooling system that humidifies and cools warm dry air by passing it though a wetted pad at the top of a tower. The cooled air, being denser, falls down the tower and into the occupied space below, drawing in more air through the pads in the process. Thus, no distribution fans are required.

DRY-BULB TEMPERATURE

The air temperature measured using a conventional thermometer. *See also Wet-Bulb Temperature.*

EARTH–AIR HEAT EXCHANGERS

A strategy of pretempering fresh air for ventilation, and in some cases, providing building cooling, by passing incoming air through buried ducts.

EARTH CONTACT

The strategy of placing building surfaces in contact with the ground to reduce the temperature difference between inside and outside, reduce infiltration, and/or use the subsurface soil temperatures to cool the building.

EARTH TUBES

See Earth–Air Heat Exchangers.

EMITTANCE/EMISSIVITY

A measure of a material's ability to emit (lose heat by) radiation at a given temperature. Range is 0–1.0. Emissivity is usually proportionally inverse to absorptance.

ENVELOPE HEAT GAIN or LOSS

Heat transferred through the skin or via infiltration/ventilation. *See also Internal Gain and Solar Gain.*

ENVELOPE LOAD

The demand for energy required at any moment to compensate for the difference between desired indoor conditions and heat gains or losses from conduction transfer through the skin, and infiltration/ventilation. *See also Total Load, Solar Load, and Internal Load.*

EQUINOX

Meaning equal light. The dates during the year when the hours of daylight are equal to the hours of darkness. The equinoxes fall on or near March 21 and September 21. On the equinox, the sun rises from the horizon at due east and sets due west.

EVAPORATION

Phase change of a material from liquid to vapor. In the process evaporative cooling occurs.

EVAPORATIVE COOLING

A heat removal process in which water vapor is added to air, increasing its relative humidity while lowering its temperature. The total amount of heat (enthalpy) in the air stays constant, but is transferred from sensible heat in the air to latent heat in the moisture. In the process of shifting from liquid to vapor (evaporating), the water must absorb large amounts of heat.

EVAPORATIVE COOLING, Direct

A cooling process where warm, dry air is moved through a wetted medium to evaporate moisture into the air. The cooler, more humid air is then used to cool a space.

EVAPORATIVE COOLING, Indirect

A cooling process where the evaporative process is remote from the conditioned space. The cooled air is then used to lower the temperature of a building surface, such as in a roof spray, or is passed through a heat exchanger to cool indoor air. The indirect process has the advantage of lowering temperatures without adding humidity to the air, thus extending the climatic conditions and regions in which evaporative cooling is effective.

EXTERNALLY REFLECTED COMPONENT

The portion of the daylight factor (at a point indoors) that is contributed by light reflected from external surfaces such as the ground and adjacent buildings. *See also Daylight Factor, Sky Component,* and *Internally Reflected Component.*

FLOOR AREA, Conditioned

The portion of a building that is heated and/or cooled. Does not include attics, unheated basements, outdoor spaces, garages, unheated buffer zones, etc. See also Conditioned & Unconditioned Spaces.

FOOT-CANDLE (fc)

An I-P measure of illuminance; specifically, the amount of direct light from one candle falling on a square foot of surface one foot away (lumens/ft²). Foot-candle x 10.764 = lux. *See also Lux.*

FOOTLAMBERT (fL)

A measure of the luminance (photometric intensity) from a light source. 1 footlambert = 0.318 candelas/ft². *See also Luminance.*

GLARE

The perception caused by a very bright light or a high contrast of light, making it uncomfortable or difficult to see. *See also Contrast.*

GLAZING

Transparent or translucent materials, usually glass or plastic, used to cover an opening without impeding (relative to opaque materials) the admission of solar radiation and light.

HEAT CAPACITY

Also known as volumetric heat capacity. A measure of the ability of an element of thermal storage mass to store heat per unit of volume. It is the product of the material's density and specific heat. Units are Btu/ft³, °F (kJ/m³, °C). Water has a heat capacity of 62.4 (4181); masonry, about 15–23 (1000–1550). *See also Specific Heat.*

HEAT GAIN

The gross amount of heat that is introduced into a space, whether from incoming radiation, air infiltration, ventilation, or from internal sources such as occupants, lights, and equipment. *See also Heat Loss.*

HEATING DEGREE DAYS (HDD)

See Degree Day.

HEAT ISLAND

The increased temperatures, relative to surrounding open land, found in center cities and areas of high development density. Heat islands are caused by concentrations of heat sources, decreased vegetation cover, increased massive and dark surfaces, decreased wind flows, and narrow sky view angles.

HEAT LOAD

A total load with net heating required. *See Cooling Load and Total Load.*

HEAT LOSS

The gross amount of heat that leaves a space, by heat flow through the building envelope, air infiltration, or ventilation.

HORIZON

All points at zero degrees solar altitude from an observing point.

HVAC

Mechanical systems for heating, ventilating, and air-conditioning that control temperature, humidity, and air quality.

HYBRID SYSTEM

A solar heating or cooling system that combines passive and active elements.

HYPOCAUST

Massive floors with channels through which solar heated air passes, giving up its heat to the mass for storage and radiation to the floor surface above and/or the ceiling below. Originally, a Roman system of underfloor heating in which combustion gases from a wood fire were passed under a massive floor. *See also Murocaust.*

ILLUMINANCE

The measure of light intensity striking a surface. Specifically, the concentration of incident luminous flux, measured in foot-candles (I-P) or lux (SI). *See also Luminance.*

ILLUMINATION

Lighting of a surface by daylight or electric light. *See also Illuminance.*

INCIDENT ANGLE

See Angle of Incidence.

INDIRECT GAIN

The transfer of solar heat into the space to be heated from a collector that is coupled to the space by an uninsulated, conductive, or convective medium; for example, thermal storage walls and roof ponds. *See also Direct Gain and Isolated Gain.*

INFILTRATION

Air exchange between interior spaces and the outdoors, resulting in heat loss or gain. It is driven by the difference in pressure between inside and outside; buildings exposed to higher wind speeds and buildings with looser construction have increased rates of infiltration. Heat transfer from infiltration is proportional to the volume of air entering and to the temperature difference between inside and outside.

INSOLATION

The total amount of direct, diffuse, and reflected solar radiation that strikes a surface. This total radiation is also known as global radiation. Insolation is usually measured in Btu per square foot per hour or per day (Btu/ft², hr—sometimes written Btu/hr ft², or Btu/ft², day). Metric (SI) units are usually kilowatt-hours per square meter per day (kWh/m², day).

INSULATION

Any low mass material with high thermal resistance used to slow the transfer of heat via conduction. May also refer to materials used to reflect radiant heat (reflective insulation). *See also Internal Sources.*

INTERNAL HEAT GAIN

Heat generated inside the building by sources other than the space-heating equipment, usually by appliances, lights, and people. *See also Internal Sources.*

INTERNAL LOAD

The demand for energy required at any moment to compensate for the difference between desired indoor conditions and heat gains from the internal sources of electric lights, people, and equipment. *See also Total Load, Solar Load,* and *Envelope Load.*

INTERNAL-LOAD-DOMINATED BUILDING (ILD)

A building with a balance point well below the desired interior temperature and having a heat load profile in which internal gains or solar gains are much larger than the envelope load. *See also Skin-Load-Dominated Building.*

INTERNALLY REFLECTED COMPONENT

The portion of the daylight factor contributed by light reflected from internal surfaces such as walls, floor, and ceiling. *See also Daylight Factor, Sky Component,* and *Externally Reflected Component.*

INTERNAL SOURCES

The sources of internal heat gain other than the space-heating equipment, such as appliances, lights, and people. *See also Internal Heat Gain.*

I-P UNITS

Inch-Pound Units, the "American Standard," system of measurement used in the United States. Also known as (English) Imperial units. *See also SI Units.*

ISOLATED GAIN

The transfer of heat into a space from a collector that is thermally isolated either by physical separation or insulation. Examples include convective loop collectors and attached sunspaces with an insulated common wall. *See Direct Gain* and *Indirect Gain.*

JOULE

A metric (SI) unit of heat; specifically, the 1/4.184 of the heat needed to raise the temperature of one gram of water by 1 °C. 1000 joules = 1 kilojoule (kJ); 1 kJ = 0.9478 Btu. *See also Btu* and *Watt.*

LATENT HEAT

A change in heat content that occurs without a corresponding change in dry bulb temperature, usually accompanied by a change of state, as when water vapor in the air condenses.

LATITUDE

The angular distance north or south of the earth's equator, measured in degrees along a meridian. The equator is 0 degrees; the North Pole is 90° North latitude. Latitudes farther from the equator have lower sun angles, less radiation and illuminance per hour, and more variation in sun path between summer and winter. *See also Longitude.*

LEE

The downwind side of a building or obstruction that faces away from the direction from which the wind blows, usually subjected to lower pressure, reduced wind speeds, and higher turbulence. *See also Windward.*

LIGHT SHELF

A horizontal reflector dividing upper and lower glazing, used to reflect light to the ceiling, even daylight distribution in a room, and reduce glare.

LIGHT-TO-SOLAR-GAIN RATIO (LSG)

A relative expression of the "coolness" of a glazing, obtained by dividing its visible transmittance (VT) by its solar heat gain coefficient (SHGC). A daylit building in a hot climate would ideally use a glazing with high VT and low SHGF.

LOAD COLLECTOR RATIO (LCR)

The ratio of the building load coefficient (Heat Load per Degree Day) to the collection area. LCR is an expression of the relationship between energy conservation and solar gain and can be used to compare buildings within the same locality.

LOAD, total

The demand for energy required at any moment to compensate for the difference between desired indoor conditions and the net of heat gains and losses from *Internal Loads, Solar Loads,* and *Envelope Loads. See also Cooling Load and Heating Load.*

LONGITUDE

Angular distance on the earth's surface, measured east or west from the prime meridian (0 degrees) at Greenwich, England, to the meridian passing through a position, expressed in degrees. St. Louis, MO, is at 90° West longitude. Range is 0–180, East or West. *See also Latitude.*

LUMEN (lm)

Unit measuring the rate of light flow (luminous flux). Each square foot (square meter) of spherical surface surrounding a one candela (candlepower) light source receives one lumen of light flux. Lumen is the unit used in both I-P and SI units. One lumen produces a 1 foot-candle (lux) illuminance.

LUMINANCE (L)

The luminous intensity (photometric brightness) of a light source or reflecting surface, including factors of reflection, transmission, and emission. Units are candelas per square foot (cd/ft^2), candelas per square meter (cd/m^2). An unobstructed sky of 1 footlambert luminance produces an illuminance of 1 foot-candle on a horizontal surface. *See also Brightness, Illuminance,* and *Footlambert.*

LUMINOUS FLUX

The flow of light from a source to a receiving surface, measured in lumens (lm).

LUX

A metric (SI) measure of illuminance; specifically, the amount of direct light from one candle (one candela) falling on a square meter of surface one meter away ($lumens/m^2$). 1 lux x 0.0929 = 1 foot-candle. *See also Foot-candle.*

MASONRY

Concrete block, brick, adobe, stone, concrete, and other similar massive materials.

MASS-AREA-TO-GLAZING-AREA RATIO

The ratio of the surface area of massive elements in a solar heated building to the total solar collection area. Massive elements include all floors, walls, ceilings, and other high-density interior objects.

MASS, Thermal

See Thermal Mass.

MEAN RADIANT TEMPERATURE (MRT)

The weighted average temperature of surrounding surfaces, based on the angular size between a person (or other surface) and those surfaces. A lower MRT of room surfaces, such as with earth contact, can give the perception of comfort at higher air temperatures than when the surfaces are near the temperature of the indoor air. Similarly, in a passively heated building, a person will feel comfortable in a room with warm thermal mass (higher MRT) at lower air temperatures than if in a room with no mass.

MET

Human metabolic rate of heat gain. A measure of the heat produced by a seated sedentary person, and therefore added to the space the person occupies. One met unit = 18.4 Btu/hr, ft^2 (58.2 W/m^2).

MOVABLE INSULATION

Operable thermal insulating shades or shutters placed over windows only at night to reduce convective and radiant losses through the glazing at night. Movable insulation greatly increases the solar savings fraction in passive solar heated buildings, because more of the heat captured during the day is retained for use during the night.

MUROCAUST

Massive walls with vertical channels through which solar-heated air passes, giving up its heat to the mass for storage and radiation to the interior wall surface(s). *See also Hypocaust.*

NATURAL CONVECTION

Heat transfer between a surface and adjacent fluid (usually air or water), by the circulation of the fluid induced by temperature differences only and not by mechanical means.

NIGHT INSULATION

See Movable Insulation.

NIGHT VENTILATION OF MASS

A cooling process where a building is closed during the hot daytime hours, its heat gains are stored during that time in the building's structure or other thermal mass, and then at night the building is opened, and cooler outdoor air is used to flush heat from the mass, lowering its temperature to prepare for another cycle.

NIGHT SKY RADIATION

A reversal of the day time insolation principle. Just as the sun radiates energy during the day through the void of space, so heat energy can travel unhindered at night, from the earth's surface back into space. On a clear night any warm object can cool itself by radiating long-wave heat energy to the cooler sky. On a cloudy night, the cloud cover acts as an insulator and prevents the heat from traveling to the cooler sky.

OPAQUE

Not able to transmit light; for example, unglazed walls.

OVERCAST SKY

The condition in which the sky is completely covered in clouds and the sun cannot be seen. Usually taken as 8–10 tenths covered in clouds. Overcast skies generally have lower luminance, lower radiation, and create weak shadows and more diffuse lighting, relative to more clear conditions. The sky is about three times brighter at the zenith than at the horizon. *See also Partly Cloudy Sky* and *Clear Sky*.

PARTLY CLOUDY SKY

The sky condition between overcast and clear conditions, which varies from mostly cloudy with patches of clearness to mostly clear with a few clouds. Partly cloudy skies are highly variable and difficult to predict. Usually taken to be 2–8 tenths covered in clouds. *See also Cloudy Sky* and *Clear Sky*.

PASSIVE SYSTEM

A system that uses nonmechanical, nonelectrical means to satisfy heating, lighting, or cooling loads. Purely passive systems use radiation, conduction, and natural convection to distribute heat and daylight for lighting.

PERCENTAGE OF POSSIBLE SUNSHINE

The total actual time that sunshine reaches the surface of the earth is expressed as the percentage of the maximum time possible from sunrise to sunset with clear sky conditions.

PROFILE ANGLE

The angle used to size overhangs or spacing between buildings for shade; specifically, the vertical shadow angle of an overhang made by the angle between a horizontal from the bottom of a window and a line between the bottom of the window and the end of the overhang. It is the geometric translation of the solar altitude of the sun at a particular time into the plane normal to the window. When the sun's azimuth is perpendicular to the window, the profile angle is equal to the sun's altitude. When the sun is at any other angle, the profile angle and solar altitude will be different. See Libbey-Owens-Ford (1974).

RADIATION, THERMAL

The transfer of heat by electromagnetic waves. It does not require material contact (as does *Conduction*) or a fluid medium (as does *Convection*). Any two surfaces with a direct line of sight between them and a temperature difference will have a radiant exchange. *See also Solar Radiation and Night Sky Radiation.*

RADIATION, SOLAR

See Solar Radiation.

RADIANT TEMPERATURE

The average temperature of surfaces surrounding a person or surface with which the person or surface can exchange thermal radiation. See also Radiation, Thermal and Mean Radiant Temperature.

REFERENCE NONSOLAR BUILDING

A building similar to a solar building but with an energy-neutral wall in place of the solar wall and with a constant indoor reference temperature. Used as a reference for assessing the performance of solar buildings.

REFLECTANCE

The ratio of radiation reflected by a surface to the radiation incident on it. Range is 0–1.0.

RELATIVE HUMIDITY

The percentage of water vapor in the atmosphere relative to the maximum amount of water vapor that can be held by the air at a given temperature.

REMOTE STORAGE

Thermal mass or other thermal storage located outside occupied spaces, such as in a rock bed. It is normally used to increase the thermal storage capacity beyond what can be stored in the building's massive walls, floors, roofs, or structure.

ROCK BED/ROCK STORAGE SYSTEM

A solar energy storage system in which the collected heat or cold is stored in a rock bin for later use. This type of storage can be used in an active, hybrid, or even passive system.

ROOF POND SYSTEM

An indirect-gain heating and cooling system in which the mass, which is water in plastic bags, is located on the roof of the space to be heated or cooled and covered with a movable insulation. A roof pond system absorbs solar radiation for heating in the winter and radiates heat to the night sky for cooling in the summer.

R VALUE (R)

A measure of the thermal resistance of a building element. *R* is the number of hours needed for 1 Btu to flow through one square foot of skin, given a temperature difference of 1 °F. The units for *R* are ft^2, °F, hr/Btu (or m^2, K/W). The reciprocal of *R* is the *U*-factor. *See also Thermal Resistance and U-Factor.*

SELECTIVE SURFACE

A surface used to absorb and retain solar heat in a solar heating system such as a trombe wall or in a solar collector. Often a dark metallic surface, selective surfaces have high absorptance and low emittance. *See also Absorptance* and *Emittance*.

SEMI-ENCLOSED SUNSPACE

A sunspace that shares three common walls with the associated building. *See also Attached Sunspace* and *Sunspace*.

SENSIBLE HEAT

Heat that results in a change in air temperature, in contrast with latent heat.

SHADING COEFFICIENT (SC)

The total amount of radiation transmitted though a glazing, relative to clear, 1/8-in (3-mm) single glass, which has, by definition, a shading coefficient of 1.0. Also used to define the fraction of incident radiation transmitted by an internal or external shading device. For glazing, SC   1.15 x Solar H eat Gain Coefficient. *See also Solar Heat Gain Coefficient (SHGC).*

SIDELIGHT

Daylight from apertures in a wall. *See also, Toplight.*

SIMPLE PAYBACK PERIOD

The time (usually measured in years) for an investment in an energy saving system or design to pay for itself by the cost of energy saved. It is determined by dividing the initial cost by the annual rate of savings.

S-I UNITS

Standard International units; the metric system. *See also I-P Units.*

SKIN-LOAD-DOMINATED BUILDING (SLD)

A building with a balance point near the desired interior temperature and having a heat load profile in which the envelope load is much larger than the solar load or internal load. *See also Skin-Load-Dominated Building.*

SKY COMPONENT

The portion of the daylight factor (at a point indoors) contributed by luminance from the sky, excluding direct sunlight. *See also Daylight Factor, Internally Reflected Component,* and *Externally Reflected Component.*

SKY COVER

A measure of the fraction of the sky covered in clouds. Range is 0–10 tenths. *See also Overcast Sky, Partly Cloudy Sky,* and *Clear Sky.*

SKY LIGHT

Daylight from the sky dome only, excluding the direct sun. *See also Sunlight.*

SKYLIGHT

A roof window, horizontal or sloped.

SKY LUMINANCE DISTRIBUTION—THE C.I.E. STANDARD OVERCAST SKY

A completely overcast sky for which the ratio of luminance at an altitude q above the horizon to the luminance at the zenith is assumed to be $(1 + 2 \sin q)/3$. This means that the luminance at the zenith is three times brighter than at the horizon.

SKY VIEW FACTOR (v)

The sector of the sky as seen from a daylight aperture or building surface. It can be measured in either section or as a three-dimensional solid angle. Specifically, for daylighting calculations, v is the angle subtended, in the vertical plane perpendicular to the window, by sky visible from the center of the window. The larger the area of sky seen by a window, the more illuminance available from the sky and the higher the daylight factor in the room. The sky view factor can be reduced by obstructions such as buildings, trees, and landforms. For a surface that needs to lose heat by radiation to the night sky, the sky view angle determines the rate of cooling. Urban streets and building facades often have their view of the sky blocked by adjacent buildings of the urban canyon.

SOLAR ABSORPTANCE

The fraction of incident solar radiation that is absorbed by a surface. The radiation not absorbed by an opaque surface is reflected. Range is 0–1.0. *See also Emittance and Absorptance.*

SOLAR APERTURE

That portion of the solar wall covered by glazing. The orientation of the opening should be within 30° of south (30° of north in the Southern Hemisphere) to be considered a solar aperture.

SOLAR ENVELOPE

The maximum buildable volume on a site that will not shade adjacent sites during specified dates and times.

SOLAR GAIN

Heat transferred to a space by solar radiation through glazing. *See also Internal Gain and Envelope Gain.*

SOLAR HEAT GAIN COEFFICIENT (SHGC)

The fraction of incident solar radiation (for the full spectrum) which passes though an entire window assembly, including the frame, at a specified angle. Range is 0–0.85. A higher SHGC is preferred in solar heating applications to capture maximum sun, whereas in cooling applications, a low SHGC reduces unwanted solar heat gain.

SOLAR HEAT GAIN FACTOR (SHGF)

The amount of solar heat transmitted though a standard glazing (single or double) per unit of glazing area, for a given latitude or location, time, date, and orientation. Depending on the source, SHGFs may be given for either single glazing or double glazing, and either by latitude, in which case average clear days are assumed, or by specific city, in which case average sky condition is used. The amount of radiation transmitted depends on the angle of the sun with respect to the window and on the intensity of the radiation incident. Units are Btu/hr, ft² (W/m²). *See also Shading Coefficient.*

SOLAR LOAD

The demand for energy required at any moment to compensate for the difference between desired indoor conditions and heat gains from solar radiation. *See also Total Load, Envelope Load, and Internal Load.*

SOLAR RADIATION

Radiation emitted by the sun, including infrared radiation, ultraviolet radiation, and visible light.

SOLAR REFLECTANCE INDEX (SRI)

A measure of a material's ability to reject solar heat, as shown by its temperature rise under full sun. It is defined so that a standard black (reflectance 0.05, emittance 0.90) has an SRI of 0 and a standard white (reflectance 0.80, emittance 0.90) has an SRI of 100. Materials with higher SRI values are cooler.

SOLAR SAVINGS FRACTION (SSF)

The percentage of annual heating energy saved by using solar energy to space heat a building, compared to a nonsolar building with similar thermal characteristics

SOLAR TIME

Time of day adjusted so that the sun is due south at noon.

SOLSTICE

The dates of the shortest and longest days of the year. Winter solstice is on or around December 21 (June 21 in the Southern Hemisphere); summer solstice is on or around June 21 (December 21 in SH). Sun altitude is lowest at winter solstice and higher at summer solstice. Daily azimuth variation is greatest at summer solstice and least at winter solstice.

SPECIFIC HEAT

A measure of the ability of a material to store heat, specifically, the amount of heat in Btus required to raise the temperature of one pound of a material 1 °F. Units are Btu/lb, °F (kJ/kg, °C). In I-P units, water, by definition, has a specific heat of 1.0. Masonry materials are about 0.2. The heat capacity of a heat storage material is a product of its density and specific heat. *See also Heat Capacity.*

SPECULAR REFLECTANCE

Reflectance is the ratio of reflected radiation to incident radiation. Specular reflection redirects incident flux like a mirror at one specific angle where the angle of incidence is equal to the angle of reflection. *See also Diffuse Reflectance.*

STACK VENTILATION

The cooling process of natural ventilation induced by the chimney effect, where a pressure differential occurs across the section of a room. Air in the room absorbs heat gained in the space, expands, and loses density, thus rising to the top of the space. When it exits through high outlet openings, a lower pressure is created low in the space, drawing in cooler outside air from low inlets.

STRATIFICATION

The tendency of fluids, like air and water, to form layers when unevenly heated. The warmer fluid rises to the top of the available enclosure, and the cooler fluid drops to the bottom.

SUNDIAL

A latitude-specific chart used with a physical model for predicting shadow patterns on a site or sun penetration for a building design.

SUNLIGHT

Beam daylight from the sun only, excluding diffuse light from the sky dome. *See also Sky Light.*

SUN PATH DIAGRAM

A latitude-specific chart mapping the apparent movement of the sun and used to determine solar altitude and azimuth angles for a given time and date.

SUNSPACE

A room that doubles as a solar collector; also called *greenhouse or solarium.* Sunspaces concentrate solar radiation collection and heat storage in one room used to heat surrounding rooms. *See also Semi-enclosed Sunspace and Attached Sunspace.*

TASK LIGHT

Lighting on a specific area used for a specific task. Task lighting is usually from an electric source and is a higher illuminance level than the surrounding ambient light level. It is a good strategy to combine task light with ambient daylight. *See also Ambient Light.*

THERMAL BREAK (THERMAL BARRIER)

An element of low thermal conductivity placed within a composite envelope construction in such a way as to reduce the flow of heat across the assembly. *See also Thermal Bridge.*

THERMAL BRIDGE

An element of high thermal conductivity within a construction of otherwise low thermal conductivity. Small areas of materials that conduct heat at high rates can substantially reduce the insulating effectiveness of an assembly. Examples are metal frame windows without thermal breaks and metal stud walls, where the metal conducts heat at a much higher rate than the insulation between. *See also Thermal Break.*

THERMAL CONDUCTANCE (C)

A measure of the ease with which heat flows though a specified thickness of a material by conduction. Units are Btu/hr, ft², °F (or W/m², °C). *See also U-Factor and Thermal Conductivity.*

THERMAL CONDUCTIVITY (k)

A measure of the ease with which heat flows though a unit thickness of a material by conduction; specifically, the heat flow rate in Btu per inch of material thickness, square foot of material area, and degree of temperature difference. Units are Btu, in/ft², hr, °F (W/m, °C). *See also U-Factor and Thermal Conductance.*

THERMAL MASS

Materials with high heat capacity, such as masonry or water, used to store heat or cool when there is an excess of a resource for use later when there is a need.

THERMAL RADIATION

Energy transfer in the form of electromagnetic waves from a body by virtue of its temperature, including infrared radiation, ultraviolet radiation, and visible light.

THERMAL RESISTANCE

A measure of the insulation value or resistance to heat flow of building elements or materials; specifically, the reciprocal of the thermal conductance. *See also R-Value and U-Factor.*

THERMAL STORAGE MASS

High-density building elements, such as masonry or water in containers, designed to absorb solar heat during the day for release later when heat is needed.

THERMAL STORAGE WALL

A trombe wall or water wall.

THERMOCIRCULATION

The circulation of a fluid by convection. For example, the convection from a warm zone (sunspace or trombe wall air space) to a cool zone through openings in a common wall.

TOPHEAT

Solar heat gain admitted from skylights, monitors, cupolas, or clerestories.

TOPLIGHT

Daylight from skylights, monitors, cupolas, or clerestories. *See also Sidelight.*

TOTAL LOAD

See Load, total.

TROMBE WALL

A solar heating system consisting of a masonry thermal storage wall placed between the solar aperture and the heated space. Heat is transferred into the space by conduction through the masonry, radiation from its inner surface, and, if vents are provided, by natural convection.

U-FACTOR (COEFFICIENT OF HEAT TRANSFER)

A measure of heat flow, specifically, the number of Btus that flow through one square foot of building skin, in one hour, when there is a 1 °F difference in temperature between the inside and outside air, under steady-state conditions. The units for U are Btu/hr, °F, ft^2 (or W/K, m^2). The U-factor is the reciprocal of the resistance or R-value. *See also Thermal Conductance and R-Value.*

VENTILATION LOAD

The energy required to bring outdoor air to the desired indoor conditions. In this book, ventilation load refers to fresh air ventilation, which may be provided either naturally or by a mechanical system. The rate of required ventilation varies with the use of the space and the number of occupants. Ventilation load depends on the rate of fresh air ventilation and on the temperature difference between inside and outside. It may be reduced by pretempering or the use of heat exchangers.

VENTILATION (NATURAL)

Air flow through and within a space stimulated by either the distribution of pressure gradients around a building or thermal forces caused by temperature gradients between indoor and outdoor air. *See also Cross-Ventilation and Stack-Ventilation.*

VISIBLE TRANSMITTANCE (VT)

The fraction of incident visible light that passes though glazing. A higher VT is better for daylighting. A low Solar Heat Gain Coefficient (SHGC) that rejects heat can reduce VT, but not necessarily. Some spectrally selective glazings have both low SHGC and high VT. Range is 0–1.0. *See also Light-to-Solar-Gain Ratio.*

VOLUMETRIC HEAT CAPACITY

See Heat Capacity.

WATER WALL

A solar heating system consisting of a thermal storage wall of water in containers placed between the solar aperture and the heated space. Heat is transferred into the space by conduction and convection through the water and by radiation from the inner wall surface to the room.

WATT (W)

A measure of power commonly used to express heat loss or heat gain or to specify electrical equipment. It is the power required to produce energy at the rate of one joule per second. 1 W = 3.412 Btu/hr. *See also Btu/hr.*

Watt/m^2, °C

Watts, per square meter, per degree centigrade of temperature difference. A measure of heat flow (thermal conductance). The SI units of U-factor. *See also, U-Factor.*

WET-BULB TEMPERATURE

The air temperature measured using a thermometer with a wetted bulb moved rapidly through the air to promote evaporation. The evaporating moisture, changing phase, lowers the temperature measured, relative to that measured with a dry bulb. Wet-bulb temperature accounts for the effects of moisture in the air. It can be used, along with the dry-bulb temperature on a psychrometric chart to determine relative humidity. *See also Dry-Bulb Temperature.*

WINDWARD

The upwind side of a building or obstruction that faces the direction from which the wind blows, usually subjected to higher pressure. *See also Lee.*

WORKING PLANE (REFERENCE PLANE)

The horizontal work surface, usually at about 30–36 inches (0.8–0.9 m) from the floor, at which illumination is specified and measured.

ZENITH

The top of the sky dome. A point directly overhead, 90° in altitude angle above the horizon.

A+U (7/1997a). "Indian Institute of Management, Bangalore India, 1977–1985," *A + U: Architecture and Urbanism,* July, No. 322, pp. 66–73.

————. (7/1997b). "Sangath, Architect's Studio, Ahmedabad, India, 1979–1981/Balrkishna Doshi," *A + U: Architecture and Urbanism,* July, No. 7 (322), pp. 80–97.

————. (5/1997). "Webler + Geissler: Götz Headquarters, Würzburg, Germany," and "An Approach to Ecological Building Design: Götz Headquarters, Würzburg," (2 articles), *A + U: Architecture and Urbanism,* May, No. 5 (320), pp. 60–79.

————. (5/1994). "Kohn Pedersen Fox: DG Bank, Frankfurt am Main, Germany, 1987+1993," *A + U: Architecture and Urbanism,* May, No. 5 (284), pp. 6–73.

————. (8/1988). "Residential Quarter at the Giudecca Island, Venice, Italy," *A + U: Architecture and Urbanism,* Aug., No. 8 (215), pp. 7–26.

————. (11/1987). "Baha'i House of Worship, New Delhi, India, 1986," *A + U: Architecture and Urbanism,* Nov., No.11 (206), pp. 11–16.

————. (1/1983). "University of Trondheim, University Center at Dragvoll, Trondheim, Norway, 1978 (stage 1), architects: Henning Larsens Tegnestue," *A + U: Architecture and Urbanism,* No. 1 (148), pp. 81–89.

A+W (9/1997). "Reihenhäuser in Egebjerggård, Kopenhagen-Ballerup," *Architektur + Wettbewerbe,* Sept., No. 171, pp. 28–29.

————. (12/1991). "Solarhaus Lützowstrasse, Berlin," *Architektur + Wettbewerbe,* No. 148, Dec., p. 17.

————. (3/1991). "Kindertagesstätte in Frankfurt-Griesheim = Children's day home in Frankfurt-Griesheim." *Architektur + Wettbewerbe,* Mar., No. 145, p. 7.

Abel, Chris (1994). "Cool High-Rise," *Architectural Review,* Sept., Vol. 194, No. 11571, pp. 26–31.

————. (1985). "Riyadh Angles: Ministry of Foreign Affairs, Riyadh, Saudi Arabia," *Architectural Review,* July, Vol. 178, No. 1061, pp. 24–39.

Abrams, Donald W. (1986). *Low Energy Cooling: A Guide to the Practical Application of Passive Cooling and Cooling Energy Conservation Measures.* New York: Van Nostrand Reinhold.

Argiriou, A., and M. Santamouris (1995). *Natural Cooling Techniques.* Series: Energy Conservation in Buildings. Athens: CIENE : University of Athens; European Commission, Directorate General XVII for Energy.

Ahmed, Khandaker Shabbir (1994). "A Comparative Analysis of the Outdoor Thermal Environment of the Urban Vernacular and the Contemporary Development: Case Study in Dhaka," *Proceeding of the 11th Passive and Low Energy Architecture (PLEA) Conference, 1994.*

AHFC (1999). *Alaska Housing Manual.* Anchorage: Alaska Housing Finance Corp.

AHS (1997). "Plant Heat-Zone Map." Alexandria, VA: American Horticultural Society.

AIA Research Corp. (1978). *Regional Guidelines for Building Passive Energy Conserving Homes.* For the U. S. Dept. of Housing and Urban Development, in cooperation with the U. S. Dept. of Energy. HUD-PDR-355, Nov. Washington, DC: U. S. GPO.

Akbari, Hashem, Susan Davis, Sofia Dorsano, Joe Huang, and Steven Winnett (1992). *Cooling Our Communities: A Guidebook on Tree Planting and Light-Colored Surfacing.* U.S. Environmetal Protection Agency, Office of Policy Analysis, Climate Changes Div., GPO Doc#055-000-00371-8. Washington, DC: U.S. GPO, Jan.

Al-Azzaui, Subhi Hussein (1969). "Oriental Houses in Iraq." In Paul Oliver, ed. *Shelter in Society.* New York: Praeger.

Allen, Isabel (1997). "BRE Building Better Than Best Practice, Office Building, Garston, England," *Architects' Journal,* Vol. 205, Apr. 10, p. 10.

Al-Megren, Khalid Abdullah (1987). *Wind Towers for Passive Ventilation Cooling in Hot-Arid Regions, Arch. D. Thesis, University of Michigan.* Ann Arbor: University Microfilms International.

Ander, G. D., and M. Navvab (1983). "Daylight Impacts of Fenestration Controls," *Proceedings of the 8th National Passive Solar Conference.* Boulder, CO: American Solar Energy Society.

Architectural Design (1–2/1995). "Nicholas Grimshaw: British Pavilion, Expo 92, Seville," *A/D,* Jan.–Feb., Vol. 65, No. 1–2, pp. 36–39.

————. (11–12/1977). "Building With Nature (Ski Slope Hotel at Borgafjall by Ralph Erskine)," *Architectural Design,* Vol. 47, No. 11/12, pp. 762–764.

Architectural Forum (2/1956). "Frank Lloyd Wright–After 36 Years, His Tower Is Completed," *A/F,* Vol. 104, No. 2, pp. 106–113.

————. (1/1948). "Akron Cyclorama for El Marting: F. L. Wright, arch.," *Architectural Forum,* Vol. 88, p. 75.

Architectural Record (5/1983). "Mere House, Flint Hill, Virginia," *A/R,* Vol. 171, Mid-May, pp. 90–93.

————. (5/1974). "Winston House, Lyme, N.H." *A/R,* Vol. 155, Mid-May, pp. 52–53.

Architectural Review (5/1995). "Raising the Revenue [Inland Revenue Offices, Nottingham, England]," *Architectural Review,* May, Vol. 197, No. 1179, pp. 30–42.

_____. (10/1992). "Courageous Criteria [Aga Khan 1992 Award winners]," *Architectural Review,* Oct., Vol. 191, No. 1148, pp. 50–65.

Features nine winning buildings, including the Entrepreneurship Development Institute, Ahmadabad, Bimal Patel, architect.

_____. (6/1976). "House in a Box (Zimmerman house, Virginia)," *Architectural Review,* Vol. 159, p. 381.

Architecture (2/1985). "Preservation: First Phase of Pension Building Renovation for Museum Finished," *Architecture: the AIA Journal,* Feb., Vol. 74, No. 2, pp. 26–27, 32.

_____. (8/1983). "India: The Offices of an Architect Who Holds to Traditional Values," *Architecture: the AIA Journal,* Aug., Vol. 72, No. 8, p. 169.

Architecture d'aujourd'hui (9/1983). "Sangath, Atelier Doshi a Ahmedabad, Inde/Balkrishna Doshi," *Architecture d'aujourd'hui,* Sept., No. 228, pp. 80–83.

Architecture in Greece (1986). "Heliako chorio 3 sten Peuke, Attikes = Solar Village 3 in Pefki, Attica," *Architecture in Greece, Architektonika Themata,* Vol. 20, p. 196–199.

Ardalan, Nader, and Laleh Bakhtiar (1973). *The Sense of Unity, the Sufi Tradition in Persian Architecture.* Chicago: Univ. of Chicago Press.

Arens, E., P. McNall, R. Gonzalez, L. Berglund, and L. Zeren (1980)." A New Bioclimatic Chart for Passive Solar Design," *Proceedings of the 5th National Passive Solar Conference,* American Section of the International Solar Energy Society.

Argiriou, A., and M. Santamouris (1995). *Natural Cooling Techniques.* Series: Energy Conservation in Buildings, European Commision Directorate General XVII for Energy. Athens, Greece: Univ. of Athens.

Arkitektur DK (1985). "Henning Larsens Arkitektur," *Arkitektur DK,* Dec., Vol. 29, No. 7, pp. 261–328.

ARS (1990). "USDA Plant Hardiness Zone Map: [North America]." Misc. publication No. 1475 (U. S. Dept. of Agriculture), GOV-DOC NO: A 1.38:1475 13-A. Washington, DC: United States Agricultural Research Service.

Aschehoug, Øyvind (1992). "Daylight in Glazed Spaces: Daylighting in Long Glazed Streets Examined With Physical Models in an Artificial Sky and Computer Calculations," *Building Research and Information,* 1992, Vol. 20, No. 4.

_____. (1986). "Daylight Design for Glazed Spaces," in Ervin J. Bales, and Ross McCluney, eds. *Proceedings II, 1986 International Daylighting Conference.* Nov. 4–7, 1986, Long Beach, CA. Atlanta: American Society of Heating, Refrigerating, and Air-Conditioning Engineers, 1989.

ASHRAE (1997). *1997 ASHRAE Handbook, Fundamentals,* Inch-Pound Edition. Atlanta: American Society of Heating, Refrigerating, and Air-Conditioning Engineers.

_____. (1989a). *ASHRAE/IES Standard 90.1-1989, Energy Efficient Design of New Buildings Except Low Rise Residential Buildings.* Atlanta, GA: American Society of Heating, Refrigerating, and Air-Conditioning Engineers.

_____. (1989b). *ASHRAE Standard 62-1989, Ventilation for Acceptable Indoor Air Quality.* Atlanta, GA: American Society of Heating, Refrigerating, and Air-Conditioning Engineers.

_____. (1988). *Active Solar Heating Systems Design Manual.* Atlanta: American Society of Heating, Refrigerating, and Air-Conditioning Engineers.

Aynsley, R. M., W. Melbourne, and B. J. Vickery (1977). *Architectural Aerodynamics.* London: Applied Science.

Bahga, Sarbjit, Surinder Bahga, and Yashinder Bahga (1993). *Modern Architecture in India: Post-Independence Perspective.* New Delhi: Galgotia.

Bakarat, S. A. (1987). "Thermal Performance of a Supply Air Window," *Proceedings of the 12th National Passive Solar Conference.* Boulder, CO: American Solar Energy Society, pp. 152–158.

Baker, N., A. Franchiotti, and K. Steemers, eds. (1993). *Daylighting in Architecture, a European Reference Book.* London: James & James.

Balcomb, J. D., and K. Yamaguchi (1983). "Heat Distribution by Natural Convection," *Proceedings of the 8th National Passive Solar Conference.* Boulder, CO: American Solar Energy Society.

Balcomb, J. Douglas, Dennis Barley, Robert McFarland, Joseph Perry, Jr., William Wray, and Scott Knoll (1980). *Passive Solar Design Handbook, Vol. II: Passive Solar Design Analysis.* DOE/CS-0127/2 Dist. Cat. UC-59. Springfield, VA: NTIS.

Balcomb, J. Douglas, Robert W. Jones, Robert D. McFarland, and William O. Wray (1984). *Passive Solar Design Analysis: A Design Manual.* Atlanta: American Society of Heating, Refrigerating, and Air-Conditioning Engineers.

Balcomb, J. Douglas, Robert W. Jones, Claudia E. Kosiewicz, Gloria A. Lazarus, Robert D. McFarland, and William O. Wray (1983). *Passive Solar Design Handbook, Vol. III: Passive Solar Design Analysis and Supplement.* Boulder, CO: American Solar Energy Society.

Bansal, Narena K., Gerd Hauser, and Gernot Minke (1994). *Passive Building Design, A Handbook of Natural Climate Control.* New York: Elsivier Science.

Barreto, Abilio (1950). *Resumo Historico de Belo Horizonte (1701–1947).* Belo Horizonte, Brazil: Imprensa Oficial.

Bastlund, Knud (1967). *José Luis Sert, Architecture, City Planning, Urban Design.* New York: Praeger.

Baumeister (1996). "Wohnanlage mit Lärmschutzwand," *Baumeister,* Oct., Vol. 93, No. 10, suppl., pp. 26–30.

Environmentally friendly apartment complex in Vienna.

Baumeister (1/1999). "Wohnhochhaus in Wien," *Baumeister,* Jan., Vol. 96, No. 1, pp. 16–21.

English captions and summary, p.19. Energy-efficient high-rise apartment tower in Vienna's new Wohnpark Alte Donau.

Bauwelt (5/1992). "Wasserschloss: Geschäftsgebäude Haans in Tilburg," *Bauwelt,* May 8, Vol. 83, No. 18, pp. 1000-1009.

Beltran, L. O., E. S. Lee, K. M. Papamichael, and S. E. Selkowitz (1994). "The Design and Evaluation of Three Advanced Daylighting Systems: Light Shelves, Light Pipes, and Skylights," In *Conference Proceedings, 19th National Passive Solar Conference.* Boulder, CO: American Solar Energy Society.

Benton, Charles C., and Marc Fountain (1990). "Successfully Daylighting a Large Commercial Building: A Case Study of Lockheed Building 157," *Progressive Architecture,* Nov., Vol. 71, No. 12, pp. 119–121.

Benton, Charles C., and Robert Marcial (1993). *PEC Solar Calculator.* San Francisco: Pacific Gas and Electric Energy Center.

PG&E Energy Center, 851 Howard St., San Francisco, CA 94103. Also aviable for free download on-line from Vital Signs Project at U.C. Berkeley: <http://www-archfp.ced.berkeley.edu/vitalsigns/index.html>.

Bhatia, Gautam (1995). "Indian Archetypes," *Architectural Review,* May, Vol. 197, No. 1179, pp. 74–77.

Features three public projects in India, inlcuding the Entrepreneurship Development Institute, Ahmadabad, Bimal Patel, architect.

Bhatt, Vikram, and Peter Scriver (1990). *Contemporary Indian Architecture After the Masters.* Ahmedabad: Mapin.

Bittencourt, Leonardo Salazar (1993). *Ventilation as a Cooling Resource for Warm-Humid Climates: An Investigation on Perforated Block Wall Geometry to Improve Ventilation Inside Low-Rise Buildings.* Doctoral Thesis, Architectural Association Graduate School, Oct. 1993.

Bosselmann, Peter, Edward Arens, Klaus Dunker, and Robert Wright (1995). "Urban Form and Climate: Case Study Toronto," *Journal of the American Planning Association,* Vol. 61, No. 2, Spring, pp. 226–239. Chicago: APA.

Also available on-line from University of Toronto, Centre for Landscape Research at: <http://www.clr.toronto.edu/PROJECTS/Toronto/>.

Bosselmann, Peter, Juan Flores, and Terence O'Hare (1983). *Sun and Light for Downtown San Francisco.* IURD Monograph No. 34. Report by Environmental Simulation Laboratory, Institute of Urban and Regional Development. Berkeley, CA: College of Environmental Design.

Bourbekri, Mohamed (1992). "Impact of Position on the Performance of a Combined Light-Shelf," in S. Burley and M. E. Arden, eds. *Conference Proceedings, 17th National Passive Solar Conference.* Cocoa Beach, Florida, June 15–18, 1992. Boulder, CO: American Solar Energy Society.

Brawne, Michael (1992). *Kimbell Art Museum: Louis I. Kahn.* London: Phaidon.

Bressi, Todd W. (1993). *Planning and Zoning in New York City, Yesterday, Today, and Tomorrow*. New Brunswick, NJ: Center for Urban Policy and Research.

Brown, G. Z., J. Reynolds, and M. S. Ubbelohde (1982). *INSIDE-OUT: Design Procedures for Passive Environmental Technologies*. New York: Wiley.

Buchanan, Peter (1995). "High Dividends," *Architecture*, July, Vol. 84, No. 7, pp. 76–83.

Buckley, Mike, Simon Burton, Allison Crompton, and John Doggart, (ECD Partnership) eds. (1991). *Solar Architecture in Europe*. Bridgeport, England: Prism Press.

Butti, K., and J. Perlin (1980). *A Golden Thread: 2500 Years of Solar Architecture and Technology*. New York: Van Nostrand Reinhold.

Büttiker, Urs (1994). *Louis I. Kahn, Light and Space*. New York: Whitney Library of Design/Watson-Guptill.

Campbell, Robert (1988). "Canada: National Gallery That Is a Symbol of National Pride," *Architecture: The AIA Journal*, Sept., Vol. 77, No. 9, pp. 98–103.

CANMET (1998). *RETScreen analysis software and Renewable Energy Technologies Project Assessment Tool Manual*. CANMET Energy Diversification Research Laboratory. Varennes, PQ, Canada: Natural Resources Canada.
Prefeasibility analysis models for Microsft Excel. Models for photovoltaics, wind, biomass, passive solar, solar ventilation air preheaters, solar hot water, small hydro, and ground source heat pumps. Includes on-line climate database for sites worldwide. Available free on-line at: <http://cedrl.mets.nrcan.gc.ca/e/412/retscreen/ retscreen_new_1.html>.

_____. (1991). *Photovoltaic Systems Design Manual*. Ottawa: CANMET.
Free from CANMET Energy, Mines, and Resources Canada 580 Booth St., Ottawa, Ontario K1A 0E4.

Carmody, John and Raymond Sterling (1985). *Earth Sheltered Housing Design*, 2nd ed. New York: VNR.

Cathey, Henry Marc (1998b). *Heat-Zone Gardening: How to Choose Plants That Thrive in Your Region's Warmest Weather*. Alexandria, VA: Time-Life Books.

Cathey, Henry Marc (1998a). "USDA Plant Hardiness Zone Map [North America]." Misc. publication No. 1475 (United States. Dept. of Agriculture). Washington, DC: U.S. National Arboretum, Agricultural Research Service, U.S. Dept. of Agriculture.
This is "The 1998 US National Arboretum 'Web Version' of the 1990 USDA Plant Hardiness Zone Map." On-line at: <http://www.ars-grin.gov/ars/Beltsville/na/hardines.html>.

Chandler, T. J. (1976). *Urban Climatology and Its Relevance to Urban Design*. Technical Note No. 149, WMO-No 438. Geneva: World Meteorological Organization.

Chandra, Subrato, Philip W. Fairey, III, and Michael M. Houston (1986). *Cooling With Ventilation*. Golden CO: Solar Energy Research Institute. SERI/SP-273-2966, DE86010701, Decnber 1986.

Changery, M. J., W. T. Hodge, and J. V. Ramsdell (1977). *Index-Summarized Wind Data*. U.S. Department of Commerce, National Oceanic and Atmospheric Administration; and Battelle, Pacific Northwest Laboratories, BNWL-220, WIND-11, UC-60, September.

CHBA (1994). *Canadian Homebuilders Association Builder's Manual*. Ottawa: CHBA.

Christiansen. Jørgen Hegner (1989). "Administrations-bygning for Unicon Beton, Roskilde," *Arkitektur DK*, June, Vol. 33, No. 6, pp. 290–298.

CIBSE (1987). *Applications Manual: Window Design*. London: Chartered Institution of Building Service Engineers.

CIE (1970). *Daylight*. CIE No. 16 (E-3.2). Paris: Commission Internationale de l'Eclairage.

Cinquemani, V., J. R. Owenby, and R. G. Baldwin (1978). *Input Data for Solar Systems*. Asheville, NC: NOAA (U.S. National Oceanic and Atmospheric Administration), Nov., 1978; revised Aug., 1979/DOE/TIC - 10193.

City of Edmonton (1985). Downtown Area Redevelopment Plan Bylaw, consolidated edition, Dec. Edmonton, AB, Canada: City of Edmonton.

CMHC (1998). *Tap the Sun, Passive Solar Techniques and Home Designs*, 2nd ed. Ottawa: Canadian Mortgage Housing Corporation.

Cofaigh, Eoin O., John A. Olley, and J. Owen Lewis (1996). *The Climatic Dwelling, An Introduction to Climatic-Responsive Residential Architecture*. London: James & James.

Collymore, Peter (1994). *The Architecture of Ralph Erskine*. London: Academy Editions.

Compagno, Andrea (1995). *Intelligent Glass Facades: Material, Practice, Design*. Zurich: Artemis.

Conserval (1998). *Conserval Solarwall Website*. Conserval Engineering, Inc. On-line at: <http://www.solarwall.com/>.
Corporate web site for the manufacturer and patent holder on transpiring collectors. Gives a graph of temperature rise as a function of solar radiation and air flow rate in the collector.

Correa, Charles (1996). *Charles Correa*. London: Thames & Hudson.

Crawford, Thomas M. (1995). *SUN_CHART, Software for Passive Solar Energy Design*. Tuscon, AZ: Optical Physics Technology.
P. O. Box 11276 Tuscon, AZ. <http://www.srv.net/~tm_crw4d/opt/ sunchrt.html>. optics@srv.net

Curtis, William J. R. (1988). *Balkrishna Doshi, an Architecture for India*. New York: Rizzoli.

Davey, Peter (1990). "School Mastery (School, Cowplain, Hampshire/Architects, Hampshire County Council)," *Architectural Review*, Nov., Vol. 188, No. 1125, pp. 43–52.

Davies, Colin, and Ian Lambot, eds. (1997). *Commerzbank Frankfurt: Prototype of an Ecological High-Rise = modell eines okologischen Hochhauses*. Combined English and German ed. Haselmere, Surrey, UK: Watermark; Basel: Birkhauser.

Davies, Colin (1995). "Green Gothic (The Queen's Building, School of Engineering and Manufacturing, De Montfort University, Leicester, England)," *Architecture*, Vol. 84, July, pp. 88–97.

_____. (1994). "Big Blue," *Architectural Review*, Oct., Vol. 96, No. 1172, pp. 26–35.

_____. (1992). *British Pavilion, Seville Exposition 1992, Nicolas Grimshaw and Partners*. London: Phaidon.

DeKay, Mark (1992). "Plan Form Implications and a Rule of Thumb for Thickness of Atria Buildings." In S. Burley and M.E. Arden, eds. *Conference Proceedings, 17th National Passive Solar Conference*. June 15–18, 1992. Boulder, CO: American Solar Energy Society.

Department of City Planning (New York) (1981). *Midtown Development*. New York: The New York Dept. of City Planning.

Department of the Interior (1974). *The National Atlas of Canada*, 4th ed. Surveys and Mapping Branch, Geography Division. Toronto: Macmillan.

Deutsche Bauzeitschrift (1/1992). "Jugendbildungsstätte in Windberg/Ndb/Thomas Herzog," [Youth Hostel in Windberg] *Deutsche Bauzeitschrift*, Vol. 40, No. 1, pp. 35–42.

Deustch Bauzeitung (8/1992). "Gastlich: Gästehaus der Jugenbildungsstätte in Windberg/Niederbayern," [Youth Hostel in Windberg], *Deustch Bauzeitung*, Aug., Vol. 126, No. 8, pp. 36–41.

_____. (11/1965). "Wohnhaus Gadelius auf Lidingo; Wohnhaus Strom in Stocksund/Schweden," *Deutsche Bauzeitung*, Vol. 70, pp. 922–923, 943.

Diamond, Richard (1988). "Enerplex Revisited and Reevaluated," *Progressive Architecture*, March, Vol. 70, No. 3, pp. 117–119.

Dixon, J. M. (4/1982). "Solar Domesticated: Bonilla and Sisko Houses, New Jersey," *Progressive Architecture*, Vol. 63, pp. 142–145.

Drew, Philip (1994). "Aboriginal Shelter: Marika House, Yirrkala, Australia, Glenn Murcutt, Architect," *Architecture*, Sept., Vol. 83, No. 9, pp. 60–63.

Duivesteijn, Adri, and Harmel van de Wal (1994). *The Hidden Assignment: At Home in the City*. Amsterdam: Netherlands Architecture Institute, NAi Uitgevers.

Dunster, D., ed. (1978). *Alvar Aalto*. Architectural Monographs 4. London.

EBN (10/1998). "*R-Value of Straw Bales Lower Than Previously Reported*," *Environmental Building News,* Oct., Vol. 7, No. 9.

_____. (1–2/1995). "Insulation Materials: Environmental Comparisons," *Environmental Building News,* Jan./Feb., Vol. 4, No. 1.

Efficient Windows Collaborative EWC (n. d.). "*Efficient Windows*" web site. <*http://www.efficientwindows.org/index.html*>.

Egelius, Mats (1977). "Ralph Erskine," *Architectural Design,* Vol. 47, No. 11/12, pp. 750–852.

Egelius, Mats, and Yukio Futagawa (1980). *Ralph Erskine: Byker Redevelopment.* Global Architecture No. 55. Tokyo: A.D.A Edita.

EIA (1994). *Energy End-Use Intensities in Commercial Buildings.* Energy Information Administration, DOE/EIA-0555(94)/2. <*http://www.eia.doe.gov/*>.

_____. (1993). *Residential Energy Consumption and Expenditures.* Energy Information Administration. Washington, DC: U.S. GPO, Oct. DOE/EIA-032(93).

_____. (1992a). *Commercial Buildings Energy Consumption and Expenditures.* Energy Information Administration. Washington, DC: U.S. GPO. <*http://www.eia.doe.gov/*>.

_____. (1992b). *Lighting in Commercial Buildings.* Energy Information Administration, Energy Consumption Series, Mar. <*http://www.eia.doe.gov/*>.

_____. (1990). *Household Energy Consumption and Expenditures.* Energy Information Administration , DOE/EIA-0321(90). <*http://www.eia.doe.gov/*>.

_____. (1989). *Commercial Buildings Consumption and Expenditures.* Energy Information Administration, DOE/EIA-0318 (89). <*http://www.eia.doe.gov/*>.

Eley Associates (1993). *Advanced Lighting Guidelines: 1993.* DOE/EE-0008. Springfield, VA: NTIS.

El-Sioufi, Mohamed M. and Soontorn Boonyatikarm (1987). "Physical Modeling for Thermal Analysis of the Urban Built Environment," *Proceedings, Solar 87.* American Solar Energy Society. Boulder, CO: ASES.

El-Sioufi, Mohamed M. (1987). *Urban Patterns for Improved Thermal Performance.* D. Arch Thesis, University of Michigan. Ann Arbor: University Microfilms International.

English, Paul Ward (1966). *City and Village in Iran: Settlement and Economy in the Kirman Basin.* Madison: Univ. of Wisconsin Press.

Environment Canada (n.d.). *Solar Radiation Data Analysis for Canada*

A 6-volume set of reports providing detailed analysis (means, frequency of occurrence) of solar radiation amounts on a horizontal surface and several tilted surfaces for 143 Canadian locations, available directly from the Engineering Climatology Section <*http://www.cmc.ec.gc.ca/climate/*>.

_____. (1995). "Terrestrial Ecoregionas of Canada Map," In Ecological Stratification Working Group (1995). *A National Ecological Framework for Canada.* Agriculture and Agri-Food Canada, Research Branch, Centre for Land and Biological Resources Research and Environment Canada, State of the Environment Directorate, Ecozone Analysis Branch, Ottawa/Hull. Report and national map at 1:7 500 000 scale. Cat. No. A42-65/1996E.

Also available on-line at: <*http://www1.ec.gc.ca/~ecozones/*>.

_____. (1994). *Canadian Monthly Climate Data on CD-ROM (CMCD).* Ottawa: Environment Canada, Atmospheric Environment Service.

_____. (1993). *Canadian Climate Normals, 1961–1990 = Normales climatiques au Canada, 1961–1990.* Ottawa: Environment Canada, Atmospheric Environment Service.

Available on-line at: <*http://www.cmc.ec.gc.ca/climate/*>.

_____. (1988). *Climatic Atlas Canada.* Ottawa: Canadian Government Publications Ctr.

5 volumes of large-format climatic maps.

EREN (n.d.). *Fact Sheet: Solar Water Heating.* Adobe Acrobat File in pdf format. <*http://www.eren.doe.gov/*>.

ESBL (1997). *Cascadia, An Energy Efficient, Affordable House Built With Stressed Skin Insulating Core Panels.* Portfolio produced by the Energy Studes in Buildings Laboratory, Center for Housing Innovation, Department of Architecture, University of Oregon. Eugene, OR: Center for Housing Innovation.

ESSA (1975). *Weather Atlas of the United States.* Originally titled: *Climatic Atlas of the United States.* U.S. Dept. of Commerce, Environmental Sciences Services Admininstration, Environmental Data Service. Detroit: Gale Research.

Hardbound, book format. See also NOAA (1993).

Evans, Benjamin H. (1981). *Daylighting in Architecture.* New York: McGraw-Hill.

_____. (1957). *Natural Air Flow Around Buildings.* Texas Engineering Experiment Station, Research Report 59, March. College Station, TX: Texas A & M Univ., Texas Engineering Experiment Station.

Evans, Martin (1980). *Housing, Climate and Comfort.* London: The Architectural Press.

Evenson, Norma (1966). *Chandigarh.* Environmental Design and Development Series. Berkeley: Univ. of California Press.

Ferriss, Hugh (1928). *The Metropolis of Tomorrow.* New York: Ives Washburn. Reprint edition, Princeton, NJ: Princeton Architectural Press, 1986.

Fisher, Thomas (1984). "Opposites Attract: Enerplex, Princeton, N.J.," *Progressive Architecture,* Aug., Vol. 65, No. 8, pp. 8–89.

Fitzgerald, Eileen, and J. Owen Lewis, eds. (1996). *European Solar Architecture, Proceedings of a Solar House Contractor's Meeting, Barcelona, 1995.* Dublin, Ireland: Energy Research Group, University College Dublin.

Flanagan, Barbara (1988). "Weather Returns to Architecture" [Lasater house, Hebbronville, Texas]. *Metropolitan Home.* Feb., Vol. 20, No. 2, pp. 68–73.

Fleig, K., ed. (1975). *Alvar Aalto.* New York: Praeger.

Fleischhacker, Bentlay and Clark (1982). "A Simplified Methodology for Thermal Design of Roof Pond Cooled Buildings." In *Progress in Passive Solar Energy Systems,* Vol. 7, *Proceedings of the 7th National Passive Solar Conference.* Boulder, CO: American Solar Energy Society.

Fleischnacker, P., G. Clark, and P. Giolma (1983). "Geographical Limits for Comfort in Unassisted Roof Pond Cooled Residences," *Proceedings of the 8th National Passive Solar Conference,* American Solar Energy Society.

Flynn, J. E., and A. W. Segil (1970). *Architectural Interior Systems.* New York: Van Nostrand Reinhold.

Freeman, Allen (1990). "Buried Treasure: Harvey S. Firestone Library Expansion, Princeton University, Princeton, New Jersey, Koetter, Kim & Association, Architects," *Architecture: the AIA Journal,* Jan., Vol. 79, No. 1, pp. 60–65.

Fry, M., and J. Drew (1956). *Tropical Architecture in the Humid Zone.* New York: Van Nostrand Reinhold.

Futagawa, Yukio, ed. (1996a). "Coop Himmelblau: Highrise With Climate Facade, Wagramerstrasse, Vienna, Austria," *GA Houses,* Mar., No. 48, pp. 140–141. Tokyo: A. D. A. Edita.

_____. (1996b). *Louis I Kahn: Margaret Esherick House, Chestnut Hill, Pennsylvania, 1959–61, Norman Fisher House, Hatboro, Pennsylvania, 1960-67.* Text by Peter Reed. Global Architecture, No. 76. Tokyo: A. D. A. EDITA.

_____. (1994). *National Capital of Bangladesh, Dhaka, Bangladesh, Louis I. Khan, 1962–83.* Text by Kazi K. Ashraf. Global Architecture, No. 72. Tokyo: A. D. A. Edita.

_____. (1975). *Millowners Association Building, Ahmedabad, India, 1954. Carpenter Center for Visual Arts, Harvard University, Cambridge, Massachusetts, U.S.A. 1961–64/Le Corbusier.* Text by Kenneth Frampton. Global Architecture, No. 37. Tokyo: A. D. A. EDITA.

_____. (1974). *Chandigarh, the New Capital of Punjab, India, 1951-/Le Corbusier.* Text by Takamasa Yoshizaka. Global Architecture No. 30. Tokyo: A. D. A. EDITA.

_____. (1973). *Terrace Houses at Flamatt Near Bern, Switzerland, 1957, 1960: Halen Housing Estate Near Bern, Switzerland, 1961; Apartment in Brugg, Switzerland, 1970-71/Atelier 5.* Text by Niklaus Morgenthaler. Global Architecture, No. 23. Tokyo: A. D. A. EDITA.

GA Document (1981). "University of Trondheim, Trondheim, Norway, 1979 (stage 1); architects: Henning Larsen's Tegnestue A/S," *GA Document,* No. 4, pp. 38–49.

GA Houses (1985). "Bart Prince Residence and Studio, Albuquerque, New Mexico, 1983–84," *GA Houses,* No. 19. Tokyo: A. D. A. Edita.

———. (1982). "R. Fernau and L. Hartman, Brodhead House, La Honda, California, 1979," *GA Houses,* No. 10, pp. 138–143. Tokyo: A. D. A. Edita.

———. (1988). "Public Housing Estate, Guidecca Island, Venice, Italy, 1980–86," *GA Houses,* Aug., No. 23, pp. 174–181. Tokyo: A. D. A. Edita.

———. (1976). Zimmerman House, Fairfax County, Virginia, 1972–75/William Turnbull, Jr. *GA Houses,* No. 1, pp. 98–103.

Gandemer, J.T. (1978). *Discomfort Due to Wind Near Buildings: Aerodynamic Concepts.* Building Research Translation Series, NBS Technical Note 710-9. U. S. Dept of Commerce.

Givoni, Baruch (1998). *Climate Considerations in Building and Urban Design.* New York: VNR.

———. (1994). *Passive and Low Energy Cooling of Buildings.* New York: VNR.

———. (1992). "Climatic Aspects of Urban Design in Tropical Regions," *Atmospheric Environment.* Vol. 26B, No. 3, pp. 397-402.

———. (1991). "Modelling a Passive Evaporative Cooling Tower." In M. E. Arden Susan M. A. Burley, and Martha Coleman, eds., *1991 Solar World Congress,* Vol. 3, Part 1. Proceedings of the Biennial Congress of the International Solar Energy Society, Denver, CO, 19–23 Aug., pp. 3067–3071. Boulder, CO: American Solar Energy Society.

———. (1989). *Urban Design in Different Climates.* World Meteorological Organization, WCAP-10, WMO/TD-No. 346, Dec.

———. (1976). *Man, Climate, and Architecture.* London: Applied Science.

Golany, Gideon, ed. (1980). *Housing in Arid Lands.* London: Architectural Press.

Goulding, John R., J. Owen Lewis, and Theo C. Steemers, eds. (1992). *Energy in Architecture, The European Passive Solar Handbook.* London: B. T. Batsford.

Guerra, Lucas H., and Oscar Riera Ojeda (1996). *Lake/Flato.* Contemporary world architects series. Rockport, MA: Rockport.

Harriman, Marc S. (1992). "Designing for Daylight," *Architecture,* Oct., Vol. 81, No. 10, pp. 89–93.

Hartman, Charles W., and Philip R. Johnson (1984). *Environmental Atlas of Alaska.* Institute of Water Resources / Engineering Experiment Station, University of Alaska. Fairbanks: Univ. of Alaska.

Haryott, Richard (1992). "Solar-Powered Pavilion/Nicholas Grimshaw," *RIBA Journal,* Oct., Vol. 99, No. 10, pp. 32–36, 38.

Hastings, Robert S., ed. (1999). *Solar Air Systems: Built Examples.* International Energy Agency, Solar Heating and Cooling Programme. London: James & James.

———. ed. (1994). *Passive Solar Commercial and Institutional Buildings: A Sourcebook of Examples and Design Insight.* International Energy Agency, Solar Heeating and Cooling, Task XI, Passive Commercial Buildings. London: James & James.

———. (1995). *Solar Low Energy Houses of IEA Task 13.* Solar Heating and Cooling Programme, International Energy Agency, January. London: James & James.

Hauvette, Christian, and Marie-Hélène Contal (1997). *Christian Hauvette.* Barcelona: Editorial Gustave Gili, S. A.

Hauvette, Christian, Jérôme Nouel, and Georges Fessy (1995). *La Boîte à Vent: Rectorat de l'Académie des Antilles et de la Guyane.* Series: Parole à; 1 Série 11/24. Paris: Sens & Tonka.
"The Wind Box," in French, an excellent monograph on the Rectorate of the Academy of the Antilles and Guiana.

Hay, J. E. (1977). *An Analysis of Solar Radiation Data for Selected Locations in Canada.* Climatological Studies Number 32, Atmospherics Environment, Fisheries and Environment Canada. Quebec: Printing and Publishing Supply and Services of Canada.

Heisler, Gordon M. (1984). "Planting Design for Wind Control," In E. Gregory McPherson, ed. *Energy Conserving Site Design.* Washington, DC: American Society of Landscape Architects, pp. 165–183.

Herdeg, Klaus (1990a). *Formal Structure in Indian Architecture.* New York: Rizzoli.

———. (1990b). *Formal Structure in Islamic Architecture of Iran and Turkistan.* New York: Rizzoli.

Herzog, Thomas, ed. (1996). *Solar Energy in Architecture and Urban Planning.* New York: Prestel.

———. (1994). *Design Center, Linz.* Stuttgart: Gerd Hatje.

Hestnes, Anne Grete, Robert Hastings, and Bjarne Saxhof, eds. (1997). *Solar Energy Houses, Strategies, Technologies, Examples.* London: James & James.
A product of International Energy Agency (IEA) Solar Heating and Cooling Programme, Task 13.

Hightshoe, Gary L. (1988). *Native Trees, Shrubs, and Vines for Urban and Rural America: a Planting Design Manual for Environmental Designers.* New York: Van Nostrand Reinhold.

Hildebrand, G. (1974). *Designing for Industry: The Architecture of Albert Kahn.* Cambridge, MA: MIT Press.

Hildon, A., and A. Seager, eds. (1989). *Passive and Hybrid Solar Commercial Buildings, Basic Case Studies.* Produced by Databuild for International Energy Agency: Solar Heating and Cooling-Task XI. Oxfordshire, England: The Renewable Energy Promotion Group (REPG), Energy Technology Support Unit, Harwell Laboratory.

Hinweise für die Bauleitplanung (1998). *Städtebauliche Klimafibel.* Stuttgart: Wirtschaftsministerium Baden-Würtemberg.

Historic Savannah Foundation (1968). *Historic Savannah.* Savannah: Historic Savannah Foundation.

Hitchcock, Henry R. (1942). *In the Nature of Materials.* New York: Hawthorn Books.

———. (1936). *The Architecture of H. H. Richardson and His Times.* New York: Museum of Modern Art.

Hoke, John Ray, ed. (1996). *Architectural Graphic Standards,* CD-edition. New York: Wiley.

Hopkinson, R. G., P. Petherbridge, and J. Longmore (1966). *Daylighting.* London: Heinemann.

Hough, Michael (1995). *Cities and Natural Process.* New York: Routledge.

Huang, Y. J., H. G. Akbari, H. G. Taha, and H. G. Rosenfeld (1987). *The Potential of Vegetation in Reducing Summer Cooling Loads in Residential Buildings.* LBL Report No. 21291. Berkeley, CA: Lawrence Berkeley Laboratory.

Hudak, Joseph (1980). *Trees for Every Purpose.* New York: McGraw-Hill.

Humm, Othmar, and Peter Toggweiler (1993). *Photovoltaik und Architektur (Photovoltaics in Architecture).* Boston: Birkhäuser Verlag.
Many PV examples with text in four languages.

IES (1993). Mark S. Rea, ed. *Lighting Handbook, Reference and Application,* 8th ed. New York: Illuminating Engineering Society of North America.

Illuminating Engineering Society of North America (IES) (1979). *Recommended Practice of Daylighting.* New York: IES.

IURD (1984). *Sun, Wind, and Comfort, A Study of Open Spaces and Sidewalks in Four Downtown Areas.* Report by Environmental Simulation Laboratory, U. C. Berkeley Institute of Urban and Regional Development. Berkeley, CA: College of Environmental Design.

Iwersen, Bob (1992). "Night Ventilation of Thermal Mass, Guidelines for Design and Retrofit." Unpublished research report, Dept. of Architecture, University of Oregon.

Jacobson, Max, Murray Silverstein, and Barbara Winslow (1990). *The Good House, Contrast as a Design Tool.* Newtown, CT: Taunton Press.

James, George Truett (1988). "Climate and Site." In R. Gene Brooks, ed. *Site Planning, Environment, Process and Development.* Englewood Cliffs, NJ: Prentice Hall.

Jensen, Martin, and Neils Franck (1963). *Model-Scale Tests in Turbulent Wind, Part 1: Phenomena Dependent on the Wind Speed, Shelter at Houses-Dispersal of Smoke.* Copenhagen: Danish Technical Press.

Johnson, Timothy E. (1991). *Low-E Glazing Design Guide*. Boston: Butterworth.

Jones, David Lloyd (1998). *Architecture and Environment, Bioclimatic Building Design*. New York: Overlook Press.

Jones Peter Blundell (1992). "Creative Kulturhalle," *Architectural Review,* Feb., Vol. 190, No. 1140, pp. 38–43.

Kahn, Louis I. (1978). *Light Is the Theme: Louis I. Kahn and the Kimbell Art Museum: Comments on Architecture*. Nell E. Johnson, ed. Fort Worth, TX: Kimbell Art Foundation.

Kaufman, John E. , ed. (1984). *IES Lighting Handbook: 1984 Reference Volume*. New York: Illuminating Engineering Society of North America.

Khan, Hassan-Uddin (1995). *Contemporary Asian Architects*. Köln: Taschen.

_____. (1987). *Charles Correa,* revised ed. Miramar Book in the series, *Architects in the Third World*. Singapore: Concept Media, with Aperture, New York. See also, Correa (1996).

Knowles, Ralph L. (1974). *Energy and Form: An Ecological Approach to Urban Growth*. Cambridge, MA: MIT Press,

_____. (1981). *Sun Rhythm Form*. Cambridge, MA: MIT Press.

Koenigsberger, Otto H., T. Ingersoll, A. Mayhew, and S. Szokolay (1973). *Manual of Tropical Housing and Building,* Part One: *Climatic Design*. London: Longman Group.

Kohn, Wendy, ed. (1996). *Moshe Safdie*. London: Academy Editions.

Kok, Hans, and Michael J.Holtz, eds. (1990). *Passive Solar Homes: Case Studies*. Design Information Booklet Number Six, International Energy Agency: Solar Heating and Cooling Progtram, Task VIII. Report No. IEA SHAC T.8.C.6. Washington, DC: U.S. GPO, Dec.

Koomy, J. G., M. Cramer, M. A. Piette, and J. H. Eto (1995a). *Efficiency Improvements in U.S. Office Equipment: Expected Policy Impacts and Uncertainties*. Berkeley, CA: Lawrence Berkeley National Laboratory.

Koomy, J. G., R. E. Brown, R. Richey, F. X. Johnson, A. H. Sanstad, and L. Shown (1995b). *Residential Sector End Use Forecasting With EPRI-REEPS 2.1: Summary Input Assumptions and Results*. Lawrence Berkeley National Labs LBL-34044. UC-1600. Springfield, VA: National Technical Information Service (NTIS), Dec.

Krewinkel, Heinz W. (1998). *Glass Buildings: Material, Structure, and Detail*. Basel: Birkhäuser.

Kusuda, T. and K. Ishii (1977). *Hourly Solar Radiation Data for Vertical and Horizontal Surfaces on Average Days in the U.S. and Canada*. Building Science Series 96, National Bureau of Standards.

Labs, Kenneth (1991). "Direct-Coupled Ground Cooling: Issues and Opportunities," *Passive Cooling '81*, International Technical Conference (Miami Beach), American Solar Energy Society, Univ. of Delaware, Newark, pp. 131–135.

_____. (1989). "Earth Coupling," In Jeffrey Cook, ed. *Passive Cooling*. Series: Solar Heat Technologies: Fundamentals and Applications, Vol. 8, pp. 197–346. Cambridge, MA: MIT Press.

_____. (1981) *Regional Analysis of Ground and Above Ground Climate*. ORNL/Sub-81/4045/. Springfield, VA: National Technical Information Service.

_____. (1980). "Terratypes: Underground Housing for Arid Zones." In G. Golany, ed, *Housing in Arid Lands*. New York: Wiley.

Lambeth, J., and J. D. Delap (1977). *Solar Designing*. Fayetteville, AR: Lambeth.

Lam, William M. C. (1986). *Sunlighting as a Formgiver for Architecture*. New York: Van Nostrand Reinhold.

LBL (1999). "Cool Roofing Materials Database." *<http://EETD.LBL.gov/CoolRoof/>*.

Lechner, Norbert (1991). *Heating Cooling Lighting, Design Methods for Architects*. New York: Wiley.

Lee, B. E., M. Hussain and B. Solliman (1980a). *A Method for the Assessment of Wind Induced Natural Ventilation Forces Acting on Low Rise Arrays*. Report No. BS50, Dept. of Building Sciences, Univ. of Sheffield, Sheffield, England.

_____. (1980b). "Predicting Natural Ventilation Forces on Low Rise Buildings," *ASHRAE Journal,* February, pp. 35–39.

Lemos, Celina Borges (1995). "The Modernization of Brazilian Urban Space as a Political Symbol of the Republic," *The Journal of Propaganda Arts,* No. 21, Brazil Theme Issue, pp. 218–37.

Libbey-Owens-Ford (1974). *Sun Angle Calculator*. Toledo, Ohio.

Littlefair, P. J. (1996). *Designing With Innovative Daylighting*. BRE CI/SfB(N). Watford, Herts, England: Construction Research Communications.

_____. (1991). *Site Layout Planning for Daylight and Sunlight: a Guide to Good Practice*. BR 209. Garston, Watford, England: Building Research Establishment.

_____. (1988). *Average Daylight Factor: A Simple Basis for Daylight Design*. BRE paper IP 15/88. Garston, Watford, England: Building Research Establishment.

Loftness, Vivian (1981). *Climate/Energy Graphics*. Washington, DC: Association of Collegiate Schools of Architecture.

Loud, Patricia Cumming (1989). *The Art Museums of Louis I. Kahn*. Durham, NC: Duke University Press.

Lundahl, Gunilla (1988). "Erskine Experience," *Architectural Review,* Mar., Vol. 183, No. 1093, pp. 52–65.

Lunde, Peter J. (1980). *Solar Thermal Engineering*. New York: Wiley.

Lynch, Kevin (1971). *Site Planning,* 2nd ed. Cambridge, MA: MIT Press.

Marion, William, and Ken Urban (1995). *User's Manual for TMY2's, Typical Meteorological Years*. Derived from the 1961–1990 National Solar Radiation Data Base, June. Golden, CO: National Renewable Energy Laboratory.

TMY files and information are available on-line from NREL: *<http://rredc.nrel.gov/solar/old_data/nsrdb/tmy2/>*.

Marion, William and Stephen Wilcox (1995). *Solar Radiation Data Manual for Buildings*. Document No. NREL/TP-463-7904, DE95009254. Sep. Golden, CO: National Renewable Energy Laboratory.

Available on-line at: *<http://rredc.nrel.gov/solar/>*.

_____. (1994). *Solar Radiation Data Manual for Flat-Plate and Concentrating Collectors*. Document No. NREL/TP-463-5607, DE93018229. Apr. Golden, CO: National Renewable Energy Laboratory.

30-year average monthly and yearly solar radiation values from the 293 stations in the National Solar Radiation Data Base, customized for common types of solar collectors: fixed tilt, flat-plate, one and two axis tracking systems, and concentrating collectors. Values for average climate data. Available from the NREL Document Distribution Service, 1617 Cole Boulevard, Golden, CO 80401-3393, phone (303) 275-4363. Available on-line at: *<http://rredc.nrel.gov/solar/>*.

Matthews, Scott and Peter Calthorpe (1979). "Daylight as a Central Determinant of Design: How It Helped Shape a New TVA Office Building," *AIA Journal,* Vol 68, Sep, pp. 86-93.

Maui Solar (2000). *PV-Design Pro* software. Kula, HI: Maui Solar Software Corp.

<http://mauisolarsoftware.com>.

Mazria, Edward (1979). *The Passive Solar Energy Book*. Emmaus, PA: Rodale Press.

McClennon, Charles, and Gary O. Robinette (1975). *Site Planning for Solar Energy Utilization*. McLean, VA: American Society of Landscape Architects Foundation.

McPhereson, E. Gregory, ed. (1984). *Energy Conserving Site Design*. Washington, DC: American Society of Landscape Architects.

Melaragno, Michele G. (1982). *Wind in Architectural and Environmental Design*. New York: Van Nostrand Reinhold.

Meteotest (1997). *METONORM, v.3.0, Global Meteorological Database*. London: James & James.

A user-friendly software for calculating solar radiation and meteorological data anywhere in the world. It works from 2000 data sites, using monthly average data; will generate hourly simulated data files using theoretical algorithms.

Millet, M., J. Lakin, and J. Moore (1981). "Light Without Heat: Daylight and Shading," *Proceedings of the Interational Passive and Hybrid Cooling Conference*. American Section of the International Solar Energy Society.

Milne, Murray (1991). *Climate Consultant* software. UCLA Department of Architecture and Urban Design.

Hourly climate analysis and graphic display from TMY2 files; also plots sundials and sunpath diagrams. Available free on-line at: <http://www.aud.ucla.edu/energy-design-tools/>.

Moholy-Nagy, Sibyl, and Gerhard Schwab (1970). *The Architecture of Paul Rudolph.* New York: Praeger.

Moffat, Anne Simon, and Marc Schiller (1994). *Energy Efficient and Environmental Landscaping: Cut Your Utility Bills by up to 30 Percent and Create a Natural Healthy Yard.* South Newfane, VT: Appropriate Solutions Press.

Montgomery, Daniel A. (1987). "Landscaping as a Passive Solar Strategy," *Passive Solar Journal,* Vol. 4, No. 1, pp. 79–108.

Moore, Fuller (1993). *Environmental Control Systems: Heating Cooling Lighting.* New York: McGraw-Hill.

_____. (1991). *Concepts and Practice of Architectural Daylighting.* New York: Van Nostrand Reinhold.

Moorhead, Gerald (1991). "Industrial Evolution: Carraro House, Kyle, Texas, Lake/Flato Architects," *Architectural Record,* Apr., Vol. 179, No. 4, pp. 86–91.

Musick, Mike, Sue Mitchell, John Woodward, Randy Nicklas, Todd Hoener, and Phil London (1999). *Alaska Housing Manual.* Anchorage, AK: Alaska Housing Finance Corp.

Myrup, L. O. (1969). "A Numerical Model of the Urban Heat Island," *Journal of Applied Meteorology,* No. 8.

Naegeli (1946). Cited in Caborn, J. M. (1957). *Shelterbelts and Microclimate.* Edinburgh, Scotland: H. M. Stationery Office. See also, Heisler (1984).

NCDC (1996). *International Station Meteorological Climate Summary,* Version 4.0 (CD-ROM). Asheville, NC: National Climatic Data Center.

NOAA (1995). *Comparative Climatic Data for the United States Through 1994.* Asheville, NC: U.S. Dept. of Commerce, National Oceanic and Atmospheric Administration, National Environmental Satellite, Data and Information Service.

For sale by the National Climatic Data Center. Also available on-line at: <http://www.ncdc.noaa.gov/ol/climate/climateresources.html>.

_____. (1994). *U.S. Divisional and Station Climatic Data and Normals,* Vol. 1. CD-ROM, Dec. Asheville, NC: National Oceanic and Atmospheric Adminstration, U.S. Dept. of Commerce.

_____. (1993). *Climatic Atlas of the United States.* U.S. Dept. of Commerce, National Oceanic and Atmospheric Admininstration, National Environmental Satellite, Data, and Information Service. Asheville: National Climatic Data Service.

Reprint of the original 1968 atlas. Large format, 18" x 24" maps, same information as ESSA (1975).

_____. (1988). Koss, James Walter, James R. Owenby, Peter M. Steurer, and Devoyd S. Ezell. *Freeze/Frost Data.* Climatography of the U.S., No. 20, Supplement No. 1. Asheville, NC: National Climatic Data Service, January.

Data from 1951 to 1980 for most U.S. weather stations. Includes 6 maps, including Alaska.

_____. (1985). *Climates of the States,* 3rd ed. Detroit, MI: Gale Research.

National Oceanic and Atmospheric Administration (NOAA) narrative summaries, tables of normals, means, and extremes, and maps for each state.

_____. (1983). *Annual Average Climatic Maps of the United States.* Environmental Information Summaries C-21. Asheville, NC: National Climatic Data Center.

Maps of temperature, precipitation, relative humidity, dew point temperature, annual solar radiation on a south-facing surface, number of thunderstorms, and annual heating degree days.

NREL (1998). *Solar Water Heating.* Series: Federal Technology Alerts. New Technology Demonstration Program, National Renewable Energy Laboratory. DOE/GO-10098-570. Washington, DC: Federal Energy Management Program. Reprinted Apr., 1988, original printing, May 1996.

Available free from FEMP (1.800.363.3732) or online at: <http://www.eren.doe.gov/femp>.

_____. (4/1998). *Transpired Collectors (Solar Preheaters for Outdoor Ventilation Air).* Series: Federal Technology Alerts. New Technology Demonstration Program, National Renewable Energy Laboratory. DOE/GO-10098-528. Washington, DC: Federal Energy Management Program.

Includes examples and sizing worksheets. Available free from FEMP (1.800.363.3732) or online at: <http://www.eren.doe.gov/femp>.

_____. (1993a). *National Solar Radiation Data Base: Version 1.1,* National Renewable Energy Laboratory.

Database contains hourly values of measured or modeled solar radiation and meteorological data from 239 stations for the 30-year period, 1961–1990. <http://rredc.nrel.gov/solar/>. See also NREL (1993b).

_____. (1993b). *Solar and Meteorological Surface Observation Network, 1961–1990, Version 1.0.* Asheville, NC: U.S. Dept. of Commerce, U.S. Dept. of Energy, National Climatic Data Center, National Renewable Energy Laboratory.

Data base on CD-ROM. NCDC can provide summary statistics for individual locations on computer diskettes. Available from NCDC, User Services, Federal Building, Asheville, NC 28801-2696, (704) 271-4994. <http://www.ncdc.noaa.gov/>.

_____. (1992). *National Solar Radiation Data Base (1961–1990), User's Manual.* Sep. Golden, CO: National Renewable Energy Laboratory.

Distributed by National Climatic Data Center, Asheville, NC. <http://rredc.nrel.gov/solar/>. See NREL (1993).

O'Connor, Jennifer, et al. (1997). *Tips for Daylighting with Windows, the Integrated Approach.* LBNL-39945. Berkeley, CA: Lawrence Berkeley National Laboratory.

Also available on-line from LBL's Building Technologies Program: <http://eetd.lbl.gov/BTP/publications.html>.

Oke, T. R., D. Yap, and R. F. Fergle (1972). "Determination of Urban Sensible Heat Fluxes," In W. P. Adams and F. M. Helleiner, eds. *International Geography, 1972: Papers submitted to the 22nd International Geographical Congress.* Toronto: Univ. of Toronto Press, pp. 176–178.

Olgyay, Adalar, and Victor Olgyay (1957). *Solar Control and Shading Devices.* Princeton, NJ: Princeton University Press.

Olgyay, Victor (1963). *Design With Climate.* Princeton, NJ: Princeton University Press.

ORNL, (1997). "Insulation Fact Sheet," DOE/CE-0180, Oak Ridge, TN: Oak Ridge National Laboratory.

Available on-line from the ORNL Buildings Technology Center: <http://www.ornl.gov/roofs+walls/>. Also available, the web-based ZIP CODE computer program, for calculating recommended insulation levels.

OSU (1988). *Closed Loop/Ground Source Heat Pumps Systems: Installation Guide.* Oklahoma State Univ. Stillwater, OK: International Ground Source Heat Pump Assn.

Owenby, James R., D. S. Exell, and Richard R. Heim, Jr. (1992). *Annual Degree Days to Selected Bases Derived From the 1961–90 Normals.* Climatography of the United States, No. 81, supplement No. 2. Asheville, NC: National Climatic Data Center, July.

Passive Solar Journal (Winter/1983). "San Francisco Residence and Remodel, San Francisco, California/Second National Passive Design Competition First-Place Winner," *PSJ,* Vol. 2, No. 1, pp. 8–13.

Peckham, R. J. (1990). *SHADOWPACK-P.C., Version 2.0 User's Guide.* Pub # EUR 12802 EN. Luxembourg: Commission of the European Communities.

MS-DOS software for calculating shading effects of buildings on outdoor space. Available from R. J. Peckham, Commission of the European Communities, Joint Research Center, I-21020 Ispra (VA).

Penwarden, A. D., and A. F. E. Wise (1975). *Wind Environment Around Buildings.* Department of Environment, Building Research Establishment Report. London: HMSO.

Peri, Ilan, Brian Kellman, and Howard Beckerman (1988). *Building the Brookhaven House.* Videocassette (25 min). N.P.: Amram Nowak Assoc. Distributed by Bullfrog Films.

Place, Wayne and Thomas C. Howard (1990). *Daylighting Multistory Office Buildings.* North Carolina Alternative Energy Corporation.

PNL (1998). *Ground Source Heat Pumps Applied to Commercial Facilities.* Series: Federal Technology Alerts. New Technology Demonstration Program, Pacific Northwest National Laboratory. Washington, DC: Federal Energy Management Program. Reprinted August 1988, original printing, September 1995.

Available free from FEMP (1.800.363.3732) or online: <http://www.eren.doe.gov/femp>.

Process Architecture (1980). TAC, The Heritage of Walter Gropius, *Process, Architecture,* No. 19.

Progressive Architecture (4/1983a). "Decorated Climate-Filtering Shed: Princeton Professional Park, Princeton, NJ," *P/A,* Vol. 64, pp. 94–97.

_____. (4/1983b). "Yankee Independence: Forest Society, Concord, N.H," *P/A,* Vol. 64, pp. 86–89.

_____. (9/1981). "State Intentions: State Office Building, Sacramento, CA," Vol. 62, pp. 76–81.

_____. (6/1981). "Dog Trot House: Logan house, Tampa, FL," *P/A,* Vol. 62, pp. 86–89.

_____. (4/1981a). "Passive Action: Milford Reservation Environmental Center, Milford, PA," *P/A,* Vol. 62, pp. 118–121.

_____. (4/1981b). "Sandia Sanity: Stockebrand Residence, Albuquerque, NM," *P/A,* Vol. 62, pp. 134–137.

_____. (4/1980). "Design Dilemma: Milford Reservation Solar Conservation Center, Milford, PA and Prototype Passive Solar Townhouses," *P/A,* Vol. 61, pp. 162–165.

_____. (1/1975). "Award: Myers and Bennett Architects/ BRW (East Bank Bookstore/Admissions and Records Facility, University of Minnesota)," *P/A,* Vol. 56, pp. 52–53.

PSIC (1998). *Energy-10 software, v. 1.2.* Washington, DC: Passive Solar Industries Council.

Originally published by PSIC, now the Sustainable Buildings Industry Council (SBIC), <http://www.sbicouncil.org/>.

_____. (1990). Passive Solar Industries Council, National Renewable Energy Lab, and Charles Eley Assoc. *Passive Solar Design Guidelines: Guidelines for Home Building.* Washington, DC: PSIC.

Originally published by PSIC, now the Sustainable Buildings Industry Council (SBIC), <http://www.sbicouncil.org/>.

Quinan, Jack (1987). *Frank Lloyd Wright's Larkin Building, Myth and Fact.* Cambridge, MA: MIT Press.

Rea, Mark S, ed. (1993). *Lighting Handbook: Reference & Application,* 8th ed. New York: Illuminating Engineering Society of North America.

Reed, R. A. (1964). "Tree Windbreaks for the Central Great Plains," *Agriculture Handbook #250,* U.S. Department of Agriculture.

Reed, R. H. (1953). "Design for Natural Ventilation in Hot Humid Weather," In *Housing and Building in Hot-Humid and Hot-Dry Climates.* Building Research Advisory Board, Research Conference Report No. 5, National Research Council, National Academy of Sciences.

Reps, John William (1991). *Washington on View: The Nation's Capital Since 1790.* Chapel Hill: University of North Carolina Press.

Reynolds, John S. and Benjamin Stein (2000). *Mechanical and Electrical Equipment for Buildings,* 9th ed. New York: Wiley.

_____. (1992). *Mechanical and Electrical Equipment for Buildings,* 8th ed. New York: Wiley.

Reynolds, John S., Doug Boleyn, Richard Britz, Brent Gunderson, Vineeta Pal, Rob Peña, and Frank Vignola (1994). *Design for PV, a Curriculum Package for Teachers and Students of Architecture.* Washington, DC: AIA/ACSA Council on Architectural Research.

Richards, J. M., Ismail Serageldin, and Darl Rastorfer (1985). *Hassan Fathy.* Singapore: Concept Media (Mimar book).

Rifkind, C. (1980). *A Field Guide to American Architecture.* New York: The New American Library.

Robbins, Calude L. (1986). *Daylighting, Design and Analysis.* New York: Van Nostrand Reinhold.

Robinette, Gary O., ed. (1977). *Landscape Planning for Energy Conservation.* Reston, VA: Environmental Design Press.

_____. (1972). *Plants, People, and Environmental Quality: a Study of Plants and their Environmental Functions.* Series: Housing and Urban Affairs; No. LA-23. Washington, DC: U.S. Dept. of the Interior, National Park Service, and American Society of Landscape Architects Foundation.

For sale by Supt. of Docs., U.S. GPO.

Rossmann, Andreas (1997). "Fingerzeige in die Zukunft: Micro Electronic Zentrum in Duisburg," *Bauwelt,* May 16, Vol. 88, No. 19, pp. 998–1003.

Rumpf, Peter (1995). "Wissenschaftspark Gelsenkirchen," *Bauwelt,* Mar. 3, Vol. 86, No. 9, pp. 424–433.

Ruttenbaum, Steven (1986). *Mansions in the Clouds, the Skyscraper Palazzi of Emery Roth.* New York: Balsam Press.

Sabinkhi, Ranjit (1987). "Temple Like a Lotus Bud, Its Petals Slowly Unfolding," *Architecture: the AIA Journal,* Sep., Vol. 76, No. 9, pp. 72–75.

Sain, A. M. (1983). "Daylighting and Artificial Lighting Control," In J. W. Griffith and John I. Yellott (1984). *Proceedings of the 1983 International Daylighting Conference,* February 16–18, Phoenix, Arizona, U.S.A. New York: Elsevier Sequoia.

_____.(1980). *Building in Hot Dry Climates.* New York: Wiley.

Saini, B. S. (1970). *Architecture in Tropical Australia.* Architectural Association Paper No. 6. New York: George Wittenborn.

Sande, T. A. (1981). "Inherent Energy Saving Features of Old Buildings." In D. Maddex, ed. *New Energy from Old Buildings,* Washington, DC: The Preservation Press.

Sandia (1991). Stand-Alone Photovoltaic Systems: A Handbook of Recommended Design Practices. Photovoltaic Design Assistance Center, Sandia National Laboratories, Albuquerque, New Mexico, Revised, November, 1991, SAND87-7023. Springfield, VA: National Technical Information Service.

A fairly accessible guide with worksheets and examples. A Spanish language version is also available.

Santamouris, M., and D. Asimakopoulos, eds. (1996). *Passive Cooling of Buildings.* London: James & James.

Saxon, Richard (1987). *Atrium Buildings, Development and Design,* 2nd ed. New York: Van Nostrand Reinhold.

Schneider, Sabine (1996). "Reihenhäuser in Egebjggård [Ballerup, Denmark]," *Baumeister,* Oct., Vol. 93, No. 10, pp. 47–51.

Schoenauer, N. (1973). *Introduction to Contemporary Indigenous Housing.* Montreal: Reporter Books.

Scully, Vincent (1962). *Louis I. Kahn.* New York: George Braziller.

Sergeant, J. (1975). *Frank Lloyd Wright's Usonian Houses.* New York: Whitney Library of Design.

Selkowitz, S., and M. Gabel (1984). "LBL Daylight Nomographs," LBL Report 13534. Berkeley, CA: Energy Efficient Buildings Program, Lawrence Berkeley National Laboratory.

Shabban, Awni Kamel (8/1981). *Thermal Performance of Double-Shell Systems in Hot-Humid and Hot-Dry Climates.* Doctoral Dissertation. College Station: Texas A & M University.

Shurcliff, William A. (1981). *Air to Air Heat Exchangers for Houses.* Cambridge, MA: W.A. Shurcliff.

_____. (1980). *Thermal Shutters and Shades.* Andover, MA: Brick House.

Sick, Freidrich, and Thomas Erge, eds. (1996) *Photovoltaics in Buildings: A Design Handbook for Architects and Engineers.* International Energy Agency, Solar Heating and Cooling Program, Task 16. London: James & James.

Siefert, Richard D. (1981). *A Solar Design Manual for Alaska.* Bulletin of the Institute of Water Resources, Vol. 1, Jul. Fairbanks: Inst. of Water Resources, Univ. of Alaska.

Slessor, Catherine (1999). "Hanging Gardens (Consorcio-Vida Offices, Santiago, Chile)," *Architectural Review,* Vol. 205, No. 1224, Sep., pp. 36–40.

_____. (1996). "Critical Mass (Office and Shopping Mall Building, Harare, Zimbabwe)," *Architectural Review,* Vol. 199 (CC), No. 1195, Feb., pp. 36–40.

Smith, B. M. (1981). "Making Buildings Work as They Were Intended." In D. Maddex, ed. *New Energy From Old Buildings,* Washington, DC: The Preservation Press.

Solinfo (n.d.). *Solar Architecture and Energy Efficient Design Portfolio, Commercial and Institutional Buildings.* Solinfo Project of the Directorate General XII for Science, Research and Development of the European Commision. Dublin: Energy Research Group, School of Architecture, University College Dublin.

Copies available from "Architecture et Climat," Place de Levant 1, B-1348, Louvain-la-Neuve.

Spirn, Anne Whiston (1984, April). *The Granite Garden, Urban Nature and Human Design.* New York: Basic Books.

Spirn, Anne Whiston, and Adèle Naudé Santos (1981). *Plants for Passive Cooling, a Preliminary Investigation of the Use of Plants for Passive Cooling in Temperate Humid Climates.* A Study by Harvard University Department of Landscape Architecture for Oak Ridge National Laboratory, Solar and Spectral Studies Section, Energy Division, Contract # W-7405-eng-26. Cambridge, MA: Harvard University Graduate School of Design.

Splittstoesser, Walter E. (1984) *Vegetable Growing Handbook,* 2nd ed. Westport, CT: AVI.

Stathopoulos, Theodore, Dominic Chiovitti, and Luisa Dodaro (1994). "Wind Shielding Effect of Trees on Low Buildings," *Building and Environment,* Vol. 29, No. 2, pp. 141–150.

Steele, James (1998). *Rethinking Modernism for the Developing World: The Complete Architecture of Balkrishna Doshi.* New York: Whitney Library of Design.

_____. (1997). *Sustainable Architecture: Principles, Paradigms, and Case Studies.* New York: McGraw-Hill.

_____. (1988). *Hassan Fathy.* Architectural Monographs 13. New York: St. Martin's Press.

Steen, Athena Swentzel, Bill Steen, David Bainbridge, and David Eisenberg (1994). *The Straw Bale House.* White River Junction, VT: Chelsea Green.

Sterling, Ramond, William T. Farnan, and John Carmody (1982). *Earth Sheltered Residential Design Manual.* New York: Van Nostrand Reinhold.

Sterling, R., J. Carmody, and G. Elnicky (1981). *Earth Sheltered Community Design.* New York: Van Nostrand Reinhold.

Szerman, M. (1992). "Daylighting in Adjacent Rooms Connected to an Atrium, by Artificial Sky Measurements," *Building Research and Information,* Vol. 20, No. 8.

Tao, William K., and Richard R. Janis (1997). *Mechanical and Electrical Systems in Buildings.* Upper Saddle River, NJ: Prentice Hall.

Taylor, Brian Brace (1985). "University, Qatar," *Mimar, Architecture in Development,* No. 16, Apr.–Jun., pp. 20–27.

TEES (1996). *SolrPath* software. Energy Systems Lab. College Station, TX: Texas Engineering Experiment Station.
<http://www-esl.tamu.edu/esl_home_page.html.

Texas Architect (1–2/1990). "South Burke Ranch Headquarters," *T/A,* Vol. 40, No. 1, p. 26.

Thomas, Michael G. (1992). *Water Pumping: The Solar Alternative.* SAND87-0804. Springfield, VA: National Technical Information Service.

Thomas, Randall (1996). *Environmental Design, an Introduction for Architects and Engineers.* London: E & FN Spon/Chapman & Hall.

Thurow, Charles (1983). *Improving Street Climate Through Urban Design.* Planning Advisory Service Report No. 376. Chicago: American Planning Association.

Tilley, Ray Don (1991). "Blueprint for Survival," *Architecture,* Vol. 80, No. 5, May, pp. 64–71.

Total Environmental Action, Inc. (1979). *The Brookhaven House.* Harrisville, NH: TEA.

Traver, X., M. Miro, F. Bonhevi, A. Trias (1991). "SAV System: Towards the Ideal Component," In Servando Alvarez, Jaime Lopez de Asiain, Simos Yannas, and É. de Oliveira Fernandes, eds. *Architecture and Urban Space, Proceedings of the Ninth International PLEA Conference,* Seville, Spain, Sep. 24–27, 1991, pp. 575–580. Dordrecht, The Netherlands: Kluwer Academic.

Turan, Mete H. (1983). "Architectural and Environmental Adaptation in Slope Settlements." In Gideon S. Golany, ed. *Design for Arid Regions.* New York: Van Nostrand Reinhold.

Turnbull, Jeff (1999). *The Griffins in Australia and India: The Complete Works and Projects of Walter Burley Griffin and Marion Mahony Griffin.* Melbourne: Melbourne University Press.

TVA (1985). *Energy Nomographs, A Graphic Calculation Technique for the Design of Energy Efficient Buildings.* Energy Design Guidelines Series. Chattanooga, TN: Tennessee Valley Authority. Sept.

U. S. Dept. of Commerce (1977). *Comparative Climate Data Through 1976.* Asheville, NC: National Climatic Data Center.

_____. (1974). *Summary of Hourly Observations, From Decennial Census of the United States Climate,* Climatography of the United States, Nos. 82–83, Weather Bureau. Washington, DC: U.S. GPO.
Available from NCDC. Monthly and annual tabulations of means on an hourly basis for cloud cover, wind speed, humidity; data for wind roses and other data.

_____. (dates vary). *Airport Climatological Summary.* National Oceanic and Atmospheric Administration (NOAA). Asheville, NC: National Climatic Data Center.
Publication available by location.

_____. (dates vary). *Local Climatological Data.* Asheville, NC: National Climatic Data Center.
Publication available by location.

_____. (dates vary). *Local Climatological Data; Annual Summary with Comparative Data.* Asheville, NC: National Climatic Data Center.
Publication available by location.

_____. (dates vary). *Revised Uniform Summary of Surface Weather Observations.* Asheville, NC: National Climatic Data Center.
Publication available by location.

U. S. Dept. of Energy (1999a). "Building Standards and Guidelines Program Web Site." *<http://www.energycodes.org/>.*
MEC materials can be ordered through the BSGP Hotline at 1-800-270-CODE or downloaded at no cost.

_____. (1999b) *COMcheck-EZ™ Compliance Guides, Commercial and High-Rise Residential, Energy Code Compliance, Version 1.1.* Mar., 1998. DOE/EE/OBT-28432. Developed by Build-

ing Energy Standards Program at Pacific Northwest National Laboratory. *<http://www.energycodes.org/>.*

_____. (1999c) *MEC Check: Prescriptive Packages Compliance Approach 1992, 1993, and 1995 Model Energy Code, Version 2.07.* June 1998. Developed by Building Energy Standards Program at Pacific Northwest National Laboratory. *<http://www.energycodes.org/>.*

_____. (1998). *Commercial and High-Rise Residential COMcheck-EZ Compliance Guides,* Energy Code Compliance, Version 1.1, Mar., DOE/EE/OBT-28432. Richland, WA: Pacific Northwest National Lab, Building Standards and Guidelines Program.
Available free on-line from BSGP: *<http://www.energycodes.org/>,* 1-800-270-CODE.

_____. (1997a). "Selecting Windows for Energy Efficiency," DOE/GO-DE-AC03-76SF00098 PUB-788, Jan.
Available from Efficient Windows Collaborative (EWC) web site: *<http://www.efficientwindows.org/index.html>.*

_____. (1997b). *COMcheck-EZ Climate Map and COMcheck-EZ Prescriptive Packages, Version 1.0.* January. Richland, WA: Pacific Northwest National Lab, Building Standards and Guidelines Program.
Available free on-line from BSGP: *<http://www.energycodes.org/>,* 1-800-270-CODE.

_____. (1989). "Fans and Ventilation," Conservation and Renewable Energy Inquiry Referral Service (CAREIRS), Information Series pamphlet, Mar.

_____. (1980). *Predesign Energy Analysis: a New Graphic Approach to Energy Conscious Design for Buildings.* DOE/CS-0171. Washington DC: Dept. of Energy, Office of Conservation and Solar Energy, Federal Energy Management Program.
For sale by the Supt. of Docs., U.S. GPO; Springfield, VA: Available from National Technical Information Service.

Utzinger, Michael, and James H. Wasley (1997a). *BPgraph.* Excel Spreadsheet. Johnson Controls Institute for Environmental Quality in Architecture, School of Architecture and Urban Planning, University of Wisconsin–Milwaukee.
Available from the authors on-line at: *<http://www.sarup.uwm.edu/JCI/vs.html>.*

_____. (1997b). *Building Balance Point.* Johnson Controls Institute for Environmental Quality in Architecture, School of Architecture and Urban Planning, University of Wisconsin–Milwaukee.
A curriculum resource package of the Vital Signs project, coordinated by the Center for Environmental Design Research at the University of California, Berkeley. Available on-line at: *<http://www-archfp.ced.berkeley.edu/vitalsigns/index.html>.*

Vale, Lawrence J. (1992). *Architecture, Power, and National Identity.* New Haven, CT: Yale University Press.

Vickery, B. J., and R. E. Baddour (1983). "A Study of the External Pressure Distributions and Induced Internal Ventilation Flows in Low Rise Industrial and Domestic Structures," University of Western Ontario, Boundary Layer Wind Tunnel Laboratory Report No. BLWT-SS2-1983 (June).

Viladas, Pilar (1982). "Under and Above: Two Virginia Buildings: An Underground Office Building and a House With Passive Design," *Progressive Architecture,* Apr., Vol. 63, No. 4, pp. 138–141.

Vine, Edward, and Drury Crawley (1991). *State of the Art in Energy Efficiency: Future Directions.* Washington, DC: American Council for an Energy Efficient Economy (ACEEE).

von Arnim, Uta (1993). "Klinikum II in Nürnberg," *Baumeister,* Oct., Vol. 90, No. 10, pp. 12–17.

Vonier, T., J. W. Griffith, and John I. Yellott, eds. (1984). *General Proceedings, 1983 International Daylighting Conference,* February 16–18, Phoenix, Arizona, U.S.A. New York: Elsevier Sequoia.

Wang, Zhuqin (1995). "Layout Improvement of Building Clusters for Better Cross-Ventilation in Southern China," *Proceedings, Solar 95.* American Solar Energy Society. Boulder, CO: ASES.

Watson, Donald, ed. (1993). *The Energy Design Handbook.* Washington, DC: American Institute of Architects.

_____. (1979). *Energy Conservation Through Building Design.* New York: McGraw-Hill.

Watson, Donald, and R. Glover (1981). *Solar Control Workbook.* Washington, DC: Association of Collegiate Schools of Architecture.

Watson, Donald, and Kenneth Labs (1983). *Climatic Design.* New York: McGraw-Hill.

Weston, Richard (1995). *Alvar Aalto.* London: Phaidon.

Willbold-Lohr, Gabriele (1989). "Daylighting in Glazed Atria," *Proceeding: 2nd European Conference on Architecture.* December, 4–8, 1989, Paris.

Williams, Anthony (1991). "Queens Inclosure Middle School," *Building,* Apr., Vol. 256, No. 15, pp. 41–48.

Wise, A. F. E. (1970). *Wind Effect Due to Groups of Buildings.* Building Research Station Current Paper 23/70. Garston, Watford, England: BRS.
> Early work exploring impacts of high rise buildings on pedestrian winds, based on wind tunnel studies. Examines case studies of negative wind environments from British development projects and proposes mitigation strategies.

Woodbridge, Sally B. (1992). *Bernard Maybeck, Visionary Architect.* New York: Abbeville Press.

_____. (1981). "Half-and-Half: Brodhead House, La Honda, California; Architects: R. Fernau and L. Hartman," *Progressive Architecture,* Apr., Vol. 62, No. 4, pp. 138–141.

Wright, David, and Dennis Andrejko (1982). *Passive Solar Architecture.* New York: Van Nostrand Reinhold.

Wright, Frank Lloyd (1956). *The Story of the Tower; The Tree that Escaped the Crowded Forest.* New York: Horizon Press.

Wu, Hanqing (1994). *Pedestrian–Level Wind Environment Around Buildings.* Doctoral Thesis, Concordia University, Montreal Canada, April.

Yannas, Simos, ed. (1995). *Designing for Summer Comfort: Heat Gain Control and Passive Cooling of Buildings, a European Handbook from the EU PASCOOL Project,* Vol. 1: *Design Principles and Guidelines.* Athens: Dept. of Applied Physics, National and Kapodistrian University of Athens.

_____. (1994). *Solar Energy and Housing Design,* Vol. 2: *Examples.* London: Architectural Association Publications.

Yeang, Ken (1994). *Bioclimatic Skyscrapers.* London: Artemis London.

_____. (1987). *Tropical Urban Regionalism. Building in a South-East Asian City.* Singapore: Concept Media/Mimar.

Yellott, John I. (1983). "Passive and Hybrid Cooling Research." In Karl Böer and John A. Duffe, eds. *Advances in Solar Energy, an Annual Review of Research and Development,* Vol. 1, 1982. Boulder, CO: American Solar Energy Society, pp. 241–263.

_____. (1981). "Evaporative Cooling," *Proceedings of the International Passive and Hybrid Cooling Conference.* American Section of the International Solar Energy Society.

Zeren, L. (1982). "Urban and Architectural Planning in Warm, Arid Zones." In Gideon Golany, ed. Desert Planning, London: The Architectural Press.

INDEXES

SUBJECT INDEX

Roofs (Continued)
    thickness, 214–217, 230–231
Rooms, See also Room design strategies
    daylighting thick buildings, 197–200
    depth for daylighting, 201–202, 256–257
    edges:
        earth edges, 203–205
        water edges, 206
    heights:
        daylighting, 201–202
        stack ventilation, 187
    layers:
        shading, 142–144
    loose organizations for ventilation, 146–150
    organizations:
        combined, 146–150
        compact, 145
        differential, 158–160
        thick, solar, 155–157
        thin, daylighting, 151–152
        thin, solar heating, 153–154
    orientation:
        outdoor rooms, 139–141
        solar heat and cross-ventilation, 167–168
    outdoor, locating, 142–144
    proportions:
        atria, 198–200
        light shelves, 255–257
        sidelighting, 201
    shape and enclosure, cooling:
        high and low openings, 185–187
        openings above roof level, 188–190
        openings on windward and leeward sides, 182–184
        open/closed mass cycles, 191–193
        towers, 194–196
    shape and enclosure, daylighting:
        toplit large room within, 197–200
    shape and enclosure, solar collection and storage:
        in ceilings, 176–177
        in glazed rooms, 172–173
        at room edges, 174–175
    size for daylighting, 201–202
    solar air collection at room edges, 178–181
        within rooms, 169–171
    solar collection, 169–171, 172–173
    width for daylighting, 202
    zoning:
        buffer areas, 163–165
        daylighting, 166
        electric lighting, 279–280
        heat producing areas, 161
        migration, 136–138
        pretempering fresh air, 290
        vertical heat stratification, 162

Rooms, design strategies:
    atrium, 197–200
    borrowed daylight, 158–160
    buffer zones, 163–165
    clustered rooms, 145
    cross-ventilation, 182–184
    daylight zones, 166
    daylit room depth, 201–202
    direct gain rooms, 169–171
    earth edges, 203–205
    east-west plan, 153–154
    evaporative cooling towers, 194–196
    heat producing zones, 161
    layer of shades, 142–144
    locating outdoor rooms, 139–141
    migration, 136–138
    night-cooled mass, 191–193
    permeable buildings, 146–150
    roof ponds, 176–177
    rooms facing the sun and wind, 167–168
    stack-ventilation, 185–187
    sunspaces, 172–173
    stratification zones, 162
    thermal collector walls and roofs, 178–181
    thermal storage walls, 174–175
    thin plan, 151–152
    water edges, 206
    wind catchers, 188–190
Rooms facing the sun and wind strategy, 167–168
R-value, see Resistance

Saint Louis, Missouri (temperate continental), climate data for,
    310–313
Sand protection, see Dust protection
Season:
    balance point and, 68
    bioclimatic chart technique, 35–37
    bioclimatic design strategies, 54–55
    courtyard and room zoning, 136–138
    courtyard shading, 211–212
    solar envelope and, 89
    window shading devices exterior, 262–269
Selective absorptance surface, 218
Sensible heat, 39
Separated or combined openings strategy, 240–241
Service hot water loads technique, 77. See also Hot water
Shade and shading, 83–85
    atria and, 199–200
    bioclimatic chart, 35
    building parts strategies, 213
    coefficients, 48, 269, 270, 273–274
    courtyards, 208, 210–212
    daylight enhancement, 260–261
    elongated solar gain, 118

external shading, 262–269
in-between glazing shading strategy, 270–271
internal shading strategy, 270–271
light shelves, 255–257
movable, 48–49, 59–60, 134, 272–275
overhead shades, 133–134
photovoltaics and, 222–223
planted areas, 121–123, 132
predicting patterns on models, 5–7
predicting patterns on site plans, 9
radiant barriers, 215
shade strategy, 83–85
site plans, 5–7, 9, 128
skylights, 233
solar access, neighborhoods, 128–129
solar envelope, 89–98
solar heat gain estimation, 48–50, 62, 66
street orientation and, 102–104
sun path diagram, 8–9, 59–61
times and dates, 57–61
topographical microclimates, 86
user control, 60
vegetation, 267–269
window and glass types, 272–275
Shading calendar technique, 57–61
Shady courtyards strategy, 210–212
Shared shade strategy, 83–85
Shell, see Skin, Double skin, Envelope
Shelterbelts, wind, 131
Sidelighting, 201, 251–253. See also, Daylighting, Toplighting
Site microclimate technique, 22–26
Sites. See also Slope locations
    area for earth-air heat exchangers, 291
    breeze access, 116–117
    daylight envelopes, 110–113
    microclimates, 17–21, 22–26
        site obstructions, 8–9
        solar envelope, 89–98
    obstructions, 8–9, 33–34, 251–253
    shadows on, 5–7, 83–85
    solar envelope and, 89–98
    sun and wind combination analysis, 22–26
    urban shadows, 6
    vegetation, 121–123, 132
    water, 88, 124, 206
    wind flow and, 17–21, 130–131
Skimming flow, 116–117
Skin. See also Envelope, Insulation
    double-skin, 225–227
    earth contact, 203–205
    east-west plan, 153–154
    heat flow, 46–47, 62, 66
    heating or cooling at walls and roof, 174–175, 176–177,
        178–181, 237–238

BUILDING INDEX

ARCHITECT INDEX

DESIGN TOOLS INDEX

TABLES, GRAPHS, AND RULES OF THUMB

378